ALSO BY CHRIS MATTHEWS

Kennedy & Nixon

Hardball

Now, Let Me Tell You What I Really Think

American

Life's a Campaign

JACK KENNEDY

ELUSIVE HERO

CHRIS MATTHEWS

SIMON & SCHUSTER

New York   London   Toronto   Sydney   New Delhi

Simon & Schuster
1230 Avenue of the Americas
New York, NY 10020

First Simon & Schuster hardcover edition October 2011

SIMON & SCHUSTER and colophon are registered trademarks
of Simon & Schuster, Inc.

For information about special discounts for bulk purchases,
please contact Simon & Schuster Special Sales at
1-866-506-1949 or business@simonandschuster.com.

The Simon & Schuster Speakers Bureau can bring authors
to your live event. For more information or to book an event,
contact the Simon & Schuster Speakers Bureau at
1-866-248-3049 or visit our website at www.simonspeakers.com.

Designed by Nancy Singer

Manufactured in the United States of America

10 9 8 7 6

Library of Congress Cataloging-in-Publication Data is available.

ISBN 978–1–4516–3508–9
ISBN 978–1–4516–3510–2 (ebook)
Photo credits can be found on p. 479.

To Kathleen

CONTENTS

CONTENTS

JACK KENNEDY

At the peak of the Cold War, an American president saved his country and the world from a nuclear war. How did Jack Kennedy gain the cold detachment to navigate this perilous moment in history? What prepared him to be the hero we needed?

This is my attempt to explain the leader Jacqueline Kennedy called "that unforgettable, elusive man."

PREFACE

I grew up in a Republican family. My own political awakening began in 1952, when I was six. I remember riding the school bus to Maternity of the Blessed Virgin Mary. One of my classmates was a boy whose father was a Democratic committeeman in Somerton, our remote Philadelphia hamlet bordering Bucks County. I felt sorry for him because he was the only kid for Stevenson. It seemed everybody I knew was for Ike.

Back then, even though we kids were small, our souls were large. We had a sense of things we weren't supposed to understand. I knew that Adlai Stevenson was an "egghead." My father said he "talked over the heads of people." There was distance between us and those like Stevenson. We were regular people.

My older brother, Bert, and I spent our days fighting World War II and the Korean War in our backyard. I knew General Eisenhower had fought in what Mom and Dad always called "the war." It made him a hero. Once I was sitting with Dad at a movie theater when a newsreel came on showing Eisenhower making his return from NATO in Europe, boarding an airplane and waving. I wondered whether he was president and turned to my right to ask my father this. "No," came the answer, "but he will be."

One outcome of World War II was to offer Catholics their opening to join the American mainstream. My mother once told us how the big milk company in Philadelphia used to ask for religion on its job application. The correct answer, she explained, was any one of the Protestant denominations. "Catholic" meant you didn't get the job. What I know for sure is that in the early 1950s we were still making an effort to fit in.

Looking back, I can't count how many times we first and second graders found ourselves marching up and down Bustleton Avenue in front of Maternity carrying little flags. I don't even know which holidays we were celebrating; maybe none. But there we were, mini–George M. Cohans offering up some endless display of our American regularness. All this actually happened, this postwar assimilation of Catholics, and it's a key part of the story I'm telling.

Those were the early boomer years. And a boom it was. We had a hundred kids in our first grade, more than would fit in a classroom, so they had to put us in the auditorium.

I remember an afternoon in 1956 that's hard to believe now. What's strange about it to me is the way it marks a before-and-after moment in time. History changed. It was July, and we were listening to the radio in our two-tone '54 Chevy Bel Air.

It was broadcasting the balloting from the Democratic Convention in Chicago. The fight to become the party's vice-presidential candidate was on between Kefauver—a name I knew from listening to the news, just as I knew the name Nixon—and now, out of nowhere, this candidate named Kennedy. We'd never heard of him. It was an Irish name.

So, because he was a known quantity—Kefauver, a brand name—I was happy when the Tennessee senator won, finally, on the second ballot. The name I knew had beaten the other name. Isn't that how most voting seems to be, voting for the name you recognize, rooting for its victory, and all the time having no real idea who the person is?

Yet, looking back on this event, that Democratic National Convention of over a half-century ago, an image from it remains frozen in my mind's eye. The truth is, it's a picture that entered my consciousness and stayed there. What I still see, as clearly as if it were yesterday, is that giant hall with its thousands of cheering delegates, its chaos then suddenly punctuated by the appearance onstage of a young stranger. It was John F. Kennedy, who had just lost the nomination to Estes Kefauver; swiftly he came through the crowd and up to the podium in order to ask that his opponent's victory be made by acclamation. He was releasing his delegates and requesting unity, and, in making this important gesture, he seemed both confident and gracious. It was the first look the country at large had had of him, a figure we would come to know so well, one who would soon mean so much to us, to me.

I was ten at the time.

I was becoming increasingly obsessed with politics. Two years later, on the midterm election night in 1958, I was backing the GOP candidates, among them Hugh Scott, who won his fight that night to be junior senator from Pennsylvania in an upset. In New York, the Republican candidate, Nelson Rockefeller, defeated the Democrat Averell Harriman, the incumbent governor. My father, a court reporter working for the city of Philadelphia, offered a kind remark about the patrician Harriman, saying he looked sad. It was one of those rare, memorable times when Dad would step out of his workaday world to make such a comment, or to quote from a poem he'd learned in school.

By 1960, I was a paperboy for the *Philadelphia Bulletin,* and suddenly, as I started reading the daily afternoon paper I was throwing onto people's lawns, my loyalties were challenged. Now I was following Jack Kennedy in that year's primaries and enthusiastically rooting for him. He was Catholic, after all, and I felt the pull. Yet all the while I followed his trail through New Hampshire, Wisconsin, and West Virginia, I knew that, in the end, I'd wind up supporting Nixon, his opponent.

That's because, by this time, I'd become not merely a member of a Republican family but a Republican myself. Yet here I found myself entranced by the spectacle of the glamorous JFK winning his party's nomination.

And not only was I cheering the idea of Jack occupying the White House for the next eight years, by the time of the Los Angeles convention I was dreaming of the "happily ever after"—the succession of his vice president, Lyndon Johnson, elected to follow JFK with his own two terms; then, after that, Bobby and Teddy. Momentarily dazzled, I was caught up by the romance of dynasty.

I'd lived my boyhood reading the biographies of great men. From a young age I'd gone from one to the next and been taken with the notion of leaders' destinies. For every birthday and Christmas, Grandmom had made it her regular practice to buy me a book on the life of a famous historic figure. First it was the Young American series, then the Landmark books. I remember ones on Davy Crockett and Abe Lincoln, while others told stories of iconic events such as the Civil War sea battle between the *Monitor* and the *Merrimack*.

The first book I got from the little public library next to Maternity was an illustrated biography of Alexander the Great. And so that's who I was in 1960—a kid who had this gut interest in history and liked reading biographies of heroes.

The Democratic Convention of 1960 was in Los Angeles. Now it was the Republicans' turn in Chicago. I followed the events gavel to gavel, either watching on television or going to bed listening to the radio. I remember the jaunty, optimistic strains of "California, Here I Come!" repeatedly erupting whenever Nixon's name was mentioned. Caught up in the Republican spirit, I once again shifted my allegiance.

Nixon had reexerted his pull over me. I saw him as the scrappy challenger. I was rooting for the underdog, who was also the one who deserved it. Nixon was tough on fighting the Russians. He'd held his ground in that Kitchen Table debate with Nikita Khrushchev over in Moscow. He and his running mate, Henry Cabot Lodge, struck me as the more solid and seasoned candidates to take on the Cold War, to stop the Communist spread around the globe.

On election night, as the returns started to come in, the early ones signaling their defeat, I was overwhelmed—and I cried. By a little after seven, I was drenched in the bad news.

Yet the Matthews house was not as united as I have so far portrayed it. I remember asking my father whom he intended to vote for. When he said Nixon without hesitation, I challenged him. Weren't we Catholic? Shouldn't we be for Kennedy? "I'm a Republican" was his simple, all-explaining response. Dad stuck to his party loyalty. He was a Catholic convert and didn't feel that tribal pull the way the all-Irish side of the family did. It was simple for him, even if he was willing to go so far as to allow how Jack Kennedy had "a touch of Churchill" about him. Interestingly, he also believed that in a fistfight between the two candidates there would be no contest: JFK would easily best Nixon, he declared. I'd raised the issue, and it seemed a matter of no little importance back then.

My mother—born Mary Teresa Shields, Irish to the core—more resembled me in her responses to the political dilemma of our household. But I could tell she was keeping her sympathies to herself, as if to make less trouble in the house. One night, when I was drying the dishes alongside her as she washed them, I offered my opinion that it might be wrong to support Kennedy simply because of religion.

It seemed to scrape a wound. She shot back that Grandmom, my father's mother, from County Antrim, had become a citizen *only* in order to be able to cast her vote for Eisenhower, a fellow Presbyterian. Mom said it defensively. Don't single me out, she was arguing, your dad's side of the family was right out there voting religion, too.

Mom's dad, Charles Patrick Shields, was a classic Irishman and local Democratic committeeman. He worked the night shift as an inspector at a nearby plant, and left the house every weekday afternoon carrying his lunchbox and thermos. When he had on his peacoat and cap, he could have been heading off to work in County Cork. On Sundays he wore a three-piece suit to church at St. Stephen's and kept it on all day, even when he'd come up to visit us in Somerton, which he called "God's country." He was right out of Eugene O'Neill's *A Touch of the Poet*.

A favorite ritual of mine, when he retired, was accompanying him for long walks through the old neighborhoods, then stopping to buy the bulldog edition of the *Inquirer* on the way home. Once he'd finished reading it, sitting there under the mantelpiece, he'd fold the paper, look up at me, and say simply, "Christopher John." I loved him and I always loved that moment, and we would talk politics forever.

This conflict between being Catholic and Republican was a constant bother to me over the years. Yes, a lot of Catholics had voted for Eisenhower, but the old loyalties were deeply Democratic. The vote at LaSalle College High School, where I was going and where I argued the Kennedy-Nixon race at lunchtime, was 24 to 9 for Kennedy in my homeroom.

Our family divisions along these lines never actually reached the level of a right-out-there dispute, but the business of voting either Republican or Catholic did raise the whole question of what we were. We could be Republican, but we were still mostly Irish. In the end, I never actually knew how Mom voted. Because of how I subsequently came to feel—and how I feel now—I hope it was Kennedy she cast her ballot for in the privacy of that curtained booth. Still, I confess that when the inauguration rolled around, on January 20, 1961, my loyalties remained with the loser.

While my mother was ironing in our basement rec room, we watched the ceremonies as they took place in snowy Washington. She seemed upbeat, quietly happy about the event we were witnessing. I think.

As for me, I moved rightward in the days of the New Frontier. I became a fan of Barry Goldwater, lured by his libertarian case for greater personal freedom. Like Hillary Clinton, herself a Goldwater Girl at the time, I would eventually change course. But even back then, I found John F. Kennedy the most interesting political figure of the day. I wanted to meet him, be in the same room with him, study him.

A half century of political life later, my fascination with the elusive spirit of John F. Kennedy has remained an abiding one. He is both pathfinder and puzzle, a beacon and a conundrum. Whenever I spot the name in print, I stop to read. Anytime I've ever met a person who knew him—someone who was there with JFK in real time—I crave hearing his or her first-person memories.

One significant opportunity to listen to firsthand Jack stories came when I spent a half dozen years in the 1980s working for Thomas P. "Tip" O'Neill, Jr., Speaker of the House of Representatives. His and Kennedy's mutual history went way back in the arena of Boston politics, that fiercest of partisan battlefields. In 1946, when young Jack Kennedy was making his first political bid, in the primary race for the 11th Congressional District of Massachusetts, Tip actually had been in his opponent's camp. Later, though, when Jack gained his Senate seat in '52 after serving three terms in the House, Tip replaced him there, serving with him companionably for the next eight years.

During the time I served as his administrative assistant—enjoying a front-row seat when Tip employed all his liberal conscience and veteran's craft against that affable ideologue Ronald Reagan—I found I could occasionally get him, when he was in the right mood and time hung over us, to reminisce about the old days. It was like talking to Grandpop under the mantelpiece.

I treasured hearing him tell how Boston mayor James Michael Curley "was corrupt even by the standards of those days" and what Richard Nixon, whom he'd helped bring down over Watergate, was like to play cards with: "talked too much; not a bad guy." I'd listen eagerly, hardly able to believe my good fortune.

Later, I got to know and became friends with Ben Bradlee, the legendary *Washington Post* editor and Kennedy chum. He quickly understood what an appreciative listener I was. And in the early 1990s, when I began to research my book on the surprising history of the Jack Kennedy–Dick Nixon relationship, with its fascinating backstory, I came to know such men as Charles Bartlett, Paul "Red" Fay, and Chuck Spalding, veteran JFK cronies all.

Yet none of those encounters were enough. I wanted to get every possible look at him, see him from any angle that would help explain him. Was he a liberal as he's been tagged, or was he a pragmatist open to liberal causes? Was he a rich boy pushed by his dad, buying into what his father had sold him on, or was he a self-made leader? Was he a legacy or a Gatsby? The hold JFK had begun to exert on my imagination and on my curiosity when I was a young boy never abated. Instead, it only increased with the passing decades.

Before he came along, politics mostly meant gray men in three-piece suits, indoor types, sexless: Truman, Taft, Dewey, Kefauver, Eisenhower, Nixon. What he did was grip the country, quickening us. From the black-and-white world in which we'd been drifting we suddenly opened our eyes, feeling alive and energized, and saw Technicolor. JFK was wired into our central nervous system and juiced us. He sent us around the planet in the Peace Corps, and then rocketing beyond it to the moon.

Most of all—and, to me, this is what matters above everything else—he saved us from the perilous fate toward which we were headed. All those ICBMs, all those loaded warheads: the Cold War Kennedy inherited was bound for Armageddon. It was just a matter of time—we thought, I thought—until there'd be nuclear war, that "World War III" dreaded in every heart.

If you were a kid you didn't have to read the newspapers to know this, for, unlike our elders, we were actually living it. Weekly drills sent us crouching under our little varnished wooden desks on command. Then, at one critical moment in the fall of 1962, a lone man, President John F. Kennedy, understood the danger clearly, pushed back against his advisors' counsel of war and got us through. The hard-liners in Moscow and Washington, their backs up, were ready to fight. The word in the air was *escalation*. JFK found a way to deliver us.

How'd he do it? What personal capability did he have? What had he learned? What combination of nature and training enabled him to see through the noise and emotions of the Cuban Missile Crisis and allowed him to grasp the root of the matter, to understand what he was up against, and what Nikita Khrushchev, his opposite number, was thinking? How did he know to overrule the experts, the angry generals and the professional Cold Warriors, whose every instinct dictated "Bombs away!"?

It goes without saying that Jack and Jacqueline Kennedy were beautiful. But don't look at the pictures; they're a distraction. Jack understood that better than anyone, using them to divert us from his own far more complex reality.

Yet look at them we did. And it's hard, now, to grasp just how brief that moment was: only seven years from 1956, when we caught the first glimpse, to 1963, when the moment was extinguished.

Whether you're politically conservative, liberal, or moderate, whatever age you are, you probably have your own responses to and your own questions about Jack Kennedy, still today. And that includes all those questions about his personal life, the ones that linger and disturb.

I began this book wanting to discover how he became that leader who, at a moment of national fear and anger, when emotions were running high, could cut so coldly and clearly to the truth, grasping the nature of the catastrophe to be averted.

Not only has that decisive vision continued to hold me and stir my admiration, it has also fed my fascination with him. So what was it about him? What brought him into the world's hearts and hopes so vividly, inspiring such fascination, leaving it, mine included, so alive behind him?

Jack himself, also an avid reader of history and the lives of history-makers, once remarked to Ben Bradlee that the chief reason anyone reads biography is to answer the simple question, "What's he like?"

Having thought about it for so long, I believe I've come to recognize, and even unearth, key clues that help explain the greatness and the enigma of Jack Kennedy. They don't come easily, however. Those glamorous images deflect us from the answers. But if you want to get Jack, you need to look for what they hide.

Among them: He was a dreamer who found his dreams as he read voraciously throughout his boyhood, all alone in one infirmary and hospital bed after another. He was a rebel who showed early the grit that would repeatedly motivate him, launching him against every obstacle in his life, not the least of which was the one presented by his own all-powerful father. He was a dead-serious student of history. In young adulthood, while finishing college, he wrote *Why England Slept,* and never was able to forget the critical lesson he took away from it—that nations die or thrive on the ability and judgment of their leaders to stir them at perilous times.

Then there was the extraordinary rite of passage made in the waters of the South Pacific during World War II, when he gained the confidence that he, always the frail boy, could meet as a man the twin tests of stamina and courage. At the age of twenty-eight, he determined to master the unforgiving art of politics and did so, with his love of that rough-and-tumble more and more an essential part of him. Finally, there was the deep revulsion he felt at the possibility of nuclear war.

Before Jack Kennedy could make himself president, he first had to make himself Jack Kennedy. We've been led to take him as, essentially, a handsome young swell, born to privilege and accepting his father's purpose along with his wealth.

What I discovered, however, was an inner-directed self-creation, an adult stirred and confected in the dreams and loneliness of his youth. I found a serious man who was teaching himself the hard discipline of politics up until the last minute of his life.

What's hardest to see clearly, though, is often what hides in plain sight. So much of this man is what he did. His life is marked by events and achievements that speak for themselves. In searching for Jack Kennedy, I found a fighting prince never free from pain, never far from trouble, never accepting the world he found, never wanting to be his father's son. He was a far greater hero than he ever wished us to know.

Lem Billings

Hymns: 490 (To the tune of 482) - (1st three verses)
502 (1st three verses)

Dean Briggs' Essay
To go on, without excuses small or great; to do the
appointed task and to do it cheerfully amid all distractions, all sorrows,
all heartaches; to make routine (not blind but enlightened routine) your
friend - thus it is that by and by when you meet the hard blows of the
world you can "Go labor on; spend and be spent." One more caution. Do
not let your ideals get shopworn. Keep the glory of your youth. A man
with no visions, be he young or old, is a poor thing. There is no place
like a School and College for visions and ideals; and it is through our
visions, through our ideals, that we keep high our standard of character
and life. No man's character is fixed; and no responsible man is over-
confident of his own. It is the part of every boy when he arrives at
manhood to recognize as one of his greatest dangers the fading of the
vision, and to set himself against this danger with all his might. It
is only the man with ideals who is founded on a rock, and resists the
rains and the floods. In and out of college the man with ideals helps,
so far as in him lies, his college and his country. It is hard for a
boy to understand that in life, whatever he does, he helps to make or
mar the name of his college. As has often been said, the youth who
loves his Alma Mater will always ask, not "What can she do for me?" but
"What can I do for her?"

From the Prophet Amos:
"Behold the days come, saith the Lord God, that I
will send a famine in the land; not a famine of bread, nor a thirst for
water, but of hearing the words of the Lord: And they shall wander
from sea to sea, and from the North even to the East, they shall run to
and fro to seek the word of the Lord and shall not find it. In that
day shall the fair virgins and young men faint for thirst. For where
there is no vision the people perish."

CHAPTER ONE

SECOND SON

History made him, this lonely, sick boy. His mother never loved him. History made Jack, this little boy reading history.
—Jacqueline Kennedy, November 29, 1963,
from notes scribbled by Theodore H. White

Certain things come with the territory. Jack Kennedy, born in 1917 in the spring of the next-to-last year of World War I, was the second son of nine children. That's important to know. The first son is expected to be what the parents are looking for. Realizing that notion early, he becomes their ally. They want him to be like them—or, more accurately and better yet, what they long to be.

Joseph Kennedy, a titan of finance, whose murky early connections helped bring him riches and power but never the fullest respect, had married in 1914, after a seven-year courtship, Rose Fitzgerald. The pious daughter of the colorful Boston mayor John F. "Honey Fitz" Fitzgerald, she launched their substantial family when, nine months later, she presented her husband with his son and heir, Joseph P. Kennedy, Jr. For the proud couple, he would be their bridge to both joining and mastering the WASP society from which they, as Roman Catholics in early twentieth-century America, were barred.

Such stand-in status meant, for the young Joe, that he had

to accept all the terms and rules put forth by those whose ranks he was expected to enter. The idea was to succeed in exactly the well-rounded manner of the New England Brahmin. Above all, that meant grades good enough to keep up at the right Protestant schools, and an ability to shine at sports as well. In this last instance, there was no doubt about the most desirable benchmark of achievement. The football field was not just where reputations were made and popularity earned, it was where campus legends were born.

Joseph Kennedy's handsome eldest boy would prove himself equal to the task. Entering Choate, the boarding school in Wallingford, Connecticut, where he was a student from the age of fourteen to eighteen, he quickly made his mark. A golden youth, he became the headmaster George St. John's ideal exemplar. Transcending his origins—which meant getting past the prejudices St. John was said to hold for his kind, the social-climbing Irish—Joe Jr., with his perfect body and unquestioning, other-directed mind, seemed to embody the Choate ethos without breaking a sweat.

A second son such as Jack Kennedy, arriving as he did two years later, finds himself faced with that old familiar tough act to follow. And, of course, embedded in the soul of any second male child is this Hobson's choice: to fail to match what's gone before guarantees disappointment; to match it guarantees nothing.

You have to be original; it's the only way to get any attention at all—any good attention, that is.

Jack Kennedy, almost as soon as he got to Choate, quite obviously put himself on notice not to be a carbon copy. He was neither a "junior," nor would he be a junior edition. He would be nothing like the much-admired Joe, nothing like the Choate ideal. What he brought, instead, was a grace his brother—and Choate itself—lacked. Even as a child of the outrageously wealthy Joseph Kennedy and his lace-curtain wife, Jack soon showed himself well able to see the humor in life. The wit he displayed cut to the heart of situations and added to life an extra dimension. He was fun.

Here, then, is where we begin to catch a glimpse of the young man who would stride decisively up to that convention stage a quarter century later, leaving behind the indelible image. Even though he's very much still a boy, he's preternaturally aware of the way life demands roles and resistant to stepping into one preselected for him.

There's the wonderful irony that comes with those surprises that second sons—Jack Kennedy included—are driven, and also inspired, to produce. Unlike his older brother, bound to a more conventional blueprint, Jack wasn't under the same pressure. There was a lightness to him, a wry Irishness that blended with the WASP manner rather than aspiring to it. With that combination, he could enter where his father, mother, and brother could not.

What happened to Jack when he got to Choate in the fall of 1931, by then already a victim of persistent ill health, was that, first of all, he had to find himself, and, to a daunting degree, simply survive. His brother Robert—the seventh Kennedy child, younger than JFK by eight years—later said of that period that any mosquito unlucky enough to bite Jack would surely have paid the ultimate price. Jean, his youngest sister, told me it was his bedridden youth that made all the difference. "I remember him being sick. I remember that he read a great deal, and why he was so smart was because during those formative years he was reading when everyone else was playing baseball or football or something like that."

So it was in the sickbed, it turns out, that he became a passionate reader, thrilling to the bold heroes of Sir Walter Scott and the tales of King Arthur. At Choate, he may have wound up the holder of a title he never trumpeted: the record for most days spent in the school's Archbold Infirmary.

The appalling reality is that no one—no doctor, nor any of the

top-drawer specialists to which his father sent Jack—could tell the
Kennedy family or the young patient why he suffered so. He'd had
scarlet fever, and his appendix removed, but what continued to plague
him was a knot in his stomach that never went away. Frighteningly,
too, his blood count was always being tested. Leukemia was one of
the grim possibilities that concerned his doctors, and Jack couldn't
avoid hearing the whispers.

What seems clear to me is that, both at home and away, this
fourteen-year-old—a big-eared, skinny kid nicknamed "Ratface"—
wasn't marked for anything in particular, as far as his father was concerned. The succession was taken care of. There was only one dukedom.

For Joseph Kennedy, his determination that his kids not be losers counted as a one-rule-fits-all. Nor did Jack seem to be of any
particular emotional interest to his mother. Rose Kennedy kept her
distance geographically as well as emotionally. Hard as it is to believe, she never once visited Jack at Choate, not even when he was
ill and confined to the infirmary. "Gee, you're a great mother to go
away and leave your children alone," he once told her at age six, as
she was preparing for a long trip to California.

Sent away to school, Jack Kennedy was a spirit marooned. Choate,
from the first, caused him to feel trapped. Chilly and restrictive, overly
organized and tiresomely gung-ho, it was a typical Protestant boarding school based on the classic British model, and as such, more suited
to his brother's nature than his own. Perhaps because he suddenly was
more aware of his Catholic identity in that setting, he faithfully went
into Wallingford to church on Sunday mornings. At night, he knelt
next to his bed to say his Hail Marys and Our Fathers.

However serious were Jack's fears about his ultimate medical
prognosis, he kept them to himself. There was no one yet in whom to
confide his secrets. What he really needed to figure out for himself was
a way to be happy there. He understood, too, the necessity of putting

forth his best effort to prove himself at the sports at which he stood a chance of excelling—swimming and golf were his choices—while doing his best in the rougher ones, football and basketball. With that covered, he was free to make his name in more inventive ways.

His great success was to find ways to have fun. Jack Kennedy knew how to have—and share—good times. Watching *The Sound of Music* decades later, a classmate was reminded of him. Like the trouble-prone Maria, he "made people laugh."

But even before he'd gotten to Choate, Jack was forming and nurturing an interior self. He had survived, even thrived in his way, as a bookish boy who soon would tolerate no interruptions when reading. While at the Catholic school where he'd boarded before coming to Choate, Jack had devoured Churchill's account of the Great War, *The World Crisis 1911–1918*. Soon he was getting the *New York Times* each day. After finishing an article, it was his habit, as he once told a friend, to close his eyes in an attempt to recall each of its main points.

There would come over his face an expression of almost child-like pleasure when he'd worked through something difficult and figured it out. We all remember those kids who knew things, and cared about them, that weren't taught at school. Jack was one of them. And it wasn't the knowledge for its own sake, it was the grander world he glimpsed through it. Such habits of mind as thinking about Churchillian views of history were the glimmerings of the man he was shaping himself to become.

Yet, early on—and this habit, too, sprang from the many solitary hospital stays, lying in bed waiting for visitors—Jack had developed a craving for company. Left to himself so often for periods of his young life, as he grew older he never wanted to be alone. Even the companionship of any single person for too long never suited him. New people, and new people's attentions, energized him, bringing out the seductive best in him—all his quickness, wit, and charm.

It was close to the end of his sophomore year at Choate that he met the first person he felt he could truly trust, and this allowed the first real crack to appear in his wall of solitude.

Boys in closed-off environments such as boarding schools are caught by the dilemma of needing one another while recognizing they must stay wary. The easily popular types and their followers don't suffer; the quirkier, harder-to-classify ones are left to feel their way more carefully into friendships. Kirk LeMoyne Billings, a year ahead of Jack, would become, to the bewilderment of many, the absolute enduring stalwart of Jack's life. Their relationship was a natural affinity that could never have been described until it happened.

Also a second son—his older brother, Fred, had, like Joe Kennedy, been a Choate superstar—Lem was a big kid, a 175-pounder. His father was a Pittsburgh physician. With all the strength of his instantly faithful devotion, Lem Billings quickly began to tend to the needs of his new pal, whom he'd met in the offices of the Choate yearbook, the *Brief*. Looking at the support this friendship quickly began to provide for Jack, one could even see it as counterbalancing the neglect by his mother. He would confide in Lem that he cried whenever his mother sent word that she was heading off on yet another extended trip. He would be equally open with Lem about his health situation.

Jack was willing to divulge to Lem, a doctor's boy, descriptions of those periods he'd spent captive to medical procedures and tests— even at their most graphic. "God, what a beating I'm taking," he wrote once to Lem from one hospital over a summer break. "Nobody able to figure what's wrong with me. All they do is talk about what an interesting case. It would be funny . . . if there was nothing wrong with me. I'm commencing to stay awake nights on that."

The thought that even the experts were stymied by his symptoms tore at him, and came to haunt him. However jaunty he might have tried to sound, it was the fears they'd planted of a shortened life that he really wanted to share with Lem.

Sidekick, confidant, and traveling companion, and, above all, a touchstone, Lem was always to be a cherished constant. When his friend became Mr. President to the rest of the world, it wasn't long before Lem Billings had his own room at the White House. As Joseph Kennedy, Sr., wryly observed at the beginning, he "moved in one day with his tattered suitcase and never moved out."

Lem's loyalty changed Jack's notion of himself. It taught him he could have followers, which he soon did.

Jack had entered Choate a vulnerable and often lonely boy, a seemingly negligible younger brother with no constituency. He would depart four years later a practiced ringleader. If his adventures before then had been vicarious ones, enjoyed among knights and princes in the pages of books, when Jack left, fealty had been sworn to him much as it would have been to Robin Hood or King Arthur.

His Merry Men were called the Muckers.

To begin with, there were just the two of them, Jack and Lem. Their chemistry was the center from which the circle grew around them. Next came Ralph "Rip" Horton, the son of a wealthy New York family. The rest followed, until there were thirteen in all. Credit, or blame, for the way the Muckers chose that impudent name must be laid directly at the door of the very authority figure to whom they were setting themselves up in opposition.

It was during one of his daily sermons in evening chapel that headmaster George St. John had gone on the attack against those students displaying what now would simply be called "bad attitude." The background is this: It was Jack and Lem's final year. Lem, a class ahead of his best friend, had elected to stay on in order to graduate with Jack, and they were uproariously, and very chaotically, rooming together. The instructor overseeing their dormitory wing was not amused by their shenanigans. Fed up not only with their mess but also with the noisy gang of disciples who gathered there each day to listen to Jack's Victrola, he complained repeatedly to the headmaster.

St. John, when he went on the attack, was clearly directing his words at Jack and Lem's little band, and it was one of those you-know-who-I'm-talking-to moments. What the headmaster couldn't anticipate, though, was the way one expression, in particular, that he chose to use—to refer to the "bad apples" he pegged as a small percentage of the student body—soon would come back to haunt him.

Mucker, the label he hung on the Kennedy-Billings gang, has several meanings. A mucker can be someone who takes important matters too lightly, who mucks about to no particular purpose—in this case, the sort of boys unwilling to uphold the time-approved, gold-plated Choate standards of decency, cleanliness, sportsmanship, piety, politeness, and, above all, respect for the powers that be. In short, the kind exemplified by Jack's and Lem's older brothers.

Yet there is another, secondary definition of *mucker* that would have been well known to a Boston boy of Irish extraction. That meaning addresses itself directly to those who traffic in muck, which is to say, mud. And in Boston, this sense of *mucker* had evolved from being a derisive term applied to Irish-Americans put to work shoveling up horse manure from the city streets during the era of carriages, to becoming an all-purpose epithet for their immigrant countrymen.

Without realizing it, then, George St. John had thrown down a gauntlet. Sitting in front of him was Honey Fitz's grandson, whose own Irish ancestry was a source of pride to him and for whom the insult hit home. But the headmaster's choice of words also, Jack realized, provided an opportunity for a memorable stunt, perhaps the cap to his career at Choate.

Troublemaking by kids at school escalates. They compete to come up with outrageous schemes, each trying to top the other. Strategically astute, Jack and Lem—already known as Public Enemies Number One and Two on the Choate campus—had recruited their followers, the ones who now were the regulars in their room, from among the "wheels." That is to say, their pals were the sons of rich fathers upon whose deep pockets the school's endowment and building programs depended. That night, after chapel, back at Jack and Lem's room, they agreed to be henceforth known, as dubbed by Jack, the Muckers.

It was a thumb in the eye to old St. John.

Then Jack was clever enough—when further inspiration struck—to conjure up a reality out of the metaphor. Here was the plan: The dining hall had been decorated for an important school dance. Just imagine, he proposed, the faces of their classmates if a large quantity of manure, imported from a nearby field, suddenly got dumped in front of them and their dates. Cue the Muckers, shovels in hand, to scoop it all up and save the day.

Glorious a prank as it was, it didn't happen. What kept it still-born was the killjoy who'd caught a whiff of what was going on and ratted them out to St. John. All thirteen would-be culprits were instantly called from their classrooms and onto the carpet of the headmaster's office, where they were reminded the punishment for forming an illegal club was expulsion. They were told they could count themselves as Choate students no longer; they would have to pack their bags and arrange for transportation home.

Almost as quickly, Joseph Kennedy, Sr., was also summoned from his office in Washington, where he was chairing Franklin Roosevelt's new Securities and Exchange Commission. Jack's fifteen-year-old sister, Kick, alarmed at hearing the news from Lem—he adored her and stayed in close touch—telegrammed her support: DEAR PUBLIC ENEMIES ONE AND TWO ALL OUR PRAYERS ARE UNITED WITH YOU AND THE ELEVEN OTHER MUCKS WHEN THE OLD MEN ARRIVE SORRY WE WON'T BE THERE FOR THE BURIAL.

However, Jack's father, a ruthless rule-breaker in his own right, seemed far more impressed than angry once he heard the story. Pretending to share the headmaster's anger, he waited until he had his son alone to tell him that if *he'd* founded the club, its name would *not* have begun with an *M*.

For the first time, I imagine, Joe Kennedy was forced to take a good look at his second son. He'd devoted a great deal of his attention to imbuing Joe Jr. with the style he wanted, but now, I think, he saw in Jack essential qualities that he recognized only too well. Just as he, Joe Sr., had been a corsair defiantly mapping his own way, now Jack was revealed to be similarly audacious.

When the furor died down and, somehow, they weren't expelled after all, the failed stunt only left Jack and Lem with a zest for defiance. On the night of a different dance, they and their dates drove off campus, chauffeured in a convertible by a friend who'd already graduated. Such behavior was strictly forbidden: no students were to leave the grounds, *ever,* during a Saturday-night dance.

Off they went—Jack and Lem in white tie and tails, the girls in long formal gowns, the Connecticut country lanes opening invitingly before them. But to their shock, just as they confidently assumed they were getting away with it, they glimpsed a car following them. Panicky, and sure it was campus security, they swerved into a farmhouse driveway, leaped out, and scattered. Jack, Lem, and one of the girls sought cover in a barn. Lem's date stayed in the car and pretended to neck with the driver. When the coast seemed clear, Jack suddenly was nowhere to be found, so the others headed back to campus without him.

A half hour later he turned up at the dance. In the end, it was all a false alarm: no one from Choate had been after them, and they were never found out. The tale is a fine example of the sort of risk Jack Kennedy enjoyed taking—dangerous on the downside, with very little on the up, except for the tremendous sensation it gave, short-lived but long-savored. It offered the promise of deliverance. It was his way of coming alive, and it would never change.

As Jack's time at Choate was drawing to an end, he and the Muckers changed course. Legitimate concerns now occupied them: directed by Jack, they began to invest their wit and energy in securing for themselves the "Most" tags featured in the senior yearbook. Jack wanted "Most Likely to Succeed" for himself, while Lem would get "Most Likeable." The rest would divide the allotted spoils. However they managed it—and the historical record persists as a bit murky about whatever vote-swapping went on—Jack's budding skill as a strategist-with-defined-set-of-goals successfully came into play.

This exercise may have involved only prep school popularity, forgotten in the crumbling album of time—except for the identity of the intelligence masterminding it all. In this long-ago microcosm, Jack, the leader, created the first of what Tip O'Neill later dubbed the "Kennedy Party," a political faction united by a personality. Their success sharing the yearbook spoils, as JFK might later say, had a hundred fathers.

Speeches do, too.

Perhaps the most significant legacy from Choate was his likely memory of a familiar refrain of George St. John. As with all the other well-loved mottoes, maxims, and homilies the headmaster delivered into the ears of his youthful charges during evening chapel, he expected this one to sink in. It's a portion of an essay by his beloved mentor, Harvard dean LeBaron Russell Briggs. "In and out of college the man with ideals helps, so far as in him lies, his college and his country. It is hard for a boy to understand that in life, whatever he does, he helps to make or mar the name of his college. As has often been said, the youth who loves his alma mater will always ask not 'What can she do for me?' but 'What can I do for her?'"

Though Jack Kennedy had rebelled against that call to higher duty in his youth, it would come to define him.

We're puttin' on our top hat,
Tyin' up our white tie,
Brushin' off our tails,
In order to
Wish you

A Merry Christmas

Rip.   Leem.   Ken.

5

6

Princeton 1935 with Ralph "Rip" Horton and Lem Billings

Jack, Bobby, Torbert Macdonald

Harvard swim team

CHAPTER TWO

THE TWO JACKS

Adversity is the first path to truth.

—Lord Byron

The self-made rich man forever remains the poor kid he once was. The short boy, no matter how tall he grows, never stops measuring himself. Jack Kennedy, for all his apparent vitality as an adult, projected the shining image we remember mostly by an extraordinary force of will. We now understand that he was beset by lifelong pain in his stomach and back. What's also clear, if you listen to those who knew him best, is that this deeper Jack, who spent so much time as the vulnerable youngster struggling toward sound health, endured over the decades.

It's this bedridden child behind the man who transcended it all to become a war hero, congressman, senator, and president.

The burden of that effort gives us insight into John F. Kennedy.

From an early age, there were *two* Jacks. He'd had to learn, from necessity, to separate his life into compartments, ones that eventually grew greater in number and more intricate in their interrelatedness as time passed and the number of his relationships increased.

At Choate he seemed to most of his classmates a sunny boy, full of good humor, always ready for fun. That was the picture he chose to present. But there were also, at school, the first signs of seriousness, and with it ambition. The young Jack revealed what would later be known as his "charisma," and also, along with his risk-taking inclination, his leadership instincts and his innate political talent. When he reached Harvard in the fall of 1936, this Jack comes into sharper focus.

The standard take on Jack Kennedy is that he never intended a political career for himself until his brother's death in World War II changed everything. But Jack was always ambitious. He was headed, one way or another, into public life. Even his father was starting to take notice of him as a leader, a kid exhibiting his own defiant spunk.

When summoned by the Choate headmaster, Joe Kennedy hadn't quashed Jack's Mucker spirit so much as honored it. You don't get to be a tycoon, one of the richest men in the country, by saying "please" and "thank you" and sticking to the script.

Despite the fact that his dad had been a Harvard man, as was Joe Jr., Jack planned to spend his first year after Choate at the London School of Economics. While the LSE was known to favor a socialist point of view, Joseph Kennedy was a capitalist who liked being ahead of the market. He wanted his sons to have an edge on what he saw coming in the world.

But as fate would have it, Jack's chronic stomach problems sent him reeling back to America after hardly more than a month there. Rather than return to London when he recovered, he chose to break a second time with Kennedy family tradition and, still shunning Harvard, entered Princeton. There were several good reasons for this decision, the main one being that his closest friend, Lem Billings, and another Choate pal, Rip Horton, were already there. It's easy to see what such friendship meant to him, and how he was learning to have—to make, to keep—the kind of friends Lem and Rip represented.

Quickly moving in with them, he began attending classes. Then, once more, illness overtook him; standing six feet tall, Jack now weighed a puny 135 pounds. The blood-count roulette he was forced to play started up again, and, as his complexion went sallow, he resembled nothing so much as a scarecrow.

Back he went to Peter Bent Brigham Hospital in Boston for two months, and then, suffering also from asthma, he spent the remainder of the school year trying to recover under the dry desert sun of Arizona. Finally, facing the inevitable, he arrived in Cambridge that September to take his room in Weld Hall. He was a Harvard man.

Scrawny as he was, he quickly went out for freshman football. Whatever illnesses dogged him, he was doing his best not to let them define him. You couldn't be the "sick kid" and still be popular the way he wanted to be. Interestingly, he followed his older brother's lead in making a football star his best pal; three years ahead of him, Joe Jr. quickly had bonded with the quarterback, Timothy "Ted" Reardon. Jack's new friend was Torbert Macdonald, his own class's football hero, and Torby, like Lem before him, would come to know both Jacks. By sophomore year they were roommates.

One thing had changed. At Choate, he'd operated outside the system. Now at Harvard, his father's and brother's school, he seemed to be looking to succeed from within it. He ran for student office in both his freshman and sophomore years, falling short of success both times. Yet he continued to emphasize his quest for campus leadership over academic excellence.

"Exam today," he wrote Lem at the end of his first semester, "so have to open my book & see what the fucking course is about." But then he chalked up a social victory when he managed to get named chairman of the freshman "Smoker," just as Joe earlier had been. Traditionally the class's most elaborate party, the Smoker was considered a hot ticket, and expectations for it ran high.

Taking his responsibilities to heart, Jack didn't disappoint, producing not one but two jazz bands for the occasion. "No matter who you were or what you did as a freshman . . . everybody went to the Smoker," one of his classmates recalled. "It was a leadership activity at Harvard . . . a big deal. It was his first political success. So by this, Jack Kennedy had made his mark."

Still, he had yet to outdo his brother. When he did, it would be a matter of beating Joe at his own game. During his sophomore year he was asked to join Spee, one of Harvard's top final clubs. With that coveted invitation, the second son now possessed entrance into circles closed to both Joes. Demonstrating what we might call his "crossover appeal," Jack, with his easy charm, had moved beyond the self-circumscribed orbit of the equally ambitious but unimaginative Joe Jr., who seemed unwilling to stride beyond the local Irish comfort zone. According to Joe's tutor, John Kenneth Galbraith, the older brother was "slightly humorless, and . . . introduced all his thoughts with the words 'Father says.' "

Quickly becoming both well known and popular, Jack didn't give off the impression that he was trying too hard, and he made good use of what his older brother never seemed to have, namely a light touch. And more than that, his conversation, friends said, ranged more widely than that of anyone else their age.

As Jack started to make a name for himself on campus, his energies at first were directed to such pursuits as arranging to meet Lem at the Stork Club in New York. Only in his "Gov," or political science courses, in which he would eventually major, was the unexpectedly serious side to him glimpsed. Before an injury sidelined him—his congenital back troubles made worse by one leg's being shorter than the other—Torby patiently threw passes for hours to help improve Jack's skills as a receiver. Undaunted, Jack, who'd competed in backstroke at Choate, transferred his hopes for varsity success to the Harvard swim team.

Just as Lem would always be, Torby turned into a Kennedy constant, there when his friend needed support. Lem and Torby were the first recruits of what would one day grow to be an unofficial reserve corps of steadfast compadres always game for the next adventure. What Jack required from any of his new best sidekicks was one thing above all else, and that was rescue: from being alone, from being bored, from being *stuck*.

After spending Jack's freshman year apart, in the summer of 1937 he and Lem crossed the Atlantic to embark on a traditional grand tour. Such an exciting trip was a way to try to erase the memories of Jack's hospital stays that February and March. Sickness continued to be one specter he couldn't charm his way past.

For two months they hit the road, having fun but also making sure they saw the best cathedrals and historic buildings. Jack showed himself willing to stay in the cheapest pensions to help keep down expenses for his friend. Being two high-spirited young Americans, they couldn't help having a terrific time. It was nonetheless a moment when Europe's dark political realities were visible even to the most fun-loving of tourists.

In France, where they stopped first, Jack wrote in his diary: "The general impression also seems to be that there will not be a war in the future and that France is much too well prepared for Germany." Later, Lem would recall that his friend "was beginning to show more interest and more of a desire to think out the problems of the world. . . . He insisted, for instance, that we pick up every German hitchhiker. This worked out very well because a high percentage of them were students and could speak English. In that way, we learned a great deal about Germany." Jack and Lem couldn't resist making fun of the Nazis they saw: "Hi yah, Hitler!" they'd cheerfully call out.

The threat of war, in fact, was now less rumor than fact. The Third Reich had been rapidly rearming, and possessed an army and air corps that couldn't help but cast a pall over Europe. When Hitler first showed his true colors and remilitarized the Rhineland, in total violation of the Treaty of Versailles, which had ended World War I, neither Britain nor France rose up to challenge him. Thoughts of war, to most Europeans, too vividly brought back the devastation wrought by World War I, when masses of young soldiers were thrown against one another in a conflict that left the continent in carnage.

Returning to Cambridge for his sophomore year, Jack soon faced an array of familiar, disturbing physical setbacks. As always, he fought against them in his own way. To remain on the swim team—as freshmen, they'd gained glory by being undefeated—was one of his goals. Thus, when he found himself in Stillman Infirmary, he relied on Torby, who brought him steaks and ice cream to tempt his appetite and build up his strength. His friend even snuck Jack out to the indoor swimming pool to get the practice time he needed. Swimming for Harvard was serious business, after all, and team members were expected to sandwich in four hours a day between classes.

Then, just before the year drew to a close, Franklin Roosevelt, now in the first year of his second White House term, threw a joker into the U.S. international diplomacy game: he named Joseph P. Kennedy, Sr., ambassador to Great Britain. It's impossible to figure out exactly what mix of motives inspired this maladroit appointment. Certainly domestic politics played a major role, for Irish-American voters made up a huge faction of the Democratic constituency. Also, given his background and connections, Joe Kennedy's presence in London might help resolve the tricky situation between Ireland and Britain. However, if Roosevelt imagined that his new envoy would act as his surrogate in trying to stiffen the spine of the British when it came to facing down Nazi aggression, he was, sadly, wrong.

The choice of Kennedy, who'd been an early, generous FDR supporter, for this ultimate plum offered the wily Roosevelt the satisfaction of making him into a retainer—a well-rewarded one, but a retainer nevertheless. Both men were well aware the job had to be entrusted to someone able to foot the extravagant costs its social traditions demanded. Ever the bold striver, Joe wanted badly to go there and was ready to spend whatever it took. Until the consequences of sending him to London would prove too large, FDR, too, was ready to weather them.

With his credentials ready to present at the Court of St. James, Joe arrived in London in early 1938, just eleven days before Hitler demanded acceptance of *Anschluss*—in effect, annexation—from the government of his native Austria. Such a relationship between the two countries had been forbidden by the allies at the end of World War I, but the Führer ignored it. Bent on expanding the borders of the great German-speaking state he envisioned, he signaled ever louder his disdain for those who considered themselves Germany's masters.

The Treaty of Versailles for him was no longer worth the paper it had been written on, and so the next territory he looked to grab was the German-speaking part of Czechoslovakia, the Sudetenland, taken from Germany by the allies in 1919.

He had only a simple goal, Hitler told the world—acting the perfect wolf in sheep's clothing—and that was to see all Germans united into one country. Hearing this, Germany's old European and

British antagonists managed, hiding their faces in the sand, to justify tolerating it as a means to preventing the continent from again morphing into a bloody battlefield. Meanwhile, to the newly arrived American ambassador to Great Britain, a new war was out of the question. In late September 1938, British, French, and Italian diplomats fatefully met in Munich and there gave in to Hitler's demands for the Sudetenland. The British delegation was led by Prime Minister Neville Chamberlain, whose reputation would ultimately be destroyed by this concession to the Germans.

Returning to Britain, he announced, "We regard the agreement signed last night and the Anglo-German Naval Agreement as symbolic of the desire of our two peoples never to go to war with one another again." Later that day, he stood outside 10 Downing Street and this time said, "My good friends, this is the second time in our history that there has come back from Germany to Downing Street peace with honour. I believe it is peace for our time."

Events would swiftly prove him wrong.

Ambassador Kennedy, as soon as he'd arrived in London, formed a close relationship with Chamberlain, and it wasn't long before they were in almost daily contact. After the Munich capitulation, Joe made widely known his approval, and gave in October a Trafalgar Day speech that spoke of the need for "democratic and dictator countries" to focus on their similarities and not their differences. "After all, we have to live together in the same world, whether we like it or not," he declared. It could hardly have been worse timing. Only three weeks later came *Kristallnacht*, or Night of Broken Glass, when across Germany and Austria state-sanctioned violence against Jews and Jewish property raged for two days, shocking the world.

Repugnant as appeasement strikes us today, Joe Kennedy wasn't that out of sync with the prevailing temper of the British

Establishment. Events were moving swiftly to force the democracies to make a stand, but the reluctance of the ruling class to engage with the Third Reich died hard. Four years earlier the Oxford Union, the legendary university debating society, after hearing arguments pro and con, had notoriously resolved *not* to fight "for King and Country," and that remained still a popular, if increasingly indefensible, position in London's drawing rooms.

Only the politician and ardent historian Winston Churchill—who was a hero, through his writings, to Jack Kennedy—had steadily been speaking out, from his backbench in Parliament, against the pacifist temper of the times. And people were beginning to listen to him.

It's very hard, looking at this now, to accept that Jack's father never seemed to feel any shame about backing appeasement. Joe's detachment from the sentiments of the times had always been his strength in business, as he invested or divested against the popular current. However, after *Kristallnacht*, when it was starkly evident that there could be no accommodation with Nazism, Ambassador Kennedy was out there on his own.

For a twenty-one-year-old American, the thought of war carried personal meaning. It brought with it both excitement and dread. Young men of Jack Kennedy's age had died by the hundreds of thousands in the century's first great European war. Now the daily press clamored the drumbeat of a second. Young Jack Kennedy was about to enter the very theater in which the question would be decided: Would Britain stand another Nazi demand for territory?

He had come to visit his family that summer of 1938, joining them on vacation in the South of France. It was decided that he'd figure out a way to spend the coming spring semester of his junior year working as his father's secretary in London; it meant he'd have to get permission to double up his classes at school in the fall term, but this was an opportunity to witness history.

Jack knew the valor Britain had shown in the Great War. He was powerfully affected by Winston Churchill's description of the willing courage of an upper-class Englishman, Raymond Asquith. Son of Herbert Asquith, the Liberal prime minister under whose leadership the British entered the Great War, Raymond was four years younger than Churchill and a much-admired, much-loved role model for his generation. His brave death on a French battle-field stood for all that was fine, and the tribute Churchill had written to him struck for Jack a resonant chord: "The War which found the measure of so many never got to the bottom of him, and when the Grenadiers strode into the crash and thunder of the Somme, he went to his fate cool, poised, resolute, matter-of-fact, debonair." In later years he would quote this passage from memory.

However, the poignancy of young death for a noble cause seemed far removed from the moral climate Jack began to sense around him as he spent more time in England beginning in February 1939, when he took up his post at the embassy. Arriving primed to enjoy the perks of the ambassador's family, he found himself distracted not just by the predictable flood of society invitations but also by the debate being waged.

By March, it was clear Hitler was looking to take more land beyond the chunk of Czechoslovakia ceded to him at Munich. All at once, with no warning, Hitler fulfilled the watching world's worst fears and defiantly laid claim to all of Czechoslovakia. Immediately, the issue turned to neighboring Poland's sovereignty. Would the British take their stand now?

Despite the increasingly alarmed warnings of Winston Churchill, the Chamberlain government had been hugging the be-lief that a second major war could be avoided. It knew that neither the British public's memory of the human devastation of the trenches of WWI nor the traumas of the returning survivors had lessened; a generation had been lost, with the country, overall, remaining shell-shocked.

For the first time in his life—as he learned the ways of a country not his own but mattering greatly to him—Jack Kennedy found himself seeing men and women wrestling with national principles. Quickly pegged as a highly desirable bachelor and invited everywhere, he grew increasingly sensitive to the atmosphere around him—and soon began to feel the disharmony unbalancing it.

On the one hand, his father continued to support Chamberlain, in direct opposition to the position fiercely held by Churchill. Churchill's assessments of German capabilities, Jack was aware, had proved—and continued to prove—startlingly accurate. He couldn't help but respect Churchill's arguments, despite knowing that his own father and the ruling-class parents of his new friends openly dismissed the former cabinet minister as a warmonger. And while Jack was intellectually open, he was still a son with a powerful father.

Jack was also convinced, as he grew to be at home in the continual round of parties and pleasures, that something vital was missing in the character of those privileged young English whose company he was so enjoying. Charming they were, and always delightful hosts, yet he found himself doubting the current state of their mettle—their fighting spirit. Even in front of them he didn't hesitate to share his observation that the once-valiant English elite seemed to have turned "decadent" over the two decades since the last war. How could they ever rally themselves and prevail against such a threat as the Third Reich?

In short, they were no Raymond Asquiths.

Mulling over what he was hearing and seeing, he began to form for himself a notion of where Britain's elected leaders had failed. He began to work out his ideas on the subject of leadership, the ones he would continue to consider for the rest of his life.

When the Nazis invaded Poland on September 1, 1939, Jack was still in Europe, having been touring again that summer, this time with Torby. Three days later, he sat with his parents and sister Kathleen in the Strangers' Gallery of the House of Commons and witnessed Prime Minister Chamberlain declare war against Germany. Returning to college at the end of September, by which time the Luftwaffe had begun dropping its bombs, he seemed a different person.

Certainly, in the opinion of Torby—who was there—his friend "had definitely changed. I don't think he really got interested in the intellectual side of academic life until perhaps his junior year when war seemed to bring a lot of us, especially Jack, a recognition that it wasn't all fun and games and that life was about to get very real and earnest."

But what was happening to Jack continued as an evolution. Then, in early June of 1940, he took a visible stand, writing a signed letter to the *Harvard Crimson*, implicitly renouncing his father's position. Even in 1940, once the war was under way, Joe had hoped the British would soon find a way to make peace with Hitler. He spoke disparagingly of Britain's and France's prospects, in a letter to Roosevelt, giving them hardly "a Chinaman's chance" of prevailing.

In his letter to the *Crimson*, Jack noted sharply: "The failure to build up her armaments has not saved England from a war, and may cost her one. Are we in America to let that lesson go unlearned?"

He'd chosen this for his Harvard senior thesis. "Appeasement in Munich" was its title, and it shows how Jack's thinking was diverging from that of his father. Reading it today, what you recognize is that it's actually a masterful political compromise, reconciling the views of his dad with the growing American consensus. Soon to be retitled *Why England Slept* and commercially published that same year, what Jack's analysis argues, to begin with, is that Britain simply had been unprepared in 1938. Had the British gone to war then, they would have lost badly. Most crucially, their defense capability was short the trained fighter pilots needed to keep at bay the Luftwaffe, the fearsome German air force.

The two years between 1938 and 1940, then, were critical, he contends, because, had the war begun at the earlier date, Britain would have been naked to its enemies. The beauty of this argument is that it mitigates the moral failure of giving away a country and its people to Adolf Hitler. Joe Kennedy, one assumes, wouldn't have forsworn appeasement based simply on a shift in the balance of weaponry. He didn't believe in fighting Hitler under any circumstances. But, while Jack makes the case that Chamberlain had no choice but to parlay and retreat, the real issue now, for him, is that the United States, his own country, must take the lesson and do better.

"I do not believe necessarily," he wrote, "that if Hitler wins the present war he will continue on his course to world domination. . . . But, in the light of what has happened in the last five years, we cannot depend on it."

In other words, America needed to get its act together and stop blaming Chamberlain, and therefore his own father, for not doing what it still needed to do. It was a masterful exercise in intergenerational politics. Here was the son, taking on, without condemning, the father's indefensible position on what would soon be revealed as the worst horror of the century. He was doing so with such a deft touch that his father took no apparent offense. In truth, he was saying that Britain should have been *morally prepared* to fight, and his father was saying Britain should still *avoid* the fight.

What Jack now proposed was that America be prepared to fight, not repeating Britain's error. "England made many mistakes; she is paying heavily for them now. In studying the reasons why England slept, let us try to profit by them and save ourselves her anguish." *Why England Slept* quickly became a best seller on both sides of the Atlantic, and Jack donated the royalties from the British edition to the fund to rebuild war-scarred Plymouth.

It is yet another manifestation of the two Jacks: the young American drawn to Churchill's mind and fearlessness on the one hand, and the son whose father was equally fearless but to a different purpose. To reconcile the lessons of these two figures was a task for which he had needed to make the effort.

Again, it was masterful politics. If Joe Kennedy had been paying strict attention, he would have spotted the end run his son was making around him here. Jack was arguing that Britain didn't fight because it hadn't rearmed. But wasn't that tantamount to saying Britain should have been ready to fight? And wasn't that a subversion of his father's own position? Jack had done more than find a middle ground with his father; he'd subtly taken that ground right out from under him.

That fall, the senior Kennedy would be forced from his job in London, a victim of his poor judgment. He had been quoted in a *Boston Globe* column saying, "Democracy is finished in England. It may be here." Jack's career would go on to be a continual balancing act between the nobility of valiant death on the battlefield, so admired by Churchill, and the horror of war itself, so understood by Chamberlain and backed by the hardnosed Joe Kennedy.

Jack felt deeply the emotional weight of the valor, commitment, and sacrifice demanded by war. Nothing makes this clearer than his beloved *Pilgrim's Way*, the autobiography of John Buchan, famous for writing *The Thirty-Nine Steps*. Published in 1940, it immediately became a favorite and would remain the best-loved book of his life. Most significant, in its pages he again encountered the widely mourned figure of Raymond Asquith, about whom Churchill had written so movingly.

"He loved his youth," Buchan wrote of Asquith. "And his youth has become eternal. Debonair and brilliant and brave, he is now part of that immortal England which knows not age or weariness or defeat."

Jack loved courage, hated war. That conflict would define his view of history's leaders. As we will see very soon, it will define how he viewed himself.

8

9

Raymond Asquith

Inga Marie Arvad

10

11

Red Fay

Chuck Spalding saluting

PT 109

12

CHAPTER THREE
SKIPPER

He had never found a circle where he was so much at home and his popularity was immediate and complete. He was an excellent battalion officer.

— John Buchan on Raymond Asquith,
from *Pilgrim's Way*

Up until he went to war, Jack Kennedy had the luxury of living two lives. There was the often bedridden young man, who, loving books and loving heroes, greatly admired Winston Churchill. Twinned with him was the popular bon vivant son of the wealthy Ambassador Joseph P. Kennedy. One lived in the quiet world where history looks back and looms forward, where tales of majesty mingle with dreams of glory. The other lived in the divine, fortunate present of Mayfair addresses and country estates, of titled hosts and society hostesses.

War, for a time, joined the two Jacks as one. Called upon in 1943 to be a leader of men, he shouldered willingly the burden that comes with taking others into harm's way and then getting them back alive and whole. His experience in the waters of the South Pacific was to be the most searing event of his life, the one that transformed him into a figure like those who previously consumed his imagination.

It would make of him a hero like those he'd read about. There is nowhere to hide any part of yourself when you face death. What's more, Jack Kennedy now would be what he'd never been before: a regular guy. He was about to enter a world where he'd be accepted for the man he was. It didn't matter where he'd come from, or what he'd done before. Finally, for the first time in his life, he was moving on to a level playing field. He proved more than up to the challenge, and the confidence that came of it would stay with him.

Look back at Raymond Asquith. Comparing the pair at this moment—two men poised on the brink of different wars—offers clear parallels. Both had been born to privilege and attended the most elite of schools. Both were tall and handsome. Both seemed, effortlessly, to gain the loyalty and devotion of friends. Both volunteered at the outset of world war. Both were assigned cushy, safe postings in intelligence—and, in each case, in locations far from the front. Both, on their own, rejected that safety and sought aggressively to get to the action, wanting to be in the thick of things, in front-line combat units. And the fact that Jack identified with Asquith—who lost his life after being shot by a sniper at the Battle of the Somme, where the British casualties were 420,000 men—was never any secret from his friends.

Jack and Lem Billings were playing touch football on the Washington Mall the Sunday Pearl Harbor was attacked. It was December 7, 1941. They heard the news on the car radio as they were heading back to Jack's apartment on Sixteenth Street. Jack had managed to join the navy earlier that fall after being rejected by the army for obvious health reasons.

In fact, the navy had turned him down, too, but he stubbornly went all out for five months, exercising to overcome the bad back problems that had caused him to flunk. Strengthened by the training regimen, he passed the physical on his second try, but he also benefited from the support of a naval captain who'd been attaché at the London embassy and was now the director of the Office of Naval Intelligence, the outfit to which Jack was immediately assigned in Washington. It was a no-sweat job that had him knocking out routine bulletins and briefing memos. While Jack considered the paper-pushing a waste of his time, it left him enough leisure to enjoy the distractions of the city's buzzing social life, to which the threat of imminent war added an extra charge of intensity.

His specific distraction at that moment was a Danish beauty he'd met through his sister Kathleen and was dazzled by. Inga Marie Arvad, or "Inga Binga," as Jack liked to call her, was working as a columnist at the *Washington Times-Herald,* where Kick was a research assistant to the executive editor. Four years older than he and European, she had just enough experience on him to be exciting. She'd acted in a couple of Danish films, and had married the director of one of them; in fact, she was still legally married to him when she was living in Washington.

Chuck Spalding, a Yalie Jack had met through Torby Macdonald the previous year and who now was one of his closest pals, watched the relationship heat up with fascination. "Her conversation was miles and miles ahead of everybody," he was to explain. "There was something adventurous about her. She'd done so much, been involved in so much. She was a fictional character almost, walking around. Of all the people that I ever saw him with I'd say she was the most compatible."

She cherished the memories of their wartime love affair for the rest of her life. "He had the charm that makes birds come out of their trees," was a description she would give.

Unfortunately, he wasn't the only one paying close attention to her. Washington was a hotbed of spies, obviously, each one masquerading as something else, and the FBI, led by J. Edgar Hoover, was keeping a close eye on all resident aliens. The Bureau's dossier on Inga contained enough to make her of serious interest to it, including one very explosive item: a photo of this gorgeous blonde in the company of the Führer himself.

That snapshot was a legacy of a stint she'd spent as a freelance reporter in Denmark, during which she'd gotten a tip, in early 1935, that the high-ranking Nazi Hermann Göring, a widower, was about to be married for the second time. Based on her scoop, she was assigned to cover the wedding that April, where she found herself being introduced to Hitler. Struck by the beautiful young Dane's embodiment of the perfect Nordic physical ideal, he invited her to come back to Berlin the following August to be his guest at the 1936 Olympics.

The FBI didn't like the looks of it. They refused to clear Arvad, suspecting her of being pro-Hitler or, worse yet, being a spy, using the *Herald-Examiner* job as a cover. They maintained surveillance of her comings and goings, being quite concerned about the company she was keeping, especially the time spent with the son of the rich former ambassador who backed appeasement.

Hoover's agents bugged Inga's rooms, and made voice recordings, with Jack clearly audible, which soon were in the files, testifying to the long weekends the couple spent together and Jack's love of risk-taking. Before long, Ensign Kennedy was given a new assignment and dispatched to a Southern naval base, more than four hundred miles away. It's likely the FBI had a hand in the transfer to Charleston, Hoover hoping to get him out of harm's way by re-moving the immediate temptation. At least, JFK thought so: "They shagged my ass down to South Carolina because I was going around with a Scandinavian blonde, and they thought she was a spy."

Away from the excitement of Washington, Jack quickly grew bored. Now, more than ever fed up with a desk job, what he wanted, above all, was to be where there was action. His pulse quickened by war fever, he could think only of getting to the front. Inga, who vis-ited him, took his grand, if still unclear, ambitions seriously. "If you can find something you really believe in, then, my dear, you caught the biggest fish in the ocean," she wrote. "You can pull it aboard, but don't rush it, there is still time."

The FBI, still on Inga's trail, found the pair sharing a February weekend at the Fort Sumter House hotel. Its agent reported the two left the hotel only for late-night meals and to attend church to-gether Sunday morning at the Catholic cathedral on Broad Street; young Kennedy was keeping up with church even as he shared a bed with Inga Binga.

Jack Kennedy, being a man of his times, felt the patriotic pull of service. His older brother had experienced the pull, too. Though Joe Jr., as in all things, had previously followed his father's lead, identify-ing with the isolationist America First movement, by the summer of 1941 he was training to be a navy pilot. It was truly a time of test-ing for such elite young men, suddenly having to square their belief systems with their consciences.

I talked to one of Joe's Choate classmates, Paul Ferber, then in his nineties, who'd never forgotten being at naval aviation school in Jacksonville, Florida, and running into young Joe there. He was deeply taken with his words. "I want to go over there and bomb the hell out of those Nazis!" Ferber, after all, was familiar with the anti-war sentiments of Joe's dad.

In July, Jack transferred to midshipman's school at Northwestern University, and from there applied to the Motor Torpedo Boat Squadron Training Center in Melville, Rhode Island. The essential conditions being looked for in the Melville recruits were exactly the ones he possessed, he told Lem. "I have applied for torpedo boat school under Lt. Bulkeley. The requirements are very strict physically. You have to be young, healthy and unmarried. As I am young, healthy and unmarried, I'm trying to get in."

Bulkeley was looking for hotshot junior officers used to handling high-powered speedboats and to the rigors of long sailing races. Fast thinking, teamwork, and endurance were everything. What this meant, then, was a group disproportionately Ivy League, ones who'd grown up summering in such places as coastal Maine or on Long Island Sound, where their families and friends belonged to yacht clubs. In other words, young men like Jack Kennedy.

Joining the PTs gave Jack the chance, finally, to command his own boat. His love of the sea is one of those things most people associate with him. Jack was proud of the Nantucket Sound sailing championship he'd earned. He and Joe had even been together on a victorious Harvard intercollegiate sailing team in '38, but now he was ready to be the skipper.

There in Rhode Island, he shared a Quonset hut with Torby Macdonald, who, with a little help from Jack's father, happily arrived to keep him company. After they completed their training and had their sights on the South Pacific, a snag arose when Jack received orders to stay stateside as an instructor. This time, political rescue came from on high in the person of Senator David I. Walsh of Massachusetts, chairman of the Committee on Naval Affairs.

Yet barely was that issue resolved when another crimp appeared in Jack's plans. It was his bad back and the pounding it could expect to suffer aboard a PT boat. While he got past muster, his health condition was precarious. No one knew this as well as Jack himself. Even going at half-speed, standing upright on these boats was as tough as riding a bucking bronco. One person this worried was Jack's father.

"Jack came home," he wrote Joe Jr., after Jack stopped for some R & R at Hyannis Port while at Melville, "and between you and me is having terrific trouble with his back." His son, ignoring all the danger signs, chose to make the best of it, preferring to get into the action rather than worry over its certain consequences for him.

He feared as much for what his sensitive gut would have to take. "I'm rather glad to be on my way," he wrote Lem, "although I understand that this South Pacific is not a place where you lie on a white beach with a cool breeze, while those native girls who aren't out hunting for your daily supply of bananas are busy popping grapes in your mouth. It would seem to consist of heat and rain and dysentery + cold beans, all of which won't of course bother anyone with a good stomach. If it's as bad as they say it is, I imagine I'll be voting Republican in '44."

Kennedy's first taste of the hazards of war came even before he reached his assigned PT base in the Solomon Islands, when his transport ship, an LST, was attacked by Japanese airplanes. A pilot, shot down and swimming off the side of his ship, was about to be picked up as a survivor. Then, just as the American crewmen prepared to begin the rescue, the flyer threw off his life jacket, pulled out a revolver he'd been hiding in the water, and fired two shots at the bridge, aiming for the ship's captain and other ranking officers.

Describing the scene to Lem, he wrote: "I had been praising the Lord and passing the ammunition right alongside—but that showed me a bit—the thought of him sitting in the water—battling an entire ship. We returned the fire with everything we had—the water boiled around him—but everyone was too surprised to shoot straight. Finally an old soldier standing next to me—picked up his rifle—fired once—and blew the top of his head off. He threw up his arms—plunged forward—and sank—and we hauled our ass out of there. That was the start of a very interesting month—and it brought home very strongly how long it is going to take to finish this war." What he'd now witnessed for himself was that the Japanese they were fighting were not only willing to risk their lives but to sacrifice them.

Lieutenant (JG) Kennedy found for himself a new world in the navy. His fellow officers posted to the South Pacific were, by the fact of their commissions, college men, and many from the Ivies. Yet there were also self-described "weed leaguers," young men from state universities. What united them all was merit; each had earned his place there. It was Jack's first time in such a company of dedicated equals, all facing the same discomforts and, of course, the same danger of getting killed.

"It's not bad here at all," he told Lem in one letter from Tulagi Island in the Solomons. "They have just opened up an Officers Club which consists of a tent. The liquor served is an alcoholic concoction which is drawn out of the torpedo tubes known as torp juice. Every night about 7:30 the tent bulges, about five men come crashing out, blow their lunch and swagger off to bed."

Soon he was collecting around himself new lifelong friends, just as he had at Choate and Harvard. One was Paul "Red" Fay, a Stanford grad whose father ran a San Francisco construction company. The two met when Fay, being instructed by Jack, ignored orders and got on the wrong PT boat. Kennedy dressed him down in powerful language Red Fay never forgot: "Do you realize that if what you did was compounded by every single person in the United States coming through training the war would be won by the Japs inside of three months!" Trust a pair of Irishmen to start a good friendship with a good fight.

One day Bill Battle, another officer on Tulagi, noticed that all the Catholics, including Jack Kennedy and Red Fay, seemed to head off each afternoon to visit the chaplain, Charlie Webster, who'd played football at Princeton and was now a Franciscan. It turned out that Father Webster was doubling as a bartender, complete with his own stock of medicinal alcohol of some kind. Kennedy, who hardly ever drank, would join them for the ritual but spend more of his time reading and writing letters. "Jack was a big letter writer," one of his crew members attested. But Jack would join other Catholics on a boat trip every Sunday to nearby Sesape Island for mass.

"Getting out every night on patrol," he wrote his parents in May 1943. "On good nights it's beautiful—the water is amazingly phosphorescent—flying fishes which shine like lights are zooming around and you usually get two or three porpoises who lodge right under the bow and no matter how fast the boat goes keep just about six inches ahead of the boat."

He had found an unexpected comfort in the South Pacific. "That laugh of his," Red later recalled, "the laugh was so contagious that it'd make everybody laugh." Jim Reed was another friend Jack made for life out there. "There was an aura around him that I've never seen duplicated in anybody else. He had a light touch and a serious side," said Reed. He once tossed a book onto an officer's bed. "Get acquainted with this damn war," he told him. "Read my favorite book by my favorite author." It was *Why England Slept*.

Kennedy loved mocking the brass that made occasional visits to the front lines. "Just had an inspection by an Admiral," he wrote Inga. "He must have weighed over three hundred, and came bursting through our hut like a bull coming out of chute three." He went on to satirize the flag officer's recent trip: the absurd questions, the vain jottings down of the obvious, the "inane" comment before he "toddled off to stoke his furnace at the luncheon table . . . That, Binga, is total war at its totalest."

Finding comedy around him always enlarged the picture. "His back was troubling him, he wasn't well," Jim Reed recalled. "But I can tell you this about Jack—he never complained. He always had a terrific humor—a really acute sense of humor. He was very self-deprecating. He claimed to me once that he'd never had an unhappy day in his life. Now, whether or not he'd had an unhappy child-hood, he'd come to fall back on his inner resources. He loved to read. He was curious—he had a natural curiosity about anything." Jack Kennedy often slept with a plywood board under him or, some-times, even stretched out on a table. In another officer's most vivid memory, he recalled a day when Jack paced worriedly, holding his torn sacroiliac belt and looking for someone who could lend him a needle and thread. He would rely on that corset for much of his life.

When he did beef, he reserved his sounding-off for the offi-cers above him and the orders they issued. Such predictable behav-ior eventually won him the nickname "Shafty." If he got handed a crappy assignment, he'd say, "I've been shafted"—although, with his accent, it came out as "shofted."

Out there in the middle of nowhere, talk was one of the only entertainments, and Jack preferred political discussions. "What's the purpose of having the conflict," Red Fay recalled him asking during one of these sessions, "if we're going to come out here and fight and let the people that got us here get us back into it again?" He was constantly asking questions. "We'd sit in a corner and I'd recall all the political problems in New Jersey and Long Island where I come from," the PT commander at the Russell Islands base would recall. "He did that with everybody. He had a way of really picking your brain if you knew something he didn't," recalled another officer. "He loved sitting around talking with a bunch of guys, and he'd come out with these remarks—remarks like you'd never forget."

There were twelve crewmen aboard Jack's command vessel, *PT 109*—the same number as the Muckers. The job of the PTs in the Russell Islands that August of 1943 was to patrol the Blackett Strait and attack Japanese convoys passing through. His trial by fire would come at 2:30 a.m. on August 2. It was pitch black. There was no radar. Only one of the three engines was running, standard procedure because the propellers stirred up the water, creating that phosphorescent light that Jack had told his parents was so beautiful, signaling their presence to Japanese planes patrolling overhead.

Barney Ross, one of his crewmen, thought he saw a shape out there in the darkness. Jack pegged it as another PT boat, and got consensus. But as it grew larger, the skipper became concerned. "Lenny, look at this," he told his executive officer. "Ship at two o'clock!" a crewman shouted. Ross, who'd believed the oncoming vessel was running parallel, now saw it turning toward him.

"Sound general quarters!" Lieutenant Kennedy ordered. He spun the wheel to the left in preparation for firing their torpedoes. But, operating on just the single engine, it was sluggish. Before a thirty-degree turn could be effected, a Japanese destroyer, heading at 40 knots, suddenly rammed them through. Jack was thrown hard to the deck, where, lying there, he thought to himself, *This is how it feels to be killed*. He then watched as the Japanese ship passed him, only a few feet away.

All this had happened in less than fifteen seconds.

In the darkness now, the only sound was the burning gasoline. Jack began to call out, "Who's aboard?" Only five crewmen answered. Spotting fire just twenty feet away, he ordered them all to abandon ship.

Pappy McMahon, the chief engineer, now in the separated stern of the plywood boat, found himself in far worse trouble. The flaming gasoline all around him had burned his face and hands, scorched his shins. Burning fuel continued to collect as he sank deeper into the water, the orange glare now above him.

Jack, having taken a place with the five others in the bow, realized what was happening and instantly headed to Pappy's rescue. Removing his shoes, shirt, and revolver, he dived into the water, wearing his rubber life belt, to search for the rest of his crew. Finding McMahon, he saw at once that his engineer was unable to use his badly burned arms. "Go on, Skipper," McMahon mumbled. "You go on. I've had it."

Jack grabbed McMahon's life jacket and began towing him to the floating bow, which had by this point drifted a fair distance away. Another crewman, Harris, was also losing heart. His leg was badly injured, making it difficult to swim. He wanted to stop trying, but Jack kept rallying him. "Come on! Where are you, Harris?" The crewman swore at his skipper, finally all but giving up. "I can't go any farther."

"For a guy from Boston, you're certainly putting up a great exhibition out here, Harris." Jack was not going to leave him behind. "Well, come on!" he kept at him, purposely ignoring Harris's bad leg. He then helped him take off the sodden sweater that was weighing him down, and that made a big difference. Harris could now move through the water.

When the two reached the part of the boat that was still afloat, Jack took roll. Ten answered this time, all but Harold Marney and Andrew Kirksey. Could anyone spot them? For the rest of the night the crew called out the two names, to no avail.

When dawn came, the hull flipped over on its back, becoming turtlelike. Slowly, it began to sink in the water, making it clear it wasn't going to last through another night. By midday, Jack announced they'd soon have to abandon what was left of *PT 109* and try to make it to land before too late in the day. He didn't want the hull to sink in the middle of the night, and knew it would if they stayed. By two o'clock in the afternoon, they were ready to go.

Each man was well aware of the gruesome stories about Japanese treatment of prisoners, which included horrific torture. The problem was, many of the islands around them were known to be occupied by the enemy.

"There's nothing in the book about a situation like this," Kennedy had told his crew that morning at daybreak. "A lot of you men have families and some of you have children. What do you want to do? I have nothing to lose." Jim Maguire, a fellow Catholic who'd gone to church regularly with Jack, found this hard to believe. The skipper, he felt sure, had a lot to live for.

There was also the question of Pappy McMahon, with his terribly seared flesh. And half the crew members couldn't swim. Their skipper's solution was to order nine of them to hang on to a floating eight-foot plank they luckily found nearby. Not only would this keep them together, but it would increase the nonswimmers' chances.

Lieutenant Kennedy then calmly pulled out his knife, cutting loose a strap of McMahon's life jacket and taking it between his teeth. He intended to tow him that way. The engineer never forgot his matter-of-fact manner. To him, the skipper seemed almost casual, as if he did it all the time. "I'll take McMahon with me," Jack told them. Next, he issued the order "The rest of you can swim together on this plank." Lenny Thom was put in charge.

When one seaman expressed aloud the fear that they'd never get out of this, Kennedy disagreed. "It can be done!"

For four hours they were out there in the water, their skipper pulling his engineer by his teeth and all the while keeping watch on his crew. Fortunately, the Pacific water was warm. For four hours

Jack Kennedy plowed on, halting his breaststroke only occasionally to rest. The man he was pulling, meanwhile, hadn't a clue his rescuer suffered from a bad back, slept on a sheet of plywood, and wore a corset for support. As McMahon floated on his back, he had nothing to do but look up at the sky. He was always aware of the rhythmic tugs of the skipper's arm strokes. He would remember most the sound of Jack's hard breathing.

Plum Pudding Island, named for its shape, was the length of a football field and two thirds as wide at the middle. It had a few palm trees on it, like an island in a *New Yorker* cartoon. When he finally made it, Jack could only lie panting on the sand. And when he went to stand, he vomited from swallowing so much seawater. Soon his crew also reached the beach, all clutching the plank.

Back at base, a very sad Red Fay was writing his sister: "George Ross has lost his life for a cause that he believed in stronger than any one of us, because he was an idealist in the purest sense. Jack Kennedy, the Ambassador's son, was on the same boat. The man who said that the cream of a nation is lost in war can never be accused of making an overstatement of a very cruel fact."

Jim Reed would recall: "The next morning we heard that *PT 109* hadn't returned and they'd seen an explosion and a fire. I was very sad. I couldn't believe it." Of Kennedy, he said, "He had many friends here, almost everybody knew him. He was very well liked."

Meanwhile, on Plum Pudding Island, Kennedy was conferring with Thom and Ross. "How are we going to get out of here?" he wanted to know. But, in fact, he already had a plan. What he intended to do, Jack told them, was to swim out on his own into Ferguson Passage that night to try to signal a ship.

Hanging his .38 pistol on a lanyard around his neck, he wrapped a flashlight in a life jacket to keep it afloat and headed off at sundown, knowing the PT boats went out on patrol then. Since no one had yet come to get them, he was thinking aggressively and taking matters into his own hands.

There was little point in just camping out there on that island, waiting for the Japanese to butcher them. If and when he spotted a PT boat, he'd try to draw attention by firing three shots in the air and signaling with the flashlight. There was no other choice.

Kennedy reached his destination at eight o'clock and stayed in place four hours. When no PT boats had appeared, he began the long swim back to the island. Unfortunately, he was caught in a powerful current that swept him past Plum Pudding. Drifting south, and after passing out several times, he stopped to sleep on a sandbar. The next morning he awoke and found his way back to his men. He arrived at noontime, looking scrawny and exhausted, with yellow skin and bloodshot eyes. He vomited again, and passed out.

Opening his eyes, he saw Barney Ross. He managed to say only, "Barney, you try it tonight," before, a second later, conking out.

The next day, Kennedy decided they needed to move to a nearby, larger island. Again, he assembled his men on that eight-foot plank. Again, he swam on, dragging the badly burned Pappy by the strap held in his teeth. Still there was no sign of rescue, and all they had to drink was the rainfall they captured in their mouths as they lay in a storm. The day after that, Kennedy and Ross swam to yet another island, Nauru.

There, they came upon some very welcome surprises—a dugout canoe, a fifty-five-gallon drum filled with freshwater, and a crate of crackers and candy. Exhausted, Ross fell asleep for the night, while Kennedy took the dugout back in the dark with the water and candy, supplies presumably left by the Japanese, to his crew.

This time he was greeted not just by his men but by two island-ers who'd unexpectedly arrived and had gotten a fire going. They were helping the Americans. Jack used his pocketknife to scratch a message on a coconut shell: NAURO ISL NATIVE KNOWS POSIT HE CAN PILOT 11 ALIVE NEED SMALL BOAT KENNEDY. Handing it to them, he told the islanders where they must take it. "Rendova . . . Rendova," he repeated.

When the *PT 109* crewmen awoke the next morning, a large canoe was just arriving on the beach. From it stepped eight islanders, who presented Lieutenant Kennedy with a letter that read: "On His Majesty's Service / To the Senior Officer / Nauru Island / I have learned of your presence on Nauru Island. I am in command of a New Zealand infantry operating in conjunction with US Army troops on New Georgia. I strongly advise that you come with these natives to me. Lt. Winscote."

Their friends waiting for them on the base at Rendova were so happy to see them they cried. Jack became angry when a fellow officer said he'd had a mass said for his soul.

"Kennedy's Son Is Hero in Pacific as Destroyer Splits His PT Boat," read the *New York Times* headline on August 20, 1943. The *New York Herald Tribune* told its readers that John F. Kennedy had written a "blazing new saga in PT boat annals."

A more personal commendation would come from a fellow officer, Dick Keresey, writing years later. "As a captain, Jack Kennedy was a man of courage, a good PT-boat man, and he was good company. Ranking the virtue of good company on a level with the other two may have been peculiar to those on PT boats. We were almost always on the front lines. We knew it was time to pack when the base got showers. When the movies showed up, we were long gone. So we were highly dependent on conversation to divert ourselves, and Kennedy was a good listener and an amusing talker. Our conversation was seldom deep and never about future plans, for this brought bad luck."

Jack had his own account, which he mailed to Inga, and it wasn't what made it into the headlines and news stories. It's a testament to his writing ability—but also to his heart.

He typed it in block letters on a navy typewriter:

The war goes slowly here, slower than you can ever imagine from reading the papers at home. The only way you can get the proper perspective on its progress is put away the headlines for a month and watch us move on the map. It's deathly slow. The Japs have dug deep, and with the possible exception of a couple of Marine divisions are the greatest jungle fighters in the world. Their willingness to die for a place like Munda gives them a tremendous advantage over us. We, in aggregate, just don't have the willingness. Of course, at times, an individual will rise up to it, but in total, no . . . Munda or any of those spots are just God damned hot stinking corners of small islands in a group of islands in a part of the ocean we all hope to never see again.

We are at a great disadvantage—the Russians could see their country invaded, the Chinese the same. The British were bombed, but we are fighting on some islands belonging to the Lever Company, a British concern making soap. I suppose if we were stockholders we would perhaps be doing better, but to see that by dying at Munda you are helping to secure peace in our time takes a larger imagination than most possess . . . The Japs have this advantage: because of their feeling about Hirohito, they merely wish to kill. An American's energies are divided: he wants to kill but he also is trying desperately to prevent himself from being killed.

The war is a dirty business. It's very easy to talk about the war and beating the Japs if it takes years and a million men, but anyone who talks like that should consider well his words. We get so used to talking about billions of dollars, and millions of soldiers, that thousands of casualties sound like drops in the bucket. But if those thousands want to live as much as the ten I saw, the people deciding the whys and wherefores had better make mighty sure that all this effort is headed for some definite goal, and that when we reach that goal we may say it was worth it, for if it isn't, the whole thing will turn to ashes, and we will face great trouble in the years to come after the war.

I received a letter today from the wife of my engineer, who was so badly burnt that his face and hands were just flesh, and he was that way for six days. He couldn't swim, and I was able to help him, and his wife thanked me, and in her letter she said, "I suppose to you it was just part of your job, but Mr. McMahon was part of my life and if he had died I don't think I would have wanted to go on living."

There are many McMahons that don't come through. There was a boy on my boat, only twenty-four, had three kids, one night, two bombs straddled our boat and two of the men were hit, one standing right next to me. He never got over it. He hardly ever spoke after that. He told me one night he thought he was going to be killed. I wanted to put him ashore to work. I wish I had. He was in the forward gun turret where the destroyer hit us.

I don't know what it all adds up to, nothing I guess, but you said that you figured I'd go to Texas and write my experiences. I wouldn't go near a book like that. This thing is so stupid, that while it has a sickening fascination for some of us, myself included, I want to leave it far behind when I go.

Inga Binga, I'll be glad to see you again. I'm tired now. We were riding every night, and the sleeping is tough in the daytime but I've been told they are sending some of us home to form a new squadron in a couple of months. I've had a great time here, everything considered, but I'll be just as glad to get away from it for a while. I used to have the feeling that no matter what happened I'd get through. It's a funny thing that as long as you have that feeling you seem to get through. I've lost that feeling lately but as a matter of fact I don't feel badly about it. If anything happens to me I have this knowledge that if I had lived to be a hundred I could only have improved the quantity of my life, not the quality. This sounds gloomy as hell. I'll cut it. You are the only person I'm saying it to. As a matter of fact knowing you has been the brightest point in an already bright twenty-six years.

"Now that I look back," he ended, "it has been a hell of a letter." He promised to visit her in L.A. when he got relieved of duty.

Jack Kennedy had endured an extraordinary rite of passage. Now there was a kinship with those he admired that went beyond just reading about them on the printed page—Churchill, for example, as a young man had escaped from the Boers, and then there was Hemingway, who'd been badly wounded driving an ambulance for the Italians—and so, in a real way, this linked him with them.

He was a young man who'd "proven himself on foreign soil," as an excited booster would soon declare. But for all that his courage and fortitude came to mean to others, it counted most with Jack himself. No other challenge he might face, he knew, would ever be as hard as had getting his men back to safety. He had met fear head-on, and it had changed him.

"On the bright side of an otherwise completely black time," he wrote his parents, "was the way that everyone stood up to it. Previous to that I had become somewhat cynical about the American as a fighting man. I had seen too much bellyaching and layout out here.

But with the chips down—that all faded away. I can now believe—which I never would have before—the stories of Bataan and Wake. For an American it's got to be awfully easy or awfully tough. When it's in the middle, then there's the trouble."

And in a letter to Lem that downplayed his individual heroism, he said: "We have been having a difficult time for the past two months—lost our boat a month ago when a Jap cut us in two + lost some of our boys. We had a bad time—a week on a Jap island—but finally got picked up—and have got another boat. It really makes me wonder if most success is merely a great deal of fortuitous accidents. I imagine I would agree with you that it was lucky the whole thing happened—if the two fellows had not been killed which rather spoils the whole thing for me."

At the same time he got off a letter to Lem's mother. He expressed his pride in what her son was doing with the American Field Service Ambulance Corps in North Africa.

Before leaving the South Pacific, Jack Kennedy made it his final task to ensure that all his crew members got back to the States. When he arrived there, too, he quickly found himself in familiar surroundings: another hospital room. The physical harm that had been done to him was immeasurable. Not only had he contracted tropical malaria, but the orthopedic diagnosis of "chronic disc disease of the lumbar area" was followed by the first of what would be many back operations. There was a second back surgery also that year, but neither that nor any subsequent one would provide the relief he sought.

Those who visited Chelsea Naval Hospital in Boston saw him lying there wracked, alternately, by chills and fever. Torby Macdonald offered his impression of Jack's case: "His skin had turned yellow. His weight had dropped from 160 pounds to about 125 pounds.

When I came into his room, he raised a bony hand and gave me a shaky wave." Jack insisted he felt "great." When Torby refused to believe him, the patient amended it to, "Great, considering the shape I'm in."

In June 1944, while still in Chelsea Naval Hospital, Jack was awarded the Navy and Marine Medal for "extremely heroic conduct." But medals don't mend bodies. Chuck Spalding, who visited him a little later after he'd gone down to Palm Beach to rest in the sunshine, gave this graphic account: "That wound was a savage wound, a big wound. It went maybe eight inches or so down his back. It would never heal and it was open and painful. He had to fight to get his back healed and I would walk up and down the beach with him with the back still open and he'd say 'How is it now?' or 'Is any stuff running out of it?' It was severe pain."

Spalding, who was himself a navy pilot, said, "I'll never forget Jack sitting at our table watching the 'home front.' All he felt was cynicism—everybody dancing, the lights, the women. It was the only time I ever saw him reacting like a real soldier. It was the rapidity of his move from the Pacific to Palm Beach, the juxtaposition."

That August, Joe Jr. was killed. He and his copilot had accepted a mission to fly a plane packed with 20,000 pounds of TNT toward a V3 site on the French coast, then parachute out before reaching the target. The idea was to create a guided missile, but before the two men could bail to safety, the deadly cargo detonated.

Jack, up at Hyannis Port when the telegram came, went out walking alone on the beach right after he heard. His brother had been the family standard-bearer and, in matters of politics, the prospective heir. The rivalry between the brothers, especially for the father's colors, had always been a part of their lives and endured right to the end.

There was a revealing story Jack heard about a farewell dinner for Joe, occurring just before Joe was sent to Britain as a naval aviator. It had taken place soon after accounts of Jack's Pacific ordeal were splashed across the front pages. One of the guests at the party, trying to do the right thing, had raised a glass to toast "Ambassador Joe Kennedy, the father of our hero, our own hero, Lieutenant John F. Kennedy of the United States Navy." However, Jack was absent. Joe was very much there.

Later that night, as it was reported to Jack, Joe was seen on his cot "clenching and unclenching his fists," saying to himself aloud, "By God, I'll show them." Jack understood that it had been his brother's desire to match, or even top, his own courage in the South Pacific that drove him to volunteer for the high-risk mission over Europe. In fact, when Joe Jr. perished in the line of duty, he'd already flown twenty-five combat missions, enough to permit him, honorably, to fly no more, but his fraternal competitive spirit was too deeply rooted: he simply couldn't stop trying to beat the younger brother who'd managed to pull ahead of him.

A month later, another terrible blow was dealt the Kennedys. In the spring, Jack's sister Kathleen, his beloved Kick, had married Billy Hartington, the elder son of the Duke of Devonshire and a major in the Coldstream Guards. Now he was declared a casualty in Belgium, causing Jack to write his grieving sister that Billy's death reminded him of Raymond Asquith, that other privileged Englishman whose promise was cut short on the battlefield.

Despite Jack's own triumph, the loss of a brother and a brother-in-law, each an aspirant to a career in the public arena, of necessity pushed his celebrated heroism into the background, at least for a time. It would soon be again prominent, however, for Joe's and Billy's deaths left him a legacy he was ready now to accept and the public would be ready to endorse. As one of Jack's supporters, himself a veteran, would later observe, World War II was Kennedy's "greatest campaign manager."

Jack fixed his sights on the 1946 U.S. congressional election. In this race, as in the British "khaki election" of 1900, civilians got the chance to reward the gallant service of the returning soldiers and sailors with their votes. The man who'd made his reputation saving men in wartime was about to test his mettle in a different theater—equally demanding but entirely different, one that would call on all the democratizing experience he'd gained in uniform.

The fun-loving Jack and the serious Jack would now find a mutual pursuit: politics.

13

14

Charlie Bartlett

Billy Sutton

15

Bunker Hill Day, 1946, with Dave Powers

CHAPTER FOUR

WAR HERO

It has been a strange experience and I shall never forget the succession of great halls packed with excited people until there was no room for a single person more, speech after speech, meeting after meeting—three, even four in a night—intermittent flashes of heat and light and enthusiasm with cold air and the rattle of the carriage in between: a great experience. And I improve every time. I have hardly repeated myself at all.

—Winston Churchill, from a
letter to Pamela Plowden, 1899

The biographies of all heroes contain common elements. Becoming one is the most important. With the physical courage of which he'd shown himself to be capable, Jack Kennedy had turned his years of frailty and private suffering into a personal and public confidence that would take him forward. In mythic terms, he'd also challenged his father's point of view on the war and bent it to his own. He'd experienced the loss not only of comrades in arms, but of the family's prince, his brother. Now, ahead of him loomed new ways for him to demonstrate the man he was becoming—and the leader he would be.

If Jack Kennedy didn't see at first the change he was undergoing when he was discharged from the navy in 1944 and then directly afterward, many around him certainly did. "It was written all over the sky that he was going to be something big," recalled one of his fellow officers.

Yet, as he was starting to look to the future, he couldn't let go of what he'd witnessed and what he'd learned. War marks you forever, and so there was one crucial idea he had grasped, which was that it was wrong. In conversations with other officers, he urged them to take the life of their country seriously when they got home, to prevent another war.

For his own part, he spoke as if he, himself, was on the brink of coming to grips with big decisions, of preparing to face them. His commanding officer, for one, commented on the changes in Lieutenant Kennedy that started to be evident at this point: "I think there was probably a serious side to Kennedy that started evolving at that time that had not existed before."

Now came the fortuitous: his secret illnesses could now be worn as public honors. His chronic bad back would from this era on be attributed to his war injuries. When the noted writer John Hersey, who chronicled Jack's South Pacific exploits for the *New Yorker*, made the assumption it was the result of the *PT 109* collision and all those hours spent hauling a helpless man through the water, Kennedy let it pass.

All of the other old troubles continued to plague him, especially his serious stomach problems, but they were now morphing into part of his new biography, or new image, just as the bad back was. Scarily thin and still sallow of complexion, Jack met new people and made new acquaintances who immediately chalked up his strange appearance to the malaria and other lingering effects of the PT-boat ordeal. What had been the hidden facts of life were now a statement to the man on the street—especially those meeting him face-to-face for the first time, as soon they would—of his very real heroism.

Everyone has written that Jack Kennedy needed to be dragooned into running for Congress in 1946. Everyone, that is, except the people who really knew him. The solitary walk he took on the beach at Hyannis after getting the news about Joe Jr. must have involved, along with the grief, recognition of a coming swerve on his life's path. The personal landscape he'd long taken for granted had rearranged itself around him, and so, too, had the expected demands. He was ready, it turned out, to welcome them.

Many aspects of the man were coming together. Jack had run for student office, majored in government. The reading interests that he'd maintained so steadily—memoirs and history, news stories and political currents, world affairs—had culminated in *Why England Slept*, his thesis-turned-best-seller. It had shown his skills as a first-hand observer of history. He'd been planning to go to law school, specializing in international law.

I should add that he liked poetry—Tennyson's "Ulysses" was a favorite, as were the poems sent from the front in World War I by a fellow Harvard man, Alan Seeger, who died on a French battlefield. Yet Jack, despite his childhood built on books, resisted the artistic sensibility. Though he was comfortable with the arts, the poetry that drew him was about mission and dedication, courage and overcoming obstacles. A great example are these several lines from "Ulysses"—

I am become a name;
For always roaming with a hungry heart

Much have I seen and known,—cities of men
And manners, climates, councils, governments,
Myself not least, but honour'd of them all;
And drunk delight of battle with my peers,
Far on the ringing plains of windy Troy.
I am a part of all that I have met;

Even in the far-off Solomon Islands—where, like Ulysses, he'd "suffer'd greatly" on a "dim sea"—he'd kept up lively conversations with his messmates about all the subjects that most fascinated him: indeed, "cities of men and manners, climates, councils, governments."

When he returned stateside and was required to put in more hospital time, with everything else on hold, the idea of attending law school continued to be his operative plan right up through early 1945. "I'm returning to law school at Harvard in the fall," he wrote Lem Billings, "and then if something good turns up while I am there I will run for it. I have my eye on something pretty good now if it comes through." That "something good" may well have been the seat for the 11th Congressional District of Massachusetts, a district that included Cambridge.

In the pre–Civil War nineteenth century, that seat had been held by John Quincy Adams, also a Harvard man, and the country's sixth president; it was the only time a president had served in the House after leaving the White House. At the moment, the seat was occupied by the old-style Irish pol James Michael Curley, now nearing the end of a legendary career that would, by its close, include not just four terms as Boston's mayor but also two stints in prison.

Curley, now, was about to abandon his congressional post to run again for mayor. Jack knew this because Joseph P. Kennedy, Sr., freshly involved in local political matters, was bankrolling the rascal.

His son knew it but he kept it to himself, as he took one last try at another career possibility.

His father wrangled him a job stringing for the Chicago *Herald-American,* a Hearst paper. His assignment was to cover the founding conference of the United Nations in San Francisco. He'd be reporting the historic event "from the point of view of the ordinary GI."

The city was hopping when he got there, with men and women on hand from all over the world. Fifty nations sent delegates to the conference, which began in late April 1945 and lasted two months. FDR had just died, leaving his vice president, Harry Truman, in the White House. Everyone knew World War II was nearing its close. Out in San Francisco the politically connected of every stripe were there to see and be seen, to hobnob and network amid the carnival-like atmosphere.

For Jack Kennedy, the U.N. Conference was the right place at the right moment, offering as it did an irresistible mix of high ideals and high life. It gave him a view of the political arena that now beckoned him. The atmosphere he found himself immersed in was electric with the sounds and sights of a new world being born.

Wherever he went, Kennedy worked contacts both old and new, honing his skills at making professional allies out of social friends, and vice versa. You never knew where you'd see him, but he seemed to be everywhere. For instance, when he hosted a briefing on Russia by the diplomat and Soviet scholar Charles "Chip" Bohlen, he found himself in distinguished company that included the British foreign minister, Anthony Eden, and the U.S. ambassador to the Soviet Union, Averell Harriman.

Along for the ride in San Francisco were two of Jack's pals: Red Fay and Chuck Spalding. For the former he'd wangled the boondoggle of acting as his aide at the conference, while Chuck Spalding somehow was hanging out on the strength of a best-selling book he'd cowritten, *Love at First Flight,* a memoir of his wartime training experience. Young men home from the front, they managed to share laughs despite all the speeches and earnestness, including one memorable moment that occurred in the midst of Bohlen's deadly serious analysis of Soviet intentions.

It was Jack who first noticed the elegant Harriman had slipped away from the room in the Palace Hotel where the briefing was taking place, and out onto the balcony with a young woman. "I give him about two more minutes, and then he's going to hang himself," Jack whispered to Fay. Focused on Bohlen, Fay wondered why his pal would say such a thing.

"I'm not talking about Bohlen," Kennedy shot back. "I'm talking about Harriman!"

Also in the group with whom Jack socialized at the conference were Cord Meyer, another young veteran with big political hopes, and his attractive, vivacious wife, Mary. Meyer, at this time, was an aide to the Republican presidential candidate Harold Stassen, but would go on to join the CIA.

For Kennedy, the business at hand was not just about filing stories or making the scene. As always, it was his curiosity that drove and excited him. He seemed particularly intrigued by the Soviet delegation, led by the coldly robotic Vyacheslav Molotov.

Along with the rest of the world, he'd seen President Roosevelt concede the territories of Eastern Europe to Josef Stalin at the Yalta Conference that February, only weeks before his death. Critics saw this concession of important strategic and autonomous lands to the Soviets as an unconscionable giveaway to a soon-to-be enemy.

FDR's failing health might have been a factor in the outcome at Yalta; there on the shore of the Black Sea, he was pushing himself hard and losing the battle with his own body. But equally at play were other factors that Kennedy, with his growing fascination with the way nations behaved, saw and grasped.

But if he didn't like the agreement Roosevelt had signed off on, he was able to assess it from more than one perspective. He knew his history, and saw clearly the unyielding strength of Russian nationalism. Napolean had invaded her in 1812. To repel the Grand Army, the Russians had been forced to burn Moscow. Now, in the middle of the twentieth century, the Russians, once again invaded, were facing the harsh fact that they'd lost 20 million people fighting the Germans mostly on Russian soil, with their Allies slow to open a second front.

Jack Kennedy was displaying an ability to regard an adversary's situation without emotion. In one of the pieces that ran in the *Herald-American* under his byline, he offered his own take on how the Soviets thought, and he ended it by reminding his readers of "the heritage of 25 years of distrust between Russia and the rest of the world that cannot be overcome completely for a good many years."

Also, true to his mission, he held the perspective of the fighting American home from the front.

When Victory in Europe Day came—on May 8, during the conference's second week—Jack responded by writing eloquently in the *Herald-American*: "Any man who had risked his life for his country and seen his friends killed around him must inevitably wonder why this has happened to him and most important what good will it do. It is perhaps normal that they would be disappointed with what they have seen in San Francisco. I suppose that this is inevitable. Youth is a time for direct action and simplification. To come from battlefields where sacrifice is the order of the day—to come from there to here—it is not surprising that they should question the worth of their sacrifice and feel somewhat betrayed."

In a letter to one of his war buddies, he phrased his message more bluntly: "We must face the truth that the people have not been horrified by war to a sufficient extent to force them to go to any extent rather than have another war."

Chuck Spalding, keeping an eye on his friend as well as on the tone of his articles, was starting to draw his own conclusions. "Either wittingly or unwittingly, he began to write as a politician." Just as in the South Pacific, he was acting more as a leader than as an observer. "The war makes less sense to me now," Jack wrote, "than it ever made and that was little enough—and I would really like—as my life's goal—in some way at home or at some time to do something to help prevent another."

While still on the job in San Francisco, Jack learned his next assignment was to be London. There he'd be reporting on the fierce political struggle taking place as the British home-front coalition broke down. The opposition Labour Party was going all out to contest Prime Minister Winston Churchill's Conservative government in the first postwar British general election. For Jack, it was a chance to see his most enduring hero fight for his political life, and yet he was stunned. How could Churchill, whose indomitable leadership had meant so much to his nation in wartime, now be in such serious trouble?

What Jack was about to learn is how quickly economic concerns replaced wartime loyalties. The war had been hard on the British working class and, suddenly, voters were remembering how the Conservatives had supported appeasement of the Germans before the war. The same Tories were now clinging to power with warnings of socialist dictatorship. But, more to the point in the postwar climate, the Tories were preaching belt-tightening. Just when the people were looking for a break from the depressed economy—the rationing, the empty cupboards—they were being promised more of the same.

Unfortunately, when the votes were counted, both Jack's front-row position and his empathy didn't help his critical judgment. Unable to imagine a Labour victory, he filed a wrap-up election piece predicting a close Tory win. He wasn't alone; Churchill's overwhelming defeat was a shock to many.

While in England, Jack took advantage of the opportunity to catch up with old friends. One of them, Alistair Forbes, registered this impression: "He struck me then that he was more intellectual than any other member of the family. He read more. He had a fantastically good instinct, once his attention was aroused to a problem, for getting the gist of it and coming to a mature judgment about it. He had a detachment which reminded me very much of Winston Churchill in the sense that his life had been protected by money."

Another friend, Hugh Fraser, who was running for Parliament himself at the time, saw him similarly. "He was always a great questioner. He always asked an enormous number of questions. He was very interested in things. For every one question I asked him he asked two at least." "Political to his fingertips" is how the British economist Barbara Ward recalled him. "He asked every sort of question of what were the pressures, what were the forces at work, who supported what." Such curiosity, such a need to inform himself and to sift carefully through what he was learning, would always form part of his m.o.

During this period, when he was pounding out stories for afternoon newspaper readers in Chicago, Kennedy also kept a personal diary. The entries in it further reveal him as unable to move past the idea of war's deadliness: "We have suffered the loss of nearly 8 hundred thousand young men—many of whom might become the leadership we will so desperately need."

What's more, he wrote presciently—somehow intuiting the existence of the atomic bomb, which wasn't yet publicly known—of what he saw in the future. "The clash may be finally and indefinitely postponed by the eventual discovery of a weapon so horrible that it will truthfully mean the abolishment of all the nations employing it. Thus science, which has contributed to much of the horror of war, will still be the means of bringing it to an end."

When it came to the ideological currents back home, he was critical of FDR. "Mr. Roosevelt has contributed greatly to the end of Capitalism in our own country, although he would probably argue the point at some point. He has done this, not through the laws which he sponsored or were passed during his Presidency, but rather through the emphasis he put on rights rather than responsibilities."

In Europe, Kennedy saw the brutality of the Russians to the vanquished Germans. "People did not realize what was going on in the concentration camps. In many ways, the 'SS' were as bad as the Russians." But he predicted the Red Army's treatment of defeated Berlin, especially its women, would leave a lasting mark.

As he was returning home from Europe—stopping briefly in London—he became alarmingly sick. His traveling companion at the time reported that it had "scared the hell out" of him, and that he'd never before seen anyone run such a high fever. It lasted for several days. When it was over, Jack claimed it had just been his malaria acting up.

Around Thanksgiving, his health improved, and he was back with his family at Hyannis Port. Rip Horton remembers watching him as he practiced with a tape recorder. "He made me speak into it and then played back the tape . . . and your voice always sounds awful to you. That was the first indication as to where his inclinations were then leading him."

Soon, though, Jack was being up front with his close friends about his intentions. "I've made up my mind," he told Chuck Spalding. "I'm going into politics."

"Geez, that's terrific," Spalding replied. "You can go all the way!"

Taken aback by such confidence from a close friend, Kennedy asked, "Really?"

"All the way!" Spalding recalls repeating.

Years later, Spalding explained that he'd believed Jack was one of those who'd come out of the war experience whole. "He was never pushed off this hard, sensible center of his being. I think he was beginning to get a kind of picture of himself. I think the picture of a public figure interested and capable in this area added to the dim outline of a successful politician."

Lem Billings, who by then was in the navy—he had used new contact lenses to get past the physical—took a similar view. "A lot of stories have been written and said about it. I think a lot of people say that if Joe hadn't died, Jack might never have gone into politics. I don't believe this. Nothing could have kept Jack out of politics. I think this is what he had in him, and it just would have come out, no matter what. Somewhere along the line, he would have been in politics. Knowing his abilities, interests, and background, I firmly believe he would have entered politics even had he had three older brothers like Joe."

When Jack asked Torby Macdonald what he thought of his running for Congress, his former college roommate—who'd grown up in a town near Boston—flatly stated that if his friend ran, he'd win.

Of all Jack's best pals, Red Fay was the sharpest in seeing Jack's inner directedness. When Jack told him of the pressure he was getting from his father—"I tell you, Dad is ready right now and can't understand why his fine son Jack isn't ready"—Fay understood that that wasn't actually the whole story. "Although Jack shammed indifference to the whole idea of a political career, there was an underlying determination to get started on what he considered a very serious obligation. I wasn't surprised early in 1946 when he made a very serious decision to run for Congress—and when he asked me to come east to campaign for him, I came."

It was about this time that he met a new friend, Charlie Bartlett, down in Florida. "We were down there after the war, and, you know, gorgeous women were all getting divorces down there, and they were really good-looking girls. It was very upbeat, the whole thing, and I went to Palm Beach. My family lived in Hobe Sound. We drove down for the evening and went to this place called Taboo. And they had an orchestra and I was with a very, very pretty girl who was getting a divorce and it turned out she knew Jack and Jack came over and sat down and started telling me about his plans to go into politics. And I said, 'Well, I'm getting ready to go into the newspaper business.' And he said, 'Well, you know, I've been there now and I haven't been very deep but I have to tell you, you don't get anything done. You can't make changes. There's no impact. I'm going to go into politics and see if you can really do anything.'"

Bartlett, a sixth-generation Yalie, would be Jack's close friend from that day forward.

Jack knew the leap he was taking in running for Congress. "I had never lived very much in the district," he admitted years later. "My roots were there, my family roots were there. But I had lived in New York for ten years and on top of that I had gone to Harvard, not a particularly popular institution at that time in the 11th Congressional District. But I started early, in my opinion the most important key to political success, in December before the primary election next June."

Charlie Bartlett recalled the conversation they had. "He was very clear about his decision to go into Congress. Sometimes you read that he was a reluctant figure being dragooned into politics by his father. I really didn't get that impression at all. I gathered that it was a wholesome, full-blown wish on his own part."

Jack Kennedy's own thoughts support his friend's memory: "A reporter is reporting what happens, he's not making it happen, even the good reporters, the ones that are really fascinated by what happens and who find real stimulus by putting their noses into the center of the action, even they in a sense are in a secondary profession. It's reporting what happens, but it isn't participating."

By the time he made his decision, Jack, at the age of twenty-eight, possessed a level of intellectual preparation for public office uncommon even to seasoned career politicians. He had wrestled with the big-picture issues of war and peace in the 1930s, had survived the most extreme hazards of war, and been a firsthand observer of major international events. What he lacked was any practical grounding in the business of politics.

The fact that his father would take care of what the political types call the "wholesale"—the media, the press relations—hardly let him off the hook. The relentless workaday demands of a campaign lay ahead. He, the candidate, had to be the one to master the "retail," which meant not just meeting voters one on one and winning them over, but inspiring them to join the effort. If you couldn't connect with voters, then your other advantages, in the end, counted for little.

With the help of a local PR firm, Jack would soon be making the rounds of community groups: VFW and American Legion posts, Lions and Rotary Club meetings, communion breakfasts and Holy Name societies. This was a new world to him. But it was a necessary part of achieving his ambition, and he did it all. Writing his stump speech himself, he drew on his recent travels as a reporter in Great Britain and Germany, but always made sure to emphasize his recent stopover in Ireland.

Simultaneously, Jack decided to teach himself about being Irish. The diary he'd been keeping in Europe now contained a number of scribbled book titles accompanied by their Dewey decimal numbers. He'd always liked to connect to knowledge through reading, and, on that score, nothing had changed. *Ireland and the President of the United States, Ireland in America, Ireland's Contribution to the Law,* and *Irish American History of the US* are some of the volumes he listed.

He was also soliciting the reactions of local political figures to his potential candidacy. But when he called on them, especially the Irish ones, he wasn't just making the mandatory courtesy visits, he was brushing up against the city's history. "For all Irish immigrants, the way in Boston was clearly charted," he dictated in a memo years later. "The doors of business were shut; the way to rise above being a laborer was politics."

His own path, he acknowledged, had been a privileged one. Being third-generation and not first makes a difference. "I had in politics, to begin with, the great advantage of having a well-known name and that served me in good stead. Beyond that I was a stranger to begin with and I still have a notebook which is filled page after page with the names of all the new people I met back there in that first campaign."

One of the new acquaintances was a fellow by the name of Dan O'Brien, who was skeptical about the young man's chances. After meeting him, Jack came away with these jotted-down impressions: "Says I'll be murdered—No personal experience—A personal district—Says I don't know 300 people personally. Says I should become Mike Neville's secretary. O'Brien says the attack on me will be—1. Inexperience 2. Injury to me: me . . . father's reputation. He is the first man to bet me that I can't win! An honest Irishman but a mistaken one."

The candidate also recorded maxims that applied to the situation. Among them:

- In politics you don't have friends—you have confederates.
- One day they feed you honey—the next will find fish caught in your throat.
- You can buy brains but you can't buy—loyalty.
- The best politician is the man who does not think too much of the political consequence of his every act.

He also noted: "The one great failure of American government is the government of critics." Making the rounds and learning the ropes, he'd quickly recognized, as every politician must, the impossibility of pleasing everyone.

Now, for the first time in his life, Jack needed to make friends on a basis other than compatibility. Living on Beacon Hill, a young bachelor with no fixed address beyond rooms in the historic Bellevue Hotel, he lacked roots in the local community and needed to establish himself. The most important task was to enlist supporters who'd spent their lives in the district and would come on board, willing to stand up for him. While you could always hire a few professionals, the vast army needed for a win had to be made up of volunteers, those who helped him because they decided to.

The first hire was Billy Sutton, four years older than Jack and just discharged from the army. His description of the Jack of those days was a thin, bright-eyed figure with his hair cut close on the sides. Billy—whom I got to know well many years later—said that Jack had reminded him of the young Charles Lindbergh.

Before the war Billy had made himself useful in local politics as a result of his job checking gas meters, which naturally put him in touch with a wide variety of people. But he was the kind of guy who loved talking to anyone, and so, with Billy as his guide, Jack began trudging up and down the three-deckers of the old neighborhoods, introducing himself and asking for support. The person most surprised by this was his father. What Joseph Kennedy had yet to realize was the way the navy had changed his second son. The young man who returned from the Solomon Islands was not the one who'd left for there in early 1943, and a large part of the reason the experience so altered him was because it offered continual exposure to people unlike himself, from all over the country and from every walk of life.

The fact that he was a returning serviceman was a key factor from the start. Working-class fellows like Sutton—and, later, Dave Powers, who'd served with the Flying Tigers—were ready to accept a young rich guy who'd been awarded the Navy and Marine Corps Medal with a citation for "extremely heroic conduct." What convinced Powers was witnessing Jack's appearance before a group of Gold Star Mothers, those women who'd lost sons fighting in the war. "I think I know how you feel," he told them, "because my mother is a Gold Star Mother, too." When Powers heard Kennedy say that and saw the reaction, he signed on and never would stop working for his new boss.

What Jack Kennedy brought to the table, besides his sterling war record and those well-known Boston names—Kennedy and Fitzgerald—was his obvious affection for the old Irish world he now was entering. He loved hearing his grandfather's stories, from "Honey Fitz" himself, the city's long-ago mayor and congressman.

Not surprisingly, the daily slog of introducing himself to constituents was not quite compatible with a chronic back problem, not when it meant going up and down the stairs of multifamily houses day after day. Come early afternoon, Jack would take a nap, then continue the trudge of one-on-one campaigning on into the night. He did this for months, and not everyone liked to see him doing it. The local politicians viewed him for what he was, a carpetbagger.

His voting address, after all, was a hotel, and he'd registered just in time to vote in the primary. Tom O'Neill, a local state assemblyman known as "Tip," wasn't impressed by the newcomer, war record or not. He was backing Mike Neville, the former Cambridge mayor, and the one whose turn it now was to hold the seat. "I couldn't believe this skinny, pasty-faced kid was a candidate for anything." He recalled the first time he met Kennedy outside the Bellevue Hotel: "He was twenty-eight but looked younger, and he still hadn't fully recovered from his war injuries. He also looked as if he had come down with malaria."

Tip's description tallies with that of other observers. To Billy Sutton, he "wasn't looking healthy then." To Mark Dalton, the young attorney who would become Kennedy's formal campaign manager, he resembled that same "skeleton" to which we've often heard him compared. His father, too, worried about his son's emaciation. "My father thought I was hopeless." Why? "At the time I weighed about 120 pounds."

Chuck Spalding suggested that Jack's precarious health, and his determination to surmount it at any cost, only added to the campaign's wild, even hectic, pace. "This impatience that he passed on to others . . . made everybody around him feel quicker." The trouble was, it didn't necessarily make for great organization.

One out-of-the-blue crisis almost derailed Jack's first run for office before it even officially had started. It seems that while he was obsessively wearing himself out walking the neighborhoods, he'd somehow overlooked a giant detail. The one to discover it was his old navy pal Red Fay, who'd come east to help out, he said, "even though I was a Republican." Arriving in Cambridge, Fay found the headquarters a shambles of unpaid bills and invitations to speak, and was soon put in charge of trying to run the campaign on a more "businesslike basis."

One of the campaign workers casually asked Fay about the candidate's filing of his nomination papers. The deadline was that very afternoon, and yet no one had thought to do it. Not only that, it was now after five o'clock, and thus, past the deadline. So there they were, with Kennedy's petitions not in, and the *Boston Globe*'s late edition already reporting the fact. Yet, incredible as it seems, given today's 24/7 news cycle and minute-by-minute reaction speeds, no one was besieging the headquarters. Or even paying any attention.

"My God," Kennedy said when he heard the bad news. It was 6:30 in the evening. "A series of frantic phone calls were made," Fay reports. "Then, very quietly, the candidate and some loyal public retainers went down, opened up the proper office and filed the papers. Another couple of hours, and all the thousands of hours of work by the candidate and his supporters would have been completely wasted."

This is a loyalist's account of an after-hours escapade that had to have been blatantly illegal. But what's remarkable is that Jack himself went into the municipal building that night and did what had to be done, putting those petitions in the right pile as if they'd been there by the deadline.

Kennedy pulled off other escapades. Early in the race, a rival candidate, Joe Russo, had run this newspaper ad: "Congress Seat for Sale. No Experience Necessary. Applicant Must Live in New York or Florida. Only Millionaires Need Apply." The Kennedy campaign didn't get mad, it got even.

Locating another Joe Russo, they paid him a few bucks to file as a candidate. The effect would be to confuse voters and skim off some of the politician Joe Russo's votes. There was an Italian vote in the district and, this way, it would be divided.

But there were other sources of resentment. A popular newspaper column authored by a "Dante O'Shaughnessy" mocked Kennedy for being "oh, so British" and for having a valet who looked after him. Tip O'Neill recalled a far more daunting, more relevant advantage. Joe Kennedy had gotten *Reader's Digest* to publish a condensed version of the John Hersey *PT 109* piece that had run in the *New Yorker*, and now the campaign was mailing out 100,000 copies of it to voters. Tip couldn't even remember a candidate before Jack Kennedy who'd had the money to pay for first-class postage.

What you did was rely on campaign workers to deliver literature.

And, even more astoundingly, Joe Kennedy, who'd made money owning chains of movie houses, had gotten local theaters to show a special newsreel recounting the story of Jack's wartime heroism. No Boston pol, or voter, had ever before seen the like in a local congressional race. Or any race, for that matter.

An important—and brilliant—clincher came just days before the primary: Jack's father and mother hosted a tony afternoon reception, a formal tea party, at the Hotel Commander in Cambridge. Women from throughout the district were invited, and all were flattered and thrilled. They'd always read about such fancy society events in the papers, but neither they nor anyone they knew had ever been to one.

Kennedy was starting to create what Tip O'Neill called the "Kennedy Party," one separate from the regular Democratic organizations. He was making it happen by asking citizens who'd never been involved before to come on board. He, the millionaire's son, was seeking the help of regular folk, not just the predictable party faithful or the machine hacks. Anyone stopping by Kennedy's storefront headquarters would be asked to volunteer, and, in agreeing, they'd become, on the spot, "Kennedy" people. Thus, as word began to get around that someone's son or niece was "working for young Jack Kennedy," the popular appeal of the campaign grew, along with its strength.

Meanwhile, Jack himself continued acting in a way that was deeply impressive for someone of his wealth and name. He was out there going door to door on foot, and it was not simply a choice but rather a necessity. While his rivals could count on their associations with other politicians to further their candidacies, he was a new-comer who, despite his hard-core Boston bloodlines, didn't have those established connections. His only means of getting to know voters was to meet them himself.

With either Billy Sutton or Dave Powers by his side, he went everywhere. "He met city workers, he met letter carriers, cabbies, waitresses, and dock workers," Billy recalled. "He was probably the first of the pols around here to go into the firehouses, police sta-tions, post offices, and saloons and poolrooms, as well as the homes, and it was probably the first Jack ever knew that the gas stove and the toilet could be in the same room." Having the gabby, comical Sutton—a gifted mimic of character high and low—with him pro-vided great company.

He deliberately made the rounds of the Cambridge city coun-cilmen, putting up with their silent responses or sometimes outright abuse. He was showing that he had the guts to do it, gaining respect, if not for this election, for the next time. He was honoring the po-litical rule of keeping his enemies in front of him, showing them he wasn't afraid and letting them know he had what it took to look them in the face.

At one candidates' event, he listened patiently to each of his rivals describe their difficult lives. When his turn arrived, he, son of one of the world's richest men, stood up and began, "I guess I'm the only one here who didn't come up the hard way."

He also did something else other candidates failed to think of, or were unable to imagine themselves doing, which was making a direct appeal to women. "Womanpower," he would tell Tip, "the untapped resource."

Red Fay reported that visiting junior colleges in the area with Jack back then was like traveling with the young, also very skinny Frank Sinatra. "They would scream and holler and touch him—absolutely, in 1946. I mean these girls were just crazy about him."

Finally, there was the undeniable stamina Kennedy poured into the race, working hard at it until the very last day. Years later he would say it was mostly a matter of getting started early. "My chief opponents . . . followed the old practice of not starting until two months before the election. By then I was way ahead of them. I believe most aspirants for public office start much too late. When you think of the money that Coca-Cola and Lucky Strike put into advertising day after day though they have well-known brand names, you can realize how difficult it is to become an identifiable political figure. The idea that people can get to know you well enough to support you in two months or three months is wholly wrong. Most of us do not follow politics and politicians. We become interested only around election time. . . . In my opinion the principle for winning a war fight or a Congressional fight is really the same as winning a presidential fight. And the most important ingredient is a willingness to submit yourself to long, long, long labor."

Ted Reardon, his older brother's close friend from Harvard, was running the get-out-the-vote effort. "We were constantly going over the voting lists to find where the Democrats were. We had four or five telephones going all the time, with volunteer girls calling up and getting out the vote. We used to stay until three or four in the morning."

Lem Billings, recalling the pace, said: "Remember, we were all amateurs and all very young. Everyone was either a young veteran or a young girl. We had people who'd lived in each district all their lives stationed at the polls. We tried to get as many volunteers with cars as we could, but we always had to hire an awful lot of taxis and these were all sent to addresses of Democrats who hadn't voted."

The big event each year in Charlestown, then a part of the 11th Congressional District, is the Bunker Hill Parade. The day before the primary, Jack marched in the parade. On this hot June day, the pressure and work of the campaign finally catching up with him, he collapsed before reaching the finish.

"I called his father," said the man whose house he was taken to. "I was instructed to wait until a doctor came. He turned very yellow and blue. He appeared to me as a man who probably had a heart attack. Later on I found out it was a condition which he picked up, probably malaria or yellow fever." In fact, it would take until the following year for Kennedy to find out the true, much more serious cause of his problem.

On the following day, Kennedy was up early and at the movies. It was a way for him to escape the early, misleading, mind-destroying tidbits of information about how the voting was going. That night, when the results were in, he'd beaten Neville by two to one. Joe Russo—the real one—finished fourth. The other Joe Russo, the one the Kennedy people had put up, managed to get nearly eight hundred votes. He finished fifth.

Jack Kennedy had started earliest and worked the hardest. He had done what was necessary, and more, and he had won. But what did he believe? And what were his loyalties? He had championed the concerns of his primarily working-class district: wages, unemployment benefits, the need for a national health care system. In deep ways, he was as Irish as his constituents. He'd run, after all, as a "fighting conservative," fearing in his heart the dark specter of Moscow, angered still by the ailing Roosevelt's giveaway at Yalta.

"What about Communism?" he asked a lawyer he knew who'd been supporting Mike Neville in the race. That fall he was already calling the Soviet Union, our wartime ally, a "slave state," clearly drawing a line between himself and his party's liberal wing.

This fighting conservative was already fighting a war that had not yet gotten its name.

The *Daily News*, McKeesport

The House class of 1946

CHAPTER FIVE

COLD WARRIOR

While the hand of fate made Jack and me political opponents, I always cherish the fact that we were personal friends from the time we came to the Congress together in 1947.

—Richard M. Nixon, from a letter written to
Jacqueline Kennedy, November 22, 1963

Jack Kennedy knew well before going to the House of Representatives that he didn't intend to stay there. He was headed for statewide office, either the governorship or the U.S. Senate. Even if he opted for the governorship first, it was only to be a stepping-stone. His goal was the Senate, since what he really wanted was to join the big national debates, especially those on foreign policy. That was where he intended to make his mark.

There were no near-term options for reaching his goal. If he ran against Senator Leverett Saltonstall in two years—in '48— he would look impetuous. Besides, he'd formed an affection for the older man. But if he waited to run against the other senator from the Commonwealth of Massachusetts, the august Henry Cabot Lodge, Jr., in 1952, it might be a suicide mission.

Lodge had sacrificed his first seat in the Senate to go off and fight in the war. Now, in '46, he'd won the second Massachusetts seat, with a smashing victory over Senator David I. Walsh, a four-term Democrat. So Jack would have to wait. Whatever and whenever he decided on for his next step he needed to prove himself with the job he'd won.

From the start, when he walked into his office on Capitol Hill, Jack Kennedy made it clear he was his own man. Arriving with a high profile, built first on his best-selling, prewar book and then on his news-making exploits in the South Pacific, he had no intention of compromising his hero's image by becoming just another Massachusetts Democrat. Out there in the Solomon Islands, he'd engineered the saving of ten men's lives; he was not about to sign on to someone else's crew. And that included the number two Democrat in the House, John McCormack, who, because he was the senior congressman from Massachusetts, expected a certain deference from his fellow Bay Staters.

He would not be getting it from young Kennedy. On the morning the about-to-be congressman was to take his oath, Billy Sutton met him at the Statler Hilton on Sixteenth Street, a few blocks north of the White House. Jack had just flown in from Palm Beach.

"You should be in a hurry," Sutton warned his boss, who showed up tanned and carrying his black cashmere overcoat. "You have a caucus meeting." In other words, McCormack was waiting for him up on Capitol Hill. "Well, I'd like a couple of eggs," Kennedy said, continuing to ignore the suggestion to get a move on. "How long would you say Mr. McCormack has been here?

Don't you think Mr. McCormack wouldn't mind waiting another ten minutes?"

The Mucker wasn't about to let a new headmaster intimidate him. At that, he went into the hotel's drugstore lunch counter to join his new top aide, Ted Reardon, for breakfast.

Kennedy's little-concealed disdain for the John McCormacks of the world was not a trait he was ready to hide. He'd made it his business to win his seat free of the entangling alliances that tied up other new lawmakers before they could even get started. Establishing his independence was his purpose from the very first day. Since he didn't plan to spend the rest of his career as one of 435 members of the House of Representatives, he wasn't going to get hitched to McCormack, for the simple reason that he intended to pass him by.

Years later, when he was headed to the Senate, Jack Kennedy would advise his successor in Congress, Tip O'Neill, to "marry John McCormack." Such different behavior from his own, he said, was the better path for a man who by then had been Speaker of the Massachusetts legislature and who, he correctly assumed, would one day want to join the House leadership ladder.

The world Jack Kennedy found in Washington that winter of 1947 was a jamboree of Republican triumphalism. On both sides of the Capitol, committees were cooking up public hearings on the two hot-stove issues Republicans had championed in the previous election: the evils of Big Labor and the threat of Communism at home and abroad. Republicans had won both houses, the first time since before the Great Depression, with a simple slogan that was more a question than an answer, more a taunt than a promise: "Had Enough?"

Its meaning was clear. It summed up two decades of Democratic rule that had comprised an era of government activism or overreach, depending on the voter's degree of resentment. And during the '46 campaign it meant everything voters didn't like after V-J day, from rationing to the recent rash of labor strikes.

The new Republican majority came with a mission. Harry Truman could sit there in the White House and veto its bills, but he couldn't stop the new Eightieth Congress from investigating him, and that meant the whole twenty-year Democratic era. They were, in the words of one Republican congressman, going to "open every session with a prayer and end it with a probe." Almost forty investigative panels were setting up schedules to dig up corruption any way they could find it, with the entire Roosevelt-Truman record as their quarry.

Congress was looking for bad guys, especially those who were seen as soft on the Communist threat. Someone had to pay for the giveaway at Yalta, and FDR, who'd agreed to it, wasn't around to take the punishment.

Jack Kennedy had brought Billy Sutton to Washington as his press secretary and jack-of-all-trades—housemate included. Being from the Boston neighborhoods, he took a street-corner guy's view of things. So much was happening so fast that the spectacle on Capitol Hill seemed to him like a "Stop 'n' Shop, a supermarket of hearings."

The very day he arrived on Capitol Hill, Jack Kennedy met the fellow member of the House freshman class of 1946 whose destiny would wind up twinned with his own. Richard Nixon had just beaten a much-admired New Dealer and five-term Democratic incumbent in the battle for California's 12th District. It had been an upset victory tinged by telephoned whispers that Nixon's opponent was a "Communist."

Kennedy, however, was impressed by the drama of the triumph itself. "So you're the guy who beat Jerry Voorhis," Kennedy exclaimed on meeting Nixon at a National Press Club reception for freshman congressmen who'd fought in the war. "That's like beating John McCormack up in Massachusetts!"

At Harvard, Jack had gravitated to Torby Macdonald, hotshot of the freshman football team. Now it was the star of the House class of 1946—this thirty-four-year-old Californian, like himself a navy man, who'd just pulled off the biggest political upset of the season.

"How's it feel?" Jack asked him. Here was the son of one of the richest men in the world showing Dick Nixon, the poor boy, true admiration. "I guess I'm elated," the Californian answered, plainly taken by the attention. In fact, Nixon's loyal presidential aide H. R. Haldeman told me decades later and just days before his own death that he'd always found Nixon's feelings toward Jack Kennedy "strange and inexplicable." It had been so from the start.

The two ex–naval officers from the South Pacific theater— Nixon had been a supply officer there—were both assigned to the Committee on Education and Labor. Now both were being thrown into the most intense battle of the season: the effort by the reenergized Republicans to rein in the power of organized labor. In those early months of 1947, it would offer Jack Kennedy his first chance for distinction.

Rather than join his fellow Democrats in simply opposing the measure, he decided to put forth his own "dissenting opinion." He had called Mark Dalton, the friend who'd managed his campaign, and asked him to join him in Washington. "John wanted to know what we—Billy Sutton was in the room—thought of the Hartley proposal and what he should do about it. We sat there and developed a position," recalled Dalton, who wound up manning the typewriter.

To Dalton, it was a billboard screaming the new congressman's ambitions. "People have always said to me, was John Kennedy running for the presidency from the start? Was he thinking of the future?" For Dalton, there was never any doubt—and certainly not from that moment forward.

But there was more still to learn about his boss, and it had to do with the way he kept his eye on the future competition. The morning Kennedy was scheduled to present his dissenting position to the Rules Committee, a congressman Dalton didn't recognize was offering the official Republican support of what would be the Taft-Hartley Act. "Listen to this fellow," Kennedy whispered as Dalton entered the cramped hearing room. "He's going places."

When the Republican member finished speaking and took the seat next to them, Kennedy introduced him. "I'd like you to meet Richard Nixon of California." In the coming years Jack would be telling his family that Nixon was "brilliant," the smartest of all his colleagues.

Kennedy, of course, was also trying to establish himself. "There were very few Democrats who would speak as strongly as he did to labor," Dalton recalled. "The reaction was 'Kennedy is courageous,' just what Kennedy wanted it to be."

Thus, when he rose on the House floor to give what would be his maiden speech in Congress, he was taking on the power of organized labor as well as big business. "I told him that day that he reminded me so much of Jimmy Stewart in *Mr. Smith Goes to Washington*," Billy Sutton remembered.

Still, not everyone in the chamber was so thrilled. "You can imagine the reaction of the congressmen who had been there for years and had worked on this problem," said Dalton, "to be told that the new congressman from Massachusetts was filing a separate report."

A few days later, Kennedy and Dick Nixon got their first chance to match talents in an arena beyond Capitol Hill. A local group had asked a freshman member from western Pennsylvania, Frank Buchanan, to pick the two standouts in his class, one from each party, and invite them home for a debate. The topic would be the new labor reform bill, to be known as Taft-Hartley. The audience would be a mixture of business and labor people.

The pair was greeted at the train station early that evening and taken to the Penn McKeesport hotel. There in the ballroom, they put on vastly dissimilar performances. Nixon was the aggressor, punching away like a hungry middleweight. Playing to the Republicans in the mixed crowd, he pummeled Big Labor. Brutally, he listed all the troubles that had been dominating the postwar headlines: the automobile strike, the steel strike, the coal strike, the railroad strike. He had picked his side in the fight and was quite willing to taunt his enemies on the other.

The younger speaker, the one with the quaint New England accent and the slight limp, offered a more nuanced performance. Watching Nixon antagonize the labor people in the McKeesport crowd, Jack worked to soften the hostility of the business folks. There was much to say for the labor reforms the Republicans were pushing, he allowed, particularly its banning of "wildcat" strikes. His concern was that the legislation might go too far and lead to more trouble between management and labor, not less.

It was Jack's charm they witnessed that night. Nixon came into the room like a club fighter, eager to win the rivalry point by point. A champion debater at Whittier College, he focused on his rival, challenging whatever he said. Kennedy, his focus on the audience, ignored his rival on the stage and concentrated on winning over the room. Knowing he had labor on his side—Nixon made sure of that—he wanted to end the evening with the business people convinced that he shared their concern for an end to the country's labor troubles.

What surprised those who greeted them and saw them off that night was the way these two partisans got along with each other personally. Before catching the *Capitol Limited* back to Washington, they grabbed hamburgers at the local Star Diner and talked over the new baseball season. Boarding at midnight, the two junior pols drew straws for the lower berth. Nixon won. Then, as the train rolled on toward Washington, they spent the early-morning hours discussing their true mutual interest, foreign policy, especially the rising standoff with the Soviets in Europe, which Bernard Baruch had just christened the "cold war."

Kennedy was drawn to those who shared his big-picture view of the world, and Nixon was one who did. Their responses to the threat posed by Communism's spread were similar, too. For both of them, it was a central issue of their generation.

In the morning-after press, it was Kennedy who scored highest. The next morning's editions of the McKeesport *Daily News* ran a front-page photo of the smiling, handsome Kennedy, one that could easily have been of a popular local college grad. The shot of Nixon, on the other hand, caught him with his eyes darting sideways with a hunted look, his defiant chin displaying a beard well beyond the five o'clock mark. Even in black and white, the charisma gap was stark.

That March, President Truman called on Congress to stop the Red advance across Europe by approving U.S. military aid to help governments in Greece and Turkey resist Communist-backed insurgencies. Speaking to a joint session, he called this move crucial to American security. To those on the political left, the new "Truman Doctrine" was an unwelcome reversal from the pro-Russian policies of FDR. But for many of the young officers back from the war, the president was speaking the language they wanted to hear.

The day after Truman had addressed Congress, Russ Nixon—no relation to Richard—of the United Electrical, Radio, and Machine Workers of America, a union known for its sizable Communist contingent, told the Education and Labor Committee that labor unions had as much right to be led by Communists as by Democrats or Republicans. That was a far from popular view in the halls of Washington.

When his own turn arrived to quiz the witness, Congressman Jack Kennedy said he'd been "impressed by the dexterity" the witness had shown in fielding the earlier questions. Nixon, a Ph.D. in economics, had been Kennedy's Harvard instructor before joining the labor movement. Now the student to whom he'd given a B-minus his freshman year got to ask the questions.

Was Soviet Communism, he asked his former instructor, "a threat to the economic and political system of the United States?" No, Russ Nixon replied, the real threat to the country was its failure to meet the "basic economic problems of the people in a democratic way" as well as its failure to expand Americans' civil rights and in that way meet "the problems of the Negro people."

Kennedy then asked his instructor to defend what he said was the Communist Party's willingness to "resort to all sorts of artifices, evasion, subterfuges, only so as to get into the trade unions and remain in them and to carry on Communist work in them, at all costs."

Russ Nixon: I didn't teach you that at Harvard, did I?

Kennedy: No, you did not. I am reading from Lenin, in which is described the procedure which should be adopted to get into trade unions and how they conduct themselves once they are in.

His clever questioning of the left-leaning witness won Kennedy positive notice from the press gallery. "A freshman House member with the coral dust of Pacific Islands still clinging to his heels," UPI's George Reedy said in a radio broadcast, "stole the show from his older colleagues yesterday."

In May, Jack outdid that performance. He won a perjury citation against a Communist labor leader, Harold Christoffel, for his role in a wartime strike against a huge defense plant in Milwaukee.

He asked the witness why the union newspaper had strongly opposed war aid to Britain prior to the Nazi invasion of Russia, only to back it strongly thereafter. Why did it condemn "Roosevelt's War Program" when Hitler was in league with Stalin, then call for "All Aid to Britain, Soviet Union" in a banner headline once the Hitler-Stalin alliance was broken?

Kennedy had harder evidence that the labor leaders were under Communist Party discipline from Moscow. A former party member had testified that the 1941 Milwaukee strike was part of a "snowballing" of such work stoppage aimed at crippling the U.S. defense buildup. The labor leaders had been lying and Kennedy had caught them.

"Would you call Russia a democracy?" Kennedy asked one. "I would not know. I do not think so," he replied. "I think I would like to inform you on what I believe to be the main difference between socialism in England and socialism in Russia," Kennedy said. "They have freedom of opposition which they do not have in Russia." When his witness said he didn't know if that was true or not, Jack went at him.

"Well, I do not think you are equipped to tell whether a member of your union is a Communist if you do not know any of the answers to any of the things that I have asked you."

Deeply impressed by his young colleague's work, the Republican chairman of the committee compared it to the opening shots at Lexington and Concord.

On June 5—two years to the day after the Allies had met in Berlin, affirming the total defeat of Germany—Secretary of State George C. Marshall was Harvard's commencement speaker. He used the occasion to unveil a massive, complex plan for the economic reconstruction of war-torn Europe, funded by U.S. dollars. Though the Marshall Plan doesn't seem controversial today in the aftermath of its great success—*Time* called it "surely one of the most momentous commencement day speeches ever made"—it had its detractors.

One of them was Joseph Kennedy, Sr., who regarded the European Recovery Plan—the Marshall Plan's official name—as a terrible idea. A shrewder plan, he calculated, would be to let the Communists grab Europe, creating economic chaos that would lead to greater opportunities for businessmen like him down the road. His son disagreed. He believed that serious efforts to halt the Soviet advance in Europe were the only way to avoid repeating the mistake made at the Munich Conference of 1938, when Hitler was allowed free rein.

Had the Third Reich been confronted at a decisive moment, it was now believed, Germany might have retreated and never come to stage a deadly attack on Poland as it did the following year. The outcome of Munich, along with the thinking behind it, meant the Allies were thrown on the defensive. The World War II generation, having lived through the prewar appeasement and its consequences, had returned from the theaters of war in the South Pacific, Europe, and Africa determined to prevent a sequel to the tragedy that had interrupted and harrowed their lives—and erased so many more. This time, the dictator bent on encroachment and annexation must be stopped in his tracks.

To young men like Kennedy and Nixon, the Yalta Conference of February 1945, which had divided up postwar Europe, carried whiffs of another Munich. It represented a buckling under to a new enemy, but one even more subversive in its methods and more pervasive in its ambitions than the one who'd died in his Berlin bunker.

This firm resolve to defend Europe from Stalin was hardly a policy Jack's father, the ruthless builder of wealth, could embrace. Joe Kennedy had gone back to the isolationism he'd preached throughout the 1930s; his son, meanwhile, was moving in his own direction. "So many people said that the ambassador was pulling the strings for Jack, and he certainly was not," said Mary Davis, the congressman's secretary at the time. "Jack was his own man."

In fact, Jack Kennedy was starting to make it known, both privately and publicly, that he and his father disagreed on important issues.

"We were all at a cocktail party in the garden of Drew and Luvie Pearson," the senior Kennedy's friend Kay Halle recalled. "Suddenly, Joe said, 'Kay, I wish you would tell Jack that he's going to vote the wrong way.' I can't even remember what bill it was, but Joe said, 'I think Jack is making a terrible mistake.'

"And then I remember Jack turning to his father and saying, 'Now, look here, Dad, you have your political views and I have mine. I'm going to vote exactly the way I feel I must vote on this. I've great respect for you, but when it comes to voting, I'm voting my way.' Then Joe looked at me with that big Irish smile, and said, 'Well, Kay, that's why I settled a million dollars on each of them, so they could spit in my eye if they wished.'"

Jack's tough stand against the Soviets abroad and Communism at home made sense to his constituents up in Boston. Growing up, I saw this myself: Catholics as a group had it in our gut that Roosevelt had sold out the country's interests at Yalta. To us, the growing threat from Moscow increasingly resembled Hitler's pre-war aggression. Supporters back home could see that Jack Kennedy, down in Washington, knew just how they felt, agreed with them, and was saying exactly what they were feeling.

Kennedy also knew he, the privileged son, was being watched back home for how he was handling the job. If he gave the cold shoulder to a single constituent, if a letter went unanswered, the word would get around. He'd be seen as having gotten too big for his britches. "He was very particular about people in his district and answering the mail," Billy Sutton recalled. "He didn't want anything to stay on your desk. If some poor soul or constituent needed help and he gave the assignment to you, you were liable to be riding home in the car and he'd say, 'Well, what about John White? What did you do for him?' And if you said, 'Well, I was going to do that tomorrow,' he'd almost tell you, you know, to get out of the car and go back to the office. He wanted you to do your job, and if you didn't, then you were in trouble."

Mary Davis understood the stakes. Her young boss wasn't down in Washington only to be a dutiful congressman. He wanted those constituents of his to help elect him senator. That meant at least doing no harm. "I would say that was always in the back of Jack's mind, and in the minds of the people who had supported him first for representative in the House. They always felt that this was a start and that he would go onward and upward."

There quickly came a time in that first year that Kennedy had to decide between going along and getting along: at issue was the man whose seat he had taken in Congress. Reelected mayor in 1945, James Michael Curley had been convicted of mail fraud; he now sat, plotting, in Danbury federal prison. Curley's daughter was passing around a petition to the Massachusetts members of Congress asking for his release on health grounds. It was feared, the petition argued, that he would die if not released. A hundred thousand Massachusetts voters had signed a citizens' petition.

Kennedy friend Joe Healey was Jack's tutor at Harvard and continued to be a trusted advisor and occasional speechwriter. "I got a call from Washington. It was Congressman Kennedy, and he said he wanted to talk with me about a petition that had been brought to his office. The person who had brought the petition to his office was Mary Curley, the daughter of the former governor."

Healey was cautious in his advice. If Curley's illness was truly fatal, he said, the old pol should be given some last time with his family. If he wasn't as sick as he advertised, he shouldn't be treated any differently than anyone else convicted of his crimes. Kennedy agreed this was exactly the way to look at it. In fact, army physicians had examined him and found his health as good as any man of his age reasonably could expect to have. Kennedy said he could not, knowing that, in good conscience sign the document.

Hearing this, Healey pointed out it was going to be "a very politically unpopular thing to do." Kennedy's refusal to sign the Curley petition was of course infuriating to the local politicians back home. It turned out he was the only Massachusetts Democratic congressman to do so. "I guess I'm going to be a one-term congressman," he told one back-home advisor.

Mark Dalton, who worked for Kennedy unpaid and picked up his own expenses, was disgusted with the Curley ploy. "My strong reaction was that he was a young man starting his political career, just on the threshold of it, and I thought that the older people who were putting the pressure on him to sign this petition had a terrible nerve."

Jack had gone against his party and the state machine regarding something he knew in his bones was wrong. It was also an issue of pride; he didn't want to be a hack. Add in the matter of style: refusing to sign showed class. But standing against the pardon was both a political and moral risk that Kennedy would sweat for weeks to come. Joe Healey never forgot the episode.

Curley, he recalled, "lived for some ten years after this event, but as a congressman, I heard Jack Kennedy say that, if anything had happened to Mr. Curley during his stay in prison, it would have been the end of his political career." For his part, Jack would cite the Curley dilemma as a case study of how political fortunes turn on the unpredictable.

Years later, to put it in perspective, Tip O'Neill, once a Curley protégé, refused to defend him on moral grounds. In the midst of one of our long backroom conversations about the old days, he had put it bluntly and succinctly, how "Curly was crooked" even by the standard of those days. "Personally crooked?" I asked.

"Personally," he said with the firmest possible pronunciation.

But Jack Kennedy's independence on matters such as the Curley petition was unsettling to political observers. He had begun to build a reputation for standing alone, a two-edged sword. Edmund Muskie, who served as governor and later senator from Maine, recalled how Kennedy's behavior scared the clubhouse types. "I don't know whether the more foresighted of them saw in young Jack Kennedy a major political force or not, but they certainly recognized his political attractions and his political potential; and they were disturbed by his apparent determination to be independent of the 'regular' party organization."

Mark Dalton remembered another moment when Kennedy stood out. "I'm going to debate Norman Thomas at the Harvard Law School," said Jack one day, surprising Dalton, who had arrived at his friend's Boston apartment to find the congressman hard at work. So now his young friend was going to take on the quadrennial candidate of the Socialist Party. "There was Kennedy sitting on the sofa. There were two or three books open there and six or seven books on the floor opened. Each one had been written by Norman Thomas. The next day I got reports from several people, and everyone was agreed that John Kennedy had won the debate with Thomas."

Again, the old dichotomy. His colleagues saw the popular bachelor who lived the good life in Georgetown, the rich kid with such a great sense of humor. Few noticed the other Jack, the occasional Cold Warrior, the autodidact who crammed for off-campus debates, who quietly but steadily was preparing himself for something greater than labor law.

Like others, his secretary Mary Davis would come to learn that Jack Kennedy was not the fop he played so charmingly. For all the fun she saw him having, she could catch that spark of brilliance. "He didn't make that many speeches, and we didn't issue that many position papers when he was here in the House, but when he wanted to write a speech, *he did it.* I would say ninety-nine percent of that was done by JFK himself.

"I can remember the first time he ever called me in—I even forget what the speech was going to be on, but it was going to be a major speech, one of his first major speeches. And I thought, 'Oh, oh, this young, green congressman. What's he going to do?' No preparation. He called me in and he says, 'I think we'd better get to work on the speech.' And I said, 'Okay, fine.' And I thought he was going to stumble around, and he'll 'er, ah, um.'

"I was never so startled in my life. He sat back in his chair, and it just flowed right out. He had such a grasp of what he was saying, and was able to put it in such beautiful language. I thought, 'Wow. This guy has a brain.' I mean, you didn't get that impression when you first met him because he looked so young and casual and informal. But he knew what it was all about. He knew about everything."

Richard Nixon had a similar epiphany. Ted Reardon recalled the time that Jack became deeply focused on an issue before the Education and Labor Committee, so much so that he went himself to the National Archives to look something up. "At the hearing, the thing I remember is when Jack started to talk, Dicky Boy sort of looked at him . . . with a look between awe and respect and fear."

Jack's greatest secret remained his bad health, the extent of which, until then, was unknown even to him. When Kennedy arrived in Washington that January, his problems had followed. "He was not feeling well," Mary Davis noticed. "I mean, he still had his jaundice, he still had his back problems."

"Emaciated!" is how his fellow congressman George Smathers of Florida remembers his frail classmate. The Florida Democrat, who had been assigned to the same hallway as Kennedy, vividly recalls that "every time there was a roll call, he'd have to come over on his crutches." Wanting to help, Smathers often would stop by Jack's office to give him a hand as his new friend made the painful journey across Independence Avenue to the Capitol to vote.

The various maladies from which he visibly suffered were being blamed on his war traumas, but that explanation, while infinitely useful spinwise, was only part of the story. For Jack the truth lay deeper, and he was about to discover it.

During the summer recess of 1947, a group of congressmen, Dick Nixon included, headed to Europe to study the impact of the Marshall Plan, which was now being implemented. For a bon voyage gesture—one that was, apparently, ignored—Kennedy had sent his married California colleague the names of a few women he might look up while in Paris. For himself, Kennedy also set off across the Atlantic, first to Ireland with his sister Kick, then to the Continent along with a Republican colleague to look into the Communist influence on European labor unions.

Arriving in London after falling ill on the first leg of his journey, he was rushed to the hospital, where he was diagnosed with Addison's disease, a serious disorder of the adrenal glands. Prior to Jack's release, the attending physician offered this grim prognosis to Jack's English traveling companion. "That American friend of yours, he hasn't got a year to live." Just as the *Queen Mary* docked in New York, a priest came aboard to administer to him the last rites.

He had lost his older brother in 1944. The husband of his beloved Kick had died the following year. Yet, on the return voyage home from England and near death, he showed himself as politically curious as ever. Much of his time was spent quizzing a fellow passenger on the new British health service created by the Labour Party.

Jack continued to keep tight the compartments of his life. Like the ship's captain he still was, he knew he couldn't sink if he kept each of them strongly secure from the other. In Georgetown, he basked in a princely life, attended by a housekeeper, Margaret Ambrose, and a valet, George Thomas, who delivered a home-cooked hot lunch to his Capitol office each day.

Meanwhile, Billy Sutton was with him 24/7, since Jack still couldn't stand to be alone. On those nights he didn't have a date for the movies, his "firecracker" provided entertainment and company. Mary Davis explained the dynamic between the two men this way: "He was someone he could completely relax with, who would be available, and who would be on call, who could do a thousand and one things for Jack, just being there, knowing that he had a friend close by."

Referring to the townhouse they shared on Thirty-first Street NW as akin to a "Hollywood Hotel," Billy cherished the memories of all the gorgeous women coming and going. "Thinking about girls is what kept Jack alive," he said.

Playing the field, rejecting any definite romantic attachments, gave him the freedom he craved. Refusing to give fealty to the Democratic leadership or to the liberal old guard gave him the independence he treasured. Being able to enter each world without the baggage from the other gave him the breezy, debonair life he wanted. Anywhere he went he could simply be Jack Kennedy, the guy he wanted to be, the one he'd made himself.

"He did have a lot of close associations," Mary Davis recalled. But not "a lot of close personal friendships." Charlie Bartlett recalls the detached way his friend regarded political colleagues, no matter their status. "He used to enjoy kidding about the personalities on the scene, and there used to be a lot of jokes about different personalities from Sam Rayburn down, and even some sort of gossiping about the foibles of some of the senior statesmen in Congress." He liked to watch what they were up to, enjoyed charting their purposes and behavior—but at a distance.

George Smathers was the rare *social* friend Jack made in the House of Representatives. A marine in World War II, and son of a federal judge in Florida, he'd gotten to know Jack's father at the Hialeah Park Race Track in Miami. Smathers, not to put too fine a point on it, was a hack, knew it, and enjoyed it—and this gave him, for Jack, a special aura of honesty. Confiding that he voted whatever way would keep him in office, this made him, in a world of hypocrites, special indeed.

Kennedy told Charlie Bartlett he liked Smathers "because he doesn't give a damn." If he judged Dick Nixon to be the "smartest" guy on the Hill in those days, his pal George was the most fun to hang out with.

Smathers knew his role: he was Falstaff. Jack was still playing Hal, a prince whose fears, in those days, were not—or not yet— of coming kingship but of mortality. Smathers remembers his pal being "deeply preoccupied by death," talking endlessly on a Florida fishing trip about the best ways to die. He remembered Kennedy deciding it had to be drowning, "but only if you lost consciousness."

"Quick"—that was the key. "The point is, you've got to live each day like it's your last day on earth," he recalled Jack telling him. "That's what I'm doing." Ted Reardon recalled a similar conversation on the way home from Capitol Hill one late afternoon in Jack's convertible. "It was a bright, shining day. We had the top down. Out of the blue he said, 'What do you think is the best way of dying?'" A new friend, the newspaper columnist and Georgetown mandarin Joseph Alsop, recalled Jack's bluntness when it came to his short-range outlook. "Unless I'm very mistaken, he said that as a matter of fact, he had a kind of slow-acting—*very* slow-acting—leukemia and that he did not expect to live more than ten years or so, but there was no use thinking about it and he was going to do the best he could and enjoy himself as much as he could in the time that was given him."

Alsop could clearly see there was cause for worry. "He used to turn green at intervals," he recalled. "He was about the color of pea soup."

As he had all his life, Jack found refuge from his health worries in the power of words and ideas. Reading remained his salvation, and not just of the newspapers that are the daily fare of most politicians. Billy Sutton recalls him staying up late at night with Arthur Schlesinger's *Age of Jackson*. Mark Dalton, perhaps the most thoughtful of the people around him back then, recalled a visit to Hyannis Port one weekend when Kennedy called him and another friend up to his bedroom.

He wanted to read them a passage by Churchill, possibly one from his magnificent study of the Duke of Marlborough, a heroic ancestor. "Did you ever read anything like that in all your life?" Kennedy demanded, thrilled again by his hero's work.

Dalton, obviously very fond of his friend in those days, believed he saw a side of Jack that rarely showed itself to others. "As I look back, the things that I liked most about John Kennedy were the small flashes of sentiment." He recalled a particular incident. "One morning I was at mass with him in the early congressional days down at the Cape, at St. Francis there. We were alone. We were about to leave the church, and John said, 'Will you wait a minute? I want to go in and light a candle for Joe.' And I was stunned at it. But it showed the deep attachment that he had for his brother Joe, and it also showed his religious nature. You know, there was a strong bond.

"Another day I can remember riding along with him in the car. He was driving. It was over by the Charles River here in Boston and he was humming a tune to himself, but he was way off. And I said to him, 'What are you thinking about?' And he said, 'I was thinking of Joe.'"

He would soon lose someone closer still. His sister Kathleen, widowed when her husband, Billy Hartington, was killed in 1945, now was being courted by another English aristocrat, Peter Fitzwilliam. In February 1948, Kick took the bold step of telling her mother about this new relationship. It was with yet another Protestant, this one married. Her mother threatened to disown her. But nothing could dissuade Kathleen. She had found true, passionate love and would not let go.

Now came tragedy. She and Fitzwilliam had left Paris on a chartered flight to Cannes. They had persisted in flying despite the bad weather, and then, in heavy rain, their plane crashed into the side of a mountain. Jack was listening to music on his Victrola when the first, preliminary call came.

When the next call confirmed the tragedy, he sat quietly listening to a recording of the Broadway musical *Finian's Rainbow*. He would never make it to the funeral of the person he loved most. Setting out for the flight to Europe, he got only as far as New York. For whatever reason, he couldn't go on.

"He was in terrible pain," Lem Billings recalled of Jack. "He couldn't get through the days without thinking of her at the most inappropriate times. He'd be sitting at a congressional hearing and he'd find his mind drifting back uncontrollably to all the things he and Kathleen had done together and all the friends they had in common."

Chuck Spalding could see the specter the deaths of his friend's brother and sister had left in their wake. "He always heard the footsteps. Death was there. It had taken Joe and Kick and it was waiting for him."

Now he started to take risks. In September 1948 Kennedy decided to make a target of the powerful American Legion, declaring that this mainstream, middle-American organization of veterans hadn't had "a constructive thought since 1918." It was one of those marks of independence—his risk-taking again—that helped make him a hero to the young.

One of those who thrilled to Jack's taking on the Legion was Kenneth O'Donnell. A Harvard roommate of Bobby Kennedy and captain of the football team, he'd served in the Army Air Corps. When Jack "took on the American Legion," said O'Donnell, "that was big to the average veteran." Veterans, O'Donnell believed, were looking for "a fresh face in politics."

Jack Kennedy fully intended to be that face. Dave Powers had put a Massachusetts map on the wall of Kennedy's Boston apartment, with colored pins indicating towns Jack had visited. "When we've got the map completely covered with pins," Jack told his aide, "that's when I'll announce that I'm going to run for statewide office."

By his second year in Congress, Jack Kennedy had committed to a cause: the Cold War. He'd already triggered a mild stir with his tough grilling of the left-leaning Russ Nixon and his indictment of Harold Christoffel. In 1948, when East Germany cut off West Berlin, Kennedy went there and saw for himself the heroic survival of its people, as well as the pro-American loyalty the situation was instilling.

As General Lucius Clay, commander of the American zone, put it, "the Russians, by their actions, have given us the political soul of Germany on a platter." The spirit of the West Berliners stayed with Jack for years to come.

Back home, the pursuit of the Communist threat continued to stir emotions. Dick Nixon had just led the successful exposure of Alger Hiss, America's top diplomat at the U.N. Conference in San Francisco. For denying that he had ever been a Communist, the well-connected Hiss now stood indicted for perjury. Jack, who saw Hiss as a "traitor," shared Nixon's indignation at the way Hiss had managed to install himself in critical government positions through the patronage of New Deal figures.

In September 1949 President Truman announced that the Soviets had exploded their first atom bomb, making it clear to the world that the United States no longer held a monopoly on the weapon that had ended World War II. Next came the declaration from China's Communist rebel leader Mao Tse-tung that he had taken control of the entire Chinese mainland. America's WWII ally Chiang Kai-shek was trapped on the island of Formosa.

Kennedy was quick with his rebuke. "The responsibility for the failure of our foreign policy in the Far East rests squarely with the White House and the Department of State. So concerned were our diplomats with the imperfection of the democratic system of China after twenty years of war and the tales of corruption in high places that they lost sight of our tremendous stake in non-Communist China." He accused the Truman administration of "vacillation, uncertainty, and confusion."

To Kennedy, America's leaders were repeating the old prewar mistake of failing to confront aggression. Kennedy believed FDR had been as derelict in failing to stop Soviet ambitions in Asia as he had been in Europe. In a Salem, Massachusetts, speech, he described how "a sick Roosevelt with the advice of General Marshall and other chiefs of staff, gave the Kurile Islands as well as control of various strategic Chinese ports, such as Port Arthur and Darien, to the Soviet Union. This is the tragic story of China, whose freedom we once fought to preserve. What our young men have saved, the diplomats and our President have frittered away."

In January 1950 came another Cold War milestone. Alger Hiss, the accused Soviet spy, was convicted on two counts of lying under oath and sent to federal prison. That same month, desperate for material to use at a Lincoln Day talk to Republican women in Wheeling, West Virginia, Wisconsin's Senator Joseph McCarthy jumped on the anti-Communist bandwagon. Cribbing from a speech Nixon had just given on the Hiss conviction, McCarthy said there were 205 Communists in the State Department. His specificity hooded the recklessness of the accusation.

That June brought a real Communist menace. North Korea attacked American-backed South Korea. President Truman sent troops as part of a United Nations force. The next month came stunning news at home: Julius Rosenberg was arrested for stealing atomic secrets for the Soviets. Suddenly the country was under assault abroad *and* at home.

Kennedy strongly allied himself with the anti-Communist activism. While facing no political contest himself in 1950, he played a small role in helping Nixon win a Senate seat: he walked to Nixon's office and left a thousand-dollar check from his father. When he got the word, Nixon was overwhelmed that his Democratic colleague had crossed the political aisle like that. "Isn't this something!" he exclaimed to an aide.

Jack wanted what Nixon now had. Since they had come to the House together, he, Nixon, and George Smathers had enjoyed running banter on which of them would graduate first to the Senate. Smathers had gotten the jump early that year, beating a fellow Democrat in a Florida campaign notorious for its Red-baiting. Nixon now used similar tactics to beat the liberal New Dealer Helen Gahagan Douglas. Kennedy had to catch up.

"This rivalry developed and they were all shooting for the future," said Mark Dalton. Billy Sutton saw it in personal terms: "I think the thing that sent him to the Senate was George Smathers and Richard Nixon." He was clear about not intending to stay in the House. Jack told his new aide Larry O'Brien, whom he recruited to begin organizing Massachusetts for him politically, "I'm up or out." And he was ready to play rough. "I'm going to run!" he told Smathers. "I'm going to use the same kind of stuff."

Jack, Ethel, and Bobby, November 1952

CHAPTER SIX

BOBBY

All this business about Jack and Bobby being blood brothers
has been exaggerated. They didn't really become close until
1952, and it was politics that brought them together.

—Eunice Kennedy Shriver

By 1951, Jack Kennedy's ambition was clear. He wanted very much to reach the Senate. Three times voted in, he'd proved himself an independent Democrat, an ardent anti-Communist, and he had been an efficient, if sometimes detached, steward of constituent services. Based upon his performance and popularity in such a heavily Democratic district, the House seat could have been his for life.

His chance at the Senate would arrive the following year when Henry Cabot Lodge, Jr., a Republican, came up for reelection. The only problem was that Governor Paul Dever, having already served two terms himself, was also considering a job change. If Dever chose to take on Lodge and run for senator, Jack's only option would be to declare for the State House. Whichever happened, he'd definitely decided he wasn't going to stay put. Thus, in January 1951, he gave Tip O'Neill a heads-up.

"I've decided not to run for a fourth term in the House," he told him. "I don't yet know whether I'll run for the Senate or governor, but you can be sure of one thing: my seat will be open. I won't be making any announcements for at least another year, so don't tell a soul. But in case you have any interest in running, I wanted to give you a head start."

Getting ahead in politics generally requires solving a pair of equations, the first being the availability of an office that matches the politician's ambitions. The other is finding the right person to run the campaign. While waiting for Paul Dever to make his decision, Jack got a lead on meeting the second challenge.

Here's how it happened: In September, Kennedy set off on a seven-week fact-finding trip to the Far East. America was at war in Korea, Asia presented the premier foreign-policy front, and the issues presented by foreign policy continued to be his primary interest. The trip would have the added merit of establishing in voters' minds his firsthand experience. However, as the trip was being planned, a family issue arose, casting a slight shadow over it. The problem was pressure from his father to take along his younger brother Bobby. Jack's reaction was that his sibling, eight years his junior, would be nothing but a hindrance, a "pain in the ass."

While Jack had been a warm, loving brother to both Joe Jr. and Kathleen, still missing them terribly, he had yet to form close ties with the younger members of the family. At the time, Bobby struck him as a very different sort from himself, a far more churchy guy, a straight arrow who spent most of his time trying to impress their father with his dutifulness. But rather than Bobby's presence being an annoyance, the opposite turned out to be true. Spending their first ever quality time together, they managed to surprise each other.

As Jack traveled with his brother all the way from Israel to Japan—from the Mediterranean to the South China Sea, stopping in India and Indochina—what they found deepened his own long-standing fascination with foreign policy. But the circumstances they encountered also opened the eyes of both men to the sparks of postwar nationalism beginning to catch fire in each country they visited. While Jack admired the nobility of General Jean de Lattre de Tassigny, the French military commander he met in Hanoi, for instance, he sensed the war he was fighting was "foredoomed."

More important than any other knowledge Jack gained over the course of their journey was the strength of heart he discovered in Robert Fitzgerald Kennedy—and the extent of his brother's love for him. The evidence came during a moment of mortal peril when Jack, thousands of miles from home, suffered a frightening new episode of his Addison's disease. The younger brother more than rose to the occasion, showing his guts under pressure and also his resourcefulness. He got things done.

As Jack was flown from Tokyo to a U.S. military hospital in Okinawa, Bobby never left his side, keeping watch over him as his temperature rose to 106 degrees and he became first delirious, then comatose. It looked like he was dying, and for the second time he was given the last rites.

The upshot of this latest brush with death was a memory an older brother would be unlikely to forget. Where Jack had once seen only the puritan, he now recognized the protector.

Back home, Jack Kennedy once again focused on his quest to leave the U.S. House of Representatives behind. In his mind he was already out of there, and even began disparaging the 435 members as "worms." He'd had it with the House. He'd already begun spending weekends campaigning statewide, and the map hanging on the wall of his Bowdoin Street apartment was starting to be thickly covered in pins. Those were Dave Powers's markers indicating where a speech had been made or where his boss had shared a coffee with a significant political leader.

The time had come to face the big challenge. For him, running for governor in '52 would only be a connecting flight to the next destination. Chuck Spalding could see his friend's determination. Eventually, "if he was going to get anywhere, he'd always have to be able to beat somebody like Lodge . . . So, I think, he made the decision, 'I've been long enough in the House. It's time for me to move ahead. If I'm going to do it, I've got to take this much of a chance.'" Pitting himself against Henry Cabot Lodge—*now* and not later— had overwhelming appeal. Above all, it showed audacity, a quality that ranked high with Jack.

On December 2, 1951, Kennedy made the admission, rare for a politician, of personal ambition. He did it during an appearance— his first—on NBC's *Meet the Press*. The moderator had wasted no time zeroing in on the hot political rumor buzzing through the Bay State.

Lawrence Spivak: When I was in Boston last week, I heard a good deal of talk about you. There were many who thought that you would be the Democratic nominee for the senatorship against Henry Cabot Lodge. Are you going to run?

Jack Kennedy: Well, uh, I'd like to go to the Senate. I'm definitely interested in it. I think most of us in the House who came in after the war—some of them have already gone to the Senate, like George Smathers and Nixon and others, and I'm definitely interested in going to the Senate, and I'm seriously considering running.

But, to anyone paying attention, it was obvious it wasn't just the intramural rivalry of his '46 House classmates driving him. His thinking about matters beyond the scope of the typical House member, his grander notions, were in every way a part of who he was, of who he had become.

The mind of Jack Kennedy, in fact, was already busy with the big picture. He'd been traveling the world since his teens. He'd witnessed Britain and Europe up close in the late '30s, he'd fought in the war and come back to see the depressing events in postwar Europe and Asia. He'd honed a personal sense of what was wrong with U.S. influence abroad.

On his trip to the Far East, for instance, he'd had an eyewitness look at the predicament of France trying to hold on to its empire after World War II, against the local resistance to colonial power. What he saw was the overriding strength of the Vietnamese people's desire for independence.

"You can never defeat the Communist movement in Indochina until you get the support of the natives," he explained in a speech on his return, "and you won't get the support of the natives as long as they feel that the French are fighting the Communists in order to hold their own power there. And I think we shouldn't give the military assistance until the French clearly make an agreement with the natives that at the end of a certain time when the Communists are defeated that the French will pull out and give this country the right of self-determination and the right to govern themselves."

He also articulated that Sunday morning a strong critique of the way America represented itself overseas. On that same *Meet the Press,* Spivak quoted back to Kennedy a remark he'd made about our diplomats being "unconscious of the fact that their role was not tennis and cocktails but the interpretation to the foreign country of the meaning of American life." Is this something, he wanted to know, Kennedy had seen for himself?

"I think something ought to be done about it. I think there are a lot of young men interested in going into the Foreign Service. I don't know where they get a lot of the ones I saw. I think we're not getting the representative, well-rounded type of young man to go to the Foreign Service that we should as a rule. . . . I was up at a college in Massachusetts two days ago, speaking, and I asked, out of five hundred students how many would be interested in going into the Foreign Service, and a surprisingly large number raised their hand. What I think is that they're not getting young men who are well-rounded, who are balanced, and who are what we like to think of as representative Americans."

This call to service for young Americans—especially as they might affect the developing world—marked the beginning of an idea that, a decade later, inspired the country. It was one of many emblematic ideas evolving in his mind even now.

That trip to the Far East had been a confidence builder. Upon his return, Jack had shared what he learned with the voters. It was a repeat of his performance in 1946 as he'd entered the political arena. Back then he'd talked mainly of his experiences in the Pacific Theater, along with the need to prevent another war like the one just ended.

Since then he'd grasped, both instinctively and intellectually, the central importance of nationalism in the new world order and how it would affect Great Power relationships, most crucially those between the United States and the emerging Communist monoliths of Russia and China. What he witnessed, and also deeply understood, was the way that people struggled to free themselves from foreign control. It was a fight that Kennedy, the Irishman and Mucker, could feel in his genes.

He was discovering his ability to absorb complexity. In understanding the dangers facing his country, he saw, too, the role he might play. He had a mission now. To survive the Cold War, his country must grasp its nature. If he could get to the Senate, he might change history.

Despite his resolve to move forward, come what may, Jack began 1952 still unsure which office he would now seek or who'd help him win it. He'd spent four years traveling the state, decorating the map with those pushpins, hitting small towns that statewide Democratic candidates rarely visited. But still he needed an organization that could deliver the vote. He needed *people*.

The very first recruit to the cause was Lawrence F. O'Brien, with whom Jack had earlier been friendly down in Washington and now got in touch with to see if he'd come on board. When Jack met him, O'Brien was on the staff of another Massachusetts congressman, Foster Furcolo. Before taking that job, he'd worked in his family's cafe and bar in Springfield. Well connected in Democratic politics in Springfield, he'd served as manager for three of Furcolo's campaigns.

One day on Capitol Hill, the two of them, Jack and Larry, had dinner, during the course of which O'Brien declared he'd had enough of Washington. Perhaps he'd also had enough of Furcolo. He was heading home.

At a later meeting in Boston, Kennedy asked him to help out with his own effort in the Springfield area, and O'Brien agreed. But it took a strong-arm play by his former boss to complete O'Brien's transition to Kennedy loyalist. O'Brien had agreed to set up a public meeting for Kennedy, only to have Jack get word from Furcolo that

Springfield was *his* turf and he wanted it called off. Jack replied, too bad, he intended to go ahead as planned and Furcolo would just have to live with it.

Larry O'Brien was impressed. The son of Irish immigrants whose dad was a local Democratic leader, he saw Jack Kennedy as a new kind of Irish politician, virtually the antithesis of the typical Democratic pol from Boston. "Republicans were respectable. Republicans didn't get thrown in jail like Jim Curley," O'Brien would write, describing the divide between the two parties as it had long been. The thing was, Jack Kennedy was "respectable" in a whole new style. And what O'Brien, a seasoned strategist, saw was how Jack Kennedy could win votes, especially in the Boston suburbs, that the Democrats had been losing because of the dishonesty of scoundrels like Curley.

"But Jack Kennedy was different. If the Yankee politicians had their snob appeal, so did the Kennedys. Those suburban sons and daughters of immigrants might not say 'I'm a Democrat,' but I hoped they could be brought to say, 'I'm for Jack Kennedy.'"

To O'Brien, his new ally, Jack made the extent of his ambition clear. Pointing at the Massachusetts State House from the window of his Bowdoin Street apartment, he put it this way: "Larry, I don't look forward to sitting over there in the governor's office and dealing out sewer contracts."

In aiming high and refusing to be satisfied with even the governor's job—when what he wanted was to be a senator—Jack was showing how much his ambitions paralleled his father's. Joe Kennedy refused to settle for what his fellow Boston Irish regarded as good enough achievement, an upper-middle-class level of success. Joe wanted more—and allowed nothing to stand in his way. In his own words: "For the Kennedys, it's either the castle or the outhouse."

Besides O'Brien, the other key recruit joined the team as a result of Bobby Kennedy's intervention. In February 1952, Bobby got in touch with his college roommate Ken O'Donnell, suggesting he join the campaign effort. "He called me and said Jack was going to run, had not decided for what, but he was going to run."

Ken O'Donnell was a hybrid—a middle-class Irish guy who'd gone to Harvard, but whose dad had been the legendary football coach at Holy Cross. Raised in Worcester, he was both town and gown. In World War II, he'd served in the Army Air Corps based in Britain and flown more than thirty missions over Germany as a bombardier, often in the lead plane. During the Battle of the Bulge he was forced to crash-land between German and Allied lines. But his most harrowing exploit came when he'd had to climb down and kick loose a bomb stuck in the doors. He'd ended up hanging on to the plane for dear life—certainly a strong memory to carry into one's postwar career, and also a character-building one. His football career at Harvard only added to his appeal. On all counts, Ken O'Donnell was the kind of guy Jack Kennedy could admire and, eventually, trust.

At their first meeting to discuss the job, just five days after the call had come from Bobby, Jack was put off by O'Donnell's questioning of him. The problem was that Ken had asked him which office he actually wanted to run for, a reasonable enough question for a prospective campaign worker. Jack didn't like it. One reason was that he didn't know the answer. But Ken O'Donnell was just the kind of guy Jack needed to win, no matter his place on the ballot.

At home in Harvard Yard and on Soldiers Field, O'Donnell was equally at ease with those "lace-curtain" Irish who'd gained wealth and social self-esteem. Yet he knew, too, the working class with all its awe of pedigreed Yankees like Henry Cabot Lodge, Jr., and its entrenched resentment of the lace-curtain types. He knew the begrudgers, those Irish who made a specialty of hating those who either had a leg up on them or acted as if they did. Winning Ken O'Donnell's steadfast loyalty, which he soon did, was one of Jack Kennedy's crowning lifetime achievements.

Ken recognized Jack's voter appeal long before he went to work for him. "He started getting our attention because he made statements and did things that weren't the norm for politicians in Massachusetts. When he didn't sign Curley's pardon petition, it didn't mean much in terms of the position, but it meant something to my generation. We quietly watched . . . and here was a guy who bore some watching. Frankly, his money had something to do with it. He was wealthy, so he could be independent of the political machine. They can't crush him the way they can somebody else, because he has both the money to stand up to them and the guts to tell them to go to hell. He was one of us. He is a veteran. He has had enough. He can afford to take them on."

"Them" was personified by the name Henry Cabot Lodge. And, to illustrate exactly the weight that name once carried in the Commonwealth of Massachusetts, consider this famous bit of doggerel penned by a Holy Cross graduate:

In the land of the bean and the cod,
The Cabots speak only to the Lodges,
And the Lodges only to God.

The current Henry Cabot Lodge was the grandson of the first Henry Cabot Lodge, who'd beaten Jack Kennedy's grandfather John "Honey Fitz" Fitzgerald for the U.S. Senate. He was the Republican who'd successfully crushed Woodrow Wilson's struggle to establish the League of Nations following World War I.

In 1936 his grandson, at the age of thirty-four, assumed the ancestral Lodge seat. Then, in 1942, the younger Lodge joined the U.S. Army and served gallantly in North Africa while remaining a senator. His outfit won the distinction of being the first American unit in World War II to make ground contact with the German army. When President Roosevelt ordered that men serving in both the military and the Congress make a choice between the two roles, Lodge left the army in 1942. But after winning reelection that year, he chose to give up his seat to rejoin the army, the first senator to do so since the Civil War.

As a lieutenant colonel, Lodge distinguished himself in Europe by once single-handedly capturing a four-man German patrol. He was decorated with the French Légion d'Honneur and the Croix de Guerre. At the end of the war, he served as liaison officer and interpreter in the surrender negotiations with German forces. In 1946, he ran for the Senate again, now a handsome war hero come back to serve the people. As such, he drew extraordinary respect, especially among the Irish, who usually voted Democratic. He was viewed by them as a man of the people, a man's man, a strong-jawed Yankee who was a regular enough guy to come have a beer at the local bar. Though times were changing, such condescension still went over well. Lodge was the kind of high-standing Brahmin the Irish looked up to.

Ken O'Donnell understood that Senator Lodge was more than the well-born patrician, more than just his name or his family tree. He recognized the reality of Lodge's very genuine accomplishment, returning from the war and in '46 beating Senator David I. Walsh, a powerful Democratic fixture on the state's political scene for nearly half a century. "Lodge, killing off Walsh, became the giant of Massachusetts politics. He had a good organization, excellent staff, and he was honest. Lodge was everything people wanted in a politician."

By early 1952, Lodge was a major figure in national Republican politics. He would soon be an even greater pillar of the party. It was he who, sticking his neck out, asked General Dwight David Eisenhower, formerly supreme commander of the Allied Forces in Europe and now supreme commander of NATO, to run for president. When Ike rebuffed his proposal, Lodge went on *Meet the Press* and promoted the idea publicly. With the general's quiet support, he soon accepted the job of Eisenhower's campaign manager, entering him in the New Hampshire primary. When his candidate beat the Ohio senator known as "Mr. Republican," Robert A. Taft, in that momentous contest, Lodge had not only pulled off a considerable coup, but was now the closest advisor to a five-star hero headed for the White House.

Mark Dalton, a good friend to Jack whose speechwriting ability was his greatest asset, had been the official "campaign manager" for that first congressional run in 1946. More a pipe-smoking intellectual than a tough, savvy strategist, Dalton was once again nominally in charge of what was happening, but with no title and no real power. Unfortunately, he possessed none of the organization-building or tactical skills necessary to get up and running the sort of statewide campaign now called for. Besides that, he was absolutely incapable of mustering the strength to withstand the meddling of Jack's father, the nature of whose influence—he was paying the bills—could never for an instant *not* be dealt with. And this was a job that needed doing.

For all his wily self-made rich man's shrewdness, the estimable Joseph P. Kennedy lacked political sense. Good at making money, he had little or no gift for democracy. He thought you got your way in this world by cozying up to people at the top, and bossing everyone else. His notion of putting together an effective campaign team was to get a squad of old political hands together and then start barking orders. That was no playbook for winning elections, certainly not the one against Henry Cabot Lodge.

Therefore, the first thing O'Donnell—whose political grasp was instinctive—looked to accomplish once he signed on to Jack's effort was to get the old man's hands out of the pudding. And not just that, but from the instant he arrived on the scene, he recognized an even bigger issue, which was that nothing had been done, throughout those early months of 1952, to build a statewide organization that could ever hope to come together to unseat the formidable incumbent. What was deadly clear to O'Donnell was the extent to which the two problems were intertwined.

No one had the nerve to stand up to Joe Kennedy when it came to naming Kennedy "secretaries" across the state. O'Donnell recalled: "I said to Dalton, 'Look, we need to name a secretary or leader in each community to be a Kennedy man, and then that person can form committees and set up events, but we can't be sitting in this office.'" Soon, Ken would conclude that Dalton simply was "too nice to be in politics." But that wasn't the same as solving the problem.

Jack himself could not make up his mind. He wouldn't fire Dalton, but at the same time he wouldn't give him the authority to do the job, not even the title. If Dalton was too weak, and he, O'Donnell, too much the newcomer, then who was there around who'd be able to short-circuit Joe Kennedy's meddling, to talk back to him and keep him on the sidelines? Only one man seemed to fill the bill, O'Donnell concluded: his old roommate, Bobby.

Bobby, O'Donnell knew, understood how to gain his father's approval, for the simple reason that he'd spent his young life doing it. It was a task that Jack, who kept his distance from his father and was always wary of him, couldn't manage. By being the good son,

Bobby had earned and could now cash in on his father's trust. If Jack was to win this election, the question of bringing in Bobby would have to be answered. And soon.

The date for Jack's big decision was April 6. That's because Governor Paul Dever had scheduled that date to announce which job he was running for. Would the governor think he might be able to beat Lodge, or would he decide to play it safe and seek a third term?

Joe Healey, Jack's Harvard tutor, went with Kennedy when he was summoned to the meeting with Dever, which took place at the grand old Ritz-Carlton across from the Boston Public Garden. "We arrived at the Ritz about three o'clock, went to a room, and waited. Governor Dever had a topcoat on, and he said—and I think these were his exact words—'Jack, I'm a candidate for reelection.' And Jack said, 'Well, that's fine. I'm a candidate for the Senate.'"

There were many factors joining together to favor Jack Kennedy's Senate run in 1952.

A keen observer, Jack saw it was now the case that, whatever they'd felt previously, Irish voters could now express pride, and not resentment, when called upon to identify with their most socially and financially successful family. His own personal charm had a great deal to do with how the Kennedy name resounded. So did all the countless hours he'd put into meeting voters and making them feel that a connection had been made and that he was, really, one of them.

The Kennedy "teas" were a smart combination of old and new. A novel concept, they served to boost awareness of Jack's senatorial campaign, and at the same time create followers who would then, they hoped, turn into volunteers. The official hosts at the kickoff tea would be the former ambassador to the Court of St. James, the

Honorable Joseph P. Kennedy, and his wife, Rose. After all, everyone knew the pair of them had spent time in London among the English. Why wouldn't they want to hold a "tea" to meet and greet the people of Massachusetts?

Thus, Kennedy's background, rather than his party, became the major element in his attractiveness to voters. What worked splendidly was the way the teas bridged the obvious gap. The invitees were excited and pleased to be there—working-class and middle-class women alike. It proved a brilliant strategy for claiming the majority of voters.

Across the state, Jack's attractive sisters Eunice, Pat, and Jean hit the hustings for him as they had in Cambridge six years earlier. Everywhere these events took place, Jack Kennedy came off as the kind of aristocratic Irishman that the public enjoying the cakes and cookies hadn't seen before—one of theirs, and yet the perfect challenger, well matched against the elegant Henry Cabot Lodge.

As David Powers would note, one basic truth about these receptions was that here was an invitation turning up in mailboxes amid envelopes normally filled only with bills. Finding themselves requested to come have tea with the Kennedys left many of the recipients astonished—and pleased. For the first tea held in his gritty hometown of Worcester, Ken O'Donnell made certain the invitations went out—specifically—to regular Catholics, rather than "lace-curtain" ones.

Here's his description of that afternoon: "It was a beautiful day. He was on crutches. He walked in and the room came to a halt. Everyone stared. He walked in and took over, and every one of those people just had hands on him, wanted to shake his hand and touch him. This little Italian lady was wearing a new dress and hat and gloves she paid $100 for and she could not get to him fast enough. They weren't the hoity-toity rich, they were the hardworking poor of

Worcester, but today, this day, they all looked hoity-toity, all dressed to shake the hands of that young congressman and his family. The place was packed, lines out the door. You could not move. Packed. I knew then, 'We've got something going here. This guy, he's got it.'

"He spoke, shook every single person's hand in the room. He was on crutches, and, by the end, it was clear his hand was swollen—and it was evident to me he was in pain, real pain. I remember being concerned about him. It was the first time I realized he had substantial health issues. I hate to say it, but I was concerned, also, from a political standpoint. I realized there was something more to his health problems and I was wondering what it was. I also was wondering whether you can elect a candidate who has to be on crutches all the time.

"He wasn't well known in Worcester. He hadn't spent a lot of time in Worcester, and hadn't gotten any good press in Worcester. It was something different. I wouldn't have gone, myself, and I didn't think my mother would go, but she was there. I was shocked to see her and all her friends. *Shocked*. I had never known them to bother with politicians. Then, I just *knew*.

"You're talking two or three thousand people on a Sunday who came out to meet him. They went through the line once and they'd go back again, then shake his hand again, then just stop and watch him, just watch him. They would not leave. Nobody would leave until he left, and even after he left they all just stood there in awe. It was just that I had never seen anything like it. I just felt this guy could go all the way."

In fact, the very visible strains of his physical infirmities caused Jack Kennedy—greeting voters as he stood there on crutches—to resemble distantly, and despite his wealth, a character like Dickens's Tiny Tim. His simple fortitude compelled people to root for him. When X-rays taken of Jack's spine in 1951 showed the collapse of support bones in his spinal column, it could hardly have been surprising to anyone who spent time with him, especially out on the road. Charlie Bartlett, who joined him on some of these trips, remembered Jack keeping a stiff upper lip through it all. "I must say, he always had a sort of stoic, sociable quality about it. He'd drive all over that damn state. With that back it must have hurt like hell, and he'd sit there with the coat collar up and drive through those cold Massachusetts evenings."

But even though Ken O'Donnell was now convinced Jack might actually have a very good shot at winning against the formidable Lodge, what was still needed was someone to run the show. "The whole operation had degenerated into a three-ring circus, with Joe Kennedy coming in once in a while disrupting things, Jack showing up only rarely, and nothing getting done the minute he left." Somebody had to play middleman.

"I knew the Kennedys well enough by then to know the only one who can talk to the Kennedys is a Kennedy. It took a Kennedy to take on a Kennedy. I knew Bobby was the only one with enough sense, who was tough enough and a regular enough guy to run the campaign. He'd be the only one able to turn to the father and say, 'No, Jack won't do it.'"

At this point Ken made his move. He phoned Bobby and laid it on the line, all but demanding he drop everything and get up to Massachusetts to run his brother's campaign. Otherwise, Jack was going to have his butt handed to him. Bobby hated what he was hearing, for the understandable reason that he wanted to build his own career as a Justice Department lawyer and thus his own life. But he could hear his friend's argument, knew it, probably, even before he heard it. Someone had to broker matters between his dad and Jack. He was the one—the only one—to do it, and do it right.

Now that Bobby seemingly was willing to leave his job and

come run the campaign, there was the problem of selling Jack on the idea. O'Donnell recalled the scene in the car when he and his boss went head to head on it. The truth was, Jack didn't like hearing Ken had talked to Bobby without going through him first, but, at the same time, and despite his irritation, he saw the point.

First, Jack sounded off. He, above all, seemed stunned to learn that there'd been any lack of action on the part of his people. As O'Donnell remembers the tongue-lashing, Kennedy couldn't believe they hadn't begun naming local secretaries across the state. "As far as I'm concerned, this moment you can go ahead and begin. I'm not interested in the nuts and bolts of who's going to run what. That's the job of the organization and not the candidate."

But, after he'd finished giving O'Donnell a taste of his anger, he'd also obviously talked his way into a decision. Ken O'Donnell had won. "That was the day that Bobby decided he would move to Massachusetts. Bobby, as I recall, went back to get his own personal affairs in order, and then he came up."

Mark Dalton had seen it coming. Though he had his own law practice, he'd been volunteering time for Jack's political career, mainly writing speeches, ever since the victorious '46 race. He'd now given up his practice and come to work full-time for the congressman. It was a change in status, from friend and unofficial counselor to paid aide, and it would matter.

For him, the decisive incident occurred at a meeting at a social club in Fall River. As he made to leave, Kennedy had to pass the bar, where was parked a convivial trio "feeling no pain." The men garrulously corralled Kennedy. Dalton, ignoring the candidate's plight, had continued alone to the parking lot.

It was the wrong move. Jack wasn't happy. "He got in the car, turned around, and stuck his finger in my belly," Dalton recalled a half century later. "'Don't you ever let that happen to me again.'"

Now he got the picture. "I was to take care of him with drunks. I was his caretaker, his bodyguard. That son of a bitch! Right in the belly! 'Don't you ever'!"

Jack's rough treatment of his old pal was a sign of something off-kilter in the relationship. For him, the problem with Dalton wasn't about getting waylaid by the Fall River drunks; rather, it was about the campaign, his father, and the way things felt stalled. The final moment for Dalton came at a meeting where Joe Kennedy tore into him for leasing a new campaign headquarters without his permission. "He didn't like the building," O'Donnell remembered. "He thought we'd paid too much for it. He didn't like the owner. He thought the location was bad, and they had a great brawl about it."

When Jack refused to stand up for his campaign manager, Dalton had no choice except to quit. Bobby made the gesture of trying to soften the blow by asking him to stay on as speechwriter, but Dalton left the office that day with his belongings and never returned. "I decided that I could no longer play a role in the Kennedy campaign in view of the feeling which had developed. I wrote John a little note saying I was through and then I told him that I was through." Listening to him so many years later, it was obvious that Dalton never got over the way he'd been discarded.

Once Bobby arrived, he began working eighteen-hour days to get the campaign workers focused and up to full speed. "I didn't become involved in what words should go in a speech, what should be said on a poster or billboard, what should be done on television. I was so busy with my part of it that I didn't see any of that." Most important, when he moved in, their father moved out.

This was, just for the record, not Bobby Kennedy's first involvement in a Jack Kennedy campaign. He had a talent for organization. In the '46 race, as a twenty-year-old, he'd asked for the toughest area, East Cambridge, territory loyal to the former Cambridge mayor Mike Neville, Jack's strongest opponent, Tip O'Neill's candidate. But Bobby took it slowly, laying the groundwork, spending time playing softball with the kids of the neighborhood, killing the notion that the Kennedys thought themselves superior. His brother ended up doing better in that community than anyone had expected.

Bobby enjoyed one advantage over Jack, and it had to do with their attitude toward Joe. While his brother was stubborn in his dealings with their father, Bobby was respectful and needy for love. This created a smooth relationship, even if one layered with guile. He proved to be the essential cog in the Kennedy machine. No one else could have done what he was now doing. There he was, having left his job in Washington, working all out in the campaign, using his father's resources—money and public-relations clout—to produce the maximum impact where it counted, on the hearts and minds of the Massachusetts voters. Charlie Bartlett remembers listening to Bobby on the phone with the senior Kennedy. "Yes, Dad," Bobby kept repeating, "Yes, Dad." However, he wasn't taking orders; rather, he was pacifying. Where Jack always took their dad with a grain of salt and didn't mind letting him know it, the younger Kennedy boy never treated him as less than the paterfamilias.

It was now May and the election was six months away. Out in the field, Larry O'Brien was helping the cause by building the organization from the ground up, one Kennedy "secretary" at a time. What this meant, at a very basic, very significant level, was the creation of a totally different political network from that of the regular Massachusetts Democrats. "Our secretaries were making weekly reports to me, and they were growing more sophisticated from week to week. . . . For a long time neither Lodge nor the Democratic regulars realized what we were doing."

At their April 6 meeting at the Ritz-Carlton, Governor Dever had made it clear that Jack was going to have to build his own organization. Meaning, if he chose to go up against Lodge, it was his show, for he wouldn't be getting any help from Dever, who had his own race to run. But such a challenge also suited the Kennedy people. They wanted solid loyalty from their people, no confusion about which candidate mattered most.

For me, Ken O'Donnell personified the old brand of politics, which the Kennedys were customizing on a family basis. From the moment he signed on, he had one vocation: helping and protecting John F. Kennedy. And right now, in the summer of 1952, his value lay in his ability to grasp and use the reality of post–World War II Massachusetts, the world he knew. As a man who'd lived between Worcester and Cambridge, between Holy Cross and Harvard, he had a natural understanding of those voters Jack Kennedy needed to pry away from Lodge. They were folks whose parents were loyal Democrats, while they, this new generation, reserved the right to cast their ballot candidate by candidate.

What Jack Kennedy was trying to do, helped by O'Donnell and others, wasn't going to be easy. They were trying to outflank Lodge, a moderate Republican, from the right and the left. In other words, Kennedy had to come off as both a tough Cold Warrior and a work-and-wages Democrat—which is precisely what he'd spent six years being. This allowed him to strike at his rival from the right for not being aggressive enough on foreign policy and from the left for not being sufficiently on the side of the average family struggling to make ends meet; that is, for not being a Democrat. It was a pincer move that was to work well again in a later Kennedy campaign. The strategy is to bash an opponent on both sides until you force him to go both ways to avoid the very charges you're making against him. The voter sees the targeted rival being pulled apart by his own hands.

Kennedy set his people digging for weak spots in Lodge's record.

"Lodge was always on the popular side of every issue, which didn't necessarily make him an awfully good statesman, but might make him a satisfactory politician," Jack told Rip Horton. To prepare for the planned bombardment of Lodge, Ted Reardon, who'd been Jack's top aide on the Hill, began assembling an inventory of his voting on the issues. This carefully documented loose-leaf binder, each page covered in sheer plastic, was soon dubbed "Lodge's Dodges"—or, more irreverently, the "Bible"—and it provided the ammunition for the coming all-out assault.

Joe Healey, Kennedy's speechwriter, found himself impressed by Reardon's attention to Lodge's every word, tracking down every discrepancy. "The major credit belongs to Ted Reardon for certainly one of the most thorough jobs in this area I have ever seen."

From this point on, the campaign's operating structure quickly fell into line. Bobby, as the campaign manager, decided where the money went. This is always the supreme power that comes with that title. "Any decision you wanted, Bobby made," O'Donnell recalled. "If you were talking about spending two hundred bucks to do such and such, Bobby would say, yes, go ahead, and that was it."

The Kennedy Party, as it continued to grow, was the perfect model of a volunteer operation. Those who came to work for Jack found themselves making a personal investment in the candidate's future, resulting in a campaign of relationship rather than transaction. In this sense, it wasn't about political payoffs, at least not in the business-as-usual way. Anyone who walked into a Kennedy headquarters was, right off the bat, given a task to do. His people knew the best method of earning and toughening loyalty was by quickly getting a newly interested citizen onto the team. Before you knew it, you were a "Kennedy person."

What happened, as in 1946, was that word would start to spread that a member of this family or that friend or neighbor was "working for Jack Kennedy." It made the campaign a kind of cement, ever expanding its hold. You pretty much *wanted* to take part. It was as simple as that for many people. And so the organization built on itself.

To enforce this, Bobby Kennedy repeatedly made it clear to one and all that there were to be *no* paid campaign workers. No exceptions. One local political veteran who'd supported Jack's campaign in '46 would learn the hard way that the campaign manager this time around wasn't about to be messed with. Here's Ken O'Donnell's account of what happened when that fellow failed to take the hint:

"'How much money is the candidate going to give us to spend in our district?' this guy called out at a meeting. When Bob Kennedy ignored him and kept to the order of business, the man then stood up and cut Bobby off. 'Listen, kid, we've been around a long time, we know politics. You're wet behind the ears and you'd be better off in Washington than here, where you don't know what you are doing. You've got to pay these people; you want campaign people out working for you, you got to pay them, and you can afford it. The Kennedys are rich.' Bobby just stared at him. Then he got up, grabbed him by his collar, and showed him the door—and, as he was throwing him out in the street, he told him, 'Would you mind getting lost . . . and keeping yourself lost.'"

When the troublemaker appealed his case to Jack, Bobby didn't like it one bit. "Look, you get one guy like that crying, then you have to pay him and his volunteers to work. Then other people hear about it, and then they want to be paid to volunteer, and then we'll end up spending a million dollars in Boston alone. I'm not going to have him around. You asked me to run this campaign. I didn't want to, but now I'm here, so I will run it my way."

Jack was actually tougher than his younger brother. When

Governor Dever began to worry that he was going to lose his race and saw Kennedy gaining strength, he offered to combine forces. Joseph Kennedy liked the idea; O'Brien and O'Donnell didn't. Jack agreed with his people, refusing to be Dever's life preserver. He gave Bobby the job of delivering the decision to his father and Dever both. "Don't give in to them, but don't get me involved with it," were the instructions. The older brother was becoming a hard-nosed, unsentimental politician. Bobby's role was to play the *part* of one.

From the beginning, the teas that started it all proved to be an excellent recruiting platform. As O'Donnell was to explain, "Nobody went to one who didn't fill out a card. We had them in every community, and . . . they allowed our organization to get going and to get our secretary in action." They became competitive events. "When Lowell had four thousand, Lawrence had to have five thousand. So the secretary had a great incentive."

Hugh Fraser, one of Jack's British friends visiting at the time, was impressed by the novelty of these occasions, referring to them as "shenanigans." "The 'tea party' technique amazed me," said Fraser, who'd never seen anything of its kind.

Anyone who organized a tea was required to provide a quota of signatures for Kennedy's nomination papers. Only 2,500 signatures statewide were required for a candidate in the Senate primary, but Dave Powers and Larry O'Brien had decided that they'd ask the regional organizers to produce a grand total of 250,000. The reason, according to O'Donnell, was not just "psychological"; it was also a way to have a quarter-million voters not only committed but actively participating in the early stages, before the real fight started up in the general election campaign. Too, it was a gauge to help them figure how the organizers were performing and which ones were particularly effective.

The teas were aimed at winning the hearts of the working class, and also as a means of identifying and organizing the Democratic voter base. But equally crucial was the need to go after those Irish and other traditional Democratic voters who'd drifted away and might very likely stay drifted with the popular Ike as the Republican candidate.

It had been customary for statewide Democratic candidates in Massachusetts to expend their major effort in the larger cities, where most of their voters lived. In other words, they counted heavily on Boston. Jack Kennedy, instead, went out and methodically hit every neighborhood, including the largely Republican suburbs, ignoring the toll this relentless, unsparing, but extraordinarily effective effort to reach voters took on his physical well-being.

O'Donnell figured that Jack Kennedy could pull votes in small suburban communities where no other Democrat might. "We appreciated the fact that there were an awful lot of Democrats throughout the state, in those small towns, who'd moved out of Boston and out of the big cities into these small communities, had bought their own homes. They were Democrats, but ashamed of some of the antics that had been associated with the party." He saw these as potential Kennedy people.

Here again, Kennedy had gotten traction from his early start in places off the standard grid for Democrats. "We'd be in those homes—in the homes with seven or eight people, who'd remember having coffee with Jack Kennedy in 1947 or '48," said O'Donnell.

The Second World War had changed a great deal in American life. In the Northeast, as elsewhere, the Irish and other ethnic groups were seeing beyond the old boundaries, and didn't want to be the pawns of the big-city political bosses. They wanted the fresh air of the suburbs, the freedom of making up their own minds at election time. Many had gone to college under the GI Bill. They no longer felt confined by the politics of the old neighborhood. "Boston" meant a certain kind of old politics, and a sort they were only too happy to leave behind. This sense of the shifting times was definitely an idea the Kennedy campaign made skillful use of.

As election day approached, Tip O'Neill, facing no real opposition in the general election, got a call asking him to lend a hand. He was to be Jack's stand-in at an election-eve radio broadcast. Tip's script from Kennedy headquarters arrived just minutes before airtime. It "kicked the living hell out of Henry Cabot Lodge," O'Neill would recall, to his chagrin. Senator Lodge, who spoke next, was outraged by what he regarded as an ambush, and told O'Neill's wife, Millie, "The Kennedys would never give a speech like that for him. And I would never say the things about Jack Kennedy that he was saying about me."

Lodge had a far bigger problem. Throughout the course of the campaign he'd been greatly distracted by his efforts, begun the year before, to promote Eisenhower. This had earned him the bitter hostility of Republican voters steadfastly loyal to Ike's opponent for the nomination, Senator Robert Taft of Ohio, "Mr. Republican." Here Joe Kennedy saw his opportunity. He convinced the pro-Taft publisher of the New Bedford *Standard-Times* to reprint in full the glowing *Reader's Digest* article on his son's *PT 109* exploits, then to break ranks and endorse the Democratic candidate, young Jack Kennedy, outright. When Jack went on the attack, criticizing Lodge's absenteeism from the Senate, the newspaper dutifully repeated those charges in its editorials. Next, when Lodge countered by citing Kennedy's own poor voting record, the *Standard-Times* refused to publish the information.

To gain the endorsement of the equally conservative *Boston Post,* Joseph P. Kennedy got out his checkbook to write its pliable publisher a loan for $500,000. About this episode, Jack would later joke that for him to win his Senate seat his father had to "buy a fuckin' newspaper."

To pound home Lodge's weakness among Taft Republicans, Jack accused him of being a "100 percent" supporter of Truman's appeasing administration policy in China and the Far East.

But if Lodge was overly committed to Eisenhower's candidacy, Jack Kennedy was undercommitted to Adlai Stevenson's. He simply could not disguise his lack of faith in the Democratic presidential nominee, and, after having breakfast with him at the 1952 Democratic National Convention, Kennedy complained about his encounter to a friend, "Well, for Christ's sake. I don't know why I allowed myself to be railroaded into *that*. That was an absolutely catastrophic breakfast."

"What happened?" asked his listener.

"Well," Jack explained, "practically nothing happened. As I saw it, he was looking at me and he knew that I didn't really think he was the best candidate. He knew that I knew that he knew."

The one man who might possibly have saved Lodge's bid for reelection refused to help. When an S.O.S. came from Lodge's campaign asking Wisconsin Senator Joseph McCarthy to come to Boston and make a speech on behalf of the incumbent senator, McCarthy demurred. He told the conservative columnist William F. Buckley, Jr., in whose Connecticut home he was staying at the time, that Lodge had always opposed him. Young Jack Kennedy, on the other hand, he counted as a covert supporter. McCarthy even told Buckley he'd made the Lodge people a counteroffer he knew would surely be refused. "I told them I'd go up to Boston to speak if Cabot publicly asked me to. And he'll never do that; he'd lose the Harvard vote!"

Richard Nixon, meanwhile, had been put on the ballot as the

Republican nominee for vice president, Ike's running mate. It was a skyrocketing leap for a congressman who'd gone to Washington the same year as Jack. The latter was gracious in a handwritten note. "Dear Dick: I was tremendously pleased that the convention selected you for V.P. I was always convinced that you would move ahead to the top—but I never thought it would come this quickly. You were the ideal selection and will bring to the ticket a great deal of strength. Please give my best to your wife and all kinds of good luck to you."

The Kennedy campaign, meanwhile, presented its own man as every inch an anti-Communist crusader as any Republican. When Adlai Stevenson made a campaign stop in Springfield, Massachusetts, Sargent Shriver—who was an employee of Joe's in Chicago and would marry Eunice Kennedy the following year— sent him a very pointed note. "Up there, this anti-Communist business is a good thing to emphasize."

Sarge Shriver also let it be known, in a briefing paper, exactly what the Kennedy people wanted the Democratic presidential candidate to say about the local boy when speaking on his behalf. Stevenson should say it was Kennedy, not his Republican colleague from California, Richard M. Nixon, who'd been the first to expose Communists in organized labor. He "was the man . . . that got Christoffel . . . not Nixon."

The pitch was legitimate. Earlier in the year, Jack had attended an anniversary dinner of the Spee, his Harvard club. There, one of the speakers told the gathering how proud he was that their college had never produced "a Joseph McCarthy *or* an Alger Hiss." Kennedy jumped from his chair. "How dare you couple the name of a great American patriot with that of a traitor!" he exclaimed, and left the dinner early.

The Kennedy family's close association with Joe McCarthy

wasn't an asset everywhere in the Commonwealth. In fact, it hurt him badly with one particular community. Jewish voters had reason enough to question the younger Kennedy's attitudes, given his father's record of unveiled anti-Semitic comments and sentiment. Now the senior Kennedy once more expressed himself outrageously and stirred up the problem anew. When a campaign aide passed around a proposed statement attacking McCarthyism, Joe Kennedy went wild. "You and your . . . sheeny friends . . . are trying to ruin my son's career." Although Jack tried to assure the campaign worker, who was not himself Jewish, about his father, the episode became notorious.

Senator Lodge saw an opening. His campaign began distributing literature spotlighting a report by Herbert von Dirksen, who'd been the last German ambassador to Great Britain before World War II. In it the author recounted Joseph Kennedy's support for Hitler's prewar actions against the Jews. Lodge then recruited Congressman Jacob Javits of New York, a Jewish Republican, to come and speak to a large Jewish gathering in Mattapan. In his talk, Javits stressed repeatedly that Jack was "the son of his father." As Tip O'Neill remembered the event, "He didn't have to be any more explicit."

But Javits, one of the smartest national legislators of his era, also had an indictment of Jack personally. Publicly critical of President Truman's spending policies, Kennedy had voted for a House amendment to cut back foreign aid. While the measure dealt with the overall Middle East spending package, the reduction affected Israel, too. Despite Kennedy's out-front backing for the creation of the Jewish state and his recent visit to the country, Javits's attack stung. As O'Neill told the story, it took Majority Leader John McCormack himself to damp down the fire by spinning it that Kennedy had voted a "token" reduction of U.S. aid to Israel in order to save it from a larger cut. It was a simple case of a respected politician—McCormack was known as "the Rabbi" for his strong support of Jewish concerns—looking out for a fellow Democrat.

The father's reputation, nastily earned as it was, would always be a problem for Jack. As Ken O'Donnell himself noted, "You can't stop a whispering campaign if it's true." If Jack could never adequately defend his father's attitudes, he certainly didn't share them. He knew that Jewish fears were legitimate. "They have problems you don't know anything about," he'd remind O'Donnell.

His health, too, continued to be an issue he could never ignore. In October he made the mistake of sliding down a fireman's pole in Everett, Massachusetts, an impulsive act that worsened the state of his already weakened back. "He was in intense pain towards the end of the campaign," his aide John Galvin recalled. "I'm convinced that there were times when he was walking around almost unconscious."

Despite such all too real medical handicaps, which couldn't be disguised, the boyish Jack continued to win fans. That summer of 1952, three hundred Capitol Hill news correspondents had voted Congressman Kennedy of Massachusetts the "handsomest" member of the House. In order to capitalize on this perception, Jack proceeded to sign up for a special course offered by the CBS network on how to use the new medium of television to best advantage; it was a savvy move, since, by then, about half the households in the country owned a set. This habit of self-improvement was a pattern he continued, going on to take other courses in subjects ranging from speed-reading to public speaking.

On November 3—the eve of Election Day—General Eisenhower, the Republican candidate for president, ended his national campaign in Boston. Ahead in the polls, he was completing his march to the American presidency bearing tribute to the man who'd led him to the fight, the noble Henry Cabot Lodge.

"'It looks like Eisenhower's going to win easily,'" Torby Macdonald recalled telling Jack as the ballots were being counted the next night, "'but I don't think that necessarily means it's going to affect you in Massachusetts.' He said, 'Why not?' I said, 'Well, I think you represent the best of the new generation, really, the newly arrived people. And Lodge represents the best of the old-line Yankees. I think there are more of the newly arrived people than there are of the old-line Yankees.'"

Macdonald never forgot what came next. "Then, out of the clear blue sky, he asked me a question. 'I wonder what sort of job Ike will give Cabot?' I just thought to myself that if I were in Jack's position, listening to these returns . . . Where do you get that kind of serenity?

"By twelve o'clock that night, there was a definite conclusion that Eisenhower had carried the state by 200,000 votes. John Barry, a well-known writer for the *Globe*, went on TV and said authoritatively: 'On the basis of the returns now received by the *Boston Globe*, it is definite that Governor Dever has been defeated for Governor of Massachusetts, that Congressman Kennedy has been defeated, and Senator Lodge has been reelected to the United States Senate.'"

"Well, all hell broke loose," O'Donnell recalled the moment. "The congressman called Bobby, furious—and Bobby cut him off and said, 'Look, on the basis of our numbers and our chart and the basis of what we have and our computations, we are winning the race. And if the trend continues with little drop-off, we will defeat Lodge. The television and newspaper predictions are wrong.'"

O'Donnell, O'Brien, and Bobby remained optimistic. Based on their calculations, the Kennedy vote was doing what it had to even as the candidate kept calling the headquarters and arguing.

"Finally, he got so frustrated he came down around midnight or so," O'Donnell said, "and began to run the slide rule himself. He went town by town, and we walked him through it. But it became confusing to him, and he just kept telling us that the reports we were getting on the television and those we gave to him simply did not square at all."

Governor Dever then telephoned and told Kennedy that, on the basis of the returns, they were both defeated and should concede together. O'Donnell recalled the dramatic response. "The congressman, who by now had learned our system—in fact, had made some improvements to it, typically, and knew it better than we did—said to the governor . . . that on the basis of our computations we were *not* defeated—and that, in fact, on the basis of our figures he was about to win by a narrow margin."

At this point, there remained a general sense Kennedy had lost. Looking beyond their headquarters, they could see what appeared to be the electoral reality. Outside there were rowdies—"Irish bums," O'Donnell called them, local fellows with various bones to pick—shouting drunkenly, "Jack Kennedy, you're a loser and a faker! You're in the shithouse with your old man!" Mainly, they were giving it to Bobby, who'd been the tough guy in the campaign.

By then, according to O'Donnell, "it was just us sitting around drinking coffee. Even most of the girls had left. It was a very disheartening moment.

"At about three or probably closer to four in the morning, only the major cities were still out . . . Worcester . . . Springfield . . . and I remember Bobby and the congressman began to give me some grief, because I'd dismissed the hand-picked Kennedy secretary the congressman had selected in Worcester—he was a faker and I'd replaced him with someone I knew and trusted. Now Bobby was saying to me, 'Everything rides on Worcester and your judgment. If we lose, it's your fault.'

"Well, it was beautiful: he hadn't completed the sentence, literally not gotten the words out of his mouth, when I got a call from our man in Worcester saying we'd carried it by five thousand votes. And that, we all knew, was the final clincher. The congressman and Bobby looked at me in astonishment. Then the congressman said to me, 'You're either the brightest or the luckiest SOB on the planet!'"

After the votes were tallied in the big cities, with Worcester and Springfield now in the Kennedy column, the candidate continued strongly, surpassing other Democrats. "Even in these little towns, we were running four, five, or six percentage points ahead of any Democrat and ahead of Dever. The margin of victory can really be found in all those small communities where he'd spent all that time and done all that work in for the past six, seven years. It was now paying off. Every weekend he could, he'd been out there meeting people, having coffee with them, handshaking—and it was now paying off as it was intended to." The Kennedy Party strategy had worked.

The proud incumbent, there in his headquarters across the street, refused to accept defeat. "We could see him sitting there in his suit coat, looking very calm, watching the returns. What's he waiting for? Why won't he concede? What does he know that we don't? The senator-elect kept asking me, 'Are you sure?' Yes, we were sure, but we were worried. At one point, he even joked, 'Is this what victory looks like?' We were sitting at the card table—the congressman, Dave, Bobby, Larry, myself, and just a few of the girls. The fair-weather types had all gone home.

"Finally, about six or six thirty, Lodge conceded. He walked across, looking dapper, and the congressman, now the senator-elect, said what a bunch of bums we all looked like. 'Put a tie on, for God's sake,' he told Bobby. Lodge came over and shook the newly elected senator's hand. He seemed very disconnected, as if he still could not comprehend that this young fellow had somehow bucked the tidal wave called Eisenhower.

"We ended up winning by seventy thousand votes in a very tight contest; I mean, we knew we were winning, but we also recognized it was very tight. The governor had lost by fourteen thousand votes at this time."

Lyndon Johnson telephoned immediately after the results were in, causing Jack to remark, "That guy must never sleep." O'Brien, though, saw the cunning: "Johnson wasn't wasting any time in courting Kennedy's support." The Senate's democratic leader had just been defeated and Johnson was gunning for the job.

The next night there was a celebration, and all the Democratic hacks and coat holders and meal tickets shamelessly showed up, driving O'Donnell and O'Brien crazy. Unfazed by the strange faces in the room, the victor performed in classic fashion. "The senator-elect got up on a table and sang a song in that famous Kennedy off-tune manner. It was pretty awful. Then it was he and Bobby singing together, in a duet. It was just awful, too."

The Eisenhower-Nixon ticket carried the country by 7 million votes. In Massachusetts, Adlai Stevenson suffered a crushing defeat. Jack Kennedy, meanwhile, had carried the state against Ike's number one man.

He'd taken on the best and beaten the best. He walked out of the race with a solid organization. He had shown his ability to cut people loose—Mark Dalton, after all, had been a close, deeply de-voted champion—who failed to meet his needs. All the while, he let his younger brother take the heat for such acts and thus gain the reputation for being the ruthless one. Bobby, Kenny O'Donnell, and Larry O'Brien were now a rare combination of ice-cold efficiency and die-hard loyalty. The skipper had a new crew, a great one. They'd been blooded by a tough battle fought against the odds and won.

Jack and Bobby—and Kenny, too—would be together for the duration, and they would stand together in the worst crisis of the Cold War, when the stakes were much higher than a Senate seat.

CHAPTER SEVEN

MAGIC

She could be amusing in a direct, caustic way; and she
understood the art of getting on with men completely . . .
never asked an awkward question.

—David Cecil, writing about
Lady Melbourne in *Young Melbourne*

In Washington, Tip O'Neill was moving into his new office in
the House of Representatives. By coincidence, his predecessor was
packing up right across the hall. As he stepped into Jack Kennedy's
outer office, Tip could hear him engaged in a heated backroom argument with his secretary, Mary Davis.

"Mary, now don't be silly. You're coming to the Senate with me."

"No, Senator, I'm not. I'm going to be working for Congressman
Lester Holtzman of New York."

"Now, Mary, you know you're coming with me."

"I am not, Senator, and that's all there is to it."

O'Neill could hear the dispute going back and forth. Finally, he heard Mary say, "And the reason I'm not going with you is that Congressman Holtzman has offered me six thousand dollars."

"Tip, can you believe this?" Jack said when he walked out and saw O'Neill.

"I'm paying her four thousand dollars, and I've just offered her forty-eight hundred. That's a twenty percent raise. But this guy wants to give her six grand the first day he's here. There's not a broad in the world worth six thousand a year."

Mary Davis had similar memories of the standoff. When Kennedy won the Senate race, she accepted the mission of building a clerical staff. To this end, she recruited a team of secretaries to assist her with managing the mail and other constituent work.

"They were all experienced, knew exactly how to do things, what to do, where to go, and they really could have been an invaluable asset to the functioning of his Senate office. But he called me one day from Palm Beach and said that he'd been discussing the situation with his father, who wanted to know: 'Did you find out exactly who they are, what they are, what the salaries are going to be?'"

Joe Kennedy, still watching the purse strings, wasn't above keeping his eye even on the funds the Senate provides its members for hiring staff. "I told him," Davis said, "what I thought the salaries should be, in line with the money we were being allocated. I thought he was going to go through the ceiling!"

She was surprised because she'd set the pay levels for the skilled staff members she'd picked based on the standard allocations from the Senate. But while this might seem routine practice, and wholly acceptable, her focus on the reality of the office's likely day-to-day needs was, in fact, shortsighted. Her eye to office management and not political strategy, she was failing to consider the larger picture. It simply wouldn't have occurred to her that the Kennedys, father and son both, intended to start right away building a wider constituency, one that would extend far beyond the Commonwealth of Massachusetts.

The money, therefore, had to stretch further.

For this reason, Jack rejected both the top-drawer hires and the top-of-the-line pay scale. According to Davis: "He said, 'Well, I don't think we're going to be able to work that out.' And I said, 'Well, why not?' He said, 'Well, number one, I have to have a Polish girl on the staff, I have to have an Italian on the staff, I have to have an Irish girl on the staff, I have to have, you know, these different ethnic groups.' And I said, 'That's ridiculous! You know, a staff member is a staff member.' He said, 'No, *you* don't understand. I've got to have these ethnic groups.'"

Rejecting the pay levels she'd determined appropriate for the newcomers, Kennedy figured sixty dollars a week about right as an upper limit. He believed Mary herself was asking for too high a weekly check.

Hearing this, she was having none of it. "Sixty dollars a week! You've got to be joking. Nobody I've lined up would be willing to accept a job at that salary. I have to have competent, capable staff who can back me up. If I don't, I won't have a life to call my own."

She remembered only too clearly what came next: "His famous reply to me was, 'Mary, you can get candy dippers in Charlestown for fifty dollars a week.' And I said, 'Yes, and you'd have candy dippers on your senatorial staff who wouldn't know beans. If that's what you want, I'm not taking charge of it.'

"He didn't believe me. And that's when I said, 'Uh-unh. Not me.'"

So Tip O'Neill's memory was on the button. She'd continued to stand up to Kennedy despite numerous attempts on his part to win her over. He'd simply pushed her past the breaking point, and his cajoling was to no avail. After six years of working for him, Davis knew the man too well. The issue, for her, anyway, wasn't the money in and of itself. It was a question of whether Jack Kennedy, born to great wealth, was going to give her, Mary Davis, what she knew the U.S. Senate had decided was owed to anyone taking the supervisor job Jack was offering her.

In the end, he didn't budge.

What can be seen here is how the financier Joseph Kennedy exerted enduring control over anything in his son's life having to do with money. Well able to maintain his independence on the matters that counted most with him—policy, politics, his personal associations—Jack was faced with the fact that his father still could tell him what to do if there were dollar signs involved.

There was another rule in play here: when you worked for the Kennedys, you quickly learned that a staffer is a staffer. You needed to understand the limits of the relationship, and also the borders. Mark Dalton had learned that the hard way. As he would tell me, all those years of dedicated volunteering for Jack were forgotten the day he went on the Kennedy family payroll. Before him, the beloved Billy Sutton—the onetime press secretary, entertainer, and live-in buddy—had suffered the same fate. It seemed that he'd asked his salary to be upped from sixty-five dollars a week, a request Jack didn't take well.

Larry O'Brien, shrewder politically than the others, understood the problem and avoided it. "If you work for a politician, he tells you what to do, but if you maintain your independence, you can now and then tell him what to do." Seeing the lay of the land, he decided to return to Springfield after helping Jack win the Senate race.

O'Brien had the situation nailed. He'd worked hard to achieve a balance of mutual respect in his relationship with Jack, and he intended not to let it get *out* of balance. Even as his loyalty grew, so did his awareness of the senator-elect's nature. The man so steadfast in his friendships, carrying along pals from prep school, college, the navy, and his social world, looked upon staff as employees. He had his needs; they had their tasks. Each was obliged to understand his place as well as his task, to honor the bounds of his role and its tenure. The Kennedys believed that anyone could be replaced. So it was, even with a onetime boon companion like Billy Sutton.

Cut loose from the role he'd so cherished and filled so well, Billy still, years later, loved revisiting spots where once he'd hung out with Jack: the diner downstairs from 122 Bowdoin, Jack's apartment, the federal buildings where Jack's offices had been, and political hangouts such as the Parker House hotel. He was like a toy soldier waiting for its young owner to come back.

There's a measure of defense to Kennedy's cutthroat approach to personnel. In Washington, a city packed with people who kiss up and kick down, Jack never kissed up. Although it may not perfectly justify the harshness of his discarding people like Dalton and Davis and Sutton, each of whom had been powerfully loyal to him for a decent number of years, it does put it in the context of the place and its morality. Isn't the definition of a just man one who treats all the same? Jack Kennedy was equally his own man in both directions, caring no more for the feelings of those of higher authority than he was of those who served—or ceased to serve—at his pleasure.

His cheapness, though imposed by his father, came at some cost. George Smathers caught sight of the chaos left in Mary Davis's wake: "I'd go down to his office and it would always seem as in so much pandemonium, such a disarray . . . Everyone in his back office was very friendly, but it didn't seem to me as though there was any organization to it, and I used to tell him so." Jack couldn't believe he was hearing this from a colleague whose own operation was hardly a model of professionalism.

Smathers, to his credit, actually saw past the seeming daily disorder to what lay behind. "His mind was on bigger things. I never did feel that he was a well-organized man either in his personal life or in just the mundane matters of running an office. If the work got done, that was all that really concerned him."

His victory over Henry Cabot Lodge had placed him on a career pedestal sufficient for most men. Yet in Jack's own mind he was merely at the foot of the mountain he now contemplated climbing. To reach the top he would need to further share his vision and also himself, to let a lot more people know who Jack Kennedy was. Even more important, he'd have to successfully signal the country he was ready to lead it.

It was simply a matter of random placement, but Jack Kennedy's new Capitol Hill office was directly across the hall from that of the new vice president. Richard Nixon was in Room 362, Kennedy in 361. Already, both their futures, at least on the surface, seemed mapped out.

The inhabitant of 362, many figured already, was tagged to be his party's nominee for president once the incoming Ike finished his two terms. Opposite him, the senator assigned to 361 was marked to spend—and end—his political career as a New England Democratic moderate, a rich man's son with a celebrated war record who'd shown himself to be a tough Cold Warrior. Being a Roman Catholic, the limitations to Senator Kennedy's political future were clear to any observer. Hadn't the country been electing Protestants to the White House since the first peal of the Liberty Bell?

Even before Kennedy moved into Room 361, he was interviewing people to sit at its desks. One of the hopefuls was a twenty-four-year-old lawyer from Nebraska. Ted Sorensen had grown up a world apart from the Ivy League, from Cape Cod, from the Stork Club, and from the U.S. Navy. He came from Scandinavian and

Jewish parents, had been a conscientious objector and a dedicated supporter of Adlai Stevenson. What grabbed Jack about him, perhaps, was a reference he presented that praised his "ability to write in clear and understandable language" and, more important, called him "a sincere liberal, but not the kind that always carries a chip on his shoulder." Jack liked him already.

The result was a five-minute meeting in the hallway outside the office of the Massachusetts senator. Of the encounter, Sorensen would write, "In that brief exchange, I was struck by this unpretentious, even ordinary man with his extraordinary background, a wealthy family, a Harvard education, and a heroic war record. He did not try to impress me with his importance; he just seemed like a good guy."

Sorensen was surprised even to have been summoned for an interview. He'd sent in his application despite hearing that Jack hired only staffers his father himself might choose. Meaning Irish Catholics, and with few exceptions to this rule. Yet it took only five minutes for Kennedy to make the decision to hire the young stranger. It was another example, one of the most important in its consequence, of Jack *not* being his father's son.

Ted Reardon, tapped to run the Kennedy senate office just as he had the House operation, understood what was happening. Jack was starting to reach beyond his old regulars and past the Massachusetts Irish. He was upgrading his team. He wasn't picking new pals; he had different criteria now. "Jack had the ability to have guys around him whom, personally, he didn't give a damn about as a buddy . . . but he was able to get what he needed from them."

Ted Sorensen was the ideal Kennedy staffer. Not only would he go on to help draft some of Kennedy's most glorious words, ones that stirred the world and resonated down through the decades, but he knew his role. In time it became hard for either man to say who had written what. Ted offered many of the lyrics, but it was always Jack's music. If they were never social intimates, theirs was a collaboration of the heart. Indispensable as he was, Ted Sorensen would write extraordinary prose under the spell of Jack Kennedy.

However, there were issues Sorensen wanted to resolve before coming on board. Although anti-Communist, he was also anti-McCarthy, and so requested a second interview with the senator-elect. It was then he voiced to him his concerns that "he was soft on Senator Joe McCarthy and his witch-hunting tactics. JFK must have thought I was a bit odd, as well as headstrong and presumptuous, a new job applicant asking questions about his political positions. But he did not resent it, calmly explaining that McCarthy was a friend of his father and family, as well as enormously popular among the Irish Catholics of Massachusetts."

Kennedy went on to tell Sorensen he didn't "agree with McCarthy's tactics or find merit in all his accusations." Hearing it all, Sorensen accepted. Now, for the first time, Jack had someone at hand whom neither his father—nor his late brother—would have hired. For Jack Kennedy, Ted Sorensen would be his "intellectual blood bank," providing him the Churchill-like phrase-making we now associate with him. "I never had anyone who could write for me until Ted came along," Kennedy would later tell Tip O'Neill. There was cruelty in the comment, and it bothered O'Neill. Before Sorensen arrived, Jack had gotten speechwriting help from his former Harvard tutor, Joe Healey, who was also a good friend of O'Neill's.

As for Sorensen, he understood the boundaries. "I never wanted to be JFK's drinking buddy; I wanted to be his trusted advisor." It was enough for him—or, at least, he protested as much to the end—to be "totally involved in the substantive side of his life, and totally uninvolved in the social and personal side."

Clearly, Jack had found a devoted ally, someone who could see through to the idealist in the politician. Sorensen knew whom he was serving. "He was much the same man in private as he was in public. It was no act—the secret of his magic appeal was that he had no magic at all. Few could realize, then or now, that beneath the glitter of his life and office, beneath the cool exterior of the ambitious politician, was a good and decent man with a conscience that told him what was right and a heart that cared about the well-being of those around him."

Yet it didn't take Sorensen long to realize he and Jack came from very different worlds. "During my first year in JFK's Senate office, when dropping me off after work to catch my bus home, he confessed that he had never ridden one in his life."

They spent an enormous amount of time together, working, thinking, and planning. Not long before his death, Sorensen wrote this: "I do not remember everything about him, because I never knew everything about him. No one did. Different parts of his life, work, and thoughts were seen by many people—but no one saw it all."

In the beginning she was Jackie Bouvier. The year was 1951. To hear the name now conjures up that early time and a young, fresh beauty untouched by fame and position.

But what was it about this young woman? Looks, certainly. Jackie was stunning, with large eyes so far apart it took two eyes to see them. Her beauty was original. She was elegant, self-contained, aristocratic. To Jack she was the only woman he "could" have married, he once confided to Red Fay.

Charlie Bartlett had been one of Jack's best friends ever since they met and began hanging out together in Palm Beach in 1945. Now living in Washington, where he was working for the

Chattanooga Times, he remained a careful observer of his pal. "The thing to remember, and that really made him special in my book, was a mind that went right to the problem. I mean, he must have inherited it from his old man. When you discussed anything with Jack, politics mainly, he'd go right to the bottom. He had a wonderful way of separating all the crap from the key issue. . . . It made him great fun to discuss things with.

"He always had a pretty clear picture of the motives of the people he was with, and he was good on that. I don't know how to say it, but Jack wasn't, sort of, in love with humanity. He was cool. His attention moved quickly. That mind would start going, and he did get bored awfully easily. This was part of his being spoiled, and I found it sometimes annoying. I mean, if you wanted to get into a long story, why, you were apt to not have Jack with you at the end of it."

When the moment came for settling on a partner, Jacqueline Bouvier managed to grab his attention and hold it. She possessed both the personality and the pedigree. She also lacked what Jack himself lacked: a childhood cushioned by a warm upbringing. She, too, had been raised by a cold, willful mother and had a father—the handsome but philandering, alcoholic stockbroker known as "Black Jack" Bouvier—who did exactly as he pleased. Whether she told him about her childhood, or he intuited it once they'd met, it could have made her intriguing. Jack was most of all driven by curiosity.

Asked once to describe Jackie in a word, he chose *fey.* Her otherworldly qualities made her unlike all the other women he'd known and dated. She was detached, elusive, like him.

Jackie, who'd spent her first two years of college at Vassar, followed by a junior year in France, was finishing her college degree at George Washington University. She felt about France the way Jack did about Great Britain. Like Jack, she'd sought escape and refuge in books when she was young, especially as she sought shelter from her parents' stormy marriage. Her father, John Vernou Bouvier III, was as unreliable as he was attractive, and her parents' 1928 marriage lasted just a dozen years. Jacqueline Lee—Lee was her mother's maiden name—was the firstborn child, in 1929; her sister, Caroline Lee, known as Lee, came four years later. Jack Bouvier was sixteen years older than Jackie's mother, Janet. Jack Kennedy, twelve years Jackie's senior, noticed that their age difference seemed to appeal to her.

Jackie's part-time job at the *Washington Times-Herald* as an "Inquiring Camera Girl" resembled the one Inga Arvad once had held, while requiring far less writing. All Jackie had to come up with were brief captions for the snapshots she took of whoever was being featured that day.

The encounter that set off the romance between Jack Kennedy and Jacqueline Bouvier occurred one evening at Charlie Bartlett's house. "I leaned across the asparagus and asked for a date," Jack would recall in a much-quoted line. A Georgetown dinner party was a perfect setting for what began—at least, in the eyes of others—as a fairy-tale union, and became an almost mythical one.

Even at the outset, though, the courtship was uneven; nothing out of the ordinary there. Jack would ask her out for a date, then disappear. Yet he always returned. Following his election to the Senate, he proposed in '53, and she accepted. The chemistry between them, however you try to analyze it, was undeniable, and they knew it.

While he was wooing her, Jack presented Jackie with copies of his two favorite books, John Buchan's autobiography, *Pilgrim's Way*, and Lord David Cecil's *Young Melbourne*. These men each expressed, in their different ways, ideals of honor, sacrifice, and political nobility that continued to inspire him. When she learned his favorite poem was Alan Seeger's "I Have a Rendezvous with Death," she memorized it. In the years to come, he would often have her recite it for him.

"Jack appreciated her. He really brightened when she appeared," Chuck Spalding recalled. "You could see it in his eyes. He'd follow her around the room watching to see what she'd do next. Jackie interested him, which wasn't true of many women."

Jackie's temperament, though, was very far from the rambunctiousness of the large and competitive Kennedy brood. "Jackie was certainly very bored by politics and very bored by the very aggressive camaraderie of the Kennedy family, which was absolutely foreign to her nature," Alistair Forbes said. "Fortunately, I think, she also spotted that it was really foreign to Jack's nature." She saw him as being more sensitive and "much less extroverted than they all were."

Jackie offered the handsome and popular young senator a social status he didn't quite have on his own. For all their recently amassed wealth, his family was still nouveau riche and thus lacked entrée to certain clubs, certain circles. Jack knew it, didn't like it, but made the best of it. His friends, mostly, were like him—the sons of the successful—but others, met at Choate and Harvard and in Palm Beach, were from old money or old bloodlines. Charlie Bartlett, himself an old-line Yalie, could see the effect the Bouvier name had on his friend.

Bartlett, however, liked to speculate, in later years, on what Jack's life would have been like had he chosen another sort of wife. "There was this beautiful girl up in Boston. Her name was K. K. Hannon. Her father was a policeman. She was gorgeous. If Jack had married her, she could have dealt with him, I think. She was Irish and tough and damned good-looking. But, no, he had to marry up."

Jackie, whose father's infidelities had helped destroy his marriage, recognized she was marrying a husband of similar habits. "Well, she knew what she was getting into when she married him," Bartlett said. "She was in love with Jack, and he had this terrible habit of going out with these other girls." As Bartlett figured it, his friend's intended bride simply made a vow that she'd "take it all on, and she did."

Jack's concern was more on the politics of his decision. "I gave everything a good deal of thought," he announced in a letter to Red Fay out in San Francisco. "So I am getting married this fall. This means the end of a promising political career, as it has been based up to now almost completely on the old sex appeal. Let me know the general reaction to this in the Bay area."

In fact, with an eye to the likely fallout from the coming change in his marital status, he managed to keep secret his engagement until after the *Saturday Evening Post* had run a long-planned feature headlined "Jack Kennedy: The Senate's Gay Young Bachelor." Later, without telling his fiancée, he invited a *Life* photographer along on a sailing trip that she'd supposed would be time alone for them.

To reap the political benefit of their boss's engagement, O'Donnell, together with O'Brien, began to plan a large event for all the "Kennedy Secretaries" from the previous year. To get the reluctant Jack to agree, they told him, "They haven't seen you since the election and they all want to give you a gift and so forth," O'Donnell recalled his pitch to the bridegroom. It was a classic, canny Kennedy event, a party to honor the engaged couple for which the guests paid admission and were more invested in their hero for having done so. "For the time and the place, it wasn't cheap. But the faithful were willing to shell out ten dollars for a chance to see the senator they'd helped elect and to meet his beautiful fiancée. They felt included, even 'related.'"

O'Donnell described the celebration he staged: "They paid for their meal, paid for their drinks, and they gave the senator and Jackie a gift. One of the few organizations in the history of mankind that were paying him instead of him paying them, but we knew he wouldn't pay for it, so we had to, or he wouldn't come—since he didn't want to, anyway. Though, once they were there, he had a great time."

The wedding party convened the weekend of September 12, 1953, in Newport, Rhode Island, where Jackie's remarried mother, now Mrs. Hugh Auchincloss, lived at Hammersmith Farm. The groomsmen included Lem from Choate, Torby from Harvard, and Red Fay from the navy, plus Chuck Spalding, Charlie Bartlett, and George Smathers. The ceremony was held at St. Mary's, a nineteenth-century church in the Gothic style. Society pages around the country pronounced it the "wedding of the year."

When Fay showed up, the ever-competitive Jack asked him as soon as the two men were alone what he thought of Jackie. "I said, 'God, she's a fantastic-looking woman.' And then I added, 'If you ever get a little hard of hearing, you're going to have a little trouble picking up all the transmission.'" Jack laughed, loving his navy pal's reaction to the classic Jackie whisper.

Jack was about to embark on a new life, yet there remained evidence that he himself, the onetime Mucker ringleader, had changed little over all those years. Fay noticed the way he enjoyed the bit of culture clash that occurred between a few of his cronies and the Newporters. "Almost across the street from Hammersmith Farm were the green fairways of the Newport Country Club," he said, "where I'd often played during the war. The gentry of Newport had opened up their club for men in uniform, but with the end of the war the doors had shut tight again."

Somehow, Fay and Kennedy's aide John Galvin—"looking more Irish than Paddy's Pig"—got themselves onto the course to play a round. At this point Fay hadn't realized that the relaxed wartime regulations were no longer in force. The club had returned to its firm rule that all nonmembers must be accompanied by a club member. "I hope you two enjoyed your game of golf," Jack teased them, "because as a result of it there was almost a total breakdown of relations between the mother of the bride and her dashing prospective son-in-law. I'm afraid that they feel that their worst fears are being realized. The invasion by the Irish Catholic hordes into one of the last strongholds of America's socially elite is being led by two chunky red-haired friends of the groom."

Still, the temporary vibe of spontaneous, unpredictable fun was welcomed by at least a few Newporters. Fay recalls a comment made by the lifeguard at a nearby beach where the Kennedy guests were swimming and playing touch football. "I want to tell you," the young man said, "this is the first time this place has had any life in it since I've been here."

The wedding weekend was not proceeding without discord. Jack had asked Red to be the master of ceremonies at the bachelor dinner. Eventually, this favoritism seemed to cause resentment among his fellow ushers, especially as the evening wore on and more alcohol was imbibed. "Torby Macdonald stood up at the other end of the table, took his water glass, and hurled it the length of the table; and it hit me on the chest. Then it fell to the table and shattered. Since I'd had a few drinks, the natural response was to start down the table after him. Luckily for me—because I'm sure Torby would have taken me apart—Jim Reed and the president, then senator, grabbed me and the thing was averted."

Also in attendance at the wedding and the dinner were Ken O'Donnell and Larry O'Brien. As the former describes it, "There were only a few political people invited, and we stayed together and talked politics. I met some of the gentlemen for the first time, like Spalding. I'd known Lem through Bobby. I met Smathers for the first time. And Charlie Bartlett. But we didn't talk to them much. The Boston political guys sat with the other Boston political guys and drank with the Boston political guys, and we mostly talked politics and what the future might be for the senator."

Lem Billings, Jack's oldest friend, felt the need to have a personal heart-to-heart with the bride. "She was terribly young, and I thought it would be best if she were prepared for any problems. So I told her that night that I thought she ought to realize Jack was thirty-six years old, had been around an awful lot, had known many, many girls—it sounds like an awfully disloyal friend saying these things—and that she was going to have to be very understanding at the beginning. I said he had never really settled down with one girl before, and that a man of thirty-six is very difficult to live with. She was quite understanding about it and seemed to accept everything I said."

Rather amazingly, Lem then reported this exchange to Jack. "Of course, later I told him everything I'd said to her—and he was pleased because he felt it would make her better understand him."

Chuck Spalding had his own telling memory of the weekend. To him, it was as if his friend were actually two people at his own wedding—one being the groom, and the other a grand observer of the entire event, watching it as if from afar, the way an outsider might see it. To Spalding, this other Jack was totally detached from what was happening, this lifetime pairing of him with another.

On the wedding weekend, one thing is sure, which is that the newlywed Jack Kennedy was clearly thinking beyond the imaginings of the ordinary groom. Sailing in the waters off Hammersmith Farm, he gazed at his wife's family's cove on Narragansett Bay and said to Bartlett, "This would be a helluva place to sail in the presidential yacht."

By the time the honeymooning couple arrived in San Francisco—they'd gone first to Acapulco and then on to San Ysidro Ranch in the hills above Santa Barbara—the reality of the union between the thirty-six-year-old Jack Kennedy and twenty-four-year-old Jackie Bouvier was asserting itself. Here's Red Fay's account of hosting the two near the end of their wedding journey: "When Jack and

Jacqueline came to the West Coast on their honeymoon, the pressures of public life too often intruded on the kind of honeymoon any young bride anticipates. For example, on their last day on the West Coast, Jack and I went to a pro football game. I'm sure this didn't seem a particularly unusual arrangement for Jack."

Jack Kennedy continually craved such fresh company. He liked the rush of excitement that came with it. Perhaps that enjoyment was rooted in those times in his youth when he'd been confined to bed. Bored easily by sameness, he preferred to keep moving, wanted the movie to stay exciting, liked people to be forever fascinating—and he wanted never to be alone, or too long with the same person.

The trouble was, as at least one friend saw it, those around him let him get away with it. In Charlie Bartlett's words, "they spoiled him. . . . They spoiled the hell out of Jack. . . . I wish they hadn't, actually." People came to understand that, attractive as he was, Jack could be coldly self-indulgent. Yet his company was magnetic and his joy in life was irresistible.

Jack and Jackie were, both of them, like characters out of Fitzgerald, two people with old-world aspirations, but like most Americans, self-inventing. Lem Billings, I think, had it right when he said: "He saw her as a kindred spirit . . . he understood the two of them were alike. They had both taken circumstances that weren't the best in the world when they were younger and . . . learned to make themselves up as they went along. Even the names, Jack and Jackie: two halves of a single whole. They were both actors, and I think they appreciated each other's performances. It was unbelievable to watch them work a party. Both of them had the ability to make you feel that there was no place on earth you'd rather be than sitting there in intimate conversation with them."

Dumbarton Oaks

McCarthy & Cohn

21

Ted Reardon

22

CHAPTER EIGHT
SURVIVAL

*The world breaks everyone and afterward many are strong
at the broken places.*

—Ernest Hemingway

Jack Kennedy had faced death often in his life. He'd spent much
of his teenage years with doctors examining him, saying what an
"interesting" case he presented. Leukemia, even, was mentioned.
He never did manage to escape the knot he felt in his stomach, a
chronic reminder of the frequent invalidism he'd lived with in youth
and which now followed him into adulthood. When the Japanese
destroyer cut through *PT 109,* barely missing him, the pounding he
took said, *This is what it feels like to die.* Once home, the surgery performed on his back left him with a pain he was forced to live with.
In London, there was the diagnosis of Addison's.

In 1954, Jack had a choice to make. He could play it one way,
living a diminished life that would lead, very likely, to worse. Or

he could risk it all—just as he'd done when he left Plum Pudding Island and swam out into that channel in hope of rescue. He was thirty-seven years old and staring at a future that promised a different sort of torture than he might have suffered at the hands of the Japanese. His steadily worsening back promised a return to the sickbed he'd endured as a boy. This time, however, his dreamed-of future would no longer be looming before him, but, rather, drifting forever into the past.

He would, of course, throw everything he had on the table. Rather than accept a lessened existence, he chose to bet his life on the operating room.

The year began with him executing a masterstroke. As a freshman congressman, he'd shown his independence by withholding his signature from the sleazy Curley petition. Now, in his second year in the Senate, Kennedy made an even bolder move, separating himself from the ranks of his fellow New Englanders. He voted for the creation of the St. Lawrence Seaway, connecting the Atlantic Ocean with the Great Lakes. This meant backing a public works project that could mean the loss of Boston Harbor's importance as a major shipping port.

That 1954 January vote made him an unpopular figure in Massachusetts. It wasn't hard to understand why. The carving out of a direct route from the Atlantic to the Great Lakes could be seen in New England only in terms of its economic threat to the region. The Northeast was already in decline, and those factories engaged in shoemaking and in textiles, especially, were moving to the non-unionized, cheap-labor South. If ships could find their way to the Midwest without docking at Boston Harbor, huge numbers of jobs would be lost. The men and families who relied on those jobs—the townies of Charlestown and other harbor areas—wondered aloud why their young Irish representative in Washington wasn't now safeguarding them.

"The story circulated around the state," said Ken O'Donnell, who was friendly with many longshoremen, "that the Seaway was being built to take care of his father's Merchandise Mart . . . that he was caught at last, paying off Joe Kennedy for all the money he spent on the election."

In 1945 Joseph P. Kennedy had purchased the Merchandise Mart, the giant Chicago landmark and, at the time, the largest building in the world. Who stood to gain more from the opening of a direct shipping lane to the Atlantic than the man reaping the profits from this giant center for retailers and wholesalers situated there near Lake Michigan?

Tip O'Neill saw a grander political motive in Kennedy's vote. He spotted it as the first clear signal that Jack Kennedy's horizons stretched well beyond the job he now held. "I knew Jack was serious about running for president back in 1954, when he mentioned that he intended to vote for the St. Lawrence Seaway project. The whole Northeast delegation was opposed to that bill, because once you opened the Seaway, you killed the port of Boston, which was the closest port to Europe. The Boston papers were against it, and so were the merchant marines and the longshoremen. But Jack wanted to show that he wasn't parochial, and that he had a truly national perspective. Although he acknowledged that the Seaway would hurt Boston, he supported it because the project would benefit the country as a whole."

The burst of vitriol directed at him spurred his historical curiosity. "After he had been in the Senate for less than a year," Sorensen would write in his late-in-life memoirs, "JFK called me into his office and said he wanted my help researching and writing a magazine article on the history of senatorial courage."

Kennedy had come upon accounts of the heat John Quincy

Adams—later the country's sixth president—had taken not quite a century and a half earlier for a transgression similar to his own. As a Massachusetts senator, Adams had voted against the economic interests of New England when he supported President Jefferson's embargo on Great Britain because of its attacks on American ships. As a result, he lost his Senate seat. Eighteen years later, though, Adams entered the White House.

Kennedy was another New Englander with wide ambitions. Still a Cold Warrior, he maintained his belief that the global struggle against Communism must remain his country's prime concern. "If we do not stand firm amid the conflicting tides of neutralism, resignation, isolation, and indifference, then all will be lost, and one by one the free countries of the earth will fall until finally the direct assault will begin on the great citadel—the United States," he would declare in a 1956 commencement speech at Boston College. He had only contempt for those men and women—and this included fellow Democrats—who refused to regard the fight against Communism as the essential struggle of the times.

Yet he worried how the struggle was being waged. A stark example was the desperate French fight in Indochina. Weakened by its humiliation in World War II, France was fighting to regain its international stature, to hold on to its colonial empire. Its conflict with the popular Vietnamese leader, Ho Chi Minh, had become a grinding war of attrition. Many on the American right, Vice President Richard Nixon included, wanted to go to the aid of the French. Communism, they felt, must be resisted on every square inch of global real estate.

When the North Vietnamese forces, the Viet Minh, surrounded the French army at Dien Bien Phu in '54, Nixon grew more hawkish still, telling news editors he supported sending "American boys" to replace them. He then backed a secret plan, code-named

"Operation Vulture," to drop atom bombs on the Viet Minh. He, other Republicans, and some Democrats like Jack Kennedy had blamed President Truman for "losing" China by not giving sufficient aid to the anti-Communist Chiang Kai-shek. The Eisenhower administration could not afford to lose Indochina.

Despite his own anti-Communism, Jack Kennedy resisted falling into line. For the first time, he broke with the Eurocentric view of the Cold War. He also challenged the Republicans' position that the United States could defend itself worldwide on the basis of its nuclear supremacy alone. We could not intimidate an adversary such as Ho Chi Minh with the threat of dropping a hydrogen bomb in the jungles of Indochina. It would not be credible.

The argument he was using was the same one he'd employed to justify Britain's failure to confront Hitler at Munich: the *capability* to fight such a war was not in place. "To pour money, material and men into the jungles of Indo-China without at least a remote prospect of victory would be dangerously futile and self-destructive. I am, frankly, of the belief that no amount of military assistance in Indo-China can conquer an enemy that is everywhere and at the same time nowhere, 'an enemy of the people' which has the sympathy and covert support of the people."

Equally important to him was the reality he'd seen for himself during his trip to Indochina three years earlier. And that reality was the power of nationalism. On this issue Jack Kennedy found common ground with the newly elected Republican senator from Arizona, Barry Goldwater, who demanded, as the price for American aid, that the French promise Indochina its independence.

But it was closer to home that Cold War issues were causing Senator Kennedy the greatest challenges. Since January 1950, Joseph R. McCarthy, the Republican junior senator from

Wisconsin, had made himself into a force to be reckoned with. His relentless effort to unearth Communists within the government and the American establishment made "McCarthyism" the one-size-fits-all label pinned to the national Red hunt. With bullying zeal, McCarthy and his Senate subcommittee unjustly tarnished and in some cases ruined reputations.

McCarthy was fueled by the temper of the times. In August 1945, the people of America had looked out upon a world dominated by the United States as by no other country in history. Within a year, the geopolitical shifts were so alarming that Winston Churchill spoke of an Iron Curtain being drawn down between free Western Europe and an Eastern Europe falling increasingly under the control of Moscow. Within two years, the victory in Europe had largely been undone. Czechoslovakia and Poland, the countries that had been the casus belli of World War II, were now under Soviet domination.

Other news from around the globe added to the sense of disillusion and insecurity across America. In 1949, the same year Mao Tse-tung claimed all of mainland China, the Soviets exploded their first atom bomb, an event that occurred shockingly in advance of American predictions—or expectations.

In 1950 came the conviction of the top American diplomat Alger Hiss, who'd presided at the United Nations Conference in San Francisco, which Jack Kennedy covered for Hearst, for his role in a Soviet espionage plot. The fear of Communism on the advance would spike violently with the coming of the Korean War. In July of that year, a thirty-two-year-old New Yorker, Julius Rosenberg, was arrested for helping to pass atomic secrets to Moscow; a month later, his wife, Ethel, was taken into custody.

This was the national mood when Joseph McCarthy entered

stage right. He'd begun his crusade in January of 1950 in a speech to a Republican women's group in Wheeling, West Virginia. There he borrowed phrases from a speech Richard Nixon had just given on the Hiss conviction. McCarthy upped the ante by declaring that Hiss was only the iceberg's tip, that the State Department actually, if unknowingly, harbored large numbers of dedicated Communists— and all committed to the sabotage of American interests in favor of those of the Soviet Union. Unchecked, he would ride high on the brazenness of such charges, reaching his zenith of popularity in January 1954. At that juncture, 50 percent of the American people held a favorable opinion of the Wisconsin senator, just 29 percent an unfavorable one.

But his downhill slide was about to begin, precipitated by CBS's Edward R. Murrow, a broadcaster who'd made his reputation reporting from London during the Blitz and who was revered for his integrity. In March 1954, Murrow aired a special entitled *Point of Order!* in which he attacked McCarthy, and dared him to present an on-air rebuttal. McCarthy's response offers a classic example of how he strung together events to craft his outrageous indictments.

"My good friends," he said, "if there were no Communists in our government, would we have consented to and connived to turn over all of our Chinese friends to the Russians? If there were no Communists in our government, why did we delay for eighteen months, delay our research on the hydrogen bomb, even though our intelligence agencies were reporting day after day that the Russians were feverishly pushing their development of the H-Bomb? Our nation may well die because of that eighteen months' deliberate delay. And I ask you, who caused it? Was it loyal Americans? Or was it traitors in our government?"

There you have it, an absurd but compelling case against those in high places. It was the old charge of rot at the top. If the Chinese Communists took over China, it was the doing of Commies in our own government. If the Russians had sprinted forward and now had flaunted their H-bomb, it was because we'd slowed down to let them catch us. In short, if anything bad happened, the reason is we were stabbed in the back.

McCarthy loved charging respected figures with bad faith, thus lending a catchy populism to his accusations of treason. In his view, it was the country's best and brightest who were selling us out. "The reason why we find ourselves in a position of impotency is not because the enemy has sent men to invade our shores, but rather because of the traitorous actions of those who have had all the benefits that the wealthiest nation on earth has had to offer— the finest homes, the finest college educations, and the finest jobs in government we can give."

To validate this belief system, he fixed in his sights on such lofty officials as President Truman himself, Secretary of State Dean Acheson, and his predecessor, George Marshall, who'd been army chief of staff in World War II. He attacked them all, famously calling Marshall the perpetrator of "a conspiracy so immense and an infamy so black as to dwarf any previous venture in the history of man."

Of course, no demagogue ever has a lifetime career, and Joe McCarthy's own downfall was determined when he decided to focus his crusade on the presence of hidden Communists in the U.S. Army. The target he selected for attack was an army major, Dr. Irving Peress, a dentist who'd been a member of the American Labor Party, believed to be a Communist Party front. When Peress's commanding officer at Camp Kilmer in New Jersey, Brigadier General Ralph Zwicker—a Silver and Bronze Star recipient who'd been a hero of the Battle of the Bulge—appeared before his committee, the senator taunted him, saying he was "not fit to wear that uniform."

That encounter showed the extent to which McCarthy was beginning to spiral out of control. His absolute fall from grace came a month later in a moment of television history. The newly launched American Broadcasting Corporation, ABC, covered gavel to gavel the thirty-six days of hearings convened. The April 1954 broadcasts of the Army-McCarthy proceedings gave the audience sitting at home the chance to examine McCarthy's own conduct as well as the wild charges he brought against army personnel.

Thus, with the entire country watching—on some days, as many as 20 million people—he self-destructed, with the help of a righteous attorney, Joseph Nye Welch, the army's chief counsel, who objected to the senator's innuendo-filled attack on one of his staff lawyers for a past membership in a left-wing legal group. Voicing his distaste, he accused McCarthy of "reckless cruelty" and then asked whether he had "no decency." It was a stunningly unexpected comeback, and one that marked McCarthy as a pure bully. For the first time, many Americans focused on Joe McCarthy's tactics and didn't like the looks of them.

Not everyone turned on McCarthy. More than a third of the country remained loyal to him after the five weeks of legal spectacle. His fellow Irish-Americans were especially defiant, seeing him as a lonely challenger to the country's political, diplomatic, and academic elites.

Within days of the Army-McCarthy hearings, Senator Ralph Flanders of Vermont, a Republican, introduced a resolution to censure his colleague and remove him from the chairmanship of his committees. It read, in part, "Were the Wisconsin senator in the pay

of the Communists, he could not have done a better job for them."
Now that public opinion had turned on him, the Democrats were
free to cast Joe McCarthy as their ultimate archvillain.

Jack Kennedy had a McCarthy problem and he knew it. Joining his
fellow Democrats, who were now calling for McCarthy's head on
a pike, put him in a serious dilemma. For one thing, up until this
moment he'd successfully managed to say nothing on the subject of
Joe McCarthy's harsh tactics. It was a silence he would, in the years
to come, always have to answer for. Outside the Senate, moreover,
he was actually known to be quite friendly with the man. The pair
of them had hung around together during Jack's early congressional
days, and McCarthy, handsome in a Black Irish way, had been out
on dates with Jack's sisters. A close friend of Bobby's wife, Ethel,
McCarthy was a kind of unofficial uncle to their two young children, especially the eldest, Kathleen. Because of his friendship with
the Kennedys, McCarthy had refrained from endorsing his fellow
Senate Republican Henry Cabot Lodge in the race he lost to Jack.
The December before, Jack had been a guest at McCarthy's wedding, as had many of the Kennedy family.

Another problem for Jack was Bobby's closeness to the senator. For half the previous year, he'd been a McCarthy staffer. Their
father, a financial supporter of the Republican senator as well as a
friend, had helped pave the way for the job. However, Bobby had
quit, smarting under the fact that he was outranked by the senator's chief counsel, Roy Cohn, a fellow whom he despised. But his
departure didn't last long. The next January he switched sides, hired
now by the investigating committee's Democratic minority as its
chief counsel.

When the time came for the Democrats to move against

McCarthy, it would fall to the twenty-eight-year-old Bobby, despite his continued personal loyalty, to write the draft of the Democratic members' report on the senator's out-of-control conduct. While it targeted Cohn's behavior, it placed responsibilities on the committee's chairman. "Senator McCarthy and Mr. Cohn merit severe criticism," and "the Senator cannot escape responsibility for the misconduct of Cohn. Nor can he excuse the irresponsibility attaching to many of his charges. The Senate should take action to correct this situation."

Still, it was one thing to staff the committee report, as Bobby, acting in his official capacity, had done. It would be a very different matter to vote for the historic censure of a colleague—a man who was also a friend—as Jack would now be asked to do.

There had actually been rumblings against McCarthy in the Senate for several years at this point, including a declaration made by his own party members that denounced smear tactics—in effect, McCarthyism—without mentioning the names of any specific lawmaker. In response, McCarthy contemptuously dubbed Senator Margaret Chase Smith of Maine, who originated the declaration, along with the six fellow Republicans who joined her, "Snow White and Her Six Dwarfs." With the Army-McCarthy hearings having weakened McCarthy and made him at last vulnerable, Senator Flanders's intention was now to deliver the coup de grâce.

Yet, even given the rising swell of condemnation, Jack Kennedy remained resistant when it came to voting to censure a man whose wedding he'd attended, for whom his brother had worked, and to whom his father had provided sizable contributions. Had Jack joined the vote against McCarthy, it would have meant a dramatic, even traitorous break with his father and brother, who'd devoted themselves so totally to his career and were not ready to abandon a fellow anti-Communist and close friend.

How was he going to handle it? Personal connections aside, there were other factors affecting his ultimate decision when it came to the McCarthy censure vote. An important one, of course, was how it played back home. The same people of Massachusetts who'd supported Jack on the basis of the old loyalties were largely—and vehemently—in McCarthy's corner. These men and women saw the battle as one pitting the Ivy League establishment against the working-class Irishman. For such Americans, here was a contest between those who seemed far too dainty, if not neutral, on exposing Communists in government and regular people who were willing to play rough.

It was bad enough Jack had gone to Harvard, but here he would be taking sides against one of his own—a fellow who happened to be the best-known Irishman in the country. It would be an act of betrayal, nothing less. Whatever Joe McCarthy's faults, most Irish-Americans viewed his motives as right, while those of his enemies were, at best, suspect.

In Jack Kennedy's own office, the enormous tribal significance of the McCarthy issue was brought home by Ken O'Donnell, whose brother Warren was then a student at Holy Cross. After Warren had delivered a strong classroom attack on McCarthy and his methods, his older brother recalled, "He was told to sit down, and the rejoinder from the priest, quite coldly, was: 'I guess I shouldn't expect anything less from someone whose brother went to Harvard and is friends with Jack Kennedy.'"

O'Donnell, who was running the Kennedy office in Boston, keeping watch on the constituents and their concerns, insisted that Jack's voting against McCarthy would be "political suicide." He never changed his mind. "The feeling was *that* strong. If he'd voted for censure, there's no question it would have ended the career of Jack Kennedy in Massachusetts."

He believed that the only course was for Jack "to avoid the vote. McCarthy was deteriorating to nothing more than the subject of barroom brawls. In time, he would fade. These haters always do, and, if you argued against him, you were a Communist. My view was that we needed to stand back and allow him to self-destruct."

The passions of that historic moment created strange alliances. O'Donnell could never forget what he'd seen one night at a favorite political hangout. "I was in the Bellevue bar, having a drink, and we were watching the hearings. Bobby Kennedy had this altercation with Roy Cohn right on television. Remember, it was a group there, watching, of Boston Irish politicians, some truck drivers, and hard-working guys, most tinged with anti-Semitism. So Cohn wasn't the type of fellow you'd think they'd like. Yet every single person in that bar cheered and yelled and hoped he'd belt Bobby one."

Jack *got* this. Despite his seeming golden-boy status, he felt the lure of the underdog throughout his life; once a Mucker, always a Mucker. For this reason, he *got* Richard Nixon, his early congressional buddy, in ways that others in his circle never did. A part of him, the stubborn part—the part still dominant—cheered just about anyone liberals loved to hate.

Two years earlier he'd walked out of that Spee event after another attendee had dared compare McCarthy with Alger Hiss. Jack, after all, had run for Congress as a "fighting conservative." His identity as a Cold Warrior was well known. Besides the all-politics-is-local aspect, there was the issue of Communism itself and what it actually meant in the context of American life and American security. There were those who took its threat seriously and those who pooh-poohed it, with Jack squarely in the vigilant camp, a position he'd arrived at long before.

He'd criticized FDR's compromises at Yalta, and blamed Truman for the losses in Asia. "I'm very happy to tell them I'm not a liberal," he'd declared in a *Saturday Evening Post* interview the year before.

Even years later, when he'd begun to identify himself as a "liberal," he would confess to having little sympathy for the people McCarthy had persecuted. "I had not known the sort of people who were called before the McCarthy committee. I agree that many of them were seriously manhandled, but they represented a different world to me. What I mean is, I did not identify with them, and so I did not get as worked up as other liberals did."

The decision would come down to the coldest calculation. Sorensen, in his memoir, summed up the situation: "JFK knew that if he voted with his fellow Democrats and anti-McCarthy Republicans on a motion to censure McCarthy, he would be defying many in his home state and family, but if he voted against such a motion, he would be denounced by the leading members of his party, by the leading liberals and intellectuals in the country and his alma mater, by the leaders of the Senate, and by the major national newspapers."

That spring of 1954, as he looked to both past and future—his entangling ties to McCarthy and what they would cost him later—Jack Kennedy found himself staring into the face of mortal danger. In April, the back pain from which he'd long suffered turned unbearable. X-rays taken showed that the fifth lumbar vertebra had collapsed, a result believed by some to be a result of steroids prescribed over the years for his Addison's disease. According to the historian Robert Dallek, he couldn't even bend down to pull a sock onto his left foot; only by walking sideways could he get up and down stairs.

Yet Kennedy managed to keep any awareness of these ever-encroaching medical setbacks from the public. Snapshots taken that May show Jack, Jackie, and Bobby Kennedy enjoying the Washington spring, playing touch football in the park behind Dumbarton Oaks. Wearing a T-shirt, Jack looks sunny and healthy. Jacqueline, still in her preregal stage, appears joyously youthful and untroubled.

The photographs reveal nothing of either's pain. You can see in these pictures neither the dire reality of Jack's health nor the sadness his infidelities were already causing the twenty-four-year-old he'd married just the autumn before. "I've often wondered if I'd do it again," Charlie Bartlett would say of the two he'd brought together after seeing the one hurt the other so. "I don't understand Jack's promiscuity at all." Yet all that's apparent in the images of those halcyon days are the skills the pair shared in their concealment.

As bad as his condition was, however, it was about to get worse. By August his weight had dropped from 180 pounds to 140. So bad was the back pain that Jack needed to remain on the Senate floor between votes rather than attempt the commute from his office across Constitution Avenue. As the days passed, with little to stimulate him except agony, he arrived at a point of existential decision: the choice was between living a life of increasingly limited mobility—ending up in a wheelchair was inevitable—or else taking an enormous risk by submitting to spinal surgery.

In describing to Larry O'Brien the operation he chose now to endure, he minced no words. "This is the one that kills you or cures you."

To John Galvin, he explained that he was going to New York, to the Hospital for Special Surgery there, because his Boston doctors had advised against the procedure. "They said the best thing to do would be to stay with the crutches and live, rather than take the chance on the operation and die. He told me then, 'I'd rather die than be on crutches the rest of my life.'"

What intensified the danger was his Addison's disease. It meant his body could not produce the adrenaline needed to deal with the shock of surgery. The steroids he was taking complicated matters still further by reducing his ability to stave off infection. Jack knew that he faced the possibility of dying on the operating table. None of this was foreign territory to him.

With this high-risk surgery now on his calendar, Kennedy had to take on two political crises. One was the McCarthy censure, the other even nastier.

The midterm elections were coming in November, and Jack's Massachusetts colleague Foster Furcolo was running for the Senate. Jack didn't like the man's ambitions, which happened to be the same as his own. In fact, he didn't like the man, marking him as an "empty suit," a politician with no other reason to seek public office than the status it accorded the winner. It didn't help that Furcolo, whose base was Springfield, hadn't endorsed Jack in '52.

The antagonism between them was at once tribal and personal. Ever since Larry O'Brien, once a Furcolo staffer, had joined up with Jack in 1950, there'd been bad blood. Six years apart in age, the two legislators were both Harvard grads, both focused on getting ahead politically. Beyond that, they were simply rivals for the same turf: one Italian, the other Irish. As far as Jack was concerned, the Commonwealth wasn't big enough for both of them.

In the summer of 1954, their simmering feud came to a boil. Furcolo was the Democratic candidate for Senate, the same job Jack already had—if Furcolo won, it would make him the junior senator—and he looked to Jack for his backing. But there was no way Jack wanted Furcolo to become his political equal either in Washington or in Massachusetts. Complicating matters even more, Jack felt affection for the incumbent Furcolo wanted to run against, the Republican Leverett Saltonstall, a Brahmin of the same stripe as the man Jack had vanquished, Henry Cabot Lodge. As the Commonwealth's pair of senators, Jack and "Salty" had built a good working relationship.

"This was the circumstance for Kennedy's oft-quoted remark that 'sometimes party asks too much,'" Ted Sorensen recalled. In fact, Jack engaged him in a secret plan to undercut Furcolo's chances. "When I had been with him barely eighteen months," the aide recalled, "JFK took me to Boston, where he decided to oppose quietly the Democratic Party's nominee for the Senate against Leverett Saltonstall, JFK's Republican Senate colleague, in the 1954 election." It was another caper, like sneaking into the Massachusetts State House after hours to file his '46 nominating petitions. It was willful deception. Kennedy needed to make it *look* like he was being the loyal party man all while his bright young brain truster would be using his skills as a researcher-writer to provide ammo for the enemy.

Lending Sorensen to Saltonstall was only part of the plan. Late that summer, Kennedy met with Ken O'Donnell and Larry O'Brien at the Ritz-Carlton Hotel and instructed them to get on board to assist the Democratic candidate Robert Murphy, who was running for governor. The scheme called for Jack to endorse Murphy for governor and Furcolo for the Senate on the same live TV program. This being the era before videotape, Furcolo would have Jack's backing but would be unable to keep showing it in TV ads.

Kennedy's mistake was his failure to keep his dislike for Furcolo as secret as he kept his plotting. When the night of the live appearance arrived, Furcolo got a prebroadcast copy of Kennedy's intended remarks and blew up.

"Furcolo told him he wouldn't go on the show unless he received a more forthright and direct endorsement," O'Donnell recalled. "The senator then gave him that famous line, 'You've got a hell of a nerve, Foster. You're lucky you're here.' The senator next, quite coldly, went on to remind Furcolo of the time he had refused to endorse him. The exchange was quite heated." The actual telecast, however, went off smoothly enough. As they were leaving, Furcolo even wished Jack well with his coming surgery—"The main thing is, take care of your back"—a gesture of goodwill that Jack saw as entirely insincere.

Then hell broke loose. Even if the papers failed to notice that Senator Kennedy neglected to offer a personal endorsement of Furcolo, one radio station—albeit with a bit of help—got it cold. "I was riding into town that next morning," said O'Donnell, "and I heard on the radio that Senator Kennedy's not naming Foster Furcolo had been a direct affront. That he'd done it on purpose and, in fact, was not endorsing Foster Furcolo. The report quoted Frank Morrissey."

Morrissey was Joe Kennedy's man, the one he'd assigned to hang around his son's political operation and report back anything his boss wanted to know. Here's O'Donnell's account of that morning-after: "I called Frank and asked him to come over immediately. When he got there, I put it right to him and asked, 'What happened here?' He told me he thought it was off the record. I just stared at him. Couldn't believe it. All our preparation out of the window. I remember my exact words. I walked over and opened the window and said, 'Frank, jump.' He looked around and then looked like he would cry."

O'Donnell, who recalled the scene in all its drama years later, had no trouble recognizing the very real damage. Every politician in the state now knew what Jack Kennedy thought of Furcolo and how he'd undercut him in their one and only joint television appearance. "We'd been building up a solid residue of party regulars, and now they pointed to this and said, 'We were right about him in '52. He and his people are a bunch of Harvard bastards who take care of themselves. They don't care about the party. Kennedy does not want Furcolo in there because he'll compete with him. Kennedy doesn't *want* two Democratic senators.'"

A tribal war now loomed. Italians in Massachusetts had been voting for Irish candidates for generations. Now one of their own, Furcolo, was seen getting the bum's rush by a prince of the Irish side. Needing both groups in order to win statewide, certainly to win big, the Kennedys recognized the cost of the screwup as well as anyone. Here, though, Jack had made himself vulnerable by allowing his feelings to get in the way of his political calculation.

On October 10, Jack checked into the Hospital for Special Surgery. The operation was postponed three times, finally taking place eleven days later, on the twenty-first. Only then, before he was taken into the operating room, did he finally address the Furcolo problem. O'Donnell recalls the effort it took. "I kept pushing and, through some process of negotiation and with Bobby's help, we finally extracted a statement from him. It was unsatisfactory, but covered the problem. What we did was disavow Morrissey."

At the same time, O'Donnell knew it wouldn't fly. He would call the snubbing of Furcolo, who lost that November, "the only wrong political move Jack Kennedy ever made."

The back operation did not go well. After more than three hours in the surgeons' hands, Kennedy was left with a metal plate inserted in his spine. At that point he developed a urinary tract infection that failed to respond to antibiotics, sending him into a coma. The news spread around the political world that the handsome Massachusetts senator's life was in jeopardy.

"The odds made by the political wise guys were that he wouldn't live," Ken O'Donnell recalled, "and that if he did live he'd be a cripple. It became 'he might not make it.'"

Evelyn Lincoln, the secretary in his Senate office, got the terrible news that "the doctors didn't expect him to live until morning." The Kennedy death watch even was reported on television. For the third time in his life, Jack was given the last rites of his church. Jacqueline Kennedy, never one to practice her religion openly, went down on her knees to pray. Richard Nixon, being driven home that night, was heard to moan: "That poor young man is going to die. Oh, God, don't let him die." His Secret Service agent never forgot it.

Rallying in the night, against the odds, Jack pulled through. "The doctors don't understand where he gets his strength," the hospital told Lincoln when she called to ask about the patient the following morning. But the ordeal left a darkness in Kennedy.

"The tenor of his voice was tinged with pain," Ken O'Donnell said. "You could detect it in his voice even over the telephone. It was the first time in my experience with him—and I'd say, in his life—when he was, in fact, disinterested completely in politics. John Kennedy was at the lowest point of anytime I'd known him in his career, physically, mentally, and politically. He was at the bottom. It seemed over."

Back in Washington, the two Teds, Reardon and Sorensen, had been left in charge. The trouble was, Jack had given Sorensen, his young legislative assistant, no guidance on what he wanted to do about the upcoming vote to censure Joseph McCarthy. Sorensen, for his part, never called his boss's hospital room to ask how he wanted to be counted on the issue. Perhaps, it was simply preferable not to ask. He said he "feared the wrath of the senator's brother and father more than the senator's" if he declared Jack in favor of the McCarthy censure. In the end, Sorensen concluded, "I . . . suspected—correctly—that there was no point in my trying to reach him on an issue he wanted to duck."

On December 2, 1954, the Senate at last brought down the

curtain on the peculiar political spectacle starring Senator Joseph McCarthy. Except for the absent Kennedy, every Democrat, joined by half the Republicans, voted for the condemnation. The controversial senator would live just two and half years longer, dying of acute hepatitis brought on by alcoholism. By that time, his anti-Communist crusade and his political significance both were long over.

The man in the New York hospital bed had missed the vote.

Kennedy tried to make light of it. "You know, when I get downstairs, I know exactly what's going to happen," he told Chuck Spalding upon leaving the hospital a few days before Christmas. "Those reporters are going to lean over me with great concern, and every one of those guys is going to say, 'Now, Senator, what about McCarthy?' Do you know what I'm going to do? I'm going to reach for my back and I'm going to yell 'Oow!' and then I'm going to pull the sheet over my head and hope we can get out of there."

Jack left it to Bobby to carry the family's continuing respect for their fallen Irish-American ally. In January, while Jack was recuperating in Palm Beach, his younger brother was honored at a Junior Chamber of Commerce dinner as one of the country's "Ten Outstanding Young Men." When the evening's speaker, Edward R. Murrow, rose to address those in attendance, Bobby walked out of the room, a silent protest against a man who'd played a significant role in bringing down McCarthy. When the senator died in 1956, Bobby Kennedy flew to Appleton, Wisconsin, for the funeral and stayed with the mourners' procession all the way to the gravesite.

Now Jack Kennedy had survived another brush with death. He was helped through the crisis by the one strong emotional reality of his life: old friendships. One name high on the list was Red Fay. "In January 1955, Bobby called to ask if I could come to Florida. The family was worried about Jack, and didn't know whether he was going to live. The doctor felt that he was losing interest, and a visit from someone closely associated with happier times might help him regain his usual optimism and enjoyment of life. I flew to Palm Beach and spent ten days with him."

It was an opportunity for someone who cared about him to realize what Jack was up against. Fay watched as his recuperating friend gave himself a shot as part of the treatment for his back. "'Jack,' I said, 'the way you take that jab, it looks like it doesn't even hurt.' Before I had time to dodge, he reached over and jabbed the same needle into my leg. I screamed with the pain."

Down in Palm Beach, with time on his hands, surrounded by Jackie and family members, he took up oil painting and spent hours playing Monopoly. His convalescence lasted for almost six months and was interrupted only by a trip back to New York for a second surgery. While in Florida he grew close to his new brother-in-law, the young Hollywood star Peter Lawford, who'd married Patricia Kennedy the year before. "I think we hit it off because he loved my business. He loved anything to do with the arts and motion pictures. It never ceased to amaze me."

The British-born Lawford, who'd been in films since he was a young boy, observed Jack with an actor's keen eye. He got as good a look at him as anybody. "I don't think anybody ever made up John Kennedy's mind for him. I don't think anybody swayed him, including his father. I think he took what he wanted and then sifted it, you know, evaluated it. Then he did what he wanted to do with it." Lawford was amazed at Kennedy's self-discipline and his will to make the most of every day, the preciousness of time to him. "He was really ill with that back, but he fought his way through that, and, as you know, wrote the book while he was lying on his back."

The book was *Profiles in Courage*. It was Kennedy's tribute to eight U.S. senators who during their legislative careers had taken positions highly unpopular with their constituents. Though Kennedy dug up the stories and sketched out his intentions, Ted Sorensen did most of the actual writing. So it's fair to call the project a collaboration. The bookish child had been father to the man. "He was enormously well read in American history and literature," Hugh Fraser, the British politician and longtime friend, recalled. "I mean, to me, staggeringly so." Charlie Bartlett saw the book as an obvious undertaking for Jack. "I think the whole concept of the really gutsy decisions made by men with seats in the Senate fascinated him. So when he had this time, I suppose it was natural for him to turn to it." Bartlett, like all the others gathered around Jack in Palm Beach, would watch him, still unable to rise from bed, writing upside down on a board suspended above him.

In his memoirs, Sorensen explained that they worked on the book by letter and telephone. The reason was, he was in Washington helping hold down the fort in Kennedy's office while his boss was on his back down in Florida. The way Sorensen explained the enterprise, Kennedy played an especially serious role composing the first and last chapters and that he, the aide, wrote the first draft of the rest.

The theme and the bulk of the content were pure Jack. As smart as Sorensen was, and even given his familiarity with politics—his Republican father had been the attorney general of Nebraska—he was nonetheless a twenty-seven-year-old. He'd arrived in Washington only four years earlier, armed with a law degree but no on-the-ground political experience. He would admit that he was nowhere as well read as Kennedy in American history.

The voice of John F. Kennedy seems to me to be noticeably audible in *Profiles in Courage*. For example, in the opening passages, you read, "Where else, in a non-totalitarian society, but in the political profession is the individual expected to sacrifice all—including his own career—for the national good?" It's a quip that, I think, captures Jack Kennedy's own ironic style. Another sentence, I believe, derives from his ability to see things from the inside out as well as the outside in: the prospect of forced retirement from "the most exclusive club in the world, the possibilities of giving up the interesting work, the fascinating trappings and the impressive prerogatives of Congressional office, can cause even the most courageous politician a serious loss of sleep."

Here's a story that comes clearly from the insider Jack: "One senator, since retired, said that he voted with the special interests on every issue, hoping that by election time all of them added together would constitute nearly a majority that would remember him favorably, while the other members of the public would never know about—much less remember—his vote against their welfare." That senator was George Smathers, his pal who'd once said he didn't "give a damn." That business about the senator being "retired" was a cover.

David Ormsby-Gore, now a member of Parliament, stayed in touch with his friend as he recovered. "He must have been getting near the end of the book—but one of the lessons he had drawn from examining these moments in American history was that there were very much two sides to each problem. Now, this didn't prevent him being capable of taking decisions, and knowing that somebody had to make decisions, but it did always prevent him saying, 'I know that I have got nothing but right on my side, and the other side is entirely wrong,' and he never would adopt that attitude.

"He said that one of the rather sad things about life, particularly if you were a politician, was that you discovered that the other side really had a good case. He was most unpartisan in that way. . . . He wondered whether he was really cut out to be a politician because he was often so impressed by the other side's arguments when he really examined them in detail. Where he thought that there was a valid case against his position, he was always rather impressed by the arguments advanced."

At the end of May, with the help of physical therapy, a corset, and a rocking chair, Jack was set to proceed gingerly with a career that had hung, along with his life, in the balance. Pale and limping, he returned to Capitol Hill more sensitive than usual to imagery. When a Senate page, Martin Dowd, saw the long-absent senator approaching on crutches and opened the Senate chamber door for him, Kennedy tore into him. "Shut that door!" Kennedy yelled to the crushed seventeen-year-old. Unwilling to drop the matter, he confronted Dowd a moment later. "Don't you touch that door until I tell you to!"

Sorensen could sense how his boss had grown tougher, not just on others but himself. The political columnist and Kennedy friend Joseph Alsop also recognized the transformation: "Something very important happened inside him, I think, when he had that illness, because he came out of it a very much more serious fellow than he was prior to it. He had gone through the valley of the shadow of death, and he had displayed immense courage, which he'd always had."

That June, Kennedy gave a party in Hyannis, inviting to Cape Cod not just his own supporters, but also a sizable group of Democrats who'd never been active for him. Ken O'Donnell helped pull it together. "Larry and I got a call saying he was coming back to Massachusetts and the first thing he wanted to do was have a political reunion of the Kennedy secretaries." Clearly, the purpose of the event was to prove to the faithful how healthy he was. It was to show others, coming out of morbid curiosity, that he remained formidable.

"The thing I remember most about the event was that he was physically able to move around. There were no crutches. They had softball games and so forth, and it was an excellent outing. A very successful political event—an all-day affair." O'Donnell could see Jack's appeal to the rank-and-file types hadn't faded. "What struck me the most and to me was critical was that he still held the same old attraction for people. All our people loved him, but you knew there was no question about that. If he'd returned flat on his back or in a wheelchair, our people would have been there. But I was watching the others. The reaction from the professional politicians that were there: *they* loved him. Loved him, despite themselves."

If Kennedy was going to go further in politics, he needed to bring all the factions of Massachusetts together. He needed to win over those who practiced politics day in and day out. "It was important for our political futures and for the senator's that if we were going to take the next step, we had to know them on an intimate personal basis. We realized how important it was that they shouldn't feel we were snobs, that we didn't look down on the 'regulars.'"

It was obvious that Kennedy's renewed vigor had stirred a healthy fear among the Massachusetts Democratic stalwarts. Abandoning him might well mean abandoning the winning side. No political regular likes being tied to a loser, and while a young senator sidelined for six months with medical problems might have the voters' sympathy for a time, what good was he? Besides, Jack Kennedy had end-run them over the years, and many had been waiting for him to get his comeuppance. His sunny reappearance at that June picnic was therefore vital to his prospects.

"Out of that affair," O'Donnell said, summing up the situation, "I think, at least in our minds, we accepted that, for Senator Kennedy, the bottom point had been reached. Now there was a solid foundation from which to build forward."

• • •

Moving into the future, the Kennedy Party needed to reach out to the wider Democratic organization and win it to the cause. It was no longer enough to woo and charm. To win the big prizes Jack now needed to master the rougher side of politics. To intimidate those he could not seduce, he'd have to play the game harder than his rivals.

23

Filing petition for senate reeletion, 1958

24

Adlai Stevenson

CHAPTER NINE

DEBUT

Politics is essentially a learning profession.
—Arthur M. Schlesinger

When 1956 began, Jack Kennedy was far from a household name. By year's end, he'd managed to step into the ring as the most exciting Democratic challenger for the American presidency. He'd gotten there by sheer audacity.

President Eisenhower, having enjoyed a successful first term, was continuing to reap the prestige earned by his wartime victory. Despite the fact he'd suffered a heart attack the previous year, he was still expected to seek and win reelection. Offering himself to the task of opposing him was Governor Adlai Stevenson. The real question was who would be the Illinois Democrat's running mate.

That was the brass ring on which Jack Kennedy, now thirty-nine, began to focus. He'd gotten the heads-up from Theodore H. White, then reporting for *Collier's* magazine, that he was on Adlai's shortlist. Though possibly no more than a signal to Catholic voters in Massachusetts that Stevenson understood their importance, the result was to get Kennedy thinking.

Why *not* make a move in '56?

But if he were to do so, Jack saw how critical it was for him to arrive at the national convention and give the right impression. As an attractive war-hero-turned-thoughtful-politico, he could easily come across as the perfect complement to Adlai: youthful, active, eastern, Catholic, well-rounded. The prospective negatives of his candidacy—his religion and his relative conservatism—could even be regarded as ticket balancers.

Such boldness is in itself a selling point. But before he could turn his attention to this exciting notion of competing on the national stage, Jack Kennedy first had to face up to serious trouble back home. The problem was a central-Massachusetts farmer whose nickname derived from his cash crop: William "Onions" Burke, chairman of the Massachusetts Democratic Party.

Onions was a John McCormack guy, and an especially tribal Irishman. He hated the academic elite, Ivy Leaguers, and liberals. He couldn't stand Adlai Stevenson. His idea of a Democratic leader was McCormack, a devoutly Catholic congressman from South Boston, who'd come to Washington in 1928 and risen to House majority leader. So Onions was a problem. For Jack to woo Stevenson, he needed to convince him he could deliver New England. Initially, he and Onions agreed to split the Massachusetts delegates going to the national convention. Burke then pulled a double cross, and organized a quiet write-in campaign for McCormack in the April primary that ended up beating Stevenson, whose name was on the ballot. McCormack won big: 26,128 votes to 19,024. It made Kennedy look like a political eunuch, a pretty boy who couldn't control his people.

If Jack Kennedy couldn't deliver his state in the primary, how could he be counted on at the convention? And if he couldn't deliver votes, why should Stevenson even consider him as a running mate? Onions had put Jack, who now wanted badly to be on the Stevenson ticket, in an embarrassing situation.

Onions now added insult to the injury. "Anybody who's for Stevenson," he declared to the press, "ought to be down at Princeton listening to Alger Hiss." The accused Soviet agent had just been released from federal prison. Invited to speak at his alma mater, he'd been celebrated as a returning hero. Translation: being for Adlai was the same as being for Alger. Joe McCarthy couldn't have phrased it better.

Burke's slur was unmistakable, intentional, and uttered with impunity, by a guy who figured he could get away with it. He'd put Kennedy in a position where he had no choice but to destroy the man who'd said what he had.

Kennedy knew he couldn't let the charge go unchallenged. Until now, he'd been content using the political process simply as a mechanism for winning office. He'd avoided involvement in local politics. That had been his father's early advice, and it still was. According to Bobby, his father had been telling his children that local Massachusetts politics was an endless morass. "You're either going to get into the problems of Algeria or you're going to get into the problems of Worcester."

But, for Jack, Onions's attack made his choice clear. Now he had to get down and dirty. He'd used the Massachusetts Democratic Party to win elections to office, but he'd never actually joined it, much less tried to lead it. He would now either prove himself a leader or be forever at the mercy of the *locals*. And that would be a problem, because, unlike him, they weren't big thinkers. Nor did they regard themselves, of course, as national statesmen. Neither were they as liberal as the national party. The reputation that Massachusetts would gain for liberalism, never fully on the mark, was not the case even then. In 1956, it was Joe McCarthy country.

To get rid of Chairman Burke and the threat he presented, Kennedy needed to switch to a new brand of politics. He had to shift back from the wholesale politics of speeches and position-taking to the retail politics of the clubhouse. And he had to be tough. He needed to beat Burke in the back room, where the television cameras weren't watching.

To this end, he ordered his staff to run a personal check on every member of the state Democratic committee. "Find out everything about them. Who do we know who knows them? What time do they get home from work at night? I'm going to ring their doorbells and talk to each one of them personally." Armed with this intelligence, Kennedy began to travel the state, visiting a sizable percentage of the eighty committeemen.

The election for state chairman that year was held at the Bradford Hotel in downtown Boston. Larry O'Brien recalled the Kennedy hardball: "We argued that Onions shouldn't be allowed to attend the meeting since he wasn't a *member* of the committee. To back up our ruling, we had two tough Boston cops guarding the door, one of whom had reputedly killed a man in a barroom fight. Burke arrived with some tough guys of his own. Just as the meeting was about to begin, he and his men charged out of the elevator and broke past our guards. One of the leaders was 'Knocko' McCormack, the majority leader's two-fisted three-hundred-pound younger brother. As shouting and shoving spread across the meeting room, I called the Boston police commissioner. He arrived minutes later.

"'I'm O'Brien,' I told him. 'You've got to get those troublemakers out of here.'

"'One more word out of you, O'Brien,' the commissioner replied, 'and I'll lock you up.' I hadn't known the commissioner was a McCormack man. The whole thing was a scene out of *The Last Hurrah*. The two candidates for state chairman almost settled matters by a fistfight. There was shouting and confusion, and as the roll call began, one member who'd gotten drunk attempted to vote twice."

The guy Kennedy had chosen as his candidate, Pat Lynch, wound up winning two to one. "He and his millions don't know what honor and decency is," Burke complained. Kennedy had risen to the occasion, done exactly what was necessary, changing his tactics to suit the situation, ambushing his complacent rival on his home turf. On the afternoon of victory, he made sure the press understood that the day marked a "new era" in Massachusetts politics.

The fact is, Jack Kennedy had no intention of staying involved in townie politics. He knew it was like quicksand: you got into the fray, picked sides, made enemies, and could never free yourself from it. He now needed to reengage himself in national politics.

As a Roman Catholic, Jack Kennedy would have been, until this moment, an unlikely candidate for national office. World War II had changed things, however, and it was obvious that now there were ways to position oneself favorably as an Irish Catholic, to take advantage of the changes. He needed to make the case that the number of Catholics Stevenson had lost in '52 could be lured back to the fold with the right running mate. Catholics liked Ike, who'd vanquished Hitler, and were turned off by the divorced Adlai, who couldn't escape the contemptuous label "egghead," attached to him not just for his shiny high forehead but also because of his intellectualism.

Kennedy gave the job of proving the case for putting him on the ticket to Ted Sorensen. It was the same sort of tricky assignment he'd handed his legislative assistant two years earlier when he'd sent him up to Boston to work on the sly for Saltonstall against Furcolo. Again, Sorensen proved equal to the task, knocking out a seventeen-page memo showing the power of the Catholic vote in fourteen key states. It demonstrated how Catholics' defection in '52 had cost the Democrats the election. It showed, too, that they had split their tickets in the election, voting for Democrats for the House and Senate, but Ike for president.

However, Kennedy also understood that such a sales pitch coming from him would be seen exactly for what it was. It might even trigger a backlash. To camouflage the effort, he had the Sorensen memo distributed by Connecticut's John Bailey, the state Democratic Party chairman, a close Kennedy ally. In any case, the "Bailey Memorandum," as it was marketed, went out to fifty top Democrats thought to have Stevenson's ear. A few days later, it showed its power. Stevenson's campaign manager, Jim Finnegan, asked for a dozen copies of "that survey" that was going around. "You know, about the Catholic vote," the Philadelphian said.

Jack went to Chicago prepared for lightning to strike. He phoned Tip O'Neill and asked him to let Bobby take his place as a Massachusetts delegate. He said his brother was the smartest politician he knew and he wanted him there on the convention floor in case the odds broke in his favor.

He, nonetheless, remained cool about his prospects. On the way home from the Hill with Ted Reardon that summer, he sounded easygoing about the whole thing. "After all this, I may actually be disappointed if I don't get the nomination. Yes, and that disappointment will be deep enough to last from the day they ballot on the vice presidency until I leave for Europe two days later." He was thinking about his coming end-of-summer cruise along the south coast of France with Torby Macdonald, George Smathers, and his youngest brother, Ted.

It was at this moment that Jack Kennedy got one of those big breaks that made so many other ones possible. After Governor Edmund Muskie of Maine, another rising young Democratic figure, turned down the opportunity, Kennedy won a big role on the first night of the national convention in Chicago. He, a freshman senator, was asked to narrate a documentary film on the Democratic Party.

It would turn out to be the highlight of the convention's opening. Hearing his distinctive New England accent echoing across the floor of Chicago's International Amphitheatre and broadcast over the country's television and radio stations, Americans discovered a new voice. *The Pursuit of Happiness*, created by Dore Schary, a Hollywood producer who'd made his name at RKO and MGM, was projected onto huge screens in the convention hall. It made Jack Kennedy the Democrats' star of the night.

The applause in the hall, swelled by his friends, was prolonged when Jack was introduced from the floor. Edmund Reggie, a Catholic delegate from Louisiana, was astonished by this young promising Democrat. "I didn't even know Senator Kennedy existed. The Louisiana delegates sat across the aisle from the Massachusetts delegation. And the first time I ever remember seeing him is in a film that he narrated."

Nothing that Jack Kennedy had done before, not the offices he'd won, the books he'd written, even the heroics in WWII, would propel him so mightily as what had just happened. Everything before was now prelude.

The sensation created by Jack's role in the convention film had an immediate effect. Stevenson picked him to be his chief nominator, Kennedy having gotten the word from Adlai himself on Wednesday morning. It came with the assurance that he was still in contention for the vice presidency.

Kennedy and Sorensen then went to work, laboring together on the speech until six o'clock in the morning. Criticized by the *New York Times* for relying too heavily on a "cliché dictionary," the speech, nonetheless, was a genuine rouser. In it Kennedy warned that the Democratic ticket would be facing fierce opposition in the fall from "two tough candidates, one who takes the high road and one who takes the low road."

The knock on Vice President Richard Nixon thrilled its intended audience. The liberals loved it, and continued throughout the campaign to repeat the line. In fact, it became a refrain, resonating throughout the months of the contest. Kennedy had understood exactly what he was saying and precisely whom he wanted to hear him. He was playing to the Nixon haters. It was a theme to which Stevenson, once nominated, would return. He wanted his fellow Democrats to keep in mind that Ike had been the first sitting president to have a heart attack. What would happen, he implied, if he died and Dick Nixon became president?

At eleven o'clock on Thursday, the convention's fourth night, Adlai Stevenson made a surprise announcement: instead of picking his running mate himself, he would let the delegates do it. Seven of the country's thirty-four presidents, he reminded them, had risen to office because of an incumbent's death. Bluntly implying it could happen again—"The nation's attention has become focused as never before on the . . . vice presidency"—Stevenson told the hundreds of assembled Democrats he wanted the decision made by the party rather than by a single man.

When the convention opened, Senator Estes Kefauver of Tennessee had been the front-runner. The field now included Senators Lyndon Johnson of Texas, Hubert Humphrey of Minnesota, and Albert Gore, Sr., of Tennessee, Mayor Robert Wagner of New York, and John F. Kennedy of Massachusetts.

Fourteen years older than Jack Kennedy, Kefauver had gained national attention for chairing a 1950 Senate committee investigating organized crime; in the '52 election he'd sought the Democrats' nomination for president but lost, in the end, to Stevenson. Trying again, this time he'd won a number of early primaries before falling to Stevenson in later big-state contests. He and the other contenders for vice president, including Kennedy, now entered upon what would be a twenty-four-hour effort to secure the honor of being Adlai's running mate.

"Call Dad and tell him I'm going for it," Jack instructed Bobby.

Reached in the South of France with the news, Joseph P. Kennedy was livid. Bellowing what an "idiot" his son was, he could be heard all the way across the room. Jack was ruining his career with this move. "Whew!" Bobby said, after the connection was broken. "Is he mad!"

To place his name in nomination, Jack picked Governor Abraham Ribicoff of Connecticut. This choice of a Jewish politician, the son of immigrants who'd begun his political career in the Connecticut state legislature back in the late '30s, was a shrewd one. Equally savvy was the next phone call he made. At one in the morning, he reached George Smathers, asking him to give the seconding speech. When the Floridian asked what a Southern conservative might say that could help, Kennedy assured him it was a no-sweat assignment. "Just talk about the war stuff," he said.

Kennedy now had to figure out how to beat the seasoned pros lined up against him. He already had a base of support in the Massachusetts delegation, and in the early days of the convention, he'd realized, during various sessions, that he'd emerged as leader of the New England region. He now had just hours to extend his support beyond it.

As his taxi headed toward the convention hall that Friday dawn, a sleepless Kennedy was clenching his fist, whispering again and again to himself: "Go! Go! Go!" Charlie Bartlett attributed it to his friend's innate love of competition. "The way Stevenson laid that challenge on the floor was what really challenged him. At that point he decided this was going to move. And, of course, everybody was all around *ready* to move. I remember the whole family was milling around, ready to go. As soon as the competition arose, he lost his reluctance. He really went for it."

For the rest of the morning, Kennedy would personally do much of the hour-to-hour campaigning. He discovered he had surprising strength in the South. Part of this was the result of antipathy toward Kefauver due to his record of civil rights support. But there was also clearly goodwill toward Kennedy himself, as a result of his war heroism and his reputation as a moderate. Many Southern delegates saw him as standing apart from the liberal pack.

Of course, he also had to face prejudice. "If we have to have a Catholic," Speaker of the House Sam Rayburn told Stevenson, "I hope we don't have to take that little pissant Kennedy." But some Catholics were themselves a problem. James Farley, the old New Deal warhorse who'd helped make FDR and then broken with him when he ran for his unprecedented third term in 1940, gave Stevenson his opinion: "America is not ready for a Catholic yet."

Kennedy also took a hit from the party's liberal wing, who knew he wasn't really one of them, who'd never forgotten, let alone forgiven, his failure to cast a censure vote against Joe McCarthy. To woo the keepers of the New Deal flame whom he'd spent his early congressional years bashing over Yalta and the loss of China—those same liberals with whom he said he did "not feel comfortable"—he now needed to do some genuflecting.

When he managed to set up a meeting with Eleanor Roosevelt in Chicago, the former first lady and Democratic grande dame didn't make it easy. She'd let it be known how "troubled" she was by "Senator K's evasive attitude on McCarthy." Her opinion wasn't changed by their get-together. Elaborately orchestrated, it turned out to be a disaster, with the rapport between them nonexistent. When Mrs. Roosevelt raised the McCarthy issue, Jack replied that it was "so long ago" it didn't help. He also quibbled that the time to censure the Wisconsin senator had been when he returned to the Senate for his second term in 1953.

FDR's widow was having none of it. In full dudgeon, she berated Jack in front of everyone present, including other politicians who came and went throughout the discussion. Mrs. Roosevelt correctly saw herself as not just Franklin Roosevelt's partner within the Democratic Party but his political heir. She regarded Kennedy's approach to her as less than sincere, which it was.

Balancing his failure to win over Mrs. Roosevelt, there now came good news. They began to get promises of support from delegates far and wide. Two or three in Nevada, one in Wyoming, one in Utah, and so forth, people who were for Jack Kennedy personally, but represented no large group of votes or delegates. They'd knock on the door of the hotel suite and say, "My name is Mary Jones. I've seen the senator on television and I think he is wonderful." Or, "I'm from Oregon, and I want to vote for him."

Winning the support of big-state delegations was a more serious challenge. Charlie Bartlett described the process of Jack going to the Democratic bosses of the country—all complete strangers to him—and asking for their backing. It was an intimidating group that included the major honchos of the New York machine. But he was breaking new ground.

"After Stevenson had thrown down the challenge, it was all beginning to accelerate, and he was obviously quite excited. I said, 'Look, there's Carmine DeSapio. You ought to go and see what you can do about him. He might be able to help you.' I wish I had a movie of that scene. There he was—this rather slight figure, and DeSapio was a rather big fellow—and the reporters were all around DeSapio, completely ignoring Kennedy. But he went up and shyly said, 'Excuse me, Mr. DeSapio, but my name is John Kennedy from Massachusetts, and I wondered if I could have a few words with you?' That was the beginning. As I remember, he got a pretty good chunk of the New York vote." It was like his old door-to-door campaigning in the Boston neighborhoods.

When the public balloting began, Kennedy mustered surprising strength, with the Southern bloc contributing to his numbers. "Texas proudly casts its fifty-six votes for the fighting sailor who wears the scars of battle," Senate Majority Leader Lyndon Johnson hollered when his state's delegation was recognized. The first ballot count was John F. Kennedy, 304 delegates; Estes Kefauver, 483; Albert Gore, 178. A total of 686 was needed for the required two-thirds majority.

With the second balloting, momentum further shifted to Kennedy. Once again, he was drawing more support than expected from the Southern states. "I'm going to sing 'Dixie' for the rest of my life," Jack promised aloud as the states reported their counts to the podium. With 646 delegates, victory seemed assured.

Kennedy and Kefauver were now the two main contenders. The other candidates were flagging. The next ballot would be the decider.

Ted Sorensen was watching the broadcast from campaign headquarters at the Stockyards Inn, as was his boss. "The second ballot was already under way, and a Kennedy trend had set in. The South was anxious to stop Kefauver, and Kennedy was picking up most of the Gore and Southern favorite-son votes. He was also getting the Wagner votes. Kefauver was gaining more slowly, but hardly a handful of delegates had left him. Bob Kennedy and his lieutenants were all over the floor shouting to delegations to come with Kennedy. Our television set showed wild confusion on the convention floor and a climbing Kennedy total. But the senator was as calm as ever. He bathed, then again reclined on the bed. The race was now neck and neck, and Kennedy knew that no lead was enough if it could not produce a majority."

The religious issue was about to intervene. The governor of Oklahoma stayed with the also-ran Gore, his candidacy now dead in the water, rather than back a Catholic. "He's not our kind of folks," he told a Kennedy pleader. With South Carolina, Illinois, and Alabama all seeking recognition to shift their delegates to Kennedy, the convention chairman, Sam Rayburn, instead recognized Oklahoma, which switched its Gore votes to Kefauver. Rayburn then called on Senator Gore, who now threw his own dwindling number of delegates to his fellow Tennessean.

Kennedy, who'd been in the lead, could see that the trend had shifted. "Let's go!" Kennedy said to Sorensen. Once inside the Amphitheatre, he began pushing his way through the crowded floor up to the podium. While some convention officials tried to stop him, urging him to wait for the balloting to be completed, Jack walked onto the rostrum, smiling. Speaking impromptu, he congratulated Kefauver, saluted Adlai Stevenson for allowing the delegates to choose his running mate, and called for making the nomination of Kefauver unanimous.

That moment up on the stage, before the national television cameras, was Jack Kennedy's unforgettable debut as a national leader.

In a matter of hours Jack had learned a slew of lessons. He'd discovered the need for state-of-the-art communications on the convention floor; the need for an ongoing, accurate delegate count; for a perfect grasp of the minutiae of convention rules. Friendships were important, too. Celebrated senators mattered less. Estes Kefauver had beaten Jack because he knew delegates personally; after all, it had been his second time around and what he himself had learned in '52 he'd put into action now. Wearing his trademark coonskin cap—a reference to his pioneer ancestors—Kefauver was a familiar figure who had shaken a lot of hands in a great many small towns. Unlike him, Jack Kennedy lacked the experience of traveling the length and breadth of the country itself and connecting with voters face-to-face.

These lessons, absorbed and put to use later, were nothing in contrast with his triumph. He had taken a near-miss for the vice-presidential nomination and converted it, at the moment he raced to the podium, into a career-changing event. He had gone to Chicago one of several Democrats looking to the White House, and now was a subject of national fascination. In an inspired gesture of magnanimity, he had, in effect, won the first national primary of 1960.

In the short run, of course, all he counted was the loss itself. Just an hour ago, his vote total was rising, seeming to clinch the deal. Now he was absorbing the defeat. As Jackie and his aides gathered around him in their hotel suite, he refused to be cheered by those who said the close defeat was the best possible outcome, that he'd made a name for himself without having to endure the thrashing in November everyone expected for the Stevenson ticket.

"He hated to lose anything, and glared at us when we tried to console him by telling him he was the luckiest man in the world," says Ken O'Donnell. The defeat brought Kennedy to a sober reckoning. He now believed that whatever lip service they paid to tolerance, the main party leaders, such as Rayburn, would simply not let him—young, independent, and Catholic—become their nominee. The 1956 experience also marked Kennedy's metamorphosis from dilettante to professional. "I've learned that you don't get far in politics until you become a total politician," he told his crew. "That means you've got to deal with the party leaders as well as with the voters."

Until that week in Chicago, the Kennedy people had been parochial in their experience and their outlook. But what had just happened to Jack—this incredible almost getting the vice-presidential nomination—was no real guide to what they'd have to do now. He, Jack Kennedy, needed to get out in the country, among the future delegates on their home ground, doing what Kefauver had done, but better.

"It was too damned close not to be disappointed," Kennedy would say years later. "Kefauver deserved it. I always thought that, with his victories in the primaries. Because I had done much better than I thought I would, I was not desolate. I was awfully tired. We had worked awfully hard, and we had come damn close."

Jackie Kennedy would recall how hard her husband had driven himself in his chase for votes: "Five days in Chicago, never went to bed."

What mattered was that John F. Kennedy now owned an edge on which he'd had no claim before. Change was stirring out in that vast territory beyond Capitol Hill. Those who'd watched on television had seen a dazzling sight. In a sea of gray faces, the camera had lingered on the handsome countenance of Jack Kennedy. It had spotted, too, his radiant spouse: anyone with Jacqueline Kennedy by his side could hardly be counted among life's losers. Moreover, by making himself so visible, even in defeat, Jack Kennedy had gained the advantage that would carry him to victory four years later— those millions of Catholics who'd seen him felt pride, then were disappointed, and now were on his side, ready for the next chance.

Yet Jack Kennedy was not, we now know, the perfect vessel for the hopes of America's Roman Catholics. Though he and his gorgeous wife seemed in public a stunning portrait of the adoring, supportive couple, the reality behind the picture was far from perfection. As planned, once the convention ended, Jack left Chicago for a sailing trip in the Mediterranean with Torby, Smathers, and his brother Teddy tagging along. Just as he'd hung out with a buddy during his honeymoon, he was defecting again at another less than ideal moment. Left behind was his wife, eight months pregnant with their first child.

During his absence, Jackie found herself faced with dangerous complications of the pregnancy, necessitating a Caesarean. But it was too late. On August 23, less than a week after the convention ended, Jackie delivered a stillborn daughter she had wanted to name Arabella. She suffered this tragedy without the presence of her vacationing husband. He wasn't even close by.

Jack had hurt his wife deeply. While he had always refused to accept his father's politics, or his selfish view of the world, when it came to his marriage he was Joe Kennedy's true son. Jackie was able to see the effect her husband had on other women, and it wasn't easy. Yet she'd given him the nickname "Magic" for his ability to walk into a room and seduce all present. Charlie Bartlett could see the effect on her of his pal's behavior in those early years of marriage. "She wasn't the carefree, happy Jackie Bouvier anymore." But Jack's behavior now traveled beyond casual infidelity. He wasn't there when she needed him. He'd shown off his wife at the convention for political gain, then left her to suffer her tragedy alone.

It was Bobby, usually politically astute, who made the decision not to alert his brother about what had happened. His reasoning seemed based on the belief that Jack's returning from a pleasure trip to console his grieving wife would be the wrong sort of reunion. It was a bad call, and the newspapers got the story. George Smathers made it his business to persuade Kennedy to return home pronto, telling him that his marriage was at stake and, along with it, his ambitions for high office.

That fall Jack Kennedy traveled the country for Adlai Stevenson. He owed him, after all. What Stevenson was giving him now was actually better than the vice-presidential nod; it was the perfect trial run. It set Jack loose on the political circuit as a Stevenson man. To the Democratic Party, still dominated by its liberal faction, this was an incalculable benefit. After August 1956 Jack knew what he possessed, and what he needed to change. He was a smart and engaging outsider, a moderate in a party still run by its liberal establishment.

To win the next prize he sought, he'd have to become part of it. He would do what was necessary.

Senate Rackets Committee, 1959

Ben Bradlee

Ted Sorensen

CHAPTER TEN

CHARM

A little touch of Harry in the night.
　　　　　　　—William Shakespeare, *Henry V*

What we are born with are our gifts. What we learn are our prizes. Jack Kennedy came into the world with good looks and wealth, and the social confidence that accompanies them. He possessed an instinctive trait for getting to the heart of a matter that enabled him to direct himself to the essence of a challenge. He possessed also an ability—rare and somewhat unsettling—to separate himself from the emotions of those around him. He was uncannily astute, moreover, when it came to seeing the motives of those he encountered. That he could know what moved others but not be moved himself brought hurt to those close to him, but it was for Kennedy himself a source of strength and provided for him an almost scary independence.

All these gifts would have been his had he never embarked on a career in professional politics. His prizes were what he picked up along the way. He now understood better than he might have before how the candidate who starts early gives himself the advantage. He saw how much simple personal contact mattered when you wanted something from people. He'd recognized the truth of that during his first race, back in '46, when he was out at dawn, campaigning at the Charlestown docks, and then staying with it until late in the evening when he sat with constituents in their living rooms. To accomplish his goal, he'd practically killed himself—and it had worked.

He'd learned, too, in that first, winning effort, that the ambitious politician such as himself needs to create his own organization; he cannot expect existing political factions to whisk him forward. And he quickly realized that the key to forging loyalty within his organization was the invitation itself. The mere act of asking someone to become a Kennedy person was the step that mattered. Nothing builds fealty like getting people out there working for you. With time, discipline, experience, and trust, Jack Kennedy had forged a strong team, one that had been blooded in battle and now was ready for a fresh attack on an even greater trophy.

At the 1956 convention, Kennedy had begun to set the course for the next four years. Above all, he had made his presence known. But the strong backing for Kefauver, known as both a heavy drinker and difficult maverick, had been a clear sign that liberals didn't see Jack as one of their own—which, of course, he wasn't. The truth is, even Stevenson himself had reservations about the Tennessean who'd been twice his rival before he was his running mate. "Kefauver has never done anything to me," he told his friend the historian Arthur Schlesinger. "I just instinctively don't like that fellow."

The pivotal revelation in Chicago for Kennedy and his budding strategists was the emerging power of the primaries. A big change had occurred in the way Americans choose presidents. Consider the difference in how Adlai Stevenson had won his party's nomination in

1952 and how he gained it again in '56. In January of '52, he'd been summoned to meet with President Truman. In that meeting, Truman had offered him the presidential nomination, as if it were a Kansas City patronage job. Stevenson, to the dismay of his host, turned it down. He said he wanted to run for reelection as governor of Illinois.

In March, Truman met with him a second time and offered the nomination again. Stevenson once more held back. Only at the convention itself, staged in Chicago, did Adlai finally bow to the "Draft Stevenson" pressure and agree to be the party's candidate against Dwight Eisenhower.

What's particularly interesting, given what came later, is that, during all those months Truman and the party were urging Stevenson to run, Senator Kefauver was out there doing his own thing, running and winning primaries, including the New Hampshire contest in which he famously upset the incumbent, Truman. So, in 1952, what mattered was not victory in the primaries, but the blessing of the president, along with the excitement Stevenson was able to stir on the convention floor by the rousing speech he gave, which started a stampede for his nomination.

Four years later, the nomination went to the same man—but by a very different route. As he had before, Kefauver again won New Hampshire, this time swamping Stevenson. He went on to secure the primaries in Minnesota and Wisconsin. But then Stevenson turned the tide, winning in Oregon, Florida, and California, where he'd retained his popularity among the Democratic faithful. By the end, he won more primary votes, overall, than Kefauver.

So, if Jack Kennedy was to win the presidential nomination in 1960, there was only one route for him. He needed to go out in the country and build the basis for winning primaries. Here he faced a set of personal challenges. One concern was his health. His Addison's disease required that he pace himself and, as needed, take time off to rest. In addition, he would have to contend with the perennial twin curses of his bad back and weak stomach. "I know I'll never be more than eighty to eighty-five percent healthy," he told Red Fay, "but as long as I know that, I'm all right."

Beyond that were more basic challenges. How could he possibly run for president of the United States? Charlie Bartlett had challenged him. After all, he didn't know the country. For all his intellectual curiosity, Jack had spent very little time in the real United States, if by that we mean the way regular Americans know it. Until he entered politics, Jack's America had been Hyannis Port, Palm Beach, and the Stork Club. The product of elite prep schools and Harvard, he'd spent summers in Europe, touring with his chums and staying with his family in the South of France. During his father's tenure in London, he was the ambassador's son, a privileged American youth among the titled.

To win nationally, Kennedy would have to get out there and stay—from now until 1960. The goal would be to build a whole national organization, just as he'd constructed a local one in the 11th Congressional District in 1946, and then across the Commonwealth of Massachusetts in the lead-up to the Lodge race in '52. He'd be required to "retail" himself the way he'd done in both those earlier races. Certainly, the countrywide scale of the enterprise was daunting, and he could hardly piggyback on any existing organization. This meant a whole new Kennedy Party from coast to coast.

Only by getting out there before everyone else could he build the sort of support he'd be able to use to dominate the Democratic big shots, especially the governors, who, he'd learned, control the bulk of the delegates. But before he could give them the Onions Burke treatment, he needed to secure his own clout.

At first, it was just him and Ted Sorensen. The two of them would head out together across the country to introduce Jack to the local political people, the ones who'd likely be chosen as delegates to the next national convention. "For Christmas that year, 1956," Sorensen recalled, "I gave him a blank map of the United States, with each state shaded or colored . . . according to a code indicating what percentage of that state's 1956 convention delegation had supported him for vice president. He pored over that little map often in the next few years, and it became a guide to our early strategy and travel priorities in his quest for the presidency."

The hosts welcoming them out there in America's cities and towns responded well to the attention of the glamorous Massachusetts senator. "The smaller states," Sorensen remembered, "were flattered by this attention; the large states were pleased to have him speak at their annual fund-raising dinners." Wherever he traveled, he was a hit, and for Sorensen, it was the hair-raising adventure of a lifetime: "To reach small towns not served by major airlines, private planes were an unavoidable part of political campaigning. Most politicians can tell stories of scary plane travels. Prior to my journeys with JFK, at least two sitting senators had been killed in small plane crashes."

He found his boss to be great company. It almost always was just the two of them, with the budding candidate giving the speeches, shaking hands, getting to know people, while his aide took down the names and details. "It was more than a list of names and addresses. I attempted to add to the file notes on which people were most influential in each state, their attitudes toward JFK, and the issues that mattered most to them. I also made certain that they received Christmas cards, personal notes, some even phone calls, from JFK, gradually building a 'Christmas card list' of thirty thousand influential Democrats across the country." With a goal of meeting every potential delegate, it meant dealing with a lot of politicians.

In those days the word *politician,* used today almost exclusively for candidates and officeholders, applied to those fellows behind the scenes as well. They were the ones calling the shots, picking the future mayors and governors. In the late 1950s and early '60s, many of those less visible pols—the party chairmen, the big-city bosses, the ward captains—were Irish Catholics. Actually, almost all of them were. "When we said good-bye to almost every Irish-American mayor, party leader, or legislator we met around the country," Sorensen recalled, "JFK would turn to me and say—depending on whether our host had been warmhearted or cold, compassionate or conservative—'Now, that's our type of Irish.'"

With some of this crowd, their mission would prove a hard sell. The city bosses from New York, Philadelphia, Cleveland, and Chicago were the people Kennedy most needed to win over. Having them on board would lay the foundation for winning over big-state governors such as David Lawrence of Pennsylvania and Pat Brown of California. Such men were skittish about Kennedy, perhaps even resentful. Why back another Al Smith, the Irish-Catholic New York governor who'd lost to Herbert Hoover in the presidential race of 1928? Based on Smith's performance, Kennedy could run and wind up bringing scores of other Democrats down with him, embarrassing Catholics like them in the process. Some begrudged the fact of Kennedy's effort itself. If he could take it on, it undercut their own egos. Why weren't they themselves running for president?

The key players the traveling duo of Kennedy and Sorensen hooked up with might include a congressman, an influential delegate, a governor, or sometimes just an old friend or relative. It was an education in national politics for both of them. "Those early trips were a way to test the presidential waters for 1960, to make friends and contacts while ascertaining whether a young, inexperienced Catholic senator would have any serious chance as a presidential candidate," Sorensen said. "We discovered that there was no true national party, only a coalition of forty-eight—later fifty—state parties. JFK set out to win them over, state by state, building grass-roots support, starting in smaller states, and encircling the big cities until we were ready to tackle them."

They also operated with a low enough profile to avoid any back-lash. Many of their stops were in remote corners of the west and Midwest where, as Sorensen put it, his man's "candidacy could make solid gains without alerting the national party and press barons to mount a 'Stop Kennedy' movement." By late in 1959, Kennedy had personally contacted half the delegates who would be headed to the 1960 Democratic Convention.

Larry O'Brien was separately traveling the country for Kennedy. His accounts of that period show what a pioneer effort the mere idea of such canvassing was at the time. "My main job, in those early months, was to go on the road, to travel around America to build a campaign organization, as seven years earlier I'd traveled through Massachusetts in search of Kennedy secretaries. I would pay special attention to the potential primary states, since we knew that Kennedy would have to score well in the Democratic primaries to have any chance for the nomination."

Indiana was a typical destination, a central state where O'Brien spent days chatting up mayors, sheriffs, state legislators, and union officials. "I introduced myself as a representative of Senator Kennedy, a potential candidate for President in 1960. I soon realized I was a long way from Massachusetts, that most often Jack Kennedy was just a name, an image on a television screen. People were polite, sometimes interested, but there was no great groundswell for him. I found some support, a sheriff here, a mayor there, but more impor-tant, I found concern about Kennedy's religion."

O'Brien's account of a trip through California revealed the prob-lem Kennedy would have with fellow Catholics. "I paid a courtesy call on Governor Pat Brown in Sacramento, who was himself considered a dark-horse possibility for the presidential nomination or, more likely, the vice-presidential nomination. He was in a difficult position. Stevenson had a great deal of support in California, and I assumed the Stevenson people were hinting that Brown might be Stevenson's running mate if he could deliver his state to their man. Brown certainly knew that, as a Catholic, he wasn't going to be on the ticket with Kennedy. We had a pleasant talk, but we both were playing our own little games."

After this, he met with Jesse Unruh, the astute Democratic leader of the California State Assembly. Unruh announced his support for Kennedy right away and stuck with him even when it got tough. "Jesse," O'Brien would tell him, "Senator Kennedy has every politician's name written in one of three books, and yours is written in Book One, in gold letters."

In this way, O'Brien worked his way across the country, finding both resistance and acceptance, but also people who were waiting to commit. What he didn't come across was the enemy doing the same thing that he and his candidate were doing: getting out there and meeting people one on one. "As I moved from state to state making friends, nailing down support, I kept waiting for the opposition to show up, but it never did. . . . It always amazed me how other politicians underestimated Kennedy. Johnson and Symington weren't taking him any more seriously in 1959 than Henry Cabot Lodge had in 1952. His opponents never discovered how tough, gutty, and ring-wise he was—until it was too late.

"We were lucky in 1959, because if his opponents for the nomination had started earlier and worked harder, they could well have blocked Kennedy's nomination," O'Brien recalled. "Instead, they sat tight, the Washington columnists kept writing about what a political genius Lyndon Johnson was, and we kept locking up delegates."

Because he had neither the party liberals nor the congressional leaders behind him, Jack was creating his own national political organization. Charlie Bartlett was amazed at his old friend's commitment. "I don't think anybody realizes, really, how much of a job that was. I mean, those weeks that he put in . . . and going into these towns where he really didn't know many people and there was no great Kennedy organization. He was traveling most of the time alone or with Ted Sorensen. It wasn't very lavish. But he traveled a long road. This was, of course, part of his strength."

Kennedy's feeling that his fate lay with a presidential run strengthened his resolve not to take a veep nomination. "He was urged to accept the vice presidential nomination to avoid a dangerous controversy," Sorensen recalled, "to which he replied, 'Oh I see, Catholics to the back of the bus.'" Kennedy still felt the sting of whatever anti-Catholic attitudes he'd come across over the years, even if they'd never been directed at him personally.

The four-year marathon taxed Kennedy to his limits. "As hard as it is on the speechwriter, a presidential campaign is even tougher on the candidate," Sorensen said. "It is impossible for him to remember the names of all the people whose hands he shakes, to remember the time of day, the day of the week, and the town in which he is speaking; to remember his own previously stated positions on issues, much less those of his opponent. All day, the press is outside his door and window, the rooms are full of sweat and smoke, his hand is bruised, scratched, full of calluses. In JFK's case, one callus burst with blood. Everyone you meet wants something from you, your time, your endorsement, your support for some local project or measure; and then you move on to three more stops in three more states before you fall into bed."

Kennedy's physical condition had improved somewhat since the surgeries of 1954 and early '55, but his suffering continued. The

pain in his back, attributed to loss of bone mass, was being allevi-
ated with numbing injections. In September of '57, an abscess was
removed from his back at New York Hospital, where he remained
a patient for three weeks. Not long after that, a bout of flu sent him
back into a hospital bed.

For everything that ailed him he was taking a daily smorgas-
bord of prescription medications, hardly the usual diet for a man of
forty. Yet they all proved nothing more than stopgaps when it came
to putting an end to his ongoing health troubles. The cortisone he
took for the Addison's, however, had the positive side effect of filling
out his face, and he didn't mind that at all. As perilous as his health
remained, he looked better than he ever had.

Ted Sorensen could do little to alleviate the strains of the road
on Kennedy. "In the late 1950's when we traveled the country together, I would ask each hotel to provide him with a hard mattress
or bed board. When that failed, sometimes we moved his mattress
onto the floor of his hotel room." It was a replay of what had taken
place in 1943 as young Lieutenant Kennedy was seen placing a piece
of plywood under his mattress when he was training for PT-boat
duty. "In retrospect, it is amazing that, in all those years, he never
complained about his ailments," Sorensen recalled. "Occasionally,
he winced when his back was stiff or pained as he eased himself into
or out of the bathtub.

"On the political circuit I assumed that his practice of eating in
the hotel room before a Democratic party luncheon was intended
to avoid the bad food and constant interruptions that characterized
his time at the head table. But now I realize after reading an analysis
of his medical file, that his many stomach, intestinal, and digestive
problems required a more selective diet." Jack, it turns out, was a
man typical of his World War II generation. He didn't complain.

As Sorensen noted, he'd committed himself to a year-upon-year commitment "best suited to fanatics, egomaniacs, and superbly fit athletes." Jack Kennedy, well-rounded, pleasure-loving, was none of these.

As a candidate, Kennedy quickly had begun to give off the glow of celebrity. No politician had ever gotten the kind of star treatment he was accorded. It had begun at the Democratic Convention in Chicago: his debut in the public eye there threw the spotlight on him and his wife as well. In April 1957, he'd been awarded the Pulitzer Prize for Biography for *Profiles in Courage*, the book he'd dedicated to Jackie. Their first child, Caroline Bouvier Kennedy, was born in November 1957.

Whenever Senator Kennedy showed up at a local Democratic dinner in some small city where there were more hands to shake, it was if a Hollywood star had come to town. It was still the age of the glossy magazines, many of them pictorials. *Look, Life,* the *Saturday Evening Post,* all weeklies back then, did spreads on Jack and Jackie, as did *McCall's* and *Redbook.*

"Senator Kennedy, do you have an *in* with *Life?*" a high school newspaper writer once asked the roving candidate. "No," he shot back, "I just have a beautiful wife." There was a professional's assessment if ever there was one. But the fuss didn't stop with the romantic-couple angle. The TV series *Navy Log* did an episode on *PT 109.* The Knights of Columbus magazine *Columbia* offered a salute to a brother knight. And at the end of 1957, in the issue of December 2, he was *Time* magazine's cover boy, painted looking thoughtful by Henry Koerner, whose unmistakable celebrity portraits were often featured there.

This ongoing stream of media attention continued into the 1960 primaries. "You could go to the A&P store," his rival Hubert Humphrey would later say, revealing his exasperation, "you could go to any grocery store. You'd pick up a women's magazine—there would be a wonderful article. He had the publicity. He had the attraction. He had the *it*."

The Jack and Jacqueline Kennedy Show had a powerful effect even on people who normally paid little attention to politics but now could not take their eyes away. Eventually, the "it" to which Humphrey referred would achieve a name: *charisma,* not a word much in popular use until the Kennedys made it so.

While the stillbirth in 1956 and Jack's absence from the country at the time caused Jackie much pain, she and her husband had made their peace with it. Celebrating their new small family, they moved into a town house in Georgetown. Again, all the public saw were the pictures. Photos of infant Caroline with her splendid-looking parents captivated the American public.

Nonetheless, the audience with which Jack most needed to make inroads wasn't falling for it. Not yet, anyway. The liberals, given life by Franklin Roosevelt and still in love with Adlai Stevenson, were looking for gravitas. Here, again, Jack Kennedy went to work, with the help of his most trusted and productive lieutenant. For several years now, Ted Sorensen had been turning out all kinds of articles under Kennedy's name. They appeared in such journals as the *General Electric Defense Quarterly,* the *Bulletin of the Atomic Scientists,* and the *National Parent-Teacher.* Their purpose, Sorensen conceded, was "to promote Senator John F. Kennedy as a man of intensive progressive thought, balancing the flood of superficial articles about his looks and his romance with Jackie."

There remained the challenge of winning over the Stevenson people. "I'm not a liberal at all," the *Saturday Evening Post* had quoted him just after his election to the senate. "I never joined Americans for Democratic Action or the American Veterans Committee. I'm not comfortable with those people."

Still, his pursuit of the intellectuals who persisted in carrying a torch for Adlai was soon to begin in full earnest. The winning of the Pulitzer for *Profiles*, in fact, had been no happy accident. Rather, it was the result of energetic lobbying by Jack's dad. Through the good offices of Arthur Krock, a *New York Times* columnist and Kennedy friend, Joe was able to approach the members of the Pulitzer screening board, one by one. Even Rose Kennedy, for a change, was clued in. "Careful spadework," she said, was the key. Joe learned "who was on the committee and how to reach such and such a person through such and such a friend."

In this way, Kennedy senior and the influential Krock were able to get the job done. Rose, not always happy with her husband's backroom activities, loved this bit of work. "Things don't happen," she said with untroubled pride, "they are *made* to happen." That May, no doubt in recognition of the Pulitzer honor, Jack was named to chair the panel to select the five greatest senators in history, their portraits to be hung in the Capitol's Senate Reception Room. The quintet chosen were Henry Clay of Kentucky, John C. Calhoun of South Carolina, Daniel Webster of Massachusetts, Robert Taft of Ohio, and Robert La Follette, Sr., of Wisconsin.

The fact that Kennedy now was being taken seriously as a historian exerted its appeal over the Stevenson crowd, as it was meant to. Meanwhile, Kennedy won another distinction, one that would carry him nearer to the goal of influencing international affairs that had motivated him since first entering politics. He found himself appointed to the Senate Committee on Foreign Relations. Now came his first curtsy to the Democratic Left, which needed to be a clear sign that he'd departed from his rigid orthodoxies of the early postwar years, a semaphore signaling that he shared the liberals' more sophisticated attitudes.

On the Senate floor in July 1957, Kennedy called boldly for revision of the Eisenhower administration's Eurocentric foreign policy. America, he said, should end its automatic alliance with its colonialist World War II allies and recognize instead the rising aspirations of the developing world. "The most powerful single force in the world today is neither Communism nor capitalism, neither the H-bomb nor the guided missile," he began. "It is man's eternal desire to be free and independent." His criticism was aimed at French colonial rule in Algeria. Kennedy explained that France's 1954 defeat at Dien Bien Phu had not resulted from a shortage of military power. France would have lost the war in Indochina, he argued, even if it "could afford to increase substantially the manpower already poured into the area."

The speech, certainly prophetic for U.S. policy, stirred up the pot, just as he intended. "His words annoyed the French, embarrassed the American administration, and almost certainly would not satisfy Algerian nationalist leaders," the London *Observer* tartly noted at the time. "But they did one thing: they introduced Kennedy the statesman." This is precisely what he intended. Lou Harris, Kennedy's new pollster, was to confess that the "Algeria speech" had, in fact, been customized to appeal to the wing of the party whose backing his client needed. It was meant to show the liberals just how far Joe Kennedy's boy had come. The irony, Harris noted, like everyone else who knew Jack, was that his boss probably read more and was a good deal more informed than those on the Democratic Left into whose political bed he was trying to climb.

Kennedy had been careful to embed his argument in sound Cold War thinking; that is, that the fight in North Africa was weakening the far more important contest with the Soviet Union. "The war in Algeria, engaging more than 400,000 French soldiers, has stripped the continental forces of NATO to the bone," he declared. "It has undermined our relations with Tunisia and Morocco." And, more directly against U.S. interests: "It has endangered the continuation of some of our most strategic airbases, and threatened our geographical advantages over the Communist orbit." Kennedy was still anti-Communist, but now he was connecting this great cause with America's revolutionary roots. "The great enemy of that tremendous force of freedom is called, for want of a more precise term, imperialism—and today that means Soviet imperialism and, whether we like it or not, and though they are not to be equated, Western imperialism."

Kennedy was remembering the compelling force of nationalism he'd seen firsthand on that trip to Indochina in 1951. He was being true to what he'd discovered himself.

The Algeria speech offered political benefit with little if any cost. It appealed to the Northern liberals, but not at the expense of the Democratic South. Algerian independence had no chance of angering those Southerners who had rallied to him in Chicago the previous summer.

Kennedy was still trying to have it both ways: he wanted to be the liberals' candidate while not giving up those he'd won over in '56. Even as he seduced the Democratic Left with urbane commentary on colonialism, he wanted to protect the popularity with Southerners that he'd demonstrated during his vice-presidential tug-of-war with Estes Kefauver. Whatever maneuvers he was slyly executing in order to win over the liberals, he wanted, at the same time, to keep himself positioned as the best hope of moderate and conservative Democrats. And this group included those Southerners still holding fast to segregation.

Such folks liked the fact he was a "moderate," and he wanted to keep it that way. In the same year he gave the Algeria speech, Kennedy voted for the amendment to the 1957 Civil Rights Act that allowed jury trials for local officials charged in civil rights cases. While passage of this amendment was viewed as critical to avoiding a filibuster, it was also seen as a way for all-white Southern juries to continue, routinely, to acquit defendants in such cases. Kennedy's position on the jury-trial question earned him a rebuke from the NAACP, but maintained the warm regard of his colleagues below the Mason-Dixon line.

The man himself was more complicated. Kennedy had an instinctive contempt toward discrimination. Speaking at the Somerset Club, a private men's club in Boston, he suffered an introduction by a member who jokingly insinuated that the Democrats were the party of "the help." After hearing this, Jack remarked to his friend Alistair Forbes: "Well, I wondered why more people weren't blushing with shame. But can you believe that such people can still be around?"

Forbes recalled, "He was a man wholly devoid of rancor, and his personality was completely well integrated so that he had no worries of any kind at all. He could see everything with a sort of detached view.

"And yet he was aware of the interplay of snobbish forces in his life. In England he could see which English people basically didn't like Americans, and he knew people who didn't like Irish people. He was always amused and interested by this sort of sin, but absolutely unaffected by it because he was his own man and happy with his money in the bank—and damn good-looking."

George Smathers agreed. He said his friend was "always greatly interested in civil rights." Then he amended that: "Put it this way—not civil rights legislation so much, but civil rights because he was against discrimination. I think he felt that, as an Irishman, somewhere along the line he had been discriminated against. I don't know, but I did get the feeling that he felt that other Irishmen had felt the sting of prejudice."

At the same time, Kennedy operated at a distinct remove from certain realities, even as he crisscrossed the country broadening his reach. Forbes, for one, was struck by his lack of awareness about black America. "I remember very late, sometime in the fifties, he'd only just heard the phrase 'Uncle Tom' and was like a man who'd just made this extraordinary discovery. 'Do you know that Clayton Powell's got this marvelous expression?' he asked me." Powell, it seems, had been talking to Jack about a black colleague in Chicago, saying, "The trouble with him is he's an Uncle Tom." Learning this new expression from Harlem's congressman delighted him.

Politically, he knew that if he wanted to make his way into liberal hearts and minds, he had to forge ties with those who cared about such issues as civil rights. He wanted very much to have the support of men such as Arthur Schlesinger, one of the co-founders of Americans for Democratic Action and a longtime Stevenson stalwart. Here's an entry in Schlesinger's journal from 1959. It displays just what kind of effort Jack Kennedy was mounting to win over a man whose support was critical.

July 19—Jack Kennedy called up around noon and asked us to come to dinner at Hyannis Port this evening. Marian could not go, so I went alone. The Kennedy place was less grand than I had imagined. I expected miles of ocean frontage with no alien houses in view; but it is a cluster of Kennedy houses, all large and comfortable but not palatial, in the midst of a settled community. Jackie Kennedy was the only other person present, and we all drank and talked about from 8 to 12:30. I only brought two cigars, one of which Jack took, having typically no cigars in the house. Jackie wanted for a moment to go and see *A Nun's Story*, which was being screened in a projection room in one of the other houses; but, though somewhat encouraged by Jack to go, finally stayed the evening out with us. She was lovely but seemed excessively flighty on politics, asking with wide-eyed naivete questions like: "Jack, why don't you just tell them that you won't go into any of those old primaries?" Jack was in a benign frame of mind and did not blink; but clearly such remarks could, in another context, be irritating. This is all the more so since Jackie, on other subjects, is intelligent and articulate. She was reading Proust when I arrived; she talked very well about Nicolas Nabokov, Joe Alsop, and other personalities, and one feels that out of some perversity she pretends an ignorance about politics larger even than life.

As for Jack, he gave his usual sense of seeming candor. I write "seeming" without meaning to imply doubts; so far as I could tell, he was exceedingly open; and this was, indeed, the freest, as well as the longest, talk I have ever had with him. As usual, he was impersonal in his remarks, quite prepared to see the views and interests of others. He showed more animation and humor than usual and, indeed, was rather funny in some of his assessments of people and situations. He seems fairly optimistic about his presidential chances. He thinks that Humphrey can't win, that Johnson will take care of Symington, and that he will go into Los Angeles with a large delegate lead. He seems to regard Stevenson as the next most likely person to get the nomination.

Then an uncomfortable subject was broached. "We had considerable talk about McCarthy. Kennedy said he felt that it would be a good idea to admit frankly that he had been wrong in not taking a more forthright position. I said that he was paying the price of having written a book called *Profiles in Courage*. He replied ruefully, 'Yes, but I didn't have a chapter in it about myself.'"

The conversation that night in July of 1959 is telling in so many ways. The invitation itself was a fine gesture, with the arranging of an intimate evening around one person, a figure Jack saw as powerfully influential. Well aware of the liberal rancor over his failure to oppose McCarthy, he now was working at being convincingly conciliatory. Schlesinger observed his efforts: "I think he genuinely thinks he was wrong about it; but says he was constrained for a long time because Bobby had joined the committee staff—over Jack's opposition, he says. He also said that his father and Joe were great friends, and that his father would defend Joe as a person to this day."

During the course of the evening, Jack showed contempt for President Eisenhower, saying he refused to hang around with his old comrades in arms from the war. "All his golfing pals are rich men he has met since 1945." He also went after Ike's willingness to drop Nixon from the ticket in '56. "He won't stand by anybody. He is terribly cold and terribly vain. In fact, he's a shit."

But he was less candid on other matters. When Schlesinger pushed him on his Addison's disease, he said the problem with his adrenal glands was caused by his wartime malaria, it had cleared up, and he was okay. "No one who has Addison's disease ought to run for President; but I do not have it and have never had it." He then claimed he was no longer taking cortisone, that, in fact, he took nothing. It was a pattern of denial that he would continue as he now campaigned for the backing of a group—the liberals—whose approval he'd never sought in the past.

Over the period from '57 to '59, Kennedy also had to build bridges with another key power in the Democratic Party: labor. Kennedy had started his Capitol Hill career on the Education and Labor Committee and made a name for himself by being tough on suspected Communist sympathizers among the union leaders. Now Bobby and he were targeting the corrupt ones.

The Senate Select Committee on Improper Activities in Labor and Management, to be famously known as the "Senate Rackets Committee," was formed in January 1957. Senator John McClellan initiated the temporary panel to investigate the rivalry between Dave Beck and Jimmy Hoffa for the presidency of the International Brotherhood of Teamsters. Both men were accused of bribery and, in Hoffa's case, fraud. McClellan brought Bobby Kennedy with him from the Government Operations Committee. He named him chief counsel and investigator. Bobby, in turn, named Ken O'Donnell, his administrative assistant, as his top aide.

Jack worried what this would do to him politically. Bobby's new job now associated his brother with the Republicans and pro-management Democrats who dominated the committee. Any attacks on organized labor by Bobby Kennedy, a bulldog in pursuit of his goals, would be seen by labor and its political friends as an attack by Jack.

Bobby understood this. "If the investigation flops . . . it will hurt Jack in 1958 and in 1960, too. . . . A lot of people think he's the Kennedy running the investigation, not me. As far as the public is concerned, one Kennedy is the same as another Kennedy."

That mention of 1958 alluded to Jack's reelection campaign. Seeing his weak opposition, Senator Kennedy begged Republican pals back home in the Commonwealth to put up a stronger candidate so he could at least prove *something*. What he ended up demonstrating was his overwhelming support among Massachusetts voters as he defeated the martyred Vincent J. Celeste, representing the Republicans, 1,362,926 to 488,318. The result of this rout was that Joe Kennedy at last saw great worth in Ken O'Donnell and Larry O'Brien. Not only had they delivered the goods; they'd done so without taking up much of Jack's precious time. The efficiency of their performance had the effect of ensuring less interference from Joe, who now trusted the pair of them, in the big contest to come.

The Rackets Committee managed to strip Dave Beck of his title as president of the Teamsters Union and also to expose, by use of wiretaps, a plot set up by Hoffa and organized crime figures to establish phony locals to vote him in as president. This was new ground Bobby Kennedy was plowing. Over at the Federal Bureau of

Investigation, Director J. Edgar Hoover still refused even to recognize the existence of the Mafia.

That November a meeting of organized crime figures in Apalachin, New York, was discovered by local police. But when Bobby Kennedy asked the FBI for records on the bosses, he discovered it had none. So he opened up his own hearings. The star witness was Salvatore "Sam" Giancana, heir to Al Capone. Kennedy interrogated him about his operations, which included hanging his victims on meat hooks and stuffing them into trunks of cars.

Robert Kennedy: Would you tell us anything about any of your operations, or will you just giggle every time I ask you a question?

Sam Giancana: I decline to answer because I honestly believe my answer may tend to incriminate me.

Kennedy: I thought only little girls giggled, Mr. Giancana.

Bobby Kennedy was both fearless and relentless. On the wall of his office, buried in the basement of the Senate Office Building, was a quotation from Winston Churchill: "We shall not flag or fail. We shall never surrender." It didn't win him any friends in the labor world, or in those political fiefdoms where union leaders freely operated. A number of big-city mayors felt the heat and didn't like it, didn't like the paths Bobby Kennedy was heading down.

Meanwhile, Jack Kennedy's performance on the Rackets Committee impressed one of Bobby's assistants. Pierre Salinger, a reporter for the *Saturday Evening Post* who Bobby hired as an investigator, saw Senator Kennedy zero in on whatever relevant issue was at hand: "John F. Kennedy had clearly done his homework. . . . In what is essentially a nebulous area, he was very incisive in his questioning. He was able, with a question or two, to do what it seemed to me to take hours to get to from other people on the committee." He was careful not to lump the clean labor executives in with the bad. "Senator Kennedy made a special effort not to join the Republicans and conservative Democrats on the committee when it came to dealing with honest union leaders like Walter Reuther of the United Auto Workers."

Yet even the UAW was held to account. In Ken O'Donnell's words, Jack "was not only good in terms of defending the union, but several times, armed by Bobby, he went right after the union and was probably tougher on them than some of the Republicans. He criticized them for the use of violence against their own men and against the company. He was tough, but tough in an appropriate way. The intellectual ability of Senator Kennedy and Bob Kennedy was established with the UAW. Reuther and the UAW saw the Kennedy brothers as not only honest, keeping their word, but also that they were both smart as hell. It wasn't an image that the union had held of either brother up until that point."

The Democratic governor of Maine, Edmund Muskie, who would enter the Senate himself in 1959, said the hearings made Kennedy a heavyweight there. It was the facing down of the criminals that impressed them. "I think that his performance in the Senate added tremendously to his stature, and to the respect which all his Senate colleagues, even those with a different political philosophy, had for him. I know that it was performances like this that enlisted the support of people like Dick Russell and other giants of the Senate. They *did* respect him. It wasn't just because they liked him, because they were attracted by his charm, because he had a way with words. They respected his guts . . . respected him as a man."

But Kennedy cited the struggle for labor reform as further proof that "the Presidency is the source of action . . . There is much less than meets the eye in the Senate." Yet his service on the Rackets Committee gave Jack another memorable victory. He'd made himself a *reputation*, as had his brother. Both were seen now as tough, independent reformers, racket busters. The image remains suspended in the mind, in black and white, of the two of them staring insolently at the crude thug there in the witness seat. We see Bob, the hot-blooded Irish cop, asking questions close into the microphone; Jack, the cool brother, tapping his fingernails on his teeth, that old habit that betrayed his cunning.

Jack Kennedy made few new personal friends from the time he entered politics. But that was about to change. On a warm winter Sunday early in 1959, Ben Bradlee, a correspondent for *Newsweek,* and his second wife, Tony, were wheeling a baby carriage along N Street in Georgetown. In it was their baby boy, Dino. Another couple, Jack and Jackie Kennedy, were also enjoying the winter sunshine, with two-year-old Caroline. The couples, similar in background, quickly became friends.

Bradlee had been a young naval officer in World War II, and his experience had included being at the helm of his destroyer as it navigated Japanese waters. The bond with Kennedy was secured further by their prep school and Harvard backgrounds. Bradlee would say that he was, in fact, higher up in the social "stud book" than Jack Kennedy, having descended from an old New England family around a lot longer than the immigrant Kennedys. Ben was the sort of guy—smart, handsome, ironic, and seemingly fearless—that Jack liked on sight. A working journalist, Bradlee now counted as a close friend a man bent on achieving the presidency. "Nothing in my education or experience had led me to conceive of the possibility that someone I really knew would hold that exalted job."

Bradlee soon saw clearly the obstacles ahead for his new pal, what he called "the mines" he'd have to navigate: "His age—at forty-three, he'd be the youngest man ever elected president, and the first one born in the twentieth century. His religion—too much of America believed that a Catholic president would have to take orders from the pope in Rome. His health—he'd been given the last rites several times. His father—Joseph P. Kennedy's reputation was secure as a womanizing robber baron, who'd been anti-war and seen as pro-German while he was ambassador to Britain during World War II, and pro-McCarthy during the fifties."

When Bradlee asked Jack if it didn't seem "strange" to him to be running for president, Kennedy offered even his friend a stock reply: "Yes, until I stop and look around at the other people who are running for the job. And then I think I'm just as qualified as they are." When he asked if he thought he could pull it off, Kennedy's answer was even more studied: "Yes. If I don't make a single mistake, and if I don't get maneuvered into a position where there's no way out."

It was, in fact, a troubled time, as the 1950s were coming to a close. The country that had proudly, gloriously led the forces that vanquished the Axis dictators now had a growing set of worries when it looked beyond its borders in almost any direction. From the earliest moments of his run for the presidency, the country that Jack Kennedy was hoping to convince he could lead was beset by an unsettling feeling. Americans sensed they were losing pace in the Cold War, and weren't sure how this had happened. The Soviets were moving worldwide; we were fading as a global power, not dramatically, but undeniably.

In October 1957, the country even became wary, suddenly, about the grandfatherly leadership of Dwight Eisenhower. The launching of the Soviet space satellite Sputnik sent an ugly shiver down the spines of complacent citizens long convinced of their country's enduring edge against the "Soviet menace." We'd been told by Wernher von Braun and Walt Disney—in 1955 more than 40 million of us had watched on TV the gung-ho film *Man in Space*, which they'd made together—that the United States would be the first to launch a satellite into orbit. Now the Russians had done it. Our leaders had committed the worst sin a politician can—as Churchill once noted: to promise success and then fail.

The second tangible sign of losing pace came on New Year's Eve 1958. That evening the Cuban president, Fulgencia Batista, a dictator who'd been up until that moment agreeably rotten, sneaked out of Havana at midnight and headed into exile. His departure allowed the bearded leader Fidel Castro, a young lawyer-turned-guerrilla clad in fatigues, to come down out of the Sierra Maestra and assume power. When Castro, who'd sold himself as a democratic reformer, announced his allegiance to Marxist-Leninism, the Soviet Union had an ally ninety miles from our coast.

There was also intangible evidence of America's failure to keep pace against the encroaching Soviet menace. As we fought the battle of the global game board, there came a creeping sense ours was not the winning side.

Kennedy had run on the spirit of the returning vet in '46, then, in 1952, had catapulted himself past the Yankee order in Massachusetts, thanks both to the creative way he again worked his own tribe and also to its own rising self-estimation.

Now, with Ike aging and the decade slowing, the candidate saw how his fellow Americans were reacting against the dullness, feeling a restless urge to *do something*. Even in their prosperity, they knew the times weren't living up to their aspirations, felt the pang of their unchallenged spirits. Jack Kennedy, having been out there in a way no one else was, sensed the mood of the country in a way uniquely his own, and now staked his claim on the task of getting us moving again.

New Hampshire Primary

West Virginia Debate

CHAPTER ELEVEN

HARDBALL

*See DiSalle and make sure he is going to meet his
commitment.*

—The candidate's instructions, October 28, 1959

At the 1956 Democratic Convention, Jack Kennedy had allowed himself to be at the mercy of the delegates. From now on, *he* was going to call the shots. He would be the one making other politicians do his bidding. He would do, on a national scale, what he'd accomplished at home, when grabbing control of the Massachusetts Democratic Party committee. This would mean wooing those he could, playing hardball with the ones he couldn't.

In early November 1958, Kennedy won reelection to the U.S. Senate for his second term by a margin of three to one. Later that month Jack stopped by Tip O'Neill's office, wanting to talk to Tip's top guy, Tommy Mullen, about how the vote had gone in their district, the one Jack himself had once represented. Tip remembered, "Together, the two of them, Mullen and Kennedy, went over the district precinct by precinct—where the Irish lived, where the Jews lived, and so on, with every ethnic group. Jack wanted to know how each one had voted because he intended to use that information on the national scene for the 1960 presidential election. I'd never seen anybody study the voting patterns of ethnic and religious groups in a systematic way before, and I don't think that most people realized then, or appreciate now, that Jack Kennedy was a very sophisticated student of politics."

Looking around, Kennedy wasn't impressed by the field he would face. "There's nothing there in 1960," he told a doubting Charlie Bartlett, who argued he should wait at least eight years. "This is really the time," Jack insisted. The Rackets Committee had made him a celebrated figure. Bobby, too. "For the couple of years there, all you heard was the name Kennedy," Ken O'Donnell recalled. Jack's tough, evenhanded treatment of both labor and management had shown "a different kind of Democratic politician." He gave the impression of being independent, fearless.

At the same time, the Kennedy brothers were creating a reputation for themselves as dangerous enemies, even when it came to fellow Democrats. Thanks to them, George Chacharis, a onetime millworker who was the mayor of Gary, Indiana, went to prison for conspiracy and tax evasion. Pierre Salinger recalls that Jack preferred killing a politician to wounding one. "'A wounded tiger,' he always said, 'was more dangerous than either a living or a dead one.'"

It was Salinger's first exposure to Jack Kennedy's ruthlessness. Up until then, Jack had appeared, on the surface, the one with the easygoing nature. Salinger was fascinated. He was learning what Ken O'Donnell and others had before him. Bobby was the one who'd gained the reputation for ruthlessness, but Jack could be pitiless.

Two important strategy meetings, looking to the immediate

future, were staged six months apart in 1959. The first, with every-one flying to the Kennedy family house in Palm Beach, was held in April. It was here Jack revealed himself as a man fully in charge of his troops and the operation upon which they were embarking.

"At Palm Beach, the senator was in full command," Ted Sorensen recounted. "He was still his chief campaign manager and strategy advisor. He knew each stage, the problems it presented, the names of those to contact—not only governors and senators but their ad-ministrative assistants as well, not only politicians but publishers and private citizens. He kept in touch with the Kennedy men in every state, acquired field workers for the primary states, made all the crucial decisions, and was the final depository of all reports and rumors concerning the attitudes of key figures."

Sorensen knew, by now, his boss's special way of dealing with "rumors." "Whenever word reached him of a politician who was being privately and persistently antagonistic, the senator would often ask a third party to see the offender—not because he hoped for the latter's support, but because 'I want him to know that I know what he's saying.'"

Ted Sorensen, now a veteran well acquainted with Jack's think-ing and his wishes, briefed the others in Palm Beach on the cam-paign to date. O'Donnell recalled, "Sorensen dominated much of this meeting—with the exception of the senator, of course. He'd done a great deal of research on each primary and the pros/cons for and against, so he talked and we listened. Then Senator Kennedy and his father would respond accordingly. Bobby, Larry, and I had little to contribute. We listened carefully.

"The main thrust of the first conversation was that the senator planned to set up some sort of organization in Washington, D.C., reasonably rapidly," O'Donnell continued. "This was the first and critical step towards putting together professional organizations.

Steve Smith, husband of Jack's sister Jean, was going to come down from New York, open and run the office in Washington, to begin organizing the campaign. Sorensen had been the record-keeper on where the candidate stood with regional party leaders. As Steve took over and became more and more familiar, he increasingly took over that role from Sorensen. He oversaw the filing system that recorded how Jack stood with the delegates and politicians across the country.

"If the senator met a delegate and the delegate said that he'd support Kennedy if he ran for president . . . then either Dave Powers or Ted would make such a notation on the card and give it a number. The numbering system began with a ten. If a delegate was a ten, that meant he was a totally committed Kennedy man." The card was then "returned to the main file in the Washington campaign office and then the senator would write the person a thank-you letter."

According to O'Donnell, "There was still an element of hush-hush: Steve Smith's headquarters bore no mention of the Kennedy campaign. They couldn't have asked for a more anonymous office without lying: the sign read simply, 'Stephen E. Smith.'" The Kennedy campaign was still, at this point, purposely under the radar.

In addition, the Kennedy team at Palm Beach had moved on to the wider issues facing the candidate throughout the country. Sorensen took notes of the questions posed. It came down to what had been learned in 1956: Who calls the shots when picking delegates, and how do we influence them? This inevitably led to the question of which state primaries the candidate would have to enter.

It was not clear if winning primaries, even a great many of them, would be enough to secure the nomination. As recently as 1952, Kefauver had won practically all of them; still, the convention had "drafted" Stevenson. The goal now was to win as many primaries as possible, meanwhile convincing the big-state governors to climb aboard the bandwagon. It was still a common practice for governors to run in their own state primaries, then arrive at the convention to broker their delegates in backroom deals.

To win, Kennedy would have to do it the hard way, dominating enough primaries that as the convention approached, those governors would go to him. Only that way could he gain the momentum he needed. Jack, after all, wasn't a party favorite with either the liberal or Washington establishments. If the old Roosevelt crowd prevailed, it could well be Adlai Stevenson again. If Lyndon Johnson proved able to leverage his sizable Capitol Hill clout, the nomination might be his.

"By taking the case directly to the people, as he intended, he felt he'd be able to pick up a great many delegates," O'Donnell said. "I think, very early, he took the position that the leaders and professionals will, in the end, follow their delegations. He believed he could succeed in building a fire under these leaders by appealing directly to the voters and to the delegates."

The governors most on his mind were a trio composed of David Lawrence of Pennsylvania, Pat Brown of California, and Mike DiSalle of Ohio. These men, so the idea went, "would begin to get nervous and, though their inclination might—or not—be for John Kennedy, in the end they would follow their delegates."

Kennedy knew he faced a problem with all his fellow Catholics. He needed to overcome their ingrained belief that one of them could not be elected president. To do that, he'd have to convince the governors to support him in the face of what many of them believed to be their own self-interest, fearing as they did that a Catholic on their state ballot would hurt the chances of their other candidates. Yet there was also something deeper at work. Any Catholic governor was at the top of the heap, as far as Catholic perception was concerned; he'd risen as high as he could up until that moment.

Maintaining that ceiling on his possibilities meant he could congratulate himself on reaching the pinnacle he'd attained.

The cold fact was that these governors feared a backlash among their states' voters. Bishop Wright, a politically savvy Catholic leader from Worcester, Massachusetts, and longtime family friend of the O'Donnells, had become the bishop of the Diocese of Pittsburgh. He warned O'Donnell that "he didn't believe Governor Lawrence would support Senator Kennedy. The bishop indicated that friends had talked to him and that the governor was still exactly in the same spot he'd been in 1956, still horribly fearful of the problem a Catholic candidate would present to the Democratic ticket nationally. The governor also believed that under no circumstances would people in the state of Pennsylvania support a Catholic at the top of the ticket." His nervousness was understandable, given that he was the first Catholic to hold his position.

Governor Pat Brown of California, also Catholic, was resisting Kennedy's approaches. His aide Fred Dutton admitted later that he'd been urging his boss to hold off backing the Massachusetts candidate. "The truth of the matter is that Brown, privately, was very strong for Kennedy at that stage. It was me arguing that it made sense in terms of California politics—and everything else—that the governor stay uncommitted. This was something between just Brown and me, but Kennedy was completely aware of it. He had it right down to the gnat's eyebrow."

Brown had a high regard for Kennedy. "There was no bullshit to the man," the former governor told me long into his retirement. He'd seen how Kennedy had come west well prepared. "His complete familiarity with California politics was incredible," Dutton recalled. "I would guess he knew more about California politicians than any of the chief California Democratic politicians of the period." But it wasn't all soft sell. "O'Donnell and O'Brien were out several times," said Dutton, "and made strong private approaches to various individuals—*threatening*, in fact, is the only accurate word."

With O'Donnell and Bobby still on the Rackets Committee through the first half of 1959, the campaign progressed at a gradual pace. In the period between Palm Beach and the second strategy meeting in October, the senator continued to travel the country seeking out delegates. O'Brien and O'Donnell, at the behest of Bobby, began accompanying him on these trips, allowing Sorensen to remain in Washington, "working on issues and speeches."

When Bobby left the committee in July in order to write his own book, *The Enemy Within*—billed as a "crusading lawyer's personal story of a dramatic struggle with the ruthless enemies of clean unions and honest management"—he also took a hiatus from the campaign. O'Donnell noted with regret the difference his absence made.

The Kennedy campaign's second crucial meeting that year was convened at Bobby's Hyannis Port house in October. Again, Jack conducted it, once more demonstrating his leadership strengths, but also the in-depth knowledge he'd gained. This time the group included influential Democrats in need of continual reassurance that they were backing the right candidate. Among them were Governor Abraham Ribicoff of Connecticut and that state's party boss, John Bailey. When they left, each man present had designated responsibilities for which he'd volunteered.

For example, Larry O'Brien would handle California, Maryland, and Indiana, and Hy Raskin, a Chicago lawyer and onetime Stevenson loyalist, took Oregon. There were no salaries; just their expenses were paid by the campaign. And now, with his book finished, Bobby was free to assume the reins of the entire effort. They needed him "to take control and get it all organized in order to be effective," said O'Donnell.

Currently looming was the decision whether to run in Ohio

or Wisconsin. Since both primaries were held at the same time, a choice had to be made. If Kennedy tried to campaign in both, he'd be spreading himself too thin. It was decided that a win in Wisconsin, where a poll by Lou Harris showed him ahead, made the most sense. It would prove he could win in a Midwestern farm state against a regional rival, Senator Hubert Humphrey of neighboring Minnesota.

Here, the great potential advantage was identical to the disadvantage: his rival's geographic edge. Humphrey had for years been a popular figure in Wisconsin. Beating him in his own territory would send a very definite signal. Here's how O'Donnell recapped Kennedy's thinking: "He said, 'I'd be running against Hubert, who practically lives in Wisconsin. Minnesota and Wisconsin have about the same economic problems, Hubert obviously being on the right side. While I—a city boy from Boston—am not going to be on the right side of some Wisconsin problems.'"

Thus, with Wisconsin obviously such a challenge, it made victory there all the more significant. "He felt it would be a great gamble and, if he lost, it would knock him out of the ballpark, totally." There was just one real danger the candidates saw to the enterprise: a battle with the Protestant Humphrey could draw unfavorable attention to Kennedy's Catholicism and thus hurt him in primaries coming after.

But if Kennedy forfeited Wisconsin to Humphrey, focusing instead on Ohio, it would be a mistake, imagewise. Forgoing Wisconsin, with its largely rural population, would leave Kennedy seeming too much the candidate destined to take only the ethnic, big-city states.

Once the decision was made to campaign in Wisconsin, then the task was to figure out how to claim Ohio through other means. What happened next is an example of just how tough a politician Jack Kennedy had become. He and Bobby were about to give

Governor Mike DiSalle of Ohio a variation on the Onions Burke routine.

DiSalle was presumed to favor Senator Stuart Symington of Missouri, who was Harry Truman's candidate to head the Democratic ticket. With DiSalle still owing a debt to Truman— he'd given him a sizable job in his administration, director of the Office of Price Stabilization, during the Korean War—the Kennedy people figured he was spoken for. That is, if the Ohio governor ran as a "favorite son" in the state's primary, he'd then be expected to hand over his delegates to Symington at the convention.

But what if the Kennedy people didn't intend to leave that option open to him? Soon, Kennedy warned DiSalle, "Mike, it's time to shit or get off the pot. You're either going to come out for me or we are going to run a delegation against you in Ohio and we'll beat you." And the truth was, Jack Kennedy was popular enough in Ohio to pull it off.

So, even if he wasn't actively campaigning there, Ohio was still hugely critical for him, especially now that he'd been acting tough and holding a club over the head of the governor. At a press event organized by Ben Bradlee, one *Newsweek* reporter challenged Kennedy by asking him what his plans were for showing the skeptics he wasn't "just another pretty boy from Boston and Harvard." According to Bradlee, Jack didn't hesitate before replying: "Well, for openers, I'm going to fucking well take Ohio."

Before getting rough with DiSalle, the Kennedys needed to mend fences with labor. Kennedy declared that the United Auto Workers convention in Atlantic City would be his next destination to, as O'Donnell put it, "stop some of this drift" toward Humphrey and Stevenson, both reliable cultivators of organized labor.

At the UAW event, Kennedy further closed the distance between himself and Humphrey. The Minnesotan delivered a rousing speech that was received with great enthusiasm. Still, according to reports, the "wild and frenzied" reception given Jack Kennedy by the convention-goers surpassed it. And that wasn't all. He'd won the support of the UAW leader, a highly regarded liberal. "The fact that Walter Reuther would walk away and say nice things about Jack Kennedy, which he did forcefully from that moment on," said Ken O'Donnell, "that was a significant breakthrough for us."

In a colorful episode, O'Donnell arranged a discreet meeting between Kennedy and Richard Gosser, "very much the old-school labor union type of fellow and not of the new-breed Reuther type." Accompanying Gosser were his handlers, who "looked like wrestlers and like they might break a few legs when called upon. The senator shot me a look."

Gosser confided to Jack that "the rank-and-file members of his locals were all without exception for John Kennedy" and that "all the resources that he could bring to bear in Ohio would be put at Senator Kennedy's behest."

O'Donnell recalled that Gosser "got very emotional, and while he was talking, his false teeth kept popping out. So, in between sentences, he'd reach up and shove them back in, with some force. The senator winced the first time, as it looked rather painful. Then, as Gosser kept doing it with every sentence, the senator would look over at me with that quizzical expression that said, 'What have you gotten me into here?'" As comic as it was, it was a politically important meeting. Jack Kennedy was making allies he never could have imagined.

In all his years in politics to date, Jack Kennedy, the opposite of a joiner, had maintained his independence, and cherished it. He took special pride in not being part of the coalition of liberals and labor leaders dominating the Democratic scene of the 1950s. Yet, as he now moved to identify himself with them—he had begun calling himself a liberal—he was determined to preserve his separateness in private. "I always had a feeling that he regarded them as something apart from his philosophy," Charlie Bartlett said. "I think he saw the liberals as the sort of people who ran like a pack." Ben Bradlee concurred, with even greater bluntness: "He hated the liberals."

Despite the fact that Vice President Richard Nixon was heavily favored to be his party's candidate for the White House this time around—it was his turn—and despite Kennedy's shots at him on the stump, friends of Jack knew he was anything but a Nixon hater. Whatever he might say out on the campaign trail, when at home he refused to join in when Nixon was being ridiculed. Ben Bradlee recalled how this annoyed Jack's "card-carrying anti-Nixon friends."

For example, one evening Jacqueline Kennedy had invited their old neighbors Joan and Arthur Gardner to dinner. There'd be just the two couples and Rose Kennedy, who was stopping by on her way to Palm Beach. Mrs. Gardner made a crack about the "dreadful" Richard Nixon, fully expecting her host to chime in with his agreement. He didn't. "You have no idea what he's been through," Kennedy defended him. "Dick Nixon is the victim of the worst press that ever hit a politician in this country. What they did to him in the Helen Gahagan Douglas race was disgusting."

Kennedy would take pains, even, to avoid hurting Nixon's feelings. Arriving at a 1959 social event at which Nixon had reason to expect him, Kennedy changed his mind at the last second and decided it would be impolitic to be seen attending. Later, he stopped by the vice president's office, with the apologetic explanation that he "did make it out there but at the last minute a crisis arose." He'd had to avoid someone who was leaving just as he was arriving, he said, a person whom he'd rather didn't know about his friendship with Dick. "Nixon is a nice fellow in private, and a very able man," he would tell a British reporter around this time. "I worked with him on the Hill for a long time, but it seems he has a split personality and he is very bad in public, and nobody likes him."

Charlie Bartlett had a memory of an especially telling moment. He and his wife, Martha, spent New Year's Eve 1959 with the Kennedys. Something his old friend said that night caused him to write a note to himself the following morning. "Had dinner with Jack and Jackie—talked about presidential campaign a lot—Jack says if the Democrats don't nominate him he's going to vote for Nixon." Bartlett told me that he figured moments like that are what get pals of famous people to write memoirs. He never did.

On January 2, 1960, John F. Kennedy stood in the Senate Caucus Room, one floor up from his office, and announced his candidacy. "The presidency is the most powerful office in the Free World," he declared. "Through its leadership can come a more vital life for our people. In it are centered the hopes of the globe around us for freedom and a more secure life. For it is in the Executive Branch that the most crucial decisions of this century must be made in the next four years—how to end or alter the burdensome arms race, where Soviet gains already threaten our very existence . . ." He was offering himself as a latter-day Churchill, warning his people that the enemy was arming while America was asleep. It was an homage to his hero and, at the same time, a son's declaration of independence from his father's support for Neville Chamberlain and appeasement.

It was also a challenge to would-be rivals. He spoke of his relentless cross-country campaigning "the past forty months." He'd been out with the people since September 1956. Where were they? "I believe that any Democratic aspirant to this important nomination should be willing to submit to the voters his views, record, and competence in a series of primary contests." He was daring Lyndon

Johnson, master of the Senate, to come out and joust in the open fields. Better yet, he was using his weakness—his lack of a power base like Stevenson's in the loyal Roosevelt cotillion or Johnson's among the Senate barons—to suggest they do what he *had* to do: build a national organization from scratch.

But he kept coy about where he intended to make his fight. He would enter the New Hampshire primary, but keep his other options open. "I shall announce my plans with respect to the other primaries as their filing dates approach." He was keeping other information hooded, too: a biography stapled to the prepared speech lightly wallpapered over significant facts.

The official handout opened with a description of his father having "served under Franklin Roosevelt," a bland portrait of that terribly bitter relationship. It described the candidate as having been "educated in the public schools of Brookline, Massachusetts," an obvious effort to democratize his elite upbringing. The document further said he'd attended the London School of Economics "in 35–36." This was an obvious effort both to claim distinction and hood the serious illness that sent him back home from the LSE within days of his arrival, not to mention his registration at Princeton that same fall and the subsequent relapse that cost him the academic year. Illness, such a powerful part of Jack Kennedy's biography, was clearly not something to be admitted in this version. Finally, the sheet highlighted the candidate's "*WAR RECORD*," something his opponents in the upcoming primaries, most particularly Hubert Humphrey, didn't possess.

The campaign was on! The season had arisen for selling strengths and diverting attention from weaknesses. Jack Kennedy was now running to be the champion of the party that had twice run Adlai Stevenson, a party still liberal at its heart, working-class in its gut. Traveling to Boston that evening, he summoned Arthur Schlesinger and John Kenneth Galbraith, two keepers of the liberal keys and Stevenson regulars, to dine with him at the grand old Locke-Ober restaurant.

"At dinner he was, as usual, spirited and charming, but he also conveyed an intangible feeling of depression," Schlesinger jotted in his journal later that night. "I had the sense that he feels himself increasingly hemmed in as a result of a circumstance over which he has no control—his religion; and he inevitably tends toward gloom and irritation when he considers how this circumstance may deny him what he thinks his talents and efforts have earned.

"I asked him what he considered the main sources of his own appeal. He said obviously there were no great differences between himself and Humphrey on issues, that it came down to a question of personality and image. 'Hubert is too hot for the present mood of the people. He gets people too excited, too worked up. What they want today is a more boring, monotonous personality, like me.' Jack plainly has no doubt about his capacity to beat Nixon and can hardly wait to take him on."

When it came to pulling out ahead of the Democratic pack, Kennedy wanted to take as many big states as he could in his fight for the nomination. He also needed to decide where to put the biggest effort, where to devote the better part of what he had: his polling, his time, his money, his family, his father. Mike DiSalle, the Ohio governor, was still holding out on him. Privately supportive, he was still withholding his public endorsement. Though he had promised to come out for Kennedy, when Christmas 1959 came and went he was still wiggling. He now explained to Kennedy that, as a Catholic, his backing would not be as beneficial to him and recommended he find some non-Catholics in Ohio to back him. Kennedy got the message: DiSalle was trying to welsh on the deal.

At a Christmas meeting among Jack, Bobby, Joe Sr., and Ken

O'Donnell, the decision was made to send Bobby out to Columbus to get Mike DiSalle on board once and for all. O'Donnell remembers Jack's teasing his brother: "You're mean and tough, and can say miserable things to Mike that I cannot. And if you get too obnoxious, then I'll disown and disavow what you said and just tell DiSalle, 'He's a young kid and doesn't know any better.'" Bobby, not amused, replied, "Thanks a lot."

Early that January, Bobby Kennedy, accompanied by John Bailey, met with DiSalle. Afterward, the indignant governor called O'Donnell and Senator Kennedy to complain. "He was furious," said O'Donnell. "He told me that Bobby was the 'most obnoxious kid he'd ever met,' that Bobby practically had called him a liar and said 'We can't trust you. You will do what you're told.'

"In essence, Bobby'd done exactly what he'd been told to, of course. And then Bailey called me privately, saying he'd been horrified at the conversation. Bobby was awfully tough, completely unreasonable, rude and obnoxious, and totally demanded that DiSalle come out for his brother immediately. And if he did not, well . . . he threatened him." To Bailey, it had sounded just like the kind of pressure mobsters applied.

According to a *Newsweek* feature, the taking of Ohio made for "a pretty dramatic story," one that pitted DiSalle's desires against the Kennedy Party's own, as well as its "six months of careful effort." Bobby had secured the endorsement and more. Jack, making good on his determination to claim Ohio's delegates at the convention, had fashioned for himself a reputation.

Not only were such rivals as Lyndon Johnson, himself no slouch at brutal manipulation, put on notice by the Kennedy brothers' maneuver, but so were the country's political bosses, such as Carmine DeSapio of New York and Richard Daley of Chicago. They saw how Mike DiSalle was now running, committed to delivering his state's delegates to John F. Kennedy at the national convention, and they were impressed.

In March, Kennedy won the New Hampshire primary with 85 percent of the vote. It was a big, if expected, victory. The Wisconsin primary, held the first week in April, was a contest between Jack's national celebrity and Hubert Humphrey, the boy next door. Democratic voters in both his own state and the one to their east were looking to him to represent their own brand of Midwestern liberalism on the national scene. He was also enormously strong on farm issues, an area where his eastern rival was something of a city slicker.

Stumping around this alien landscape brought the fighter in Jack into sharp relief. "You think I'm out here to get votes?" he said, sitting in a Wisconsin diner one morning early in the campaign. "Well, I am, but not just for their vote. I'm trying to get the votes of a lot of people who are sitting right now in warm, comfortable homes all over the country, having a big breakfast of bacon and eggs, hoping that young Jack will fall right on his face in the snow. Bastards."

Hubert Humphrey was, within his own realm, a uniquely well-respected Democratic figure, having stood up to anti-Semitism when he was Minneapolis mayor in the late 1940s. He'd also called upon his fellow party members to commit themselves to taking on the issue of civil rights at the 1948 convention. It was the speech he gave supporting this conviction that led to the Dixiecrat walkout there and to the third-party nomination of the segregationist candidate Strom Thurmond of South Carolina.

Because Wisconsin's economy mirrored that of Minnesota, and because its Catholic population was low, the primary could be seen as Humphrey's to lose. Facing these facts, the Kennedy people started early and hit hard. At the beginning of January, Bobby dispatched

Kenny O'Donnell there to live full-time in the lead-up to the primary. "He knew we had to run the same type of campaign we'd run in Massachusetts—therefore we needed to have someone full-time from the Kennedy organization giving actual day-to-day direction," O'Donnell said. Soon Bobby and Teddy Kennedy—whose first child, Kara, was born in February—followed O'Donnell, living with their wives and families at the Hotel Wisconsin in Milwaukee for seven weeks. Bobby, by this time, was the father of seven.

Pat Lucey, a former Wisconsin assemblyman who'd go on to the governorship, was an early supporter of Kennedy in the state. Watching the candidate, Lucey was impressed with his well-disciplined retail politics. As Lucey describes it, Senator Kennedy's day began early and kept to a "grueling" pattern. "He was campaigning at six o'clock in the morning and probably at a shopping center at ten o'clock that night. Finally, he started running out of steam and thought he'd made enough of the right impression to let up a little bit." The purpose had been achieved. The image of Jack Kennedy standing in freezing dawn weather at the factory gates was now fixed in the mind of the voter. For Pat Lucey, the result could be summed up as the "effective presentation of a celebrity."

Humphrey, for his part, tried to portray the smart Kennedy operation as a negative. "Beware of these orderly campaigns," he declared. "They are ordered, bought, and paid for. We are not selling corn flakes or some Hollywood production." To imply further shallowness, Humphrey took aim at what he saw as his opponent's superficial appeal. "You have to learn to have the emotions of a human being when you are charged with the responsibilities of leadership." And then, if that wasn't enough: Jack Kennedy had "little emotional commitment to liberals," he took pains to remind his listeners. There was truth to this, of course. Kennedy's newfound liberalism had been neatly packaged since the 1956 Democratic Convention.

But Kennedy enjoyed a state-of-the-art edge. Using Lou Harris's polling data on local attitudes and concerns, Jack knew what people had on their minds, which arguments would win their interest. It was a breakthrough technique, and one that would change modern campaigning in the years to come.

By this point Jack was becoming keenly attuned to the image he projected. Having encouraged Charlie Bartlett to fly to Wisconsin to watch the reaction he drew from the crowds, he quickly revealed this self-awareness, even if he wasn't about to make any adjustment to fit in with the local scene. When they'd finished dinner after his arrival, Bartlett was startled to hear the candidate ask: "Shall I wear this blue overcoat?" He was indicating his usual coat. "Or shall I wear this?" Now he was holding up a sporty brown herringbone. "Why not wear that one?" Bartlett suggested, pointing to the second. "It looks like Wisconsin." This brought a swift retort: "Are you trying to change my personality?"

Bartlett also put effort into trying to convince him to wear a hat. "It was as cold as the devil up in Wisconsin. I bought him one of those fur hats with the flaps on it and tried to get him to wear that. But he wouldn't." In Bartlett's phrase, as time went on, it was his old friend who "killed the hat."

With loudspeakers throughout the state blaring the Oscar-winning song "High Hopes," sung by Frank Sinatra—its lyrics now specially tailored for Kennedy's candidacy—the presidential hopeful put on a dazzling show in Wisconsin, especially in its ethnic communities. He made a lasting impression when he appeared at a Polish event in Milwaukee, mainly because Jackie took the stage briefly and addressed the gathering in their native language. "I have great respect for the Polish people. Besides, my sister is married to a Pole," she told them. Then she said, pronouncing the words carefully and correctly, "Poland will live forever." Her listeners went wild.

A moment later, her husband caught the attention of Red Fay, asking over the tumult with a pleased grin: "How would you like to try and follow that?" Yet Jackie wasn't her husband's sole secret weapon in Wisconsin. Working for him there was a fellow who stayed under the radar and away from crowds. Paul Corbin was a campaign operative with a flair for dirty tricks. Later to be legendary in some political circles, Corbin began a close and lasting friendship with Bobby Kennedy during that push to win the 1960 Wisconsin primary. Probably his most famous stunt at the time had him distributing anti-Catholic material—ostensibly written by fearful Protestants—throughout largely Roman Catholic neighborhoods. Nothing incites voters to support their own kind like hard evidence they're under assault from others.

For their own campaign song, the Humphrey people had chosen the tune of "Davy Crockett," the jaunty theme of a hit Disney TV show. The problem was that their man was no more "king of the wild frontier" than he could claim to have "killed himself a b'ar when he was only three." It was Jack Kennedy, who'd proven his grit and courage in his youth, who was plausibly heralding a new frontier.

While Kennedy believed his hard work would pay off, he also knew he had to win. "You have to keep coming up sevens," he said, admitting, implicitly at least, that the outcome of the Wisconsin primary remained a crap shoot. However, on April 5, the balloting day, he admitted to Ben Bradlee the confidence he felt. "On the day Wisconsin voters went to the polls, he flew to some town in northern Michigan in the *Caroline* for a midday political rally before coming back for the returns, and I went with him. During the flight, I asked him for his prediction in each of the ten Wisconsin election districts. He wouldn't tell me, but agreed to write them down and put them in a sealed envelope, if I'd do the same. We did, and Kennedy put them casually in a drawer on the plane, and switched the subject. Two or three days later, I was back on assignment on the Kennedy family plane and remembered the envelope. He pulled it out and showed me the predictions. I'd put down 'Kennedy 7, Humphrey 3,' out of an abundance of caution; I really thought it would be eight to two. Kennedy himself had put down, 'JFK 9, HHH 1.'"

Despite a surprise attack from liberals trying to make last-minute political capital of the thousand-dollar contribution he'd delivered from his father to Nixon in 1950—an episode Kennedy aides were under instructions to deny—the Massachusetts senator had scored a big victory. The final count was 478,901 votes for John F. Kennedy to Hubert Humphrey's 372,034.

But the results, the way they were presented, were inconclusive for two reasons. First, the press covered the Wisconsin Democratic vote in terms of congressional districts, of which there were ten: Kennedy took six, Humphrey four. Calling it that way made it appear a far narrower victory than a comparison of total votes for each candidate. This is because three of Humphrey's four victorious congressional districts lay along his home state's border and could have been expected to go his way. Kennedy's friend Lem Billings had run the campaign in one of those districts and would later comment on the outcome there, saying, "In all fairness to myself, Humphrey was a very beloved figure in that district."

Another reality helping, spinwise, to offset Humphrey's loss was his victory in the congressional district that included Madison, the state capital, where the University of Wisconsin campus was also located. It was the single district Humphrey carried that was *not* on the Minnesota border, and for that reason it was judged to be a clear and unexpected upset of Jack Kennedy. Madison was the center of liberalism in the state, and even though Kennedy lost the district only narrowly, it looked bad. Why couldn't Jack persuade the liberals he so needed to win the nomination that he should be their candidate?

The election-night coverage harped on the religion issue. Kennedy had won in six of the state's ten congressional districts, the commentators decreed, mainly because Wisconsin's Republican Catholics, rallying to their own, had crossed over to vote for him on the Democratic ballot.

"Kennedy is, of course, Roman Catholic, Humphrey a Congregationalist, and Nixon a Quaker," Walter Cronkite reminded listeners. "And some observers think that the election has resolved into a religious struggle." Sitting on a couch and smoking a small cigar, Kennedy watched Cronkite make this assessment with simmering rage, furious at seeing his victory recast along the very lines that represented a truth about himself that he could never change.

"One of the most elaborate and intense campaigns in the state's history will end up achieving nothing," another broadcaster intoned. After all the trudging through the snow, the hand-shaking, and the speechmaking, Jack was being denied the proper credit for snatching Wisconsin out of Humphrey's grasp. Now the only choice was heading to heavily Protestant West Virginia, where the Democratic primary was scheduled for one month and five days later.

Adversity had again presented Jack Kennedy with a truth and a test. Wisconsin reminded the country of the hazard posed by his religion. He had predicted this himself at the April strategy meeting the previous year. Now the press was rehashing the same old story. Kennedy resented it, and to his sister Eunice, he spelled out the consequences of Wisconsin: "It means that we've got to go to West Virginia in the morning and do it all over again. And then we've got to go on to Maryland and Indiana and Oregon and win all of them." He had to keep coming up sevens.

In deciding to throw his hat in the West Virginia primary, Jack Kennedy again had to overrule his father. Ben Bradlee recalled the two of them knocking heads over it. "When the question of West Virginia came up for discussion, Joe Kennedy argued strenuously against JFK's entering, saying, 'It's a nothing state and they'll kill him over the Catholic thing.' A few minutes later JFK spoke out. 'Well,' he said, 'we've heard from the ambassador, and we're all very grateful, Dad. But I've got to run in West Virginia.'"

Lem Billings saw it as his old school friend's drive, his compulsion to rise to the occasion. "He knew that if he dropped West Virginia, particularly for a Catholic reason, it would be interpreted as meaning that a Catholic could never be president of the United States."

Upon entering West Virginia, Kennedy must have felt his initial determination had bordered on bravado. The focus on his Catholicism was having an effect. Lou Harris's numbers, which had been giving Kennedy a 70–30 lead in West Virginia, now showed Humphrey ahead 60–40. Pierre Salinger knew exactly what the turnabout boiled down to. "The reversal was, of course, produced by the addition of a single word to his poll. Harris had neglected to tell the people in West Virginia in his first one that John F. Kennedy was a Catholic. So we were right up against it there. But if we lost in West Virginia, we were gone."

It suddenly didn't look good. The unthinkable—an anti-Kennedy turnaround, a building backlash—might well be looming ahead. In Washington, the oddsmakers—including the self-interested Nixon, whose own future was tied to whomever the Democrats finally nominated—were betting that Jack couldn't pull it off. Now it appeared that the nomination would have to be brokered, after all, at the convention in Los Angeles, a scenario that squared with Lyndon Johnson's own game plan. The Senate leader imagined getting together with the delegates and wooing them in the same tried-and-true manner he used on senators before a key vote. He'd work the states one at a time, using his allies from the Hill as local kingmakers. Then, when the time came to pick the party's nominee, the convention would choose a candidate who could actually win in November—not a Catholic, not a young backbencher who'd yet to do much of anything where it counted: on Capitol Hill.

Around this time, Lyndon Johnson called on Tip O'Neill in his office. The Senate leader said he understood O'Neill's first loyalty was to his Massachusetts colleague, but that "the boy" was obviously going to falter after not getting the nomination on the first ballot. He lobbied O'Neill for his commitment on the second.

In West Virginia, Humphrey pressed the advantage he'd gained in Wisconsin. With the strains of "Give Me That Old Time Religion" coming from his campaign bus, he tried to play the faith advantage over Kennedy to the hilt. There was nothing subtle about it. Its verses had featured prominently—and ominously—in the film *Inherit the Wind,* a stirring drama based on the 1925 "Scopes Monkey Trial." In the movie, released that year, the song comes to stand for the beliefs of the rural Christian fundamentalists opposed to any teaching of evolution, and in West Virginia its message was clear: Humphrey understood who the voters were, and Roman Catholic wasn't part of the description.

Cannily—and what choice did he have?—Kennedy himself began citing his Catholicism at every opportunity, but often in the same context as his navy service. If his critics wanted to make his religion, rather than his political experience, the issue, he was willing to play their game. It was the game of politics at its most masterful. His brother Bobby would call this ploy "hanging a lantern on your problem." Lem Billings recalled how, of necessity, the strategy had shifted. While in Wisconsin Jack had "pretty well avoided the religious question," in West Virginia he "jumped into it with both feet. He pounded home day after day about religion." There it became the issue, out in the open.

Kennedy showcased his service record in World War II to extinguish voters' fears about possible conflicted loyalties; his allegiance was to the United States, it always had been and always would be. Why else had he risked his life in the Pacific? "Nobody asked me if I was a Catholic when I joined the United States Navy. Nobody asked my brother if he was a Catholic or Protestant before he climbed into an American bomber plane to fly his last mission."

William Battle, who'd served in the PT boats with Kennedy, introduced him to a much-respected Episcopal bishop, Robert E. Lee Strider, with strong political influence in the Charleston area. "Young man, I should tell you right off the bat the only time I have ever voted Republican was when Al Smith ran for the Democratic nomination," was the churchman's opener to Kennedy, as Battle recalled. "And it was because of the Catholic issue. The way he handled it."

Battle remembered the look Jack shot him, basically "What the hell did you bring me up here for?" And then Strider smiled. "That's the way he handled it," the bishop told his visitor. "Smith would not discuss it. You've handled your religion entirely differently. I'm satisfied, and I'd be delighted to work with you." The next morning local papers throughout the coalfields region ran stories headlined: "Bishop Strider Supports Kennedy!"

Ken O'Donnell noted the way Kennedy was affected by what he saw in West Virginia. "Here right in our midst was a great mass of people totally ignored, yet they didn't complain as he talked to them. They didn't like it; they weren't lazy, they were just people who'd been in poverty so long they didn't know a way out." Pierre Salinger saw the same thing. "I believe West Virginia brought a real transformation of John F. Kennedy as a person. He came into contact, really for the first time, with poverty. He saw what had happened as a result of the technological changes in coal mining. He saw hundreds of people sitting around the city with nothing to do. It affected him very deeply. It really, in my opinion, changed his whole outlook on life."

What now made a difference to the campaign's fortunes in West Virginia was the inherited prestige of Franklin Delano Roosevelt, Jr. The president's son and namesake was brought in to strike at the Minnesotan's soft underbelly, his failure to fight in World War II. From here on in, the gloves were off. The conclusion of that conflict was just fifteen years in the past, and memories of its horrors and its casualties, along with its many great acts of heroism, hadn't faded. Ben Bradlee knew how Jack always wanted to know where a fellow of his generation had been in the "wor-ah." It was a key for him, a key to sizing up other men.

Humphrey was vulnerable, and the wartime president's son spread the news. Humphrey twice had attempted to enlist only to be rejected for medical reasons. But to guarantee that no voter remained unaware of who'd served and who hadn't, the Kennedys undertook a comprehensive education program. Souvenir *PT 109* insignia emblems of Jack Kennedy's wartime heroism were put on sale at the affordable price of a dollar. A letter from FDR Jr. endorsing the young candidate, was mailed to West Virginia voters. It was postmarked Hyde Park, New York, unmistakably signaling its connection to America's greatest Democrat.

Out on the campaign trail, Kennedy made it clear to the curious crowds that came to hear him that here was a chance for little West Virginia to choose the country's top leader. "The basic strategy was a psychological one," Pierre Salinger recalled. "That is, let West Virginia play a role in selecting the next president of the United

States. If Hubert Humphrey wins the West Virginia primary, he will never receive the nomination of the Democratic Party. Therefore, you are throwing your vote away. If John F. Kennedy wins the West Virginia primary, you will have selected the next president of the United States."

Salinger confessed the campaign's subtext. The state had a lot to gain from electing a president. "West Virginia, the fiftieth state in the union in defense contracts, wanted to be with a winner who would remember it. John F. Kennedy sold West Virginia on the fact that if he became president he would never forget West Virginia."

Money also played a crucial role. The county political people expected to be paid for their election efforts, and the Kennedys would do what was expected. West Virginia was a state, after all, where the facts of political life weren't overseen by reformers. The decisive swing came on election eve, when the largest amounts yet of Kennedy cash started falling into outstretched hands. Humphrey could do little but complain. "I'm being ganged up on by wealth. I can't afford to run around this state with a little black bag and a checkbook."

Salinger didn't argue with the assessment. "We were running the campaign there as if you were running a campaign to elect a ward leader in New York or Chicago. We whipped this campaign down to the sheriffs, the district attorneys, and the councilmen because this is the way you win elections in West Virginia."

The Nixon backer Charles McWhorter, a native of the state, saw it as a daunting preview of the general election. "They went through West Virginia like a tornado, putting money—big bucks!—into sheriffs' races. You were either for Kennedy or you weren't. The Kennedy people just wanted the gold ring. They were ruthless in that objective. That scared the shit out of me."

In the last days, Kennedy was campaigning so hard that he lost his voice. Trying to rest it, he scribbled a note to Charlie Bartlett just as the final showdown at the polls was about to occur. What he wrote said it all: "I'd give my right testicle to win this one."

But, as he had told Ben Bradlee, he would not be maneuvered into a corner. He would not let the entire campaign hang on winning one difficult primary. His mind was racing ahead to whatever the West Virginia results might require. He warned his old college friend, and now U.S. congressman, Torby Macdonald, who was running the Kennedy campaign in Maryland, that he might need him more than ever. The primary there was to take place that Friday.

"If Jack were beaten in West Virginia," Macdonald said, "then this would be a bail-out operation, in which he'd win so overwhelmingly in Maryland that everyone would forget about West Virginia. It may have been wishful thinking, but that was the point—and that's why I worked as hard as I did in Maryland."

Just as Jack Kennedy had refused to sit on that little island in the Solomons, awaiting a rescuer for him and his men, just as he'd swum again and again out into the water looking for help, just as he'd sent Barney Ross when he couldn't do it, now he was sending an S.O.S. to his buddy Torby. When it came to survival, he was not a pessimist, but he was seized by the fear that West Virginia had slipped from his hands.

He made sure to fly back to Washington, D.C., as the actual election was getting under way. He'd look even more a loser should the results go against him and he was there, hanging around in West Virginia, on primary night.

To pass the time while the votes came in, the Kennedys, joined by the Bradlees, went out to dinner. Getting away from the action and the teasing hints from the early returns is standard political practice. For his sanity, a candidate needs to remove himself, however momentarily, from the minute-to-minute rumblings and false reports bringing alternating euphoria and gloom. It's also a pleasure to find yourself alone with good friends after weeks of craziness with strangers.

Bradlee remembers: "The Kennedys asked us to sweat the vote out with them at dinner, but dinner was over long before any remotely meaningful results were in. After a quick call to brother Bobby at the Kanawha Hotel in Charleston, we all got into their car and drove to the Trans-Lux theater to see *Suddenly Last Summer*. Bad omen. It was a film with a surprise ending, whose publicity included a warning that no one would be admitted after the show started."

They ended up at a film showing around the corner from the White House. To Bradlee it seemed like porn. "Not the hard-core stuff of later years, but a nasty little thing called *Private Property*, starring Kate Manx as a horny housewife." Bradlee said he and Kennedy "wondered aloud if the movie was on the Catholic index of forbidden films"—it was—and "whether or not there were any votes in it either way for Kennedy in allegedly anti-Catholic West Virginia if it were known he was in attendance."

"Kennedy's concentration was absolutely zero," Bradlee recalled. "He left every twenty minutes to call Bobby in West Virginia. Each time he returned, he'd whisper 'Nothing definite yet,' slouch back into his seat and flick his teeth with the fingernail of the middle finger on his right hand, until he left to call again."

Word suddenly came that Kennedy had won. The foursome headed to National Airport and boarded the *Caroline* for the short hop to the state that had just defied all the doomsayers, all the experts, all the Democrats backing the wrong horse.

The moment of Kennedy's victory speech, O'Donnell recalled, was both ecstatic and poignant. "He gave the usual speech—about the hard work, and about what wonderful people they all were, and that he would keep his word to them. . . . And if he won the presidency he intended to come back to West Virginia and keep his word. That all the things he'd seen there that disturbed him so much, as president of the United States he'd do something about. That hadn't just been campaign talk. It was a commitment. And then he moved in and worked the room and shook everyone's hand."

What a night! "The place was jammed and it was around two a.m., and he came over and thanked us," O'Donnell continued. "He pulled me aside and shook his head and said, 'What the hell happened? We won!' I just laughed and shook my head, looked at Bobby, who was exhausted. He nodded." For his part, Salinger could see a weight had lifted: "He was elated. He knew he'd been nominated."

Ben Bradlee, though, was stunned to see how little attention the exhilarated victor showed his wife that night. "Kennedy ignored Jackie, and she seemed miserable at being left out of things. She was then far from the national figure she later became in her own right. She . . . stood on a stairway, totally ignored, as JFK made his victory statement on television. Later, when Kennedy was enjoying his greatest moment of triumph to date, with everyone in the hall shouting and yelling, Jackie quietly disappeared and went out to the car and sat by herself, until he was ready to fly back to Washington."

The candidate was alone in his triumph.

KENNEDY
FOR PRESIDENT

CHAPTER TWELVE
CHARISMA

How does Jack get them girls to squeal that way?
—Senator Herman Talmadge of Georgia

Jack Kennedy's singular personal appeal was recognized by Ken O'Donnell for the first time at the Worcester tea in 1952. He noticed how women simply stared at the candidate. The effect Kennedy had on people, most noticeably women, is visible today in films from the Wisconsin primary. You see high-school-age girls racing down the sidewalk merely to capture a glimpse of him. As the campaign entered the general election phase in 1960, and the crowds around Kennedy grew deeper, these young women—"jumpers" they were called—would leap into the air to see over the heads of those in front of them.

It takes more than sex appeal, however, to win the American presidency. To gain the Democratic nomination, those victories in Wisconsin and West Virginia were necessary, but not sufficient. Jack still needed to conquer the resistance of pivotal governors, many of whom were Catholic like himself. It was not about whom they liked, or with whom they felt comfortable; the decisive question was whether they could be pushed to do what they didn't want to do: commit, put their own political careers on the line for a guy who might well be stopped short of the nomination, halted for the sin of having the same religion as their own. These men had their own ambitions, too. They wanted the leverage, the clout that comes to a governor who arrives at a national convention with a bevy of delegates under his control.

But Jack Kennedy wanted those delegates under his control. He wanted the nomination locked up before he reached Los Angeles for the basic, understandable reason that he'd seen what could happen in the middle of a Democratic Convention roll call. People who don't want you to win can stop you in your tracks, just at the very moment when you and your people think you've got it in the bag. Just four years before, he'd seen it unfold like that in Chicago.

So, to prevent it from happening again, he was taking certain steps, of a sort familiar to the Onions Burkes of this world.

It had started with Ohio. Bobby's strong-arm treatment of Mike DiSalle had ensured that the Ohio governor was headed to L.A. on the Kennedy bandwagon. Next had been Maryland, whose primary came the Friday after West Virginia's. Bobby, now an expert at strong-arm tactics, had taken care of the dirty work there, from the moment the campaign learned that Governor J. Millard Tawes planned on running unopposed on the primary ballot as a "favorite son." He wanted to arrive in California with the state's delegates under his personal control. The Kennedy brothers, however, thought otherwise. Just as he had in Ohio with DiSalle, Bobby went to meet with Governor Tawes personally. Here's Ken O'Donnell's account:

"We talked to the governor and suggested that the governor might want to talk to Bobby Kennedy alone, that he'd acquaint him with what our desires and our intentions were, and that he'd relay back to the senator what Governor Tawes's intentions and desires were. We ushered the governor into a bedroom and Bobby went in and the governor was not happy, looking over his shoulder for some assistance. But there was none forthcoming. We closed the door."

Once the door opened again, Tawes had agreed to what the Kennedy forces wanted: an open run for the primary in Maryland.

The Kennedy treatment of Governor Pat Brown of California was cordial, if only in comparison. Brown, after much prodding from Jack himself, O'Donnell, and O'Brien, worked out a deal. It was simple enough: he'd run on the ballot unopposed in his home state and then hand over his delegates at the convention if Kennedy continued to sweep the primaries and lead in the Gallup poll. Even with this agreement between Brown and Jack, Bobby continued to put pressure on the California governor. Although Senator Kennedy had agreed not to run in the California primary as long as Pat Brown was the only candidate on the ballot, Bobby filed a last-minute delegation. It was an insurance policy against the possibility of Hubert Humphrey attempting a comeback in delegate-rich California, where loyalties to the old liberal crowd ran high. Bobby agreed to withdraw the Kennedy slate of delegates only after Humphrey gave his personal guarantee he wouldn't try to sneak in at the wire.

Fred Dutton, who was Pat Brown's top political guy, thought this final move showed moxie on the Kennedy side. "It was a pretty good example of the sort of hard-boiled game that the Kennedy group was playing. They were just protecting themselves, they said."

Even after the California primary, the Kennedy campaign wouldn't let up. According to Dutton, "The Kennedys, as soon as the primary was over with, ran a very aggressive war of nerves to try to get Brown to come out for them and to pull over as many California delegates as they could. Bobby was in the state a half-dozen times;

Larry O'Brien came out and met with me. They had every right to be worried, since a strong pro-Stevenson contingent made it increasingly difficult for Pat Brown to support Kennedy if he was going to protect his own skin in local politics. Liberals loyal to Adlai were beginning to make an eleventh-hour run for their twice-nominated hero. He'd taken on the challenge of Ike, went the argument. Didn't he deserve the chance to beat the now far more beatable Nixon?"

Bobby again refused to allow any possibility of this romance with the past taking hold. He was keeping his fingers around Brown's throat. "He was calling up and was impatient, a little petulant, and not at all understanding of why Brown couldn't make up his mind." Dutton figured he either didn't understand Brown's political problems or, if he did, he wasn't going to show he did. Bobby Kennedy was not the sort to see it from the other guy's point of view. Besides, his job was not to be convinced. "I'm not running a popularity contest," he told *Time*'s Hugh Sidey. "It doesn't matter if they like me or not. If people are not getting off their behinds and working enough, how do you say that nicely? Every time you make a decision in this business, you make somebody mad."

Next in line was Pennsylvania. Jack Kennedy knew that Governor David Lawrence feared a backlash if he supported him. Having been the first of his religion to rise to this position there, he was uneasy about endorsing a fellow Catholic. To win Lawrence over, Jack needed an inside man. He found him in U.S. congressman William Green, who chaired the Democratic Party in Philadelphia. Green was a consummate big-city political boss. Two years earlier he had used his clout to get Lawrence the nomination for governor. After West Virginia, he was convinced his fellow Irish-Catholic had proven himself the strongest candidate. He believed no other Democrat would stand a chance of beating Richard Nixon. With the bulk of Pennsylvania's delegates in his control, he began putting pressure on Lawrence to drop his loyalty to Stevenson and lead the delegation to Kennedy.

Despite Green's backing, the governor remained stubborn. Lawrence remained neutral even after Kennedy's impressive victory in the Pennsylvania primary as a write-in on the ballot. Time was starting to run short, and the deal needed to be closed. Thus, at the invitation of Governor Lawrence, Kennedy spoke at a luncheon in Pittsburgh that included the county leaders in the western part of the state. Lawrence himself introduced Kennedy, but wasn't very warm. Implying in his remarks that Kennedy's write-in triumph still wasn't the last word, the governor seemed to have asked Jack to Pittsburgh to audition for a job he'd already won.

Understanding that he'd been set up, Kennedy strode to the stage. "I could tell, as Governor Lawrence was speaking, that the senator was very angry," O'Donnell recalled. "He got up and laid it out cold and hard to them, that these political leaders better think what was going to happen to the Democratic Party if the candidate who'd won all the primaries and amassed all the delegates could be denied the nomination simply for being an Irish Catholic. He told them they'd better think long and hard about what might be left of the Democratic Party should they follow this course.

"Then he ended with a tough—and I mean *tough*—attack on Lawrence, kicking him good and hard where it hurts the most. All the color drained from Governor Lawrence's face. He was stunned. There was a muttering in the room and a nodding of heads in agreement, along with chilly looks directed at Lawrence . . . who got up suddenly, almost knocked his chair over, and rushed out the door, claiming he had a meeting to go to. He didn't even say good-bye to the senator, just fled the room. The rest of the people at the meeting got up and cheered and swarmed the senator."

New York was a different story. There Kennedy had all the Irish bosses working for him. As Daniel Patrick Moynihan, former aide to Governor Harriman, described the situation: "It was still the last moment in history where Irish political leaders had that much power." Rip Horton, Kennedy's Choate classmate and Princeton roommate, was a New York volunteer who saw Kennedy's religion pay dividends in the cities. "This organization, this Kennedy-for-President movement, encompassed everywhere: Albany, Syracuse, Rochester, and Buffalo. So the politicians were responding to the electorate," seeing he might be a help to local candidates in their elections. His momentum was starting to be infectious.

Preparing for a possible power play at the convention, the Kennedy campaign began shuttling through the Midwest attempting to tie down delegates. Adlai Stevenson, presidential nominee of 1952 and 1956, was not ready to accept a changing of the guard in the Democratic Party. Moving into May, Kennedy still had received no support other than neutrality from Stevenson. "God, why won't he be satisfied with secretary of state?" he demanded of a Stevenson loyalist.

On the eve of the convention, Jack asked Adlai, one last time, to back him. Again, the answer was no. When Kennedy made it clear he had the votes for the nomination, Stevenson still refused. Now came the threat: "If you don't give me your support, I'll have to shit all over you. I don't want to do that, but I can and I will if I have to." Nothing worked. The old campaigner wasn't ready to give up his one last chance for glory. Eleanor Roosevelt would arrive in Los Angeles still bearing the torch for Adlai, but it was a flame that burned, just as brightly, against this younger favorite. The year before, Jack had sent a young ally, Lester Hyman, to secretly test her attitude toward him. Asked her opinion of a potential Kennedy presidency, and not knowing Hyman's loyalties, Mrs. Roosevelt let loose with a broadside. "We wouldn't want the Pope in the White House, would we?" Hyman, who is Jewish, told me he almost fell off his chair.

To Kennedy, the more formidable presence at the convention would be Lyndon Johnson. Kennedy kept his opinion of the Senate majority leader well guarded. To Ben Bradlee, he would refer to Johnson as a "riverboat gambler," although leaving the impression that that wasn't necessarily a bad thing.

Jack Kennedy had demonstrated over the years two vital capabilities that would now come into play. First, he was, generally, able to view situations without having his vision distorted by anger or any other emotion. Second, he could see through to the essence of a problem. Like Harry Hopkins, the FDR advisor Churchill once dubbed "Lord Root of the Matter," Jack Kennedy was focused, shrewd, and incisive when it came to his basic interests.

And what he now knew, perfectly clearly, about Lyndon Johnson was that he'd beaten him. He understood that when Johnson went over his list of supporters at the Democratic Convention in Los Angeles, the proud man would have only senators, and that was if they were lucky enough to be there themselves. Jack, on the other hand, had delegates. After four years crossing and recrossing the country, he not only had them but knew a good number personally.

Johnson's only hope lay in lassoing together a large enough herd of western delegates to add to his base in the South. Ted Kennedy, working for his brother in the mountain states, was able to shatter that strategy. And, with the help of Stewart Udall, a Tucson lawyer, he got half the Arizona delegation to declare early for his brother. It was a shocker right there in LBJ's southwestern backyard, and the press play it got contributed significantly to the waning of the Texan's chances.

Nonetheless, Kennedy flew to the Los Angeles convention still concerned with LBJ's plans as well as Adlai's. Tony Bradlee was on the same plane and had been given a list of questions by her husband to ask him. "He was having throat problems, and to save his voice, he took the list and wrote in his answers. The first question was 'What about Lyndon Johnson for vice president?' His tantalizing answer was 'He'll never take it.'"

Jack Kennedy arrived in California far better prepared than he'd been four years earlier in Chicago. This time around he had the organization ready and backing him up as he entered the convention hall, and all the technology he'd been missing before, such as the walkie-talkies that would keep his operatives in continual contact. The country had been divided into "six regions, and every region was manned and they had a telephone and they were in touch with the Kennedy Shack which served as the command post. Pierre Salinger published a daily convention journal designed to look like an impartial newspaper." All their efforts to build a "Kennedy Party," starting back in early '46 for that first congressional race, were now paying off. This time Bobby was masterminding its tactics, while, above him, Jack, the consummate political professional, was in command.

In the beginning, Kennedy looked a shoo-in. But then, Lyndon Johnson threw down the wild card of Kennedy's health. "It was the goddamndest thing," he said with mournful relish, "here was this young whippersnapper . . . malaria-ridden, yallah . . . sickly, sickly." The wily Texan was well aware that the young front-runner rolling up his delegate total in the Los Angeles Memorial Sports Arena was suffering from health problems far worse than malaria, and, riverboat gambler that he was, he had no desire to keep that knowledge to himself.

For Jack Kennedy, who'd come so far, truth posed the greatest threat to him. By hook or crook, LBJ had learned the name of Jack's most dreaded weakness. His staff, led by John Connally, were now ready to deploy what they knew: namely that, living as he did with Addison's disease, the Massachusetts senator was perpetually at risk for new infections while also dependent on cortisone injections to keep him functioning. When Connally daringly called a press conference to lob this grenade, the Kennedys were enraged. Pierre Salinger had only one word for the maneuver: *despicable.*

As it had been in the past—in the Wisconsin primary, for example, when the issue was the thousand-dollar check hand-carried by Jack to Dick Nixon—the response was all-out self-protection. To scotch the accusation of ill health, Kennedy's physician, Dr. Janet Travell, was thrown into action, on the principle that what they couldn't defend, they would deny.

The release of a complete medical workup on the candidate would have handed Kennedy's rivals, including Richard Nixon, enough to bury him. Given the closeness of the election, his Addison's disease would undoubtedly have proven decisive. What if the public had learned of his regular intake of steroids, the degeneration in his bones that it caused, the corset he wore for his congenital back problem, his lifetime of stomach illness? What if they knew his constant tanning was to cover up the sickness that gave his skin a yellowish tint? What if the voters knew Kennedy and his people were engaged in a massive cover-up? Would they have responded as well as they did to his great call to arms?

Lyndon Johnson now took unerring aim at another of Kennedy's vulnerabilities, this one a matter of public record: namely, his father's backing of appeasement. "I wasn't any Chamberlain-umbrella policy man . . . I never thought Hitler was right," the majority leader reminded his listeners.

Kennedy kept his cool—and his cunning. And so, when Johnson challenged him to speak with him before the combined Texas and Massachusetts delegations, he accepted. "We seized on the opportunity to push it into a debate situation," recalled Pierre Salinger. Kenny and Bobby, however, were worried not just about what theatrics Johnson might pull, but about the possibility of an embarrassing brawl between the two delegations. "There were a few rough Irishmen in the Massachusetts delegation, as well as Kennedy men who wouldn't mind hitting a few Texans after some of the slurs they'd made against Kennedy, Catholics, and especially the Irish," said O'Donnell. "So our concern, Bobby's and mine, was that here we'd be on nationwide television and the potential for the best ruckus show of the year was there. We could be guaranteed that if it were to happen the Republicans would play it over and over again."

"I was really digging at Johnson pretty hard," Salinger remembered. He was angry, still, at the attacks on his candidate's health—accurate as they were. He'd chosen to fight back by accusing Johnson of lacking guts, claiming he was afraid of Kennedy, and so forth. Then he got a phone call. "I heard the voice on the other end of the line say, 'Young man, this is Phil Graham.' I'd never met Phil Graham before in my life." Of course, he knew who the *Washington Post* publisher was.

"And he said, 'I just want to say one thing to you. Don't tear something apart in such a way that you can never put it back together again.' I said, 'Okay,' and hung up the phone. Of course, it immediately dawned on me what he was trying to say to me. It was that there was a chance of a Kennedy-Johnson ticket." Graham, it turns out, was pushing Johnson to accept the vice presidency if Kennedy offered it, and was pushing the idea of the ticket to LBJ as being for the good of the country.

With Lyndon Johnson's arrows having failed to hit their mark, the next rival Jack needed to render impotent was Adlai Stevenson. He'd retained scattered loyalists, but his support since '56 had rusted, even on his home turf, Illinois. Despite some packing of the galleries, there was no demand for Adlai on the convention floor or in the deal-making back rooms.

Still Stevenson's supporters persisted, keeping up the drumbeat, hoping the scene they were creating on the television screen would stir the delegates. Senator Eugene McCarthy of Minnesota gave the convention perhaps its most memorable oratory. "Do not turn away from this man. Do not reject this man. . . . Do not reject this man who has made us proud to be Democrats. Do not leave this prophet without honor in his own party."

But nothing happened. The Kennedy "operation was slick, well financed, and ruthless in its treatment of Lyndon Johnson's Southerners and the uncredentialed mob that was trying to stampede the convention for Stevenson," noted John Ehrlichman, then a young campaign worker for Richard Nixon secretly scouting the opposition.

Beating Vice President Nixon was not going to be easy. Jack was going to need support in the once-reliable Democratic South. His decision to offer the job of running mate to Lyndon Johnson was a model of cold-blooded politics. The fact was, no one else brought to the table what LBJ did, which was Texas and much of the South. The big surprise was that he might accept the prize if offered. But such was the case. And one person who found himself a go-between, helping to seal the deal, was Tip O'Neill.

Johnson's mentor was Sam Rayburn—a fellow Texan and the powerful Speaker of the House—who made it his business to contact Tip, saying, "If Kennedy wants Johnson for vice president, then he has nothing else he can do but to be on the ticket." Instructing O'Neill to find Kennedy and tell him what he'd just said, he even passed on the phone number for Jack to call.

Tip located Jack that night at a legendary Hollywood hangout, Chasen's. When the two met on the sidewalk outside the restaurant, O'Neill gave Jack the phone number and told him what Rayburn had said: Lyndon would accept if offered. "Of course I want Lyndon," Kennedy replied. He said to tell Rayburn he'd be making the call that night.

The full story of what lay behind John F. Kennedy's selection of Lyndon Baines Johnson remains murky to this day. When Salinger asked his boss for "some background" on the making of the decision, Jack was unforthcoming. "He said, 'Well, I'd just as soon not tell you. I don't think anybody will ever really know how this all really came about.'" Bobby, opposing the choice, had urged him to withdraw Johnson's name. Jack himself appears to have wavered.

What remains impressive is his ability to absorb the attack he took from Johnson and his people and keep his political bearings. "It was a case of grasping the nettle," Schlesinger wrote in his journal for July 15, 1960, "and it was another evidence of the impressively cold and tough way Jack is going about his affairs." Indeed, in putting the Johnson assault in its place, Jack was simply sorting matters into compartments, as he often did. Fending off a last-ditch challenge to his nomination was one matter. Finding someone to help him in November was totally another. Whether Johnson had played tough to try to secure the presidential nomination for himself was no deterrent to his running as Jack's vice president. Not in Jack's eyes. Not now. Rather, it was an indicator of how tough Johnson was prepared to fight by his side.

Charlie Bartlett could sense Jack was brooding about the necessity of picking Johnson, just as he'd brooded four years earlier over the need to back the less than fresh Pat Lynch as his Massachusetts party chief in 1956. But he also remembers Joe Kennedy standing there in his smoking jacket and slippers saying, "Don't worry, Jack, in two weeks, they'll be saying it's the smartest thing you ever did." For once, the father's political judgment was on the money.

With the issue of his vice-presidential choice resolved, and the waves of history lapping at his feet, now came Kennedy's speech accepting the nomination.

What most people recall is the debut of his presidential signature. "Today some would say that those struggles are all over—that all the horizons have been explored—that all the battles have been won—that there is no longer an American frontier . . . But I tell you the New Frontier is here, whether we seek it or not. Beyond that frontier are uncharted areas of science and space, unsolved problems of peace and war, unconquered pockets of ignorance and prejudice, unanswered questions of poverty and surplus.

"For the harsh facts of the matter are that we stand on this frontier at a turning point in history. We must prove all over again whether this nation—or any nation so conceived—can long endure; whether our society—with its freedom of choice, its breadth of opportunity, its range of alternatives—can compete with the single-minded advance of the Communist system."

Kennedy was really harking back to the same question that presented itself just before World War II, the one that had gripped him and driven his interest in foreign policy. It had not lost its relevance, for what he was asking was, could the democracies match the dictatorships when it came to responding to a dire threat? While we see the allusion to Lincoln in the wording, the question itself is pure twentieth century—only it was now Khrushchev, not Hitler, in opposition to us.

But it wasn't just America's Democrats who had their attention focused on the convention concluding in Los Angeles. The about-to-be Republican candidate, Richard Nixon, was watching television that night, viewing it carefully with the eye of a professional, and deciding, when all the shouting was over, that he was encouraged by what he'd seen.

Theodore White, then doing the reporting for his landmark book *The Making of the President, 1960,* described the response of the Republican cohort this way: "They sat rapt, then content, then pleased. The rapid delivery, the literary language, the obvious exhaustion of the Democratic candidate . . . all combined to invite in them a sense of combative good feeling." Nixon told those with him that he thought Kennedy had turned in a poor performance, his speech above people's heads and delivered too rapidly. He could take this man, his longtime colleague, now a known quantity, on TV—or so he felt.

So Nixon, made confident by what he'd seen, and trusting his judgment, was in a mood receptive to the idea of televised debate. Kennedy, when the moment came, jumped at the opportunity. "I took the telegram to him," Pierre Salinger said. The networks were proposing a candidates' debate, and, in the Kennedy camp, the decision to agree was quickly made. "The feeling was that we had absolutely nothing to lose by a debate with Nixon. If we accepted right away, we'd put Nixon in a position where he *had* to accept."

No one, least of all Jack, could have predicted the vice president's psychology or realized that Jack's performance at the convention had allayed Dick Nixon's worries about going head to head with him in front of the cameras. But by saying yes to a debate, what Nixon was handing his opponent was, in fact, a platform of such value that not even the senior Kennedy's wealth could have purchased it. Here was an opportunity for Jack to face the American people and claim for himself a measure of the recognition already Nixon's. Eight years in the vice presidency had given his rival a mammoth edge. TV would now hand it to the challenger.

The Kennedy themes, devised to differentiate his candidacy from Nixon's, all looked to the future. While the one man was so closely associated with both the long-standing positives and the more recent negatives of the Eisenhower era, the other could recast the country's complacency as a trap. Elect him, Jack Kennedy promised, and he'd arouse citizens to a new urgency, a new determination to face up to the challenges ahead. The United States was slowing down; everyone knew that. But he, John F. Kennedy, would get it moving again. He'd take on the Soviet threat, close the "missile gap," and bring the enemy to the bargaining table. He would arm America, not to fight, but to parlay. In short, he'd do what Winston Churchill might have done to prevent World War II, had his own countrymen listened to him back in the 1930s.

Meanwhile, Kennedy had a vibrant domestic agenda as well. He vowed to be a Democratic activist in the tradition of Franklin Roosevelt, bringing medical care to the elderly, federal aid to education, and strong enforcement of civil rights.

When the two came together face-to-face, the strategy was for Nixon to be squeezed, maneuvered into appearing both weak on defense and inactive on the home front. The tactic had worked against Henry Cabot Lodge in 1952, and, since you repeat what works, Kennedy intended to deny Nixon any chance to benefit as a moderate-sounding Republican. Not hard enough on defense, not soft enough on taking care of people: Kennedy would keep up the punches and send his rival into a defensive crouch, trying to match point for point every charge made against the Eisenhower record.

However, before he could go head to head with Nixon, Kennedy first needed to deal once again with the religion issue, which, despite his facing it head-on in West Virginia, had never really gone away. The need to do so once again came in early September, as he was whistle-stopping his way down the Pacific coast from Portland to Los Angeles. Suddenly, at one stop, he was peppered with questions about a meeting of 150 ministers just held at Washington's Mayflower Hotel. The purpose of the gathering, called Citizens for Religious Freedom, had been to band Protestant clergymen together to work against the election of a Roman Catholic president.

The meeting's organizer, Norman Vincent Peale, the longtime pastor of New York's Marble Collegiate Church and author of the best-selling *The Power of Positive Thinking*, also hosted his own radio program, *The Art of Living*. Thus, he was a popular and influential figure, now committed to using his clout against Jack Kennedy. "Our freedom, our religious freedom," he proclaimed, "is at stake if we elect a member of the Roman Catholic order as president of the United States." He worried that the pope was poised to assert his authority over any Catholic aspirant to the White House. His mission was convincing his fellow Americans of that risk.

As the waiting reporters clamored for a statement, Kennedy's initial response was curt: "I wouldn't attempt to reply to Dr. Peale or to anyone who questions my loyalty to the United States." Later, though, he'd remark to Ted Sorensen—after hearing Peale had claimed "the election of a Catholic president would change America"—"I would like to think he was complimenting me, but I'm not sure he was."

Yet, as he traveled on, it was becoming increasingly apparent that his responses to date still weren't enough to put the issue to rest. He decided to accept an invitation to speak to the Protestant ministers of Houston. When he stood there in front of them, he intended to address thoughtfully what he'd actually come to view as legitimate questions about his loyalty. The effect of it, he hoped, would be enough to arouse the loyalty of all Americans, not only Catholics, who'd felt the sting of prejudice. Though it's true he was sending mixed signals, telling Protestants not to vote their religion at the same time he was courting the Catholic vote, still, the eloquence he brought to bear upon bigotry cut deep and created a watershed moment in American politics.

The math, in fact, was straightforward enough. Kennedy understood the electoral power his religion actually gave him. While just one voter in four was Catholic, these citizens had sizable leverage in the states with the most electoral votes. So he needed, first off, to minimize the anti-Catholic vote by hanging the "bias" tag on any Protestant vote against him. Jews and other minorities would then get the picture, he hoped, and rally to the cause.

He also had to keep it light; he couldn't allow himself, ever, to get publicly defensive. When Harry Truman, campaigning for Kennedy and sounding only like himself, let loose at Nixon-loving Southerners, telling them they could "go to hell," the profanity earned him a pious rebuke from the Republican candidate himself. Kennedy, though, dispatched a clever telegram to the highly partisan, and also Nixon-hating, former chief executive. "Dear Mr. President," he wrote, "I have noted with interest your suggestion as to where those who vote for my opponent should go. While I understand and sympathize with your deep motivation, I think it is important that our side try to refrain from raising the religious issue."

En route to address the Greater Houston Ministerial Association, he made a stop in El Paso. *Look* magazine's Bill Attwood, who was friendly with Jack, saw him there and has recounted a telling exchange. "It was night and we were late, and a crowd of 7,000 people had been waiting at the airport for hours. They wanted to yell and cheer, and they wanted him to wave his arms and smile and say something about the Texas sky and stars. But he just strode out of the plane and jabbed his forefinger at them and talked about getting America moving again. And then he turned and climbed into a car and drove away.

"A few days later . . . I told him the crowd had felt let down and suggested that the next time he should at least wave his arms the way other politicians did and give people a chance to get the cheers out of their throats. Kennedy shook his head and borrowed my notebook and pencil—he was saving his voice for the day's speeches—and wrote, 'I always swore one thing I'd never do is' and he drew a picture of a man with his arms in the air." There were limits to what he would do to win votes.

But someone else was impressed—and extremely so—that night at the El Paso airport. According to Ken O'Donnell, Sam Rayburn, the legendary "Mr. Democrat," told him "ten times after we got to the hotel he had never seen such a crowd in El Paso and certainly not at that hour of the night. He didn't quite understand it, saying 'This young fellow has something special. I just didn't realize until now.'"

While the Kennedy advisors all agreed that a speech on his religion was necessary, they were equally against their candidate's accepting the Houston invitation. Jack Kennedy himself was the sole voice in favor. "In the end, he alone made the decision to go," O'Donnell recalled. "It came about casually; he was in shaving . . . and came out of the bathroom and said, 'Notify them we're going to do it. I'll give the speech. This is as good a time as any. We might as well get it on the record early; they're going to be asking this throughout the rest of the campaign. So, I'm going to do it.'"

In the hours leading up to the speech, Kennedy continued to wonder aloud if he'd made the right decision. Then, just before leaving his hotel room in his black pinstriped suit, a nonpolitical issue arose. "Look!" he told the ever-present Ken O'Donnell, pointing at his shoes. "They're brown!"

Finally, Dave Powers, the staff guy in charge of wardrobe, was located. His response brought common sense to bear: "I think, Senator, you'll be behind a podium and nobody will notice it on television. . . . I think this once you'll be okay."

"Really, Dave," Kennedy replied, "so you don't think anyone will notice that I have brown shoes with a crisp black suit?"

"Nah, nobody will notice. I mean, come on, Senator, most people in America only have one set of shoes—and, Senator, those shoes! Those shoes are brown! You know what you did tonight, Senator! You know what you did! You sewed up the brown shoe vote." At this, even Jack began to see the humor.

Kennedy walked into the meeting room alone. To make sure the audience viewing clips at home got the message, the advance man, Robert S. Strauss, had picked the "meanest, nastiest-looking" ministers to put in the front row. Assuming the role of defendant in the argument, Jack offered respect to these serious citizens with doubts about his loyalties. The invited ministers had a perfect right to question him, he said. But once having satisfied themselves as to his sincerity, they also had a responsibility to move on to other issues.

Kennedy's opening presentation in Houston was, perhaps, the finest of the campaign. "So, it is apparently necessary for me to state once again not what kind of church I believe in, for that should be important only to me, but what kind of America I believe in. I believe in an America where the separation of church and state is absolute, where no Catholic prelate would tell the president—should he be a Catholic—how to act, and no Protestant minister would tell his parishioners for whom to vote."

O'Donnell described Senator Kennedy's performance there as "dancing on a needle." On the one hand, he had "to satisfy this audience with regard to a Catholic in the presidency; and yet at the same time he had to be careful not to jeopardize his position with the Catholics across the country, the Catholic Church, or the Catholic priests." If he "came across as too conciliatory to these people, some of whom were outright bigots, it would destroy his candidacy and his position."

Not only did Kennedy speak eloquently; he presented himself

with careful dignity, at the same time displaying an elegant pugnacity when roused. This was especially true in the long question-and-answer period that followed his speech. One focus of attention was Kennedy's rejection of a 1947 invitation to address a dinner in Philadelphia to raise funds for a Chapel of the Chaplains. It had been intended as an interfaith house of worship honoring the four chaplains who went down with the *Dorchester* in World War II. Kennedy had, at first, accepted the invitation, only to later turn it down. He'd done so at the request of the local archbishop, Dennis Cardinal Dougherty.

Kennedy's answer was that he had lacked the credentials to attend the dinner "as a spokesman for the Catholic church." When pushed further on the question again, he'd finally had enough. "Is this the best that can be done after fourteen years? Is this the *only* incident that can be charged?" But in the end, he'd been respectful, made all his points, stood his ground, and came away looking like a winner.

There are many ways of preparing for a life on the political stage. To the usual list—remembering the names of people you meet once, smiling at proven enemies—Jack Kennedy now added making noises like a seal. Given to bouts of self-improvement—his famous speed-reading is an example—he had been concerned about the timbre of his voice, how he sounded to listeners when he spoke in public. His performance at the Los Angeles convention had not been that strong and he knew it. The loud daily barking, then, was an exercise assigned to him by the vocal coach David McClosky, one that Jack chose to practice in the bathtub. Unexpectedly hearing him emit these very peculiar sounds caused even the most loyal of his aides to wonder if there wasn't, perhaps, a new health problem.

Jack's ongoing transformation had other aspects, with one significant physical change being inadvert, a side effect of the medication he was taking for his Addison's. More than saving his life, the cortisone he'd been taking had transformed his face, fleshing out his features. Billy Sutton, who'd lived with him during those early years in Washington, would remark that he'd never looked better than he did in those months of running for president against Richard Nixon.

But cosmetic advantages didn't guarantee elections. True enough, Dick Nixon had looked old even when he was young—he was, in fact, just four years the senior of his Democratic rival—but he'd also spent two terms as vice president in the shadow of the prize they both were after. He was no one Jack could take for granted.

Throughout that fall, Dave Powers, Kennedy's campaign "body man," used the specter of Nixon to motivate his boss each morning. He once told me that he'd walk into Jack's room, in whatever town they happened to be in, pull open the curtains, and begin, tunelessly, to serenade the candidate: "I wonder where Dick Nixon is this time of day. I wonder how many factories he's been to, how many events he's had already."

The coming debates were, of course, of far greater importance than a typical day on the campaign trail, and Jack Kennedy knew it. Hadn't Nixon won his original seat in Congress by stomping on a first-rate New Dealer, Jerry Voorhis? It had been a no-holds-barred assault when he'd run against Congresswoman Helen Gahagan Douglas, defeating her in the even nastier 1950 Senate race, in which her lone success was in hanging on him a lasting nickname, "Tricky Dick."

But as much as Jack had to be wary of Nixon, there was also the fact that they'd be facing each other in front of a huge audience, bigger than any in history. That year, 1960, wasn't the first one in which television coverage had to be taken into account by presidential campaigns. It was, however, the first one in which *nearly every voter* had a television.

There were to be four debates, the first scheduled for September 26 in Chicago.

"Kennedy took the thing much more seriously than Nixon," recalled Don Hewitt, the CBS producer assigned to direct the candidates' first encounter. The Democrat had asked Hewitt to meet with him a week early in a hangar at Chicago's Midway Airport. "Where do I stand?" Jack kept asking, eager to get an idea of what the setup would be in the WBBM studio. On the afternoon of the debate, wearing a terry-cloth robe, Kennedy lay in bed in his hotel room, clutching a fistful of cards in his hand, each with a probable question and its staff-prepared answer. Drilling him was Ted Sorensen and his other legislative assistant, Mike Feldman. After each card had been dealt with, Kennedy would throw it on the floor. Additionally, there was the "Nixopedia," which Feldman had prepared—in a binder like the once-invaluable "Lodge's Dodges"—to track and detail Nixon's positions.

The pollster Lou Harris recalled Kennedy standing on his Ambassador East Hotel balcony with the sun on his face. "He was nervous, and would hit his fist. There he was, walking back and forth, hitting his fist." To pass the time, Kennedy kept asking his pollster how he went about the business of calculating public opinion.

Also there with Kennedy was a veteran of the new camera-driven politics. Bill Wilson had been a young television producer when hired by Adlai Stevenson's campaign in 1956. His role was to help the TV-shy candidate perform as best he could in the new medium, since, for all his eloquence as a platform orator, Stevenson was a primitive as far as TV was concerned. When the set in his hotel room went on the blink, for example, he telephoned Wilson to come fix it. He saw no difference between a television advisor and a TV repairman. Nonetheless, Stevenson had kept Wilson through the primaries and into the general election, although never quite sure what the point was. Such basic resistance was not the case, though, with Wilson's new employer, who understood very well the importance of the tiny screen that sat there in voters' homes.

As the two participants arrived at the studio, there was a moment of mutual appraisal that gave a harbinger of what was to come: Jack looked like a million bucks and Nixon knew it; Nixon looked terrible and Kennedy knew it. In the tapes from their prebroadcast rehearsal, you can see Nixon's confidence shatter the instant Jack walked onto the set.

"He and I were standing there talking when Jack Kennedy arrived," Hewitt recalled. Tanned, tall, lean, in a dark, well-tailored suit, the Democratic candidate positively gleamed. Photographers, seizing their chance, abandoned Nixon and fluttered about their new prey like hornets. The senator bore no resemblance to the emaciated, jaundiced, wounded figure he'd been. "He looked like a young Adonis," Hewitt said simply.

Bill Wilson recalled his candidate's strategy: "The design was that we attack Nixon and everything he was saying. He had to get the floor. He had to be the one that had the control and had the sense of command on the stage, which he did. I told him the things that counted in terms of his body language and when you look at the camera, you're only talking to one person. When you're doing a debate or sitting, you're talking to one person and that's the lens."

Once the two men were on the stage together, going through the rehearsal, the psychological battle was on. Asked to pose with his rival, Kennedy appeared barely to notice him. They could have been total strangers for all the interest Jack Kennedy showed in the colleague with whom he'd enjoyed cordial terms since 1947. Nixon, for his part, seemed intimidated. From the moment Kennedy strode in, hijacking the attention of the photographers, he was not the same man. Visibly deflated by his rival's matinee-idol aura and seeming nervelessness, Nixon slouched in his chair, his head turned away, as if in retreat.

Pierre Salinger recalled Nixon's pale, unhealthy appearance. The vice president had injured his leg in August, with a subsequent knee infection forcing him off the campaign trail and into Walter Reed Hospital. He did not yet seem entirely recovered from the ordeal. "Nixon looked awful off camera. He really did. Kennedy went back to his dressing room and remarked how awful he looked." It seemed to Salinger that Nixon's ghastly appearance boosted Kennedy's confidence. "I think he thought that Nixon was afraid."

"Do you want some makeup?" Hewitt asked Kennedy. Hearing the Democrat's "no," Richard Nixon also declined it, ignoring the fact that his opponent had just spent days campaigning in the California sun and that he, himself, hadn't fully regained his health. Kennedy's people were taking no chances. "I was in the greenroom," recalled Wilson, "and they were playing with him, asking him all kinds of questions. Bobby was there. Anyway, I said okay, we've got to close it down, he needs about ten minutes before he goes on to get quiet and I've got to put some makeup on him.

"Ted Rogers, who was Nixon's guy, said, 'When's your guy going to get makeup on?' And I said, 'Well, after your guy's going to get it.' Rogers was wary. If the other guy didn't ask for it, his guy wasn't going to. 'Nixon's not going to get his makeup,' he said, 'until John Kennedy does.' And I said, 'Well, it looks like it's a Mexican standoff.'"

Both candidates now retired to their separate rooms. Wilson understood the dangers of going on without makeup, even for the already telegenic Kennedy. "So I went back and I said, 'You know, we've got to do makeup. You've got a great tan; you look fine.' But the lights in 1960 in studios were just broad and heavy, not like anything you see in studios today. They were just hot as hell. And if you put a little bit of makeup all over the face, it closed the pores. They wouldn't sweat."

Finally, Wilson quietly ran out to get makeup, and when he returned, cleared the room of the others. "And the last thing Bob Kennedy said after I said everybody's got to get out, was 'Kick him in the balls, Jack.' It was a beautiful moment, because that was the whole strategy."

The Kennedy guys had one more trick up their sleeve. Nixon was nervously waiting for the clock to tick down to the debate's starting time. The countdown commenced over the loudspeaker. "Five minutes to airtime." Nixon was staring at the studio door. Now there were only three minutes left. As Wilson described it, "Nixon was still watching the door, as tense a man as I had ever seen. By then, I was sure that no one had summoned Kennedy, and I was about to dash after him, when the door swung open. Kennedy walked in and took his place, barely glancing at Nixon. Kennedy had played the clock perfectly. He had thrown his opponent off stride. He'd set him up for the kill."

In fact, Nixon may have arrived already off his stride, for reasons other than his impaired health. His running mate, Henry Cabot Lodge—Jack's old opponent, who should have known better—had warned him to try to "erase the assassin image." In other words, Nixon was not to be his hardfisted self, but rather more of a gentleman, a Nixon who'd be unrecognizable, say, to those citizens of California who'd seen him in action against Voorhis and Helen Douglas. "Kick him in the balls" would have been more useful counsel to him as well.

"The candidates need no introduction," the moderator, Howard K. Smith, announced to 70 million watching Americans. Richard Nixon, for his part, looked ill at ease, unshaven, middle-aged. Jack Kennedy, by contrast, seemed poised, with his legs crossed and his hands folded on his lap. Nixon sat in his chair awkwardly, his legs side by side, his hands dangling from the chair arms. He was wearing a gray suit that didn't flatter him in the harsh light, and soon he would be perspiring profusely.

By agreement, the focus of this first encounter was domestic policy. Believing the size of the audiences would grow with each debate, the Nixon people had insisted on saving foreign policy until last. In his opening statement, Kennedy showed he was intent on playing the game strictly by his rules, but hardly by Nixon's plan. "Mr. Smith, Mr. Nixon," he began, slyly equating the status of a two-term vice president and a television newscaster. "In the election of 1860, Abraham Lincoln said the question is whether this nation could exist half slave and half free. In the election of 1960, and with the world around us, the question is whether the world will exist half slave and half free, whether it will move in the direction of freedom, in the direction of the road that we are taking, or whether it will move in the direction of slavery."

Kennedy then pushed the detonator. "We discuss tonight domestic issues, but I would not want . . . any implication to be given that this does not involve directly our struggle with Mr. Khrushchev for survival." What he was doing was introducing precisely the topic Nixon had thought was postponed.

The United States needed to be strong economically, Kennedy declared, not just to maintain the American standard of living but because economic strength buttressed our fight against the Communists. "If we do well here, if we meet our obligations, if we are moving ahead, I think freedom will be secure around the world. If we fail, then freedom fails. Are we doing so much as we can do?" he asked an anxious country. "I do not think we're doing enough."

Kennedy's words struck home for his largest audience ever. In eight minutes he'd shown himself as infinitely more appealing than the fellow who'd been vice president of the United States for eight years. There wasn't a word of his opening presentation anyone could have argued with, not a sentiment his fellow citizens couldn't share. No, the country was not meeting its potential. No, we were not the same nation of doers who'd, heroically and with such sacrifice, ended World War II. Yes, we could do better. And, yes, with the right leadership, it was in our power to "get the country moving again."

After observing this tour de force, Nixon took his turn with the look of a man dragged from a five-dollar-a-night hotel room and thrust before the unforgiving glare of a police lineup, a man charged with a crime of which he knew, if not he himself, his political cohorts were guilty. Afraid to project the "assassin image," he was stymied. "Mr. Smith, Senator Kennedy, there is no question but that we cannot discuss our internal affairs in the United States without recognizing that they have a tremendous bearing on our international position. There is no question that this nation cannot stand still, because we are in a deadly competition, a competition not only with the men in the Kremlin but the men in Peking." Then, finally: "I subscribe completely to the spirit that Senator Kennedy has expressed tonight, the spirit that the United States should move ahead."

Incredibly, Nixon was agreeing with his challenger. Yes, domestic policies affect the country's foreign situation. Yes, we cannot afford to "stand still." Yes, Kennedy has the right "spirit" to lead. His only concern was that Kennedy's statistics made the situation appear bleaker than it was.

He gave a similar response on Kennedy's call for medical care for the aged: "Here again may I indicate that Senator Kennedy and I are not in disagreement as to the aim. We both want to help old people." Minutes later: "Let us understand throughout this campaign that his motives and mine are sincere." And, after a small reminder that he knew "what it means to be poor," he offered yet another genuflection to Kennedy's goodwill. "I know Senator

Kennedy feels as deeply about these problems as I do, but our disagreement is not about the goals for America but only about the means to reach those goals."

Only? The race for the presidency is "only" about "means"? With staggering humility, Nixon was telling the largest American political audience ever assembled that his rival was not only a man of unquestioned sincerity but one of unassailable motive. It was merely a matter of method that separated the two applicants for the world's most towering position. To avoid coming off as his nastier self, Dick Nixon was presenting himself as Jack Kennedy's admiring, if somewhat more prudent, older brother.

Throughout, he kept his attention fixed exclusively on Kennedy. Just as he had at McKeesport, Pennsylvania, thirteen years earlier, Nixon was ignoring the audience. He seemed to crave his opponent's approval, even to the point of rebuking his own administration. "Good as the record is," he averred, "may I emphasize it isn't enough. A record is never something to stand on. It's something to build on."

As the sitting vice president of the United States dealt with each of his opponent's points, he tried desperately to elevate himself to an Ike-like pedestal, one from which Kennedy was just as determined to knock him. Asked about Nixon's campaign charges that he was "naïve and sometimes immature," Kennedy explained how the two men had come to Congress together in 1946 and how both served on the Education and Labor Committee. "I've been there now for fourteen years, the same period of time that he has, so our experience in government is comparable." He went on to quote the unassailably noble and beloved sixteenth president: "Abraham Lincoln came to the presidency in 1860 after a rather little-known session in the House of Representatives and after being defeated for the Senate . . . and was a distinguished president. There is no certain road to the presidency. There are no guarantees that if you take one road or another that you will be a successful president."

But more than either contestant's words, it was their images, projected on millions of black-and-white Admiral and General Electric televisions, that affected the American judgment. Each time Kennedy spoke, Nixon's eyes darted toward him uneasily, the same look that Kennedy's aide Ted Reardon had spotted more than a decade before at a House committee meeting. When Nixon was on, Kennedy sat, sometimes professorially taking notes, at other moments wearing a sardonic expression as he concentrated on his rival's answers. Sargent Shriver later noted that it was his brother-in-law's facial language, more than anything he said, that in the end decided the results. By raising an eyebrow at Nixon, Jack had shown he had the confidence to lead the country.

In the hours that followed, the challenger was convinced he had won. "Right after the debate, he called me up at the hotel," Lou Harris recalled. "'I know I can take 'im. I know I can take 'im!'" Kennedy had exulted. He was not alone in the assessment. A despondent Henry Cabot Lodge, who had given Nixon the misguided advice to go easy on his rival, watched the last minutes of the debate with dismay. "That son of a bitch just lost the election." On the other side of the case, those hearing the debate on radio—a much smaller audience—were more favorable to the Republican. Lyndon Johnson, listening in his car, was one of them. He thought Nixon was the winner.

But it was a debacle for the vice president. After weeks of parity in the polls, one candidate now moved into a clear lead. A Gallup survey taken in the days following the first debate found Nixon with 46 percent approval and Kennedy pulling ahead to 49 percent. Who had "won" the debate? Forty-three percent said Kennedy; 29 percent called it even. Just 23 percent gave it to Nixon. Kennedy's captivating but also commanding performance in the first debate now made him the country's number one box office attraction.

Nursing his wounds, Nixon sought a weapon with which to make his fighting comeback. He found one in a current Cold War issue, counting on it to be the club with which he might beat his rival. Since the Communist takeover of China in 1949, the two offshore islands of Quemoy and Matsu had been occupied by the forces of Chiang Kai-shek's government on Formosa. The Chinese Communists had been shelling Quemoy and Matsu, demanding their evacuation. In an interview with NBC's David Brinkley, Kennedy had questioned the U.S. policy of helping Chiang's forces defend them, saying they weren't essential to the defense of Formosa.

If his opponent was willing to back down in the face of Communist aggression, as Nixon saw it, he was going to call him on it. How could any American leader allow the other side to annex even a small chunk of global territory and not see it as an invitation to further aggression? He was ready to attack.

Nixon's people, meanwhile, recognized they had other fronts to deal with as well. How their candidate looked mattered as much, obviously, as anything he said. This time Nixon was prepared to wear makeup. There'd be no macho hesitancy as before. He had his own dark suit to wear, and he'd been downing several milk shakes a day to give him the bulk he'd lost in those weeks in the hospital. But none of this would matter, his aides realized, if he showed the same sweaty look he had in that first, disastrous encounter with Kennedy in Chicago.

On the evening of October 7, Bill Wilson arrived with the Kennedy brothers at NBC's Washington bureau for the second debate. They walked into the studio to realize that someone had set the temperature practically to freezing. It felt like a meat locker. "What the hell is this?" Jack asked. After complaining loudly to no avail,

Bobby darted in anger to the control room. Bill Wilson remembers racing down to the basement of the building, looking for the air-conditioning unit. "There was a guy standing there that Ted Rogers had put there, and he said don't let anybody change this. I said, 'Get out of my way or I'm going to call the police.' He immediately left and I changed the air-conditioning back. Ted wanted to keep his job because of the fuck-up in the first debate."

That night, Nixon showed that he'd been preparing himself not simply to look better than in the first encounter with Kennedy but to fight better as well. There was no more of agreeing in principle. He knew he needed to draw a line. "I should point out here that Senator Kennedy has attacked our foreign policy. He said that it's a policy that has led to defeat and retreat, and I'd like to know, where have we been defeated and where have we retreated? In the Truman admin-istration, six hundred million people went behind the Iron Curtain, including the satellite countries of Eastern Europe and Communist China. In this administration we've stopped them at Quemoy and Matsu. We've stopped them in Indochina. We've stopped them in Lebanon. We've stopped them in other parts of the world."

Nixon's reference to Quemoy and Matsu was impossible to ig-nore. Kennedy's response was tortured. "We have never said flatly that we will defend Quemoy and Matsu if it's attacked. We say we will defend it if it's a part of a general attack on Formosa, but it's extremely difficult to make that judgment." Then he started to backpedal. "I would not suggest the withdrawal at the point of the Communist gun; it is a decision finally that the Nationalists should make, and I believe that we should consult with them and attempt to work out a plan by which the line is drawn at the island of Formosa."

Kennedy was now in Nixon's Cold Warrior target zone. Fighting Communism, Nixon charged, wasn't about being wishy-washy. "The question is not these two little pieces of real estate—they are unimportant. It isn't the few people who live on them—they are not too important. It's the principle involved. These two islands are in the area of freedom. We should not force our Nationalist allies to get off them and give them to the Communists. If we do that, we start a chain reaction. In my opinion, this is the same kind of woolly thinking that led to disaster for America in Korea. I am against it. I would not tolerate it as president of the United States, and I will hope that Senator Kennedy will change his mind if he should be elected."

For the first time, Nixon had scored a hit. He'd wounded Kennedy where the Democratic candidate himself knew his own party was vulnerable. The point of contention, after all, was one at which Kennedy himself had taken aim back in the "Who lost China?" period. He knew firsthand the potential firepower of the issue: if the Democrats found themselves positioned again as the party of "appeasement" in Asia, they were finished. In the days ahead, Nixon continued to hit Kennedy for a craven willingness to cede territory to the enemy. "I think it is shocking for a candidate for the presidency of the United States," he said in speech after speech, "to say that he is willing to hand over a part of the Free World to the Communist world."

However, what Nixon portrayed as strength, Kennedy saw as brinkmanship. Why would we risk war with the Chinese Communists over such a slight point as this? It made no sense. What it seemed to be about was Nixon wanting to fight the Communists on their own terrain and at significant peril of it going global. "Mr. Nixon is not interested in policies of caution in world affairs," he told a partisan audience at the Waldorf-Astoria. "He boasts that he is a 'risk-taker' abroad and a conservative at home. But I am neither. And the American people had caught a sufficient glimpse of the kind of risks he would take when he said in 1954, 'We must take the risk now of putting our boys in Indochina on the side of the French if needed to avoid further Communist expansion there.' That is a foolhardy and reckless decision. How much wiser it would be to follow the president's original recommendation—to persuade the Chinese Nationalists to evacuate all military personnel and any civilians who wish to go—now, when we would not be seeming to yield under Communist pressure, before real pressure is put on again."

There were now two hurdles facing Jack Kennedy as he headed into the third debate, on October 13. One was that he continued to be pegged as the squeamish candidate, ready to pull back from Quemoy and Matsu, while Nixon remained the vigilant champion, loudly prepared to hold the line. Helping to prepare him that day, Arthur Schlesinger observed his jitters. "I had the impression that he was a little nervous about the Q-M issue."

The other problem was the new debate format, which separated the candidates physically, the Democrat in a studio in New York and his Republican opponent 2,500 miles away in Los Angeles. With an entire country between them, Kennedy's ability to intimidate his rival, so crucial a factor in their first encounter, would be gone.

NBC's Frank McGee posed the first question, asking Kennedy about his charge that Nixon was being "trigger-happy" in regard to Quemoy and Matsu. If that was so, would Kennedy be willing to take military action to defend Berlin? Ignoring the Asia reference, Kennedy limited his answer only to a commitment regarding Berlin. But when Nixon took his turn, he swiftly moved the issue back to the now notorious offshore Chinese islands. "As a matter of fact, the statement that Senator Kennedy made was, to the effect that there were trigger-happy Republicans, that my stand on Quemoy and Matsu was an indication of trigger-happy Republicans. I resent that comment."

On the attack now, Nixon challenged Kennedy to come up with

the name of a Republican president who'd led the country into war. "I would remind Senator Kennedy of the past fifty years. I would ask him to name one Republican president who led this country into war. There were three Democratic presidents who led us into war."

Boldly, Nixon cited the pre–World War II legacy of Munich, comparing Kennedy's position on Quemoy and Matsu to the appeasement policy toward Hitler's Germany that his father had supported as ambassador to Britain. "This is the story of dealing with dictators. This is something that Senator Kennedy and all Americans must know. We tried this with Hitler. It didn't work. He wanted, first, we know, Austria, and then he went on to the Sudetenland, and then Danzig, and each time it was that this is all he wanted." Before a national television audience of millions, Richard Nixon was calling Jack an appeaser. He was reminding him of his father's disgrace.

"Now what do the Chinese Communists want?" he asked, building dramatically to his climax. "They don't want just Quemoy and Matsu. They don't just want Formosa. They want the world."

With the third debate over, Kennedy took off for Michigan. He was scheduled to spend the night in Ann Arbor and then begin a whistle-stop train tour of the state the next day. Arriving late at the University of Michigan campus, he found nearly ten thousand students waiting for him. Speaking in front of the Michigan Union building, he suddenly, out of nowhere, made a proposition. "How many of you who are going to be doctors are willing to spend your days in Ghana? Technicians and engineers? How many of you are willing to work in the Foreign Service and spend your lives traveling around the world? On your willingness to do that—not merely to serve one year or two years in the service—but on your willingness to contribute part of your life to this country, I think will depend the answer whether our society can compete."

The speech lasted barely three minutes. He told Dave Powers

he'd "hit a winning number" with it. He'd said it all before, pretty much, in that 1951 appearance on *Meet the Press* after he'd come back from the Far East. He'd talked then about sending off smart and idealistic young Americans to represent their country around the world. This time, however, he was speaking as a candidate for president. This time he was talking about something he would *create*. He was talking about the Peace Corps.

There on the steps of the Michigan Union, at two in the morning, he'd imagined out loud the genesis of a phenomenon that would change American lives. An idea that had not before existed in the minds of his countrymen now did: that of non-military service on foreign soil. Harris Wofford, a campaign aide and early civil rights activist, along with other Kennedy staffers, felt he'd been so angered by Nixon's taunt about the Democratic habit of starting wars that he determined to push in a totally different direction. In the closing weeks of the campaign, Jack began to pair the call for nuclear disarmament that he'd been making with his vision of a "peace corps of talented young men and women, willing and able to serve their country."

As for Quemoy and Matsu, Kennedy wanted it dropped, and to this end, he sought out Secretary of State Christian Herter, a former Massachusetts governor, to help broker a deal. The idea was that he, the Democratic candidate, as a point of national solidarity, felt it unwise to give the impression America was divided on the China issue. Kennedy's people told Herter their candidate was even prepared to change his position in order not to appear out of step with administration policy.

Hearing this, Nixon, surprisingly, agreed to a moratorium on discussions of the disputed Chinese islands. Whatever the vice president's posturing, as far as Kennedy himself was concerned, if there was ever to be a Cold War showdown, such an escalation made sense only when the value of the ground being fought over was indisputable.

And he knew of a hot spot near home, approximately ninety miles off the southern tip of Florida. On the night before the second debate with Nixon, Jack gave a major speech in Cincinnati attacking what he called "the most glaring failure of American foreign policy today . . . a disaster that threatens the security of the whole Western Hemisphere . . . a Communist menace that has been permitted to arise under our very noses." In short, he blamed the Republicans for losing Cuba, just as he and others had once blamed the Truman administration for the loss of China. He reminded his audience that two recent American ambassadors to Cuba—Arthur Gardner and Earl Smith—had warned about the danger of Fidel Castro and his brother Raul.

Castro, he said, "with guidance, support, and arms from Moscow and Peiping, has made anti-Americanism a sign of loyalty and anti-Communism a punishable crime, confiscated over a billion dollars' worth of American property, threatened the existence of our naval base at Guantánamo, and rattled Red rockets at the United States, which can hardly close its eyes to a potential enemy missile or sub-marine base only ninety miles from our shores."

He ended the speech by directly addressing the people of Cuba. "Be of stout heart. Be not dismayed. The road ahead will not be easy. The perils and hardships will be many. But here in America we pledge ourselves to raise high the light of freedom—until it burns brightly from the Arctic to Cape Horn—and one day that light will shine again."

Nixon felt the pressure. How could he be sounding alarms about Chinese islands and not defend one just a short boat ride away? He began to push the administration to take action against Castro. His greatest hope was that it would expedite the attack of armed anti-

Castro Cubans on the island, a clandestine CIA-backed operation already under way for several months. But the most he could accomplish, to show his muscle, was the Eisenhower administration's declaration of a trade embargo perfectly timed for the eve of the last debate.

Quick to respond, Kennedy termed the embargo an "empty gesture . . . which will have so little impact on Castro as to be almost meaningless." All it would do, he said, was speed up Cuban reliance on trade with the Communist countries. Without clearing it with Kennedy, speechwriter Richard Goodwin put out a statement raising the ante. "We must attempt to strengthen the non-Batista democratic anti-Castro forces in exile and in Cuba itself, who offer eventual hope of overthrowing Castro. Thus far, these fighters for freedom have had virtually no support from our government."

Kennedy was calling for an armed assault on Cuba by anti-Castro forces backed by the United States. It was an extraordinary proposal to make in the middle of a campaign, and it enraged Richard Nixon. That's because he was aware of top secret American plans to do exactly what Kennedy was proposing. He suspected that Kennedy was as well. Dean Acheson, who'd served as Truman's secretary of state, later warned that Kennedy had gone too far. "He was likely to get himself hooked into positions which would be difficult afterwards."

As he prepared to meet Kennedy for their fourth debate, Nixon continued fuming over that "fighters for freedom" statement. To follow such a recommendation, he declared disingenuously, would cause key Latin American countries to denounce not only the United States, but the U.N., too. What's more, such aggression would serve as "an open invitation for Mr. Khrushchev to come in, to come into Latin America and to engage us in what would be a civil war and possibly even worse than that."

To find new ground during their last televised meeting, Kennedy zeroed in on another area of dissatisfaction with Republican governance. And that was Americans' growing sense they were falling behind the Soviets in space and strategic weaponry. At the same time, the economy was slowing. From 5.9 percent in August, the nation's jobless rate rose to 6.4 percent in October. Between the conventions and Election Day, 330,000 people were thrown out of work. Not many of those hundreds of thousands of workers could ignore that their pink slips had been handed to them while Ike sat in the Oval Office, with Dick Nixon as his second in command.

On October 19, a group of African-Americans politely asked for service at the Magnolia Room in Rich's, the grand Atlanta department store. The lunch counters at drugstores and other downtown businesses were strictly whites-only. Coretta King described how it was in those days: "There was hardly a place outside our own neighborhoods where a Negro could even get a soda except by going to the side door and having it handed out." Among those arrested and charged with trespassing at Rich's that great day was the Reverend Martin Luther King, Jr. While the other sit-in demonstrators soon were released, a judge denied King bail, sentencing the civil rights leader to six months at hard labor in Reidsville State Prison. The defendant, he said, had violated probation on an earlier charge of driving in Georgia with an Alabama license.

Coretta, pregnant at the time, was naturally horrified—and very frightened—when she learned her husband had been roughly awakened at night, placed in handcuffs and leg chains, hurried into a car, and driven two hundred miles into rural Georgia. She shared her worry with a longtime friend, Harris Wofford. After discussing the situation with his fellow Kennedy aide Louis Martin, Wofford persuaded Sargent Shriver to take the case for action to the candidate, seizing a moment when Ken O'Donnell and the other political aides were out of the room.

"Why don't you telephone Mrs. King and give her your sympathy," Shriver suggested to Jack. "Negroes don't expect everything will change tomorrow no matter who's elected, but they do want to know whether you care. If you telephone Mrs. King, they'll know that you understand and will help. You will reach their hearts and give support to a pregnant woman who is afraid her husband will be killed."

"That's a good idea," Kennedy said. "Why not? Do you have her number? Get her on the phone." Mrs. King would later recount to Wofford what Jack had said. "I want to express my concern about your husband. I know this must be very hard on you. I understand you are expecting a baby, and I just wanted you to know that I was thinking about you and Dr. King. If there is anything I can do to help, please feel free to call me."

Afterward, the press quickly learned from Mrs. King about John Kennedy's having reached out to her. "It certainly made me feel good that he called me personally and let me know how he felt. I had the feeling that if he was that much concerned, he would do what he could so that Dr. King was let out of jail. I have heard nothing from the vice president or anyone on his staff. Mr. Nixon has been very quiet."

Beyond the hearing of any reporters, however, Kennedy worried out loud that even his little gesture had been too much. When asked about the call to Mrs. King, he appeared irritated at the leak. The campaign manager, Robert Kennedy, was downright furious. "Do you know that three Southern governors told us that if Jack supported Jimmy Hoffa, Nikita Khrushchev, or Martin Luther King, they would throw their states to Nixon? Do you know that this election may be razor close and you have probably lost it for us!" he scolded Wofford and Shriver.

But Bobby soon transferred his anger to the "son of a bitch" judge who'd thrown the book at King. He called Governor Ernest Vandiver of Georgia, and then, taking his advice, called the judge himself, who ordered King released on bail.

Louis Martin, an African-American, was elated when his friend Bobby Kennedy phoned in the early-morning hours with news of his successful mission. "You are now an honorary brother," he said.

Meanwhile, Kennedy's opponent had remained silent on King's predicament. The baseball hero Jackie Robinson tried and failed to get him to say something. "He thinks calling Martin would be grandstanding," Robinson said mournfully. "Nixon doesn't understand."

For this he would pay dearly. Martin Luther King, Sr., like his son a prominent Atlanta minister, now decided to endorse Kennedy publicly despite the religious difference between them. "I had expected to vote against Senator Kennedy because of his religion," the elder King somberly told his flock in the Ebenezer Baptist Church during the exultant welcome-home service held for his rescued son. "But now he can be my president, Catholic or whatever he is. It took courage to call my daughter-in-law at a time like this. He had a moral courage to stand up for what he knows is right. I've got my votes, and I've got a suitcase, and I'm going to take them up there and dump them in his lap."

Up at Kennedy headquarters in Washington, Wofford and Louis Martin were about to make history. Collecting all the appreciative and admiring comments pouring in from black leaders and others praising the Kennedys' efforts on behalf of the Kings, they found a pair of Philadelphia ministers willing to sponsor publication of a pamphlet, "The Case of Martin Luther King," which laid out the story of the Kennedy-King episode in bold language.

"No-Comment Nixon versus a Candidate with a Heart: Senator Kennedy," one caption read. "I earnestly and sincerely feel that it is time for all of us to take off our Nixon buttons," the Reverend Ralph Abernathy, a King ally, was quoted in the document. "Since Mr. Nixon has been silent through all this, I am going to return his silence when I go into the voting booth."

The pamphlet, two million copies of which were printed on light blue paper and delivered to black churches the Sunday before the election, would be dubbed "the blue bomb." Though it never stirred even the mildest alarm among conservative white voters, who'd remain loyal to the national Democratic ticket, it moved black America overnight to the Democratic side of the ballot, from the party of Lincoln to that of the Kennedys. Martin Luther King, Jr., summing up the episode's meaning, was eloquent: "There are moments when the politically expedient can be morally wise."

On November 2, Kennedy gave a major address at the Cow Palace in San Francisco. He spoke on two topics: the importance of nuclear disarmament and his plans for the Peace Corps. That afternoon, sitting in the bathtub at the Palace Hotel, he talked to Red Fay about how the campaign was going. "Last week, Dick Nixon hit the panic button and started Ike speaking. He spoke in Philadelphia on Friday night and is going to make about four or five speeches between now and the election. With every word he utters, I can feel the votes leaving me. It's like standing on a mound of sand with the tide running out. I tell you he's knocking our block off. If the election was tomorrow I'd win easily, but six days from now it's up for grabs." Then, suddenly, he changed the subject and began to tell his old friend, who'd been to war with him, what he intended to talk about that night: his great plans for this new corps of Americans working for peace throughout the world.

But the tide was clearly turning. Ike was out there drawing enormous crowds, and Nixon was playing rough. "You know, it's not

Jack's money they're going to be spending!" The debates were yesterday's news, and voters were fickle.

To a Nixon accusation that he was a "bare-faced liar," Kennedy retorted: "Having seen him in close-up—and makeup—for our television debates, I would never accuse Mr. Nixon of being bare-faced." Away from the microphones and reporters' notebooks, he could be vicious. "He's a filthy, lying son of a bitch and a dangerous man," his aide Richard Goodwin heard him say once. To Red Fay, he articulated his dislike: "Nixon wanted the presidency so bad that there were no depths he wouldn't sink to, to try to achieve his goal. How would you like to have that guy deciding this country's problems when it became an issue of what was best for the country or what was best for Dick?"

Fay called it a "180-degree reversal from what it was back in the Congressional years when Jack Kennedy wrote me on November 14, 1950, about how glad he was to see Nixon win big in his Senate race." Kennedy also was worried about last-minute dirt, waiting for Nixon's people to hit him with evidence of his "girling," as he referred to it. He never did. Perhaps the voters would not have believed it if he had. How could they? One Nixon aide, watching news footage of Jack and Jackie in the final hours of the campaign, suddenly was struck by the power of the beautiful couple's allure. *Good God,* he remembered thinking to himself, *how do you run against that?*

Yet, all the time, the momentum of the 1960 campaign, the reality of the here and now, was shifting about him. He sensed he was losing California and wanted desperately some more days of campaigning, especially in the farm-rich Central Valley. But the schedule had been set. Promises had been made to the bosses of New York. The men who'd helped him win the nomination were now calling in their chits. They wanted him *there*.

It's hard to know how a campaign is going from the stump, Ken O'Donnell knew. Being in the bubble skews your perception. Unlike Jack, Bobby was at headquarters, getting phone calls and detecting very strongly that the question of religion was now back with a vengeance. "They're much more concerned back at the headquarters because they're seeing it. We've been to the Philadelphias and the Chicagos, Oklahoma—with big crowds across California, Arizona, New Mexico, Texas. Wild crowds. So we don't see it."

O'Donnell said that he, along with the rest of the staff, now feared that the "silent bigot" would emerge as the decider, the voter who'd never voice his anti-Catholicism but would cast his or her ballot accordingly.

New York on the final weekend proved disastrous. Kennedy was increasingly convinced that he had blown his chance at the presidency by not going back to California. His time would be split between pleasing the city's powerful bosses and its equally important liberal groups. To get where he was, he'd needed both. Now, facing Election Day, he especially needed the bosses. It was like a comedy in which the hero's on a date with two different people, simultaneously zipping back and forth to keep both appeased. Jack was forced to move from one hotel, the Carlyle, to another, the Biltmore, for breakfast, then back to the Carlyle for still another breakfast.

The exhausted candidate's simmering frustration finally rose to a dangerous boil when he was expected to ride in a New York City parade organized by the local Democratic strongman Carmine DeSapio. It was pouring rain, and as he was driven back to Manhattan from an appearance on Long Island, Jack finally had had enough. His breaking point reached, he kicked everyone out of the car, insisting that his driver abandon the motorcade and return to his Upper East Side hotel. En route, however, the driver took some wrong turns. "I was beginning to panic now," O'Donnell recalled. "I was soaking wet, angry. Our motorcade had also gotten lost—and I'd lost the senator."

When he reached the Carlyle, the drenched Kennedy was forced to wait for his suitcase, which had been mistakenly taken to the Biltmore. Disgusted, he commandeered O'Donnell's bedroom and once again threw everyone out. Lyndon Johnson, unaware of the meltdown, wanted to greet his running mate. Said O'Donnell, "Well, the next thing I see is Lyndon being literally thrown out of the room by a rather irate young Irishman from Massachusetts." The shock was enough to make Johnson worry about the political bed he'd made.

Next, Kennedy demanded that O'Donnell set about canceling the parade DeSapio had planned. "I don't give a shit if they have five million people out there. Cancel it. Either you tell them, or I will. If you don't have the balls to tell them, I'll tell them. Send them in," he instructed O'Donnell.

"Look, Senator, this is my fault. I'll tell them. But you're not going to lose." O'Donnell couldn't change his boss's mood. Jack's reply: "Just cancel the fucking thing."

On November 8, as Americans went to the polls to vote for their thirty-fourth president, early returns showed a big Kennedy victory. Connecticut's results came in quickly and strongly. Philadelphia gave Jack a plurality of 330,000 votes. Then, the news began to shift. "It started out like gangbusters," Pierre Salinger recalled. "It started out like we were going to win by a landslide. In fact, the computer said we were. Then, everything started to go bad all over the place. By midnight it was a real dog race." The religious issue was doing its damage.

The news from Ohio was devastating. Kennedy, watching TV at Bobby's Hyannis Port house with the others, rolled up his sleeve to show how much his hand had swollen. "Ohio did that to me.

They did it there." But as upsetting as it was, it was also unexpected. "All those people now say they knew we would lose Ohio," said O'Donnell. "Well, if they did, they kept it to themselves until election night, when returns showed we lost it. Ohio was one that came as a shock to all of us."

Nixon was picking up Midwestern states in landslide fashion: Iowa, Indiana, even Wisconsin, where Kennedy had campaigned so hard that recent winter. As election night turned to morning, Jack saw the heartland turning against his candidacy. They were rejecting him. "I'm angry," the author Teddy White heard him say.

Though Kennedy would later insist the words he'd spoken were "I'm hungry," the situation suggests that the word White recorded might be taken as the more reliable. Nebraska was another wipeout. "Nebraska has the largest Republican majority of all fifty states," Rip Horton, who'd run the campaign there for his old Choate classmate, recalled. "His religion was definitely a handicap out there. They used to have meetings in churches. They'd advertise these meetings, various denominations, telling people to come to a mass meeting on why they shouldn't vote for a Catholic for president."

Yet even with these losses, Kennedy was managing to stay in front. "If the present trend continues," Richard Nixon told a loyal crowd waiting in the Ambassador Hotel in Los Angeles, "Senator Kennedy will be the next president of the United States." As supporters shouted out for him not to concede, Nixon doggedly kept on. "Certainly, if the trend continues and he does become our next president, he will have my wholehearted support."

"Does this mean you're president, Bunny?" Jackie Kennedy asked her husband. "Why don't you give up?" someone else in the room exhorted the face on the television screen. "Why should he?" Kennedy jumped in. "I wouldn't in his place."

Jack was done for the evening. "What am I going to tell the

press?" Pierre Salinger asked. "Tell them I went to bed," came the answer. "Wake me up if anything happens." With that, he walked out into the Cape Cod night, headed for his own house. When he awoke, he was the next president.

Ted Sorensen beat Salinger to him with the news. That morning they watched intently as Herb Klein, Nixon's press secretary, read the telegram Nixon had sent from California, before flying at dawn back to Washington. "I want to repeat through this wire the congratulations and best wishes I extended to you on television last night. I know that you will have the united support of all Americans as you lead the nation in the cause of peace and freedom during the next four years."

Nixon wasn't playing by the rules and Jack resented it. It had been a close election, yet here was his opponent denying him the courtesy of a televised concession. It was part of the ritual, and yet he'd ducked out at the climax, leaving his press secretary to do the job. He, Jack Kennedy, would never have behaved in such an unsportsmanlike manner. Once he'd known he'd lost the vice-presidential race in 1956, he'd *raced* to the podium.

As he greeted and thanked his top political aides O'Donnell and O'Brien, he now struck them both as a different man. The battle had been hard fought and won.

When the Secret Service detail arrived at Hyannis Port at 5:45 a.m., the agents knew the names, faces, and roles of each of Kennedy's people. Seeing Ken O'Donnell at the Kennedy compound that Wednesday afternoon, the chief of the Secret Service unit approached him as he got out of his car. "Mr. O'Donnell, the president has informed the Secret Service that we will now be reporting to you and that you are now our boss, in charge of the Secret Service for the length of the president's term of office. What would you like us to do right now?" It was the first indication that Kennedy intended him to come to Washington.

President-elect Kennedy's plans did not include appointing a chief of staff. He, Jack Kennedy, was going to be at the center. Everyone else, including O'Donnell, now a special assistant, and Sorensen, special counsel, would be arrayed around him, each spoke of the wheel competing for his attention. Jack would design a White House operation to match his compartmentalized personality. No one would control him. He would, in that fashion he loved, have things under control.

Still, before he could relax in his triumph and enjoy his cresting euphoria, Kennedy needed to secure the victory against any doubters. The problem was that the historically close tally had left questions about certain state results. Those in dispute were in Illinois—especially Cook County, where Chicago is located—and in Lyndon Johnson's Texas. It remained unclear in the first days after the election whether Richard Nixon intended to demand recounts or otherwise challenge the results. In order for John Kennedy to be able to move forward as chief executive, an extraordinary measure was required: someone must indicate, clearly and convincingly, that he had, without question, won the election. The person who needed to do so was Dick Nixon.

It fell to Joseph P. Kennedy, a master at the deal and knowing whom to call, to figure out the way. A longtime friend of Herbert Hoover, he was able to pick up the phone and quickly reach the eighty-six-year-old former president. The message he delivered to Hoover was a straightforward one: it was in the country's interest for the newly elected president and the defeated Nixon to get together. Hoover listened and understood. He'd once lost a presidential election himself, and survived. Plus, over the years Nixon had come to regard him as a political father figure. For both these reasons, Nixon would listen to him and respect his counsel.

The Saturday after the election, the excitement and fatigue of the campaign had faded from the fallen candidate. Defeat, both dull and cruel, had taken hold. The loyal Herb Klein could see it plainly. "Nixon was, in my opinion, more unresponsive than at any time I had known him. He was completely depressed and had finally realized, four days later, that he'd lost the election."

Nixon and his retreating corps of advisors were assembled that night in Key Biscayne, Florida. It was there he took the call from Hoover and heard the big-picture case for getting together with Kennedy. "I think we are in enough trouble in the world today that some indications of national unity are not only desirable but essential."

But, as always in such moments, there were dimensions that existed beyond the easy explanations. After talking to Hoover, Nixon's glum mood suddenly lifted. "It was the difference between night and day," Klein said. While Nixon was on another phone calling President Eisenhower for guidance, Klein took a call from Kennedy, who hadn't wanted to wait for Nixon to ring him. The upshot was the two men agreed to meet the following Monday in Key Biscayne.

The meeting accomplished just what the Kennedys intended: providing a photo op to showcase the image of loser meeting winner. "Ladies and gentlemen," Jack Kennedy told the press, "I just wanted to say that the vice president and I had a very cordial meeting. I was delighted to have a chance to see him again. We came to the Congress the same day fourteen years ago, and both served on the Labor Committee of the House of Representatives. So I was anxious to come here today and resume our relationship, which had been somewhat interrupted by the campaign." Had the two discussed the campaign during their hour-long meeting? "I asked him how he took Ohio, but he did not tell me," Kennedy joked. "He is saving it for 1964."

The vote count would turn out to be incredibly tight—Kennedy: 34,226,731; Nixon: 34,108,157. But now the results had been validated by the face-to-face meeting on Nixon's own turf.

Jack Kennedy's ultimate trophy had been won by virtue of the truth he'd grasped about his country, one that Richard Nixon had failed to see. "He had done it by driving home the simple message of unease," *Time* reported, addressing "the things left undone in the world, where a slip could be disastrous." The historian Arthur Schlesinger enlarged on the same point in his diary. "He wisely decided to concentrate on a single theme and to hammer that theme home until everyone in America understood it—understood his sense of the decline of our national power and influence and his determination to arrest and reverse this course. He did this with such brilliant success that, even in a time of prosperity and apparent peace, and even as a Catholic, he was able to command a majority of the votes."

Victory confirmed, Jack could focus anew on those ideals of peace and heroic leadership that had inspired him since youth. The new president had a favorite quote from Lincoln that he liked to carry with him on a scrap of paper. He'd used it in speeches, but now it spoke to him personally. "I know there is a God, and I know He hates injustice. I see the storm coming and I know His hand is in it. But if He has a place and a part for me, I believe that I am ready."

Inauguration

Meeting with Khrushchev

CHAPTER THIRTEEN

LANDING

He who learns must suffer, and, even in our sleep, pain
that cannot forget falls drop by drop upon the heart, and in
our own despair, against our will, comes wisdom to us by
the awful grace of God.

—Aeschylus

John F. Kennedy, the youngest man ever elected to the White House, understood how incredibly close the race had been. He also recognized the meaning of his slender margin, a victory that was far from a mandate. Both he and his rival had sought to show the strength and the will with which they would confront the Soviets. Now that he'd triumphed, little, really, had changed. Except that now the task was at hand.

A critical first endeavor involved the reassurance of two important government officials: both J. Edgar Hoover and Allen Dulles—the FBI and CIA directors, respectively—had to be told their jobs were safe. To have done otherwise would have unsettled the country. Therefore, urgent phone calls were placed to each man in the earliest hours of the interregnum. For JFK, retaining Hoover offered the premium of putting a lid on, among other prospects, the troublesome "Inga Binga" material in his files.

President-elect Kennedy put a pair of Republicans in top cabinet posts, naming Douglas Dillon, who'd been Eisenhower's undersecretary of state, to run the Treasury Department and placing the Ford Motor Company president, Robert McNamara, at Defense. The clubby Dillon, with his old-money connections, appealed to Kennedy the man. McNamara, showing no lack of toughness, made a point, when they discussed the job, of asking Jack whether he'd written *Profiles in Courage* himself. An air corps lieutenant colonel by the end of World War II, McNamara had a Harvard MBA and at Ford had been one of the famous "Whiz Kids," a group of ten returning veterans who came in and revitalized the company.

Looking to the liberal faction, which he needed both to acknowledge and include, the president tapped Adlai Stevenson to be his United Nations ambassador, Walter Heller as chief economic advisor, and Arthur Schlesinger as all-around Renaissance man.

Now, as always, concessions needed to be made to the senior Kennedy. It was, after all, the tribute Joe's money and support deserved. Since his sons' futures were of the utmost importance to him, posts for both younger Kennedy brothers were part of the bargain: Bobby would be attorney general, Ted would get Jack's senate seat once he turned the required age of thirty.

Jack laughed with Ben Bradlee at the absurdity of the youngest president ever elected picking his brother, eight years younger than he, as attorney general. When Bradlee asked him how he planned to deliver the news to the press, his probable course of action had a familiar ring. Kennedy said, "I think I'll open the front door of the Georgetown house some morning around two a.m., look up and down the street, and if there's no one there, I'll whisper, 'It's Bobby.'"

There was no getting around the appointment for what it was: sheer, unadulterated nepotism.

"I think he hadn't really thought about how to run the government until he got elected," Ken O'Donnell said. "He was a very single-minded person. Politically, each battle he fought one at a time. There were very few things that were clear when he was elected."

Kennedy's "spokes of the wheel" approach had been championed by the presidential scholar Richard Neustadt, but such an organizational principle, in fact, followed his natural inclination. Unlike the former army officer Eisenhower, who appointed a strong chief of staff to run his agenda and team, Kennedy refused to have anyone between him and his advisors. Shrewdly, he set up two doors to the Oval Office, one manned by O'Donnell, the other by his secretary, Evelyn Lincoln. This system worked well: cabinet members had to fight their way past O'Donnell, while pals could whiz past Lincoln.

There was little camaraderie among Jack's chosen men, and several ongoing rivalries. O'Donnell resented the partnership Sorensen assumed with Jack. Ben Bradlee, the Washington sophisticate, failed to see the appeal of Lem or Red. Bobby, meanwhile, resented how much his brother reached out to Torby. As couples, the Bradlees and the Bartletts hardly ever saw each other for the simple reason that as couple-to-couple friends to Jack and Jackie, to invite them at the same time would create a redundancy. Thus, they were asked over on different nights. Together, of course, all of them had a purpose, to keep Jack company, to ensure that he was never alone, never bored, never stuck.

Harris Wofford, Kennedy's civil rights advisor, described insightfully how he and the others fit in. "The president-elect was a complex political leader in a complex situation. He was not anyone's man—not Stevenson's or Bowles's, and not Mayor Daley's or John Bailey's, not the Civil Rights Section's, and not the Southern senators'; not his father's and not Bobby's. He had one foot in the Cold War and one foot in a new world he saw coming; one hand in the old politics he'd begun to master, one in the new politics that his campaign had invoked."

Kennedy picked Clark Clifford, who'd been President Truman's counselor, to be his liaison with the outgoing Eisenhower staff. An astute observer of men and power, Clifford recognized early on John Kennedy's ability to detach himself *from himself*. You'd see him sitting at meetings, Clifford once told me, and you could almost imagine JFK's spirit assuming a form of its own and rising up, the better to look down on the group and assess its various members' motives and agendas. It was the same uncanny detachment Chuck Spalding had seen in Jack on his wedding day.

Not all the people in the U.S. government, even at the top, owe their positions to the president. This remains one of the challenges of being chief executive in the American system. The reality of that limited control over people dawns eventually, if not right away. There's also the need to lay down clear presidential orders.

Take the time JFK and his aides gathered around a swimming pool in Palm Beach, with dark-suited agents wearing sunglasses crouched protectively around them. JFK told O'Donnell, the White House official he'd personally posted to oversee the Secret Service, to have the agents back off. He wanted them to change to sports shirts and lose the fighting stance. "Nobody's going to shoot me, so tell them to sit down and relax a bit."

More than one Kennedy friend commented how happy he seemed in those days, making decisions while enjoying the Florida weather and waiting for Inauguration Day. Feeling buoyed up as he did—so thrilled and excited about his new circumstances, and proud to have pulled off what he had—he determined to stay fit as president. Said Charlie Bartlett: "I remember he told me, 'From now on I'm really going to take care of myself.'" Bartlett also heard him make a different sort of commitment to the future. It had to do with his marriage. "'I'm going to keep the White House white.' He said it right out there on that terrace."

Kennedy and Ted Sorensen had been devoting a good deal of that Palm Beach time to writing Jack's inaugural address. Composed in the tropical air, it was delivered on January 20, 1961, when the Washington temperature hovered in the low twenties and eight inches of snow had fallen that morning.

Given the ongoing challenge of the United States–USSR relationship and its immense significance in the election, that theme would command the heart of the speech. Its focus was on strength— not as a prelude to war, but as an instrument for peace. "Man holds in his mortal hands the power to abolish all forms of human poverty and all forms of human life."

The Churchillian notion of peace through strength had echoed throughout Jack's adult life. "We dare not tempt them with weakness. For only when our arms are sufficient beyond doubt can we be certain beyond doubt that they will never be employed." America would arm not to fight, but to parlay its power into protection. "Finally, to those nations who would make themselves our adversaries, we offer not a pledge but a request: that both sides begin anew the quest for peace, before the dark powers of destruction unleashed by science engulf all humanity in planned or accidental self-destruction."

Those decisive phrases have not lost their resonance. "Let both sides, for the first time, formulate serious and precise proposals for the inspection and control of arms—and bring the absolute power to destroy other nations under the absolute control of all nations. Let both sides seek to invoke the wonders of science instead of its terrors. Together let us explore the stars, conquer the deserts, eradicate disease, tap the ocean depths, and encourage the arts and commerce."

The one domestic policy reference would be Kennedy's commitment to "human rights" at home as well as abroad. At the end came the words that passed into the world's consciousness: "And so, my fellow Americans, ask not what your country can do for you—ask what you can do for your country."

To some who'd once been at Choate and paid attention in chapel to the words of Headmaster St. John, a lightbulb flickered. The irony is that Jack Kennedy, the Mucker now grown up, was appropriating the very rallying cry from which he'd felt so alienated as a rebellious student.

The act of asking, in fact, marked the passage of John Kennedy through his public life. Most politicians make promises. They tell people what they will do for them, dangling the prospect of jobs, or government spending, with elections and "pork" irrevocably intertwined. That approach was certainly politics-as-usual for Lyndon Johnson, who always sought ways to find a person's "button"— that thing he wanted, or feared—that would put him in his power. Kennedy was never like that. From the very start, he called on people to come out, to join, to be active, to be part of something larger than themselves. At the beginning, when Jack was little known, it had been a necessity, but it evolved into a grander vision, one that changed lives exactly as George St. John once had preached.

In Moscow, the Soviet leader, Nikita Khrushchev, had been sounding a different call to arms, in his case a boastful one. The progress of the international Communist cause, he'd told his countrymen on January 6, had "greatly exceeded the boldest and most optimistic predictions and expectations." Encouraging "wars of liberation" such as the one under way in South Vietnam, he then emphasized the crucial position of Berlin in the struggle being waged against Marxism's enemies. "The positions of the USA, Britain, and France have proved to be especially vulnerable in West Berlin. These powers . . . cannot fail to realize that sooner or later the occupation regime in that city must be ended. It is necessary to go ahead with bringing the aggressive-minded imperialists to their sense, and compelling them to reckon with the real situation. And would they balk, then we will take resolute measures. We will sign a peace treaty with the German Democratic Republic."

Once he'd heard those declarations, Jack Kennedy's sense of purpose—mission, really—was focused on their possible consequences. Did Khrushchev actually intend to sign a treaty with East Germany that would throw the USA, Britain, and France out of West Berlin, where they'd governed as allies since 1945? According to Arthur Schlesinger, Kennedy couldn't stop reading and re-reading those words. Did they mean war? And would the United States be forced to escalate to nuclear war if the Soviets made good on their threat? Could an American president let the Communists grab West Berlin, the very symbol of Cold War defiance?

This is the specter Jack Kennedy was forced to contemplate in those early days of his presidency: the real chance that he alone would have to choose between nuclear war over Berlin or a historic capitulation to a European aggressor, a second "Munich." Somehow he was able to greatly enjoy these early weeks after the inauguration. Living, as he did, in compartments, he didn't let the worry show. He found comfort where he had since youth, in the close company of old friends.

During those early weeks after they'd moved into 1600 Pennsylvania Avenue, the Bartletts came to visit and the First Couple took them on a stroll down the streets surrounding the White House. Escaping through the guard gates was a way of testing his freedom. That night both Jack and Jackie spoke of their commitment to saving the buildings surrounding Lafayette Park, just across Pennsylvania Avenue. The Eisenhower administration had considered leveling the historic townhouses to put up government office buildings. They also mentioned their desire to restore the White House itself. When they found their way up to the ornate Indian Treaty Room in the Old

Executive Building, Kennedy practiced using the microphone used by Ike during press conferences. Charlie sat in the back, listening to how the new president sounded from there. The brand-new president was having fun in his discovered world and sharing it with a beloved pal. He wasn't letting his hidden dread affect the occasion. As Chuck Spalding once told me, even amid crisis, "Jack's attitude made you feel like you were at a *fair* or something."

Lem Billings arrived on Friday and stayed a week. He was the Kennedys' first houseguest and their most frequent. Soon he'd have his own room, and would show up unannounced and stay as long as he liked. He was never issued a White House pass, but the Secret Service agents all knew him. He joined the couple, too, on weekends at Glen Ora, their retreat in the Virginia horse country. Often, Jackie was the one inviting him. She wanted Jack to have someone to hang out with when she was out riding. The presence of Jack's old Choate roommate ensured there'd always be company to lighten the mood.

Lem never took for granted Jack's friendship, cherished it, and was always there for him. "Jack was the closest person to me in the world for thirty years," he said, and no one doubted it. Still, even he found it difficult to explain Jack's enduring loyalty. "I've often wondered why, you know, all through the years, we continued to be such close friends, because I never kept up on politics and all the things that interested him. What he really wanted to do, on weekends, was to get away from anything that had to do with the White House."

In fact, escaping the White House even on weeknights appealed greatly to its new occupant. One time he had Red Fay buy tickets ahead of time for *Spartacus,* allowing them to slip into the nearby movie theater unnoticed once the lights were down. Fay never forgot an incident that occurred a few nights later, walking across Lafayette Park. A fellow standing in the shadows caught the attention of the Secret Service agents, who checked him out by shining their flashlights at him. "What would you do now if that man over there pulled a gun?" Kennedy suddenly asked his buddy from the PT boat days. "What would you do to help your old pal?"

As they walked on, they began talking about assassination, the word itself rather antiquated, given that there'd been none since McKinley. "You know, this really isn't my job, to worry about my life," Kennedy said. "That's the job of the Secret Service. If I worry about that, I'm not going to be able to do my own job. So I have just really removed that from my mind. That's theirs to take care of. That's one of the unpleasant parts about the job, but that's part of the job."

Fay had moved from California to work at the Navy Department. Once he was on the federal payroll, Jack teased him. "Listen, Redhead, he'd say, I didn't put you over there to be the brightest man that ever held the job of Undersecretary." He said that he wanted him there for his honest judgment about what he saw. But, clearly, the president wanted Fay's company as well. Jack had arranged for another PT buddy, Jim Reed, to be made assistant secretary of the treasury, and for Rip Horton to go to the Army Department. "The presidency is not a good place to make new friends," Jack said. "I'm going to keep my old friends."

The Peace Corps—once an idea that seemed, spontaneously, to create itself—was now in the process of becoming a reality. Not sure exactly how the logistics of the visionary but also highly practical project might work, Kennedy put it in the hands of Sargent Shriver. As the founding director, Shriver got it off the ground, with the first volunteers overseas by the end of the year in countries such as Ghana and Tanganyika, Colombia and Ecuador. "The president is counting on you," he told one early group on the eve of their departure. "It's up to you to prove that the concepts and ideals of the American Revolution are still alive. Foreigners think we're fat, dumb, and happy over here. They don't think we've got the stuff to make personal sacrifices for our way of life. You must show them."

But then, Washington bureaucratic jealousy threatened the enterprise. Shriver sought help from Vice President Johnson, named by JFK to chair the advisory council. "You put the Peace Corps into the Foreign Service," he told Shriver, "and they'll put striped pants on your people when all you'll want them to have is a knapsack and a tool kit and a lot of imagination. And they'll give you a hundred and one reasons why it won't work every time you want to do something different. If you want the Peace Corps to work, friends, you'll keep it away from the folks downtown who want it to be just another box in an organizational chart."

Like a high priest in cowboy boots, Johnson knew the secrets of life and death in the capital. Thanks to him, the Peace Corps remained independent.

Having first talked about it when she entered the White House, Jackie Kennedy now wanted to start making good on her desire to redecorate the Executive Mansion. To help her, she asked her friend Rachel "Bunny" Mellon, married to the Pittsburgh banking heir and philanthropist Paul Mellon, whose high-patrician style she admired. According to Bunny, "When he became president, Jackie changed—she became just as royal as could be. She said, 'Will you come now? Jack's president. Will you come now and help me fix up this house? It's terrible. And don't call me "First Lady" ever, because I just work here. This is a job. I've got to do it for Jack.'"

But in addition to her work with Jackie on the public and private rooms, Bunny Mellon made another singular and lasting contribution to the Kennedy-era White House. In this case, it was Jack himself who asked for her expert knowledge. Knowing her to be a celebrated garden designer and horticulturalist, he requested that she renovate the Rose Garden, which he could see from his Oval Office window and called "a mess."

Established in 1913 by Mrs. Woodrow Wilson, it continues to

this day to be the scene of ceremonial events. The layout Bunny Mellon created for JFK, often following his specific instructions, comprises the admired Rose Garden layout still seen today.

On April 12, 1961, the Soviet cosmonaut Yuri Gagarin orbited the earth. It was the first time in human history that man had gone beyond our planet's atmosphere. Having beaten the United States into space with their first unmanned craft, the satellite *Sputnik 1,* back in 1957, the Russians once again had surpassed us. That first victory had come on President Eisenhower's watch, but this one was on Kennedy's.

But April, the "cruelest month," held further setbacks, ones that would leave even more serious political scars. On April 17, more than 1,400 anti-Castro Cuban exiles—trained, equipped, transported, and given limited air cover by the CIA—landed on a Cuban beach bordering an inlet now known as the Bay of Pigs on the island's south side. The disembarking Cubans had been assured by Agency officials they'd have full U.S. military support were they to encounter trouble on landing, but this turned out to be a false promise.

As Kennedy famously quoted at the time, "Victory has a hundred fathers; defeat is an orphan." The best way to look back with full understanding at the debacle known as the "Bay of Pigs" is to get an idea of how it appeared going forward.

There were several factors contributing to the pressure put on the new president to approve this ostensibly secret plan. Kennedy had himself called for such an action during the campaign, having gotten a tip-off from, if not others, Governor John Patterson of Alabama, who knew his National Guard units were helping the CIA invasion effort. He felt another spur to action. Once he'd taken the oath of office, and had it confirmed that the operation was already well into its planning stages, he understood that to back off and shut down the preparations would paint him as a soft-liner.

Driving him the hardest were his new colleagues. Somehow, the people directing "Operation Zapata," the invasion's CIA code name, fully believed their plan could succeed. They were encouraged by the success Allen Dulles, the brother of the late John Foster Dulles, President Eisenhower's secretary of state, had had in pulling off what was regarded as a similar scheme back in 1954, when a coup d'état had been stage-managed in Guatemala.

Richard Bissell, Dulles's chief of operations, had slyly arranged, while Kennedy was still a candidate, to meet him at a Georgetown party, and the two Ivy Leaguers had hit it off. Not only was Bissell a persuasive and convincing supporter of Operation Zapata, but so were key Kennedy people, such as Secretary of Defense Robert McNamara and National Security Advisor McGeorge Bundy.

But what really clinched it for those men sitting safely in faraway Washington was the escape hatch many were led to believe was built into the plan: if the exiles found themselves unable to hold a beach-head once they landed, they could then retreat to the Escambray Mountains only eighty miles away, where they'd be able to join up with counterrevolutionary forces hiding out. Unfortunately, it was a *very* long eighty miles, across nearly impassable swamp—and getting even to that point meant eluding a Castro force vastly larger than the exile group. Obviously—had he known, and he *should* have known this—instead of signing off on it, Kennedy should have shut Zapata down while it was still possible.

Instead, there on the sands of that Cuban bay, every member of the invading Brigade 2506—mostly middle-class professionals re-cruited in Miami with little idea how to defend themselves against Fidel's soldiers—was captured or killed. Quickly, in the aftermath, Kennedy asked for the resignations of both Dulles and Bissell. "In a parliamentary government, I'd have to resign," JFK told Bissell. "But in this government, I can't, so you and Allen have to go."

In the end, even from this distant vantage point, nothing is perfectly clear about that ill-conceived CIA operation except for the fact that, once it was launched, it was bound to fail.

It's hard to say just why Kennedy went along with his advisors, most of whom seem to have either had their heads in the sand or were otherwise enacting agendas of their own. Yet what does a president have such military and intelligence experts for if not to listen to them? JFK had been in office only three months, and however quick a study he was, he was still learning on the job. He was also used to being entirely his own boss, his own skipper, his own engine of accomplishment—from the Muckers to *PT 109* to his extraordinary campaigns. The scope and scale, the sheer bulkiness of the apparatus around him made a difference to his sense of maneuverability. Now he'd signed on, not just to an operation, but to a government. He was surrounded by a government establishment he himself had no hand in forging.

But the contradictions buried in the Bay of Pigs scheme echoed Kennedy's own. It was the old "two Jacks" problem. He was an idealist pursuing a new foreign policy he hoped would transcend the Cold War. He was also a Cold Warrior who had promised in the recent campaign to back "fighters for freedom" against Fidel Castro. Here he was caught going down the one road while signaling the other.

Just a month earlier, at a White House reception for Latin American diplomats, Kennedy had delivered his "Alliance for Progress" speech. In it he'd vowed to abandon the gunboat diplomacy engaged in by the "Goliath of the North" for generations, as the United States intervened at will in countries such as Cuba. This declaration of Pan-American mutual respect would be tarnished by U.S. efforts to overthrow Castro. Only too aware of the hypocrisy it revealed, Kennedy insisted that the Cuban invasion be carried out in the absence of direct U.S. military action, on the principle of what's known in dark diplomacy as "plausible deniability."

To achieve this goal, Kennedy had instructed the CIA's Bissell, whose baby the operation really was, to see that it was carried out with the minimum of "noise." For this reason he ordered the landing point shifted from Trinidad, a busy port city, to the desolate Bahía de Cochinos. As a result, the invasion inevitably lost what chance it might have had of triggering a countrywide rebellion, with citizens coming out to join the "liberators."

Kennedy's conflict in purpose continued as he sought to reconcile his aggressive Cold Warrior stance, which had seen him denouncing the Truman administration's "loss" of China, with his newly emerged recognition of postwar nationalism. The incredibly tricky challenge of toppling a despot on foreign soil by supporting an invasion was dealt another blow when Kennedy called off two of the planned air strikes in the midst of the operation. For the anti-Castro force to hold the beachhead, the small Cuban air force needed to be knocked out of action. In the event, it suffered only limited damage.

By the third day, the battle was lost. The mountains with their promise of sanctuary were little more than a mirage, real but impossible to reach. The eyes of the world were watching as Castro rounded up the poorly served and even more poorly supported surviving combatants, who would not return home to Florida for twenty more months, not until the United States bartered for their freedom with more than $50 million worth of medicine and baby food.

In the aftermath, there was certainly enough blame to go around, as JFK ironically suggested. But that mattered little in the face of such headlines as the one that ran in the *New York Times* on April 21: "CUBA SAYS SOVIETS SCARED OFF U.S.; Asserts Washington Feared 'Superior' Russian Arms."

The question must be asked: What *was* Kennedy thinking? Why did he sign off on an invasion offering so slender a possibility of success? What about the thought he never seemed even to take into account: What would success actually look like? Could anyone seriously imagine the people of Cuba overthrowing Fidel Castro—or attempting to—upon hearing news of a 1,400-man invasion force landing on a remote beach? And given the strong chance of the mission's failure, how did he imagine the United States would then appear to the world, both in Latin America and around the globe?

Those questions having been put on the table, there are others equally important. Why didn't Dulles or Bissell tell JFK he was compromising the invasion by changing the landing area, and that the air strikes—all of them—were essential? Why had they maintained that there would be a widespread Cuban uprising against Castro? Why did they lie in saying the members of Brigade 2506 could escape into the mountains if they failed to secure a beachhead? Bissell, the chief instigator, would later admit to having misled Kennedy into believing that option was a viable one. But why hadn't General Lyman Lemnitzer, chairman of the Joint Chiefs of Staff, spoken up to warn the president that the invasion plan was a fool's game? Why had Secretary of State Dean Rusk not expressed his own doubts about the Cuban people's willingness to embrace a general revolt? Far more important, why hadn't Kennedy asked the right questions, and made sure to have the solid answers such a risky undertaking demanded? Beyond the human toll, the collateral damage, after all, would be to his administration's credibility.

To his credit, Kennedy kept disaster from becoming calamity. He decided at the most critical moment to cut his losses, refusing to send in U.S. forces, and that may have been the crucial decision of the entire episode. He took charge—far too late, admittedly—but with executive firmness. He told the military and the intelligence brass that the United States would not openly attack the island of Cuba. He would let those men meet their fate on the beach rather than commit his country to possible direct confrontation with the Soviet Union. Who knew how many Russians were on the island, how many would be killed by a U.S. air attack on Castro's forces?

The Bay of Pigs cast a long shadow over the Kennedy White House, but the value of the early lessons it provided for Kennedy cannot be underestimated. One of them involved one of his very first presidential acts. "I probably made a mistake in keeping Allen Dulles on," the president told Arthur Schlesinger just two days later. "It's not that Dulles is not a man of great ability. He is. But I have never worked with him and therefore I can't estimate his meaning when he tells me things. We will have to do something about the CIA. I must have someone there with whom I can be in complete and intimate contact—someone from whom I know I will be getting the exact pitch. I made a mistake in putting Bobby in the Justice Department. He is wasted there. Bobby should be in the CIA. It's a helluva way to learn things, but I have learned one thing from this business—that is, that we will have to deal with the CIA."

In a statesmanlike gesture, he soon met with Richard Nixon, who hawkishly urged him to "find a proper legal cover and go in." Nixon's idea was to use the defense of our naval base at Guantánamo as a possible excuse. Hearing this, Kennedy pointed to the inherent danger in that plan. "There is a good chance that if we move on Cuba, Khrushchev will move on Berlin," he said. The former vice president, always touched by any sign of respect from Jack, came away ready to rally support for him. "I just saw a crushed man today," Nixon told his allies after the encounter, asking them to resist taking easy shots at the demoralized president.

President Eisenhower was more hard-nosed, wanting to know why Kennedy had called off the air strikes. When the younger man said it was to conceal the country's role in the operation, Ike was contemptuous. The very concept was obviously contradictory. Here was the United States offering training, equipment, transportation, and air cover to a military operation in which it intended to deny involvement. "How could you expect the world to believe that we had nothing to do with it?" When Kennedy said he feared how the Russians might retaliate in Berlin, Ike's response was to tell his successor that the Soviets didn't react to what we did. Rather, they "follow their own plans." The general, now a partisan proud of his presidential service, refused to allow that Soviet strength and belligerence had grown toward the end of his watch. The new president had to.

Accustomed to success, Jack took the defeat hard. For the first time, witnesses actually saw him in tears. Yet, recognizing that he'd backed a military effort requiring greater resources than he was ready to commit and greater risks than he, in the end, wanted to take, he accepted the responsibility. "I'm the responsible officer of the government," JFK assured reporters and the country.

The American people decided they liked the fact that Kennedy, whatever his failings heading into the disastrous mission, had acquitted himself as a true commander in chief at its conclusion. The record shows that he gained his highest job approval rating—scoring 83 percent in a Gallup poll—in the weeks thereafter.

Close friends such as Red Fay could see the toll it had taken. "In the months that followed, no matter how you tried to avoid touching on the subject, by one route or another it seemed to find its way back into the President's conversation." Even on vacation in Hyannis Port, it obsessed him, much to the distress of Jackie, who was ready to put the nightmarish scenes on that Cuban beach that haunted her husband behind them.

One of those Cape Cod evenings provided an outpouring Fay never forgot. It was when Jack outlined for him what he believed in: "I will never compromise the principles on which this country is built,"

JFK told him, "but we're not going to plunge into an irresponsible action just because a fanatical fringe in this country puts so-called national pride above national reason." Then he went on, "Do you think I'm going to carry on my conscience the responsibility for the wanton maiming and killing of children like our children we saw here this evening? Do you think I'm going to cause a nuclear exchange—for what? Because I was forced into doing something that I didn't think was proper and right? Well, if you or anybody else thinks I am, he's crazy."

When his host reached for his crutches, Fay understood he was finished with him for the evening. "He started up the stairs, straining with every step. He stopped me in the middle of the stairs and looked down at me, his face still inflamed. 'By God, there will be no avoiding responsibility—nor will there be any irresponsibility. When the decisive time for action arrives, action will be taken.' Turning, he lifted himself painfully up the rest of the stairs and to his room."

Meeting with the leaders of the Cuban Revolutionary Council, the main exile group, Jack spoke of his own wartime losses, even sharing a photograph of his brother Joe. One of the leaders, who'd lost his son in the invasion attempt, said the exiles had been "taken for a ride." He suggested Kennedy had been taken for one as well.

With the wounds from the Bay of Pigs still smarting, another Communist threat suddenly loomed on the horizon. It presented the likelihood of a far more dangerous crisis. Premier Nikita Khrushchev, who'd been making dark utterances for several years about changing the balance of power in Berlin—a city that had become such a symbol—demanded a showdown with President Kennedy in Vienna in early June.

Before heading to the summit in Austria, JFK took his first foreign trip, to Ottawa, where he and Jackie were welcomed by Prime Minister John Diefenbaker. Fifty thousand people turned out to watch the Kennedys' arrival. After addressing jointly both houses of Parliament, Jack took part in a tree-planting ceremony. As he lifted a silver shovel of dirt, he suddenly wrenched his weak back so painfully that he grabbed his forehead in anguish. Upon his return to Washington, he needed his crutches—which he used now only in private, in front of family and friends—to walk from the helicopter landing pad on the South Lawn to the White House.

Jack Kennedy had spent the past decades stoically rising above extreme physical discomfort, and he wasn't about to change, having now reached the White House. Less than two weeks after their return from Canada, the First Couple flew off to France, where one of the highlights was a luncheon at the Elysée Palace hosted by President Charles de Gaulle. Throughout her stay, beautiful Jackie, with her fluent French and stunning wardrobe, was an unqualified success, both fascinating and delighting the French public. People would remember that her husband joked to the traveling press corps, "I'm the man who accompanied Jacqueline Kennedy to Paris, and I have enjoyed it." But fewer will know that de Gaulle, an entirely formidable figure, had been captivated enough by her on a trip to Washington the previous year to have commented, "If there were anything I could take back to France with me, it would be Mrs. Kennedy."

The two leaders got along surprisingly well. During the war, de Gaulle had headed the Free French, symbolizing their country's resistance to the Nazi occupation. With regard to the American's coming engagement with Khrushchev in Vienna, de Gaulle was both thoughtful and candid. Urging Kennedy to keep his priorities in perspective, the French president expressed doubts about the ultimate sustainability of the Soviet system. He put little faith in their economic model, and so the Russian tide, he predicted, eventually would recede from Europe. Until that happened, the West, he reminded JFK, must stand firm. The greater threat, he predicted, would come decades later from China.

De Gaulle, like Kennedy, was able to put himself in the other man's shoes. Yet even as he could see beyond the immediate conflict to three decades down the road, de Gaulle recognized that such foresight little helped the predicament now. His practical advice, when it came to dealing with Khrushchev over the fate of Berlin, was to avoid even the *appearance* of negotiating. To do so would mean playing the Soviets' game.

Yet, as Eisenhower had been, de Gaulle was somewhat out of step with the times when it came to assessing the Russian mood. It had been one matter to not take the Soviets seriously when Russia, despite its immense size, seemed to lag behind the West. Now, just sixteen years after the war had ended, leaving devastation and demoralization in its wake, the Soviets were gunning their engines, trying to race ahead of the European powers and the United States. Their numerous gains—from their first-in-space status to their successful backing of "wars of liberation" in Africa, Asia, and Latin America—had left them confident, ready to flaunt their new standing vis-à-vis the West.

Moreover, if the size and power of the Soviet military forces weren't sufficiently frightening, the fact that the Soviet defense system had come to include a sizable nuclear arsenal surely was. What was bringing President John Kennedy to Vienna with such uncertainty—and foreboding—was Khrushchev's announced intention to sign a separate treaty between the Soviet Union and East Germany that would have the effect of stranding the city of Berlin 110 miles within the Russian-allied German Democratic Republic. Berlin, split by the Allies into sectors at the end of the war, had become the main escape route for millions fleeing west to escape Communist dictatorship. Ambassador Llewellyn Thompson told the president that the Soviet leader was so personally committed to a solution to the Berlin problem that the chances for either war or an "ignominious" retreat by the West were "close to fifty-fifty."

Kennedy's arrival in Vienna resembled a campaign stop of the year before. As they had in Paris, adoring crowds greeted the American First Couple at the airport. Khrushchev—who'd become first secretary of the Russian Communist Party in 1953 after the death of Josef Stalin and consolidated his power, ascending to premier five years later—had taken the train west from Moscow. He arrived to no fanfare. The glamour of Jack and Jackie Kennedy, and their excited reception, undoubtedly stirred resentment.

The meetings were scheduled for alternating sessions in the Soviet and American embassies. On the first day Khrushchev took the role of teacher, lecturing Kennedy on the case for socialist inevitability. Kennedy was no match for his ideological fervor. Both Ken O'Donnell and Dave Powers would write in their joint memoir how the bull-necked Soviet leader paced circles around his slender, youthful listener, "snapping at him like a terrier and shaking his finger."

That vivid description also paints a picture of Jack Kennedy having to endure the far outer limits of his comfort zone. When Evelyn Lincoln asked the president how the meeting had gone, "Not too well" was his reply.

Khrushchev's performance was a far cry from an American politician's usual encounters—except, perhaps, his use of the filibuster. But it seemed to have the effect the Soviet premier desired. Kennedy believed he meant business. Nixon and all the others back home could sound off about the need to call the Soviets' bluff. Nikita Khrushchev looked and sounded nothing like a bluffer.

The second day turned out to be worse. Khrushchev, having had his ideological warm-up, was now ready for the main event. JFK had come to Vienna hoping to build on what he saw as a recent major diplomatic breakthrough. In April, the United States and the USSR had reached an agreement that each would stop supplying military aid to Laos, a little landlocked kingdom north of Thailand

and Cambodia and west of Vietnam. Its significance lay entirely with its central Indochinese location. Kennedy hoped that he and Khrushchev could jointly see the Laos cease-fire as a starting point for broader negotiations.

Unfortunately, Khrushchev himself was there to talk about Berlin, and only Berlin. The Soviet Union, he reiterated, was planning to sign a treaty with East Germany that gave it total authority to control access to West Berlin. What this meant—and Khrushchev made it sharply specific—was that the Americans, the British, and the French would have to end their historic shared occupation of the divided city. The Russians had been edging up to this land grab, then backing away, for several years. This time, however, they seemed ready to proceed.

"The USSR will sign a peace treaty, and the sovereignty of the GDR will be observed," Khrushchev said in a formal pronouncement. "Any violation of that sovereignty will be regarded by the USSR as an act of open aggression. If the U.S. wants to start a war over Germany, let it do so."

Kennedy argued, to no avail, for the opposite approach. Instead of heightening Cold War tensions, why not try to lessen them? If Berlin was going to change, why not see it as a model for the future and not as a relic of the past? He tried to interest the Russian in a topic that meant more to him than just about anything else: a treaty over nuclear testing. He tried everything he could think of that might touch the man who was his opponent. He even invoked their shared losses in World War II. For, in the same way Jack mourned his brother Joe, so Khrushchev grieved, still, for his downed fighter-pilot son. But all the efforts the American made to light some spark of commonality between them produced no results.

Desperate, Kennedy requested a third meeting. In the last encounter with Khrushchev, he tried separating the two issues, suggesting that the Soviets might sign a treaty with East Germany while still allowing open access to West Berlin. That way, peace, at least, could be maintained. But the whole idea of the USSR-GDR agreement was to shut down the steady drain of East German workers through the city. Again, Khrushchev dug in his heels.

The new East German government, he said, would have full authority to deny access. Any effort to resist by either America or its allies would be met with the full force of the Red Army, which greatly outnumbered American and allied forces. When Kennedy pushed Khrushchev to acknowledge the right of the United States to continue to have access to West Berlin, Khrushchev held firm. "It is up to the U.S. to decide whether there will be war or peace."

At this final session Kennedy's companion made it clear, if it wasn't already, that his decision was "irrevocable" and "firm." In the end, all Jack was able to offer in reply to Khrushchev's threat of war was this grim prediction: "If that's true, it's going to be a cold winter." He left Vienna and returned to Washington, crushed by the experience. The Bay of Pigs had tainted him, he saw, allowing Khrushchev to treat him so contemptuously.

Jack Kennedy now understood he *had* to find a way to convince Khrushchev he was someone who would fight. But, even before that, he needed to understand exactly why the Soviet leader had talked to him that way, hectoring him. Was Khrushchev, in fact, crazy? He hadn't thought so, but what else explained why he was talking about war between two countries armed with nuclear weapons? "I never met a man like this," he told *Time*'s Hugh Sidey. "I talked about how a nuclear exchange would kill seventy million people in ten minutes, and he just looked at me as if to say, 'So what?' My impression was that he just didn't give a damn if it came to that."

To Ken O'Donnell he spelled out his own deeper belief, one he'd never share with a reporter, that not even Berlin was worth the possibility now threatened. "It will have to be for much bigger and more important reasons than that. Before I back Khrushchev against the wall and put him to a final test, the freedom of all Western Europe will have to be at stake." It fell to Lem Billings to record that Jack Kennedy had told him he'd "never come face to face with such evil."

Jack knew the order of battle for any conflict over Berlin. The United States had 6,500 troops in the city, for a combined American, British, and French force of 12,000. The Soviets had 350,000. Once the first shot was fired, the choice he'd be facing would be Armageddon or Munich. Long his greatest fear, it was now what he saw before him. Worse still, his adversary refused to acknowledge their mutual humanity.

He heard the voices—the chorus was always there—that exhorted him to "stand tough," the voices that encouraged him to ignore the signals he was getting from Khrushchev in favor of a different party line. "Our position in Europe is worth a nuclear war, because if you are driven from Berlin, you are driven from Germany. And if you are driven from Europe, you are driven from Asia and Africa, and then our time will come next. You have to indicate your willingness to go to the ultimate weapon." Hadn't he said that, himself, to a Milwaukee radio interviewer during the campaign?

So, he knew how to talk like a war hawk. But what did it actually mean—words like that, all the threats and gun-cocking—if you're the first American president to come into office aware of your enemy's rival nuclear stockpile? It's one thing to use words such as *appeasement* and *surrender* and *vital principle* with regard to Berlin when someone else is making the decisions.

It was the old "Munich" argument—the one that had so obsessed him that he'd written a book about it—adapted to the nuclear age. The Berlin conflict would endure through much of the summer. As the months went on, Kennedy seemed sapped of initiative. "He's imprisoned by Berlin," members of the cabinet told Sidey. "That's all he thinks about." On June 21, he would suffer another flare-up of his Addison's disease, with his temperature spiking to 105 degrees. For several days he was sick in bed, ministered to by Jackie and Lem.

On July 25, Kennedy gave a pivotal speech on the conflict in Europe. "We cannot and will not permit the Communists to drive us out of Berlin, either gradually or by force. . . . We will at all times be ready to talk, if talk will help. But we must also be ready to resist with force, if force is used upon us." He spoke of West Berlin as a "showcase of liberty, a symbol, an island of freedom in a Communist sea." But he also made concessions. Suggesting that it might be possible to remove "irritants" from the conflict, he then made a conciliatory statement about Soviet security concerns regarding Germany, the country that cost it 20 million lives in World War II.

Throughout the speech, he made a point of referring to "West" Berlin. The message was that his country did not care what the Soviets and East Germans did in the rest of the city. They had a free hand in that regard. Five days later, Senator William Fulbright, chairman of the Foreign Relations Committee, told a Sunday-morning TV audience that it was in the Russians' power to shut down the West Berlin escape route if they wished. They could end their problem without war. It was an assessment of American policy, quickly cheered by the East German government, that Kennedy never denied.

On August 3, the Soviets made their long-threatened move on West Berlin. Fortunately for the world, the Soviets and East Germans had found a solution to stop the tide of refugees to the West—a wall. To the man in the White House, it came as a secret relief. "Why would Khrushchev put up a wall if he really intended to seize West Berlin? There wouldn't be any need of a wall if he planned to occupy the whole city. This is his way out of his predicament. It's not a very nice solution, but a wall is a hell of a lot better than a war."

33

President Kennedy with the Joint Chiefs (L to R): Gen. David M. Shoup, Marine
Corps; Gen. Thomas P. White, Air Force; Gen. Lyman Lemnitzer, chairman;
Kennedy; Adm. Arleigh Burke Navy; Gen. G. H. Decker, Army

34

James Meredith with U.S. Marshals after
enrolling in the University of Mississippi,
October 1, 1962

35

Sargent Shriver, Peace Corps Director

CHAPTER FOURTEEN

ZENITH

*I felt I was walking with destiny and all my past life had
been but a preparation for this hour and for this trial.*
—Winston Churchill, May 10, 1940

Jack Kennedy's victories had taught him essential lessons. He recognized the edge a candidate receives when he's made the earliest start and kept at it. He realized the importance of the vital energy gained by building a trusted team. He discovered the power derived when a politician grasps the nature of the times and wields that understanding.

But failures also offer education. The Bay of Pigs taught him something more critical: When the stakes are the highest and most desperate, there must be both clarity and completion. Know the enemy *and* your goal, and hold fast to what you're attempting. Should any oppose your course, fight them with all your resolve.

Throughout the summer of 1961, Jack Kennedy had managed to sustain his hopes for a ban on nuclear arms testing to which the

Soviets would agree. At the very heart of his presidency was his mission to keep his country from nuclear war. It would be, he knew, a battle from which no winners could emerge. In 1946, the young journalist John Hersey had published in the *New Yorker* his account of the survivors of the attack on Hiroshima; no one who'd read it would ever forget it.

We'd agreed, as had the Soviets, to halt nuclear testing in 1958. Yet, in July, a Gallup poll had indicated that public support for the resumption of U.S. nuclear testing stood at two to one. The other side, exhibiting its greater aggression, suddenly showed its hand. August brought Moscow's shocking announcement of its unilateral decision to resume nuclear testing in the atmosphere. Kennedy's reaction— "fucked again!"—was deep and personal. Even before this horrifying news hit the headlines, Americans had gotten reports that the milk drunk by Russian children across the country contained detectable traces of radioactivity. Had the Russians treacherously been testing underground all along, even if they'd sworn not to? And was this a clue? And, if so, what were we going to do about it?

Over the next three months the Soviet Union would go on to conduct thirty-one such tests, including the exploding of the largest bomb in history—58 megatons, four thousand times more powerful than the one dropped over Hiroshima in 1945. Despite partisan pressure to respond by resuming U.S. testing, Kennedy resisted. He persisted in believing in the possibility of a comprehensive ban on all forms of nuclear arms testing, atmospheric and underground as well. "Mankind must put an end to war—or war will put an end to mankind." Yet as the leader of the Free World, he couldn't allow the Soviets to proceed without a U.S. response. With this in mind, the president instructed Defense Secretary McNamara to begin testing underground.

The United States had tested its first nuclear weapon at the White Sands Proving Ground in New Mexico in July 1945, a month before the U.S. fighters flew off to drop the atomic bombs on Hiroshima and Nagasaki. Those attacks, of course, brought about the Japanese surrender and ended World War II. Seven years later, the United States tested the first hydrogen bomb in the isolated Marshall Islands in the western Pacific in early November 1952. It was one of the last acts of the Truman administration before the election on November 4 ushered in the Eisenhower era.

Truman himself had presided over the dawn of the nuclear era by signing off on the Hiroshima and Nagasaki missions. Other peacetime nuclear explosions—military tests of new, far deadlier weapons—followed on his watch. Then, under President Eisenhower, the number doubled or even tripled. For a dozen years, from 1946 to 1958, the Marshall Islands, a U.S. Trust Territory until 1986, bore the brunt of America's experimentation. For the Soviets, the testing of their nuclear weapons secretly in their vast territory had begun in 1949. They had selected sites in remote Kazakhstan and later in Novaya Zemlya, a chain of islands in the Arctic Ocean at Russia's northern edge.

The history of the Cold War is written in the long lists of these many tests. During this period, our allies France and Great Britain were intent on developing their own nuclear arsenals. But distinctions such as "atomic" and "hydrogen," "nuclear" and "thermonuclear" mean little to the average citizen. Americans accepted the basic contradiction. The United States could keep the Soviets from aggression in Europe by the threat of nuclear retaliation. At the same time, neither side would dare use nuclear weapons, knowing the other would as well.

Even after Kennedy issued the directive for underground nuclear tests, he continued to be pressured by his own experts. They wanted more. In November, the National Security Council delivered a blunt assessment: "If we test only underground and the Soviets tested in

the atmosphere, they would surely pass us in nuclear technology."
Still, Kennedy persisted in trying to negotiate. Following a further
failure to bring the Soviets around to the American position, he
let it be known that the United States was now prepared to begin
atmospheric testing again. Though he did nothing beyond indicate
American willingness to resume, it was a necessary step in getting to
the negotiating table. With it came a new pressure: Prime Minister
Harold Macmillan of Britain, considered by JFK a personal as well
as an official friend, urged the United States to put off any such
activity for six more months.

As 1962 began, Kennedy hadn't given up on his hope of bringing
the Russians around to his idea of a peaceful rivalry, not a nuclear one.
What he cared about, above all, was making sure the nuclear genie
got put back in the bottle; for him, arriving at a mutual test ban would
be the first step. "A journey of a thousand miles begins with one step,"
he liked to quote.

Nothing mattered more to him.

In February he and Prime Minister Macmillan jointly wrote
a letter to Khrushchev, calling for a "supreme effort" to stop the
arms race and avert a nuclear apocalypse. Kennedy, in a phone call
with Ben Bradlee not long after sending it, shared his frustration
with what he called this "hard-boiled" conflict over nuclear weapons
testing between the United States and the USSR, but also the "soft-
boiled" one with the British.

Kennedy's national security team now voted unanimously to
resume atmospheric testing. But with the next round of international peace talks scheduled for March in Geneva, he wanted to
delay the announcement. It would get in the way, he felt, of offering
Khrushchev another chance.

It didn't matter. Once again, his approaches were refused, his
aims thwarted—and, as a result, he saw himself gradually pushed

toward brinkmanship. At this point, with the Russians intransigent and any attempts at persuasive diplomacy a failure, Jack felt it was time to present his case to the country. On March 2, speaking on television and radio for forty-five minutes, he made the case for deterrence, explaining the strategic necessity.

He wanted to explain to millions of worried Americans why he'd agreed to resume atmospheric testing. "For all the awesome responsibilities entrusted to this office, none is more somber to contemplate than the special statutory authority to employ nuclear weapons in the defense of our people and freedom." He needed to test, he said, in order to maintain the country's deterrent strength. "It is our hope and prayer that these . . . deadly weapons will never be fired." Red Fay, at the White House for dinner that night, recalled how deeply delivering the speech had affected his friend. "It was about 9:30 when the President finally arrived. Jackie had placed me so that when he came in, I'd be sitting on his left. He was flushed . . . really worn from the whole experience. Everybody sensed that he was very tense. His hands shook. . . . Everybody else, because of his tension, all started to talk among themselves. He directed his conversation to me and said, 'God, I hope you've been enjoying yourself over here, because I've been over there in that office, not knowing whether the decision I made . . .'" His voice trailed off, and Fay was left to imagine the agonizing weight of the responsibility that he felt.

Kennedy had dark forebodings. "Ever since the longbow," he would tell a trusted visitor to the oval office, "when man has developed new weapons and stockpiled them, somebody has come along and used them. I don't know how we can escape it with nuclear weapons."

Still Kennedy clung to the fading notion he might be able to shift the two-power rivalry between the United States and the

Soviets to peaceful pursuits. He understood that the real contest between the USA and the USSR was over authority in the "Third World." The rising peoples of Africa, Asia, and Latin America were looking to see who was winning, which system—democracy or Communism—best suited their needs and their hopes.

The ability to conquer space mattered greatly in this quintessential Cold War struggle to be top gun. The way to win was by looking like a winner. Unfortunately, through 1961 the Soviets had held the competitive edge. The launch of *Sputnik* four years earlier in 1957 had thrown America off stride, and the flight of Yuri Gagarin in April 1961 had done the same again, making the Russians seem invincible by virtue of their superior technology.

But on February 20, 1962, the balance of power, when it came to achievement in space, was restored. On that day, John Glenn became the first American to orbit the earth, circling the globe three times in *Friendship 7*. A marine among the original seven American astronauts picked by the National Aeronautics and Space Administration in 1959, Glenn met with President Kennedy at the White House both before and after the flight. Even space—*especially* space—isn't free of politics, John Glenn well understood. Kennedy knew "we were actually superior to the Soviets and that that's what we were out to prove."

Glenn's triumphant space flight proved the boost NASA needed. What it had lacked before were bragging rights. "I think one reason my flight got so much attention was that we sort of turned the corner in public opinion at that point." In fact, conquering space offered an unprecedented thrill for the American public. Suddenly it seemed as if all things extraordinary were possible under the young president's leadership. The dark shadows cast by the unchecked arms race were forgotten for the moment. Yet, however urgent the question of nuclear disarmament was, it was far from the only crisis facing John F. Kennedy.

• • •

In the fall of 1961, Walter Heller, who chaired the president's Council of Economic Advisers, came to tell him that it was crucial to the economy that steel prices get brought under control. Because the industry's high prices drove up costs across the board, they had the effect of crippling America's ability to compete with foreign producers.

Kennedy acted. To keep American steel in the game, Kennedy went in and won an agreement from the United Steelworkers to cut back their wage demands. In March 1962, industry executives and top union officials gathered at the White House and emerged from the meeting having agreed to defer increases. While the president had no right to tell the steel companies how much to charge, the deal was clear: labor would keep down salaries, the executives would hold back on prices. Afterward, JFK called both sides to thank them for making concessions in the national interest. The union men, when he talked to them, seemed especially pleased to hear the president praising them for their sacrifice.

Then came trouble. Roger Blough, chairman of United States Steel, requested a meeting. From across the cabinet table he handed Kennedy a press release. His company was raising the price of steel 3.5 percent. "Mr. Blough," JFK said, "what you are doing is in the best interest of *your* shareholders. *My* shareholders are every citizen of the United States. I'm going to do everything in the best interest of the shareholders, the people of this country. As the president of the United States, I have quite a bit of influence."

Blough, Jack realized, had already released the announcement. "You have made a terrible mistake," he said. "You have double-crossed me."

To Ken O'Donnell, it was a shocking episode. "These guys felt they were so powerful they could stiff the president of the United

353

States without consequences." He also saw how livid his boss was. "He was white with anger." Big steel had betrayed its workers and "made a fool of him." Discussing it with Ben Bradlee, Jack explained he wasn't about to take a "cold, deliberate fucking."

The president's credibility was now on the line because he'd acted as broker. Labor leaders, he knew, would never trust him again. The steel industry, meanwhile, assumed, "wrongly, he could not or would not do anything." O'Donnell, who'd watched him at work in Massachusetts, knew what sort of surprise they were in for. "You find out about these guys in these steel companies, where they have been on vacation, who they have been with on vacation," he instructed.

His instincts told him where the corporate chiefs were vulnerable. "I don't think U.S. Steel or any other of the major steel companies wants to have Internal Revenue agents checking all the expense accounts of their top executives," Kennedy told Red Fay, who, before becoming undersecretary of the navy, had himself been a Republican businessman. "Too many hotel bills and nightclub expenses would be hard to get by the weekly wives' bridge group out at the Country Club."

The next day, Attorney General Robert Kennedy announced that, under the antitrust laws, a grand jury investigation into the steel industry's pricing had been ordered. Subpoenas to produce documents were served on U.S. Steel. Defense Secretary Robert McNamara instructed the Pentagon to purchase steel "where possible" from companies that had not raised prices. Later that day, in a press conference, Kennedy addressed the issue: ". . . the American people will find it hard, as I do, to accept a situation in which a tiny handful of steel executives whose pursuit of private power and profit exceeds their sense of public responsibility can show such utter contempt for the interests of 185 million Americans." By the next night, eight steel companies that had announced price hikes canceled them.

The president's response to the pullback was to congratulate the steel companies for honoring the public good. "Kennedy's style of politics: you never paint a guy into a corner," O'Donnell later observed. "You give the other fellow as much credit as you can. So, he wants a statement thanking the steel companies for realizing their commitment to the United States Government was more important than their commitment to their stockholders."

But the swords were sheathed only when the mission was accomplished. America's competitiveness was restored, but revenge had also been extracted. Robert Kennedy later confessed the rough tactics employed. "We looked over all of them as individuals . . . we were going to go for broke . . . their expense accounts and where they'd been and what they were doing. I picked up all their records . . . I told the FBI to interview them all, march into their offices the next day! We weren't going to go slowly. . . . So, all of them were hit with meetings the next morning by agents. All of them were subpoenaed for their personal records. I agree it was a tough way to operate, but under the circumstances, we couldn't afford to lose."

When the action settled, Jack Kennedy didn't like being left alone. If no one else happened to be around for the evening, he'd ask Dave Powers—now, like Ken O'Donnell, a presidential special assistant—to stay and have supper with him. They'd then spend the evening together until it was time for Dave to escort him to his bedroom. When he was finally ready to sleep, it'd be: "Good night, pal. Will you please put out the light?"

What's curious—and fascinating—are the fixed orbits JFK assigned to this circle of friends. He always exhibited great fondness for his "Irish mafia" of O'Donnell, O'Brien, and Powers, but they were never part of his social life. With the exception of Powers, who'd join him when nothing else was going on, these men formed an indispensable support team that could be dismissed at sundown. The same went for Ted Sorensen, who'd spent those four years with him in close quarters day after day, flying around the country. They'd become so attuned that Sorensen was practically an alter ego, yet he was never invited for an evening out with his boss.

Novelty and turnover mattered in Jack's personal world. And, naturally, there were rules. Chuck Spalding liked to say that nobody got as much as forty-eight hours with him. If you bored him, you got less. Anyone ever imagining he was an equal colleague soon knew better. Even social friends might step across invisible boundaries and pay the price. Ben Bradlee was "banished," to use his word, for several months in 1962 for daring to mention to another reporter how sensitive Kennedy was to critical reporting. Proving Bradlee to be right, Jack gave him a protracted cold shoulder—a kind of grown-up's "time out"—until eventually the Bradlees were returned to his good graces.

In the White House, he didn't leap up at dawn like some presidents, but read the newspapers in bed over breakfast. He regularly went for a swim before lunch, took a nap afterward, and then would have another swim before dinner. Kennedy was far from the healthiest president on record, but, clearly, he wanted to come across as that. In photographs, especially, he projected a smiling vitality. When it came to his ongoing medical problems—above all, the intractable back pain—he didn't complain. Nor did he explain.

As a married man, he'd decided not to forgo his bachelor pleasures. It seems not to have occurred to him. Lem had been right to try to warn Jackie at the wedding. But one of his affairs had an abrupt ending not of his own choosing. In March of 1962, he was visited by J. Edgar Hoover. The FBI, which had kept tabs on him during his Inga Arvad days, had now been chronicling his current relationship with a woman "of interest" to the Bureau. "Information has been developed that Judith E. Campbell, a freelance artist, has associated with prominent underworld figures Sam Giancana of Chicago and John Roselli of Los Angeles. Went on to note the phone calls back and forth between the White House and Campbell." President Kennedy broke off the liaison with Campbell, who'd been introduced to him by Frank Sinatra, later that day.

His affair with the free-spirited Washington socialite Mary Meyer was very different. This was a relationship of equals. Divorced at the time of their relationship, she'd been married to a top CIA strategist, Cord Meyer, and was the sister of Tony Bradlee. So well did Jack segment his life, he could be good friends with her brother-in-law at the same time he was sleeping with her. He'd regularly see Meyer, who was legendarily attractive and also unpredictable, at Georgetown and White House parties. Sometimes he'd even be the one inviting her to White House functions. "She'd be difficult to live with," he once noted to pal Ben. But, then, he didn't have to.

Now that they'd been settled in the White House for more than a year, Jack had grown accustomed to being no longer able to avail himself of the absences necessitated by the campaign trail. His response was to start arranging his time to avoid being alone socially—even alone with Jackie, it seems—for any extended period. He used New York overnights, Palm Beach weekends, campaign trips, and Jackie's summer-long departures to the Cape for "girling" with pals Chuck, Torby, or George Smathers invited along for company. If they went away together for a weekend, he invariably asked one or more of his pals along. Whether it was the Virginia hunt country, Camp David, Hyannis Port, or Palm Beach, he made a point to start calling around Tuesday to fill up the guest list. His nature seemed to render him unable to look forward to a weekend alone with his wife, or even a dinner, without the addition of outside company.

Rachel "Bunny" Mellon was the close friend who helped Jackie restore the White House, close enough to have Jackie confide in her.

"Jackie knew that he had this . . . feeling. But she sort of said, 'Well, Jack's got these girlfriends.' She never griped about it, she said he could do what he wants."

Part of it, she believed, was that Jackie had a very "old world" view of men.

"She was a Bouvier and, how can I put it, I think she was strange enough not to be small. It was her fault to marry Jack Kennedy. I mean, she was attracted by him. She was fascinated by him. Regular, decent kind of guys, they would come down the road. She didn't care who, but she married him. She married him because he was different."

The presidency offered Jack the chance to act on his old schoolboy's love of heroes. In August, he invited General Douglas MacArthur to visit. Jack was entranced by the old soldier, respectful even when the eighty-two-year-old wartime general showed what the years and Korea had done to him. He told of his recommendation that his infantrymen each be issued "some kind of cartridge that would clear ten or fifteen yards in front of him." He was talking about nuclear weapons carried in holsters! "If you could get me this type of atomic cartridge so that every soldier will have that," he told of his frustrated efforts to win production of this new serviceman's hardware, "one hundred men could stop a division." Awestruck at the preposterous idea, Kennedy was true to form. He asked for details. "Let's say that the cartridge would be fired, let's say, at some man, or group of men, coming across a field at a hundred and twenty yards. It would hit one man and what? You just explode in a puff?"

It must have occurred to the young president how much war had changed. Here was a revered military hero, a general for the ages, who'd come back to liberate the Philippines and win the war in the Pacific. Here was the genius behind the Inchon Landing in the Korean War, totally unaware of the menace posed by a minor nuclear explosion. Kennedy, the junior officer from World War II come back to lead his country, could not afford such anachronistic thinking, even if it survived among the top military men who now commanded the services.

At the University of Mississippi as that fall semester began, a new student was under extraordinary scrutiny. The air force veteran James Meredith was seeking admission. He would be the first African-American to enroll—and in a rigidly segregated state, it wasn't going to happen without trouble.

Washington efforts to end discrimination were another issue on the Kennedy administration's agenda. The main task up to this point, however, had been to encourage government contractors to hire more minorities. But even more radical social change was on the minds of civil rights leaders, and across the South, the educational system at all levels was under assault. Ernest Green and eight other African-American students had made history by integrating Little Rock's Central High School in 1957. In early May 1961, the first Freedom Riders—seven black, six white—had begun courageously riding buses throughout the South, challenging the rules of segregation.

Now it was Ole Miss's turn to join the late twentieth century, however unwillingly.

On September 10, the U.S. Supreme Court ruled in favor of Meredith. Supported by the NAACP—the pioneering civil rights organization founded in 1909 by W. E. B. Du Bois, among others—Meredith petitioned the university to admit him. The school continued to refuse, making it increasingly clear that the federal government might need to use force. As the crisis escalated,

President Kennedy feared he was heading for a showdown, not just with one school or even one state, but with the entire South.

Here is the recorded conversation between Kennedy and Mississippi governor Ross Barnett:

Kennedy: Can you maintain this order?

Barnett: Well, I don't know. That's what I'm worried about. I don't know whether I can or not. I couldn't have the other afternoon.

Kennedy: You couldn't have?

Barnett: There was such a mob there. It would have been impossible. There were men in there with trucks and shotguns and all such as that. Certain people were just enraged. Would you be willing to wait awhile and let the people cool off on the whole thing? It might be ... two or three weeks, it might cool off a ...

Kennedy: Would you undertake to register him in two weeks?

Barnett: You know I can't undertake to register him myself.

Governor Barnett continued to be intransigent. His stance put him in a long succession of Southern governors such as Orville Faubus, who'd summoned the Arkansas National Guard to "protect" Central High. "I won't agree to let that boy get to Ole Miss," Barnett told Attorney General Kennedy. Jack and Bobby both were hoping they'd get James Meredith into Ole Miss without using federal troops, but Jack was also determined not to be caught unprepared. Aware of the shellacking he'd taken over the Bay of Pigs, what he intended to avoid was trusting anyone to share his agenda when their own was what mattered to them.

Jack was now involved in checking out every detail, scanning the aerial photographs of the university's campus and ascertaining such details as where military helicopters might land. When two thousand demonstrators, students and nonstudents alike, showed up on September 30 to protest Meredith's registration, Kennedy, on the phone with Barnett, pressed him either to take charge or defer to the president. The university president was evasive and came across as increasingly unstable.

The problem was whom they could trust to protect Meredith. As the day wore on, the U.S. marshals guarding him were being attacked by the crowd. Governor Barnett, claiming he couldn't control the Mississippi state troopers—in fact, he'd secretly taken them off duty—refused to guarantee Meredith's further safety. Kennedy had federalized the Mississippi National Guard but was reluctant to rely on them; he'd also positioned U.S. Army backup in Memphis.

By late that night, the hostilities had increased to a level of violence that saw two men—one a journalist from Agence France-Presse—killed. Military intervention was urgently needed. There was now little option but to summon the waiting troops and pray they arrived in time. Nicholas Katzenbach, the deputy attorney general representing the Justice Department at the campus, confessed to his boss Bobby Kennedy his doubt that the marshals could hold off the rioting protesters until the U.S. soldiers appeared.

If they didn't manage to arrive in time, Katzenbach worried "neither Meredith nor any of those men have a chance." Moreover, the reliability of the Mississippi National Guard remained a real question. In Ken O'Donnell's words, "we knew that most of the National Guard members were students, former students, or else ninety percent in sympathy with the mob." When the president issued the order to the marshals to protect Meredith at all costs, it was with the knowledge that it might be their last. In Washington, all they could do now was sit and wait. Kennedy and his advisors were on tenterhooks. Some of them feared the next news they'd hear was that Meredith was dead and Katzenbach a prisoner being held by out-of-control students and townie hooligans.

Kennedy was responsible for all the lives that hung in the balance. It was critical that the army not fail him. Yet, here again, as in the Bay of Pigs operation, Kennedy discovered the difference between command and control. Those troops stationed in Memphis, it turned out, had yet to be mustered. When the soldiers finally landed at the Rebels' football field, it was quickly evident they weren't mobilizing fast enough. Communicating with them by phone, staying on top of their positions minute by minute, Jack began issuing orders as their commander in chief. As they at last made their way onto the central campus, their presence had an immediate effect. By dawn on October 1, the situation was stabilized. That day, James Meredith became the first black student at the University of Mississippi.

It had been a very long night.

In the aftermath, JFK felt pretty unforgiving toward the military. "They always give you their bullshit about their instant reaction and their split-second timing, but it never works out. No wonder it's so hard to win a war." And he had even harsher thoughts about the local officialdom. It was simply incredible to John Kennedy that not a single elected Mississippi authority had stepped in to attempt to restore civil order. The siege of Ole Miss—like his experience as skipper of the foundering *PT 109*—had forced him to assume a lone command and grab tight his own destiny. What it also had done was give him the satisfaction of enforcing, to the best of his abilities and with all the conviction he had, the law of the land.

To be the American president at this moment in history was to sense the edge of the precipice. Jack Kennedy's deepest fear was that he might somehow take the step that would send the United States toppling over it. And when he looked out at the world beyond Washington, what he saw was a single place—West Berlin—that, in the flash of an instant, could provide the setting. The balance between the two superpowers was now so precarious that a single stumble there would be all that it took.

The German Democratic Republic, or East Germany, as it was commonly known, was determined to take back full control of its capital, the largest city in Germany. In pursuit of this aim—a land grab completely unacceptable to the Free World—the German Communists had their Russian patron's full support. In July, Premier Khrushchev had once again thumped his chest, demanding the end of "the occupation regime in the West Berlin."

The American, British, and French troops billeted there since the end of World War II were to be replaced by a newly organized police force, Khrushchev insisted. This constabulary's members would be recruited from the three Western powers, as well as from neutral and Warsaw Pact countries. Four years down the road, the new force would be composed entirely of East Germans.

The Soviet leader sent word to Kennedy that he would put off pressing his demands until after the American midterm elections in November. As Khrushchev made clear, this was just a temporary reprieve. Alluding to West Berlin as the "bone in my throat," he wasn't about to let it remain there. Rumors of an increased Soviet military presence on the island of Cuba were also disturbing the peace of mind at the Kennedy White House.

Khrushchev, very certain that he had the upper hand and meaning to keep it, had Interior Secretary Stewart Udall, who was visiting Moscow, flown to his Black Sea dacha. There the startled American was entrusted with a warning to pass on to the president. "We will not allow your troops to be in Berlin." He then added an even more specific threat that he wished relayed. "War over Berlin," he said, "would mean that within the space of an hour, there would be no Paris and no France."

Then, having issued this horrifying message, he told Udall that he wanted to meet the president at the United Nations General Assembly meeting in New York in the second half of November. The main topic would be Berlin.

With the Americans continuing, nervously, to monitor Russian activity in Cuba, the Soviet leader once again issued an ultimatum. He sent JFK a letter bluntly informing him that any U.S. attack on Cuba would bring a retaliatory strike at West Berlin. The Russian behavior was so provocative as to be puzzling. Two days later, Kennedy told his close friend David Ormsby-Gore, now British ambassador to the United States, and Secretary of State Dean Rusk that he thought Khrushchev might actually be encouraging him to invade Cuba so he could grab West Berlin. Why else would he be tying the two together?

Suddenly it came, the real threat of war over Berlin. It came in a fight, once again, over Cuba. A bit after eight a.m. on Tuesday, October 16, 1962, McGeorge Bundy carried to Jack Kennedy the news that the latest U-2 spy flight had brought back photographic evidence of Soviet offensive missile sites under construction in western Cuba. Kennedy quickly called his brother, who now hurried to the White House, studying the photos even before the president did.

Though running the Justice Department, Bobby had decided to moonlight in the area of intelligence. He'd done so because of the numerous dissatisfactions with the ill-conceived Bay of Pigs scenario. He was now running the administration's secret anti-Castro operation himself. Code-named "Operation Mongoose," this enterprise involved an array of secret plots to topple the Cuban dictator, all doomed to be pathetically unsuccessful.

In the Senate, Kennedy was already under attack from two

Republicans—New York's Kenneth Keating and Indiana's Homer Capehart—with both insisting on the fierce reality of those now verified Soviet missile installations. "Ken Keating will probably be the next president!" Jack commented as he looked at the three large photographs Bundy had carried to him. The Republicans who had been mounting the attacks may have lacked hard evidence, but at the moment it didn't matter. They were right.

Squeezed between his soon-to-be-gloating critics on the right and the Soviets, whom he now realized had deceived him, Kennedy was suddenly in an extremely tight spot with little breathing room. The wily Khrushchev had made use of the delay he initiated for the American election to arm his Cuban allies with nuclear weapons—SS-24 Scalpels, medium-range ballistic missiles with a range of a thousand miles—able to reach well into the United States.

The only question on which the CIA had no intelligence at that moment was how rapidly the weapons on that site could be equipped with nuclear warheads. Summoned to the White House, the top cabinet officials and military advisors began to weigh in, making their case for immediate action to destroy the missiles. Such a response, Kennedy was told, would entail either an air strike on the missile sites alone or else a full-scale invasion.

The latter option, General Maxwell Taylor, chairman of the Joint Chiefs of Staff, told him, would mean an involvement of up to 150,000 troops—a hundredfold increase on the ragtag Bay of Pigs invaders. Attacking Cuba was serious military business, and for the Joint Chiefs, what they'd been lobbying for all along. As he listened to his people, one thing was clear: the overall consensus in the room held that the least delay would allow the Soviets the time needed to ready the missiles for use.

Kennedy now assembled an expert panel to decide on what steps to take. The purpose of this group, called ExComm—for Executive

Committee—was to keep all intelligence regarding the Soviet missiles at San Cristobal limited to a smaller group than the National Security Council.

"Virtually everyone's initial choice, at that first October 16 meeting, was a surgical air strike against the nuclear missile sites before they could become operational," said O'Donnell. "U.S. bombers could swoop in, eliminate the sites, and fly away, leaving the problem swiftly, magically ended. But further questions—JFK always had further questions—proved that solution illusory. First, no cruise missiles or smart bombs existed in those days to assure the precision and success of the strike. The air force acknowledged that it could be certain of eliminating only sixty of the missiles, leaving the others free to fire and destroy us."

With each question he now asked, Kennedy gained more knowledge. It would be highly risky to send bombers over Cuba unless its surface-to-air missile sites were destroyed, along with its antiaircraft sites, its fighter planes, and its bombers, which might head off to Florida. But an invasion would pit American fighting men against Cubans defending their homeland, a recipe for long casualty lists on both sides, a guarantee of a bitter occupation. It would also mean killing countless numbers of Russians.

Time was of the essence. But so was taking the time—even if it was in short supply—to weigh all the options. Every so often, JFK would leave the room during the deliberations, allowing the others to express themselves more freely. One statement that must have played and replayed in his head was General Taylor's "It'll never be one hundred percent, Mr. President." In other words, an air strike could never be guaranteed to wipe out all the missiles. But Berlin was also central to his thinking. Any attack on Cuba could give Khrushchev his chance. He was only too aware that, back in 1956, when the British, French, and Israelis had gone to war with Egypt, it gave the Soviets the opportunity to crush the Hungarian revolution. If Khrushchev was attempting the same ploy this time, using a U.S. attack on Cuba as a pretext for rolling through West Berlin, Britain and France might well blame the Americans for this mortal breach in the West's defense.

By Thursday, Bobby was starting to have second thoughts of his own about a raid on Cuba. The issue of America's moral standing had become part of the debate. After one meeting he passed a note to Sorensen: "I now know how Tojo felt when he was planning Pearl Harbor." It was a serious consideration. Despite the photographic evidence, there would be many around the world who would regard any military strike against Cuba as aggression, pure and simple. For the United States to attack such a tiny neighbor would wind up in the history books as a classic example of imperialism.

Friday marked the fourth day since Bundy had shown the president the surveillance pictures. Now the stakes were raised even higher, with new aerial photographs revealing more sites in Cuba, ones serving intermediate-range missiles. Such weapons could travel nearly three thousand miles, all the way to New York. The hawks were now screaming for action. The most ferocious was the air force chief of staff, General Curtis LeMay, the former head of the Strategic Air Command, who, during World War II, had led brutal incendiary attacks over Japan.

Kennedy challenged LeMay's thinking. Might not an American attack on Cuba quickly start a nuclear chain reaction? We attack their ally, they grab for Berlin. Then, confronted by the overwhelming force of the Red Army, the only resort of the United States would be to use tactical atomic weapons right there in the middle of Europe. The next escalation, involving an exchange of each side's nuclear arsenals, was not, after that, hard to imagine.

This was all unfamiliar language to the cigar-smoking LeMay, who'd entered the air corps in 1929. His interest was simply spelling out the strategic facts. The United States enjoyed a huge advantage in intercontinental missiles. Why weren't we playing our strength? A naval blockade of Cuba, the only alternative to an attack on the missile sites, would be a sign of weakness. It would be like "appeasement at Munich," LeMay said. He'd dared—though he may not have entirely realized what he was doing—to imply that Jack Kennedy was his father's appeasing son.

Yet, to his credit, Kennedy realized to whom he was talking, understood the mind-set of what he was confronting in this frightening moment. LeMay was telling him that the smart move for the United States was to engage in a nuclear test of strength, as if it were an arm wrestle. We lose tens of millions but we end up winning the test of strength, since the Russians will get the worst of whatever planetary horror is inflicted. "You're talking about the destruction of a country," Kennedy said simply. That led to the following exchange:

LeMay: You're in a pretty bad fix at the present time.

Kennedy: What did you say?

LeMay: You're in a pretty bad fix.

Kennedy: Well, you're in there with me. Personally.

Tapes of the discussions among the Joint Chiefs after their civilian commander left the room show them united against the president. "You pulled the rug right out from under him," Chief of Staff General David Shoup of the marines applauded LeMay. The military men agreed that anything short of an all-out invasion was "piecemeal."

Kennedy, fortunately, knew whom he was dealing with. He knew that LeMay and others in the high strategic command leaned toward a "first strike" option, especially in the case of a Soviet move on

Berlin. This meant an "obliterating" nuclear attack on all Communist countries, three thousand weapons aimed at a thousand targets. "And we call ourselves human," Kennedy said after a briefing.

Out campaigning in Chicago, fulfilling his obligation to attend a Democratic fund-raiser for Mayor Richard J. Daley, Jack received a call from Bobby. His brother didn't mince words. The time had come to make a decision, he said. Flying back to D.C. on *Air Force One*, Jack warned Pierre Salinger: grab your balls.

A phalanx of powerful men now was allied against him. The Joint Chiefs, McGeorge Bundy, John McCone, Douglas Dillon—all supported an air strike. Here was the Establishment—intelligence, military, and finance—mutually agreeing that the best move was to send in the bombers. And other influential voices were about to join the chorus. On Monday, Senator Richard Russell of Georgia, chairman of the Armed Services Committee, stood by LeMay, urging an air strike followed by an all-out invasion. The time for the showdown with the Soviets had arrived. Yet, still, Kennedy persisted in disagreeing.

Here was a perfect affirmation of the Founding Fathers' reasoning, which had led them to place ultimate constitutional authority in the hands of the person elected by the American people. As the French statesman Georges Clemenceau more recently had observed, "War is far too important to be left to the generals." Thus, even after hearing the expert arguments, Kennedy rejected the air-attack option, ordering instead a blockade on all offensive weapons headed to Cuba, a suggestion earlier made by Dean Rusk. He would announce it three days later in a nationally broadcast address.

"This government, as promised, has maintained the closest surveillance of the Soviet military buildup on the island of Cuba," he told American listeners, the aerial photographs in hand. "Within the past week, unmistakable evidence has established the fact that a series of offensive missile sites is now in preparation on that imprisoned island. The purpose of these bases can be none other than to provide a nuclear strike capability against the Western Hemisphere."

The missiles had to go, Kennedy declared, decreeing a naval blockade of all ships carrying offensive weapons or missile-firing equipment to Cuba. Any such vessel would be stopped and turned back. "It shall be the policy of this nation to regard any nuclear missile launched from Cuba against any nation in the Western Hemisphere as an attack by the Soviet Union on the United States, requiring a full retaliatory response to the Soviet Union." He then recited the Cold War canon: "The 1930s taught us a clear lesson: aggressive conduct, if allowed to go unchecked and unchallenged, ultimately leads to war."

Now began the waiting. During this period he distracted himself, as usual, by having his buddies to dinner at the White House. "I think the pressure of this period made him desire more to have friends around," recalled Charlie Bartlett. "I think I was over there for dinner three times in the week . . . just small groups, which he would break up about nine thirty and go back to the cables."

He shared what he could. On one of those nights, Bartlett was climbing into bed around eleven thirty when the phone rang. Kennedy told him, "You'd be interested to know I got a cable from our friend, and he says that those ships are coming through, they're coming through tomorrow." To hear such information gave his listener a very clear notion of what kind of pressure Jack was under. Bartlett realized "it was on that kind of a note that he had to go to sleep. But I must say that the president's coolness and temper were never more evident than they were that week."

Under the careful supervision of Robert McNamara, the navy enforced the blockade without attacking the Soviet ships, which retreated from the Cuban sea channels. Within the Department of the Navy, however, it was an unpopular decision. That's because, as Red Fay explained it, his friend was stepping all over what the navy brass saw as the right of a captain to run his own ship. "The President said, 'Any communication with any skipper of our ship when coming in contact with a Russian ship, I will make the decision as to exactly what he is to say, when he's to say it, and how he's to say it.'" He was running the operation, but it wasn't what they wanted to hear.

Nor was the young president's operation like any they'd known before. He wasn't fighting a war but acting to prevent one, signaling to the other side the terms on which peace could be maintained.

Two letters arriving from Premier Khrushchev marked the beginning of the conclusion to the crisis. They were sent to the U.S. embassy in Moscow on consecutive days, October 26 and 27. The first letter proposed the removal of missiles and Soviet personnel in exchange for a promise not to invade Cuba. The second asked for the added concession of the removal of Jupiter missiles from Turkey.

The text of the second letter, sent on the following day, was broadcast on Moscow radio at the same time it was delivered to the U.S. embassy.

Kennedy resolved to answer Khrushchev's first letter, agreeing not to invade Cuba. He then instructed Bobby to tell the Soviet ambassador, Anatoly Dobrynin, in confidence that the Jupiter missiles in Turkey would be withdrawn later. Bobby gave Dobrynin a timetable of one day to accept.

Arriving at the Justice Department, Dobrynin was taken aback by Bobby's conduct. In the past he'd come to expect the same rough treatment the president's brother had meted out to Mike DiSalle and other resistant Democrats two years earlier. He had prepared himself to be castigated for the Soviets' deception. Instead, he came face-to-face with an upset young father trying desperately to prevent a nuclear war. "He didn't even try to get into fights," the envoy cabled his superiors in Moscow. The United States would remove the missiles from Turkey, as Khrushchev had requested, within four or five months, Bobby assured him, but couldn't let it look like a concession. "He persistently returned to one theme: time is of the essence and we shouldn't miss the chance."

Still, the entire perilous and exhausting adventure wasn't going to be over, Bobby told Dobrynin, until the Russian missiles were actually removed from Cuban soil. That was "not an ultimatum, just a statement of fact." Khrushchev *must* commit to doing so. It worked. Within the week, Kennedy had won the Soviet leader's agreement. The crisis had ended. A country that had lived for days with the prospect of nuclear war could now breathe easy.

Though Curtis LeMay would call the decision to not invade Cuba "the greatest defeat in our history," it was a minority view. "If Kennedy never did another thing," said the British prime minister, Harold Macmillan, "he assured his place in history by this single act."

It was later learned that the Soviets had deposited in Cuba a disturbing cache of nuclear weapons in early October, well before the Kennedy administration had the photographic evidence that spurred it into action. There were ninety nuclear warheads in all. Thirty of them possessed sixty-six times the explosive power of the bomb dropped on Hiroshima. There was an equal number of warheads with the firepower of the Hiroshima atomic bomb, plus an assortment of other, smaller ones.

Would Khrushchev have fired them? Here's what he said afterward in his memoirs: "My thinking went like this: If we installed the missiles secretly, and then the United States discovered the missiles after they were poised and ready to strike, the Americans would think twice before trying to liquidate our installations by military means. I knew that the United States could knock out some of our installations, but not all of them. If a quarter or even a tenth of our missiles survived—even if only one or two big ones were left—we could still hit New York, and there wouldn't be much of New York left. I don't mean to say everyone in New York would be killed—not everyone, of course, but an awful lot of people would be wiped out . . . And it was high time that America learned what it feels like to have her own land and her own people threatened."

But if America had attacked those missile sites, killing the Soviet soldiers and technicians there to deploy them, Khrushchev had in mind another target: West Berlin. "The Americans knew that if Russian blood were shed in Cuba, American blood would surely be shed in Germany."

The bitter coldness of that statement would have surprised the American president only in tone. It's precisely what Kennedy had on his mind when everyone else was thinking Cuba. It's hard to imagine any other president—let alone the youngest one ever elected—resisting the pressures the way Jack Kennedy had managed to. Despite the many buddies he relied upon, despite his brother's indispensability, despite the curiosity about the world that drove him, the Bay of Pigs had taught him whom he could best rely upon: himself.

Bobby Kennedy offered the sharpest assessment of what his brother had done. "The final lesson of the Cuban missile crisis is the importance of placing ourselves in the other country's shoes. During the crisis, President Kennedy spent more time trying to determine the effect of a particular course of action on Khrushchev and the Russians than on any other phase of what he was doing. President Kennedy understood that the Soviet Union did not want war."

It was his detachment that saved us. Another man would have reacted with force to the Soviet treachery. He would have shared in the righteousness of the cause, been stirred to attack by the saber rattling. Jack resisted. He was not moved by the emotion of others around him. He knew his course and stayed to it. Thank God. The boy who had read alone of history's heroes was now safely one of them. He had done it not by winning a war, but by averting one far more horrible than any leader in the past could have imagined.

President Kennedy in West Berlin

"I have a dream." Dr. King in Washington, DC,
August 28, 1963

Caroline and John Jr. in the Oval Office

CHAPTER FIFTEEN

GOALS

Blessed are the peacemakers.

—Matthew 5:9

Politicians are, at different times, driven by grand notions and near necessity. Speak of the next election when they're dreaming loftily, and you risk being dismissed as a hack. Speak of high purpose when they're hearing the footsteps of a rival, and you invite instant dismissal.

Jack Kennedy was both an original and a consummate politician. Yet his stewardship of priorities still resembled those of a college student. With a number of classes on his schedule, he gave most of his attention to some, did the best he could with others, and let a few slide. It's common enough. He was always most committed to what interested him. What made all the difference was the love of history that never failed to engage him.

In the first two years of his presidency, he had been making history. His accomplishments were linked in a singular way to what he most highly valued: his commitment to the Peace Corps, to peaceful competition in science and space travel, to containment of nuclear arms, to civil rights. But he also needed to be reelected. He began his third year in office pushing for a tax cut. It was an attempt to court a constituency that was resisting him: a previous year's poll had shown that 88 percent of businessmen viewed him as hostile to their interests. However, many of them didn't even go for his idea of a tax cut. The view then from Wall Street and Main Street both was that balanced budgets were the best thing for business.

Kennedy had campaigned on just such a principle, only to grow concerned over time that the economy simply wasn't growing as it should. His chief economic advisor, Walter Heller, believed tax cuts would stimulate spending and investment, thereby increasing employment. Eisenhower's commitment to fiscal conservatism had spiked the jobless rate in the fall of 1960, hamstringing Nixon's quest to succeed him. Looking ahead to November 1964, Kennedy wanted that rate heading downward—and believed a slash in taxes would do the trick.

He also sought to correct the unfairness he saw in the tax code. Why, for example, had H. L. Hunt, the oil baron, paid just $22,000 in taxes the previous year? Why had J. Paul Getty, another ridiculously wealthy oilman, forked over only $500? When Ben Bradlee told him he paid the same amount, Kennedy said it made his point. "The tax laws really screw people in your bracket." Hearing this, Bradlee suggested it would surely help the cause of reform if he'd release the figures on those oilmen's tax levels. Kennedy paused before replying. "Maybe after 1964." All he wanted at the moment was a tax cut that would juice the economy enough to get it moving before voters had their next chance to weigh in at the polls.

President Kennedy delivered three epochal addresses in June of 1963. The first was the commencement address at American University. It became known as his "Peace" speech. In it he spoke of his desire for a limited nuclear test ban treaty with the Soviet Union. The Cuban Missile Crisis, he knew, had been a terrifyingly close call.

"What kind of peace do I mean? Not the peace of the grave or the security of the slave. I am talking about genuine peace, the kind of peace that makes life on earth worth living, the kind that enables man and nations to grow and to hope and to build a better life for their children—not merely peace for Americans, but peace for all men and women—not merely peace in our time, but peace for all time."

He was calling on the Soviet Union to join with the United States to prove that peace was possible, conflict not inevitable. "The problems of man are man-made; they can be solved by man. And man can be as big as he wants. No problem of human destiny is beyond human beings. Man's reason and spirit have often solved the seemingly unsolvable—and we believe they can do it again." With these words, he revealed that his highest commitment was not to arms control alone but to human hope.

Kennedy then expressed thoughts new to an American president, ideas especially startling coming from a man who'd once been a committed Cold Warrior. What he pointed out was the obvious but unspoken fact that the peoples inhabiting the two countries, the USA and the USSR, are not that different in their needs and dreams. "For in the final analysis, our most basic common link is that we all inhabit this small planet; and we are all mortal." He went on to offer a gesture of respect that was even more unexpected. "As Americans, we find Communism profoundly repugnant as a negation of personal freedom and dignity. But we can still hail the Russian people for their many achievements—in science and space, in economic and industrial growth, in culture and in acts of courage."

He continued, powerfully, to make his case. "Among the many traits the peoples of our two countries have in common, none is stronger than our mutual abhorrence of war. Almost unique among the major world powers, we have never been at war with each other. And no nation in the history of battle ever suffered more than the Soviet Union suffered in the course of the Second World War. At least twenty million lost their lives. Countless millions of homes and farms were burned or sacked. A third of the nation's territory, including nearly two thirds of its industrial base, was turned into a wasteland—a loss equivalent to the devastation of this country east of Chicago.

"The one major area of these negotiations where the end is in sight, yet where a fresh start is badly needed, is in a treaty to outlaw nuclear tests. The conclusion of such a treaty, so near and yet so far, would check the spiraling arms race in one of its most dangerous areas. It would place the nuclear powers in a position to deal more effectively with one of the greatest hazards which man faces in 1963, the further spread of nuclear arms. It would increase our security—it would decrease the prospects of war. Surely this goal is sufficiently important to require our steady pursuit, yielding neither to the temptation to give up the whole effort nor the temptation to give up our insistence on vital and responsible safeguards.

"To make clear our good faith and solemn convictions on the matter, I now declare that the United States does not propose to conduct nuclear tests in the atmosphere so long as other states do not do so. We will not be the first to resume. Such a declaration is no substitute for a formal binding treaty, but I hope it will help us achieve one. Nor would such a treaty be a substitute for disarmament, but I hope it will help us achieve it."

Finally came the radical commitment: "Our primary long-range interest in Geneva, however, is general and complete disarmament—designed to take place by stages, permitting parallel political developments to build the new institutions of peace which would take the place of arms."

What Kennedy had said would quickly become known to the men and women of the Soviet Union—but only because Nikita Khrushchev had dictated that it be so. According to a *New York Times* piece three days later, headlined "Russians Stirred by Kennedy

Talk About Cold War," the Communist daily *Izvestia* had published the speech in full. Reported the *Times,* "The decision to make the speech available to the Soviet people through the government newspaper was interpreted here as an indication that the speech had made a favorable impression in the Kremlin."

The story then quoted a Soviet intellectual: "The speech and its publication in *Izvestia* show that there can be mutual understanding." While a young woman worker was "overheard to ask a friend: 'Have you read the Kennedy speech? It is all about peace.'"

The previous month, however, most Americans had witnessed something they wanted no one in the world to see. It had been in their newspapers and on their television sets. The incident had occurred in Birmingham, Alabama, in early May, when Eugene "Bull" Connor—the unrepentantly racist commissioner of public safety, just elected for his sixth term—had unleashed dogs and ordered fire hoses turned on peaceful African-American civil rights demonstrators.

Now, on June 11, the day after Kennedy's American University speech, two black students, Vivian Malone and James Hood, had attempted to enroll at the University of Alabama. Their way was blocked by order of Governor George C. Wallace, who'd campaigned on a promise to do just that. Watching the eleven o'clock news two weeks earlier with Jackie and the Bradlees, the president had grown solemn at clips of Wallace promising—in the face of a federal court order—personally to "bar the door" against any attempts at desegregation. "He's just challenging us to use the marshals . . . that's going to be something."

He'd once met Wallace—whose recent campaign slogan had been "Segregation now—Segregation tomorrow—Segregation forever"—and was disgusted by the man. "Make him look ridiculous. That's what the president wants you to do," Attorney General Robert Kennedy instructed his deputy, Nicholas Katzenbach.

There in Tuscaloosa, flanked by an enormous contingent of National Guardsmen—his earlier experience at Ole Miss had taught him about strength in numbers—Katzenbach instructed Wallace to allow the two students to be admitted. When the governor remained immovable in the door of Foster Auditorium, the commander of the Alabama Guard, General Henry Graham, told him to "stand aside," which Wallace then did.

Thanks to a documentary shot at the time by Robert Drew, we can see much of what happened next. Titled *Crisis: Behind a Presidential Commitment,* it shows Kennedy standing in the Oval Office and asking his top aides—Ken O'Donnell, Larry O'Brien, Ted Sorensen, Pierre Salinger, and his brother Bobby—to join him around a small coffee table. Kennedy assumed the captain's seat, in this case a rocking chair. He did so with a subtle, two-thumbs-up gesture as if he were still a young skipper calling his crew to quarters. General Graham's success, acting on his behalf, obviously had energized Kennedy. At that moment he made the call to deliver a major speech that night, giving Sorensen only three hours to prepare it.

In his State of the Union that January, President Kennedy had affirmed that the "most precious and powerful right in the world, the right to vote . . . not be denied to any citizen on grounds of his race or color. In this centennial year of Emancipation, all those who are willing to vote should always be permitted." He'd followed it by endorsing a push for voting rights, backing an end to all discrimination in hiring and supporting full access to public accommodations. Now, with his own deepening conviction heightened by the confrontation in Alabama he'd just seen on television, he was ready to further speak his thoughts.

Calling civil rights "a moral issue . . . as old as the Scriptures and . . . as clear as the American Constitution," he framed it in the context of the Cold War. "Today we are committed to a worldwide struggle to promote and protect the rights of all who wish to be free. And when Americans are sent to Vietnam or West Berlin, we do not ask for whites only. We preach freedom around the world, and we mean it."

The commonsense truths he spoke that night were framed in the idiom of everyday American conversation.

"It ought to be possible, therefore, for American students of any color to attend any public institution they select without having to be backed up by troops.

"It ought to be possible for American consumers of any color to receive equal service in places of public accommodation, such as hotels and restaurants and theaters and retail stores, without being forced to resort to demonstrations in the street, and it ought to be possible for American citizens of any color to register to vote in a free election without interference or fear of reprisal.

"It ought to be possible, in short, for every American to enjoy the privileges of being American without regard to his race or his color. In short, every American ought to have the right to be treated as he would wish to be treated, as one would wish his children to be treated. But this is not the case.

"If an American, because his skin is dark, cannot eat lunch in a restaurant open to the public; if he cannot send his children to the best public school available; if he cannot vote for the public officials who represent him; if, in short, he cannot enjoy the full and free life which all of us want, then who among us would be content to have the color of his skin changed and stand in his place? Who among us would then be content with the counsels of patience and delay?"

Martin Luther King, Jr., declared that the speech he'd heard represented "the most sweeping and forthright ever presented by an American president."

But it was one thing to speak eloquently in one's own language, and another to confront an audience on foreign land. Driving through the streets of West Berlin later that month, on June 26, Ben Bradlee watched Kennedy struggling to rehearse the German sentences he intended to use in a speech. Bradlee knew his friend was no linguist. In fact, Jack was secretly taking French lessons, having resented Bradlee's own fluency, which he'd gained years before as a press attaché with the American embassy in Paris. "Two thousand years ago the proudest boast was '*civis Romanus sum.*' Today, in the world of freedom, the proudest boast is '*Ich bin ein Berliner.*'"

Twenty-two months earlier, the East Germans had stepped back from the edge of conflict and constructed the Berlin Wall, taking the city—and the watching world—by surprise. Overnight, the twelve-foot concrete-and-barbed-wire symbol of totalitarianism had taken shape as a scar on the landscape of European history. More than a hundred miles long, one section of the Wall divided East and West Berlin, while a much larger one encircled the American, British, and French sectors, cutting them off from the rest of East Germany. Where once there had been reasonably free passage between the halves of the politically bifurcated city, now there were checkpoints and guards with guns.

Kennedy tackled the problem of addressing the beleaguered West Berliners straightforwardly. He and his country stood for democracy, and everything else derived from that simple reality. "There are many people in the world who really don't understand, *or say they don't*, what is the great issue between the Free World and the Communist world. Let them come to Berlin. There are some who say that Communism is the wave of the future. Let them come to Berlin. And there are even a few who say that it is true that Communism is an evil system, but it permits us to make economic progress. *Lass' sie nach Berlin kommen!* Let them come to Berlin. Freedom has many difficulties, and democracy is not perfect, but we have never had to put a wall up to keep our people in to prevent them from leaving us. All free men, wherever they may live are citizens of Berlin, and, therefore, as a free man, I take pride in the words '*Ich bin ein Berliner.*'"

A million Germans lined the parade route, with 300,000 jamming into the square fronting West Berlin. Two thirds of the population had come out to greet JFK. His speech that day was—for both his listeners and for all those who lived in that time—the greatest of the Cold War. Seeing the Wall itself affected the president physically, shocking him probably even more than he'd expected. He looked "like a man who has just glimpsed Hell," Hugh Sidey observed.

Jack called the time he spent in Berlin and then in Ireland, where he flew next, the happiest days of his life. There, in the country of his ancestors, the first Irish-Catholic American president was welcomed with near ecstatic enthusiasm. Accompanied by his sisters Eunice Shriver and Jean Smith, he made a stop in Dunganstown in County Wexford, site of his Kennedy roots, and then, in Galway, was honored with the Freedom of the City. At the port town of New Ross, he told the crowd gathered to hear him, "When my great-grandfather left here to become a cooper in East Boston, he carried nothing with him except two things—a strong religious faith and a strong desire for liberty. I am glad to say that all of his grandchildren have valued that inheritance."

In England, before going to Birch Grove, Harold Macmillan's residence, to meet with the prime minister, he traveled to Derbyshire to visit the grave of his sister Kathleen. The current Duchess of Devonshire remembers how the presidential helicopter affected one resident of the small rural village: "The wind from that machine blew my chickens away, and I haven't seen them since," the woman complained. At St. Peter's Church there, Jack went to the gravesite and, carrying some flowers for his sister, carefully and painfully went down on his knees to pray.

The fact that Jack Kennedy achieved this historic hat trick— the "peace speech" on nuclear arms, the epic address on civil rights, and the "*Ich bin ein Berliner*" moment—while enduring chronic back pain enhances the nobility of it all. You can see in the documentary footage of the Oval Office scene during the Birmingham crisis a tinge of the torture in the careful way Kennedy carries himself, the deliberate way he rocks his chair. There's nothing easy in his manner.

For ten days in July, Averell Harriman, who'd been the U.S. ambassador in Moscow in the 1940s, negotiated with Nikita Khrushchev a treaty to ban the testing of nuclear weapons in the atmosphere. During those negotiations, recalled Ted Sorensen, "Khrushchev told Harriman that more than anything else, Kennedy's 'Peace Speech'—which the chairman allowed to be rebroadcast throughout Russia and to be published in full in the Moscow press—had paved the way for the treaty."

The treaty outlawed nuclear testing by the USA, USSR, and Great Britain in the atmosphere, outer space, and underwater. On July 25, 1963, envoys from the three powers signed the document, making it official. John Kennedy considered this his greatest achievement.

David Ormsby-Gore, the British ambassador in Washington, traced Kennedy's determination to secure the treaty and his courage in pursuing it to his good friend's own biography. "With all human beings, one of the things that gives confidence is to have been in extreme peril and come well out of it, perhaps on some occasions to have been near death and come back from the brink. I have always noticed that people who have had that kind of experience have a sort of calm; not quite a detachment from life, but a calm attitude to anything that life can throw at them, which is rather significant. Of course, he had had the experience on more than one occasion of being faced by death."

During that summer, as Jack had been traveling, Jackie Kennedy had remained at home pregnant, expecting to deliver her third child in September. Their second, John Fitzgerald Kennedy, Jr., born right after the 1960 election, was now twenty months old. Caroline was almost six. On August 7, Jackie gave birth, five weeks early, to a boy whom they named Patrick. Never strong to begin with, two days later he began to fail. The father held his tiny fingers for two hours as the infant tried to breathe. He was holding them when Patrick died. "He put up quite a fight." Then, "He was a beautiful baby."

Afterward, the president went to his room, having asked to be given time alone. Through the door, Dave Powers could hear him sobbing. Later he would kneel beside Jackie's bed and tell her about the son he'd loved that they now, together, had lost.

There was never a good time to try to come to grips with the situation in Vietnam, and Kennedy had been delaying it. Within days of taking office, he'd signed a national security directive stating that it was our country's policy to "defeat Communist insurgency" in South Vietnam. By 1963 there were twelve thousand U.S. "military advisors" there. However, JFK had resisted calls from South Vietnam's president, Ngo Dinh Diem, to send in combat troops, seeing no merit to that idea. Fully aware that there were gung ho American officers hoping he'd upgrade our status there from "advising" to actually fighting, he had no intention of letting that happen.

"I can remember one particular case," Red Fay recalled. "We were out, I believe it was off of Newport. I think the Blue Angels had just flown over. The president was sitting in his swivel chair in the back of the *Honey Fitz*, and the phone rang next to him. There were some marines that wanted to lead their unit into combat. The situation, they thought, was ideal for an attack, and so, therefore, they wanted to lead it. And, evidently, the standing orders of the president at that time were that our advisors over there were not there to lead Vietnam troops into battle. Fay heard his old navy buddy make it crystal clear that he wanted that order enforced to the *letter*.

But he couldn't abandon Saigon to the Communists and expect

to win a second term. He couldn't afford to be the president who "lost" South Vietnam, just as he'd accused Harry Truman of doing with China. The problem was President Diem. A Roman Catholic, Diem had enjoyed strong support from American Catholics, including Kennedy, since taking command when Vietnam was divided at the Geneva Convention in 1954. Diem was now conducting a campaign of repression against the country's Buddhist majority. In June a seventy-three-year-old Buddhist monk had lit himself on fire in a main Saigon thoroughfare, having moments earlier handed a statement to reporters. "Before closing my eyes to Buddha, I have the honor of presenting my word to President Diem, asking him to be kind and tolerant toward his people and to enforce a policy of religious equality."

President Kennedy realized he could no longer support a regime that was fighting the Communist guerrillas *and* Buddhist monks. Besides this, the Diem government was viewed as hopelessly corrupt, totally under the control of Diem's brother and sister-in-law, the notorious "Dragon Lady," Madame Nhu. Feeling stymied, he had the idea to name his onetime political rival Henry Cabot Lodge as U.S. ambassador. There were clear advantages to this. Lodge lacked any sentimental feelings toward Diem. He was arrogant enough to act decisively. Most important, he wanted a victory, personally as well as nationally. He had the added advantage, for Kennedy, of making the hellish situation in South Vietnam bipartisan.

Something had to be done. Diem and his brother Nhu were leading the country's special forces in raids on Buddhist pagodas in Saigon and other cities, arresting monks and nuns alike. Lodge now represented a group within the Kennedy administration who wanted to back a military coup to topple Diem. The leader of that faction was Averell Harriman, who'd proven himself to Kennedy by winning Khrushchev's agreement in July to the limited nuclear testing ban.

On August 24, Kennedy approved a cable to Saigon authorizing

American support for a military coup against President Diem. It was a cold decision, certainly a stark shift in loyalty. Kennedy had been a backer of Diem from the earliest days of the country's division, and had been a supporter of the American Friends of Vietnam, a lobbying group. Now he was approving his former ally's overthrow. Inside his administration, his decision was never truly cleared by either McNamara or Rusk, and it met with disfavor from Lyndon Johnson.

The cable said: "U.S. Government cannot tolerate situation in which power lies in Nhu's hands. Diem must be given chance to rid himself of Nhu and his coterie and replace them with the best military and political personalities available. If, in spite of your efforts, Diem remains obdurate and refuses, then we must face the possibility that Diem himself cannot be preserved. You will understand that we cannot from Washington give you detailed instructions as to how this operation should proceed, but you will also know we will back you to the hilt on action to achieve our objectives." It was precisely what Lodge wanted: a death warrant.

August was also the month of the extraordinary, epoch-making March on Washington, with its unforgettable "I have a dream" speech delivered with Moses-like fervor by Martin Luther King, Jr., to the crowd of 250,000. The president had done what he could to stave off the possibility of conflict at the event. His efforts had helped swell the numbers of marchers, especially whites, because he'd encouraged Walter Reuther to bring his UAW members. He'd taken steps to accommodate the crowd, reducing the chances of discord by making sure there was both food and bathroom access. And, sensibly, he drew the route from the Washington Monument to the Lincoln Memorial—not to the gates of the White House.

Meeting with the leaders after the speech, Kennedy immediately quoted the most memorable line to show his admiration: "I have a dream," he repeated.

Ben Bradlee accompanied Kennedy when he went the following month to visit Jackie at her mother's house in Newport, where she'd been staying since the loss of their infant boy. It was the Kennedys' tenth wedding anniversary. "This was the first time we'd seen Jackie since the death of little Patrick, and she greeted JFK with by far the most affectionate embrace we had ever seen them give each other. They were not normally demonstrative people, period."

Also in September, Jack attended the Harvard-Columbia football game. He left at halftime to head off for a secret visit to the grave of his lost son, Patrick. He told Ken O'Donnell to make sure no press people were around. When he got to the grave in Brookline, he knelt down and prayed.

It's always difficult to penetrate another person's religious beliefs. This would be especially the case with someone as complex as Jack Kennedy.

Back in his younger years Jack would stay in his pew during Communion because he wasn't in a state of grace. Now, as president, he'd go to mass weekly, but also to confession. When a priest once signaled he'd recognized his distinctive accent, he had a way to evade detection. In future visits to the confession booth, he took a place in line among the Secret Service agents, assuming the confessor would not be quite sure who was telling him what.

When it came to family and loss, his faith regularly showed itself. Mark Dalton was always touched, he said, when Jack stopped by a church to light a candle for Joe Jr. There were often times when friends would catch him losing himself briefly in reveries about the older brother who'd so much paved the way for him. Dave Powers, who saw Jack off to bed so many nights, said that the president would kneel and pray before retiring. One wonders whether he ever echoed St. Augustine's famous prayer: "Give me chastity and continence, but not just now."

Ted Sorensen offered this moral verdict on Jack. "An American President, commander in chief of the world's greatest military power, who during his presidency did not send one combat troop division abroad or drop one bomb, who used his presidency to break down the barriers of religious and racial equality and harmony in this country and to reach out to the victims of poverty and repression, who encouraged Americans to serve their communities and to love their neighbors regardless of the color of their skin, who waged war not on smaller nations but on poverty and illiteracy and mental illness in his own country, and who restored the appeal of politics for the young and sent Peace Corps volunteers overseas to work with the poor and untrained in other countries—was in my book a moral president, regardless of his personal misconduct."

On October 4, Jackie left on a Caribbean cruise aboard Aristotle Onassis's yacht, the *Christina*. The trip offered her a chance to regain her spirits. Jack took her absence as a chance to get to know his children better, and put in time as their babysitter. Pictures taken in the Oval Office show John Jr. peeking out from under the front of his father's desk.

In late October, Kennedy was pounding away for passage of the civil rights bill. At one point, he called Mayor Richard Daley to put pressure on a Chicago congressman who was holding up the measure. Their conversation, packed with old-school politics, was picked up on the White House taping system:

Kennedy: Roland Libonati is sticking it right up us.

Daley: He is?

Kennedy: Yeah, because he's standing with the extreme liberals who are gonna end up with no bill at all. I asked him, "If you'll vote for this package which we got together with the Republicans, [it] gives us about everything we wanted," and he says, "No."

Daley: He'll vote for it. He'll vote for any goddamned thing you want.

Kennedy: (laughs) Well, can you get him?

Daley: I surely can. Where is he? Is he there?

Kennedy: He's in the other room.

Daley: Well, you have Kenny. Tell Kenny to put him on the wire here.

Kennedy: Or would you rather get him when he gets back to his office? That's better. Otherwise, he might think . . .

Daley: That's better. But he'll do it. The last time I told him, "Now look it. I don't give a goddamned what it is. You vote for it, for anything the president wants and this is the way it will be and this the way it's gonna be."

Kennedy: We have a chance to pull this out. Billy [Green] in Philadelphia got Toll. If you can get Libonati.

Using the muscle of his political pals, the same bosses who helped get him to the White House, Kennedy nailed down Democratic members of the House Judiciary Committee. By November, he had gotten it out of the committee, though stymied by the segregationist chairman of the Rules Committee, who refused to bring it to the House floor.

On November 2, Ngo Dinh Diem was killed in the military coup that the United States had signed off on in August. When he learned of the death, and the brutal manner of it, Kennedy bolted from the room in horror. Hearing the coup leader's claim that Diem had taken his own life, Kennedy rejected it outright. He never believed that a fellow Roman Catholic would commit suicide. Ted Sorensen would later say: "Perhaps he should have guessed that, in that part of the world, the overthrow of Diem by the South Vietnamese army could well lead to Diem's death. But I could see from the look of shock and dismay on JFK's face when he heard the news of Diem's assassination that he had no indication or even hint that anything more than Diem's exile was contemplated."

After retreating from the cabinet room, Jack called up Mary Meyer, his sometime mistress and friend. Not wanting to be alone, he spent the rest of the day with her.

Back at his desk after the weekend, he dictated a memorandum of what had happened.

"Monday, November 4, 1963. Over the weekend the coup in Saigon took place. It culminated three months of conversation about a coup, conversation which divided the government here and in Saigon.

"Opposed to the coup was General Taylor, the attorney general, Secretary McNamara to a somewhat lesser degree, John McCone, partly because of an old hostility to Lodge, which causes him to lack confidence in Lodge's judgment, partly as a result of a new hostility because Lodge shifted his station chief. In favor of the coup was State, led by Averell Harriman, George Ball, Roger Hilsman, supported by Michael Forrestal at the White House.

"I feel I must bear a good deal of responsibility for it, beginning with our cables of early August in which we suggested the coup. In my judgment that wire was badly drafted; it should not have been sent on a Saturday. I should not have given my consent to it without a roundtable conference at which McNamara and Taylor could have presented their views. While we did redress that balance in later wires, that first wire encouraged Lodge along a course to which he was in any case inclined."

On the tape, the listener can hear the voices of John Jr., who was almost three, talking with his father. Caroline, six, joins in at the very end:

Kennedy: You want something? Say something. Hello.

John: Hello.

Kennedy: Why do leaves fall?

John: Because it's winter.

Kennedy: No, autumn.

John: Autumn.

Kennedy: And why does the snow come on the ground?

John: Because it's winter.

Kennedy: Why do the leaves turn green?

John: Because it's winter.

Kennedy: Spring. Spring.

John: Spring.

Kennedy: And why do we go to the Cape? Hyannis Port?

John: Because it's winter.

Kennedy: It's summer!

John: It's summer.

Kennedy: Say your horses . . .

Caroline: Your horses.

"I was shocked by the death of Diem and Nhu," Kennedy continued his dictation.

"I'd met Diem with Justice Douglas many years ago. He was an extraordinary character. While he became increasingly difficult in the last months, nevertheless over a ten-year period he'd held his country together, maintained its independence under very adverse conditions. The way he was killed makes it particularly abhorrent. The question now is whether the generals can stay together and build a stable government, or whether . . . the intellectuals, students, et cetera, will turn on the government as repressive and undemocratic in the not too distant future."

The following day he gave Maxwell Taylor, the chairman of the Joint Chiefs, a clear signal of his intentions in Vietnam, offering what he viewed as the limits of American commitment in-country. "He is instinctively against introduction of U.S. forces," Taylor would report. Jack made a similar comment to Arthur Schlesinger. "They want a force of American troops. They say it's necessary in order to restore confidence and maintain morale. But it will be just like Berlin. The troops will march in, the bands will play, the crowds will cheer, and in four days everyone will have forgotten. Then we will be told we have to send in more troops. It's like taking a drink. The effect wears off, and you have to take another."

Yet his exact thoughts about Vietnam remain a mystery. What we do know is his early understanding of the fighting. Motivated by nationalism, the Viet Minh had fought the French, and he'd grasped what was at stake. Why would he make a different assessment of the Viet Cong war against the pro-American Diem? Ken O'Donnell said Kennedy told him he was determined to get out once the election-year politics were behind him. But it's not that simple. Ted Sorensen believed his boss could never have the cynicism about war and human lives that the conflict in Vietnam would turn out to mandate. "I do not believe he knew in his last weeks what he was going to do."

At about this same time, Kennedy called members of the House Rules Committee to the White House. He was interested in getting their insider knowledge about why his legislation, which included the Civil Rights bill, was stalled. Tip O'Neill remembered being asked to come for a drink afterward when Jack spotted him stranded without a ride. The two of them chatted about the old days. Jack was curious about how some of his old boys were doing, the ones who'd been with him in the beginning. He asked about Billy Sutton, Mark Dalton, Joe Healey, John Galvin, and the others. He asked Tip to make sure Billy had a job up in Massachusetts.

The Kennedys spent the Veterans Day weekend with the Bradlees down at their friends' new getaway in Virginia. Jack told Ben he didn't like what he'd heard about Dallas, where he was soon headed, about the way Adlai Stevenson had been spat on, heckled, and jeered when giving a United Nations Day speech there. He felt, he told his friend, that the "mood of the city was ugly." In a front-page editorial, the *Dallas Times Herald* had pronounced the city "disgraced. There is no other way to view the storm-trooper actions of last night's frightening attack on Adlai Stevenson." Governor John Connally called the affair "an affront to common courtesy and decency." And Mayor Earle Cabell pointed out that the demonstrators were "not our kind of folks." Jack allowed White House photographers to take pictures of the family that weekend. One film shows Jackie rehearsing with John Jr. a salute he was practicing, perhaps for when he joined his father that Monday at the Tomb of the Unknown Soldier.

The following Thursday, Jack had invited the film legend Greta Garbo to the White House. Lem Billings had met her on a recent European trip and was thrilled at the prospect of introducing her to his pal. Jack, meanwhile, ever the practical joker, had hatched a plan. The evening was arranged so that Garbo would arrive before Lem, giving Jack a chance to chat with her and lay the groundwork for his scheme.

Kennedy's idea was to convince her to act as if she'd never before set eyes on Billings. The pair of them carried it off for a quite some time before finally taking Lem out of his misery. It is a perfect example of Jack's taking the time, as he often did with his closest friends, to give them a little trouble. Though mildly sadistic—Lem devoted himself to trying to get Garbo to remember the various outings they'd had together, only to have her stare at him blankly—the prank also showed, in an odd way, that Jack cared. And cared enough—he, a president of the United States—to concoct a scheme that was at once so silly and yet so intimate. He'd done such things all his life.

It was a dinner to remember: Jackie, Jack, and Lem—and Garbo. But it would always be a sad memory for Lem. It had taken place on November 13, 1963.

That month, Kennedy hosted his first major campaign meeting for 1964. Included were Bobby, Ted Sorensen, Ken O'Donnell, and Larry O'Brien. It was the same team that had met in Palm Beach and later in Hyannis Port in 1959. Once again, his brother-in-law Steve Smith was to take charge, overall. The effort would be run from the White House, and the theme would be "peace and prosperity."

Kennedy looked forward to running against Senator Barry Goldwater. He was convinced that the conservative Arizonan was just too candid for a presidential candidate and would quickly self-destruct. His bigger worry was Governor Nelson Rockefeller of New York. Told that "Rocky" liked him, Kennedy said it didn't matter. Politics would change that. "He'll end up hating me. That's natural," he said, remembering, perhaps, his own change of heart over Nixon.

President Kennedy was confident. But he also knew that he needed Texas and, perhaps, Georgia—not easy states to get in his corner, given the growing rage of white Southerners against him for his strong stand on civil rights. The polling showed that two thirds of them were deeply hostile, not an easy situation for a man looking to nail down Southern support. It was going to be a tough election. He needed to begin raising money and rousing those yellow-dog Democrats who'd been raised with the party and might still be won over.

Jack spent the next weekend in Palm Beach with Torby Macdonald, now in his fifth term as a Massachusetts congressman. It was a bachelor party fueled by enough bonhomie to induce JFK to croon "The September Song" with extra feeling. That Monday, November 18, he traveled with George Smathers to Miami and Tampa to deliver speeches denouncing Castro and his regime.

"A small band of conspirators has stripped the Cuban people of their freedom and handed over the independence and sovereignty of the Cuban nation to forces beyond the hemisphere. This, and this alone, divides us. As long as it is true, nothing is possible. Once this barrier is removed, everything is possible."

With the trip to Texas ahead of him, Kennedy worried about the South. "I wish I had this fucking thing over with," he complained to Smathers. He also told him, "You've got to live each day like it's your last day on earth."

On November 22, having spent the night in Fort Worth, he agreed to meet outside, before breakfast, with a good crowd of union people. Despite the early morning drizzle, the crowd was warm and enthusiastic. Inside, as the business leaders sipped their coffee, he gave a tough speech on Vietnam. "Without the United States, South Vietnam would collapse overnight."

Whatever concerns he had in the long run, whatever hesitation kept him from committing combat troops, he had those eighteen thousand "advisors" there on the ground. He was also thinking about an exit strategy. The day before, he'd asked his national security aide Michael Forrestal to "organize an in-depth study of every possible option we've got in Vietnam, including how to get out of there."

On the way from Fort Worth to the airport later that morning, Jack grilled Congressman Jim Wright and Governor John Connally about the strange difference in politics between the city he'd just left and the one he was about to enter. Why is Fort Worth so Democratic and Dallas so angrily right-wing? It was his usual curiosity abetted here by fresh reason to wonder. After all, he'd just been given a hero's welcome by the people of one city but remembered only too well Richard Nixon carrying Dallas with 65 percent in 1960. Now, there was the pall cast by the recent ugly treatment of Adlai Stevenson.

While Wright laid some of the blame on the conservative press, especially the *Dallas Morning News,* Connally offered a more so-phisticated assessment of the difference between the two Texas cit-ies. He said it could be traced to their different economies. Fort Worth was still a cowboy town. Dallas, on the other hand, was a white-collar town where people worked in high-rise office build-ings. They identified with the folks on the floor above them, not the guy or woman working next to them in the stockyard or factory. They voted like their managers because they wanted to join them. This explained the shift of the city to the Republicans, a change that Connally understood and that was a precursor of his own ambitions.

Jack was just trying to figure it all out. He was out there in the American landscape, doing what he'd come very much to love, per-haps even more than the public service it allowed. He was on the road, doing the work of an American politician. He had goals, and he needed to be president to reach them.

39

40

Bobby, Jack, Joe Sr., Teddy, and Joe Jr.

41

At the London embassy

42

4

44

Sister Kathleen "Kick" Kennedy

4

CHAPTER SIXTEEN

LEGACY

He was acutely responsive to the romance of history in
the making, to the drama of great events; and to national
sentiment.

—David Cecil, *Young Melbourne*

On a cold Friday night in late November 1963, Teddy White of *Life* magazine traveled through a driving rainstorm from New York to Cape Cod. When he arrived at Hyannis Port, he was received at the main house, Joseph P. Kennedy's. He found the president's widow fully composed despite the horror of the week before. Chuck Spalding was there, Dave Powers and a few others, but they quickly left the guest alone with the woman who had so earnestly invited him.

White would remember her appearance vividly. She wore trim slacks and a beige pullover sweater. Yet it was her eyes he most recalled. "They were wider than pools." She was, of course, beautiful. Her voice, as she spoke to him, was low, and what she said seemed to offer almost total recall.

Jacqueline talked and talked for nearly four hours. Her companion was mesmerized and could barely write fast enough. The story that ran in *Life* was a careful selection from what she told him. He'd been summoned in a situation of the utmost distress as a respected journalist. But he was also a friend, and his instinct was to protect this woman whom he cared about when he dictated on deadline during those first hours of Saturday morning. She was listening to his every word as he called it in, he would confess years later, and she'd pushed hard for the idea of Jack Kennedy's presidency being like Camelot.

Not surprisingly, what was left out of White's story was far more fascinating than the narrative she'd designed. Her monologue had been simultaneously art and accident, and White was an expert assembler of information. But when you see his actual notes, the raw material, what you find is telling.

The piece quotes her as saying to White that "men are a combination of good and bad." Yet it isn't, in fact, how she'd phrased it. "Comb. of bad and good" is what sits there in White's scribbled notes. Why would he transpose it for the magazine? Why did he transcribe it correctly later on? "His mother never really loved him," she said, and that, too, is in the typescript of the handwritten interview, but again, not in the article. "She likes to go around talking about being the daughter of the mayor of Boston, of how she's the ambassador's wife. She didn't love him," Jackie had repeated.

She wanted to explain Jack Kennedy, not as a president, not as a husband, but as a man. It may not have been what she thought she intended, but it was what gripped her. "History made him what he was. He sat and read history." She mentioned his scarlet fever. "This little boy in bed, so much of the time. All the time he was in bed, this little boy was reading history, was reading Marlborough. He devoured the Knights of the Round Table. And he just loved that last song."

She was talking about *Camelot* now, the musical that was a hit on Broadway. The final song was the reprise of "Camelot," and in it was the image that soon came to haunt a nation: "Don't let it be forgot that once there was a spot / for one brief shining moment that was known as Camelot."

Here are more of White's raw notes, jotted quickly as he tried to keep up with her: "History is what made Jack. He was such a simple man. He was complex, too. He had that hero, idealistic side, but then he had that other side, the pragmatic side. His friends were all his old friends. He loved his Irish mafia." She knew his compartmentalized way of living better than anyone.

She also said this: "And then I thought, I mustn't think that bad way. If history made Jack that way, made him see heroes, then other little boys will see." In the shock of tragedy, she was telling her husband's story, as she put it, both the "bad and good."

Aided and abetted by Jackie Kennedy, White produced a thrilling evocation of the fallen president, bringing home the immense loss. Around the world, everyone old enough to this day remembers exactly where they were when they heard the news of the assassination. When the story ran, the readers of *Life,* and then millions more, accepted his widow's vision; they took to their hearts the notion of Camelot—that vanished, shining place presided over by a noble, merry hero.

It was her gift to him. She'd wanted only two monuments to her husband. First, there would be an eternal flame to mark his grave at Arlington National Cemetery. She told White about how, driving across Memorial Bridge to Virginia at night, you can see the Lee Mansion lit up on the side of the hill from "miles and miles away." When Caroline was little, she said, that immense white building had been one of the first things she recognized. Now, below it, there would be the small twinkling light for her father.

The other commemoration she requested was quite different. She'd clearly given it careful thought. NASA's *Apollo 5* mission was set for takeoff in January 1964. The president had mentioned the launch in recent speeches. She asked that her husband's initials be placed on a tiny corner of the great Saturn rocket where no one would even see them.

To White, she also talked about Jack's last look at life, that instant when the end came, out of nowhere during that Dallas motorcade. "You know when he was shot, he had such a wonderful expression on his face," she told him. "You know that wonderful expression he had when they'd ask him a question about one of the ten million gadgets they have on a rocket, just before he answered? He looked puzzled."

I think we know that expression. It was a look he gave when he'd conjured up a witty answer at a press conference. It was the startled but pleased expression of a guy who's just figured something out. His friends as far back as Choate knew it well and remembered it.

Jacqueline Kennedy had come a long way that week. A short piece of film recently unearthed shows us a slender, dark-haired young woman—seemingly no more than a girl—racing to catch up to a gurney. She is a woman chasing after her love.

Within hours she'd assumed the reins of command, designing and staging a magnificent funeral. It was Lincolnesque with its horseless rider, the boots of the lost hero turned backward. There were the drums, relentless, insistent, hammering their bleak reality. Soldiers die to the sound of drums.

"Jackie was extraordinary," Ben Bradlee would write after watching her from close up that weekend. "Sometimes she seemed completely detached, as if she were someone else watching the ceremony of that other person's grief." Still at the age Jack had been when he married her, she was observing the whole scene as if, really, she weren't a part of it.

Jack had, as Arthur Schlesinger described it, "to an exceptional degree, the gift of friendship." As Jim Reed, his navy friend, put it: "each of us had a certain role we were cast into, whether we knew it or not." The night they lost their leader, Ken O'Donnell, Dave Powers, and Larry O'Brien had headed up Wisconsin Avenue to Gawler's Funeral Home to pick out a coffin. The Irish mafia, the men Jack loved, were doing what their people do. The Irish are good with death. That Saturday night—the day after the horror—Dave delighted Jackie with stories of her husband before she knew him, of his endless climbs up the stairs of those wooden "three-deckers" in the old 11th Congressional District. Dave said he'd hoped that Jack would have one day come to *his* wake up in Charlestown.

Ken O'Donnell would be haunted by what he saw as his role in the tragedy. Before Jack had given anyone else a job, he'd handed him his: to protect him. It was impossible to forget that he, Ken O'Donnell, had been in charge of the Secret Service covering his friend, and he'd been the one urging Jack to make the trip to Texas.

I would get to know some of these men who'd been part of Jack's story. Billy Sutton was one, the first guy hired, just off the train from the army. One day in the 1980s, I walked into a back room in Speaker Tip O'Neill's suite of offices up in Boston. There was this little fellow sitting at a table. Moment by moment he would transform himself. One instant, he'd be Adlai Stevenson, gravely addressing the General Assembly. Next, he'd be Rose Kennedy, her voice high and churchy. It was as if she were standing there before me. No wonder Jack had called Billy his "firecracker."

Tip O'Neill, as you can tell from this book, was rich in stories, each shining with a love of the game that bonded him and Kennedy.

Jack's closest friends have helped me answer that question he himself gave for the reason people read biography. What was *he* like?

Once, when I got Charlie Bartlett remembering his friend, he took his glasses off to dry his eyes as he thought back. Here's what Charlie himself wrote in November 1963, upon first hearing the news:

"We had a hero for a friend—and we mourn his loss. Anyone, and fortunately there were so many, who knew him briefly or over long periods, felt that a bright and quickening impulse had come into their life. He had uncommon courage, unfailing humor, a penetrating, ever-curious intelligence, and over all a matchless grace. He was our best. We will remember him always with love and sometimes, as the years pass and the story is retold, with a little wonder."

Chuck Spalding and Jack had been buddies since the year before the war. It was a matter of "chemistry," Chuck said. When I asked him my question, "What was he like?" he said he'd answer by way of a story. It was back when he and his then-wife, Betty, were getting ready to go through divorce, not a good time for them. Still together, though, they were out on the dock one day when Jack joined them for a sail. Spotting their two faces, he said, "Ah, the agony and the ecstasy." That's what one of his closest lifetime pals said Jack Kennedy was like.

I loved hearing Sally Fay, Red's daughter, speak of the joy in her house each time the phone rang and it was Jack Kennedy. "The most charming man I ever knew," George Smathers told me. His old Senate pal was thrilled when I told him how Jack explained liking him, saying the reason was because "he doesn't give a damn." Ben Bradlee, a good friend of mine as well, described Jack as having an "aura of royalty about him."

Robert Kennedy carried on, we know, never stopped trying to keep his brother's spirit alive, until he, too, was stopped. Teddy surprised everyone. Jack had said his kid brother wanted to spend his life "chasing girls in the South of France." But it didn't happen that way. Jack was once asked to pick the greatest senators in history. Of course, he could only look backward. Had he been able to look forward, he might well have included his youngest brother.

Daniel Patrick Moynihan, who served Kennedy as assistant secretary of labor, was the one who said, "There's no point in being Irish if you don't know the world's going to someday break your heart." He carried on Jack's plan to make Pennsylvania Avenue, the presidential inaugural route, a corridor of grandeur. "Make it like Paris," he'd said. Pat once remarked to me, in a very personal way, his feeling about the events of November 1963: "We've never gotten over it." Then, looking at me with generous appreciation, he added, "You've never gotten over it." I saw it as a kind of benediction, an acceptance into something warm and Irish and splendid, a knighthood of the soulful.

In a 2009 national poll, people were asked to say which American president deserves to be added to Mount Rushmore. It's a good question, because it really gets to heroic stature. Who should be there with Washington, Jefferson, Lincoln, and, especially the old "Rough Rider" himself, Teddy Roosevelt? They chose John F. Kennedy.

In July 1969, a fellow volunteer of mine sat on a hillside in Swaziland with a group of local villagers looking at the night sky. He wanted them to sit and watch with him. Finally it arrived overhead, what they were looking for: a small light moving in the distance. It was his countrymen heading to the moon. That Saturn rocket Jack so loved had done its job; so had his Peace Corps.

Twenty years later, the Berlin Wall came down. I was there on a drizzly night that November with the beaten-down East Germans, waiting for the Brandenburg Gate to open. When I asked what "freedom" meant to him, a young man answered, "talking to you." Jack Kennedy would like to have heard that, deserved to, I think.

The Iron Curtain was being ripped aside. Communism was in its death throes. The Cold War was ending without the nuclear war we so feared. We had gotten through it alive, those of us who once hid under those little desks of ours.

Thanks to him, I'd say. He'd come a long way from the kid who caused trouble at boarding school, from being Joe Kennedy's son. In the time of our greatest peril, at the moment of ultimate judgment, an American president kept us from the brink, saved us really, kept the smile from being stricken from the planet.

He did that. He, Jack Kennedy.

ACKNOWLEDGMENTS

The person I owe most for this book's completion is my son Michael Matthews. At a critical juncture, he transformed a mountain of historic material—chapter themes, interview transcripts, oral histories and citations from other sources—into coherent notes. He has a beautiful historic sense.

I want to thank Michele Slung for an editing and literary craft that gave shape and life to my narrative.

I owe my TV producer Tina Urbanski for her role at every stage of *Jack Kennedy*. Taking on this project amid the schedule of six television programs a week is a chore no one can accomplish alone.

I want to thank Helen O'Donnell for providing me with the vast oral history recorded by her father with correspondent Sander Vanocur. Kenneth O'Donnell was at Jack Kennedy's side from that first senate race in 1952 to the end. His sharp political mind is well on display here. It took a reporter of Vanocur's moxie to ask him just the right questions, and ask them he did.

I want to thank the inimitable Vincent Virga for the design and selection of the photographs that give this book its artistic completion. He is a visual choreographer. I want to thank U.S. Congressman

Edward Markey of Massachusetts and Mark Johnson, a teacher of history, for reviewing my manuscript with sharpness and intelligence.

In an important way, this book emerges from my decades of real-time interest in Jack Kennedy. It benefits, of course, from the foundation of research I did for *Kennedy & Nixon*. Two other books have provided sturdy scaffoldings: Nigel Hamilton's *JFK: Reckless Youth*, the best-ever work on Kennedy's early life, and Robert Dallek's *An Unfinished Life*, which reveals for the first time his full medical history.

I need to credit Jon Meacham, author of *Franklin and Winston*, for the inspiration on how to craft this biography from the perspectives of those around him.

Jack Kennedy lived his life in a golden circle of friends and close associates. By bringing together their firsthand memories, I've sought to bring to life the man at their center. For the first-person accounts in this book I interviewed many witnesses to the life of Jack Kennedy: Letitia Baldridge, Charles Bartlett, Benjamin Bradlee, Mark Dalton, Fred and Nancy Dutton, Red Fay, Paul Ferber, John Glenn, Lester Hyman, Peter Kaplan, Patrick Lucey, Rachel "Bunny" Mellon, Thomas P. "Tip" O'Neill, Jr., Dave Powers, Terri Robinson, Tazewell Shepard, George Smathers, Ted Sorensen, Chuck Spalding, Billy Sutton, Bill Wilson, Christopher Lawford, and, especially, Ambassador Jean Kennedy Smith.

For those I could not interview—Torbert Macdonald, James Reed, and Rip Horton—I depended on the oral histories archived at the John F. Kennedy Library. I owe the personal accounts of Lemoyne Billings to the excellent *Jack and Lem: The Untold Story of an Extraordinary Friendship* by David Pitts, as well as the wonderful chapter on the Jack-Lem relationship in *Best of Friends* by David Michaelis.

I benefitted greatly from Thomas P. O'Neill's *Man of the House*, Lawrence F. O'Brien's *No Final Victories*, Red Fay's *The Pleasure of His Company*, Ben Bradlee's *Conversations with Kennedy*, Ted Sorensen's *Counselor*, Deirdre Henderson's *Prelude to Leadership: The European Diary of John F. Kennedy: Summer 1945*, and Arthur Schlesinger's *Journals*.

Other books on John F. Kennedy are essential to any understanding of him. *Jack: The Struggles of John F. Kennedy* by Herbert Parmet, *Kennedy* by Theodore Sorensen, *President Kennedy: Profile of Power* by Richard Reeves, *Mrs. Kennedy* by Barbara Leaming, and *A Thousand Days* and *Robert F. Kennedy and His Times* by Arthur Schlesinger.

I need to thank Lorraine Connelly and Judy Donald of Choate Rosemary Hall for the great help in understanding Jack's early years; David McKean, Tom Putnam, Laurie Austin and Maryrose Grossman of the John F. Kennedy Library and Christopher Peleo-Lazar who did the excellent research there for me.

I also want to thank Phil Griffin, President of MSNBC; *Hardball* executive producer John Reiss; Nancy Nathan, executive producer of *The Chris Matthews Show*; and the committed production teams of both programs.

I want to express my strong gratitude to Jennifer Walsh of William Morris Endeavor for her tremendous professional talent in bringing this project to completion. At Simon & Schuster, I want to thank Nicholas Greene, Jonathan Evans, Nancy Singer, Alexis Welby, Emer Flounders, Rachelle Andujar, Jackie Seow, Elisa Rivlin and Richard Rhorer. Most vital of all, I want to express my esteem for Editor-in-chief Jonathan Karp as editor, friend, pathfinder.

For *Jack Kennedy*, like all the projects and hopes before, I thank Kathleen, to whom this book is dedicated, for forming the loving world in which this project was undertaken and completed.

NOTES

The sources for this book include my interviews for *Kennedy & Nixon*, published in 1996 (Simon & Schuster). In a number of cases—Charlie Bartlett, Ben Bradlee, Ted Sorensen—I returned to the same people for fresh interviews that centered on Jack Kennedy himself. With the passage of time, many of those I interviewed earlier—Billy Sutton, Dave Powers, Mark Dalton, Paul "Red" Fay, George Smathers, and the warmhearted Tip O'Neill—have died. I treasured the opportunity to know them and benefit from their generous accounts of life with Jack. I was able to add to their memories with new interviews with Jean Kennedy Smith, John Glenn, Rachel Mellon, and others.

An extremely powerful resource for this book is the extraordinary collection of taped interviews with Kenneth O'Donnell made available to me by his daughter Helen. I refer to his sourcing as KOD. He was Jack Kennedy's political strategist from the first Senate race in 1952 to the end. He offers a colorful account that gives this book a spine and spring it would not have otherwise. His leads a long list of oral histories (abbreviated herein as "OH"), most of them archived at the John F. Kennedy Library, that cover the man's life from his teenage years onward.

The key documents exhibited in this volume include a binder of chapel notes kept by George St. John, who was headmaster in the years Jack Kennedy attended Choate. Also vital to me are the scribbled and typed notes Theodore H. White kept of his historic interview with Jacqueline Kennedy on the night of November 29, 1963.

A far more expansive source for me is the collection of great books written about John F. Kennedy, works I have come to respect enormously. Each section of this book relies on these remarkable efforts that have come before. Together they provide a scaffold for the new material I have been able to assemble and develop. I want to give full credit to the part these earlier works, some of them truly majestic, played in building the story of Jack Kennedy's rise from rich kid to national hero.

. . . .

CHAPTER ONE: SECOND SON

The greatest achievement in chronicling Jack's younger years is *JFK: Reckless Youth* (New York: Random House, 1992) by Nigel Hamilton. It is a treasure trove of research up to and including his first political race. He did more than anyone to unearth the great story of Jack and his "Muckers Club" at Choate.

There were two other valued sources for this early chapter. The first is Robert Dallek's *An Unfinished Life: John F. Kennedy, 1917–1963* (Boston: Little, Brown, 2003), which reveals Jack Kennedy's medical history. The second is David Pitts's equally revealing *Jack and Lem: John F. Kennedy and Lem Billings: The Untold Story of an Extraordinary Friendship* (Cambridge, MA: Da Capo Press, 2008), which tells the wondrous story of Kennedy's friendship with LeMoyne Billings, his Choate roommate and lifelong companion. I have relied here as before on Herbert Parmet's *Jack: The Struggles of John F. Kennedy* (New York: Dial Press, 1980). Barbara Leaming alerted me in *Jack Kennedy: The Education of a Statesman* (New York: W. W. Norton, 2006) to the power of Winston Churchill in young Jack's imagination and ambition.

. . . .

14 *Joseph Kennedy's handsome eldest boy:* Parmet, p. 31.

14 *Jack Kennedy, almost as soon as he got to Choate:* Examples of JFK's early, wry sense of humor appear in Hamilton, pp. 83–84, 93.

15 *What happened to Jack when:* Robert Kennedy's recollection of his brother's illnesses appears in his foreword to the 1964 edition of John F. Kennedy's *Profiles in Courage* (New York: Harper, 1956), p. 8.

15 *So it was in the sickbed:* Reading King Arthur and Sir Walter Scott, Leaming, p. 17.

16 *Leukemia was one of the grim possibilities:* Dallek, *An Unfinished Life,* p. 77.

16 *"Ratface":* Joan Meyers, ed., *John Fitzgerald Kennedy—As We Remember Him* (New York: Atheneum, 1965), p. 15.

16 *"Gee, you're a great mother":* Rose Kennedy, *Times to Remember* (Garden City, NY: Doubleday, 1974), p. 93. Francis Kellogg, a classmate of Jack's, responded to a Choate class survey and wrote: "I remember clearly one thing which surprised me during my four years at Choate: to the best of my knowledge, I do not believe Jack was ever visited during those four years by either his mother or father."

16 *Chilly and restrictive:* Choate's English influence, Parmet, p. 29.

16 *Perhaps because he suddenly:* JFK's going to church, Hamilton, p. 146.

16 *At night, he knelt next to his bed:* David Michaelis, *The Best of Friends: Profiles of Extraordinary Friendships* (New York: Morrow, 1983), p. 137.

16 *He understood, too:* Parmet, p. 33.

17 *While at the Catholic school:* Leaming, p. 21.

17 *Soon he was getting:* Ralph "Rip" Horton, John F. Kennedy Library Oral History Program.

17 *There would come over his face:* Maurice A. Shea, John F. Kennedy Library Oral History Program.

18 *Lem was a big kid:* Pitts, p. 8.

18 *With all the strength of:* Kennedy and Billings meeting at the *Brief,* Michaelis, p. 132.

18 *He would confide in Lem:* LeMoyne Billings, John F. Kennedy Library Oral History Program.

18   *Jack was willing to divulge:* Lem's family background, Pitts, p. 9.

18   *"God, what a beating I'm taking":* Hamilton, p. 111.

19   *As Joseph Kennedy, Sr., wryly observed:* "As Dad liked to say, with some exasperation, Lem Billings and his battered suitcase arrived that day and never really left . . ." This is taken from Edward Kennedy's published eulogy, May 30, 1981.

19   *Next came Ralph:* Parmet, p. 34.

19   *The rest followed:* Shea OH.

20   *Yet there is another:* Story of the "Muckers Club," Hamilton, pp. 122–32.

20   *Troublemaking by kids:* Public Enemies Number One and Two, Michaelis, pp. 131–32.

20   *Strategically astute:* Muckers as "wheels," Class of 1935 survey conducted in 1985, courtesy of Choate Rosemary Hall Archives. Robert Beach, a classmate of Kennedy's, recalled in a class survey that "the main thesis was that we were such 'wheels' your father couldn't kick us out."

22   *Jack, Lem, and one of the girls:* The barn story, Michaelis, pp. 138–40.

23   *Jack wanted "Most Likely to Succeed":* Shea OH.

23   *In this long-ago microcosm:* Tip O'Neill with William Novak, *Man of the House: The Life and Political Memoirs of Speaker Tip O'Neill* (New York: Random House, 1987), p. 76.

Headmaster George St. John kept a number of loose-leaf binders over the years containing selected choral hymns and sermon notes. Choate archivist Judy Donald allowed me to study and copy from an early page in the binder that contained the essay written by Dean LeBaron Russell Briggs of Harvard, who was St. John's mentor and lifelong hero. It's from this essay, marked "Dean Briggs Essay," that St. John would recite the "Ask not" lines once or twice a year (more on this in Chapter Thirteen notes).

Tom Hawks, a bank president, was a '35 classmate of Jack's. He wrote in a class survey taken in 1985 how angry he was at hearing those familiar words in Jack's January 20, 1961, inaugural address. "What bugged me most was the way he plagiarized (the Head) in his inaugural address. I boil every time I hear the 'ask not' exhortation as being original with Jack. Time and again we all heard the Head say that to the whole Choate family. Jack did not even have the decency to give him credit—and now it is engraved in marble at his final resting place."

CHAPTER TWO: THE TWO JACKS

27   *The blood-count roulette:* Kennedy's health diminished at Princeton, Hamilton, pp. 144–45.

27   *Back he went to:* JFK's stay at Peter Bent Brigham Hospital, Pitts, p. 45.

27   *he spent the remainder:* Parmet, p. 43.

27   *Interestingly, he followed:* Ibid., p. 159.

27   *Jack's new friend was:* Jack and Torby as friends and roommates, Torbert Macdonald, John F. Kennedy Library Oral History Program.

27   *Now at Harvard:* JFK placed poorly in Harvard freshman student election, Rose Kennedy, p. 186.

27   *But then he chalked up:* Chairman of the Smoker, Macdonald OH.

28   *"It was a leadership activity at Harvard":* Said Harvard classmate Jimmy Rousmaniere about the Smoker, Parmet, p. 50.

28   *During his sophomore:* Besting Joe Sr. by being accepted to Spee Club, Hamilton, pp. 205–9.

28   *Demonstrating what we might:* Joe Sr.'s group of Boston friends as described by Ralph Pope in ibid., p. 207.

28   *According to Joe's tutor:* John Kenneth Galbraith said Joe Sr. was "slightly humorless," ibid., p. 165.

28   *And more than that:* Observations of JFK's inquisitive mind at Harvard, Parmet, p. 49.

28   *As Jack started to make:* Meeting Lem Billings at the Stork Club, Pitts, p. 48.

28   *Only in his "Gov":* Initially only serious about government classes, Hamilton, p. 175.

28   *Before an injury sidelined him:* Macdonald practices throwing passes with JFK, Parmet, p. 45.

29   *After spending Jack's freshman year:* Pitts, p. 65.

29   *Jack showed himself willing:* Ibid., p. 54.

30   *"Hi yah, Hitler!":* Dallek, *An Unfinished Life,* p. 51.

30   *His friend even snuck Jack:* Description of Macdonald trying to keep JFK in shape for the swim team is detailed in Parmet, p. 47.

34   *Jack knew the valor Britain:* As late as May of 1963, Jack Kennedy recited verbatim Churchill's lines about Raymond Asquith, surprising Asquith's sister, Violet Bonham Carter, Leaming, pp. 431–32.

35   *Even in front of them:* "decadent," ibid., p. 57.

36   *When the Nazis invaded:* Macdonald OH.

36   *"I don't think he really":* Macdonald on JFK, Hamilton, p. 242.

36   *"The failure to build up":* Parmet, p. 68.

37   *"I do not believe necessarily":* John F. Kennedy, *Why England Slept* (New York: W. Funk, 1940), p. xxiii.

38   Why England Slept: On donating the British royalties, Michael O'Brien, *John F. Kennedy: A Biography* (New York: Thomas Dunne Books, 2005), p. 105.

38   *"Democracy is finished in England":* Joseph P. Kennedy quote, Evan Thomas, *Robert Kennedy: His Life* (New York: Simon & Schuster, 2000), p. 33.

39   *"He loved his youth":* John Buchan, *Pilgrim's Way: An Autobiography* (New York: Carroll & Graf, 1984), p. 60.

CHAPTER THREE: SKIPPER

In this chapter I have relied on the accounts of Jack's navy exploits in Robert Donovan's *PT 109: John F. Kennedy in World War II* (New York: McGraw-Hill, 1961), p. 39.

42   *Look back at Raymond Asquith:* On the life and death of Asquith, Buchan, pp. 49–60.

42   *Jack and Lem Billings were:* Pitts, p. 83.

43   *In fact, the navy had turned:* For a chronology of JFK's struggles to enter the military, the intervention of Joe Sr.'s former London attaché, Captain Alan Kirk, and his entry into Naval Intelligence, Hamilton, pp. 405–6.

43   *His specific distraction:* Inga Arvad's background, Doris Kearns Goodwin, *The Fitzgeralds and the Kennedys* (New York: St. Martin's Press, 1987), pp. 729–30.

43   *"Her conversation was miles":* Hamilton, pp. 684–85.

44   *"He had the charm that makes birds":* Leaming, pp. 122–23.

44   *Struck by the beautiful:* Goodwin, pp. 731–32.

44   *They maintained surveillance:* FBI surveillance on Inga Arvad, Pitts, p. 85.

44   *Hoover's agents bugged:* Pitts, pp. 85–86.

45   *"They shagged my ass back down":* Geoffrey Perret, *Jack: A Life Like No Other* (New York: Random House, 2001), p. 98.

45   *Now, more than ever:* Goodwin, p. 734. "He had become disgusted with the desk jobs . . . and as an awful lot of the fellows that he knows are in active service, and particularly with you in fleet service, he feels that at least he ought to be trying to do something."

45   *"If you can find something you really believe in"*: Inga wrote to Jack, Leaming, p. 131.

46   *"I want to go over"*: Author interview with Paul Ferber.

46   *"I have applied for torpedo boat school"*: Pitts, pp. 95–96.

46   *Bulkeley was looking:* The makeup of the PT officers, Goodwin p. 747.

46   *He and Joe had:* Harvard intercollegiate sailing team, O'Brien, *John F. Kennedy,* p. 80.

46   *After they completed:* JFK orders to stay stateside, Goodwin, p. 749.

46   *This time, political rescue:* Senator David I. Walsh, Dallek, *An Unfinished Life,* p. 89.

47   *Even going at half speed:* Goodwin, p. 748.

47   *"I'm rather glad to be on my way"*: Jack letter to Lem, Pitts, p. 96.

47   *"I had been praising the lord"*: Ibid., pp. 96–97.

48   *Lieutenant (JG) Kennedy found:* United with fellow officers in South Pacific, Hamilton, p. 534.

48   *"Do you realize that if what you did"*: Red Fay quote, ibid., p. 516.

49   *One day Bill Battle:* Visiting the chaplain, William Battle, John F. Kennedy Library Oral History Program.

49   *"Jack was a big letter writer"*: Johnny Iles quote, Goodwin, p. 751.

49   *But Jack would join other:* Account of going to church near Sesape Island, Donovan, p. 39.

49   *"Getting out every night on patrol"*: Letter from JFK to parents, Goodwin, p. 752.

49   *"That laugh of his"*: Red Fay quote, Hamilton, p. 629.

49   *"There was an aura around him"*: Jim Reed quote, ibid., p. 544.

49   *"Get acquainted with this damn war"*: JFK to Johnny Iles, ibid., p. 518.

50   *"Just had an inspection by an Admiral"*: Letter to Inga, Dallek, *An Unfinished Life,* p. 93.

50   *"His back was troubling him, he wasn't well"*: Jim Reed quote, Hamilton, p. 629.

50   *Jack Kennedy often slept with a plywood board:* Johnny Iles quote, ibid., p. 518.

50   *In another officer's:* Recalling Jack's corset, Joan and Clay Blair, Jr., *The Search for JFK* (New York: Putnam, 1974), pp. 179–81.

50   *"I've been shafted"*: Dick Keresey quote, Kennedy Library Panel, June 27, 2005.

50   *"What's the purpose of having the conflict":* Red Fay recalled, Hamilton, p. 629.

50   *"We'd sit in a corner and I'd recall":* Blair, p. 191.

51   *"He had a way of really picking":* Goodwin, p. 752.

51   *"He loved sitting around talking":* Hamilton, p. 543.

51   *There were twelve crewmen:* Description of Jack's command vessel, thirteen men including JFK on *PT-109,* Donovan, p. 128.

51   *"Lenny, look at this":* JFK tells executive officer, ibid., p. 210.

51   *"Sound general quarters!":* JFK quote, ibid., p. 212.

51   *"Who's aboard?":* JFK quote, Goodwin, p. 758.

52   *"You go on":* Pappy McMahon quote, Hamilton, p. 578.

52   *When dawn came:* Goodwin, p. 759.

53   *Each man was well aware:* Japanese treatment of prisoners, Donovan, p. 160.

53   *"There's nothing in the book":* Maguire account, ibid., p. 158.

53   *Their skipper's solution:* Ibid., p. 162.

53   *"The rest of you can swim together":* Ibid., p. 162.

54   *As McMahon floated on his back:* McMahon's account of JFK saving his life, ibid., p. 166.

54   *Plum Pudding Island:* Ross description, Hamilton, p. 582.

54   *And when he went to stand:* Vomiting source, Donovan, p. 165.

54   *"George Ross has lost his life":* Red Fay's prematurely eulogizing JFK, ibid., pp. 169–70.

54   *"The next morning we heard":* Jim Reed quote, Hamilton, pp. 575–76.

54   *"How are we going to":* JFK quote, Donovan, p. 170.

55   *Hanging his .38 pistol:* Going on patrol, ibid., p. 172.

55   *Kennedy reached his destination:* Out on patrol, ibid., p. 177.

55   *He arrived at noontime:* Ibid., p. 177.

55   *"Barney, you try it tonight":* Ibid., p. 177.

55   *The day after that:* Ibid., p. 181.

55   *There, they came upon:* Finding canoe, water, crackers, Goodwin, p. 760.

55   *Exhausted, Ross fell asleep:* Hamilton, pp. 587–88.

55   *This time he was greeted:* Donovan, p. 191.

56   *NAURO ISL NATIVE:* Goodwin, p. 760.

56   *"On His Majesty's Service":* Ibid., p. 761.

56   *"As a captain":* Dick Keresey quote, Keresey, "Farthest Forward," *American Heritage* 49, no. 4 (July/August 1998).

56   *Jack had his own account:* Letter to Inga, Hamilton, pp. 616–17.

59   *"proven himself on foreign soil":* Hometown booster quote, Red Fay, *The Pleasure of His Company* (New York: Harper & Row, 1966), pp. 156–57.

59   *"On the bright side":* Letter from JFK to his parents, Hamilton, p. 611.

60   *"We have been having a difficult time":* Letter from JFK to Lem, Pitts, p. 99.

60   *At the same time he got off a letter:* Jack letter to Lem's mother, ibid.

60   *Before leaving the South Pacific:* Describe getting crew members back to States, Hamilton, p. 646.

60   *"chronic disc disease":* Thomas Fleming, "John F. Kennedy's PT-109 Disaster," *Military History Quarterly,* February 8, 2011.

60   *"His skin had turned yellow":* Macdonald description, Hamilton, p. 655.

61   *"extremely heroic conduct":* Parmet, p. 121.

61   *"That wound was a savage wound":* Ibid., p. 122.

61   *"I'll never forget Jack sitting":* Spalding quote, Hamilton, p. 640.

61   *That August, Joe Jr. was killed:* Ibid., pp. 659–60.

61   *Jack, up at Hyannis Port:* Ibid., p. 662.

62   *"clenching and unclenching his fists":* Ibid., p. 660.

62   *A month later, another terrible:* Leaming, pp. 161–62.

63   *"greatest campaign manager":* Author interview with Billy Sutton.

CHAPTER FOUR: War Hero

This chapter benefits from a diary Jack Kennedy kept of his travels through Europe in 1945 and the early weeks of his race for Congress. It was published and edited by Deirdre Henderson as *Prelude to Leadership: The European Diary of John F. Kennedy, Summer 1945* (Washington, DC: Regnery, 1995). The jotted-down notes contained here are priceless clues to Jack's postwar thinking, also a wonderful clue to his studious approach to his new career in politics. I cite it as *Diary*.

The topic is Jack Kennedy's first race for Congress. Here again, as in preceding chapters, I have relied on Nigel Hamilton's remarkable reporting.

. . . .

66   *"It was written all over the sky":* Hamilton, p. 543.

66   *"I think there was probably a serious side to Kennedy":* Ibid., p. 623.

66   *All of the other old troubles continued:* Parmet, p. 151.

68   *Curley, now, was about to abandon:* Joe Sr. used former Boston police chief Joseph Timilty as his go-between, Hamilton, p. 674.

69   *His father wrangled him a job:* Parmet, p. 131.

69   *"from the point of view of the ordinary GI":* Diary, p. 85.

70   *"I'm not talking about Bohlen":* Author interview with Paul Fay.

72   *"We must face the truth that the people":* JFK letter to war buddies, Arthur M. Schlesinger, Jr., *A Thousand Days: John F. Kennedy in the White House* (Boston: Houghton Mifflin, 1965), p. 88.

72   *"Either wittingly or unwittingly":* Hamilton, p. 703.

73   *"He asked every sort of question":* Barbara Ward Jackson, John F. Kennedy Library Oral History Program.

73   *"We have suffered the loss of nearly 8 hundred thousand young men":* Diary, p. 3.

74   *"The clash may be finally and indefinitely postponed":* Ibid., pp. 7–8.

74   *"Mr. Roosevelt has contributed greatly to the end of Capitalism":* Ibid., p. 10.

74   *"People did not realize what was going on in the concentration camps":* Ibid., p. 58.

74   *But he predicted the Red Army's treatment:* Ibid., p. 56.

74   *"scared the hell out":* Hamilton, p. 722.

74   *"He made me speak into it":* Horton OH.

75   *"I've made up my mind":* Hamilton, p. 689.

75   *"He was never pushed off ":* Ibid., pp. 702–3.

75   *"A lot of stories have been written":* Ibid., p. 673.

75   *When Jack asked Torby Macdonald:* Macdonald OH.

75   *"I tell you, Dad is ready right now":* Hamilton, p. 679.

76   *"Although Jack shammed indifference":* Fay, pp. 2–4.

76   *"I had never lived very much in the district":* Presidential recordings, John F. Kennedy Library.

77   *"He was very clear about his decision":* Charles Bartlett, John F. Kennedy Library Oral History Program.

77   *"A reporter is reporting what happens":* Presidential recordings, John F. Kennedy Library.

77   *Writing his stump speech himself:* Ibid. "The first speech I ever gave was on 'England, Ireland, and Germany: Victor, Neutral, and Vanquished.' It took me three weeks to write and was given at an American Legion post."

78   *"For all Irish immigrants":* Ibid.

78   *"I had in politics, to begin with"*: Ibid.

78   *"Says I'll be murdered"*: Diary, pp. 79–80.

79   *In politics you don't have friends:* Ibid., p. 80.

79   *"The one great failure of American government is the government of critics"*: Ibid., p. 83.

79   *The shrewd first hire was Billy Sutton:* Billy Sutton, John F. Kennedy Library Oral History Program.

80   *The person most surprised by this was his father:* Goodwin, p. 828.

80   *The fact that he was a returning:* Dave Powers in the Flying Tigers, Bart Barnes, "JFK Aide David Francis Powers Dies at 85," *Washington Post*, March 28, 1998.

80   *"I think I know how you feel"*: Jack's appearance before a group of Gold Star Mothers, Goodwin, p. 823.

80   *Not surprisingly, the daily slog of introducing:* Sutton OH.

81   *"I couldn't believe this skinny"*: O'Neill, p. 73.

81   *"wasn't looking healthy"*: Sutton int.

81   *"skeleton"*: Mark Dalton description of JFK, Hamilton, pp. 747–48.

81   *"My father thought I was hopeless"*: John F. Kennedy's January 5, 1960, interview with Ben Bradlee.

81   *"This impatience that he passed on"*: Spalding quote, Hamilton, p. 690.

82   *"even though I was a Republican"*: Red Fay quote, ibid., p. 745.

82   *"My God"*: JFK had forgotten to file his nomination papers, Fay, p. 147.

82   *Kennedy pulled off other escapades:* Joe Russo newspaper ad, *Boston* magazine, June 1993.

83   *Tip O'Neill recalled a far more daunting:* O'Neill, p. 77. "During the campaign, the Kennedys flooded the district with copies of that article [John Hersey's on *PT-109*] and sent reprints to every returning veteran. Using the mails to send out campaign literature was a new and expensive proposition. Normally, a volunteer would give it out on the street or hang a flyer on your door. Naturally, the Hersey article served as a good reminder that only one of the candidates has much of a war record."

83   *Jack's father and mother:* Tea party at Hotel Commander, Goodwin, p. 830.

83   *Kennedy was starting:* O'Neill, p. 76. "Jack Kennedy, of course, was a Democrat. But looking back on his congressional campaign, and on his later campaigns for the Senate and then for the presidency, I'd have to say that he was only nominally a Democrat. He was a Kennedy, which was more than a family affiliation. It quickly developed into an entire po-

litical party, with its own people, its own agenda, and its own strategies."

84 *"He was probably the first":* Hamilton, p. 756.

85 *"I guess I'm the only one":* Peter Collier and David Horowitz, *The Kennedys: An American Drama* (New York: Summit Books, 1984), p. 153.

85 *"Womanpower":* O'Neill, p. 78.

85 *"They would scream":* Fay quote, Hamilton, p. 767.

85 *"My chief opponents":* Presidential recordings, John F. Kennedy Library.

85 *"We were constantly":* Reardon quote, Hamilton, p. 757.

86 *"Remember, we were all":* Billings quote, ibid., p. 769.

87 *"fighting conservative":* Diary, p. 10.

87 *"What about Communism?":* Hamilton, p. 774.

CHAPTER FIVE: COLD WARRIOR

89 *Jack Kennedy knew well before:* Parmet, p. 147.

89 *Besides, he'd formed:* Joseph P. Healey, John F. Kennedy Oral History Program. "I know he had felt a particularly warm regard and feeling for Senator Saltonstall, who had been very helpful to him in his years in Washington."

91 *"Don't you think":* Sutton OH.

92 *"Stop 'n' Shop":* Sutton int.

92 *Richard Nixon had just beaten:* Roger Morris, *Richard Milhous Nixon: The Rise of an American Politician* (New York: Holt, 1990), p. 293.

92 *"So you're the guy":* Sutton int.

93 *"How's it feel?":* Ibid.

93 *"John wanted to know":* Author interview with Mark Dalton.

94 *"People have always said":* Ibid.

94 *"Listen to this fellow":* Ibid.

94 *"I'd like you to meet Richard Nixon of California":* Ibid.

94 *In the coming years Jack would be:* Author interview with Ambassador Jean Kennedy Smith.

94 *"'Kennedy is courageous'":* Mark Dalton, John F. Kennedy Library Oral History Program.

94 *"I told him that day":* Sutton OH.

94 *"You can imagine":* Dalton OH.

94 McKeesport debate: *McKeesport Daily News*, April 17 and 25, 1947; July 21, 1960.

100 *"So many people said":* Mary Davis, John F. Kennedy Library Oral History Program.

100 *"And then I remember":* Kay Halle, John F. Kennedy Library Oral History Program.

101 *"He was very particular":* Sutton OH.

101 *"I would say that":* Davis OH.

102 *"I got a call from":* Healey OH.

102 *"I guess I'm going":* Ibid.

102 *"My strong reaction":* Parmet, p. 183.

103 *"lived for some ten years":* Healey OH.

103 *"Curley was crooked":* Author conversation with Thomas P. O'Neill, Jr.

103 *"I don't know whether":* Edmund S. Muskie, John F. Kennedy Library Oral History Program.

103 *"I'm going to debate":* Dalton int.

104 *"I was never so":* Davis OH.

105 *"At the hearing":* Author interview with Timothy J. "Ted" Reardon.

105 *"He was not feeling well":* Davis OH.

105 *"Emaciated!":* Author interview with George Smathers.

105 *For a bon voyage:* Jonathan Aitken, *Nixon: A Life* (London: Weidenfeld and Nicolson, 1993), p. 136.

106 *"That American friend":* Leaming, p. 192.

106 *On those nights:* Davis OH.

106 *"He was someone":* Ibid.

106 *"Thinking about girls":* Sutton int.

107 *"He did have a lot":* Davis OH.

107 *"He used to enjoy":* Bartlett OH.

107 *Confiding that he voted:* Ted Sorensen, *Counselor: A Life at the Edge of History* (New York: Harper, 2008), pp. 146–47. Ted Sorensen reveals that in *Profiles in Courage* Kennedy was referring to Smathers and "decided, for reasons of senatorial courtesy, not to identify in his opening chapter the name of the fellow senator 'who acknowledged to him one day during a roll call that he voted with the special interests on every issue, hoping that, by election, all of them added together would constitute nearly a majority that would remember him favorably while the other members of the public would never know about it, much less remember his vote against their welfare.' I see no reason for anonymity now: It was his close friend, the late Senator George Smathers of Florida. Maybe Smathers was joking when he said that; maybe not."

107 *"because he doesn't give a damn"*: Bartlett OH.

108 *"deeply preoccupied by death"*: Smathers int.

108 "Quick": Ibid.

108 *"It was a bright, shining day"*: Reardon int.

108 *"Unless I'm very mistaken"*: Joseph W. Alsop, John F. Kennedy Library Oral History Program.

108 *"He used to turn green"*: Ibid.

108 *Billy Sutton recalls:* Sutton OH.

109 *"Did you ever read"*: Dalton OH.

109 *"As I look back"*: Ibid.

109 *"Another day I can"*: Ibid.

110 *"He was in terrible pain"*: Goodwin, pp. 742–44.

110 *"He always heard the footsteps"*: Collier and Horowitz, pp. 207–9.

110 *One of those who thrilled:* Kenny O'Donnell background, Thomas, p. 50.

110 *"took on the American Legion"*: KOD.

110 *"When we've got the map"*: Kenneth P. O'Donnell and David F. Powers with Joe McCarthy, *"Johnny, We Hardly Knew Ye": Memories of John Fitzgerald Kennedy* (Boston: Little, Brown, 1973), pp. 77–79.

111 *"the Russians, by their actions"*: General Lucius D. Clay quote, Perret, p. 156.

111 *Back home, the pursuit:* Nixon's exposure of Hiss, account of Hiss case, drawn from Stephen E. Ambrose, *Nixon: Volume I: The Education of a Politician 1913–1962* (New York: Simon & Schuster, 1987), pp. 169–72, and Allen Weinstein, *Perjury: The Hiss-Chambers Case* (New York: Random House, 1997), pp. 5–7.

111 *For denying that:* Parmet, p. 245. In February 1952, a speaker at an anniversary evening at Kennedy's Harvard club told the gathered alumni how proud he was that their college had never produced "a Joseph McCarthy or an Alger Hiss." Kennedy jumped to his feet. "How dare you couple the name of a great American patriot with that of a traitor!" Angry, he left the dinner early.

111 *"The responsibility for the failure"*: Congressional Record, January 29, 1949.

112 *"a sick Roosevelt"*: Parmet, p. 210.

113 *"Isn't this something"*: Bill Arnold, *Back When It All Began: The Early Nixon Years* (New York: Vantage Press, 1975), p. 14.

113 *Jack wanted what Nixon now had:* George Smathers, John F. Kennedy Library Oral History Program. "I think Jack was that competitive. When

I won, he figured he could do it. And at the same time in 1950 when I won my race—my big race was in the primary in May—Nixon ran for the Senate in California against Helen Gahagan Douglas. . . . And I think all of that worked on Jack and started him with the idea that when the time came he would run."

113   *"This rivalry developed":* Dalton OH.

113   *"I think the thing":* Sutton OH.

113   *"I'm up or out":* Lawrence O'Brien, *No Final Victories: A Life in Politics— from John F. Kennedy to Watergate* (Garden City, NY: Doubleday, 1974), p. 17.

113   *"I'm going to use":* Smathers int.

CHAPTER SIX: BOBBY

115   *Whichever happened:* Healey OH. Joseph Healey: "I remember him saying to me flatly that regardless of what was going to happen in terms of what the then incumbent governor of Massachusetts, Paul Dever, was planning to do, that he was not going to run for another term as congressman. He said to me one day, and I think that these are his exact words, 'I would rather run for governor or the Senate and lose and take the shot, than to go back and serve another term as congressman.'"

116   *"I've decided not to run":* O'Neill, p. 105.

116   *"pain in the ass":* Collier and Horowitz, p. 155.

117   *As Jack traveled with his brother:* Schlesinger, *A Thousand Days*, p. 120.

117   *More important:* Getting to know RFK on Indochina trip, Arthur M. Schlesinger, Jr., *Robert Kennedy and His Times* (Boston: Houghton Mifflin, 1978), pp. 90–93.

117   *As Jack was flown from Tokyo:* Addison's complications and evacuation to Okinawa, Collier and Horowitz, p. 156, and Bobby Kennedy's foreword, *Profiles in Courage*, pp. xv–xvi.

117   *"worms":* Referring to members in Congress, O'Brien, *No Final Victories*, p. 17.

117   *He'd already begun spending:* KOD.

118   *"if he was going to get anywhere":* Charles Spalding, John F. Kennedy Library Oral History Program.

118   *"So, I think, he made":* Ibid.

118   *When I was in Boston last week: Meet the Press*, December 2, 1951.

119   *"You can never defeat the Communist":* Ibid.

120 *"unconscious of the fact":* Boston Globe, November 20, 1951.

121 *The very first recruit:* O'Brien, *No Final Victories,* pp. 11–14.

121 *One day on Capitol Hill:* Ibid., p. 18. ". . . [O]n a Sunday in March we had dinner at Kelly's Lobster House in nearby Holyoke. Kennedy was not long in getting to the point. 'Larry, I'm not going to stay in the House,' he told me. 'I'm not challenged there. It's up or out for me. I'm definitely going to run for state-wide office next year. I don't know many people in western Massachusetts and I'd like your help.' 'What are you running for?' I asked. 'I don't know yet,' he admitted. 'I want to run against Lodge, but if Dever makes that race I'll run for governor.'"

122 *Larry O'Brien:* "Republicans were respectable. Republicans didn't get thrown in jail like Jim Curley . . . ," ibid., p. 29.

122 *"Larry, I don't look forward":* Ibid., p. 27.

122 *"For the Kennedys":* Jack Newfield, *Robert Kennedy: A Memoir* (New York: Dutton, 1969), p. 42.

123 *"He called me and said":* KOD.

123 *"lace-curtain":* Ibid.

124 *"He started getting our attention":* Ibid.

125 *"Lodge, killing off Walsh":* Ibid.

126 *Mark Dalton:* Campaign manager of 1946, O'Brien, *John F. Kennedy,* p. 193.

127 *Therefore, the first thing:* KOD. O'Donnell: "I had said to Dalton, look we need to name a secretary or leader in each community to be a Kennedy man and then that person can form committees and set up events, but we can't be sitting in this office doing it from 10 Post Office Square. Well, Mark Dalton would not even ask either the father or candidate if we could begin to do it, he was too afraid of them. I had nobody to get any action from. I would tell this [to] Dalton, Dalton would agree and say he would ask the old man or Jack, but he never would. He'd go to Morrissey, who'd bury it and nothing ever happened."

127 *He wouldn't fire Dalton:* Dalton OH. "The major thing at the time which came as a very grave disappointment and a very grave blow to me was that a release had been prepared by John Galvin announcing that I was the campaign manager of John Kennedy's campaign for the Senate. John Kennedy never spoke to me, but John Kennedy would not issue that release."

127 *If Dalton was too weak:* KOD. "I had told Bobby you got to come up here,

this is just chaos. Dalton can't handle it, he's got to go and you've got to take over."

128   *"We arrived at the Ritz":* Healey OH.

128   *a smart combination:* The teas, Parmet, p. 250.

129   *As David Powers would note:* KOD. Dave Powers, as said to Sander Vanocur, saw that "the success of these receptions was because the only thing these poor working ever get in the mail was a bill. He said when some of these people got an invitation to have tea with the Kennedys, they were amazed. It was great, because these are all very poor people."

130   *"You're talking two or three":* Ibid.

130   *X-rays taken of Jack's spine:* X-rays are available for December 14, 1944, and November 6, 1950, medical records of Dr. Janet Travell at the John F. Kennedy Library.

131   *"I must say":* Bartlett OH.

131   *"The whole operation":* KOD.

131   *"I knew the Kennedys well enough":* Ibid.

131   *He phoned Bobby:* Ibid.

131   *Bobby hated what:* Ibid. "He [Bobby] had no intention of coming up. He gave me the devil. He was really mad, he wanted me to do it, but it had to be him. It had to be someone with the authority to take on the father."

131   *Now that Bobby seemingly:* Ibid. In a car ride meeting in mid-April, "he [Kennedy] threw Frank Morrissey out of the car . . . it was Bob Kennedy, the congressman, and myself and I had really, this was the closest I'd really seen him, in my life to this moment, or had substantive discussion with him. I recollect he was irritated and as I look back I think he was irritated because he felt I had in a sense been telling tales out of school to his brother, who was reporting to his father, perhaps instead of telling him, who I really worked for."

132   *"As far as I'm concerned":* Ibid.

132   *"That was the day that Bobby":* Ibid.

132   *"Bobby, as I recall":* Ibid.

132   *"He got in the car":* Dalton int.

133   *"He didn't like the building":* KOD.

133   *"I decided that I could":* Dalton OH.

133   *"I didn't become involved":* Schlesinger, *Robert Kennedy and His Times,* p. 94.

133 *This was, just for the record:* Bobby's work on 1946 campaign, ibid., p. 64.

134 *"Yes, Dad":* Thomas, p. 60.

134 *"Our secretaries were making":* O'Brien, *No Final Victories,* p. 36.

134 *At their April 6 meeting:* KOD.

136 *"Lodge was always on the popular side":* Horton OH.

136 *"Lodge's Dodges":* Ted Reardon took down the leather loose-leaf binder from the top shelf of his closet to show me it. It was nearly a half century since it had been put to very good political use.

136 *"The major credit belongs":* Healey OH.

136 *"Any decision you wanted":* KOD.

137 *"How much money":* Ibid.

138 *"Don't give in to them":* Ibid.

138 *"Nobody went to one":* Ibid.

138 *"The 'tea party' technique":* Fraser OH.

138 *The reason, according to O'Donnell:* KOD.

139 *"We appreciated the fact":* Ibid.

139 *"We'd be in those homes":* Ibid.

140 *"kicked the living hell":* Matthews, p. 88.

140 *Here Joe Kennedy:* Ibid., p. 87.

141 *"buy a fuckin'":* Ibid.

141 *"100 percent":* Ibid.

141 *"Well, for Christ's sake":* Alastair Forbes, John F. Kennedy Oral History Program.

141 *"I told them I'd go up":* William F. Buckley, Jr., *Boston Sunday Globe,* September 30, 1962.

142 *"Dear Dick: I was tremendously":* Letter courtesy of Richard M. Nixon Library and Birthplace.

142 *"was the man":* Parmet, p. 250.

142 *"a Joseph McCarthy or an Alger Hiss":* Ibid., p. 245.

143 *"You and your . . . sheeny friends":* Ibid., p. 251. Transcript, Mutual Broadcasting Network, February 6, 1951, Pre-Presidential Papers, Box 95, John F. Kennedy Library.

143 *"He didn't have to":* O'Neill, p. 119.

144 *"the Rabbi":* Parmet, p. 248.

144 *"You can't stop a whispering":* KOD.

144 *"They have problems":* Ibid.

144 *In October he made:* Ibid.

144   *"He was in intense pain":* John Galvin, John F. Kennedy Oral History Program.

144   *"handsomest":* United Press International report in *Boston Globe,* July 2, 1952.

145   *"'It looks like Eisenhower's'":* Macdonald OH.

145   *"John Barry, a well-known writer":* KOD.

145   *"Well, all hell broke loose":* Ibid.

145   *"Finally, he got so frustrated":* Ibid.

148   *"That guy must never sleep":* Robert Caro, John F. Kennedy Oral History Program.

148   *"The senator-elect got up":* KOD.

CHAPTER SEVEN: MAGIC

151   *"Mary, now don't be silly":* O'Neill, pp. 117–18.

152   *"They were all experienced":* Davis OH.

154   *"If you work for a politician":* O'Brien, *No Final Victories,* p. 40.

155   *"I'd go down to his office":* Smathers OH.

156   *"His mind was on bigger things":* Ibid.

157   *"ability to write in clear":* Sorensen, *Counselor,* p. 96.

157   *"Jack had the ability":* Reardon int.

158   *"he was soft on Senator Joe McCarthy":* Sorensen, *Counselor,* pp. 98–99.

159   *"He was much the same":* Ibid., pp. 102–3.

159   *"Few could realize":* Ibid., p. 109.

159   *"During my first year":* Ibid., pp. 103–4.

159   *"I do not remember":* Ibid., p. 102.

160   *"The thing to remember":* Author interview with Charles Bartlett.

160   *"Black Jack" Bouvier:* Leaming, pp. 4–5.

160   *Jackie, who'd spent:* Ibid., pp. 5–8.

161   *While he was wooing her:* Ibid., pp. 8–9.

162   *"Jack appreciated her":* Dallek, *An Unfinished Life,* p. 193.

162   *"Jackie was certainly very":* Forbes OH.

162   *"There was this beautiful girl":* Bartlett int.

162   *"Well, she knew what":* Ibid.

163   *"I gave everything a good deal":* Fay, p. 160.

163   *In fact, with an eye:* O'Donnell and Powers, p. 95.

163   *"They haven't seen you since":* KOD.

164   *"I said, 'God, she's a fantastic-looking woman'":* Red Fay, John F. Kennedy Oral History Program.

164 *"Almost across the street from":* Fay, p. 152.

165 *"I want to tell you":* Ibid., p. 153.

165 *"Torby Macdonald stood up":* Fay OH.

165 *"There were only a few political":* KOD.

166 *"She was terribly young":* Pitts, p. 137.

166 *Chuck Spalding had his own telling:* Spalding OH.

166 *"This would be a helluva":* Thomas Reeves, *A Question of Character: A Life of John F. Kennedy* (New York: Free Press, 1991), p. 114.

166 *"When Jack and Jacqueline":* Fay, p. 151.

167 *"they spoiled him":* Bartlett int.

167 *"He saw her as a kindred spirit":* Collier and Horowitz, p. 233. Based on interview with Lem Billings.

CHAPTER EIGHT: SURVIVAL

171 *"The story circulated":* KOD.

171 *"I knew Jack was serious":* O'Neill, p. 90.

171 *"After he had been in the Senate":* Sorensen, *Counselor,* p. 145.

171 *Kennedy had come upon accounts:* John Quincy Adams story, Kennedy, *Profiles in Courage,* 29–50.

172 *"If we do not stand firm":* Remarks of Senator John F. Kennedy at Boston College, Chestnut Hill, Massachusetts, February 1, 1953.

173 *He also challenged the Republicans':* Parmet, p. 282. "Under these circumstances, we must ask how the new [Secretary of State Jim Foster] Dulles policy and its dependence upon the threat of atomic retaliation will fare in these areas of guerilla warfare. At what point would the threat of atomic weapons be used in the struggles in Southeast Asia—in French Indochina—particularly where the chief burden is carried on the one side by native communists and on the other by the troops of a Western power, which once held the country under colonial rule?"

173 *"To pour money, material":* JFK speech on the Senate floor, April 6, 1954.

175 *"My good friends":* Joseph R. McCarthy in response to Edward R. Murrow, CBS, April 6, 1954.

176 *"The reason why we find":* Joseph R. McCarthy speech, Wheeling, West Virginia, February 9, 1950.

177 *"not fit to wear that uniform":* McCarthy quote, Zwicker hearing, February 1954.

178 *A close friend of Bobby's:* Sorensen, *Counselor,* p. 152.

179 *"Senator McCarthy and Mr. Cohn":* Schlesinger, *Robert Kennedy and His Times,* p. 113.

180 *"He was told to sit down":* KOD.

180 *"political suicide":* Ibid.

180 *"to avoid the vote":* Ibid.

181 *"I was in the Bellevue bar":* Ibid.

182 *"JFK knew that if he voted":* Sorensen, *Counselor,* p. 152.

182 *According to the historian:* Dallek, *An Unfinished Life,* p. 196. "He could not bend down to pull a sock on his left foot and he had to climb and descend stairs moving sideways."

183 *"I don't understand Jack's":* Bartlett int.

183 *"This is the one that kills":* O'Brien, *No Final Victories,* p. 45.

183 *"They said the best thing":* Galvin OH.

184 *"empty suit":* Sorensen, *Counselor,* pp. 127–28.

185 *"'sometimes party asks'":* Ibid.

185 *Late that summer:* KOD.

185 *"Furcolo told him":* Ibid.

186 *"We'd been building up":* Ibid.

187 *On October 10:* Dallek, *An Unfinished Life,* p. 196.

187 *"I kept pushing and":* KOD.

187 *"the only wrong political move":* Powers and O'Donnell, pp. 85–86.

187 *The back operation:* Dallek, *An Unfinished Life,* p. 196.

187 *The odds made by the political wise guys:* KOD.

188 *"the doctors didn't expect him":* Evelyn Lincoln notes.

188 *"That poor young man is going to die":* Conversation with Rex Scouten, Aitken, p. 137.

188 *"The doctors don't understand":* Evelyn Lincoln notes.

188 *"The tenor of his voice":* KOD.

188 *"feared the wrath":* Sorensen, *Counselor,* p. 154.

189 *"You know, when I get downstairs":* Parmet, p. 310.

189 *Junior Chamber of Commerce dinner:* Schlesinger, *Robert Kennedy and His Times,* pp. 115–16.

189 *When the senator died:* Ibid., p. 173.

189 *"In January 1955, Bobby":* Fay, p. 159.

190 *Oil painting and Monopoly:* JFK's oil painting described, Rose Kennedy, p. 127; Monopoly playing, Jean Kennedy Smith int.

190 *"I think we hit it off"*: Peter Lawford, John F. Kennedy Oral History Program.

190 *"I don't think anybody ever"*: Ibid.

190 *"He was really ill"*: Ibid.

191 *"He was enormously well read"*: Fraser OH.

191 *"I think the whole concept"*: Bartlett OH.

191 *"Kennedy played an especially serious role"*: Sorensen, *Counselor,* p. 146.

191 *The theme and the bulk:* Ibid., p. 38.

191 *nowhere as well read:* Author interview with Ted Sorensen.

191 *"Where else, in a non-totalitarian society"*: Kennedy, *Profiles in Courage,* p. 7.

192 *the prospect of forced retirement:* Ibid.

192 *"One senator, since retired"*: Sorensen, *Counselor,* pp. 146–47.

192 *"He must have been getting"*: Ormsby-Gore quote, Lord Harlech, John F. Kennedy Oral History Program.

193 *"Shut that door!"*: Martin Dowd interview.

193 *"Larry and I got a call"*: KOD.

CHAPTER NINE: DEBUT

198 *Onions was a John McCormack guy:* Parmet, pp. 347–51, 354.

198 *For Jack to woo:* Ibid.

199 *"Anybody who's for Stevenson"*: O'Donnell and Powers, p. 109.

199 *"You're either going to get"*: Schlesinger, *Robert Kennedy and His Times,* p. 131.

200 *"We argued that Onions shouldn't be allowed"*: O'Brien, *No Final Victories,* p. 50.

201 *"He and his millions"*: Parmet, pp. 347–51, 354.

202 *To camouflage the effort:* Ibid., p. 359.

202 *"You know, about the Catholic vote"*: Finnegan quote, Sorensen, *Counselor,* p. 160.

203 *The applause in the hall:* Parmet, p. 356.

203 *"I didn't even know Senator Kennedy existed"*: Edmund Reggie, John F. Kennedy Oral History Program.

204 *Kennedy and Sorensen then:* Parmet, p. 359.

204 *The knock on Vice President:* Ibid., p. 372.

205 *"Call Dad and tell him I'm going for it"*: Schlesinger, *Robert Kennedy and His Times,* p. 132.

205 *Bellowing what an "idiot"*: Joe Sr. to Jack, O'Donnell and Powers, p. 140.

205   *"Just talk about the war stuff"*: Smathers int.

206   *"If we have to have"*: Parmet, p. 362.

206   *"America is not ready"*: Schlesinger, *Robert Kennedy and His Times*, p. 132.

207   *"troubled"*: Eleanor Roosevelt quote, Matthews, p. 108.

207   *"My name is Mary Jones"*: KOD.

207   *"After Stevenson had thrown"*: Bartlett OH.

208   *"Texas proudly casts its fifty-six"*: Robert Dallek, *Lyndon B. Johnson: Portrait of a President* (New York: Oxford University Press, 2004), p. 96.

208   *"I'm going to sing 'Dixie'"*: JFK quote, Collier and Horowitz, p. 181.

208   *"The second ballot was already under way"*: Reeves, p. 466.

209   *"He's not our kind of folks"*: Oklahoma governor quote, Sorensen, *Kennedy*, p. 89.

210   *"He hated to lose anything"*: O'Donnell and Powers, p. 142.

211   *"I've learned that you don't"*: JFK quote, ibid., p. 144.

211   *"It was too damned close"*: Kennedy interview with Ben Bradlee, January 5, 1960.

212   *"Magic"*: Nickname given to Jack by Jackie, Parmet, p. 194.

212   *"She wasn't the carefree"*: Pitts, p. 142.

CHAPTER TEN: CHARM

216   *"Kefauver has never done"*: Stevenson to Schlesinger, Arthur M. Schlesinger, *Journals: 1952–2000* (New York: Penguin Press, 2007), p. 8.

218   *"I know I'll never be more"*: JFK to Fay, Perret, p. 238.

219   *"For Christmas that year"*: Sorensen, *Counselor*, p. 172.

219   *"The smaller states"*: Ibid.

219   *"It was more than a list"*: Ibid., p. 175.

220   *"When we said good-bye"*: Ibid., p. 174.

220   *"Those early trips were"*: Ibid., p. 178.

221   *Many of their stops:* Ibid.

221   *By late 1959:* KOD.

221   *"My main job, in those early months"*: O'Brien, *No Final Victories*, p. 60.

221   *"I introduced myself as a representative"*: Ibid.

221   *"I paid a courtesy call"*: Ibid., p. 61.

222   *"Senator Kennedy has every"*: Ibid., pp. 61–62.

222   *"As I moved from state"*: Ibid., p. 62.

223   *"I don't think anybody realizes"*: Bartlett OH.

223   *"He was urged to accept"*: Sorensen, *Counselor*, p. 160.

223 *"As hard as it is":* Ibid., pp. 186–87.

223 *Kennedy's physical condition:* Medical records of Janet Travell at the John F. Kennedy Library.

224 *For everything that ailed him:* For a list of Kennedy's treatments in 1955, see Dallek, *An Unfinished Life,* pp. 212–13.

224 *The cortisone he took:* Sutton int. More than save his life, the cortisone he had taken during the 1950s had transformed his face, fleshing out his features until they coalesced into the radiant handsomeness, the familiar JFK image, that would linger in the nation's fantasy years later. Billy Sutton, who had lived with Kennedy those early years in Washington, would remark that he never looked better than he did in those months of running for president against Richard Nixon.

224 *"In the late 1950's":* Sorensen, *Counselor,* p. 106.

224 *"In retrospect, it is amazing":* Ibid.

224 *"On the political circuit":* Ibid.

225 *"best suited to fanatics, egomaniacs":* Ibid., p. 187.

225 *It was still the age:* Dallek, *An Unfinished Life,* p. 225.

225 *"Senator Kennedy, do you have":* Ralph Martin and Ed Plaut, *Front Runner, Dark Horse* (Garden City, NY: Doubleday, 1960), pp. 461–62.

225 *"You could go to the A&P Store":* Hubert Humphrey, John F. Kennedy Oral History Program.

226 *While the stillbirth:* Pitts, pp. 150–52.

226 *"to promote Senator John F. Kennedy as a man of intensive":* Sorensen, *Counselor,* p. 145.

227 *"Careful spadework":* Rose Kennedy quote, Laurence Leamer, *The Kennedy Women: The Saga of an American Family* (New York: Villard Books, 1994), p. 467.

227 *"who was on the committee":* Ibid.

227 *"Things don't happen":* Ibid.

228 *"The most powerful single force":* JFK on Senate floor, July 2, 1957.

228 *"The war in Algeria":* "Facing Facts on Algeria" speech, p. 3.

229 *In the same year he gave:* Taylor Branch, *Parting the Waters: America in the King Years, 1954–63* (New York: Simon & Schuster, 1988), p. 221.

230 *"Well, I wondered why more people":* Forbes OH.

230 *"always greatly interested":* Smathers OH.

230 *"I remember very late":* Forbes OH.

231 *July 19—Jack Kennedy called up around noon:* Schlesinger, *Journals,* p. 56.

232 *"I think he genuinely thinks he was wrong about it"*: Ibid., p. 58.

233 *"All his golfing pals are rich men he has met since 1945"*: Ibid.

233 *"He won't stand by anybody"*: Ibid.

233 *"No one who has Addison's disease ought to run for President"*: Ibid.

233 *The Senate Select Committee*: Schlesinger, *Robert Kennedy and His Times*, pp. 147–60.

234 *"If the investigation flops"*: O'Donnell and Powers, p. 132.

234 *The result of this rout*: KOD. On the 1958 elevating of O'Donnell and O'Brien in eyes of Joe Sr.: "We had had some disagreements with him during the campaign. Mr. Kennedy has never been noted for his willingness to brook disagreements from someone whom he considered young kids who are hardly wet behind the ears. In addition, his sources of information about our conduct during the campaign had not always been friendly to us . . . The test had always been the score at the end of the game as far as he was concerned . . . He was very profuse in his congratulations to both of us. He could not have been warmer, kinder, or more grateful now that everything had turned out."

234 *The Rackets Committee managed*: Schlesinger, *Robert Kennedy and His Times*, pp. 147–60.

235 *"Would you tell us anything"*: RFK interrogates Giancana, ibid., p. 165.

235 *"We shall not flag or fail"*: RFK banner, Thomas, p. 83.

235 *"John F. Kennedy had clearly done his homework"*: Pierre Salinger, John F. Kennedy Library Oral History Program.

236 *"was not only good in terms of defending the union"*: KOD.

236 *"I think that his performance"*: Muskie OH.

236 *"the Presidency is the source of action"*: Kennedy Transcript, January 5, 1960, Bradlee, 16.

237 *The image remains suspended*: Photo of RFK and JFK in the Rackets Committee, courtesy of John F. Kennedy Library.

237 *Jack Kennedy made few new personal friends*: Ben Bradlee, *Conversations with Kennedy* (New York: Norton, 1975), p. 21.

237 *"Nothing in my education"*: Ben Bradlee, *A Good Life: Newspapering and Other Adventures* (New York: Simon & Schuster, 1995), p. 206.

238 *"the mines"*: Ibid.

CHAPTER ELEVEN: HARDBALL

Ken O'Donnell's oral history provides the dominant source for the Kennedy presidential campaign's hardball tactics. It gives a strategist's look at the methods used to organize what was a breakthrough political effort. Where not otherwise identified, this chapter is based on O'Donnell's account.

241　*"Together, the two of them":* O'Neill, p. 86.

242　*"There's nothing there in 1960":* Bartlett OH.

242　*"'wounded tiger'":* Salinger OH.

242　*It was Salinger's first exposure:* Ibid. "John F. Kennedy had the exterior façade of such an easygoing nature, and yet with this one remark he revealed something to me that I was later to find in him in other situations."

243　*"At Palm Beach, the senator was in full command":* Sorensen, *Kennedy,* p. 120.

246　*"The truth of the matter is that Brown":* Frederick Dutton, John F. Kennedy Library Oral History Program.

246　*"There was no bullshit to the man":* Author interview with Pat Brown.

246　*"His complete familiarity with California politics":* Dutton OH.

249　*"Mike, it's time to shit or get off the pot":* Dallek, *An Unfinished Life,* p. 247, from Abraham Ribicoff Oral History, Columbia University.

249　*"just another pretty boy":* Ben Bradlee, *Conversations with Kennedy,* pp. 17–18.

251　*"I always had a feeling":* Bartlett int.

251　*"He hated the liberals":* Author interview with Ben Bradlee.

251　*"You have no idea":* Author interview with Joan Gardner.

251　*"did make it out there":* Ralph Martin, *A Hero for Our Time: An Intimate Story of the Kennedy Years* (New York: Macmillan, 1983), p. 221.

251　*"I worked with him on the Hill":* Ibid.

252　*"Had dinner with Jack and Jackie":* Bartlett int.

253　*The official handout opened:* Candidate's biography that was stapled to prepared remarks, courtesy of John F. Kennedy Library.

254　*"I asked him what he considered":* Schlesinger, *Journals,* p. 63.

256　*"You think I'm out here":* Reeves, *A Question of Character,* p. 159.

256　*Hubert Humphrey:* Robert Caro, *Master of the Senate* (New York: Knopf, 2002), p. xiii.

257　*"He was campaigning":* Author interview with Governor Pat Lucey.

257 *"effective presentation of a celebrity":* Patrick Lucey Oral History, John F. Kennedy Library.

257 *Using Lou Harris's polling data:* Author interview with Louis Harris.

258 *"Shall I wear this blue overcoat?"* Bartlett OH.

258 *"I have great respect for the Polish people":* Fay, p. 17.

259 *Probably his most famous stunt:* Craig Shirley, *Rendezvous with Destiny: Ronald Reagan and the Campaign that Changed America* (Wilmington: ISI Books, 2009), p. 424.

259 *"On the day Wisconsin voters went to the polls":* Bradlee, *Conversations,* pp. 16–17.

260 *thousand-dollar contribution he'd delivered from his father:* Arnold, p. 21. A March 3, 1960, note from Rose Mary Woods to Vice President Nixon recalls the Kennedy campaign contribution, also Nixon's "flabbergasted" reaction.

260 *"In all fairness to myself":* Pitts, p. 160.

261 *"Kennedy is, of course, Roman Catholic":* Cronkite's broadcast on primary night is included in the Robert Drew documentary *Primary.*

261 *"It means that we've got to go":* O'Donnell and Powers, pp. 159–60.

261 *"When the question of West Virginia":* Bradlee, *Conversations,* p. 26.

262 *"He knew that if he dropped":* Pitts, p. 161.

262 *"The reversal was, of course":* Salinger OH.

263 *Around this time:* O'Neill int.

263 *"Give Me That Old Time Religion":* Humphrey quote, Dallek, *An Unfinished Life,* p. 253.

263 *"pretty well avoided the religious":* Billings quote, Pitts, p. 161.

264 *"Nobody asked me if I was a Catholic":* O'Donnell and Powers, pp. 166–67.

264 *"Young man, I should tell you":* Battle OH.

264 *"I believe West Virginia brought":* Salinger OH.

265 *had been in the "wor-ah":* Bradlee int.

265 *Ben Bradlee knew:* Ibid.

265 *"basic strategy was a psychological one":* Salinger OH.

266 *"We were running the campaign":* Ibid.

266 *"They went through West Virginia":* Author interview with Charles McWhorter.

267 *"I'd give my right testicle to win this one":* Bartlett OH.

267 *"If Jack were beaten in West Virginia":* Macdonald OH.

268 *"The Kennedys asked us to sweat":* Bradlee, *Conversations,* p. 27.

269 *"Kennedy ignored Jackie":* Ibid., p. 28.

CHAPTER TWELVE: CHARISMA

272 *"We talked to the governor"*: KOD.

273 *The Kennedy treatment:* Dallek, *An Unfinished Life,* p. 247.

273 *Even with this agreement:* Dutton OH.

274 *"I'm not running a popularity contest"*: Schlesinger, *Robert Kennedy and His Times,* p. 213.

275 *After West Virginia he was convinced:* Author interview with William J. Green III.

275 *"I could tell, as Governor Lawrence"*: KOD.

276 *"It was still the last moment"*: Moynihan OH.

276 *"This organization, this Kennedy-for-President"*: Horton OH.

276 *"God, why won't he be satisfied"*: Bill Blair, John F. Kennedy Library Oral History Program.

277 *Eleanor Roosevelt would arrive:* Author interview with Lester Hyman.

277 *"riverboat gambler"*: Bradlee, *Conversations,* p. 18.

277 *"He was having throat problems"*: Ibid., pp. 30–31.

278 *"six regions, and every region was manned"*: KOD.

278 *"looked like an impartial newspaper"*: Salinger OH.

278 *"It was the goddamndest thing"*: Robin Cross, *J.F.K.: A Hidden Life* (Boston: C. E. Tuttle, 1992), p. 78.

279 *"I wasn't any Chamberlain-umbrella"*: Robert Dallek, *Lone Star Rising: Lyndon Johnson and His Times, 1908–1960* (New York: Oxford University Press, 1991), pp. 573–74.

279 *"We seized on the opportunity"*: Salinger OH.

279 *"There were a few rough Irishmen"*: KOD.

280 *"I was really digging at Johnson pretty hard"*: Salinger OH.

280 *With Lyndon Johnson's arrows:* KOD. "Adlai called Daley and said to Daley, 'I have a lot of support in the convention and I am going to place my name before the convention. I would like to know from you how many votes I can count on out of the Illinois delegation?' Mayor Daley said, 'Well, Governor, you know I have always been for you. I supported you for the governorship. However, it is too late now, I think you are making a mistake. In answer to your question, Governor, in all candor the answer is none. You will not get one vote from the Illinois delegation.'"

280 *Despite some packing of the galleries:* Bradlee, *Conversations,* p. 31. "At first glance it looked as if everyone on the floor was screaming and waving

something. But a careful look showed most of the delegates sitting quietly, half-hidden by demonstrators."

281 *"operation was slick"*: Author interview with John Ehrlichman.

281 *"If Kennedy wants Johnson"*: Dallek, *Lone Star Rising*, p. 575.

282 *"'Well, I'd just as soon'"*: Salinger OH.

282 *"It was a case of grasping"*: Schlesinger, *Journals*, p. 75.

282 *"Don't worry, Jack, in two weeks"*: Joe Sr. to JFK, Bartlett OH.

284 *"They sat rapt, then content"*: Theodore White, *The Making of the President, 1960* (New York: Atheneum, 1961), p. 178.

284 *"I took the telegram to him"*: Pierre Salinger, *P.S.: A Memoir* (New York: St. Martin's Press, 1995), p. 89.

285 *"meeting of 150 ministers"*: Account of the organized religious campaign to defeat Kennedy drawn from Shaun A. Casey, *The Making of a Catholic President: Kennedy vs. Nixon 1960* (New York: Oxford University Press, 2009), pp. 146–49.

287 *"It was night and we were late"*: William Atwood, "In Memory of John F. Kennedy," *Look*, December 31, 1963.

288 *"ten times after we got"*: KOD.

288 *"In the end, he alone made"*: Ibid.

289 *"meanest, nastiest-looking"*: Author interview with Robert S. Strauss.

289 *"to satisfy this audience"*: KOD.

290 *The loud daily barking*: Richard Reeves, *President Kennedy: Profile of Power* (New York: Simon & Schuster, 1993), p. 41.

291 *Jack's ongoing transformation*: Sutton int.

291 *"I wonder where Dick Nixon"*: Author interview with Dave Powers.

292 *"Kennedy took the thing"*: Author interview with Don Hewitt.

292 *"He was nervous"*: Harris int.

292 *Bill Wilson had been a young*: Author interview with Bill Wilson.

293 *"He and I were standing there"*: Hewitt int.

293 *"The design was that we attack"*: Wilson int.

293 *Once the two men were*: Description of candidate rehearsal based on CBS recording of the event.

294 *"Nixon looked awful off camera"*: Salinger OH.

294 *"Ted Rogers, who was Nixon's"*: Wilson int.

295 *"Five minutes to airtime"*: Ibid.

295 *"erase the assassin image"*: White, p. 285.

299 *"That son of a bitch"*: Fawn Brodie, *Richard Nixon: The Shaping of His*

Character (Cambridge, MA: Harvard University Press, 1983), p. 427.

300 *"What the hell is this?":* Wilson int.

303 *"I had the impression that":* Schlesinger, *Journals,* p. 88.

307 *"He was likely to get himself":* Dean Acheson, John F. Kennedy Library Oral History Program.

308 *"There was hardly a place":* The account of Martin Luther King's arrest and the Kennedys' effort to free him is drawn from Harris Wofford, *Of Kennedys and Kings: Making Sense of the Sixties* (Pittsburgh: University of Pittsburgh Press, 1992), p. 16.

311 *"Last week, Dick Nixon hit":* Fay, p. 60.

312 *"He's a filthy, lying son of a bitch":* Goodwin, p. 105.

312 *"Nixon wanted the presidency so bad":* Fay, 9.

313 *"They're much more concerned":* KOD.

313 *"I was beginning to panic now":* Ibid.

314 *"It started out like gangbusters":* Salinger OH.

314 *"Ohio did that to me":* JFK quote, White, p. 21.

315 *"All those people now say":* KOD.

315 *"Nebraska has the largest Republican":* Horton OH.

315 *"Does this mean you're president":* Matthews, p. 179.

315 *"What am I going to tell the press?":* Salinger OH.

316 *"I want to repeat through this wire":* Telegram courtesy of Richard M. Nixon Library and Birthplace.

316 *"Mr. O'Donnell, the president has":* KOD.

318 *"Nixon was, in my opinion":* Author interview with Herb Klein.

318 *"I think we are in enough trouble in the world today":* Richard Nixon, *Six Crises* (New York: Simon & Schuster, 1962), p. 404.

318 *"It was the difference between":* Klein int.

319 *"He had done it by driving home":* Time, November 16, 1960.

319 *"He wisely decided to concentrate":* Schlesinger, *Journals,* p. 93.

319 *"I know there is a God":* Jack Kennedy quoted these from Abraham Lincoln during a speech in Muncie, Indiana, on October 5, 1960.

CHAPTER THIRTEEN: LANDING

321 *urgent phone calls were placed:* Bradlee, *Conversations,* pp. 33–34.

322 *President-elect Kennedy put a pair of Republicans:* Schlesinger, *A Thousand Days,* pp. 131–36.

322 *McNamara, showing no lack of toughness:* Ibid., p. 133.

322 *Looking to the liberal faction:* Reeves, *President Kennedy*, pp. 26–27.

322 *Now, as always, concessions needed to be made:* Bartlett OH. "I always had the feeling that the decision on Bobby was not made by the President-elect, but I think by his father. I think he took his father's position on it. I never had the feeling that Bobby had any great burning desire to be attorney general, that this was really almost forced upon him."

322 *"I think I'll open the front door":* Bradlee, *Conversations*, p. 38.

323 *"I think he hadn't really thought":* KOD.

323 *Kennedy's "spokes of the wheel":* Ibid. "Roosevelt wanted them competing amongst themselves for what was best for him; at least in reading, this is what I gathered and the president gathered. President Kennedy did not want that; he did not want fighting amongst his staff. He did not want jealousy and infighting; he realized that there would be some competing for presidential favor, that is human nature. But, this was not a goal."

323 *There was little camaraderie:* Parmet, p. 47.

323 *Ben Bradlee, the Washington sophisticate:* Bradlee int.

323 *"The president-elect was a complex":* Wofford, pp. 67–68.

324 *You'd see him sitting:* Clifford quote, KOD.

324 *"I remember he told me":* Bartlett OH.

325 *"'I'm going to keep the White House white'":* Sally Bedell Smith, *Grace and Power: The Private World of the Kennedy White House* (New York: Random House, 2005), p. 173.

325 Kennedy and Ted Sorensen working on inaugural speech in Palm Beach: Thurston Clarke, *Ask Not: The Inauguration of John F. Kennedy and the Speech That Changed America* (New York: Henry Holt and Co., 2004), pp. 23–27.

326 *To some who'd once been at Choate:* Hearing President Kennedy's historic call to "Ask not what your country can do for you; ask what you can do for your country," several of his Choate classmates recalled headmaster George St. John's use of a quite similar phrase. These included some of his Class of '35 classmates, at least one of whom charged plagiarism in a survey taken by the school in 1985. Putney Westerfield, Choate '47, volunteered this account to me:

"For five years I attended compulsory chapel five evenings a week after dinner. Usually the headmaster would quote from the Bible, or literature, or political figures, and make a point concerning how a Choate student should think or act. It was in this context that he would say, once every year or two: 'Ask not what your school can do for you; ask what you can do for your school.' Sometimes it might be mundane, like, 'Be well-dressed and don't smoke cigarettes when on the train to New York or Boston for vacations.' Or: 'Pick up a paper carelessly thrown on the grass.' Or the campaign for a Christmas gift to each member of the school's support staff. It took many forms.

"Listening to the inaugural address in 1961 I immediately related the two 'Ask not's.

"Many years later, when St. John's 'quote books' (three volumes of them) were found, there was a quotation from Harvard dean LeBaron Briggs who wrote: 'The youth who loves his alma mater will always ask not "What can she do for me?" but "What can I do for her?"' Clearly this was the inspiration source for George St. John who knew Briggs from his own Harvard days in the late 1890s. In 1911, as headmaster, he asked Briggs to give the commencement address at Choate."

In *Counselor*, on p. 29, Ted Sorensen cited St. John as the "most credible theory" on the derivation of the "Ask not" exhortation. For whatever reason, he was not able to get Choate administrators to produce St. John's "quote book" for him. On a visit to Choate in 2010, archivist Judy Donald showed me the "quote book" that contained the Briggs essay. It was right there on an early page of St. John's loose-leaf binder, right below the hymns to be sung that day.

326 *"greatly exceeded the boldest"*: Schlesinger, *A Thousand Days*, p. 114.

326 *"The positions of the USA, Britain, and France"*: Ibid., p. 303.

327 *During those early weeks:* Mary Van Rensselaer Thayer, *Jacqueline Kennedy: The White House Years* (Boston: Little, Brown, 1967), pp. 103–6.

328 *Lem Billings arrived on Friday:* Pitts, pp. 191–92.

328 *He joined the couple, too:* Ibid., p. 212.

329 *"What would you do now":* Fay OH.

329 *"Listen, Redhead":* Ibid.

329 *But, clearly, the president:* Pitts, p. 184.

329 *for Rip Horton to:* Horton OH.

329 *"The presidency is not a good place":* Pitts, p. 184.

329 *"The president is counting on you":* The account here of the early organization of the Peace Corps is taken from Wofford's *Of Kennedys and Kings*.

330 *"When he became president, Jackie changed":* Author interview with Rachel Mellon.

331 *"Victory has a hundred fathers"*: Schlesinger, *A Thousand Days*, p. 289.

331 *The disembarking Cubans had been assured by Agency officials:* An "Official History of the Bay of Pigs Operation," revealed in 2011, said the CIA task force in charge did not believe it could succeed without becoming an open invasion supported by the U.S. military. The task force met on November 1960 to prepare a briefing for President-elect Kennedy. It failed to share with him its assessment that an invasion plan limited to the brigade of Cuban exiles could not succeed. The revelation came through a Freedom of Information request by the National Security Archive.

332 *"Operation Zapata"*: Jim Rasenberger, *The Brilliant Disaster: JFK, Castro, and America's Doomed Invasion of Cuba's Bay of Pigs* (New York: Scribner, 2011), pp. 138–40.

332 Background on Guatemala coup: Ibid., pp. 61–62.

332 Kennedy and Bissell meet during campaign: Harris int.

332 Bundy and McNamara support Zapata: Rasenberger, p. 159.

332 *But what really clinched it:* Ibid., pp. 136–40.

332 *"In a parliamentary government"*: Thomas Powers, *The Man Who Kept the Secrets: Richard Helms and the CIA* (New York: Knopf, 1979), p. 115.

334 *landing point shifted from Trinidad:* Rasenberger, p. 139.

334 *Castro rounded up:* Ibid., pp. 323–25.

334 Prisoner exchange: Ibid., pp. 361–78.

336 *"I probably made a mistake"*: Schlesinger, *Journals*, 112.

337 *"How could you expect the world"*: Reeves, *President Kennedy*, p. 103.

337 *For the first time:* Ibid, p. 95.

337 *"I'm the responsible officer"*: Schlesinger, *A Thousand Days*, p. 290.

337 *83 percent in a Gallup poll:* Dallek, *An Unfinished Life*, 386. (That April 1961 number would be the highest in his administration.)

337 *"In the months that followed"*: Fay, p. 171.

337 *Even on vacation in Hyannis Port:* Ibid.

337 *"I will never compromise the principles"*: Ibid., pp. 172–73.

339 *The French president expressed doubts:* KOD.

340 *His practical advice:* Ibid.

340 *even the* appearance *of negotiating:* Ibid.

341 *"snapping at him like a terrier"*: O'Donnell and Powers, p. 296.

341 *"Not too well"*: Leaming, p. 309.

342 *He tried everything:* KOD.

342 *Kennedy requested a third meeting:* Dallek, *An Unfinished Life*, p. 402.

343 *"If that's true, it's going to be a cold winter"*: Reeves, *President Kennedy*, p. 171.

343 *"I never met a man like this"*: Hugh Sidey, "The Presidency," *Time*, October 15, 1984.

343 *"It will have to be for much bigger"*: JFK to O'Donnell, Dallek, *An Unfinished Life*, p. 430.

344 *"never come face to face with such evil"*: Pitts, p. 220.

344 *"Our position in Europe"*: Ibid., p. 55.

344 *"He's imprisoned by Berlin"*: Hugh Sidey, *John F. Kennedy, President* (New York: Atheneum, 1964), p. 218.

345 *On June 21, he would suffer*: Leaming, pp. 321–22.

345 *"showcase of liberty, a symbol"*: Kempe, p. 423.

345 *Five days later, Senator William Fulbright*: Reeves, *President Kennedy*, p. 204.

345 *"Why would Khrushchev put up a wall"*: Kempe, p. 379.

CHAPTER FOURTEEN: ZENITH

348 *We'd agreed, as had the Soviets*: Leaming, p. 337.

348 *"fucked again!"*: David Halberstam, *The Best and the Brightest* (New York: Random House, 1972), p. 84.

349 *"If we test only underground"*: Dallek, *An Unfinished Life*, p. 462.

350 *With it came a new pressure*: Leaming, pp. 378–80.

350 *"A journey of a thousand miles begins with one step"*: Reeves, *President Kennedy*, p. 551.

350 *"hard-boiled . . . soft-boiled"*: Bradlee, *Conversations*, pp. 52–53.

350 *Kennedy's national security team*: Leaming, pp. 378–80.

352 *"we were actually superior to the Soviets"*: Author interview with John Glenn.

353 *In the fall of 1961*: Dallek, *An Unfinished Life*, p. 482.

353 *Afterward, JFK called both sides*: KOD.

353 *His company was raising the price of steel*: Ibid.

353 *"what you are doing is in the best interest"*: Fay int.

353 *"You have made a terrible mistake"*: Reeves, *President Kennedy*, p. 296.

353 *"These guys felt they were so powerful"*: KOD.

354 *"cold, deliberate fucking"*: Bradlee, *Conversations*, p. 76.

354 *"wrongly, he could not or would"*: KOD.

354 *"You find out about these guys"*: Fay int.

354 *"I don't think U.S. Steel or any other":* Dallek, *An Unfinished Life,* p. 486.

354 *"where possible":* Fay int.

354 *"the American people will find it hard":* Dallek, *An Unfinished Life,* p. 485.

355 *"Kennedy's style of politics":* KOD.

355 *"We looked over all of them as individuals":* Robert F. Kennedy, John F. Kennedy Library Oral History Program.

355 *"Good night, pal":* To Dave Powers, Smith, p. xiv.

355 *He always exhibited great fondness:* Bradlee, *Conversations,* p. 148.

356 *Even social friends might step:* Ibid., pp. 114–15.

356 *He regularly went for a swim:* Nancy Tuckerman and Pamela Turnure, John F. Kennedy Library Oral History Program. Nancy Tuckerman: "Yes, twice a day."

356 *"Information has been developed":* Perret, p. 346.

357 *He'd regularly see Meyer:* Bradlee, *Conversations,* p. 54.

359 *Washington efforts:* "Summary of Civil Rights Progress," Box 63, Papers of the President, John F. Kennedy Library.

359 *On September 10, the U.S. Supreme Court:* KOD.

360 *"I won't agree to let that boy get to Ole Miss":* Ibid.

360 *Jack and Bobby both were hoping:* Ibid.

361 *Jack was now involved in checking:* Ibid.

361 *When two thousand demonstrators:* Dallek, *An Unfinished Life,* p. 515.

361 *"neither Meredith nor any of those men":* KOD.

361 *"we knew that most of the National Guard":* Ibid.

362 *Kennedy was responsible:* Reeves, *President Kennedy,* pp. 359–64.

362 *"They always give you their bullshit":* Ibid, p. 363.

363 *"the occupation regime":* Letter from Khrushchev to JFK, July 5, 1962, ibid., p. 41.

363 *"bone in my throat":* Ibid., p. 168.

363 *"We will not allow your troops to be in Berlin":* From State Department, *Foreign Relations of the United States: Cuba, 1962–1963,* pp. 1045–57.

364 *he told Udall that he wanted to meet:* Frederick Kempe, *Berlin 1961: Kennedy, Khrushchev, and the Most Dangerous Place on Earth* (New York: Putnam, 2011), p. 493.

364 *He sent JFK a letter:* Leaming, pp. 378–80.

364 *Suddenly it came:* Ibid., p. 413.

365 *Kennedy now assembled:* Sorensen, *Counselor,* p. 286.

366 *"Virtually everyone's initial choice":* Ibid., pp. 288–89.

367 *If Khrushchev was attempting:* Dallek, *An Unfinished Life,* p. 554.

367 *"I now know how Tojo felt":* Schlesinger, *Robert Kennedy and His Times,* p. 507.

367 *Might not an American attack on Cuba:* On January 15, 1992, the *New York Times* reported that the Soviet Union had 43,000 troops in Cuba during the 1962 Cuban Missile Crisis, not 10,000 as was reported by the Central Intelligence Agency. This was according to Robert McNamara, who had just returned from a conference on the crisis in Havana. He said Soviet officials had told him that Moscow had sent short-range nuclear weapons to Cuba and that Soviet commanders there were authorized to use them in the event of an American invasion.

369 *Grab your balls:* JFK to Salinger, Salinger, p. 115.

370 *"I think the pressure of this period":* Bartlett OH.

370 *"You'd be interested to know":* Ibid.

371 *"Any communication with any skipper'":* Fay OH.

371 *He then instructed Bobby:* Sorensen, *Counselor,* p. 302.

372 *"the greatest defeat in our history":* LeMay quote, Dallek, *An Unfinished Life,* p. 571.

372 *"If Kennedy never did another thing":* Macmillan quote, O'Donnell and Powers, p. 284.

372 *There was an equal number of warheads:* Michael Dobbs, *One Minute to Midnight: Kennedy, Khrushchev, and Castro on the Brink of Nuclear War* (New York: Knopf, 2008), p. 98.

372 *"My thinking went like this":* Nikita Khrushchev, *Khrushchev Remembers* (Boston: Little, Brown, 1970), p. 494.

373 *"The final lesson of the Cuban missile crisis":* Robert Kennedy, *Thirteen Days: A Memoir of the Cuban Missile Crisis* (New York: W. W. Norton, 1969), p. 95.

CHAPTER FIFTEEN: GOALS

376 *"The tax laws really screw people":* Bradlee, *Conversations,* p. 218.

379 *"The decision to make the speech available":* New York Times, June 13, 1963.

379 *"The speech and its publication in Izvestia show":* Ibid.

379 *"He's just challenging us":* Bradlee, *Conversations,* p. 195.

379 *"Make him look ridiculous":* Dan T. Carter, *The Politics of Rage: George Wallace, the Origins of the New Conservatism, and the Transformation of American Politics* (New York: Simon & Schuster, 1995), p. 149.

380 *"most precious and powerful right in the world":* Public Papers of the Presidents: John F. Kennedy: 1963, p. 14.

381 *"the most sweeping and forthright ever":* Martin Luther King, June 20, 1963, Box 97, President's Office Files at John F. Kennedy Library.

382 *Driving through the streets:* Bradlee, *Conversations,* pp. 95–96. "Just before his trip to Berlin in June, 1963," wrote Bradlee, "he spent the better part of an hour with the Vreelands (Frederick 'Frecky' Vreeland, a young foreign service officer and the son of *Vogue* editor Diana Vreeland, and his wife) before he could master 'Ich bin ein Berliner.'"

382 *In fact, Jack was secretly:* Ibid., p. 84. "For some reason it bugs Kennedy that I speak French."

383 *A million Germans lined the parade route:* Michael Beschloss, *The Crisis Years: Kennedy and Khrushchev, 1960–1963* (New York: Edward Burlingame Books, 1991), pp. 604–8.

383 *"like a man who has just glimpsed Hell":* Hugh Sidey, Reeves, *President Kennedy,* p. 535.

383 *Jack called the time he spent in Berlin:* Sorensen, *Counselor,* p. 325.

383 *"When my great-grandfather left here to become a cooper in East Boston":* President Kennedy to the people of New Ross, Ireland, June 1963, John F. Kennedy Library.

383 *"The wind from that machine blew my chickens away":* Duchess of Devonshire, *The House: A Portrait of Chatsworth* (London: Papermac, 1987), p. 222.

384 *During those negotiations:* Sorensen, *Counselor,* p. 327.

384 *On July 25, 1963, envoys from the three:* Leaming, p. 435.

384 *John Kennedy considered this his greatest achievement:* Sorensen int.

384 *"With all human beings, one of the things":* Ormsby-Gore quote, Lord Harlech OH.

385 *"He put up quite a fight":* Leaming, p. 298.

385 *"defeat Communist insurgency":* Reeves, *President Kennedy,* p. 50.

385 *"I can remember one particular case":* Fay OH.

386 *He had the added advantage:* Schlesinger, *A Thousand Days,* pp. 988–89.

386 *The leader of that faction:* Ibid., p. 985.

387 *Now he was approving his former ally's:* Leaming, p. 309.

387 *"U.S. Government cannot tolerate situation in which power lies in Nhu's hands":* Reeves, *President Kennedy,* pp. 562–63.

387 *August was also the month of:* Schlesinger, *A Thousand Days,* pp. 972–73; Schlesinger, *Robert Kennedy and His Times,* pp. 350–52.

388 *"This was the first time we'd seen Jackie":* Bradlee, *Conversations,* p. 206.

388 *He left at halftime:* O'Brien, *John F. Kennedy,* p. 779.

388 *In future visits to the confession booth:* Fay, pp. 222–23.

388 *light a candle for Joe Jr.:* Dalton OH.

388 *There were often times when friends:* Ibid.

388 *president would kneel:* Dave Powers int.

389 *"An American President, commander in chief":* Sorensen, *Counselor,* p. 123.

389 *On October 4, Jackie left:* Leaming, p. 314.

391 *"Perhaps he should have guessed that":* Sorensen, *Counselor,* p. 354.

391 *After retreating from the cabinet room:* Leaming, p. 323.

391 *"Over the weekend":* Presidential recordings, John F. Kennedy Library.

393 *"He is instinctively against introduction":* United States State Department, *Foreign Relations of the United States: Vietnam, 1961,* pp. 532–33.

393 *"They want a force of American troops":* Schlesinger, *A Thousand Days,* p. 547.

394 *"I do not believe he knew":* Sorensen, *Counselor,* p. 359.

394 *At about this same time:* O'Neill, p. 177.

394 *"mood of the city was ugly":* Bradlee, *Conversations,* p. 237.

394 *"disgraced. There is no other way":* *Time,* November 1, 1963.

394 *The following Thursday, Jack had invited:* Pitts, pp. 205–6.

395 *He was convinced:* Bradlee, *Conversations,* p. 190.

395 *"He'll end up hating me":* Reeves, *President Kennedy,* p. 465.

396 *Jack spent the next weekend:* Barbara Leaming, *Mrs. Kennedy: The Missing History of the Kennedy Years* (New York: Free Press, 2001), pp. 326–27.

396 *"A small band of conspirators":* JFK speech to the Inter-American Press Association, November 18, 1963, John F. Kennedy Presidential Library and Museum.

397 *"organize an in-depth study":* William J. Rust, *Kennedy in Vietnam* (New York: Da Capo Press, 1985), pp. 4–5.

397 *While Wright laid some of the blame:* Author interview with Jim Wright.

CHAPTER SIXTEEN: LEGACY

399 *"They were wider than pools":* Theodore White's notes on his interview with Jacqueline Kennedy are at the John F. Kennedy Library.

402 *Within hours she'd assumed the reins:* Tuckerman/Turnure OH.

402　*"Jackie was extraordinary"*: Bradlee, *Conversations*, p. 244.

403　*"to an exceptional degree"*: Schlesinger, *A Thousand Days*, p. 78.

403　*"each of us had a certain role we were cast into, whether we knew it or not"*: Jim Reed, John F. Kennedy Library Oral History Program.

404　*"We had a hero for a friend"*: William Manchester, *The Death of a President: November 20–November 25, 1963* (New York: Harper & Row, 1967), p. 446.

404　*"chemistry"*: Author interview with Chuck Spalding.

404　*"The most charming man I ever knew"*: Smathers int.

404　*"aura of royalty about him"*: Bradlee int.

404　*"chasing girls in the South of France"*: Bartlett int.

405　*"There's no point in being Irish if you don't know the world's going to someday break your heart"*: Moynihan, said to columnist Mary McGrory.

405　*In a 2009 national poll:* National survey conducted for CBS's *60 Minutes* and *Vanity Fair*, published in January 2010.

INDEX

John F. Kennedy *(cont.)*

campaign "teas" held for, 128–29, 138, 139

Canada trip of, 338–39

charisma of, 26, 225–26, 271, 288

cheapness of, 151–55, 163

Choate school and, 14–23, 26, 27, 29, 162, 326

Churchill as hero of, 17, 33, 34–35, 41, 59, 108–9, 235, 239, 252, 285, 325

civil rights address of (1963), 380–81, 383

civil rights and, 229–31, 309–11, 323, 359–62, 375, 379–81, 384, 389–90, 394, 396

companionship as need of, 17, 29, 106, 167, 323, 355, 357

compartmentalization of life by, 25–26, 38, 106, 159, 282–83, 317, 327, 357, 401

congressional race of 1946 and, 7, 63, 67, 76–87, 133–34, 185, 216

Cuba and, 9, 306–8, 331–38, 363, 364–73, 396

Curley petition and, 101–3, 124, 170

dating and flirtations of, 106–7, 160, 162, 166

decision to enter politics of, 75–77

de Gaulle and, 339–40

Democratic Convention of 1956 and, 2–3, 202–11, 216, 225, 229, 241

Democratic Convention of 1960 and, 4, 277–84

Democratic nomination and, 271–84

Democratic primary races of 1960 and, 252–69

diary of, 73–74, 78–79

dirty tricks and, 259

discharge from Navy of, 66

Eisenhower disliked by, 233

Eisenhower policy criticized by, 227–29

Eleanor Roosevelt and, 206–7, 276

election of 1956 and, 213

election of 1958 and, 234, 241

election of 1964 and, 395–96

engagement of, 161, 162

European trips of, 29–30, 33–34, 36, 105–6, 202, 212–13, 218, 339–40, 382–83

failure to file congressional campaign papers by, 82, 185

Far East fact finding trip of, 116–17, 119, 120, 173, 229, 305

foreign policy as prime interest of, 116, 119–21, 283–84

funeral of, 402

Furcolo and, 121–22, 184–87, 202

Garbo White House visit and, 394–95

gravesite of, 401

Harvard and, *24,* 26, 27–29, 30, 36, 46, 97, 142, 162, 180, 184, 218, 237

PHOTO CREDITS

Evaluating
Pupil Growth

5th edition

Evaluating Pupil Growth

Principles of Tests and Measurements

J. STANLEY AHMANN
Colorado State University

MARVIN D. GLOCK
Cornell University

Allyn and Bacon, Inc.
Boston, London, Sydney, Toronto

LIBRARY OF CONGRESS CATALOGING IN PUBLICATION DATA

Ahmann, J   Stanley.
  Evaluating pupil growth.

  Includes bibliographies and indexes.
  1. Grading and marking (Students) I. Glock,
Marvin David, joint author. II. Title.
LB3063.A43 1975   371.2'6   74-26552

ISBN 0-205-04497-2

Third printing . . . July, 1976

CONTENTS

v

PREFACE

A person who has worked hard for a goal wants to find out to what degree that goal is realized. So it is with teachers, regardless of subject matter or grade level. Clearly, evaluation of the degree to which educational goals have been achieved is a basic part of teaching and concerns everyone associated with the school.

It follows, therefore, that teachers, counselors, supervisors, administrators, and other educational specialists need the following:

1. *Appreciation of the usefulness of measuring instruments in education.*
2. *Knowledge of the characteristics of a satisfactory measuring instrument.*
3. *Ability to construct measuring instruments capable of showing to what degree pupils have attained pertinent educational objectives.*
4. *Knowledge of common achievement and aptitude tests and also personal-social adjustment inventories, which are often included in a schoolwide program of evaluation.*
5. *Ability to select appropriate measuring instruments for use in a continuous evaluation program.*
6. *Ability to interpret properly the data yielded by measuring instruments, to use them in diagnosing and remedying pupil deficiencies, and to report them efficiently and accurately to the pupils, their parents, and possibly the entire community.*

The fifth edition of *Evaluating Pupil Growth* is written for a one-term college course, whether at the undergraduate or "fifth-year" graduate level, that is designed on the basis of developing attainments such as these. Each of its five parts contributes directly to one or more of the six needs and indirectly to several others. These relationships are often self-evident. In Part One, "Evaluation in Education," the role of pupil evaluation in education is defined, the use of educational objectives as a basis of evaluating is established, and a number of measurement procedures are introduced. Part Two, "Measuring Achievement in the Classroom," contains discussions of teacher-built objective and essay tests, methods by which such tests can be evaluated, and teacher-built instruments recording pupil performance. Part Three, "Characteristics of a Good Measuring Instrument," is devoted to validity, reliability, and means of reporting a pupil's relative test performance. In Part Four, "Standardized Tests, Scales, and Inventories," careful attention is given to commercially available tests and batteries of achievement, aptitude, and personal-social adjustment. In the concluding section of the book, Part Five, "Using Evaluation to Improve Learning," the use of measurement data in diagnosis and remediation is explained, and methods of determin-ing and reporting pupil growth are discussed. Finally, characteristics of a comprehen-sive schoolwide program of evaluation are listed.

Underlying this book are three significant and, indeed, axiomatic principles. In the first place, the measuring procedures of elementary and secondary school teachers are very similar. Moreover, in those instances in which the procedures differ, the secondary school teacher can profit from knowledge of the unique measuring prob-lems and procedures of the elementary school teacher, and vice versa. This book is designed to serve both groups. Secondly, to be competent in educational measure-ment, a teacher must have a speaking knowledge of common statistical techniques such as the arithmetic mean, the standard deviation, and the correlation coefficient. He does not need to be skilled in the theoretical aspects of statistics, helpful as that would be. To fill the need for a limited command of statistical procedures, descrip-tions of statistical techniques are included in the appendices. Each step to be followed when solving for one of these values is shown. The computations are so planned that no prior training in mathematics beyond fundamental arithmetic is needed in order to follow them with ease. Thirdly, before a teacher can successfully build his own measuring instruments or select appropriate commercial instruments for classroom use, he must be thoroughly familiar with basic principles of measurement and evaluation. For this reason an entire chapter is devoted to the topic of validity and another to the topic of reliability. Understand, however, that these chapters, as well as all of the others, are not written for the theorist. The treatment is such that the teacher can make practical use of it in his classroom.

Most of the chapters in this book are interrelated. It is recommended that Part One and Part Two be studied first and in that order. At this point the instructor may vary his choice as he wishes. If possible, the chapters in Part Three (that is, Chapters 8, 9, and 10), which deal with norms, validity, and reliability, should be kept together as a group. The same is true of Part Four (that is, Chapters 11, 12, and 13), which deals with standardized tests and inventories.

Scattered within each chapter are discussion questions, usually about nine or ten in number. They are designed to challenge the student in that no readily determined answers are available. Often the question requires the student to apply what he is learning. Supporting references to educational and psychological literature are regu-larly given.

At the end of each chapter is a list of suggested readings that, in the opinion of the authors, provide suitable extensions of the material included in the chapter and are written at an appropriate level. These references will provide a more complete view of many of the important topics. In addition, a list of free and inexpensive materials concerning educational measurement and evaluation is given in Appendix B.

Like all such books, this is the product of the efforts of many people. The authors are indebted to the many students at Colorado State University and at Cornell University, and to the school personnel in Colorado and New York and other states who directly or indirectly provided ideas and illustrative material for this book. In addition, the authors are grateful to Professor Helen L. Wardeberg of Cornell University, who provided numerous suggestions for the improvement of the first edition of this book, and to the stenographers who typed various parts of the manuscript, particularly to Miss Grace Roetker of Colorado State University. Finally, many publishers have granted permission to reproduce parts of their publications in this volume. These are acknowledged as they occur.

J. Stanley Ahmann
Marvin D. Glock

PART ONE

Evaluation in Education

Many years ago, it is reported, Speaker Joe Cannon was asked by an anxious freshman congressman to evaluate his maiden speech. Cannon's response was a masterpiece of honest diplomacy:

"Well, son," he said, "much of what you said was good, and some of what you said was new. But what was good was not new, and what was new was not good."

This is a clear-cut example of the evaluation that is an integral part of our everyday activities. The merchant periodically inventories his stock to see whether he has realized a profit or a loss on his transactions and to evaluate the merits of his present merchandising practices. The golfer carefully tabulates the strokes needed to play eighteen holes of golf, checks the results against the listed par or perhaps his total of last Saturday, and on this basis he then appraises the quality of his game. The surgeon examines his patient for postoperative developments so that he may better assess the success of the operation he performed and hence the well-being of his patient. The financier regularly reviews his portfolio of stocks and bonds, checks their values and earnings, and thus draws conclusions on the soundness of his present investment program.

Notice that in each of these illustrations a goal has been identified. For the merchant it is a successful merchandising policy; for the golfer, an improved skill; for the surgeon, a more healthy patient; for the financier, a productive portfolio of stocks and bonds. Notice also that, to evaluate the effectiveness of the endeavor, information is necessary on which a value judgment may be made. In the illustrations cited, a variety of information is needed. The merchant computes the amount of his sales and his expenses; the golfer counts strokes; the surgeon examines temperature charts, blood pressure readings, blood counts, and laboratory reports; the financier, like the merchant, is interested in dollars and cents as well as the trends of the stock market. After weighing the information with respect to a known goal, the individuals judge the current situation as successful, with little or no change necessary, or unsuccessful, with recommended changes to be made in the hope of improvement in the future.

1

Education has a direct parallel. Goals are identified on the basis of pupils' and society's needs. Educational programs are established so that pupils can reach these goals and do so in a reasonably efficient manner. Finally, after the program has begun, information such as test scores and reports of observation of pupil behavior is periodically gathered. The success of the pupil in reaching the goal, and hence the success of the educational program, is evaluated in terms of the objectives. This is the core of educational evaluation.

In Part One we have described in limited detail the nature of the purposes and procedures of educational evaluation. Chapter 1, "The Role of Evaluation in Education," discusses the scope of educational evaluation (particularly pupil evaluation), its purposes, the principal types of testing procedures, the heterogeneous nature of these procedures, and problems resulting from lack of accuracy of the information produced by these instruments. Chapter 2, "Educational Objectives in Pupil Evaluation," is concerned with the nature of educational objectives, taxonomies used to classify them, their degree of specificity, and their role in the development of instruments used in evaluating pupil growth.

These two chapters survey the entire field of pupil evaluation by identifying its perimeter and its principal parts, and also offer a basic vocabulary for this complex field. Part One can be compared to the large piece of heavy cardboard on which a young child is to assemble the various pieces of an inlay jigsaw puzzle. On it, the outline of the puzzle and of each piece is traced so that the child can speedily recognize the relationship of one piece to all the others. As a result, he can assemble the pieces much more rapidly than would otherwise be possible. These chapters provide similar outlines, so that detailed descriptions in later chapters of some of the topics mentioned can be easily grasped and their position in the total outline of pupil evaluation quickly recognized.

1

THE ROLE OF
EVALUATION IN EDUCATION

A trip to a crowded beach in the summer is a revealing experience. Anyone but the most indifferent observer is impressed by this fascinating view of more or less undraped humanity. Some try to capture the sight on canvas or film; few forget it. Summer reminds us how unique each human body is.

We can easily identify the most obvious characteristics that contribute to individuality. Differences in height and weight, and the sometimes phenomenal distribution of that weight, are prominent. Hair or lack of it, size of feet and hands, and posture are equally noticeable. So are characteristics of the various parts of the head—ears, eyes, chin, and mouth. Other aspects of the physiological entity called man, which remain unseen but are nonetheless important, are visual and auditory acuity, breathing patterns, strength of grip, and sense of smell.

Most of the bathers are not acquainted with each other. If they were, an entirely new constellation of individual differences would reveal itself. These differences are psychological in nature. Variations in interests, attitudes, motives, and values certainly exist, and so do differences in aptitude, be they scholastic, mechanical, musical, artistic, or clerical. In terms of achievements, there are literally thousands of additional dimensions that are sources of individuality. Achievement in the common subject matter areas is just one part of the picture. To it must be added achievement in the multitude of additional everyday activities ranging from skill in driving an automobile to the art of making and keeping friends.

The picture is staggering. Small wonder that psychologists have spent lifetimes identifying sources of individuality and developing means of measuring the amount of a given characteristic a person might have at a given moment. These efforts have clearly established the principle that each person possesses a profile of traits, both physiological and psychological, that are the result of the unique heredity (except for identical twins) and environment of each individual.

Teachers are seldom surprised when the factors of individuality are listed. Each succeeding class brings many new pupils before the teacher; no pupil is exactly like any other in this class or any in one of the preceding classes. The appearance of new and refreshing changes in the educational "raw material" each year is one of the joys of teaching. It is also the source of one of the most perplexing problems of teaching—learning to know your pupils so that educational experiences can be planned to capitalize on the individual differences.

3

In view of this pupil heterogeneity, how can we succinctly describe the teacher's role in expediting the formal educational process? Actually, this role can be conveniently reduced to four points (Tyler, 1969, p. 1). In the first place, the teacher must identify the educational objectives sought. He must know the nature of the pupil behavior that will be displayed when the educational objectives have been achieved. Secondly, he must determine what educational experiences the pupils must have to achieve the objectives. Thirdly, he must know his pupils so well that he can design and order the education experiences according to their varied interests, aptitudes, and prior experiences. Lastly, he must evaluate the degree to which the desired changes in pupil behavior have taken place, that is, the degree to which the educational objectives have been achieved. By means of the last step, the effectiveness of the various educational experiences can be inferred. Within the last two steps lie the purposes of pupil evaluation.

USES OF EDUCATIONAL EVALUATION

Educational evaluation is the systematic process of determining the effectiveness of educational endeavors in the light of evidence. For our purposes, evaluation can be thought of as formative or summative (Scriven, 1967). The former is "midstream" evaluation–evaluation of pupil progress or program effectiveness at some intermediate point. The latter is evaluation at some logical terminal point, for instance, at the end of a unit of instruction or an academic term.

The differentiation has been refined still further (Bloom, Hastings, and Madaus, 1971, pp. 91–92), in the realm of pupil evaluation. Formative evaluations provide feedback to teacher and pupil about the latter's progress, or lack of it, early enough for any needed changes in the instructional effort to be made. The degree of mastery of a certain learning task is discovered, and those aspects of the task not mastered are identified. In contrast, summative evaluations are determinations of the degree of achievement of major outcomes of a pupil's course of study. The purpose of these evaluations is often the assignment of final marks ("grades"). As we shall see, the types of evaluation instruments typically used change according to the nature of the evaluation.

The uses of educational evaluation are broad and diverse. Four subgroups have been identified (Tyler, 1966):

1. *Appraisal of academic achievement of individual pupils.*
2. *Diagnosis of learning difficulties of an individual pupil or an entire class.*
3. *Appraisal of the educational effectiveness of a curriculum, instructional materials and procedures, and organizational arrangements.*
4. *Assessment of the educational progress of large populations so as to help understand educational problems and develop sound public policy in education.*

The first two uses constitute pupil evaluation that is based on the rationale of individual differences mentioned in the foregoing paragraphs. It focuses primarily on the pupil as an individual. Judgments about his educational growth are based on pertinent data, which may then be compared with similar data about him obtained at an earlier date, or with similar data from his peer group obtained concurrently. This is the type of evaluation of greatest concern to us, and is described in detail later (see page 8). On the other hand, considerable attention is being given to the third use, that is, evaluation of programs and products, and to the last, that is, assessment of educational progress on a national scale. An examination of them, however brief, is in order.

Evaluation of Programs and Products

Just as there are pronounced individual differences among pupils, so there are differences of similar magnitudes among curricula, teaching methods, administrative organizations, flexible class scheduling plans, textbooks, school physical plants, teacher's guides, films, and even projectors, tape recorders, and encyclopedias. "Over-the-coffee-cup" opinions about these and other aspects of the educational scene are usually easy to obtain. But can a systematic determination of their worth be made? Most certainly yes.

Scriven (1967), Stake (1967, 1974), and Stufflebeam (1971) have described in detail how this can be done. Their models are not concerned with pupils as individuals. Only group response is needed, and sometimes not even that. They can encompass both formative and summative evaluations of programs and products.

One useful model is that designed by Stake (1967). As an initial step in evaluation of an educational program, perhaps a new curriculum, a rationale is first established. This designates the purpose of the evaluation—the decisions about which you need data. Should the curriculum be adopted permanently or not? Should it be modified in certain respects? Is it an improvement over others designed for largely the same purposes? With questions like these in mind, the evaluator completes data matrices such as those in Figure 1.1. Both the description and the judgment matrix have the same rows, which are defined as follows:

1. *Antecedents: Any conditions existing prior to the beginning of the program that may influence the outcomes of the program, for instance, the qualifications of the teachers and pupils as well as the quality of the facilities and equipment.*
2. *Transactions: The countless encounters between pupils and staff, that is, discussions, individualized instruction, lectures, demonstrations, etc.*
3. *Outcomes: The impact of the program on pupils, teachers, and others, for example, the pupils' changes in abilities, achievements, and attitudes resulting from the educational experiences.*

For the description matrix, the columns are:

1. *Intents: The planned-for end products such as the planned-for demonstrations, environmental conditions, and coverage of subject matter.*
2. *Observations: Descriptions of the situation as it is found, such as results*

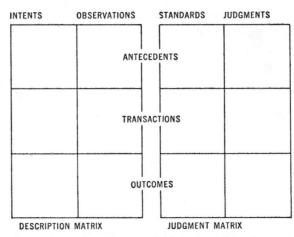

FIGURE 1.1. Matrices for Statements and Data Collected by the Evaluator of an Educational Program.

From Stake, 1967, p. 529; reproduced by permission of the *Teachers College Record.*

yielded by data-gathering devices such as tests, inventories, diaries, interviews, logs, etc.

Lastly, the columns for the judgment matrix are:

1. *Standards: Acceptable and meritorious levels of antecedents, transactions, and outcomes, often arbitrarily established.*
2. *Judgments: The decisions as to what is good, bad, and indifferent in each situation, that is, a degree of importance of any discrepancies found between features of the actual programs and the standards listed for them.*

Note the broad scope of this model as well as the sizable degree of subjectivity incorporated within it. Also keep in mind that use of such a model leads to systematic evaluation, which in turn enhances efforts to make decisions based on pertinent data. The application of sound principles of program evaluation certainly will improve the meaningfulness of the educational accountability movement as we now know it (Wrightstone et al., undated).

Should we evaluate programs and products only in terms of their effectiveness in meeting their *stated* goals? Certainly not—to do so would be dangerous. After all, there might be side-effects that would be overlooked. On the other hand, should evaluations be conducted without thought of the stated goals? No—this too would be dangerous. Yet some advocates of "goal-free" evaluation (Scriven, 1972) would respond differently. This evaluation strategy emphasizes the evaluation of the actual effects of a program or product, whether or not they are intended. Attention to stated goals, it is argued, might actually be a contaminating step that partly masks the presence of unanticipated effects. For our part, a more balanced position is to assume that goal-free evaluation is a supplement—not an alternative—to goal-based evaluation, whether it be formative or summative in nature.

National Assessment of Educational Progress

Rather than being concerned with the educational achievement of individual pupils, or even groups of pupils in a school, school system, or state, the National Assessment of Educational Progress (NAEP) is designed to determine the educational attainments of young Americans at four crucial points in their educational careers: at the end of their elementary school years (age 9); during their intermediate school years (age 13); during their secondary school years (age 17); and following the completion of all degree-seeking efforts (ages 26–35). The major goals of NAEP are:

1. *To obtain census-like data on the educational attainment of large portions of our national population.*
2. *To measure the growth or decline in educational attainment that takes place over time in key learning areas.*

Serious efforts to achieve these goals began in 1963 and continue today. NAEP has identified ten learning areas to be assessed: reading, mathematics, writing, science, social studies, citizenship, literature, art, music, and career and occupational development. Review panels of teachers, specialists, and laymen interested in each area assist in the identification of the general and specific objectives for that area. They also determine the suitability of the exercises (i.e., test items) to be used. Each exercise is designed to be a direct reflection of a specified objective. In other words, data regarding group success or failure when responding to an exercise can be used with reasonable safety as a basis for inferring the degree to which the objective in question is being achieved.

The exercises vary considerably. Some are short-answer in nature, others are of the essay type, and still others require interviews, observations of pupil behavior (e.g., in citizenship), questionnaires, performance tasks (e.g., in music), and appraisal of work products (e.g., in art). NAEP's exercises are not grouped to form tests from which total scores are computed. Instead, each exercise is scored separately and the percentages of subgroups of respondents giving correct and incorrect answers are reported.

Data gathering started in 1969, and has continued annually. Each year a national sample of almost 100,000 individuals is tested. Revision and replacement of objectives and exercises continually occur, a new assessment cycle for each learning area taking place about every four to eight years (NAEP, 1974).

For reporting purposes, a number of subgroups of the national sample are used, such as:

1. *Four age levels.*
2. *Four geographic regions of the nation.*
3. *Seven sizes and types of communities.*

4. *The two sexes.*
5. *Four levels of parental education.*
6. *Two major ethnic groups.*

Literally thousands of pieces of information already have been obtained regarding the educational attainment of young Americans, many of which are highly specific. For instance, in the reading assessment are reported the percentages of various subgroups of respondents who are able to read and understand a TV schedule, and who can follow directions for a recipe or an application form; the mathematics assessment reveals the ability of young Americans to perform such common tasks as balancing a checkbook; in the citizenship and social studies assessment, responses to several exercises show the degree of support for the principle of freedom of speech. In general, NAEP has found sizable regional and community differences in achievement, as well as very large differences between respondents of the two major ethnic groups. Furthermore, a striking and consistently positive relationship exists between the level of educational achievement of young Americans and the level of education of their parents (Ahmann, 1972).

Supporters of NAEP believe that the information being gathered is descriptive enough to tell us what the younger segment of the population is learning and to provide a solid basis for taking intelligent action to improve our educational system, even to the point of helping those preparing curriculum revisions and teaching materials designed for widespread use. Some critics disagree. For instance, Katzman and Rosen (1970, p. 584) believe that NAEP " . . . can be criticized on several grounds: (1) measuring questionable educational outcomes with questionable techniques; (2) classifying student subpopulations on largely irrelevant dimensions and/or insufficient detail; and (3) neglecting to collect any information on school characteristics which would identify policy-performance relationships." Other critics fear that the findings of NAEP will ultimately lead to a highly centralized and nationalized educational system (Hand, 1965; Saylor, 1970).

To be sure, NAEP is a unique and most ambitious project. Its true worth can be determined after it has assessed each of its ten learning areas at least twice, thereby measuring the degree of change in educational achievement on a national basis.

PURPOSES OF PUPIL EVALUATION

At this point, our focus on educational evaluation is restricted to pupil evaluation; it concentrates on the pupil as an individual and as a member of a classroom unit. Such evaluation has two purposes: (1) to help the teacher determine the degree to which educational objectives have been achieved, and (2) to help the teacher know his pupils as individuals. The first purpose is basic; changes in pupil behavior are always evaluated in terms of the goals of education. The second purpose is subsidiary to the first, since, naturally, if the teacher is intimately familiar with his pupils, he will be better able to plan educational experiences for them and determine the degree to which educational objectives have been achieved. It is important to realize this fundamental relation between the two purposes. In practice, information on the degree of achievement of educational objectives is always augmented by additional information on the pupil's earlier interests, values, aptitudes, and achievements. Thus the second purpose supports the first.

Determining the Achievement of Educational Objectives

Educational objectives stem from the needs of youth as they are guided and molded by the democratic society in which they live. Suggestions for educational objectives commonly come from three sources: study of the pupil, study of the democratic society in which he lives, and judgment of the informed educational specialist. Certainly the knowledge and skills a pupil already has, as well as his inter--ests and goals, should influence the educational objectives of the class he is attending. Hence, objectives should be based on pupil needs. By the same token, the democratic society in which the pupil lives has needs; it must be improved and perpetuated. Finally, the informed specialist in a subject matter area can, after intensive study, identify important trends and interrelations that, when translated into new objectives or allowed to influence old ones, may ultimately improve the breadth and direction of the educational program as a whole.

STATING EDUCATIONAL OBJECTIVES. The modern way of expressing educational objectives is in terms of desired pupil behavior, that is, in terms of the behavior that the pupil should exhibit if he has achieved certain objectives. Often cited are specific behavioral patterns related to the pupil's knowledge, understanding, attitudes, appreciation, abilities, and skills in a specified subject matter area. The following shows the type of statement used in expressing specific objectives:

Curriculum area: Science
Grade levels: 3–5
The pupil should be able to construct a system of pulleys by means of which approximately 100 grams could lift 300 grams (Fors, 1969, p. 26).
Curriculum area: Mathematics
Grade levels: 4–6
Given a protractor marked in degrees, and the measure of an angle between 0° and 180°, the pupil will draw the angle accurately to within five degrees (Michigan Department of Education, 1973, p. 81).

From the point of view of pupil evaluation, objectives stated in terms of outwardly observable behavior are most suitable. Determining the degree to which objectives have been met is finding out how the pupil is observably different after the educational experiences from what he was before them. Stating the objectives of education in these terms is deceptively difficult.

IDENTIFYING CHANGES IN BEHAVIOR. There are many ways to discover what changes, if any, in pupil behavior have occurred as a result of educational experiences.

By means of a few liberal interpretations, the multitude of methods can be classified into two groups: testing procedures and nontesting procedures. The testing procedures can be the common paper-and-pencil tests, oral tests, or performance tests. Nontesting procedures include teacher-pupil interviews, anecdotal records, sociometric techniques, general information questionnaires, and ranking and rating methods that summarize the results of observing samples of pupil behavior or products of that behavior. Properly or otherwise, the most commonly used is the paper-and-pencil achievement test.

No matter which of the suggested methods is used to identify changes in pupil behavior, the teacher needs considerable information in addition to knowledge of the technique. That information is a thorough grasp of the typical and atypical behavioral patterns of pupils he is teaching. Standardized testing devices attempt to provide these reference points by means of norms, that is, lists of typical scores made by a sample of pupils thought to be representative of a larger population of pupils for whom the test is designed. Nontesting procedures customarily require a full knowledge of what pupils in a given class or age group are like. The more complete this knowledge, the more adequate will be the evaluation of changes in pupil behavior.

Two notable obstacles prevent a comprehensive evaluation of the degree to which educational objectives have been achieved. First of all, certain educational goals, such as those pertaining to attitudes and interests, are difficult to translate into observable pupil behavior, and changes can be identified only crudely, if at all. Consequently, it has not been possible to construct evaluation instruments that can adequately measure the degree to which the pupil has achieved all of the many and varied educational objectives. Secondly, in some instances the total desired change in pupil behavior may not be observable until months or years following the educational experience. Of course, the teacher will not be on the scene at this auspicious moment. However, he may be able to observe changes in pupil behavior indicating partial achievement of an educational objective. For example, one of the broad educational objectives often mentioned is that the pupil will prepare himself adequately for a suitable vocation. The complete achievement of this objective may not be observable for some time. Yet the classroom teacher may observe partial achievement as the pupil masters, for example, verbal and mathematical skills.

Helping a Teacher to Know His Pupils

Every teacher subscribes to the obvious truth that, to be successful, he must know his pupils. He can begin by inquiring about their names, addresses, previous academic experiences, parents, and the occupations of their parents. By observation he may be able to appraise crudely the socioeconomic level from which the pupil comes, his physical vigor, his social training, and even his enthusiasm concerning the anticipated educational experiences.

But what lies beneath the surface? A teacher is more than curious about the pupil's aptitudes, the complete story of his previous academic achievements, and the degree of his personal-social adjustment. These aspects of a pupil cannot be assessed without relying on some of the many techniques here classified as a part of pupil evaluation. Considered guesses based on informal observations are not sufficient. Appraisals need to be based on objective data and organized in a systematic pattern.

Consider for a moment a given pupil about whom a teacher is questioned. Let's call him Mike. According to the teacher, Mike is a "fair" pupil who is "moderately bright" and who seems to be "rather well-liked" by most of his classmates. In general, Mike is not very highly motivated, but appears to be content and causes little trouble. You may have often heard such a description. Undeniably it is a helpful thumbnail sketch. Yet it could be infinitely more helpful if it were more specific and less subjective. One might ask how "fair" is "fair" and how "bright" is "moderately bright"? Test scores from achievement tests and a scholastic aptitude test could underpin this description to a sizable degree. Furthermore, according to the teacher's remarks, Mike seems to be an underachiever. Why? Test scores and teacher ratings of earlier academic achievements may shed light on this question, as may various aptitude test scores. Home conditions should not be ignored even though they can only be casually evaluated. Lastly, how "well-liked" is "rather well-liked"? What kind of trouble is "little trouble"? Sociometric devices and anecdotal records may jointly illuminate these questions.

The list of suggested evaluation techniques could be continued, but the point has been made. The picture of Mike can be brought into focus only by better evaluation techniques. These will never paint a complete profile of a pupil, but they will reveal enough of that profile to justify the time and money their use demands.

Knowing a child is a prolonged, complex process. Ideally, it combines the skill of the teacher as an impersonal, astute observer, the skill of the test technician who constructs and validates the standardized measuring instruments, and the skill of a clinician, who carefully amalgamates all the above information and ferrets out likely causes and effects. Although not confronted by the ideal situation, the average classroom teacher can, through extensive effort, attain useful though typically imperfect results. The rewards for such effort are rich.

PROBLEMS

1. Using for illustrative purposes a class level and subject matter familiar to you, cite the chief arguments for and against the contention that pupil evaluation is most successful when based on limited, well-defined educational objectives.

2. It is argued that an effective teacher is one who, in a minimum amount of instructional time, can help the pupil reach pertinent educational objectives commensurate with his abilities. In the light of this statement, to what degree should there be interaction between pupil evaluation and the evaluation of teacher effectiveness? Why?

3. Some critics of the National Assessment of Educational Progress believe that this program will result in centralized control over the curriculum of public schools (Hand, 1965; Saylor, 1970). Evaluate this claim in terms of the procedures used in the assessment (Merwin and Womer, 1969, pp. 305–334).

DIFFERENCES BETWEEN MEASUREMENT
AND EVALUATION

Differentiating between the terms "measurement" and "evaluation" is sometimes difficult. The two terms are related, yet decidedly different. Evaluation is a more inclusive term than measurement. Measurement is only a part, although a very substantial one, of evaluation, providing information on which an evaluation can be based.

Characteristics of Measurement

Educational measurement is the process that attempts to obtain a quantified representation of the degree to which a pupil reflects a trait. The use of a paper-and-pencil test to discover the scholastic aptitude or achievement of a pupil is an illustration of educational measurement. In the case of scholastic aptitude, for example, one can easily visualize it as a continuum, that is, as a trait that logically varies from much to some to none and that is theoretically capable of being divided into an infinite number of degrees. Each pupil has a specific position on the continuum. Educational measurement tries to represent that position by means of a numerical value, a scholastic aptitude test score, and to do so in as objective a manner as possible.

The measurement process is fundamentally descriptive of the degree to which a trait is possessed by a pupil and uses numbers rather than words. A teacher can characterize a fourth-grade pupil as "tall," "gifted," or "underweight." These are word descriptions of traits that are continuous. Measuring instruments can change "tall" to "61.5 inches," "gifted" to "*Wechsler (WISC)* IQ of 128," and "underweight" to "85 pounds." The advantage of reporting numbers rather than adjectives is obvious. The meaning of any adjective varies from teacher to teacher. Carefully executed measurement data do not change. They are notably less ambiguous than verbal descriptions.

Educational measurement tends to concentrate on a specific, well-defined trait and then strives to determine with precision the degree to which that trait is possessed by an individual pupil. This is in many ways comparable to the methods of a photographer who, in trying to capture the individuality of a physique, photographs each part separately, first the hand, then the foot, perhaps then the nose, and so forth. Such a photographer would hope that the result of his work would be a series of revealing photographs, each displaying clearly the status of the physique with regard to the particular part. If totally successful, he could assemble all photographs and recreate a picture of the total physique.

A teacher acts like a photographer when he examines specific pupil traits, such as reading comprehension, vocabulary, and scholastic aptitude, with a series of measuring instruments. Each test measures a certain pupil trait, just as each photograph pictures a part of the physique. Unfortunately, the teacher's task is not so simple as the photographer's. Whereas it is possible that some of the photographer's pictures might be blurred because his camera was out of focus or might have poor black and white contrast because they are underexposed, such lapses are unlikely, especially if he is a professional photographer. In contrast, the teacher using even the best measurement devices may have nothing but somewhat blurred and underexposed "photographs." Worse than that, some traits of the pupil cannot be "photographed" at all since no measuring instruments are available. Hence the total picture of a pupil yielded by combining the results of many measurements of various pupil traits is often somewhat unclear, due to the failure of the instruments to yield precise, unequivocal results, and is invariably incomplete, due to the scarcity of suitable measuring instruments, particularly in the area of personal-social adjustment.

The statement that a measuring instrument fails to yield precise, unequivocal results means that the instrument does not adequately serve the purposes for which it is intended, and that it does not measure with perfect consistency. The failure of an instrument to serve the purposes for which it is intended is known as lack of validity; the failure of an instrument to measure consistently is known as lack of reliability. The concepts of validity and reliability are described and illustrated in Chapters 9 and 10 respectively.

Characteristics of Evaluation

Pupil evaluation is a process in which a teacher commonly uses information derived from many sources to arrive at a value judgment. The information might be obtained by using measuring instruments as well as other techniques that do not necessarily yield quantitative results, such as general information questionnaires, direct observation, and teacher-pupil interviews. An evaluation may or may not be based on measurement data, though appropriate measurements are customarily used if they are available. Data from good measuring instruments can provide a sound basis for good evaluation.

The differences between measurement and evaluation can be easily illustrated. Suppose that you are about to buy a new four-door automobile and have decided to restrict your choice to three makes. Now you face the happy problem of determining which of the three automobiles to buy. Your investigation probably starts with measurements of each: the cost, the horsepower of the engine, the length of wheelbase, the gasoline consumption at various speeds, and the weight are useful measurement values. Perhaps then you test-drive demonstration cars, forming judgments on riding ease, maneuverability, rapidity of acceleration, and interior and exterior beauty. Finally, you choose one of the three automobiles. The choice results from a careful consideration of quantitative evidence, qualitative evidence, and highly subjective impressions, and is the end result of an evaluation process.

Within the field of education a common example of the differences between measurement and evaluation can be found in the practice of assigning final marks to pupils at the end of a unit of work. Measurements of a pupil's prior achievement and aptitude may have been made before the unit began, and measurements of the changes in pupil behavior follow the termination of the unit. To these pieces of information the teacher frequently adds his reactions to the pupil's attitudes, cooperativeness, motivation, and possibly even his punctuality. The final result is generally a single letter or numerical mark that supposedly indicates the relative success of the pupil as he experienced the unit of work. As in the case of the choice of automobile, an evaluation process has taken place; a value judgment has been made.

PROBLEM

4. In his criticism of the importance placed on final marks, Milton (1968) quotes St. Augustine who wrote:

"For so it is, O Lord, my God, I measure it;
But what it is that I measure I do not know."

Explain Milton's point of view with this question in mind: Should final marks be considered measurements?

EDUCATIONAL TESTING

Educational measurement is usually considered to include educational testing. Whether this is true depends, of course, on the manner in which educational testing is defined. "Test" is, paradoxically, a simple and widely used term and yet one of somewhat vague meaning. It can be defined in such a broad manner as to include some evaluation procedures that yield only verbal descriptions of pupil traits. For instance, it can be defined as any systematic procedure for observing a person's behavior and describing it by means of a numerical scale or a category system (Cronbach, 1970, p. 26). Some of these procedures cannot be included within the definition of educational measurement. On the other hand, educational testing can be defined in a more restricted manner so that, practically speaking, all tests can be called measuring instruments.

It is convenient for the purpose of this book to define the word "test" in the more restricted manner. In the first place, a test is nothing more than a group of questions or tasks to which a pupil is to respond. The questions might require the pupil to give the correct meaning of a word, solve an arithmetic problem, or identify missing parts in a picture of an animal. Tasks might require the pupil to thread beads on a string, assemble a small piece of apparatus, or arrange blocks in a prescribed design. These questions and tasks might be presented to the pupil orally or in writing; some are even presented by means of pantomine under certain circumstances. The questions and tasks are known as test items. They are intended to be a representative sample of all possible questions and tasks related to the trait measured by the test that are of suitable difficulty. A pupil's responses to the test items are scored in such a way that, ideally, the results indicate the degree to which he possesses the specified trait. The principal purpose of a test is to produce a quantitative representation of the pupil trait that it is designed to measure. Certainly educational testing is included within educational measurement when this restricted definition of a test is used.

Types of Tests

Tests can differ from each other in many ways. Some contain items of nearly constant difficulty, whereas others contain items of varying difficulty. Some require that rigid time limits be maintained; others do not. Some demand that the pupils to whom the test is to be administered have a complete command of the English language; others do not. Some can be administered to large groups of pupils simultaneously; others to only one pupil at a time. These and other variations have been used to subdivide tests into a relatively restricted list of eighteen types.*

In the following discussion, two and sometimes three types of tests are grouped together, as in the case of oral, essay, and objective tests. This grouping is made because the types are more or less contrasting. Sometimes the relative merits of each are vigorously debated by both teachers and testing specialists. In any event, it is a useful way of remembering the types and their general characteristics.

Notice also that a test can simultaneously be classified as more than one type. For example, one popular achievement test used in schools today is a group, verbal, objective, standardized, norm-referenced test. Such a multiple classification of a test is actually a highly informative thumbnail description. Mastery of such terminology is a necessary prerequisite to an understanding of this part of educational evaluation.

Individual and Group Tests

INDIVIDUAL TESTS. Individual tests are tests that can be administered to only one pupil at a time. The examiner has an opportunity to establish rapport with the pupil and to gain insight into the pupil and his reaction to the testing situation. He can even ascertain possible reasons for many of the pupil's answers. Furthermore, the examiner practically always has the responsibility of making a written record of the pupil's answers. A common illustration of an individual test is the *Wechsler Intelligence Scale for Children.*

GROUP TESTS. Group tests can be administered to more than one pupil at a time. The number of pupils can range into the hundreds if sufficient test proctors are available. In elementary and secondary school situations, however, pupils are often tested as a class. Because of its simplicity and low cost, this type of test is far more popular than the individual test.

You have no doubt repeatedly experienced the impersonal atmosphere in which group tests are typically given. As the group of pupils becomes larger, this problem increases. Certainly, a number of the desirable aspects of the individual test are found only to a reduced degree in group tests, since they have been sacrificed for economy of time and money.

Classroom and Standardized Tests

CLASSROOM TESTS. Classroom tests are sometimes called teacher-made tests or "informal" tests. They are tests constructed by a classroom teacher for use in his particular classes under conditions of his choosing. In practically all instances these tests are group tests and measure pupil achievement. More of these tests are adminis-

---

* Brief descriptions of these and other types of tests can be found in the third edition of Good's Dictionary of Education (New York: McGraw-Hill, 1973).

tered than any other kind. Unfortunately, they often are carelessly constructed and interpreted.

The value of classroom achievement tests stems from one major consideration— the individual nature of every class. This individuality can be traced primarily to the kind of educational objectives involved in the class and also to the relative emphasis each receives. It also can be traced to the quality of the pupils who compose the class. The teacher certainly knows better than anyone else the exact nature of these characteristics of his class. Since the appropriateness of any achievement test item is determined by the educational objectives of the class, the teacher is in an excellent position to build test items that measure suitable areas of the pupils' achievements and that are of suitable difficulty. Thus classroom achievement tests, if properly prepared, are tailor-made for a certain class of pupils taught in a certain manner (see Chapter 2). On the other hand, standardized achievement tests are designed for many classes of a certain type; these tests attempt to cover those achievement areas thought to be common to all classes for which they are designed.

STANDARDIZED TESTS. Standardized tests are constructed almost invariably by teams of individuals rather than by a single person. In the case of standardized achievement tests, teachers qualified in the area tested work with measurement specialists by helping to identify the scope of an achievement test and its appropriateness. Often they contribute possible test items. In the case of standardized aptitude tests, the role of the teacher is considerably reduced, if not nonexistent.

Characteristically, standardized tests are carefully designed. They are pretested in order to determine the level of difficulty of the test items, the amount of testing time required, the sizes of typical scores made by various types of pupils, and so forth. The manuals accompanying the test contain information concerning the method of developing the test, its purposes, directions for its proper administration, directions for scoring, techniques for interpreting the scores, and reports of research in which the test was involved. In order that any standardized test be used properly, it must be administered only to those pupils for whom it is designed and strictly in accordance with the manual's directions. Furthermore, the scoring of the instrument and the interpretation of those scores must be performed in the manner prescribed for that test.

Oral, Essay, and Objective Tests

ORAL TESTS. Although common in the early history of achievement testing, oral tests are not popular today. Their use as a means of testing the knowledge and understanding of a candidate for an advanced degree is no doubt their principal single function now. Even in this situation they often are not used alone but in conjunction with paper-and-pencil tests.

The disadvantages of oral testing are not difficult to identify. First of all, it tends to be somewhat unplanned in total. The first questions asked by the teacher can be selected with care; after that, however, the nature of the responses of the pupils often influences the nature of later questions. Soon the sampling of the pupil's knowledge and understanding becomes quite narrow. Consciously or unconsciously, the teacher may be grossly unfair to the pupil. Secondly, pupils, like actors, are affected by their audience. The tension created by a face-to-face contact with an examiner has caused many a pupil, even though he actually knows the correct answer, to blurt out the most unusual conglomeration of words, complete with fractured syntax. Thirdly, oral tests generally require too much time from both teacher and pupil. Fourthly, there is no written record of the pupil's responses.

A principal advantage of oral testing is that it can be diagnostic. Probing questions can reveal the causes of a pupil's error. Such information, needless to say, is extremely useful to a teacher. Oral testing has a further advantage in that it reveals how well a pupil can apply his knowledge to novel situations, though this can be tested by paper-and-pencil tests as well. To this end, specialists in medicine have designed standardized role-playing situations for the purpose of assessing certain complex skills of gathering data and making judgments as demonstrated by candidates for certification (Levine and McGuire, 1968). Simulated diagnostic interviews, proposed treatment interviews, and patient-management conferences have been used successfully. In the first two instances, the candidate plays the role of a physician and an examiner plays the role of a patient, while a second examiner uses standard rating scales to record his impressions of the interview. In the third situation, five candidates play the role of physician and their conference is rated by examiners.

ESSAY TESTS. Since many of the difficulties associated with oral tests disappear when paper-and-pencil tests are used, essay testing has replaced oral testing in part. Instead of asking the pupil to answer a question orally, he is asked to write his answer. This simple change affects the testing situation drastically. Now many pupils can be tested simultaneously; each can answer the same questions, except for an optional question or two which some teachers offer. Since only one set of questions is to be used for many pupils, extensive efforts to obtain a cross-sectional sampling of the subject matter in those questions are certainly justified. Moreover, each pupil has an opportunity to compose himself as he attacks each question. Tension is noticeably reduced, but scoring problems are still serious (see Chapter 5).

OBJECTIVE TESTS. Objective tests are tests that can be scored in such a manner that subjective judgment is eliminated when determining the correctness of a pupil's answers. True-false tests, matching tests, and multiple-choice tests are objective tests in the true sense of the definition. Supply tests (for example, completion tests) are sometimes considered to be objective tests even though the subjective judgment is not entirely eliminated. Occasionally, these are called "semiobjective" test items (see Chapters 3 and 4).

Objective tests are very common: classroom as well as standardized achievement tests are so constructed, and paper-and-pencil aptitude tests are almost invariably of this type. Clearly, objective scoring is in keeping with the whole purpose of using a standardized test. After all, a standardized test tries to be a universal "yardstick" to measure a specified pupil trait. To prevent the "yardstick" from changing its units, such precautions as uniform testing conditions are required. Uniform scoring procedures are equally vital. The test results obtained by a pupil should never be affected positively or negatively by the person who happens to score his paper.

Speed, Power, and Mastery Tests

SPEED TESTS. A speed test is one in which a pupil must, in a limited amount of time, answer a series of questions or perform a series of tasks of a uniformly low level of difficulty. The near-constant level of difficulty of the questions or tasks is such that, if the pupil had unlimited time, he could easily answer each question or perform each task successfully. The average pupil finds that he does not have sufficient time to attempt all test items. The intent of a speed test is to measure primarily the rapidity with which a pupil can do what is asked of him rather than whether he can do it at all.

Excellent illustrations of speed tests can be found in the case of some clerical aptitude tests. One such test requires the pupil to determine whether two numbers or two names are the same or different. In another the pupil must match combinations of two letters, a letter and a number, or two numbers. Rigid time limits that allow too little time for completion of the test are enforced. If this were not the case, any alert person would certainly have a perfect score.

Speed tests in the pure sense are not common in educational measurement. Usually, not only are comfortable (though controlled) time limits allowed, but also the level of difficulty of the test items is not uniformly low. However, in achievement testing, some instruments tend to be speeded because of poorly chosen time limits. So little time is allowed the pupils that the number of unattempted test items becomes excessive. On the other hand, tests designed to measure speed of reading are closely timed and properly so.

POWER TESTS. In contrast to a pure speed test is a power test. The items of a power test are more difficult and, technically, time limits do not exist. In reality, they frequently do exist. Little is to be gained by giving a pupil unrestricted time for writing a test. There seems to be a point in time after which further contemplation of the test items yields practically no profit. Builders of standardized instruments generally agree that a power test should be so timed that a very large percentage of the pupils for whom it is designed will have ample time to attempt all of the items. Although estimates vary as to the proper size of this percentage, ninety percent seems to be an acceptable minimum. Hence, the test is slightly speeded.

Power tests are widely given, particularly when testing achievement. Teachers and pupils alike feel that minimizing the speed factors in a testing situation is desirable. This feeling no doubt stems from the conviction that knowing one's level of maximum achievement as indicated by a power test is more useful than knowing the rapidity with which one can perform simple tasks as indicated by a speed test.

MASTERY TESTS. In a mastery test the level of difficulty of the items is quite low, and the time limits allowed are generous. Its purpose is to measure the knowledge and skill that every pupil of the class should have acquired. Hence it is expected that virtually all of the pupils (about eighty-five to ninety percent) will perform perfectly on the test. No attempt is made to discover how much a pupil may have acquired over and above the minimum everyone should have reached.

Mastery tests are customarily teacher-constructed. A spelling list, a vocabulary list, or a series of arithmetic computations may constitute such a test. Teachers have used them as quizzes with considerable effectiveness. However, when used alone as an end-of-unit or end-of-term achievement test, their usefulness is less than that of power tests, particularly at the secondary school level.

Sometimes we underestimate the usefulness of mastery tests. For instance, they can serve as end-of-unit achievement tests when used in conjunction with an appropriately designed classroom power test (Trow, 1968). By means of the mastery test, the teacher could determine pupil command of the essentials of the subject matter. Then the power test would be used to sample that material that remains.

Furthermore, emphasis by teachers on learning for mastery (Bloom, Hastings, and Madaus, 1971, pp. 43–57) means testing accordingly. Here mastery tests are part of a formative evaluation program; in other words, they show the points of difficulty for pupils who lack mastery and help the teacher to prescribe remedies for him. Frequent "midstream" use of mastery tests in this context helps ensure that each group of learning tasks is mastered before subsequent tasks are begun. Pupils are motivated to put forth the necessary effort at the appropriate time.

Also, the National Assessment of Educational Progress uses various levels of test items, one of which samples knowledges and skills that practically all examinees know. The same point of view is used with criterion-referenced tests (see page 21) when reporting of test results is "on-off" in nature, for instance, either a ninety percent minimum level of proficiency has been achieved by the pupil or it has not. Finally, mastery tests are used for units of programmed instruction in order to find out whether a pupil should proceed to new material, repeat the material completed, or study remedial material.

Verbal, Nonverbal, and Performance Tests

VERBAL TESTS. A verbal test is one in which the responding pupil utilizes written or spoken language. This use of language can occur in the directions needed by the pupil, in his responses to the test items, or in both cases. The widespread use of paper-and-pencil achievement tests in the typical classroom situation clearly illustrates the popularity of verbal tests.

NONVERBAL TESTS. Not all persons can be given a verbal test, however. Illiterates, mentally deficient children, and very young children are incapable of understanding written, and sometimes even oral, directions. Some tests are so constructed that the instructions are given orally and the persons tested respond without use of language. These have been called nonverbal tests, although strictly speaking a nonverbal test does not require the use of language by either the examiner or the person taking the test. Pantomime is used as a means of giving directions. The person may only point to indicate his answer. Geometric drawings and three-dimensional materials have been used in this type of test.

PERFORMANCE TESTS. In a discussion of performance tests, it is necessary to differentiate between aptitude performance tests and achievement performance tests. In aptitude testing, performance tests are often nothing more than nonverbal tests. They are designed to measure the aptitudes of those persons unfamiliar with the English language. For example, the manipulation of blocks and the tracing of a maze have been used to assess general mental ability. In achievement testing, performance tests are not devoted primarily to the illiterate. Performance tests attempt to appraise the degree to which a skill has been achieved. For example, a typing speed test is a performance test. The pupil's performance during a specific period of time is scored in terms of quantity and accuracy of the material typed. Athletic events, musical performances, food preparation, laboratory exercises, and machine operations can serve as performance tests (see Chapter 7).

Readiness and Diagnostic Tests

READINESS TESTS. Readiness tests are designed to determine the ability of a pupil to undertake a certain type of learning. They resemble aptitude tests in that they try to forecast the achievement that would occur if appropriate training were given. They differ from aptitude tests in that they deal with a highly specific kind of achievement, such as reading.

Readiness tests are designed to discover whether a pupil is sufficiently advanced to profit from formal instruction in a subject area. To accomplish this purpose, reading readiness tests may use tests of visual discrimination, auditory discrimination, vocabulary, and sometimes motor coordination. Tests of pupil readiness in mathematics and language are also given in secondary school; these are called aptitude or prognostic tests for a given subject matter area.

DIAGNOSTIC TESTS. Whereas readiness tests are administered to pupils before formal instruction is given, diagnostic tests are administered after formal instruction has taken place. The purpose of a diagnostic test is to reveal specific deficiencies in a pupil's background. This information could also point to specific deficiencies in the instruction given. The alert classroom teacher tests in this manner continually, often using mastery tests of his own design.

One outstanding characteristic of diagnostic tests is that any total test scores they might give are of limited value. The desired information comes from part scores based on a few related test items or from an item-by-item analysis of the pupil's responses. Each individual item or small group of items tests the pupils with regard to a particular part of the materials taught. Thus a pupil's answers are studied on that basis.

Norm-Referenced, Criterion-Referenced, and Objective-Referenced Tests

NORM-REFERENCED TESTS. Test norms are representations of average or common performance based on the results of testing a typical group of pupils for whom the instrument is designed (see Chapter 8). Thus a pupil's score can be compared with tables of norms such as those for percentile ranks; his relative performance can be determined in terms of his rank in a standard group of 100 pupils, for example, seventy-third from the bottom of the group.

A norm-referenced test, then, finds a pupil's performance level in relation to levels of others on the same test. This is the usual approach taken in educational testing. Many standardized achievement and aptitude tests are norm-referenced instruments.

CRITERION-REFERENCED TESTS. In contrast, criterion-referenced tests are those used to ascertain a pupil's status with respect to some criterion, for instance, an established performance standard. We want to know what the pupil can do, rather than how he compares with others. An example of this type of test is the Red Cross Senior Lifesaving Test, in which an individual must demonstrate certain swimming skills in order to pass. How well others perform is not important. Individual mastery is the primary issue (Popham and Husek, 1969).

On the basis of its appearance, you will not be able to differentiate between a norm-referenced test and a criterion-referenced test in a subject matter area such as mathematics. Yet the test items in a norm-referenced test are selected in order to produce variability among the test scores, whereas those for a criterion-referenced test are designed to be an accurate reflection of a given criterion of behavior. Thus these two types of tests differ in terms of purpose.

They also differ in the manner in which they are constructed and the kind of information produced by pupil responses. Note that test items in a criterion-referenced achievement test must be a representative sample of the tasks identified by the specific educational objectives of the instruction given. This is most easily accomplished if the objectives are stated in terms of the explicit performance to be demonstrated by the pupil. There needs to be an analysis of the structure of the task (say, ability to add integers accurately) so that components of it and criteria of performance with respect to them are described carefully. The scoring of pupil responses to test items is such that it provides detailed information about which tasks a pupil can perform (Glaser and Nitko, 1971). The desired end product is generally a descriptive statement of the pupil's behavior, like "Frank's performance on the test was such that we believe he can accurately add eighty percent of a universe of pairs of positive integers, none of which has more than three digits."

A well-designed criterion-referenced test, in short, provides a great deal of information about the behavior repertoire of a pupil. We discover what he can and cannot do, that is, whether or not he achieved some of the immediate outcomes of a learning situation. His performance, as measured by one or more test items, is compared with an external standard representing a specific educational objective (Gagné, 1970, pp. 340–343). This type of testing is highly compatible with a teacher emphasis on mastery learning, and can provide information helpful in both pupil evaluation and program evaluation (Cronbach, 1963).

OBJECTIVE-REFERENCED TESTS. The primary difference between criterion-referenced tests and objective-referenced tests is the presence of a clearly defined

TABLE 1.1. Comparison of Norm-Referenced Achievement Tests with Criterion-and Objective-Referenced Tests.

Test characteristic	Norm-referenced achievement tests	Criterion- and objective-referenced tests
Planning the test	The test is typically planned on the basis of general descriptions of subject matter topics and process skills.	The test is typically planned in terms of specific, behaviorally stated objectives, each providing the basis for one or several related test items.
Preparing the test items	Test items are constructed to maximize discrimination among pupils.	Test items are constructed to measure proficiency for a specified task.
Types of test items	All types are used.	All types are used.
Level of difficulty of test items.	Test items are of medium difficulty, i.e., about thirty to seventy percent of the pupils answer correctly (see p. 153).	Test items vary widely in difficulty, but regularly are of the mastery type, i.e., most pupils respond correctly after training.
Criterion for mastery	No criterion for mastery is customarily specified.	Objectives for criterion- and objective-referenced test items designate a criterion for mastery or it sometimes can be inferred.
Interpreting the test results	A total score or several sub-scores are computed and a pupil's relative standing in a group or class is ascertained (see p. 202).	A pupil's success or failure on a test item or small group of similar test items is determined, and a statement is prepared that describes his performance solely with reference to certain performance objectives.
Common uses of the test	1. To determine the relative standing of a pupil within a normative group (see p. 214).	1. To ascertain a pupil's status with respect to established standards of performance, thereby determining what he knows and can do.
	2. To assist in selection of individuals for educational programs, employment, etc.	2. To diagnose specific pupil deficiencies in achievement.
	3. To provide a more-or-less global representation of pupil achievement in a specified learning area.	3. To evaluate the success of an instructional program.
Availability of standardized tests	Many tests are available covering most of the common curriculum areas.	An increasing number are becoming available, many of which focus on the basic skills.

standard of performance. For instance, in the case of the National Assessment of Educational Progress, achievement test items are constructed to be a direct reflection of a specified objective, but often no performance standard is inherent in the objective. Like criterion-referenced test items, the purpose of these test items is to describe the tasks a pupil can perform. However, in view of the absence of a clearly stated criterion, they are better called objective-referenced than criterion-referenced.

The differentiation among norm-, criterion-, and objective-referenced tests is not always clear-cut. Sometimes norm-referenced tests are capable of producing criterion-referenced interpretations (Fremer, 1972). Also, the terms "criterion-referenced" and "objective-referenced" are often used interchangeably. In any event, all types have powerful roles to play in pupil evaluation and should be thought of as supplemental to each other.

COMPARISON OF TEST TYPES. The major differences and similarities between norm-referenced tests on the one hand and criterion- and objective-referenced ones on the other are delineated in Table 1.1. This table summarizes many of the ideas contained in the foregoing paragraphs. It can be most easily interpreted when one restricts its scope to achievement testing. Even in this context, however, further elaboration is sometimes needed as designated by the page references to sections of other chapters that follow.

PROBLEMS

5. According to the definition of a test used in this chapter, can the following standardized instruments be called tests? (For information about these instruments, see *The Seventh Mental Measurements Yearbook* by O. K. Buros, 1972.)
    a. *Mooney Problem Check List*
    b. *Kuder Preference Record*
    c. *Fundamental Achievement Series*
    d. *Thorndike Dimensions of Personality*
    e. *Stanford Achievement Test*
For each of the foregoing considered to be a test, identify its classification according to the eighteen types of tests described.

6. What are the important differences between criterion-referenced testing for mastery of relatively simple learning outcomes, and testing at the developmental level, that is, where learning outcomes are complex and each pupil is encouraged to achieve maximum performance (Gronlund, 1973, pp. 22–23)?

INDIRECT NATURE OF
MEASUREMENT PROCEDURES

When a carpenter builds a house, he engages in direct measurement. When he measures the length of a board or the size of the angles at which it is to be cut, he does not need to infer the characteristic being measured. It is clearly and obviously present and measurable. By contrast, the teacher must frequently engage in indirect rather than direct measurement. For example, a pupil's general mental ability is inferred by measuring, by means of a test, what are considered to be the *effects* of general mental ability and not by measuring general mental ability as such. Let us examine this situation more closely.

The expression "general mental ability" (or its near synonym "general intelligence") is widely used today. But exactly what does it mean? One writer defines intelligence as a summation of learning experiences (Wesman, 1968, p. 267). Another says that this term "characteristically designates that combination of abilities required for survival or advancement within a particular culture or subculture" (Anastasi, 1968, p. 293). Still another believes that, along with the strictly cognitive aspects of general mental ability, one must consider heavily "two additional factors; namely, (1) creativity and (2) resistance to emotional or other forces that distort the process of reasoning" (Stoddard, 1966).

These are but three of the multitude of definitions that have been proposed. The fact that they differ at least slightly among themselves and that other definitions differ to some degree from them does not now concern us. The important factor is their similarity. No matter which definition one may choose as most suitable, general mental ability is clearly a less obvious human trait than others (such as height and weight). In short, it cannot be seen, touched, or handled in a direct manner.

To appreciate the relatively obscure nature of general mental ability, we need only recall how most individuals estimate informally, without the use of instruments, the general mental ability of their acquaintances. Rare is the person who has not identified a number of his acquaintances as having less mental ability than himself. Possibly (and with less certainty, perhaps) this same person also has classified a few of his acquaintances as having more mental ability than himself. How does he arrive at these decisions? Obviously he examines each acquaintance in terms of those aspects and products of his behavior that seemingly reflect the amount of general mental ability present.

Ordinarily, informal estimates of general mental ability are based on such information as the academic or financial accomplishments of the person, his facility for quickly and correctly identifying the salient point of a humorous story, or perhaps his ability to carry on an interesting conversation. Although these pieces of information may not be representative of a person's behavior, nor directly and completely related to variations in general mental ability, judgment is nevertheless rendered.

Formal attempts to measure general mental ability resemble these informal attempts in one respect. They too evaluate general mental ability in terms of its effects. Observable behavior thought to be directly related to general mental ability is identified, and the trait is measured indirectly by evaluating the observable behavior in some way.

A few of the common types of behavior sometimes used in this measurement are the ability to solve arithmetic problems, to identify the meanings of English words, spatial ability,* and the ability to solve number series problems.† If a pupil is "gifted,"

---

*Spatial ability can be evaluated by determining whether a pupil can visualize how a geometric figure will look after it has been rotated, or how it will look after it has been divided and the parts reassembled in different positions.

†A typical number series problem is the following:

The numbers in the following series proceed according to some rule. Select the next number from among the five possibilities listed.

Series	Next number
6 7 10 11 14 15 18	17 18 19 20 21

he should be able to answer correctly difficult questions concerning areas such as those mentioned. If he is "average," he should be able to answer correctly many of the questions but not the very difficult ones. If he is "dull," he should be able to answer correctly only the very easy questions and may find even these troublesome.

Observe that in this approach an important assumption is made. It is assumed that there is a direct and unchanging relationship between the general mental ability of a pupil and his ability to answer questions in the areas mentioned. If this assumption is not true, the indirect measurement procedure is worthless. Moreover, if the ability to answer these questions is an effect of only certain aspects of general mental ability, then any measurement of general mental ability based only on the type of questions mentioned is incomplete.

Indirect measurement procedures are common. Temperatures are ordinarily measured indirectly by means of a mercury thermometer and dangerous highway conditions by means of automobile speed limits. Aspects of a pupil's personal-social adjustment are inferred from his written answers to questions about himself. For example, he may be asked to respond with a "Yes," "Uncertain," or "No" to a question such as: "Are you frequently afraid of adults?" Attempts have even been made to determine how well a pupil can apply what he has learned by asking him to recite what he has learned. Presumably, the more information he can recall, the better he can apply it. Changes in a pupil's attitudes and appreciations have been estimated by rating changes in the pupil's overt behavior in the classroom or on the playground. Changes there have been interpreted to represent deep-seated, perhaps permanent, changes, which will be manifested in the home or, in later years, in a vocation.

Indirect procedures should be used only when direct procedures cannot be applied. The repeated use of indirect measurement procedures in education stems from the fact that direct ones are often impossible or at least impractical. Measurement of such characteristics of a pupil as general mental ability, interests, attitudes, and many aspects of achievement is therefore complicated.

PROBLEM

7. Which of the following can be best classified as direct measurement and which as indirect measurement?
   a. Determining the quality of a university library by counting the number of volumes it contains.
   b. Determining the adequacy of a pupil's vision with a letter chart.
   c. Determining the teaching effectiveness of an instructor with a paper-and-pencil opinionnaire administered to his pupils.
   d. Determining a pupil's ability to subtract two whole numbers (with a minuend less than ten) by means of a criterion-referenced test (Hively, Patterson, and Pope, 1968).

ACCURACY OF MEASUREMENT PROCEDURES

A carpenter building a new house continually varies the accuracy of his measurement according to the need, and chooses his measuring instruments on that basis. For instance, as he assembles rough scaffoldings to assist in the construction, he probably cuts the board needed at points found by estimating the desired lengths. When cutting the joists, however, he uses a steel rule to measure lengths, and no greater than one-eighth of an inch error is allowed. Finally, when cutting the interior trim, he now uses the most precise of steel rules to measure length, allowing no more than one-sixteenth of an inch error.

Typically, the classroom teacher also varies the degree of accuracy of his measurement procedures as his purposes change. The measurement of general mental ability again offers a convenient illustration. In the first place, a teacher certainly wants to know whether each pupil in his class has a certain minimum amount of this trait so he can profit from the learning experiences offered. This need be only rough measurement for most pupils. Later the teacher may want to know whether each pupil is achieving in proportion to his capacity to learn. Such a classification of each pupil as an underachiever, normal achiever, or overachiever requires considerably greater accuracy of measurement of general mental ability as well as academic achievement. Determination of *amount* of overachievement or underachievement demands still greater accuracy.

Finally, certain pupils may be in competition for a highly specialized and technical training program to be started after completion of secondary school. Assume that the majority of pupils who are not qualified or interested are initially eliminated, and that only a few of the remaining pupils are to be chosen. Under these conditions, selecting those pupils who, because of their talents and earlier successes, have the greatest chance of success in such a program will demand even more sensitive measurements of general mental ability, prior achievement, and probably other factors.

The carpenter has an important advantage over the teacher in his accuracy of measurement. His accuracy, through the use of modern tools, comfortably surpasses the minimal accuracy required. He could determine the length of a joist to one-sixteenth or one thirty-second of an inch if it were necessary. The teacher is confronted with a relatively low ceiling above which his accuracy of measurement has not, as yet, reached. For example, when measuring general mental ability, a teacher must be satisfied with identifying a pupil's mental ability test score, which *probably* does not differ from his true mental ability score by more than five or six points. We simply do not possess instruments that can measure psychological traits with refined accuracy.

Level of Measurement Accuracy

What then, you may ask, is the level of accuracy teachers typically encounter in their measurement attempts? In the first place, the accuracy of measurement procedures varies with pupil traits being investigated. Secondly, although the accuracy available to teachers is considerably less than ideal, it is often sufficient to account the procedure highly useful.

ACCURACY VARIES WITH TRAITS. That the level of accuracy should vary with the pupil trait being investigated is certainly understandable. Some traits are reasonably well-defined. Perhaps they have been studied more intensively than others, or perhaps they lend themselves more readily to measurement. Accordingly, mental ability is repeatedly mentioned as an area in which the accuracy of measurement procedures is relatively high, though far from perfect. Somewhat the same is said of the procedures used for measuring academic achievement, especially the measuring of a pupil's ability to recall information. After all, it is not difficult to determine a pupil's ability to recall the year in which the Battle of Hastings was fought, to spell properly the word "parallel," or to find the product of seven and eight.

The accuracy of the measurement procedures used in such relatively simple instances as those above is superior. Furthermore, well-developed standardized tests permit assessment in quantitative units that are of equal or near-equal size. In other words, a difference of one unit between two amounts is the same or essentially the same as a difference of one unit between any other two amounts, just as a difference of one pound between two given weights is the same as a difference of one pound between any other two given weights. Measuring instruments yielding scores that have equal units are classified as interval scales.

In contrast, consider efforts to measure aspects of a pupil's personal-social adjustment or the degree to which educational objectives pertaining to changes in attitudes and appreciations have been achieved. Now the pupil traits are subtle, almost nebulous. Such irrelevant factors as "lip service" and tendency to conform to majority opinion on the part of the pupil cloud the measurement attempts. Accuracy here is appreciably less than in measurement of general mental ability. To determine the amounts of some of these traits possessed by a pupil is often impossible. Our measuring procedures may yield information of such a crude nature that ranking the pupils within a group is the most accurate representation of the individual differences that is justified. For instance, Sammy's ability to cooperate willingly with his peers in completing various projects of mutual interest may be observably superior to Sandra's; her ability in this respect may be judged to surpass Jimmy's. Hence Sammy is ranked first, Sandra second, and Jimmy third. Unfortunately, we are not at all certain that Sammy surpasses Sandra to the same degree that she surpasses Jimmy. The intervals between successive ranks are not necessarily equal; thus ranking (that is, the ordinal scale of measurement) is clearly a less precise representation of individual differences than determination of amounts.

All too frequently, the crudeness of the information produced by measuring procedures prevents us from even ranking pupils. Instead we must be content with a somewhat general verbal description. For example, instead of ranking Sammy first with respect to his ability to cooperate willingly with his peers, our measuring procedures may be so imprecise that the teacher can say only that he "cooperates frequently," or "usually displays little reluctance when the opportunity to cooperate is presented." Verbal descriptions of this type obviously are less precise representations of individual differences than the ranking of members of a group. Classifying pupils in terms of categories that have no apparent sense of order is known as the nominal scale of measurement.

USEFULNESS OF AVAILABLE ACCURACY. Certainly lack of absolute accuracy is disturbing. Yet sufficient accuracy may exist to justify the statement that measuring procedures are some of the most useful tools a teacher has. To obtain a realistic picture of accuracy of educational measuring instruments and utility of these instruments for classroom teachers, let us examine a comparable situation in meteorology.

In many respects, the teacher views his measurement results as the farmer views the weather forecasts. The success of both parties depends in part on accurate and timely evaluation results. Both recognize that their information is not totally accurate nor even timely in all instances. Both can supplement the reports with their own judgments and speculations, according to their experience.

The farmer generally follows the weather forecasts closely. They help him select dates for planting, cultivating, and harvesting his crop. He is quite aware of their inaccuracies, particularly in the case of the thirty-day forecasts, which predict the temperature and precipitation for the following month. Short-term forecasts of one or two days are doubtful enough and, in the case of measurable precipitation, are often stated in terms of probabilities. And the thirty-day forecasts are considerably less accurate despite the fact that they claim to predict only general trends. Even knowing this, the farmer rarely ignores them, for they represent a sizable improvement over his own forecasts made without the help of the meteorologist. Their utility is unquestioned.

The informed classroom teacher is in much the same position as the farmer, and recognizes the inaccuracies of the results produced by educational measurement procedures. But he must ask himself the question: "Can the information yielded by these procedures, inaccurate though it is, tell me more about the pupil than I can discover by any other means?" Frequently the answer is in the affirmative. Many instruments can reveal consistently more accurate information than the most popular alternative method, namely, informal judgments by the teacher. Teacher judgments of pupils, like the farmer's own weather predictions, can be exceedingly accurate in a given instance and should be continually made, but they should be used in conjunction with, rather than independently of, evaluation procedures. As a teacher searches for information about his pupils, he should use every means at his disposal, such as standardized tests, interviews, and rating scales, and he should be keenly aware of the accuracy of the information that each furnishes.

PROBLEMS

8. Classify each of the following in terms of the level of measurement (that is, nominal, ordinal, or interval) that they represent.
   a. Temperature in terms of the centigrade scale
   b. Scores from a well-developed achievement test
   c. Zip code numbers
   d. Dog show results
   e. Social security numbers

9. There is a fourth level of measurement known as the ratio level. In addition to having equal intervals, like the interval level, it is characterized by an absolute zero. A zero reading means that zero amount exists of the characteristic being measured. Cite illustrations of this level of measurement within the realm of educational measurement.

PUPIL EVALUATION TODAY

Pupil evaluation as we practice it today can be conveniently divided into two areas; namely, evaluation of achievement and evaluation of aptitudes. The former is the larger of the two and, in many ways, much more complex.

Evaluation of Achievement

Pupil achievement is subdivided into three categories or domains: cognitive, affective, and psychomotor. The first is typically called academic achievement, the second the development of personal-social adjustment, and the third the development of motor skills.

Academic achievement means pupil achievement in all curriculum areas except physical development, emotional development, and ethical behavior. It has a very heavy verbal and mathematical orientation. Hence its evaluation procedures include a wide variety of paper-and-pencil tests, performance tests, and nontesting procedures. Evaluation of academic achievement should be as broad and varied as the educational objectives from which it springs, yet in practice it relies heavily on paper-and-pencil tests, most of which are classroom rather than standardized tests. Improving these tests by significant degrees is one of the most serious tasks of the classroom teacher.

The importance of the evaluation of academic achievement cannot be over-estimated. Considerable attention has been given to achievement evaluation problems by measurement specialists, and properly so. Tens of standardized achievement test batteries have been developed for all grade levels with the exception of the primary grades.

Evaluating a pupil's personal-social adjustment is not the same as evaluating his personality. Personality is an all-encompassing entity, the sum total of all the individual's psychological characteristics. Thus it includes his abilities, emotions, motives, attitudes, interests, and whatever remains of all his past experiences. Evaluating a pupil's personality, then, includes evaluation of the other two categories of achievement and evaluation of aptitudes. In contrast, the evaluation of personal-social adjustment is intended to represent a miscellaneous category containing those evaluation activities not included in the classifications mentioned.

Useful techniques in the evaluation of personal-social adjustment include attitude inventories, interest inventories, any teacher ratings of such pupil characteristics as "emotional maturity," and "cooperativeness," any paper-and-pencil personality inventories, sociometric devices, and self-rating scales. Projective techniques, such as Murray's *Thematic Apperception Test* and the *Rorschach Inkblot Test*, definitely belong in this category, but receive minor mention in this book because they are essentially clinical instruments. Home visitations, interviews, and analyses of autobiographies and anecdotal records are also a part of this area of evaluation.

Evaluation of Aptitudes

An aptitude is a person's capacity to learn. Hence, the instruments included in the evaluation of aptitude are designed to predict the achievement that would occur if a pupil were given proper training. Both general and specific aptitudes have been the focal points of testing attempts, many of which produced paper-and-pencil instruments. Tests of general mental ability are the most common of the general aptitude tests; a clerical aptitude test, a nursing aptitude test, or a musical aptitude test typify testing for a more specific aptitude.

Occasionally there is some confusion about the titles of aptitude tests. For instance, when considered in a broad sense, the expression "scholastic aptitude test" cannot be considered as synonymous with the expressions "general mental ability test" or "general intelligence test." However, within the realm of paper-and-pencil aptitude testing, these expressions can be considered as essentially the same. Such tests often have highly similar content and the same primary purpose, namely, to predict future academic success in school work.

Also, there is some doubt about the difference between scholastic aptitude and academic achievement tests. In terms of the definitions, the evaluation of scholastic aptitude and the evaluation of academic achievement are distinctly different. Whereas the purpose of the latter is to reveal a pupil's accomplishments as of a particular moment, the purpose of the former is to predict those that the pupil can achieve with suitable training. From this point, the differentiation becomes fuzzy. For instance, the difference between an achievement test and an aptitude test in terms of *test content* is virtually nonexistent. The best way to predict how well a pupil will perform in the future in a given area is to adopt the time-proven procedure of examining how well he performed in the past in that area or a similar area. Thus a scholastic aptitude test designed to predict future academic achievement might contain test items that could be found in an arithmetic achievement test or an English vocabulary test. Moreover, it is evident that a given test could serve both functions. For example, a reading test measuring level of comprehension may be used as an achievement test for sixth-grade pupils or as an aptitude test to predict their achievement in junior high school in such subjects as English and social studies. In short, aptitude tests differ from achievement tests in terms of purpose, but not necessarily in content. Both measure what a pupil has learned, and they often measure with similar process and content (Wesman, 1968).

Today we have tests designed to measure verbal and quantitative aspects of scholastic aptitude, others designed to measure primary mental abilities, such as memory, reasoning, and word fluency, and still others to measure differential aptitudes such as verbal reasoning, numerical ability, mechanical reasoning, and clerical speed and accuracy. Add to these the many stenographic and mechanical aptitude tests, as well as aptitude tests for academic subject matter areas such as reading and mathematics, which often are identified as readiness tests or prognostic tests. Such is the list of tools available to help the teacher know his pupils better.

The Evaluation Movement Today

The principal developments that have contributed to pupil evaluation today have occurred since 1900. This fact more than any other clearly reveals the relative immaturity that characterizes the evaluation movement in psychology and education. Admittedly, modern efforts are less accurate and consistent than we might wish. The physical sciences far outstrip the behavioral sciences in ability to measure the phenomena being studied. Now time can be measured by means of a thallium-beam clock, which is even more accurate than the cesium-beam clock developed only a few years ago. Lasers can make automatic length measurements with an accuracy of 1.8 parts in 10^9. Such refinements as these allow us to make even greater technological advances in the space age. Educational advances are less impressive by far. Yet, instead of being disappointed in the inability of behavioral sciences to match physical sciences in measuring, we should be impressed by the fact that evaluation in the behavioral sciences has progressed so far in so short a time.

Pupil evaluation is now an important activity of the school and of most teachers who compose its permanent staff. No one knows how many standardized tests are administered each year in the schools of the United States, but the number probably exceeds 200 million per year. The number of teacher-constructed tests given annually cannot even be estimated, but must be many times the foregoing figure.

The merits of pupil evaluation are by no means universally acclaimed today. The history of the movement displays the familiar "pendulum" process. The popularity and general acceptance of the movement wax and wane, and the net result is that well-read teachers have come to realize that these tools are but means to an end and are imperfect even though indispensable. Thorough knowledge of the basic principles of evaluation is not only a necessary prerequisite to understanding and capitalizing on today's tools but also a necessary preparation for tomorrow's progress.

SUMMARY

The principal ideas in this chapter can be summarized as follows:

1. *Educational evaluation is the systematic process of determining effectiveness of educational endeavors in the light of evidence. Its four principal uses are (a) to appraise academic achievement of the individual pupil, (b) to diagnose his learning difficulties, (c) to appraise the effectiveness of educational programs and products, and (d) to assess the educational progress of a large population. The first two uses constitute pupil evaluation.*

2. *The purposes of pupil evaluation are twofold: first, it helps the teacher evaluate the degree to which educational objectives have been achieved; secondly, it helps the teacher know his pupils to such a degree that educational experiences can be planned according to their varied interests, aptitudes, and prior experiences.*

3. *The procedures used in pupil evaluation include paper-and-pencil tests, ranking and rating scales, performance tests, anecdotal records, questionnaires, interviewing techniques, autobiographies, and sociometric procedures.*

4. *Educational measurement and educational evaluation are not synonymous expressions. Measurement is the process that attempts to obtain a quantitative representation of the degree to which a pupil reflects a trait. Educational evaluation is a process in which a teacher commonly uses information derived from many sources to arrive at a value judgment. The information may be*

   obtained by using measuring instruments and also other techniques that do not necessarily yield quantitative results, such as questionnaires and interviews.

5. *Eighteen common types of tests are: individual and group tests; classroom and standardized tests; oral, essay, and objective tests; speed, power, and mastery tests; verbal, nonverbal, and performance tests; readiness and diagnostic tests; and norm-referenced, criterion-referenced, and objective-referenced tests. A given test can be simultaneously classified in more than one of these subgroups.*

6. *Educational measurement methods can be characterized by two features. First, they are primarily indirect rather than direct. The pupils' traits are appraised in terms of their effects, rather than in terms of the traits themselves. Secondly, measurement procedures are not remarkably accurate in terms of any absolute standards, but are dependable enough to reveal more information about pupils than other techniques at the teacher's disposal.*

7. *Pupil evaluation can be conveniently divided into two areas: evaluation of achievement and evaluation of aptitudes. Evaluation of achievement includes those techniques designed to measure the degree to which educational objectives have been achieved. Included are objectives pertaining to the cognitive, affective, and psychomotor domains. Aptitude evaluation is designed to predict achievement that would occur if the pupil were given proper training.*

SUGGESTED READINGS

BLOOM, B. S., J. T. HASTINGS, and G. F. MADAUS. *Handbook on formative and summative evaluation of student learning.* New York: McGraw-Hill, 1971. Chapters 3, 4, and 6.
> Chapter 3 is an excellent discussion of mastery learning. Summative evaluation is covered in Chapter 4, formative evaluation in Chapter 6.

CRONBACH, L. J. *Essentials of psychological testing.* (3rd ed.) New York: Harper & Row, 1970. Chapters 1 and 2.
> The first chapter is devoted to a brief discussion of the use of psychological tests. The second chapter includes a definition of a psychological test and a classification of tests into main types.

DUBOIS, P. H. *The history of psychological testing.* Boston: Allyn and Bacon, 1970.
> The development of psychological and educational tests is traced from the civil service tests in ancient China and the oral tests in medieval European universities to the present.

EBEL, R. L. Measurement in education. In R. L. Ebel (ed.), *Encyclopedia of educational research.* (4th ed.) New York: Macmillan, 1969. Pp. 777–785.
> This article has broad scope. Included are such subtopics as history of educational measurement, measurement literature, nature and method of measurement, and public and professional attitudes toward measurement in education. A useful bibliography of 170 references has been compiled.

POPHAM, W. J. (ed.). *Criterion-referenced measurement.* Englewood Cliffs, N.J.: Educational Technology Publications, 1971. Chapters 1, 2, and 3.
> The first three chapters of this short book provide a succinct, readable introduction to criterion-referenced tests and the manner in which they differ from norm-referenced tests.

TYLER, R. W. (ed.). *Educational evaluation: New roles, new means.* Sixty-Eighth Yearbook of the National Society for the Study of Education, Part II. Chicago: University of Chicago Press, 1969. Chapters 2, 3, 13, and 16.
> The topic of evaluation is treated in the broadest terms in this volume. A historical review is given in Chapter 2, whereas certain theoretical issues are reviewed in Chapter 3. Chapter 13 is a description of the National Assessment of Educational Progress. Lastly, ways of strengthening program and product evaluation are considered in Chapter 16.

TYLER, L. E. *Tests and measurement.* (2nd ed.) Englewood Cliffs, N.J.: Prentice-Hall, 1971. Chapter 1.
> The first chapter of this paperback has two major topics: the need for quantification in the study of human behavior and the four levels of measurement. The discussion of each is brief but effective.

REFERENCES CITED

AHMANN, J. S. National Assessment of Educational Progress: The first results. *Compact,* 1972, 6, 13–17.

ANASTASI, A. *Psychological testing.* (3rd ed.) New York: Macmillan, 1968.

BLOOM, B. S., J. T. HASTINGS, and G. F. MADAUS. *Handbook on formative and summative evaluation of student learning.* New York: McGraw-Hill, 1971.

BUROS, O. K. *The seventh mental measurements yearbook.* Highland Park, N.J.: Gryphon Press, 1972.

CRONBACH, L. J. Evaluation for course improvement. *Teachers College Record,* 1963, 64, 672–683.

CRONBACH, L. J. *Essentials of psychological testing.* (3rd ed.) New York: Harper & Row, 1970.

FORS, G. (ed.). *Science guide.* Bismarck, N.D.: North Dakota Department of Public Instruction, 1969.

FREMER, J. *Criterion-referenced interpretations of survey achievement tests.* Test Development Memorandum. Princeton, N.J.: Educational Testing Service, 1972.

GAGNÉ, R. M. *The conditions of learning.* (2nd ed.) New York: Holt, Rinehart and Winston, 1970.

GLASER, R., and A. J. NITKO. Measurement in learning and instruction. In R. L. Thorndike (ed.), *Educational measurement.* (2nd ed.) Washington: American Council on Education, 1971, chapter 17.

GRONLUND, N. E. *Preparing criterion-referenced tests for classroom instruction.* New York: Macmillan, 1973.

HAND, H. National assessment viewed as the camel's nose. *Phi Delta Kappan,* 1965, 47, 8–13.

HIVELY, W., H. L. PATTERSON, and S. H. POPE. A "universe-defined" system of arithmetic achievement tests. *Journal of Educational Measurement,* 1968, 5, 275–290.

KATZMAN, M. T., and R. S. ROSEN. The science and politics of national educational assessment. *Teachers College Record,* 1970, 71, 571–586.

LEVINE, H. G., and C. MCGUIRE. Role-playing as an evaluative technique. *Journal of Educational Measurement,* 1968, 5, 1–8.

MERWIN, J. C., and F. B. WOMER. Evaluation in assessing the progress of education to provide bases of public understanding and public policy. In R. W. Tyler (ed.), *Educational evaluation: New roles, new means.* Sixty-Eighth Yearbook of the National Society for the Study of Education, Part II. Chicago: University of Chicago Press, 1969, 305–334.

MICHIGAN DEPARTMENT OF EDUCATION. *Minimal performance objectives in mathematics education in Michigan.* Lansing, Michigan: Author, 1973.

MILTON, O. "What it is . . . I measure I do not know." *Educational Record,* 1968, 49, 160–165.

NATIONAL ASSESSMENT OF EDUCATIONAL PROGRESS. *Music and social studies: General information yearbook.* Denver: Author, 1974.

POPHAM, W. J., and T. R. HUSEK. Implications of criterion-referenced measurement. *Journal of Educational Measurement,* 1969, 6, 1–9.

SAYLOR, G. National assessment: Pro and con. *Teachers College Record,* 1970, 71, 588–597.

SCRIVEN, M. The methodology of evaluation. *AERA Monograph Series on Curriculum Evaluation,* 1967, No. 1, 39–83.

SCRIVEN, M. Pros and cons about goal-free education. *Journal of Educational Evaluation,* 1972, 3, 1–4.

STAKE, R. E. The countenance of educational evaluation. *Teachers College Record*, 1967, *68*, 523–540.

STAKE, R. E. Program evaluation, particularly response evaluation. In *New trends in evaluation*, Report No. 35. Göteborg, Sweden: University of Göteborg, 1974, 1–20.

STODDARD, G. D. On the meaning of intelligence. *Proceedings of the 1965 Invitational Conference on Testing Problems*. Princeton, N.J.: Educational Testing Service, 1966, 3–11.

STUFFLEBEAM, D. L. (ed.). *Educational evaluation and decision-making*. Itasca, Illinois: F. E. Peacock, 1971.

TROW, W. C. Grades and objectives in higher education. *Educational Record*, 1968, *49*, 85–91.

TYLER, R. W. The objectives and plans for a national assessment of educational progress. *Journal of Educational Measurement*, 1966, *3*, 1–4.

TYLER, R. W. *Basic principles of curriculum and evaluation*. Chicago: University of Chicago Press, 1949 (1969 impression).

WESMAN, A. G. Intelligent testing. *American Psychologist*, 1968, *23*, 267–274.

WRIGHTSTONE, J. W., et al. *Accountability in education and associated measurement problems*. Test Service Notebook 33. New York: Harcourt Brace Jovanovich, undated.

2

EDUCATIONAL OBJECTIVES IN PUPIL EVALUATION

In one of his many public statements, Oliver Wendell Holmes once mused:

> ... Men often remind me of pears in their way of coming to maturity. Some are ripe at 20 ... and must be made the most of, for their day is soon over. Some come into their perfect condition late, like the autumn kinds, and they last better than the summer fruit. And some, that, like Winter-Nelis, have been hard and uninviting until all the rest have had their season, get their glow and perfume long after the frost and snow have done their worst with the orchards. Beware of rash criticisms; the rough and stringent fruit you condemn may be an autumn or a winter pear, and that which you picked up beneath the bow in August may have been only its worm-eaten windfalls.

So it is with the achievement of life's goals. Each of us organizes his life around them. A few are attained comparatively early in life, some later, and still others not at all.

The sources of these goals are difficult if not impossible to trace. It is clear, however, that they stem from the needs that each of us experience. The goals are direct outgrowths of social needs such as the need for recognition, prestige, power, security, and companionship; and physiological needs such as hunger and thirst.

The nature of personal goals and also their relative importance will vary among individuals, but practically all can be classified into categories such as vocational, recreational, social, educational, and religious. This should not suggest that a goal in one category is independent of goals in any other. For example, an educational goal of acquiring a bachelor's degree from a first-class university may be closely related to a vocational goal of becoming a licensed physician. Again, a recreational goal of raising a bowling average to 175 pins per game may well be a part of a social goal of enlarging one's circle of friends.

At least for his more important goals, each person organizes, formally or informally, programs that should lead him ever closer to them. Some may have tentative termination dates; others may not. They may differ in terms of the degree to which they are structured. Programs for educational and vocational goals are, for the most part, based on formal schooling. Those for recreational and social goals may be designed by the individual and be quite casual.

It is only reasonable that a person following a program would be concerned about his progress toward the intended goal. He may search for evidence that will identify his present position. For example, in the case of the educational goal mentioned, evidence would include number of college credit hours accumulated and the grade-point average achieved; in the case of the bowling goal, it would be the bowling average for the past several games. With pieces of evidence such as these in mind, he can compare his present position with his initial position when the program began and with his goal. These two reference points allow him to evaluate the growth he has made.

TRANSLATING NEEDS
INTO EDUCATIONAL OBJECTIVES

At one time the primary purpose of formal education was to teach each new generation all the knowledge that had been accumulated by all previous generations. This conception resulted in a highly rigid school curriculum that made the textbook the strongest single element in the classroom. At the present time this concept of the primary purpose of formal education has been largely superseded by another: to train pupils in such a way that they are better able to satisfy their needs (Tyler, 1953, p. 216). The kernel of this idea has been expressed by other writers in various ways. For instance, one writer said that "schools were created for the sole purpose of helping children to grow up properly" (Havighurst, 1953, p. 159). Another stated that the "major function of education is to foster, develop, and preserve democracy as a way of life" (Ahrens, 1953, p. 104). All three statements say in effect that the objectives of American schools must be derived from the needs of youth living in a democratic society.

The pertinent needs of youth are translated into educational objectives by identifying the new patterns of behavior that they must acquire to satisfy their needs. These involve development of new knowledge, intellectual abilities and skills, affective patterns, and psychomotor skills. Knowledge includes pupil behaviors that emphasize the remembering, either by recognition or recall, of ideas, material, or phenomena (Bloom, 1956, p. 62). If a pupil can comprehend the meaning of the pieces of information to the point that he can grasp the relationships among them, restate them in his own words, and take action intelligently on the basis of them, then he has developed his intellectual abilities and skills to an important degree. Affective patterns include changes in interests, attitudes, and values. These pertain to a pupil's predisposition to react in a particular manner to certain ideas, objects, people, and events. He now has "points of view"; he has feelings of attraction or aversion toward aspects of his environment. Finally, psychomotor skills are motor skills of the kind that are so vital to achievement in physical education, music, art, and industrial education, and vocations based on them.

For purposes of convenience, the entire array of educational objectives is divided into three domains—cognitive, affective, and psychomotor. Taxonomies for classifying objectives have been established for each domain (see page 38) and greatly assist in reducing communication problems so often associated with objectives.

Classroom teachers and other education specialists have to examine each area of need and decide the nature of the new behavioral patterns that each pupil must develop to be able to satisfy his needs. Then they must make decisions as to how and when each pupil will be taught. These decisions should produce a curriculum in which attainable goals, carefully keyed to the maturity levels and various backgrounds of the pupils in question, have been selected for each area of instruction.

Whether goals should be established for each grade level of each curriculum area is another question, since the grading system can be thought of as little more than a convenient administrative device for grouping pupils. In any event, within a framework of educational goals, every teacher should still find sufficient flexibility so that he can exploit all the learning possibilities in his field, and can do so in terms of the individual needs of his pupils as he recognizes them.

The goals of education are pupil-oriented rather than teacher-oriented. The manner in which they are stated should reflect this fact. In the not-too-distant past, educational objectives were stated in terms of the activities that the teacher was to perform. A certain topic was to be taught at a certain time in a certain manner. The modern way of stating educational objectives reflects the fact that they stem from pupil needs. To be consistent, therefore, educational objectives must be stated in terms of desired pupil behavior rather than in any other way.

Types of Objectives

Efforts to translate the needs of youth into educational objectives are typically directed toward producing precise statements that identify the observable changes in pupil behavior that should take place if the learning experience is successful. Unquestionably, such objectives are excellent starting points for development of the curriculum, planning of teaching strategies, and construction of testing and nontesting instruments. Nevertheless, we must recognize that the very preciseness that is so valuable may also be detrimental, in that it is difficult to identify measurable pupil behaviors in certain subject matter areas like the fine arts.

Recognition of this possibility causes some to feel that, in reality, two types of objectives exist, namely, instructional and expressive (Eisner, 1969, pp. 14–17). The former specify unambiguously the particular pupil behavior to be acquired as a result of learning. The latter do not. Expressive objectives describe "educational encounters," for instance, a situation in which pupils are to work or a problem they are to solve. These encounters are, in essence, tasks that yield pupil products—a poem, art object, or report.

Unsurprisingly, expressive objectives are most common in curriculum areas such as art, music, drama, dance, creative writing, and speech. Illustrative of this type of objective are the following:

1. *The pupil will compose a poem depicting his personal impression of a brilliant sunset over the desert.*

2. *The pupil will interpret the meaning of Alexander Pope's* Essay on Man *and prepare a written summary of his interpretation.*
3. *The pupil will build an original mobile having at least five moving parts.*

In each instance, the primary means of evaluating pupil performance would be the evaluation of the merits of the product he develops.

Both types of objectives are needed. On the one hand, the teacher may find that expressive objectives provide a kind of outreach for his teaching efforts that is exciting to him and his pupils. On the other hand, instructional objectives are the solid base on which he can plan his teaching and pupil evaluation. As educational outcomes become prescribable, expressive objectives are not needed and instructional objectives receive their proper emphasis. In this and the following chapters, instructional objectives are given primary attention.

PROBLEMS

1. Select two school systems that you know well, preferably one in a metropolitan center and one not in such a center, and compare them in terms of the role the schools must play in the process of helping pupils learn how to satisfy their needs.

2. In your opinion, are instructional objectives or expressive objectives more important in each of the following teaching situations:
   a. Elementary school science unit on climate.
   b. Junior high school carpentry shop.
   c. Senior high school English literature class.
   d. Senior high school marriage and family living class.

TAXONOMY OF EDUCATIONAL OBJECTIVES

Educational objectives have been classified into three domains, namely, the cognitive, affective, and psychomotor. The cognitive domain includes those educational objectives related to the recall of knowledge and the development of intellectual abilities and skills. The affective domain includes those objectives concerning changes in a pupil's emotional state, or degree of acceptance or rejection of some entity—it is the domain of personal-social adjustment. The psychomotor domain includes objectives that involve primarily muscular or motor skills, some manipulation of material and objects, or some act that requires a neuromuscular coordination (Krathwohl, Bloom, and Masia, 1964, p. 7).

Cognitive Domain

The taxonomies organized for each domain represent well the hierarchical nature of each. In the case of the cognitive domain, the main organizing principle used is degree of complexity of the cognitive process involved in the objective. Comparatively simple cognitive behaviors could combine with others of a similar nature and yield more complex pupil behaviors.

The taxonomy for the cognitive domain contains six subdivisions, and these in turn are subdivided as needed. The subdivisions are as follows (Bloom, 1956, pp. 201–207):

KNOWLEDGE

1.00 KNOWLEDGE
> The recall of specifics and universals, the recall of methods and processes, or the recall of a pattern, structure, or setting. The knowledge objectives emphasize most the psychological processes of remembering.
> 1.10 Knowledge of specifics
> 1.20 Knowledge of ways and means of dealing with specifics
> 1.30 Knowledge of the universals and abstractions in a field

INTELLECTUAL ABILITIES AND SKILLS

2.00 COMPREHENSION
> A type of understanding or apprehension such that the individual knows what is being communicated and can make use of the material or idea being communicated without necessarily relating it to other material or seeing its fullest implications.
> 2.10 Translation
> 2.20 Interpretation
> 2.30 Extrapolation

3.00 APPLICATION
> The use of abstractions in particular and concrete situations. The abstractions may be in the form of general ideas, rules of procedures, or generalized methods.

4.00 ANALYSIS
> The breakdown of a communication into its constituent elements or parts such that the relative hierarchy of ideas is made clear and/or the relations between the ideas expressed are made explicit. Such analyses are intended to clarify the communication, to indicate how the communication is organized, and the way in which it manages to convey its effects, as well as its basis and arrangement.
> 4.10 Analysis of elements
> 4.20 Analysis of relationships
> 4.30 Analysis of organizational principles

5.00 SYNTHESIS
> The putting together of elements and parts so as to form a whole. This involves the process of working with pieces, parts, elements, etc., and arranging them in such a way as to constitute a pattern or structure not clearly there before.
> 5.10 Production of a unique communication
> 5.20 Production of a plan or proposed set of operations
> 5.30 Derivation of a set of abstract relations

6.00 EVALUATION

Judgments about the value of material and methods for given purposes. Quantitative and qualitative judgments about the extent to which material and methods satisfy criteria.

6.10 Judgments in terms of internal evidence

6.20 Judgments in terms of external criteria*

The claim that the six levels represent a hierarchical order, that is, vary from the simple to the complex, has some empirical support (Krathwohl and Payne, 1971). Evidence verifies the ordering of the first three levels better than that of the last three.

Affective Domain

The main organizing principle used to develop the affective domain taxonomy is the process of internalization. This process is defined as "incorporating something within the mind and body; adopting as one's own the ideas, practices, standards, or values of another person or of society" (English and English, 1958, p. 272). In the case of the taxonomy, internalization is viewed as a process through which there is at first an incomplete and tentative adoption of only the overt manifestations of the behavior in question and later a more complete adoption. Hence the taxonomy represents a continuum of the behaviors implied by objectives in this domain.

Five chief categories have been identified, each of which has two or three subdivisions as follows (Krathwohl, Bloom, and Masia, 1964, pp. 176–185):

1.00 RECEIVING (ATTENDING)

The sensitization of the learner to the existence of certain phenomena and stimuli. He is willing to receive or to attend to them. This is the first and crucial step if the learner is to be properly oriented to learn what the teacher intends that he will.

1.10 Awareness

1.20 Willingness to receive

1.30 Controlled or selected attention

2.00 RESPONDING

Pupil responses that go beyond merely attending to the phenomenon. The pupil is sufficiently motivated that he is not just willing to attend but to attend actively. This is the category that many teachers find best describes their "interest" objectives.

2.10 Acquiescence in responding

2.20 Willingness to respond

2.30 Satisfaction in response

3.00 VALUING

Recognition that a thing, phenomenon, or behavior has worth. This abstract concept of worth is in part a result of the individual's own valuing or assessment, but it is much more a social product that has been slowly internalized or accepted and has come to be used by the pupil as his own

* Adapted from Taxonomy of educational objectives, handbook I—cognitive domain, by B. S. Bloom, Ed., copyright 1956 by David McKay Co. Used with permission of the publisher.

criterion of worth. This category is appropriate for many objectives using the term "attitude" and, of course, "value."

3.10 Acceptance of a value

3.20 Preference for a value

3.30 Commitment (conviction)

4.00 ORGANIZATION

The beginnings of the building of a value system. As the learner successively internalizes values, he encounters situations for which more than one value is relevant. Thus necessity arises for (a) the organization of the values into a system, (b) the determination of the interrelationships among them, and (c) the establishment of the dominant and pervasive ones.

4.10 Conceptualization of a value

4.20 Organization of a value system

5.00 CHARACTERIZATION BY A VALUE OR VALUE COMPLEX

Integration of beliefs, ideas, and attitudes into a total philosophy or world view. The values already have a place in the individual's value hierarchy, are organized into some kind of internally consistent system, have controlled the behavior of the individual for a sufficient time that he has adapted to behaving this way; and an evocation of the behavior no longer arouses emotion or affect except when the individual is threatened or challenged.

5.10 Generalized set

5.20 Characterization*

The utility of the affective taxonomy is influenced by a number of factors. One of these is the lower level of emphasis often placed on these objectives as compared with cognitive ones. This is perplexing since, in keeping with the major objectives of education, we want pupils not only to have cognitive skills, but also to *want* to use them. Another factor is the comparatively limited knowledge we have about the affective domain in general. Such terms as *attitude, adjustment, appreciation,* and *interest* are used without being precisely defined. The range of meaning for each is so great that objectives using such terms may be classified in a variety of categories in the taxonomy.

Psychomotor Domain

The difficulty of classifying objectives according to a taxonomic framework is most apparent in the psychomotor domain. Several major efforts have been made to develop a suitable taxonomy. One significant contribution was made by Harrow (1972) in which six major classification levels were arranged along a continuum from the lowest level of observable movement behavior to the highest level, as follows.

1.00 REFLEX MOVEMENTS

Those movements which are involuntary in nature. They are functional at birth, developing through maturation.

* *Adapted from* Taxonomy of educational objectives, handbook II—affective domain, *by D. R. Krathwohl, B. S. Bloom, and B. B. Masia; copyright 1964 by David McKay Co. Used with permission of the publisher.*

       1.10 Segmental reflexes
       1.20 Intersegmental reflexes
       1.30 Suprasegmental reflexes

2.00 BASIC-FUNDAMENTAL MOVEMENTS
Those inherent movement patterns which form the basis for specialized complex skilled movements.
       2.10 Locomotor movements
       2.20 Nonlocomotor movements
       2.30 Manipulative movements

3.00 PERCEPTUAL ABILITIES
All of the learner's perceptual modalities where stimuli impinge upon him to be carried to the higher brain centers for interpretation.
       3.10 Kinesthetic discrimination
       3.20 Visual discrimination
       3.30 Auditory discrimination
       3.40 Tactile discrimination
       3.50 Coordinated abilities

4.00 PHYSICAL ABILITIES
Those functional characteristics of organic vigor which, when developed, provide the learner with a sound, efficiently functioning instrument (his body) to be used when making skilled movements a part of his movement repertoire.
       4.10 Endurance
       4.20 Strength
       4.30 Flexibility
       4.40 Agility

5.00 SKILLED MOVEMENTS
The result of the acquisition of a degree of efficiency when performing a complex movement task. This classification level includes movements which require learning and are considered reasonably complex. All sports skills, dance skills, recreational skills, and manipulative skills fall into this classification.
       5.10 Simple adaptive skill
       5.20 Compound adaptive skill
       5.30 Complex adaptive skill

6.00 NONDISCURSIVE COMMUNICATION
Behaviors that can be labeled forms of movement communication. These encompass a wide variety of communicative movements ranging from facial expressions, postures, and gestures to sophisticated modern dance choreographies.
       6.10 Expressive movement
       6.20 Interpretive movement*

The foregoing taxonomy is not as "clean" as the other two, particularly the cognitive. Cognition can occur with a minimum of motor activity, and perhaps little feeling. In contrast, psychomotor activity involves both cognitive and affective influences. This seriously complicates work in the third domain.

Value of the Taxonomies

The impact of the taxonomies on educational thinking is indeed powerful. As foreseen, they do assist appreciably in the task of helping teachers and other educational specialists discuss their curricular and evaluation problems with greater precision. We gain a better perspective of the relative importance of our objectives and their interrelationships by using the taxonomies as classification schemes. Also, terminology is standardized to a greater degree than ever before.

The three taxonomies represent the total framework of educational objectives for all types of educational institutions. They also represent, therefore, the total framework within which evaluation procedures are functioning. Hence, after careful study, a teacher can classify objectives pertinent to his teaching in appropriate categories, and devise a set of measurement procedures, some of which are tests, to obtain appropriate data on the basis of which evaluations can be made. Use of the taxonomies in this way adds meaning to the educational objectives and defines more sharply the limits of the scope of the pupil evaluation attempted.

Learning Hierarchies

For some purposes, the taxonomies are not sufficiently precise. For instance, the categories of the cognitive taxonomy deal with mental processes and do not recognize other significant aspects of a well-stated instructional objective. Such an objective identifies the specific overt behavior to be performed by the pupil, the conditions under which he is to perform, and the criteria of acceptable performance. Tools other than the taxonomies are needed if this kind of objective is to be formulated easily.

A categorizing system with a finer mesh has been designed by Gagné (1970, pp. 35–65). He identifies eight types of learning—eight sets of conditions under which changes in pupil behavior are brought about. They are ordered as follows:

1. *Signal learning: Making a general, diffuse response to a signal.*
2. *Stimulus-response learning: Acquiring a precise response to a discriminated stimulus.*
3. *Chaining: Combining two or more stimulus-response connections.*
4. *Verbal association: Learning chains that are verbal.*
5. *Discrimination learning: Learning to make n different identifying responses to as many different stimuli, which may resemble each other.*
6. *Concept learning: Acquiring a capacity to make a common response to a class of stimuli that may differ from each other widely.*
7. *Rule learning: Acquiring a chain of two or more concepts.*
8. *Problem solving: Learning that requires thinking; combining two or more previously acquired rules to produce a new capability of a higher order.*

The hierarchical nature of the breakdown is unmistakable. Achievement in each class depends on learning the preceding one. Thus these varieties of learning can serve as a means of conceptualizing a wide range of educational objectives.

This and other works by Gagné are basic to the preparation of a "learning hierarchy," that is, a set of component tasks that lead to the achievement of a certain educational objective. In other words, the behavioral pattern of a "major" objective of an instruction program is analyzed in terms of the pattern of tasks that must be mastered by the pupil. The tasks are ordered to form a hierarchy that can then guide teaching and pupil evaluation. Observe that the hierarchy of component tasks can be considered a hierarchy of specific objectives. We know "what comes first" when the pupil behaviors identified are ones known to exist among the pupils when instruction is to begin. Certainly this type of backward analysis is highly useful for pupil placement and for diagnosis and remediation of learning difficulties. In this regard, criterion-referenced tests are able to play a significant role (Glaser and Nitko, 1971).

The analysis of learning hierarchies, otherwise known as component task analysis, is highly complex. Its rewards are well illustrated by the results of its application in an elementary school science program known as *Science—A Process Approach* (Walbesser, 1968). The author has listed "action verbs" to be used in the formulation of instructional objectives in science. They are:

1. *Identify: Select the correct object from a set of objects.*
2. *Name: Specify what an object, event, or relationship is called.*
3. *Order: Arrange three or more objects or events in a sequence based on some stated property.*
4. *Describe: State observable properties sufficiently to identify an object, event, or relationship.*
5. *Distinguish: Select an object or event from two or more with which it might be confused.*
6. *Construct: Make a physical object, drawing, or written or verbal statement.*
7. *Demonstrate: Carry out a sequence of operations necessary for a stated task.*
8. *State a rule: Provide a relationship or principle that can be used to solve a problem or complete a task.*
9. *Apply a rule: Determine the answer to a problem by using a relationship or principle.*

Use of these nine terms serves to sharpen the thrust of instructional objectives in traditional subject matter areas. It can be argued that only six are needed, namely, *identify, name, describe, construct, order,* and *demonstrate,* provided such highly specific verbs as *add, spell,* and *conjugate* are also used when appropriate (Sullivan, 1969). Be that as it may, the intent of action verbs is to focus attention directly on pupil behavior. The list should be so heterogeneous that practically every pupil behavioral pattern with heavy cognitive features could be classified under one of the terms.

PROBLEMS

3. Classify each of the following objectives in terms of the six principal levels of the taxonomy for the cognitive domain:

   a. The pupil can distinguish between related scientific concepts such as speed
      and acceleration, kinetic and potential energy, and mass and weight.
   b. The pupil can list the order of the steps normally followed for a bill to be
      passed by the U.S. Congress and become law.
4. Classify each of the following objectives in terms of the five principal levels
of the taxonomy for the affective domain:
   a. The pupil finds pleasure in the investigation of natural phenomena such as
      the activity of an ant colony or tankful of tropical fish.
   b. The pupil develops awareness of aesthetic aspects of his style of dress.
5. Classify each of the following objectives in terms of the six principal levels
of the psychomotor domain:
   a. The pupil can type "smooth-copy" prose at a minimum speed of 40 words
      per minute (after adjustment for errors) using an electric typewriter.
   b. The pupil can assume the proper body stance for driving a golf ball.

LEVELS OF EDUCATIONAL OBJECTIVES

Even the most casual examination of educational objectives reveals that they
vary widely in terms of their degree of specificity. Some are "general" objectives, that
is, statements of the main aims or ultimate goals of the educational system. One
example is the goal that every pupil become a good citizen and function as such
throughout his life. In contrast to the global nature of this, consider the myriads of
subobjectives that such a goal can generate. These can be highly specific as in the case
of those dealing with a pupil's ability to distinguish among *to, too,* and *two,* or to add
accurately any combination of two integers, neither of which is greater than ten.

At least three main levels of objectives can be established (Krathwohl and Payne,
1971). The first is the most abstract and deals with long-term goals like vocational
efficiency or self-realization. The second level, derived from the first, is more concrete
and represents objectives to be attained by pupils successfully completing a course of
study. For example, "the pupil can distinguish among a chemical element, compound,
and mixture." Finally, the third level contains highly specific objectives derived from
ones at the second level, which state not only the pupil performance desired, but also
the situation that initiates the performance, the criteria of acceptable performance,
and, if appropriate, any special conditions related to the performance. For example,
"the pupil distinguishes among *to, too,* and *two* with ninety percent accuracy when
provided short written sentences that can be completed by inserting one of the three
words at a designated position."

First-Level Objectives: General Objectives

A number of the attempts to formulate first-level objectives have been quite
ambitious. Committees as well as individuals have produced impressive lists most often
delineating the ultimate goals of the educational system without direct reference to
traditional subject matter areas. Of greater interest to us are first-level objectives
organized along curricular lines.

PRIMARY OBJECTIVES FOR NATIONAL ASSESSMENT. In the late 1960's and continuing into the 1970's, advisory committees composed of educators, subject matter specialists, and laymen wrote the primary objectives for the National Assessment of Educational Progress in ten curriculum areas. This procedure was used to ensure that every objective should meet three criteria: (1) it be considered important by scholars, (2) it be accepted as an educational task by the educational system, and (3) it be considered desirable by laymen. The following are samples of this work for the second assessment of four learning areas (National Assessment of Educational Progress, 1972a, 1972b, 1972c, 1974):

SCIENCE

1. Know the fundamental aspects of science.
2. Understand and apply the fundamental aspects of science in a wide range of problem situations.
3. Appreciate the knowledge and processes of science, the consequences and limitations of science, and the personal and social relevance of science and technology in our society.

WRITING

1. Demonstrate ability in writing to reveal personal feelings and ideas.
2. Demonstrate ability to write in response to a wide range of societal demands.
3. Indicate the importance attached to writing skills.

CITIZENSHIP

1. Show concern for the well-being and dignity of others.
2. Support just law and rights of all individuals.
3. Know the main structure and functions of government.
4. Participate in democratic civic improvement.
5. Understand important world, national, and local civic problems.
6. Approach civic decisions rationally.
7. Help and respect one's own family.

READING

1. Demonstrate behavior conducive to reading.
2. Demonstrate word identification skills.
3. Possess skills for reading comprehension.
4. Use a variety of approaches in gathering information.

To be sure, this work is not complete. In some ways, such primary objectives as these are moving targets. Therefore, review and revision occurs every assessment cycle, this is, about every five to eight years.

STATE GOALS FOR ELEMENTARY AND SECONDARY EDUCATION. Increased interest in educational accountability has caused most states to re-examine their major objectives for elementary and secondary education. Existing statements of goals have been carefully reviewed, then revised, and new goals added. Extensive participation by educators and citizens has been common.

A study of the goals of thirty-five states revealed that the learner outcome goals fall into eleven categories as follows (Zimmerman, 1972):

1. *Basic skills*
2. *Cultural appreciation*
3. *Self-realization*
4. *Citizenship and political understanding*
5. *Human relations*
6. *Economic understanding*
7. *Physical environment*
8. *Mental and physical health*
9. *Creative, constructive, and critical thinking*
10. *Career education and occupational competence*
11. *Values and ethics*

Within each of these categories are classified a variety of objectives. For instance, within the basic skills area are objectives in reading, writing, speaking, listening, viewing, mathematics, science, art, and humanities. The affective domain is heavily represented in the self-realization, human relations, and values and ethics areas.

Second-Level Objectives: Subobjectives

The first important subdivisions of first-level objectives are often called subobjectives. Illustrations are countless; here are several widely used examples representing both elementary and secondary education.

ELEMENTARY EDUCATION. A prominent statement of objectives at the second level for elementary education is the one prepared by the Mid-Century Committee on Outcomes in Elementary Education (Kearney, 1953). Each objective included in the list is thought to be attainable by average children at some time prior to age fifteen or sixteen. No matter how defensible a proposed objective might have been on a purely philosophical basis, it was not included unless it was also deemed attainable during the first fifteen years of the child's life, regardless of whether the school, the home, or some other community agency was instrumental in helping the child reach this goal.

Nine curriculum areas are considered. They are:

Physical development, health, and body care
Individual social and emotional development
Ethical behavior, standards, and values
Social relations
The social world
The physical world
Esthetic development
Communication
Quantitative relationships

Within each curriculum area, four types of behavioral patterns are cited:

Knowledge and understanding
Skills and competences
Attitudes and interests
Action patterns

The objectives of elementary education are not listed for each grade level. Instead, three points in time, called age-grade periods, are selected somewhat arbitrarily and the objectives are listed for each. The primary period corresponds to the end of the third grade, the pupils having attained an age of about nine years. The intermediate period corresponds to the end of the sixth grade, or an age of about twelve years. The upper-grade period corresponds to the end of the ninth grade, or an age of about fifteen years.

To illustrate the nature of the intermediate-period objectives reported (Kearney, 1953, pp. 68–73, 113–120), a few from two curriculum areas are listed below:

ETHICAL BEHAVIOR, STANDARDS, AND VALUES

A. Knowledge and understanding
The pupil develops an awareness of property rights and of truth and falsehood.
B. Skills and competences
The pupil is able to like a person in spite of disliking his behavior in specific instances.
C. Attitudes and interests
The pupil is interested in altruistic club activities.
D. Action patterns
The pupil tends to be analytical in evaluating behavior.

QUANTITATIVE RELATIONSHIPS

A. Knowledge and understanding
The pupil knows how numbers apply to time, weight, and dry and liquid measures.
B. Skills and competences
The pupil can add, subtract, and multiply decimals.
C. Attitudes and interests
The pupil respects accuracy and arithmetical orderliness.
D. Action patterns
The pupil is able to search for meaning behind the number of numerical relationships he uses.*

SECONDARY EDUCATION. Similar to the foregoing effort, a study was made of the objectives of the secondary school (French et al., 1957). Only the objectives for the general education program in the secondary school are included in this report. The

---

* *Paraphrased from Part II of* Elementary School Objectives, *by Nolan C. Kearney, A Report Prepared for The Mid-Century Committee on Outcomes in Elementary Education,* © *1953 by Russell Sage Foundation, New York.*

basic purposes of this program are to help pupils realize their fullest potentialities and meet civic responsibility.

The lists of educational objectives are classified under three maturity goals and four areas of behavioral competence. The maturity goals are:

1. *Growth toward self-realization. (Self-realization is described as the development of "the common kinds of behaviors indicative of such personal growth and development as will enable them [the pupils] within the limits of their native environments, to live richer, more satisfying, more productive lives consonant with our ethical, aesthetic, and social standards and values.")*
2. *Growth toward desirable interpersonal relations in small groups.*
3. *Growth toward effective membership or leadership in large organizations.*

The four areas of behavioral competence are:

1. *Attainment of maximum intellectual growth and development.*
2. *Cultural orientation and integration.*
3. *Physical and mental health.*
4. *Economic competence.*

Combining the three maturity goals and the four areas of behavioral competence establishes twelve broad groups of behavior. In other words, a chart with twelve cells is formed. Each cell contains a group of related educational objectives. The cells are not considered mutually exclusive.

The educational objectives given below are classified under the maturity goal of self-realization within the area of behavioral competence called attaining maximum intellectual growth and development. These objectives are typical of those mentioned in the three major subgroups included in this cell (French et al., 1957, pp. 92–102).

1.111 (d) The pupil uses common sources of printed information efficiently; e.g., dictionary, encyclopedia, Readers' Guide, card catalog in a library.

1.121 (a) The pupil adjusts his reading rate and method to the material.

1.123 (f) The pupil demonstrates that he can read and understand mathematical reports, charts and graphs, and simple statements of financial accounts.

1.131 (e) The pupil analyzes a problem and can follow the recognized steps involved in scientific thinking. *

These objectives are designed to be reasonable goals for the most mature high school seniors. This means that, for each pupil, some of them will seem to be too high a standard. To assist the teacher in those instances in which they may seem to be too high, "developmental equivalents" are provided for each of the major subgroups of educational objectives. These are less mature behavioral patterns; they are indicative of the stages of development that we would expect as the younger pupils progress toward the mature behavior of the older pupils.

* *From Part III of* Behavioral Goals of General Education in High School *by Will French and Associates, © 1957 by Russell Sage Foundation.*

SUBOBJECTIVES FOR NATIONAL ASSESSMENT. For each of the main objectives prepared for the National Assessment of Educational Progress, second-level objectives were also prepared. The following are illustrative of these from the science and citizenship areas (National Assessment of Educational Progress, 1972a, 1972c):

SCIENCE

First level
> Understand and apply the fundamental aspects of science in a wide range of problem situations.

Second level
1. Understand and apply facts and simple concepts.
2. Understand and apply laws and principles.
3. Understand and apply conceptual schemes.
4. Understand and apply inquiry skills.
5. Understand and apply the scientific enterprise.

CITIZENSHIP

First level
> Show concern for the well-being and dignity of others.

Second level
1. Treat others with respect.
2. Consider the consequences for others of their own actions.
3. Guard safety and health of others.
4. Offer to help others in need.
5. Support equal opportunity in education, housing, employment, and recreation.
6. Be loyal to country, friends, and other groups whose values are shared.
7. Be ethical and dependable in work, school, and social situations.

Often the subobjectives are further refined for each of four age levels, namely, nine, thirteen, seventeen, and adult. These refinements are a series of suggestions of the kinds of pupil behavior that, if present, indicate that the subobjectives and hence the primary objectives are being achieved. Typically the suggested behaviors serve as a fine introduction to third-level objectives.

Third-Level Objectives: Specific Instructional Objectives

The various published statements of educational objectives at the first and second levels are most helpful to the classroom teacher. They point out the kinds of goals that should be achieved by all American youth, regardless of the family of which they are members, the schools in which they are enrolled, or the communities in which the schools are located. In so doing, these statements tend to keep the curriculum of all schools more or less aligned without necessarily specifying the nature of all of its parts.

The formal statements of educational objectives cited in the preceding sections have at least two common characteristics not mentioned previously. None of the statements suggests the relative importance of the objectives listed. The order in which they are mentioned is not intended to reflect their order of importance. Nor do any of them suggest the particular objectives that are to guide the instruction by a specific teacher on a stated day with a certain group of pupils.

As a result, the teacher becomes the most prominent person involved in the process of identifying instructional objectives for the classroom. It is he who must amalgamate the first-level and second-level objectives with a variety of pertinent local factors to arrive at the proper third-level objectives for his class, and to give each its proper emphasis. Local factors usually considered are the instructional objectives of the courses previously completed by the pupils, their success in achieving these objectives, the educational philosophy of the school, the facilities of the community, the vocational goals of the pupils, and the nature of their homes. In other words, difficult as it is, the teacher must become acquainted with the individualized needs of the pupils in his class. The influence of all local factors should yield a set of realistic and pertinent third-level objectives for classroom use.

Third-level objectives are highly specific. One can imagine literally thousands of them. Certainly the teacher needs for each learning experience a series of very concisely stated objectives that are direct outgrowths of second-level objectives, which in turn are direct outgrowths of those from the first level. When this occurs, we are truly able to understand and interpret all levels of interrelated objectives.

How does a classroom teacher go about preparing his own third-level objectives? Considerable attention has been given to this question (Mager, 1962; Gronlund, 1970). Mager (1962, p. 12) believes that three basic steps must be taken to prepare the specific objectives. These are the following:

1. *Identify specifically the kind of pupil behavior which is acceptable as evidence that he has achieved the objective in question. In other words, the objective must state explicitly what the pupil must be able to do in order to achieve it.*
2. *Describe the important conditions which influence pupil behavior. In other words, any support provided the pupil or any restrictions placed upon him when he must demonstrate his competence should be mentioned.*
3. *Specify the criteria of acceptable performance by describing at least the lower limit of such performance.*

An illustration of the results of this procedure is the following taken from an elementary mathematics unit:

When provided with accurate drawings of a variety of triangles, each having all needed dimensions shown, the pupil can compute the area of each correctly to the nearest whole number, at least 75% of the time.

Note that an attempt has been made to follow each of the three steps. First of all, the pupil behavior is concisely described; that is, he must "compute the area of each correctly to the nearest whole number." Secondly, a condition is introduced; that is, the pupil is "provided with accurate drawings of a variety of triangles, each having all needed dimensions shown." Finally, the lower limit of performance is established; that is, answers must be correct to the nearest whole number "at least 75% of the time."

The manner of preparation here described will produce specific instructional objectives of considerable utility, especially in the cognitive domain. As one fractionates first- and second-level objectives in order to formulate third-level ones, he gains an excellent insight into the problems of providing good instruction and designing sensitive measuring instruments. (For information about systems for sharing objectives, see page 59.)

PROBLEM

6. Using the NAEP second-level science objective "understand and apply facts and simple concepts," formulate a third-level objective for each of three age levels: nine, thirteen, and seventeen years.

EVALUATING IN TERMS
OF EDUCATIONAL OBJECTIVES

Does a fourth level of objectives exist? Yes, in a sense it does. Have you heard of "mini-objectives"? They are statements "representing performances observed when an individual is responding to a particular frame in an instructional test or program" (Smith and Shaw, 1969, p. 137). Often each can be represented by a single test item. In other words, test items and instructional materials can be thought of as the fourth and most specific level of all. They are direct expressions of objectives and, in reality, are operational definitions of them (Krathwohl and Payne, 1971). Thus, using testing and nontesting procedures in the process of evaluating pupil behavior is a logical extension to the development and use of specific instructional objectives. This is the central core of criterion- and objective-referenced testing.

Eliciting Pupil Behavioral Patterns

Rarely is it a simple matter to determine the degree to which a pupil's behavior has changed so that it conforms more closely to that defined in an objective. In the first place, the pupil must be given an opportunity to demonstrate that he has or has not reached the goal. Secondly, this demonstration must occur under circumstances that will allow critical evaluation in terms of the appropriate objectives. To accomplish this, a trained observer equipped with suitable measuring tools is needed. This is the only truly meaningful way of evaluating pupil growth. All other methods are indirect and, by this very fact, tend to be somewhat inadequate. The practical importance of these inadequacies varies considerably. In some cases they are so serious that the measurement results are practically worthless; in other cases their presence only modestly reduces the effectiveness of the measuring methods.

BEHAVIOR IN A NATURAL SITUATION.   The first step requires that goal behavior by a pupil be elicited within a natural situation. The pupil involved feels no compulsion to say the "proper" thing or to behave in the "proper" manner. He is behaving as he truly has learned to, rather than in a feigned manner he might adopt if required to exhibit a pattern of behavior for teacher evaluation. In the natural situation, the true, unvarnished products of his educational experiences are voluntarily displayed.

This description of natural situations actually points out one of the chief difficulties encountered in pupil evaluation. Since the very essence of natural situations prevents the teacher from controlling them, his efforts at evaluation are often hampered. Some natural situations will not occur in the classroom; in fact, some will not occur until after the formal education of the pupil has been completed. For example, it is reasonable to expect that pupil behavior related to aspects of educational objectives pertaining to citizenship, home membership, and vocational proficiency is best shown in natural situations, most of which occur outside the classroom. The natural situations that do occur during the pupil's school career may take place at haphazard times and sundry places. Needless to say, the teacher should capitalize on them whenever possible, although evaluative efforts in natural situations are at times impractical, if not impossible.

To be sure, direct observation of pupil behavior in a natural situation can be made of the degree to which pupils have achieved some of the specific objectives of education. For example, a teacher can observe with relative ease and frequency whether a pupil consistently covers his nose and mouth with a handkerchief when sneezing or coughing, whether he can tell time and make change with accuracy, whether he enjoys active games, whether he uses conventional courtesies in his oral communications, whether he can read silently with little or no lip movement, or construct charts and graphs with only minor errors. These and other direct observations of pupil behavior can be made in lifelike situations outside the classroom or in connection with normal classroom routine. Class projects, teacher-pupil interviews, field trips, social functions, and other activities may be suitable opportunities for observation even though not necessarily designed for them.

SKILLFUL OBSERVATION. Although direct observations may be made in an informal atmosphere, the observation process cannot be as casual if it is to be successful. The skilled observer is intimately familiar with the goals to be reached, the characteristics of pupil behavior that fall short of the goal to various degrees and in various ways, and the methods of reporting observations. This suggests that he should have a full knowledge of human development, psychology of learning, methods of educational evaluation, and subject matter areas in which instruction takes place. The observer must know what he is looking for and must be able to search for it as systematically and objectively as possible. Vague "impressions" are not enough. Ranking and rating procedures, check lists, anecdotal records, and even sociometric devices are tools that can be used.

ARTIFICIAL SITUATIONS AND EVALUATION METHODS. Evaluative attempts conducted in artificial situations are far more common than those conducted in natural situations. The teacher establishes artificial situations as similar to the natural situations as time and convenience will allow. It is hoped that the behavior exhibited by the pupil in the artificial situation is closely related to that he would have exhibited in a comparable natural situation if given the opportunity. Evaluation devices used in these situations are frequently paper-and-pencil achievement tests, but could be performance tests, written assignments, or work samples of a multitude of types.

The artificial situations and the evaluative devices used with them vary greatly in the degree to which they elicit pupil behavior closely related to that found in the corresponding natural situation (Lindquist, 1951, pp. 146–152). Some are quite successful in this respect. For example, paper-and-pencil tests, such as reading speed and comprehension tests, and performance tests, such as typing and shorthand tests, allow the pupil to demonstrate whether he has acquired the behavioral patterns described as objectives, and to do so in rather realistic settings. The same is true of performance tests given pupils in home economics, industrial art, and distributive education classes. The products of the pupil's behavior as well as the behavior itself can be evaluated. A typed business letter, a meat roast, or a wooden bookcase could serve this purpose. Note that in these instances the teacher does not wait until the pupil's behavioral patterns occur in the natural course of events, nor is he certain that the material involved in the evaluation is completely representative of that present in the natural situation.

On the other hand, there are countless other evaluation attempts involving artificial situations that do not elicit pupil behavior essentially the same as that the pupil would display in a natural situation. For example, attitude and interest inventories allow the pupil to indicate how he would (or should) behave in situations described to him, but do not actually place him in the situations so that he can overtly display his behavior. Is there a strong relationship between what he says he would do and what he actually would do if given the opportunity? Probably not, and so these inventories are unsatisfactory.

Additional illustrations of the importance of the foregoing assumption are easily found. For instance, paper-and-pencil tests are sometimes used as a basis for evaluating the pupil's ability to perform laboratory and shop activities. In a physics class, test items may describe the apparatus and materials necessary for laboratory experiments in electricity and magnetism. After the steps of the experiments have been recounted, the pupil is required to predict the outcome of each experiment and give reasons why this is the case. In an auto mechanics class, the test items may describe symptoms of an automobile engine that is not functioning properly. The pupil is required to diagnose the trouble by interpreting the symptoms, then select from a list of tools those necessary to repair the engine, and list the steps he would follow when making repairs. In an English class, artificial situations have been used to evaluate a pupil's writing ability. Rather than ask the pupil to write a composition, the teacher gives him a poorly written passage that he must improve by deleting or adding words, phrases, and punctuation marks.

In each of the three examples mentioned above, the response to the artificial situation is not the same as that which would have been elicited in a natural situation. The test items in physics and in auto mechanics do not allow the pupil to display his skill in the actual manipulation of laboratory apparatus and tools. It is conceivable that he could answer the test items correctly and still not be able to perform the tasks. The same is true of the English composition test. Writing ability involves more than correcting the punctuation and rearranging the words of a passage written by someone else. It also includes selection and arrangement of ideas and style of expression.

Elements of originality so important in superior writing ability are scarcely tapped by the test. Nevertheless, in the case of all three examples, the teacher must make the assumption that the abilities of the pupil measured by the paper-and-pencil test items are related to his abilities to perform the tasks as they occur in natural situations.

Planning the Paper-and-Pencil Achievement Test

No doubt the most common measurement method used in schools today is the norm-referenced paper-and-pencil achievement test. In several respects its prominence is undeserved. Nevertheless, it shows the way in which measuring methods are designed in terms of a set of selected instructional objectives.

The teacher need take relatively few steps when constructing a paper-and-pencil achievement test. First of all, he must separate from among his objectives those that have verbal and mathematical aspects, thereby excluding many objectives of considerable merit. Secondly, he must determine the relative importance of the verbal and mathematical objectives, a purely subjective process. Teachers with the same objectives differ noticeably with respect to the relative importance they assign to each. As the relative importance varies from teacher to teacher, so does the nature of the instruction. The relative emphasis that an objective receives in the process of instruction is a crude but effective indicator of the emphasis to be given that objective when an achievement test involving it is constructed. Finally, the teacher must build a group of test items, either of the essay or objective type, that constitute a representative sample of all subject matter topics and behavioral patterns included within the objectives. This can be summarized by means of a two-way grid or table of specifications (see following section). The importance of each cell in the table is roughly equivalent to the number of test items related to it, the difficulty of these test items, the amount of credit allotted to right answers to the test items, or several or all of these simultaneously.

TABLES OF SPECIFICATIONS.   As an illustration of the foregoing process, consider the case of the secondary school chemistry teacher who is conducting his educational program in terms of a number of second-level objectives, three of which are the following:

1. *The pupil can recall certain facts, definitions, laws, and theories of chemistry.*
2. *The pupil can comprehend the scientific method in its relations to the theories and principles of chemistry.*
3. *The pupil can apply the principles of chemistry in making predictions, explanations, and inferences.*

When teaching a unit devoted to oxygen and some of its common compounds, he stresses the first and third objectives insofar as this subject matter is concerned. From these he derives a large series of third-level objectives, each of which establishes, for the most part, the criterion behavior which the pupil must display if he has achieved the objective, any restrictions placed on him when he demonstrates his competence, and the lower limit of acceptable performance. The following three statements, based on the first second-level objective, show the kind of objectives used.

1. *When given a list of twenty common compounds containing oxygen, the pupil can properly classify at least fifteen of them as to whether each, at normal temperature and pressure, is a gas, a liquid, or a solid.*
2. *Of the ten oxides studied, the pupil can accurately identify each as an acidic oxide or a basic oxide at least seventy percent of the time.*
3. *When provided with an incomplete equation showing the ingredients and the conditions needed to synthesize each of twenty common compounds containing oxygen, the pupil can complete the equation and balance it properly at least sixty percent of the time.*

The next step is to group the specific objectives as needed. Notice that the foregoing three deal with recall of chemical information, but each is concerned with a different subject matter topic. Although each deals with common compounds of oxygen, the first speaks of their physical properties, the second of their chemical properties, and the third of their preparation.

A convenient way of gathering and organizing the specific objectives is a table of specifications. In its simplest form, the table of specifications is a two-way table, one dimension of which is a breakdown of behavioral changes, and the other of subject matter topics. The behavioral changes can be classified into many categories, for example, the six principal categories of the taxonomy of educational objectives for the cognitive domain. Less than six are commonly used in teacher-constructed tests. For the chemistry test, three categories were considered significant, namely, the first three principal categories of the cognitive domain taxonomy—knowledge, comprehension, and application.

The subject matter topics are subdivisions of the verbal and mathematical material included in the unit. Normally, many topics are listed. For example, the unit devoted to oxygen and some of its common compounds might be first subdivided into general topics—their physical properties, chemical properties, preparation, and uses. Each could be again subdivided into as many minor topics as the teacher deems necessary.

To build a table of specifications the teacher must decide the relative importance of the behavioral changes and the topics and represent them as percentages. The following decisions may be reached for the oxygen unit:

I. *Behavioral changes*
  1. *Knowledge*   35
  2. *Comprehension*   35
  3. *Application*   30
     Total   100

II. *Subject matter topics*
  1. *Physical properties of oxygen and its common compounds*   20
  2. *Chemical properties of oxygen and its common compounds*   30
  3. *Preparation of oxygen and its common compounds*   10

4. Uses of oxygen and its common compounds	*40*
Total	*100*

The two breakdowns and the assigned percentages are then combined into a simple table, as illustrated in Table 2.1. The entries in the twelve cells of the table are based on the best judgment of the teacher, and are arranged so that the row and column totals are not changed.

The percentages included in the table are rough approximations of the importance of each behavioral change in each topic. Therefore, if an objective test is to be constructed, the percentages could be used as rough approximations of the percentage of test items in the test devoted to the behavior changes of each topic. In actual practice, however, circumstances force the test builder to deviate somewhat from this point of view. For instance, a given test item may refer to more than one cell in the table. On the other hand, items for some cells might be extremely difficult to construct. Because of the short supply that results, the test may not reflect the designated importance of each cell as accurately as we might hope. Finally, it must be remembered that the percentage weights in the table are, at best, very crude. As the test is being constructed, the builder will sometimes gain better insight into his table of specifications and change it accordingly. The end result is a realistic view of the testing situation. The teacher knows which ideas are measurable and which are not, and thus what the test scores *do and do not* reveal about pupil behavior. After undergoing this agonizing appraisal, more than one teacher has *contracted* the scope of his interpretation of classroom test scores!

In spite of the crudeness of a table of specifications and the difficulty of constructing a sufficient number of test items for all of its cells, the use of such a table for building paper-and-pencil achievement tests produces tests vastly superior to those yielded by a casual, unsystematic skimming of lesson plans and textbooks. Furthermore, the effort invested in the development of a table of specifications can pay dividends for a prolonged period of time. With revision as needed, the table may materially assist the construction of paper-and-pencil achievement tests for a number of years.

To use the percentage weights contained in the table of specifications, the teacher must first decide how many essay or objective items the test will contain. This in turn depends on the time available for testing, the type of test item to be used, and the anticipated difficulty of those items. The time factor is frequently determined by

TABLE 2.1.   Table of Specifications for a Chemistry Unit Devoted to Oxygen and Its Common Compounds.

Subject matter topic	Behavioral changes			
	Knowledge	*Comprehension*	*Application*	*Total*
Physical properties	6%	10%	4%	20%
Chemical properties	10	10	10	30
Preparation	6	4	0	10
Uses	13	11	16	40
Total	35	35	30	100

the administrative routine of the school. A class period may be the maximum amount of time available. The maturity level of the pupils and the possibility of the test's causing excessive fatigue may be sufficient reasons for the teacher to reduce the time interval even more. In any event, knowing the testing time available, the teacher can estimate on the basis of past experience the number of test items of a given kind and difficulty that pupils can answer in the number of minutes allotted.

The techniques for constructing test items of various types are described in detail in the following chapters. Strict adherence to the rules given will yield test items of good technical quality. In spite of this, you will find that objective test items are difficult to build for the analysis, synthesis, and evaluation levels of the cognitive taxonomy. Essay tests, performance tests, and even product and procedure evaluation are used to supplement objective test items.

CONTENT VALIDITY. Clearly, the central purpose of the procedure just described for building paper-and-pencil achievement tests is to develop a high-quality test, that is, one that will satisfactorily serve the purposes for which it is intended. An achievement test such as the oxygen test has the purpose of determining, as of the moment it is administered, how well a pupil recalls, comprehends, and applies the cross-section of the total amount of subject matter studied that it contains. The degree to which the achievement test serves this purpose is its content validity (American Psychological Association, 1974). This is one of three types of test validity (see Chapter 9).

The degree of content validity of a test rises and falls in accordance with (1) the extent to which its table of specifications accurately reflects the relative importance of the various subject matter topics in relation to the various pupil behavioral changes stemming from verbal and mathematically oriented instructional objectives, and (2) the degree to which the test items built on the basis of the table of specifications accurately mirror the balance of the cells. A high degree of content validity is customarily attained when carefully contrived tables of specification, or some similar device, are used, and when the many rules of test item construction described in Part Two are conscientiously followed.

Criterion- and Objective-Referenced Tests

Increasingly, criterion- and objective-referenced tests are being used to measure pupil achievement. Like the common classroom tests previously described, their most important attribute is a high degree of content validity. Yet this is accomplished without the use of a table of specifications. Instead, third-level objectives such as those mentioned are used directly as a base for building test items. Each test item needs to be an obvious outgrowth of the objective.

PREPARING TEST ITEMS. By way of illustrating the steps for preparing test items, consider the following mathematics objective for middle school pupils:

Given (1) a list of articles for sale and their unit prices, and (2) a fixed amount of money to spend, the pupil can select those he can afford to buy, compute their total cost including sales tax, and determine accurately his change at least eighty percent of the time.

No doubt a wide variety of paper-and-pencil test items could be developed for this objective. Catalogs, price lists, and newspaper advertisements could be used as commonly available source materials. The nature of the prices and the sales tax rate to be applied could cause the level of difficulty of possible test items to vary widely. Furthermore, does the learner purchase several items each having the same price (for example, swimming pool tickets) or a group of dissimilar items (for example, groceries)? Such decisions about the test item would be determined in large measure by whether one wishes to test for mastery for a specified group of pupils. In any event, the source material must be realistic to the pupil, that is, something within his realm of experience. For instance, consider this sample test item:

The following is the menu at a drive-in restaurant where you wish to eat lunch:

Hot Dogs	*50¢ each*
Hamburgers	*60¢ each*
French Fried Potatoes	*35¢ per bag*
Soft Drinks	*25¢ per glass*
Ice Cream Cones	*25¢ each*
Pie	*40¢ per slice*
Cake	*35¢ per slice*

List the food you wish to eat, find its total cost, and then add 5% sales tax. If you gave the waitress a $5 bill to pay for your meal, how much change would you receive?

Note how this test item (as well as others that could be constructed) follows directly from the behaviorally stated objective. Certainly there is a set of potential test situations in which pupil behaviors can be displayed. If desired, one could set up a sampling plan to select a subset of test tasks to be used. Finally—and of great importance—the pupil's performance can be described objectively and meaningfully. A family of similar test items can be designed and administered so as to determine whether each pupil has reached the eighty percent level of proficiency.

COMPUTER-ASSISTED TEST CONSTRUCTION. The conscientious teacher faces a herculean task: he must design innumerable third-level objectives and prepare at least one evaluation method for each. To help him, systems for sharing objectives have been established by commercial and nonprofit organizations, and occasionally by a group of school districts or a university. Associated with each objective is one or more evaluation technique, usually a test item.

Such systems have much potential. Literally thousands of specific objectives and their associated test items have been compiled. In one instance (SCORE, Westinghouse Learning Corporation), teachers can study catalogues of objectives in areas such as reading, mathematics, science, or social studies, then select an appropriate part of them for test development. Test items associated with these objectives are retrieved by computer and assembled into a machine-scorable test booklet. After administration, the tests are scored and reported, if desired, in a variety of ways. Reports for each pupil, for each objective, are available in a relatively short period of time. Thus, the test and the reports it produced are tailored to the needs of the teacher and his class.

The Instructional Objectives Exchange (IOX) also provides a reservoir of cognitive and affective objectives from which teachers can select appropriate parts for local use. About fifty sets are available, covering all grade levels and practically every subject matter area. Each objective is accompanied by one or more illustrative test items. In addition, short objectives-based tests (five or ten items) have been designed for language arts, social studies, and mathematics (Popham, 1972).

Role of Paper-and-Pencil Tests

The acknowledged purposes of elementary and secondary education have expanded greatly since the turn of the century. As they increased, the usefulness of the traditional paper-and-pencil test as a measuring instrument has steadily declined. For a curriculum based on the idea that a school must, above all, serve as a vehicle for transmitting to the new generation all of the knowledge accumulated by previous generations, this kind of test would serve admirably. For a curriculum based upon the idea that a school must help a pupil learn how to meet his many needs as a member of a democratic society, this kind of test still is of major importance, but by no means should it dominate pupil evaluation to the degree that it now does.

The unjustified popularity of paper-and-pencil tests as measuring instruments can be most disconcerting to pupils, parents, and teachers alike. After everyone assures everyone else that the objectives of education should reflect the needs of the "whole" child, the teacher usually evaluates the behavioral patterns of his pupils on a highly restricted basis. The pupil and his parents are understandably confused; the teacher usually feels unduly frustrated. No doubt he recognizes the possibility of injustices when this method is followed, but he also knows that he does not have sufficient data-gathering tools and that many of those he has lack the respectability of paper-and-pencil tests.

This dilemma in which teachers repeatedly find themselves has no convenient solution. To use paper-and-pencil instruments to the point where most other techniques are ignored, however, is not the answer to the problem. Instead, consider the following (Lindquist, 1951, p. 157):

> For many objectives of the type suggested, measuring or observational devices concerned with the student's overt behavior while he is yet in school, even though of a rough and opportunistic character, are perhaps much more worthwhile than any written type of tests. The actual behavior of the student in school elections, for example, however fragmentary or limited in sampling, may provide a better clue to his future behavior than anything he professes that he will do in a written test; books actually read by the pupil in his free time may constitute a truer indication of his literary tastes than his score on a literary appreciation test; anecdotal records may be more meaningful than scores on personality tests; etc. The problem of deriving comparable measures from such opportunistic observational data now seems to present almost insuperable difficulties, but perhaps no worse than have been resolved before through determined and persistent effort.

The foregoing remarks should not be interpreted as a general denunciation of written tests or a recommendation that they be abandoned completely. On the contrary, paper-and-pencil tests should be a sizable part of any pupil evaluation program. These tests should be used in conjunction with, rather than in the absence of, other methods. The very nature of many educational objectives requires that this be so.

PROBLEMS

7. Prepare several third-level objectives of a unit you are teaching or soon will be teaching. On the basis of these objectives, build at least one table of specifications suitable for the construction of a classroom achievement test.

8. Using the cognitive and affective taxonomies, Metfessel, Michael, and Kirsner (1969) developed verbal guidelines for formulating specific instructional objectives. For each taxonomic category, behaviorally oriented infinitives (for example, *to recognize, to translate,* or *to classify*) and direct objects (that is, subject matter properties like *facts, terminology,* and *theories*) are given. Study these "key words" and use combinations of them to prepare three cognitive and three affective third-level objectives for a teaching situation you know well.

9. Attempts have been made to use the cognitive taxonomy to build sets of test items that hold content constant and systematically vary process from simple (that is, knowledge) to complex (that is, evaluation). Evaluate the eight interrelated test items in the physical sciences prepared by Smith (1968) and suggest changes, if any, that you would make.

SUMMARY

The following are the main ideas included in this chapter:

1. *The primary purpose of formal education is to teach youths in such a way that they are better able to satisfy their needs. The objectives of elementary and secondary education are developed on this premise.*
2. *The objectives involve the development of new knowledge, intellectual abilities and skills, affective patterns, and psychomotor skills. Thus the objectives of education are pupil-oriented rather than teacher-oriented and are stated in terms of desired behavioral patterns in the pupil.*
3. *Taxonomies for objectives in the cognitive, affective, and psychomotor domains are now being used.*
4. *Three levels of objectives are often used. The first contains statements of major goals. The second is a refinement of the first, whereas the third includes highly specific instructional objectives. A number of formal statements of objectives have been prepared by committees for the first and second levels. Third-level objectives are direct outgrowths of these, and are usually prepared by teachers.*
5. *Having taught pupils with the guidance of his instructional objectives, of course the teacher must evaluate their achievement in terms of them. Ideally this should be done by direct observation of the pupil's behavior in a natural*

situation. At times this is impractical, if not impossible. Instead, the teacher establishes artificial situations that are as similar to natural situations as time and convenience will allow, and evaluates the pupil's achievement indirectly within these situations by means of a variety of data-gathering devices.

6. *The artificial situations and the data-gathering devices used with them vary greatly in the degree to which they elicit pupil behavior closely related to that found in the corresponding natural situation. Performance tests are quite successful in this respect, as are some paper-and-pencil tests. However, many paper-and-pencil tests are considerably less successful, obvious illustrations being tests designed to measure pupil behavior in many areas in the affective and psychomotor domains.*

7. *Ordinarily, the construction of a paper-and-pencil achievement test involves three steps. First, the educational objectives with verbal and mathematical aspects must be separated from all others. Secondly, the relative importance of these objectives and their subparts must be identified. Finally, a group of test items must be constructed. These should constitute a representative sample of all subject matter topics and behavioral patterns included within the objectives. The second and third steps can be facilitated by using a table of specifications, and a high degree of content validity can be attained.*

8. *Above all else, criterion-referenced and objective-referenced tests must also have a high degree of content validity.*

9. *Evaluating pupil behavior in terms of educational objectives is a complex task. Many methods are used, including paper-and-pencil tests (both classroom and standardized), performance tests, rating scales, inventories, questionnaires, and anecdotal records. Pupil evaluation ordinarily is centered around paper-and-pencil tests to an unrealistically high degree.*

SUGGESTED READINGS

BLOOM, B. S. (ed.). *Taxonomy of educational objectives: Cognitive domain.* New York: David McKay, 1956.
> This book provides an excellent basis for building evaluation instruments in the cognitive domain. By classifying objectives, it offers a framework for improving the chances that achievement tests in this area will have acceptable content validity. Illustrative objectives and test items are shown.

EBEL, R. L. What are schools for? *Phi Delta Kappan,* 1972, 54, 3–7. (Also in *Education Digest,* 1972, *38,* 2–5).
> A challenging article which states that schools are, in the last analysis, places where the young should learn useful knowledge—rather than places serving as custodial institutions, personal adjustment centers, recreational facilities, or social research agencies.

HARROW, A. J. *A taxonomy of the psychomotor domain.* New York: David McKay, 1972.
> Classification levels for psychomotor behaviors have been arranged along a continuum from the lowest level of observable movement behavior to the highest. The usefulness of the taxonomy when writing behavioral objectives is discussed in Chapter 4.

KRATHWOHL, D. R., B. S. BLOOM, and B. B. MASIA. *Taxonomy of educational objectives: Affective domain.* New York: David McKay, 1964.
> The first part of this book is an explanation of the rationale behind the taxonomy of educational objectives in the affective domain, including a discussion of internalization, the major organizing principle underlying the taxonomy. Following is a full description of the taxonomy and illustrative educational objectives and evaluation procedures classified in the various levels.

KRATHWOHL, D. R., and D. A. PAYNE. Defining and assessing educational objectives. In R. L. Thorndike (ed.), *Educational measurement.* (2nd ed.) Washington: American Council on Education, 1971. Chapter 2.
> A well-written chapter providing significant information regarding levels of objectives, their sources, and their taxonomies. Suggestions are given for utilizing third-level objectives.

MAGER, R. F. *Preparing instructional objectives.* San Francisco: Fearon Publishers, 1962.
> Techniques for stating objectives explicitly in behavioral terms are presented. Examples of well stated and poorly stated objectives are included.

POPHAM, W. J., E. W. EISNER, H. J. SULLIVAN, and L. L. TYLER. Instructional objectives. AERA *Monograph Series on Curriculum Evaluation,* 1969, No. 3.
> The four chapters often take quite different views about the sources of objectives and the manner in which they are stated and used. Discussions among the four authors follow each chapter and are well worth reading.

REFERENCES CITED

AHRENS, M. R. Developing a plan of action for improving programs for youth. In N. B. Henry (ed.), *Adapting the secondary-school program to the needs of youth.* Fifty-Second Yearbook of the National Society for the Study of Education, Part I. Chicago: University of Chicago Press, 1953, 102–117.

AMERICAN PSYCHOLOGICAL ASSOCIATION. *Standards for educational and psychological tests.* Washington: Author, 1974.

BLOOM, B. S. (ed.). *Taxonomy of educational objectives: Cognitive domain.* New York: David McKay, 1956.

EISNER, E. W. Instructional and expressive objectives: Their formulation and use in curriculum. AERA *Monograph Series on Curriculum Evaluation,* 1969, No. 3, 1–31.

ENGLISH, H. B., and A. C. ENGLISH. *A comprehensive dictionary of psychological and psychoanalytical terms.* New York: David McKay, 1958.

FRENCH, W., et al. *Behavioral goals of general education in high school.* New York: Russell Sage Foundation, 1957.

GAGNÉ, R. M. *The conditions of learning.* (2nd ed.) New York: Holt, Rinehart and Winston, 1970.

GLASER, R., and A. J. NITKO. Measurement in learning and instruction. In R. L. Thorndike (ed.), *Educational measurement.* (2nd ed.) Washington: American Council on Education, 1971, chapter 17.

GRONLUND, N. E. *Stating educational objectives for classroom instruction.* New York: Macmillan, 1970.

HARROW, A. J. *A taxonomy of the psychomotor domain.* New York: David McKay, 1972.

HAVIGHURST, R. J. *Human development and education.* New York: David McKay, 1953.

KEARNEY, N. C. *Elementary school objectives.* New York: Russell Sage Foundation, 1953.

KRATHWOHL, D. R., B. S. BLOOM, and B. B. MASIA. *Taxonomy of educational objectives: Affective domain.* New York: David McKay, 1964.

KRATHWOHL, D. R., and D. A. PAYNE. Defining and assessing educational objectives. In R. L. Thorndike (ed.), *Educational measurement.* (2nd ed.) Washington: American Council on Education, 1971, chapter 2.

LINDQUIST, E. F. Preliminary considerations in objective test construction. In E. F. Lindquist (ed.), *Educational measurement.* Washington: American Council on Education, 1951, 119–158.

MAGER, R. F. *Preparing instructional objectives.* Palo Alto, California: Fearon Publishers, 1962.

METFESSEL, N. S., W. B. MICHAEL, and D. A. KIRSNER. Instrumentation of Bloom's and Krathwohl's taxonomies for the writing of educational objectives. *Psychology in the Schools,* 1969, 6, 227–231.

NATIONAL ASSESSMENT OF EDUCATIONAL PROGRESS. *Science objectives for the 1972–73 assessment.* Denver: Author, 1972a.

NATIONAL ASSESSMENT OF EDUCATIONAL PROGRESS. *Writing objectives for the 1973–74 assessment.* Denver: Author, 1972b.

NATIONAL ASSESSMENT OF EDUCATIONAL PROGRESS. *Citizenship objectives for the 1974–75 assessment.* Denver: Author, 1972c.

NATIONAL ASSESSMENT OF EDUCATIONAL PROGRESS. *Reading objectives for the second assessment.* Denver: Author, 1974.

POPHAM, W. J. *Procedural guidelines for developing IOX objectives-based tests.* Los Angeles: Instructional Objectives Exchange, 1972.

SMITH, R. B. A discussion of an attempt at constructing reproducible item sets. *Journal of Educational Measurement,* 1968, 5, 55–60.

SMITH, T. A., and C. N. SHAW. Structural analysis as an aid in designing an instructional system. *Journal of Educational Measurement,* 1969, 6, 137–143.

SULLIVAN, H. J. Objectives, evaluation, and improved learner achievement. AERA *Monograph Series on Curriculum Evaluation,* 1969, No. 3, 65–99.

TYLER, R. W. Translating youth needs into teaching goals. In N. B. Henry (ed.), *Adapting the secondary-school program to the needs of youth.* Fifty-second Yearbook of the National Society for the Study of Education, Part I. Chicago: University of Chicago Press, 1953, 215–229.

WALBESSER, H. H., Jr. *An evaluation model and its application, a second report.* AAAS Miscellaneous Publication 68-4. Washington: American Association for the Advancement of Science, 1968.

ZIMMERMAN, A. *Education in focus: A collection of state goals for public elementary and secondary education.* Denver: Cooperative Accountability Project, 1972.

PART TWO

Measuring Achievement in the Classroom

For the homeowner, the do-it-yourself movement usually dominates such activities as carpentry, painting, and landscaping. The novelty of being your own designer, contractor, and artisan contributes to the popularity of this movement. The self-satisfaction experienced at the completion of a project is virtually matchless.

The do-it-yourself idea is a familiar one to the teacher, both within the scope of his professional position and outside of it. Early in his training program, he discovers that recipes for teaching are few, that prefabricated teaching techniques do not exist, and that hiring someone to perform part of his duties is seldom possible. In short, he learns that he must rely on his own skill and ingenuity practically all of the time. The unique characteristics of each teaching situation are too important to permit a standardization of the teaching art.

As one step in the teaching process, pupil evaluation offers an excellent opportunity for a teacher to display his skill and ingenuity. Although outside assistance is available in the form of standardized measuring instruments and measurement specialists who serve as consultants, the lion's share of the evaluation program must be shouldered by the classroom teacher. Frequently it is he who must design the instrument, administer it, score it, interpret the results, and, finally, appraise the worth of these activities. His responsibilities here are as clear as those related to the identification of his educational objectives and, on the basis of them, the determination of suitable learning experiences for his pupils.

The teacher's measuring efforts are often centered around the paper-and-pencil achievement test, either objective or essay type. Chapter 3, "Measuring Knowledge Objectively," is devoted to discussions of the construction and use of objective test items to be used as a classroom achievement test, with emphasis on those test items that measure recall of information. Chapter 4, "Measuring Complex Achievement

Objectively," emphasizes those test items that measure the pupil's ability to use his fund of knowledge. Successful performance means that the pupil can locate appropriate information and manipulate it to solve new problems. Chapter 5, "Preparing Essay Achievement Tests," identifies the role of essay test items in achievement testing and compares it with that of objective test items. Chapter 6, "Appraising Classroom Achievement Tests," contains descriptions of various methods of appraising paper-and-pencil tests, particularly those that are objective in nature.

Not all of the data-gathering instruments built by the classroom teacher are paper-and-pencil tests. Many are ranking and rating scales, check lists, product scales, and the like, that are used to evaluate pupil performance. Chapter 7, "Judging of Procedures and Products," describes and illustrates these methods.

The classroom teacher generally cannot build measuring instruments as technically perfect as those produced by teams of testing specialists. On the other hand, he has a decided advantage over the specialists in that he is far better informed concerning the quality of the pupils whose achievements are to be measured and the nature of the learning experiences they have had. This in turn means that the classroom instruments that he builds with care will often compare favorably with standardized instruments designed to accomplish the same purpose.

The role of the classroom teacher is particularly pronounced when preparing criterion- and objective-referenced tests. No one is better qualified to select appropriate specific objectives to be used as a basis for building test items. Also, the number of standardized tests of this type has increased significantly only in recent years.

Instead of being discouraged about the likelihood of building useful measuring instruments, you should be optimistic. The expenditure of reasonable amounts of effort coupled with careful observance of a group of simple rules is all that is really needed. If you have a creative flair, the task is simpler and the product better.

3

MEASURING KNOWLEDGE OBJECTIVELY

As consumers, each of us repeatedly samples various products on the market and, on the basis of our reaction, we draw conclusions about the quality of the product. Consider for a moment any of the purchases of food we commonly make. Suppose that we enter a supermarket to buy three items—candy, bakery goods, and breakfast cereal. In the first instance we select a pound of gum drops. Within the pound are individual pieces of a variety of colors. A nibble of one of each color may quickly convince us to favor the green gum drops over those of all other colors. For the second purchase, we choose one dozen glazed doughnuts. These we find to be fresh and tasteful, and, as a result, our opinion of the bakery is favorable. Finally, we select a well-known brand of breakfast cereal. If at breakfast on subsequent mornings we conclude that, as advertised, the cereal is indeed a "taste treat," we probably will continue to buy the product; if not, we will no doubt refuse to buy another box no matter how persuasive the exhortations of well-known motion picture personalities and professional athletes.

How sound are these judgments? This question is difficult to answer. To the degree that our taste sensibilities are reasonably normal at the time we tested the product, and to the degree that the sample of the product we consumed is reasonably representative, the judgments are sound. If these two conditions are not met, the soundness of the decision is certainly in doubt. For example, had we been ill shortly before or during the trial, the first condition would very likely not be satisfied. Had the gum drops, doughnuts, or breakfast cereal been accidentally contaminated in some way, they would hardly be representative of these products when properly handled, and the second condition would not be satisfied.

When acting as a consumer of food products, the classroom teacher samples and judges them just like anyone else. When evaluating the achievement of his pupils, he follows essentially the same procedure. He is actually making the same two basic assumptions. In the first place, he believes that the ability of his pupils to reveal the knowledge and more complex intellectual skills they possess and their willingness to do so are not seriously impaired by any unusual factors. Such factors might be emotional disturbances, greatly reduced teacher-pupil rapport, physical fatigue, or any of a multitude of minor distractions.

Secondly, he concludes that the samples of pupil behavior that he observes are

67

typical of much unobserved pupil behavior both present and possibly future. In the case of achievement testing, the samples of pupil behavior are elicited by the questions or tasks included in a test. Hence, to obtain a representative sample of all the possible variations of the pupil behavior in question, the teacher tries to find a representative sample of all the possible questions or tasks that might be presented to the pupil.

The justification for the use of samples for evaluating food products as well as achievement is essentially one of practicality. It is not feasible or necessary that a person eat all gum drops in sight before deciding that the green ones are the most pleasing. In the same manner, it is not feasible or necessary that a teacher ask a pupil all possible questions or provide opportunities for him to perform all possible tasks to determine the degree to which he has achieved certain educational objectives.

Demanding that a paper-and-pencil achievement test contain a representative group of test items is equivalent to demanding that the test have a high degree of content validity. Notice again that content validity is inherently tied to educational objectives; in the case of paper-and-pencil achievement tests, it is tied to specific objectives with verbal and mathematical aspects. Thus, procedures such as the use of a table of specifications that are known to improve the degree of content validity of a paper-and-pencil test are important to us here.

PROBLEM

1. Writing test items often helps to clarify the table of specifications. This may cause one to modify table headings and even cell percentages while in the middle of his efforts to build test items (Tinkelman, 1971). In your opinion, does the failure of the table to remain fixed tend to reduce or increase the degree of content validity of the resulting achievement test?

TYPES OF OBJECTIVE TEST ITEMS

An efficient and convenient way to measure the pupil's ability to recall the information identified by a table of specifications is to build and administer a series of pertinent objective test items. An objective test item is one that can be scored in such a way that judgment is for all practical purposes eliminated when determining the correctness of a pupil's answer. To be sure, this is a broad definition. It is not surprising, therefore, to find many different types of test items identified as objective test items yet seemingly quite dissimilar in form.

Objective test items may be usefully designated as the supply type of item or the selection type of item. When responding to a supply type of item, the pupil has to provide the words, numbers, or symbols. Possible answers are not listed as part of the item. An illustration of the supply type is the short-answer item, two varieties of which are shown below:

Short-answer question:
Directions: *Within the space provided, write the word or phrase that correctly answers the question.*
What is the name of the author of the novel entitled *Pickwick Papers?* (Charles Dickens)

Completion test item:
Directions: *Within the space provided, write the word or phrase that correctly completes the statement.*
The name of the author of the novel entitled *Pickwick Papers* is (<u>Charles Dickens</u>).

The selection type of item allows the pupil to choose the correct response from the information provided. The well-known true-false test item, multiple-choice test item, matching test item, and countless variations of them typify this category.

True-false test item:
Directions: *Determine whether each of the following statements is true or false. If the statement is true, circle the "T" preceding the statement; if the statement is false, circle the "F."*
Ⓣ   F   *The novel entitled* Pickwick Papers *was written by Charles Dickens.*

Multiple-choice test item:
Directions: *For each of the following questions choose the correct answer from among the four possible answers listed. Write the number of your choice in the blank to the left of the question.*
<u>(2)</u>   *Who wrote the novel entitled* Pickwick Papers?
                        (1) William Thackeray
                        (2) Charles Dickens
                        (3) Anthony Trollope
                        (4) George Eliot

Matching test item:
Directions: *Match the title of each novel with its author by writing the letter identifying the author in the blank to the left of the title. It is possible that some authors have written more than one of the novels listed.*

Novels		Authors
<u>(F)</u>	1. Barchester Towers	A. *Jane Austen*
<u>(B)</u>	2. David Copperfield	B. *Charles Dickens*
<u>(B)</u>	3. Great Expectations	C. *Alexandre Dumas*
<u>(B)</u>	4. Oliver Twist	D. *George Eliot*
<u>(B)</u>	5. Pickwick Papers	E. *William Thackeray*
<u>(A)</u>	6. Pride and Prejudice	F. *Anthony Trollope*
<u>(D)</u>	7. Romola	
<u>(B)</u>	8. Tale of Two Cities	
<u>(E)</u>	9. Vanity Fair	
<u>(F)</u>	10. The Warden	

The similarities and differences in form among these types of objective test items are obvious. There are, however, important similarities and differences in ease of construction, applicability, and ease of scoring. These and related topics are discussed and illustrated in the following sections.

PROBLEM

2. Some teachers argue that the differences among the various types of objective test items are seemingly large but actually small. In the case of the three chief variations of the selection type of item, defend their point of view.

CONSTRUCTING OBJECTIVE TEST ITEMS

Building a paper-and-pencil test in terms of tables of specifications is, as we have seen, an important step toward assurance that the test will have high content validity. The value of this procedure, however, is noticeably lessened if the test items are carelessly devised. Even though the item may be carefully classified in terms of the subject matter topics and behavioral changes listed in the table of specifications, the test as a whole may lose some content validity if the teacher fails to apply properly a myriad of relatively simple, obvious, and seemingly unimportant rules when he builds the test items. Many "dos and don'ts" govern the construction of objective test items.

Supply Test Items

The supply test item can be crudely defined as an essay test item demanding a highly abbreviated answer. This answer is often only a single word or number, seldom more than several words or numbers. The pupil responds to a direct question or incomplete declarative statement by writing his answer in the space provided. Notice that there is little difference between these two. By means of a simple rearrangement of words, a short-answer question becomes a completion test item, or a completion test item becomes a short-answer question. They are sometimes haphazardly inter-mixed in classroom achievement tests; however, a better practice is to separate them, especially when young pupils are being tested.

SUGGESTIONS FOR CONSTRUCTING SUPPLY TEST ITEMS. *Design the supply test item so that it has only one correct answer, which is short and definite.* This is unquestionably the most difficult problem a teacher encounters when building supply test items. Although he has but one short and definite answer in mind for each item, he will be amazed at the pupils' facility for thinking of synonyms or near-synonyms of his answers, which in many instances must be considered as correct answers. For example, consider the following test item written in two different ways.

Poor: *The novel entitled* Pickwick Papers *was written by (Charles Dickens).*
Improved: *The name of the author of the novel entitled* Pickwick Papers *is (Charles Dickens).*

The first version of this completion test item could elicit such responses as "a man," "an Englishman," "an adult," "a novelist," or "a genius." All of these are technically correct, but none is the answer expected—"Charles Dickens." If a teacher wishes to avoid much needless quibbling over answers, he must exercise great care in the development of test items. Some proposed supply test items cannot be convenient-ly changed to avoid wrong or half-wrong answers—the desired answer might be too obvious and the item practically worthless because of too low a level of difficulty. Changing the item form from a supply to a selection type sometimes helps in these cases.

Avoid removing statements verbatim from textbooks or other sources and trying to use them as short-answer test items. This practice will, of course, give an advantage to that pupil who can somehow detect a textbook expression and select his answers at least partially on the basis of whether they have a textbook flavor. Moreover, the use of verbatim statements may make the item ambiguous since they are used out of context. For example, the first of the following statements is taken directly from a history textbook and one word is deleted to make it a completion item.

Poor: *The power to declare war is vested in* (Congress).
Improved: *In the United States the power to declare war is vested in* Congress.

Since the test covered aspects of the governments of many other countries, the pupils were understandably confused by the first version of the test item. Obviously, the teacher quickly recognizes the trouble when it is called to his attention; however, he is less likely to anticipate this problem if he continually takes statements out of context and uses them as short-answer test items. In summary, each test item should be able to stand alone unless deliberately related to other items.

When building completion test items, avoid mutilating the statement until its meaning is all but lost. In an effort to increase the level of difficulty, or test for several pieces of information by means of one item, some teachers greatly increase the number of blanks in a completion item. The temptation to do so is rather strong at times, but seldom is the procedure successful. Using a very small number of well-chosen blanks is more satisfactory. Notice how the following item is improved by reducing the number of omitted words:

Poor: *The process by which* (petroleum) *is separated into various component* (parts) *having different* (boiling points) *is known as* (fractional distillation).

Improved: *The process by which petroleum is separated into various component parts having different boiling points is known as* (fractional distillation).

To the pupil, the second version is a well-defined problem, whereas the first is not. In fact, the first statement would discourage anyone but the person who originally deleted the words.

When building completion test items, try to place the blank or blanks near the end of the statement rather than the beginning, and provide sufficient space for pupil answers. Often it is a simple matter to place the blanks at either the beginning or end of the test item. Placing the blanks at the end prevents the test item from acquiring a noticeable awkwardness, as well as a degree of artificial difficulty. Less time is needed to arrive at the correct answer, particularly in the case of elementary school tests.

Avoid the use of extraneous hints designed to help the pupil identify the correct answer. On occasion, teachers try to help the pupil find the correct answer to a short-answer test item by inserting the first letter of each word of the answer, by drawing the length of the answer, or by drawing several lines of appropriate length when the correct answer contains several words. The following short-answer test item in an elementary school geography test is typical of this procedure:

Poor: *In which state is the most important seaport on the eastern seaboard located?* N(ew) Y(ork)

Improved: *In which state is the most important seaport on the eastern seaboard located? (New York)*

The first version of the test item encourages guessing more than the improved version. In addition, offering such hints as these is not realistic; if a pupil were required to recall this information outside of the testing situation he undoubtedly would not be offered this assistance. The difference between the testing situation and the natural situation is increased, and therefore the form of the test item is open to criticism.

Also, the hints help him to use processes of elimination otherwise unavailable. In attempting to answer the test item, a pupil not knowing the correct answer could quickly eliminate possibilities by remembering that "N———" must mean "New" or "North." Therefore, the correct answer is New Jersey, New Mexico, New York, New Hampshire, North Dakota, or North Carolina. Of these states, only New York has the second word beginning with the letter "Y." This, then, is his answer.

Always indicate the units in which the answer is to be expressed for those supply test items that could have several answers depending upon the units chosen. For computational exercises, this can be an annoying problem for both the pupils writing the test and the person who must later score it. For instance, the correct answer to the following exercise can be expressed in three different ways.

Poor: *A four-foot piece of wire is to be cut into two pieces so that one piece will be six inches longer than twice the length of the second piece. What is the length of the longer piece? (2ft., 10 in.)*

Improved: *A four-foot piece of wire is to be cut into two pieces so that one piece will be six inches longer than twice the length of the second piece. What is the length of the longer piece? Ans. (2) ft. (10) in.*

The correct answer is 34 inches, 2 5/6´feet, or 2 feet and 10 inches. Demanding one type of unit rather than another can change the difficulty level of the exercise as well as the amount of time needed to solve it.

ADVANTAGES AND LIMITATIONS OF SUPPLY TEST ITEMS. There are two advantages in using the supply test item rather than other kinds of objective test items. First of all, the supply form reduces the likelihood that the pupil will guess the correct answer. Whereas in the case of the selection form, he need only recognize the correct response from among a relatively small number of given possibilities, in the case of the supply test item, he is confronted with a situation that is not so highly structured. As a result, some pupils argue that this type of item is more difficult for them.

A second advantage often attributed to supply test items is that they are relatively easy to construct. This is, in a sense, a deceptive statement. Although some teachers find them easier to build than the selection type of item, supply test items are by no means so simple to construct as a casual investigation might indicate. The foregoing suggestions for constructing supply test items offer ample supporting evidence.

Of all of the limitations of using supply test items usually cited, two are outstanding. In the first place, such items are more difficult to score than other kinds of objective test items. Despite the best efforts of the teacher building such a test item, often a variety of answers are totally or partially correct. Assigning total or partial credit can only be done by someone intimately familiar with the test items, the background of the pupils, and the teaching situation. In other words, it must be done by the teacher, and even he finds it to be a difficult and time-consuming task. The scoring of pupil response is complicated by legibility of handwriting and faulty spelling. The latter may or may not be sufficient cause for reducing the amount of credit a pupil receives for an otherwise correct response. If one of the purposes of the test is to determine whether a pupil can spell the correct answer after he has recalled it, then loss of credit can be justified. If this is not the case, loss of credit for faulty spelling cannot be defended.

The second limitation is the kind of behavioral change involved in the item. Typically these items demand only recall of information rather than more complex aspects, such as the application of principles in new situations. This tendency is traceable in part to the fact that no matter what type of objective test item is to be used, test items requiring only recall of information are usually easier to construct. When building supply test items, the teacher strives to find items with correct answers that are short and clear, and in so doing, he often selects test items involving primarily factual details. Vocabulary is heavily emphasized.

On balance, supply test items leave something to be desired. They cannot be considered a versatile, efficient means of measuring a wide variety of pupil achievements. As a result, they are not commonly used except for teacher-built tests, and even for those their popularity is less than that of selection test items.

PROBLEM

3. In the light of the foregoing suggestions to be followed when constructing supply test items, improve each of the following:
   a. A hogan is an almost round structure with walls made of (logs) and (mud plaster).
   b. Selling price equals cost plus (profit).
   c. (Sun) is the source of most of our heat.
   d. A diameter that is (perpendicular) to a chord (bisects) the chord.

True-False Test Items

The true-false test item is nothing more than a declarative statement to which the pupil responds in one of two ways—the statement is true or it is false. Occasionally, the statement is so worded that it is more convenient to ask the pupil to respond with "Right" or "Wrong" rather than "True" or "False." Moreover, changing the declarative statement to a question need not necessarily increase the number of possible responses. In these instances, the question can be phrased so that a "Yes" or "No" response is requested.

The most common type of true-false test item has already been illustrated. Less common variations are the following:

Correction variety:

Directions: *Determine whether each of the following statements is true or false. If the statement is true, circle the "T" following the statement. If it is false, circle the "F" and write in the blank provided the word or words that, when substituted for the word underlined, will make the statement true.*

1. The earth is essentially <u>spherical</u> in shape   Ⓣ   F
2. The sun is a <u>planet</u>.   T   Ⓕ   (star)
3. The earth spins on its axis once each <u>month</u>.   T   Ⓕ   (day)

Cluster variety:

Directions: *The following statements pertain to the location of various European countries. Determine whether each statement about each country is true or false. If it is true, circle the "T" following the statement. If it is false, circle the "F."*

Switzerland has a common border with
a. Italy on the south.   Ⓣ   F
b. France on the west.   Ⓣ   F
c. Austria on the east.   Ⓣ   F
d. Czechoslovakia on the north.   T   Ⓕ

T-F-CT-CF variety:

Directions: *Determine (1) whether each of the following statements is true or false, and (2) whether the converse of the statement is true or false. If it is true, circle the "T" preceding the statement; if it is false, circle the "F." If the converse of the statement is true, circle "CT"; if the converse is false, circle "CF."* Two correct answers must be given for each statement.

Ⓣ F   CT Ⓒ̲Ⓕ̲   1. A square is always a quadrilateral.
Ⓣ F   Ⓒ̲Ⓣ̲   CF   2. An equilateral triangle is also an equiangular triangle.
T Ⓕ   CT   Ⓒ̲Ⓕ̲   3. A right triangle is necessarily an isosceles triangle.

T-F-TF variety:

Directions: *Determine whether each of the following statements is true, false, or true under some circumstances and false under other circumstances. If the statement is true under all circumstances, circle the "T" preceding the statement; if it is false under all circumstances, circle the "F"; if it is true under some circumstances and false under others, circle the "TF."*

T F Ⓣ̲Ⓕ̲   1. If a person is living at a latitude of 40° he is living north of the equator.
Ⓣ F   TF   2. The prime meridian is an imaginary line at 0° longitude.

SUGGESTIONS FOR CONSTRUCTING TRUE-FALSE TEST ITEMS. When constructing a test item requiring a response of either "True" or "False" and only that, search for statements that are true or false without additional qualifications. All too commonly a true-false test item is *essentially* true or false rather than absolutely true or false. This is perplexing to the pupil. Should he mark statements as true only if they are true under all possible circumstances, and mark all others false even though some might be essentially true? On the other hand, should he mark those statements that are in general true and those false that are in general false, thus ignoring specific and perhaps minor qualifications that might be pertinent? If his method of attack fails to be the one the teacher has in mind, his answer will be wrong even though his knowledge of the subject matter is superior.

The following test item illustrates the problem. The intended answer is "True."

Poor: *The water vapor in the air will condense when the air is cooled.*

Improved: *If the temperature of the air in this room is progressively lowered, a temperature will ultimately be reached at which the water vapor in the air will start to condense.*

The first version of the test item may trouble the pupil because the degree of cooling, the amount of water vapor in the air, and the temperature of the air are not stated. Slight cooling may or may not cause condensation; drastic cooling probably would. Hence, the statement is true under certain circumstances and false under others. A pupil who knows the information normally required to answer the test item correctly may fail to receive credit for his knowledge because he remembers too many facts. Incidentally, copying statements verbatim from textbooks or study guides customarily produces true-false items that are not absolutely true or absolutely false.

Avoid the use of specific determiners. Specific determiners are words or expressions that frequently identify a statement containing them as true or false. Words often found in false statements are "only," "never," "all," "every," "always," "none," and "no." Those often found in true statements are "usually," "generally," "sometimes," "customarily," "often," "may," "could," and "frequently." The testwise pupil recognizes the situation. If he does not possess the knowledge necessary to answer correctly a true-false test item, he searches for a specific determiner. Should he find one and answer accordingly, his chances of having identified the correct answer are good. Consequently, the test item may discriminate among pupils on a basis other than their ability to recall information, and thus its usefulness is impaired.

In an effort to construct true-false test items that are absolutely true or absolutely false, teachers repeatedly resort to the use of specific determiners. The weakening of the test item that customarily occurs is illustrated in the following:

Poor: *None of the people of Switzerland is engaged in farming.*

Improved: *The mountains of Switzerland prevent the Swiss people from raising grain extensively.*

A clever but ill-prepared pupil would quickly mark the first version of the test item as false. The second version demands a knowledge of the geography of the country as well as the nature of its agriculture. It contains no specific determiners to provide hints as to its correct answer.

The teacher need not always avoid the use of such words as "all," "never," and "usually" because they can serve as specific determiners. On the contrary, they can be deliberately used, and with success, by including them in true-false test items that have correct answers the opposite of those suggested by the words in question. For example:

1. *All planets revolve around the sun of our solar system.*
2. *The sum of the angles of a plane triangle is always 180°.*

Try to keep the true-false test items reasonably short, and restrict each to one central idea. True-false test items that are extremely long require undue amounts of response time. The pupil must search out the truth or falsity of each phrase and dependent clause. Moreover, long true-false test items are more often true than false since the length is sometimes caused by the qualifying remarks needed to make the statement true. Strive to balance the true-false statements in terms of length. If lengthy statements are used, they should be false about as often as they are true.

A serious problem that is sometimes accentuated by lengthy true-false items is that several ideas become involved. If one part of the test item is true, whereas another part is false, the pupil customarily labels the test item as false. But this can be confusing to him, not only when he responds to the test item, but also when he reviews his test at a later time. Misinformation may result.

An illustration of a true-false test item that is partially true and partially false is shown below:

Poor: *Although today the members of the United States House of Represen-*
tatives are elected by popular vote of the people of the districts they
represent, the members of the United States Senate are selected by the
state legislatures of the states they represent.

Improved: *The members of the present Senate of the United States were selected*
by the state legislatures of the states they represent.

The clause at the beginning of the statement is unnecessary and should be eliminated, as illustrated by the second version of the test item. This deletion serves the additional purpose of reducing the scope of the item to one central idea, which can be judged as true or false.

If true-false tests are used regularly, be certain that the percentage of test items requiring a "True" answer, and hence the percentage of test items requiring a "False" answer, are not relatively constant from test to test. Some pupils quickly sense any tendency on the part of a teacher to maintain approximately the same percent of true and false statements from test to test. This is true regardless of whether an even balance between the two statements is maintained or an overbalance of one type is used. If a noticeable consistency is detected, the pupil may use it as a basis for guessing the answers of some of the test items that baffle him. Moreover, some pupils quickly discover any pattern that the correct answers may take, such as, F-T-F-T-F-T or T-T-F-F-T-T. Occasionally a teacher arranges the test items so that the correct answers form a systematic pattern, thereby simplifying scoring. Such an arrangement also simplifies the task of the alert pupil when he responds to the test items. An otherwise good true-false test can be seriously damaged by this procedure.

ADVANTAGES AND LIMITATIONS OF TRUE-FALSE TEST ITEMS. The advantages accrued by using true-false test items are outweighed by the limitations. The popularity of these test items is unjustified—a popularity that can be traced primarily to the fact that true-false test items allow the teacher to sample widely a large amount of subject matter without needing a great amount of testing time. Most pupils can respond quickly to well-constructed items of this type. A second and less obvious advantage sometimes cited in the case of true-false test items is that they are essentially a realistic task for the pupil. Frequently, in everyday life, he is called upon to judge a statement as true or false in the manner required of him by the test items. A third advantage of even more doubtful merit is the claim that true-false test items are easy to build. As in the case of the supply test items, the true-false test item is by no means so easy to construct as you might suppose.

One of the most serious limitations of the true-false test item is that many are concerned only with small, relatively unimportant pieces of information. Like the supply test item, the true-false item serves best as a means of measuring the pupils' ability to recall information. Because of the teacher's efforts to find statements that are absolutely true or false, the information needed to answer the items correctly is frequently highly specific. It is difficult to build good true-false test items that involve generalizations, broad principles, and relationships, all of which may be notably more important than the pieces of information involved in the usual true-false test items.

A second serious disadvantage is that true-false test items encourage some pupils to try to guess the correct response. They argue that, after all, they have a fifty-fifty chance of identifying the right answer without even bothering to read the statement. The use of specific determiners, the tendency of long statements to be true statements, and the practice of arranging the correct responses in a systematic pattern encourage guessing and increase the likelihood of that guessing being successful. Means of correcting for guessing are discussed later in this chapter (see page 101).

Finally, true-false test items can be criticized on the basis that many of them are ambiguous. Careful construction of true-false test items reduces ambiguity, but does not necessarily eliminate it. Words like "several," "many," "some," "frequently," "important," and "principal" can hardly be avoided. But what do they mean? Variations in the meanings of these and similar terms can mean variations in the pupils' responses to the statements containing them. Hairsplitting distinctions may be necessary, to the distress of teacher and pupil alike.

PROBLEM

4. In the light of the foregoing suggestions to be followed in construction of true-false test items, improve each of the following:
   a. If we feel heat traveling through a steel bar at a certain rate, we can assume that heat will travel through another kind of bar at that rate.
   b. Heat can do work.
   c. The *Reader's Guide* is the best source to use when looking for current material on a subject.
   d. If (+) times (+) equals (+), then (−) times (−) equals (−).

Multiple-Choice Test Items

A multiple-choice test item is one in which a direct question or incomplete statement is presented and a number of possible responses are given. The pupil chooses the response that is the correct (or best) answer to the question or that is the correct (or best) expression for completing the statement. The question or incomplete statement introducing the test item is known as the *stem*. Any undesired answer is called a *distracter* or *foil*. Generally four or five responses are listed and all but one is a distracter.

Some multiple-choice test items require a correct answer, others a "best" answer. This difference can be traced to the subject matter. For instance, when selecting the name of the author of a book among four names listed, the pupil searches for the correct answer; all distracters are completely wrong. However, when selecting the principal reason from among four possible reasons that Ulysses S. Grant was elected to the presidency of the United States, the pupil searches for the "best" answer. It should be clearly the most outstanding of those listed. As you can easily see, in this illustration the distracters can be actual reasons, but relatively unimportant. Both of these kinds of multiple-choice test items are commonly used.

Introducing a multiple-choice test item by means of an incomplete statement seems to be equally as satisfactory as introducing it by means of a direct question. Often the factor governing the choice of stem is the length of the test item. If the direct question approach yields a short, easily understood test item, it is customarily used; should it not do so, the incomplete statement approach replaces it. For a person inexperienced in building multiple-choice test items, however, the direct question is recommended, since fewer technically weak items result (Wesman, 1971).

There are numerous variations of the multiple-choice test item. The most familiar form is that illustrated earlier in this chapter. Four additional variations are shown below.

Multiple-response variety:
Directions: *For each of the following questions, select the correct answer or answers from among the four listed. Note that for each question there may be as few as one and as many as four correct answers. Write the number(s) of your choice(s) in the blank to the left of the question.*
(2, 3)   *Which of the following compounds are gases when at room temperature and under normal pressure?*
   (1) Benzene
   (2) Ammonia
   (3) Carbon dioxide
   (4) Silicon dioxide

Incomplete-response variety:
Directions: *Solve each of the following mathematics exercises and express your answer in the units designated. Identify the digit of your answer that occupies the second place to the left of the decimal point. Find that digit in the list of five shown with each exercise. Write the letter identifying it in the blank to the left of the exercise.*
(D)   *Four neighbors are to be assessed by their city for special repairs to the street in front of their houses. The amount to be paid is to be prorated among the neighbors according to the property frontage of each (i.e., the width of property along the street). The total assessment is $690, and the respective frontages are 50, 50, 60, and 70 feet. How much (to the nearest dollar) will the owner of the 60-foot frontage have to pay?*
   (A)   1
   (B)   2
   (C)   7
   (D)   8
   (E)   9

Combined-response variety:

Directions: *Each of the following exercises contains a group of objects, people, or events, the members of which are to be arranged in proper order according to the principle stated. Select the correct order for those listed and write the number of your choice in the blank to the left of the exercise.*

(1)   *Arrange the following British statesmen in terms of the dates of their careers, starting with the most recent.*

        a. Robert Walpole
        b. Stanley Baldwin
        c. William Pitt, Jr.
        d. Winston Churchill
        (1) d, b, c, a
        (2) b, d, a, c
        (3) b, a, d, c
        (4) d, c, b, a

Degree-of-certainty variety:

Directions: *For each of the following questions select the correct response from among the four listed. Write the number of your choice in the blank to the left of the exercise. Then indicate your degree of certainty for your choice by selecting the most descriptive of the three statements shown, and writing its number in the blank provided.*

(4)   *Which of the following cities in the United States is located west of the Mississippi River?*

        (1) Chicago
        (2) Detroit
        (3) Washington
        (4) Salt Lake City

___   *How certain are you of your choice?*

        (1) very certain
        (2) fairly certain
        (3) quite uncertain

SUGGESTIONS FOR CONSTRUCTING MULTIPLE-CHOICE TEST ITEMS. *Select the distracters so that all of them are reasonably plausible and appealing to those pupils who do not possess the knowledge demanded by the item.* Your experiences as an examinee are no doubt sufficient to convince you of the importance of this suggestion. When you are confronted with a multiple-choice item to which you do not know the answer, you probably attack by a process of elimination. Any response that appears to be extremely unlikely you eliminate, even though you may have little or no knowledge of it. Often you are able to reduce the number of possibilities to two, sometimes to only one. If some of the distracters are implausible, the possibility of identifying the correct answer is greatly improved.

    The following test item shows the ease with which the correct answer to a multiple-choice test item can be found when the distraters are implausible.

Poor: *Which of the following men was at one time the Chief Justice of the Supreme Court of the United States?*

        (1) Charles Evans Hughes

> *(2) Nikolai Lenin*
> *(3) Chiang Kai-shek*
> *(4) John Paul Jones*

Improved: *Which of the following men was at one time the Chief Justice of the Supreme Court of the United States?*
> *(1) Charles Evans Hughes*
> *(2) William E. Borah*
> *(3) Oliver Wendell Holmes*
> *(4) William Jennings Bryan*

If a pupil does not know the answer to the test item as stated in the first instance, a few miscellaneous pieces of information can help him find it. After all, responses 2 and 3 are unlikely possibilities. Names such as these hardly sound "American," so they probably should be eliminated. John Paul Jones will no doubt be remembered as a military hero, perhaps as a Revolutionary War naval hero. Since it seems improbable that a military hero would ever be elevated to the position of Chief Justice of the Supreme Court, this response is eliminated. Response 1 is therefore correctly selected despite the fact that the pupil knows nothing of Charles Evans Hughes, Nikolai Lenin, and Chiang Kai-shek, and very little about John Paul Jones and the Supreme Court.

The second statement of the test item is greatly improved. All of the persons listed were citizens of the United States and were prominent in public life. They were also contemporaries. All had sufficient qualifications to be considered for such a post as Chief Justice; one of them, Oliver Wendell Holmes, was a prominent associate justice of the Supreme Court but never the Chief Justice. This should be a plausible and attractive distracter to the partially informed pupil. The distracters used in the second version of the test item are more homogeneous than those used in the first version. Increasing the homogeneity of the responses tends to increase the difficulty of the multiple-choice test item.

Plausible distracters are often difficult to find. What is plausible to the teacher may not seem so to the pupils, yet the teacher must decide which distracters are used. With sufficient planning, however, an alternative technique can be used. By tabulating wrong answers to supply test items, the teacher can amass much helpful information for determining plausible distracters for future testing. Multiple-choice questions can be substituted for supply test items and wrong answers from earlier classes used as distracters.

Vary the number of options included in the multiple-choice test item as needed, anticipating that ordinarily there will be at least three and not more than five. How many options should the typical multiple-choice item have? To answer this question, consider first the test-sophistication of the pupils. Four-option and even five-option test items are commonly used in achievement tests for pupils at the junior high school level and above. Certainly this is too many for pupils in the primary grade levels. Often two-option or three-option test items are used in an effort to avoid reading problems and excessive fatigue.

Another important factor influencing the number of options is the quality of distracters available. Sometimes we slavishly adhere to a fixed number of distracters for all multiple-choice items in a given test. This is unnecessary. The effectiveness of the distracters rather than their number determines the quality of the test item

(Wesman, 1971). Instead of having a fixed mold (for example, one correct answer plus three distracters for each item), reduce the number of distracters when few good ones are available. Distracters that are nothing but "fillers" complicate the testing effort without improving our ability to differentiate among pupils in terms of achievement.

If the number of options varies somewhat from item to item in a test, the pupils should be told about it at the beginning of the test. Should variation occur frequently, group the test items according to the number of options they have, or even consider changing the item form, for example, to one of the true-false varieties.

Be certain that the length of the responses of a multiple-choice test item is not related to their tendency to be the correct (or best) answer. Because of the need to qualify to make one response the correct (or best) answer, the desired answer would regularly be the longest unless precautions are taken. Notice how obvious this is in the following illustration:

Poor: *Sliced oranges are an excellent source of*
          (1) protein.
          (2) starch.
          (3) vitamin A.
          (4) vitamin C, if the oranges are freshly sliced.

Improved: *Freshly prepared orange juice is recommended for the diet because it is an excellent source of*
          (1) protein.
          (2) starch.
          (3) vitamin A.
          (4) vitamin C.

If given the first version of the multiple-choice test item, the ill-prepared pupil will select response 4 more frequently than any other. Its length probably means that it is the correct answer.

If a multiple-choice test item requires a "best" answer, make certain that one and only one is clearly the best. "Hairsplitting" is a problem in practically all objective test items. This is especially true of "best" answer multiple-choice test items, for a judgment is involved. It is a matter of opinion as to which of many is the *most important reason why* a phenomenon occurred, or which of many is the *chief* result for a given cause. There are many counterparts to such possibilities, and they all too frequently appear in otherwise respectable multiple-choice tests. For example:

Poor: *The most serious health problem in the United States today is*
          (1) cancer.
          (2) mental illness.
          (3) heart disease.
          (4) the common cold.

Improved: *Of the following diseases, which hospitalizes the most people at the present time?*
          (1) pneumonia
          (2) mental illness
          (3) poliomyelitis
          (4) tuberculosis

On the basis of the prevalence of the illness, the possibility of its being fatal, or the difficulty of relieving it, any one of the responses to the first version of the test item can be judged the "best." Unanimity or even near unanimity of opinion may be difficult to obtain. However, the test item as revised offers no such problem.

Whenever convenient, design the multiple-choice test item so that the stem includes as much of the item as possible. Multiple-choice test items are usually improved if the stem is relatively long and the responses are relatively short; then the stem more clearly defines the problem on which the test item is based, and less response time is needed by most pupils. On the other hand, it is sometimes awkward to build each multiple-choice test item with a long stem and short responses. The rule can be ignored to ensure clarity.

Examination of the following two versions of a multiple-choice item from a sixth-grade social studies test shows the advantages of relatively long stems coupled with short responses.

Poor: *Yugoslavia*
         (1) is larger in area than France.
         (2) borders on the Adriatic Sea.
         (3) is located in western Asia.
         (4) contains the Ural Mountains.

Improved: *In which of the following continents is Yugoslavia located?*
         (1) Europe
         (2) Asia
         (3) Africa
         (4) South America

The first version is more difficult to understand than the second. With the revised version, based on a single problem explicitly stated in the stem of the item, the pupil should have no trouble grasping it and can devote his time to selection of the correct answer.

Express the responses to a multiple-choice test item so that grammatical consistency is maintained. In other words, if the stem of the multiple-choice item is an incomplete sentence, each response must be worded so that it is a grammatically correct completion of the introductory statement. If the stem is a direct question, the responses should be brief statements of parallel construction. Failure to maintain grammatical consistency is often due to carelessness; happily, this defect can be easily corrected in most instances. The following test item illustrates this point:

Poor: *If the north pole of one bar magnet is brought very near the south pole*
         of another bar magnet, the two poles will
         (1) repel each other.
         (2) attract each other.
         (3) no effect.
         (4) an electric spark will be produced.

Improved: *If the north pole of one bar magnet is brought very near the south pole*
         of another bar magnet, the two poles will
         (1) repel each other.
         (2) attract each other.

(3) have no effect on each other.
(4) produce an electric spark.

The two versions of this test item make it clear that the teacher can avoid grammatical inconsistency by simply checking each response with the stem. If this is done and any appropriate changes in wording are made, the test item is not only more impressive from a grammarian's point of view but it is also less confusing from a pupil's.

Minimize the use of negative expressions in a multiple-choice test item. Such expressions reduce the clarity of an item and may artificially add to its difficulty. This problem can become serious for less mature pupils. For instance, consider the following:

Poor: *Which of the following is not true of Puerto Rico?*
           (1) It is an island.
           (2) Its principal language is Spanish.
           (3) It is not a state in the U.S.A.
           (4) It does not have a warm climate.
Improved: *What is the political status of Puerto Rico?*
           (1) It is a state in the U.S.A.
           (2) It is an independent country like the U.S.A.
           (3) It is an unincorporated territory of the U.S.A.
           (4) It is a commonwealth under the U.S. government.

The intended correct answer to both versions is the fourth response. In the case of the first version, notice how awkward—and time-consuming—it is to arrive at this conclusion and to confirm it. The second version is much more straightforward and aims directly at one central point, namely, the political status of Puerto Rico. No negative expressions are needed or desired.

ADVANTAGES AND LIMITATIONS OF MULTIPLE-CHOICE TEST ITEMS. The advantages of multiple-choice test items are much more impressive then the limitations. The outstanding feature of the multiple-choice item is its versatility. It can be used to determine how well a pupil can recall the most specific pieces of information as well as his ability to apply the most important principle in a novel situation.* Moreover, it can do so without introducing the problems of subjective scoring, which weakens the short-answer test items, or ambiguity, so noticeable when true-false test items are used. Successful guessing by the pupils is reduced but not eliminated. Any teacher with a reasonable amount of patience and ingenuity can build and use multiple-choice items with favorable results. As illustrated by the various test items concerning novelists (see pages 68–69), he can often convert supply, true-false, and matching test items to multiple-choice form without undue difficulty.

Multiple-choice test items are used at all grade levels with the possible exception of the primary. Even there they can be orally administered if practice test items correctly answered are shown. Multiple-choice test items can also be successfully used

* *The usefulness of objective test items for measuring a pupil's ability to apply information and principles in a novel situation is discussed in Chapter 4.*

in all subject matter areas when verbal and mathematical aspects are being tested. An objection is occasionally raised, however, to the use of these items in testing achievement in mathematics. A pupil may correctly answer the test item by using the four or five responses given as a basis for solving the problem backwards. This can be circumvented by using a variation of the standard multiple-choice form, such as the incomplete-response variety already illustrated.

Multiple-choice test items are not, of course, the panacea for the difficulties of achievement testing. They have distinct limitations, some of which have been mentioned in earlier discussions. They are difficult to build, and suitable distracters are hard to find. Although a teacher's ingenuity can produce many, and others can be found among the wrong answers given to supply test items administered to preceding classes, surpluses are rare. More often than not the teacher lacks at least one distracter. He may try to fill the void by adding the response "none of the foregoing," "not given," or "can't tell." These cannot be used for "best" answer multiple-choice test items; also, they customarily weaken the correct answer variety if used consistently as a distracter, since they are recognized by the pupil as more often the wrong answer than the correct one. Such responses need not be avoided but they must be carefully presented. For instance, do not use them as the *answer* to an item when it may include a *large of number of incorrect responses* as in the case of most questions requiring mathematical computations to arrive at a numerical answer.

Another limitation of multiple-choice test items is the response time they require. For a given amount of testing time, pupils can complete fewer multiple-choice test items than true-false items. This is particularly noticeable when the multiple-choice test items demand fine discriminations and fundamental understandings.

PROBLEMS

5. Attempts to improve the quality of "best" answer multiple-choice test items may actually change the test item to the "correct" answer variety. Examine the test item concerning diseases on page 81 and decide whether this has occurred.

6. Evaluate the degree-of-certainty variety of multiple-choice test items as (1) a measurement device and (2) an instructional device (Echternacht, 1972, pp. 217–223).

7. Because some objective test items are considered more important than others, some teachers believe more points (for example, 2 rather than 1) should be given for each correct answer. Does this practice improve the quality of the test (Ebel, 1972, pp. 258–260)?

Matching Test Items

The matching test item in its simplest form consists of two lists of items and a set of instructions for matching each of the items in the first with one in the second. The first is known as a list of *premises*, the second as a list of *responses*. The instructions explain how the pupil is to match each premise with one or more of the responses. Premises and responses may be statements, names of people or places, titles of works of art, dates, formulas, symbols, or even parts of a picture or drawing. They may vary greatly but will tend to be homogeneous within a given list. Usually the length of each premise or response is (and should be) relatively short, perhaps no longer than a word or two.

In some matching exercises, the number of premises and responses is the same and each response can be used only once; this is a "perfect matching" exercise. In other instances, some of the responses do not match any of the premises; this is an "imperfect matching" exercise. An "imperfect matching" exercise can be constructed by making the list of responses longer than the list of premises or, if the lists are of equal length, by including some responses that must be used more than once. Earlier in this chapter an example is given of an "imperfect matching" test item having a shorter list of responses than premises; two responses are used more than once and one is not used at all.

In addition to the types of matching test items mentioned in the foregoing paragraph, there are a number of other variations. Two promising ones are illustrated here:

Compound matching variety:
Directions: *Below is a list of nineteenth century and early twentieth century novelists. For each novelist identify the title of one of his works that is listed in the second column by writing the letter opposite the title in the first of the two blanks to the left of the author's name. Identify his nationality from among those listed in the column below by writing the number opposite it in the second blank.*

		Authors		Novels
(H)	(3)	1. *Alexandre Dumas*	A.	The Adventures of Tom Sawyer
(G)	(2)	2. *George Eliot*	B.	Barchester Towers
(F)	(3)	3. *Victor Hugo*	C.	Call of the Wild
(C)	(1)	4. *Jack London*	D.	David Copperfield
(E)	(1)	5. *Herman Melville*	E.	Moby Dick
(J)	(2)	6. *William Thackeray*	F.	Notre Dame of Paris
(B)	(2)	7. *Anthony Trollope*	G.	Romola
(A)	(1)	·8. *Mark Twain*	H.	The Three Musketeers
		Nationalities	I.	Uncle Tom's Cabin
		1. *American*	J.	Vanity Fair
		2. *English*	K.	War and Peace
		3. *French*		

Classification variety:
Directions: *Each of the following statements is a complete sentence. Determine whether the sentence is a simple, complex, compound, or compound-complex sentence. Using the list below, find the letter corresponding to your choice and write it in the blank to the left of the sentence.*

A. *simple sentence*
B. *complex sentence*
C. *compound sentence*
D. *compound-complex sentence*

(C) 1. *During the winter the days are short and the nights are long.*
(A) 2. *Jane rode to school on her bicycle.*
(B) 3. *If Mary Lou had been home she could have visited with her grandparents and their friends.*

SUGGESTIONS FOR CONSTRUCTING MATCHING TEST ITEMS. *Make lists of premises and responses as homogeneous as possible.* Each list should be confined to one type of subject. Then, a title including every member can be placed above the list. In contrast, some poorly constructed matching test items are unnecessarily heterogeneous. Suppose that a certain list of premises contained names of inanimate objects, insects, animals, and people. For many pupils this simplifies the task of answering the test item correctly. They can eliminate many of the possible responses to a given premise not because they know much about the premise and response, but because there is no conceivable basis for matching some responses to a given premise.

Notice how this process of elimination is possible in the first version of a matching test item intended for use in a junior high school social studies achievement test.

Poor:
Directions: *Match each description in the first column with one of the names in the second column by writing the letter identifying the name in the blank to the left of the description.*

	Descriptions	Names
(C)	1. A river in southeastern Europe	A. Bucharest
(F)	2. One of the largest countries in the world	B. Czechoslovakia
(G)	3. Mountains in Russia	C. Danube
(D)	4. A level country	D. Poland
(A)	5. The capital of a country near Czechoslovakia	E. Romania
		F. Russia
		G. Ural

Improved:
Directions: *Match each river with the body of water into which it flows by writing the letter identifying the body of water in the blank to the left of the name of the river. It is possible that several of the rivers flow into the same body of water.*

	Rivers	Bodies of Water
(C)	1. Danube	A. Adriatic Sea
(G)	2. Rhine	B. Bay of Biscay
(F)	3. Rhone	C. Black Sea
(E)	4. Seine	D. Caspian Sea
(G)	5. Thames	E. English Channel
(F)	6. Tiber	F. Mediterranean Sea
		G. North Sea

Both lists of the first test item are quite varied in content. This lack of homogeneity certainly will help the relatively uninformed pupil find correct answers by a process of elimination.

The revised version of the matching test item is greatly improved. Notice that the titles "rivers" and "bodies of water" are much more accurate and definitive than those used in the first version. Any pupil, especially one with only sketchy knowledge of the topic, would find it difficult to use the process of elimination in this test item. Additional matching items dealing only with the location of various European cities, mountain ranges, or countries can also be constructed. In other words, several matching test items are needed to lessen the variation of the premises and responses in the first version without excluding any of that information from the test.

Always indicate as clearly as possible the basis on which the matching of premises and responses is to be made. Every effort should be made to clarify the task the pupil is asked to perform by improving the directions and the titles of the lists. It is not the purpose of a matching test item to find out if a pupil understands the basis for matching, but rather to see if he can accurately match each premise with a response after he understands the basis of matching.

Below is a matching test item intended for an achievement test in elementary school science. Although it is not mentioned in the first version of the test item, the teacher wants the pupil to match each animal with the kind of food it ordinarily eats.

Poor:

Directions: *Match each animal with grass, insects, or other animals. Write the number in the box next to the name of the animal.*

	Animal		Food
1	cow	1.	grass
1	sheep	2.	insects
3	fox	3.	other animals
3	lion		
2	robin		

Improved:

Directions: *Here is a list of animals. Each of these animals eats many different things each day. However, each animal will most often eat grass, or insects, or other animals. If an animal most often eats grass, write "1" in the box next to the animal's name. If it most often eats insects, write "2" in the box next to the animal's name. If it most often eats other animals, write "3" in the box next to the animal's name.*

	Animals		Food
1	cow	1.	grass
1	sheep	2.	insects
3	fox	3.	other animals
3	lion		
2	robin		

When confronted with the faulty version of this test item, even the most sophisticated elementary school pupil will at first be uncertain as to how the matching should be done. Some of the less sophisticated may never understand it and consequently skip the test item; or they may unknowingly establish a false yet semi-plausible basis for matching. For instance, several will choose the response "other animals" each time, arguing that each animal is more like other animals in terms of its activities and structures than it is like insects or grass.

The directions accompanying the improved version of the test item are long and may need to be read to the pupils. Perhaps an illustration of one animal correctly matched with the food it ordinarily eats should be shown. Either or both of the steps should be taken if the teacher suspects that the pupils are confused about the mechanics of the test item.

Arrange the premises and responses in a logical order. If the premises or responses are names or titles, they should be arranged alphabetically. If they are dates, they should be in chronological order; if numbers, they should be arranged according to size. Unless there is an excellent reason for doing otherwise, any logical order should be followed. This will noticeably reduce the amount of response time needed for answering matching test items.

In every matching test item always include responses that do not match any of the premises, or responses that match more than one premise, or both. In other words, always construct "imperfect matching" test items rather than "perfect matching" ones. The latter have the serious disadvantage of increasing the likelihood of the uninformed pupil guessing one of the correct responses. Since in the "perfect matching" test item there are as many responses as premises, and each response can be used only once, the pupil answering it can determine the last response by a process of elimination.

The following is a "perfect matching" test item; each elementary school pupil is to identify each word in terms of the part of speech it normally is.

	Words		Parts of Speech
(E)	1. with	A.	Noun
(B)	2. am	B.	Verb
(C)	3. red	C.	Adjective
(A)	4. car	D.	Adverb
(D)	5. always	E.	Preposition
(F)	6. and	F.	Conjunction

Should a pupil have trouble matching a response with such a premise as "always" he can pair all other premises and responses, thereby discovering that it matches the fourth response. Of course this is not possible if additional premises are included and hence some responses used more than once.

Keep the list of responses relatively short. When attempting to answer matching test items, the pupil reads a premise and searches the list of responses. If this list is long, he may spend considerable time in spite of the fact that he may have a rather clear notion as to what the response should be. Thus, valuable test time is wasted. Incidentally, observe that a lengthy list of premises may likewise increase the amount of time needed to respond to a matching test item. This cannot be called wasted time, however, unless some of the premises cannot be justified.

There is no well-established limit to the list of responses; however, the following is a good rule of thumb: Allow the list to exceed ten only when the maturity of the pupil and the nature of the subject matter in the test item permit; for younger pupils restrict the list to about half this number. Should you find the list of responses becoming almost endless, consider the possibility of constructing more than one test item. This will allow you to sample a number of different subject matter topics and will simplify the job of finding lists of homogeneous premises and responses.

ADVANTAGES AND LIMITATIONS OF MATCHING TEST ITEMS. The primary advantage of using matching items in an achievement test is that a lot of factual information can be included in the test without much testing time being required. Such items are useful for seeing if a pupil can associate words with their definitions, events with their places and dates, results with their causes, concepts with their designated symbols, authors with their published works, statesmen with their countries and contemporaries, and so forth. Although it is not commonly done, matching test items can be used to measure a pupil's ability to apply the information he has learned. Notice the illustration given on page 85 in which the premises are a list of novel sentences that the pupil is to classify as simple, complex, compound, or compound-complex sentences. The classification variety can be successfully used to measure products of learning other than simple recall of information.

The main limitation in measuring achievement with matching test items is that good items are difficult to build. Sometimes the subject matter is insufficient in quantity or not well suited for matching test items; in either case, homogeneous premises and responses are extremely hard to find. In others, the subject matter may seem to lend itself to this type of test item but the teacher has great difficulty in finding plausible but wrong responses as well as correct responses that are not completely obvious because of the terminology used.

PROBLEM

8. Using a teaching situation you know well, construct a matching test item involving two lists in which at least one response matches more than one premise.

APPRAISING AND EDITING OBJECTIVE TEST ITEMS

Before any newly constructed objective test items can be incorporated into an achievement test, they should undergo a critical reexamination—essentially an appraising and editing procedure. It consists in verifying the relationship between each test item and the table of specifications, rechecking it for any ambiguity or irrelevant clues, and estimating its level of difficulty and reading load. The reexamination of test items in terms of these characteristics may simply reconfirm the worth of many well-constructed items; in some cases, it may reveal grammatical weaknesses; in others, it may uncover glaring faults in test items previously thought to be sound. Regardless of the outcome, the procedure is profitable. When building the test item, the teacher is often preoccupied with details and in the process loses sight of basic features. A later review customarily allows the teacher to see with a new perspective, so he can readjust any features out of balance.

Appraising and editing objective test items can be done by the person who constructed the test items or, preferably, by someone competent in the subject matter. If the second possibility is not feasible, then the original item builder should make the review, but only some time after the building of the items.

No matter who is involved, a useful technique for appraising and editing is for that person to administer the test items to himself. He is now playing the role of the pupil. The answers he gives should then be compared to the answers as originally listed. Any lack of agreement between any two answers is a certain danger signal. It no doubt means that the test item is ambiguous. Perhaps a qualifying statement is missing, or some of the phraseology should be changed. Disagreement between two answers may be traced to the excessive difficulty of the test item. This flaw may be minor and easily corrected; it could be so serious that the item must be discarded.

The fact that the original answer to a test item and an independent answer later determined are the same, on the other hand, is no guarantee that the item is satisfactory. There may be other flaws in it that may not affect the answers arrived at by a reviewer but that could seriously affect the role of the test item in a test and the pupil's response. The teacher should therefore review each test item by checking it in terms of five questions:

1. *Is the test item properly identified with one or more cells of the table of specifications (or, in the case of objective-referenced test items, with a specific objective)?*
2. *Is the test item ambiguous in any respect?*
3. *Does the test item contain any irrelevant clues?*
4. *Does the test item have an appropriate level of difficulty?*
5. *Does the test item have a suitable reading level?*

After a test item has been so examined and any differences corrected, a smooth copy of the test item is made. A highly useful and successful procedure is to type each test item on a 5 X 8-in. card. Generally there is ample room on the card to add additional pertinent information such as the correct answer to the test item, the name and page of the section of any book or outline on which it is based, and, at a later date, a summary of the responses pupils made when answering it. As a result, the teacher has all important information neatly summarized in a single place, and his test item file is enlarged (see page 162).

Relationship Between Test Item and Table of Specifications

When building test items in the conventional way, the teacher uses his tables of specifications as blueprints to guide his selection of subject matter and behavioral changes to be included in each test item. The relationship between each test item and the part of the table of specifications from which it arose can be recorded by means of a simple coding technique. For example, the cells in the table are numbered, and the numbers of those related to the test item are listed on a card containing a statement of the test item.

The first attempt to establish the relationship between a test item and the cells of a table of specifications is usually successful. Since the teacher began to build the test item with one or more cells in mind, he has little difficulty cross-referring it and the cells. However, practically all test items undergo revisions. Perhaps the technical imperfections are corrected without regard to the manner in which these corrections might affect the relationship between the test items and the table of specifications. Sometimes they do not disturb this relationship. Many times they do. For instance, recall the differences between the two versions of many of the test items shown earlier in this chapter. Correcting a technical imperfection repeatedly may have necessitated a fundamental change in the test item. After revision, the test item may be primarily related to a different cell in the table of specifications. Clearly, if these changes are numerous and go unnoticed, the test loses much content validity.

When building objective-referenced test items, the same problem exists. The relationship between each test item and a specific objective must be identified, recorded, and rechecked after all known technical imperfections of the test item have been removed.

Presence of Ambiguity

Many suggestions for constructing objective test items concentrate on one central weakness—ambiguity. The dangers of using verbatim quotes from textbooks and the difficulty pupils encounter when denied some relevant qualifications have already been stressed. Proper phraseology in the test item as well as in the directions to the pupil is also important.

Individually, these suggestions for avoiding ambiguity can usually be followed with ease. Yet they must be applied in harmony with other suggestions not directly concerned with the problem—not always easy to do. In some instances, a teacher building an objective test item will find two suggestions working more or less at cross-purposes. Following one by making a certain revision violates another. Escape from the dilemma may be difficult. No doubt a more common situation is the automatic adoption of the most recently considered suggestion. If the revision happens to violate another suggestion, this is not noticed.

Since ambiguity is one of the chief weaknesses of objective test items, the teacher should make a final check by rereading each test item with one question in mind: Is it possible to word this test item more clearly and directly? In trying to answer his own question, the teacher may find himself improving test items he previously thought to be as polished as he could make them.

The importance of avoiding ambiguity in objective test items is primary. The pupil should never experience difficulty in trying to understand the question. We are trying to find out if a pupil can answer a question he understands, not if he understands the question.

Presence of Irrelevant Clues

The presence of irrelevant clues assists pupils to varying degrees, thereby giving some an unfair advantage. These are the "testwise" pupils. That is, a pupil's ability to capitalize on the characteristics and format of a test and/or a testing situation to obtain a high score is called "testwiseness" (Millman et al., 1965). Some aspects of testwiseness are independent of the test builder or the purpose of the test, for example, the pupil's ability to distribute effectively the testing time available among the various test items, to pay attention to directions, and to adopt a good guessing strategy based on the method of scoring. Others are directly dependent on the mistakes of the teacher when building test items, for example, the pupil's ability to identify correct answers on the basis of any consistent idiosyncrasies or specific determiners used by the teacher.

The second category emphasizes the potentially influential role of irrelevant clues. This must be reduced at all costs.

The existence of pupil testwiseness is a simple fact of life with which a teacher must contend. Reasonably even amounts of this trait within a given group of pupils can actually simplify test planning since the teacher can anticipate with some accuracy the kind of test format, terminology, time limits, and so forth, that are appropriate for an achievement test. Of concern are wide differences among pupils in this regard, which can cause important test score differences not related to pupil achievement.

Proper Level of Difficulty

An important characteristic of objective test items sometimes overlooked by the teacher is the level of difficulty. Obviously this is not determined exclusively by the idea on which the test item is based, for the manner in which it is stated is also important. A single variation of a word or phrase can change it noticeably. Obtaining the proper level for each item and then the test as a whole is a perplexing problem.

The first consideration for the teacher about level of difficulty is the type of test he is building. In a mastery test the level of difficulty is uniformly low; in a norm-referenced test, it varies somewhat, but concentrates in a zone around the fifty percent level of difficulty after correction for chance. In other words, this is the level at which half of the pupils have responded correctly to a test item after allowance has been made for successful guessing (see page 101). For a number of reasons, the target zone should be slightly above fifty percent rather than below.

A highly successful way of obtaining estimates of the level of difficulty of test items is to pretest them on a group of pupils similar to those for whom they are designed. Their answers to the test items can be tabulated and analyzed. On the basis of this analysis, the level of difficulty of each test item is determined. Unfortunately, this procedure is frequently impossible. Without pretesting data, the teacher must depend on his subjective judgment.

Subjective judgment yields only a rough approximation, even when the teacher is completely familiar with the situation, the maturity of the pupils, and many of their past experiences. At best, he can rate the test items on only a five-point scale: "very difficult," "moderately difficult," "average," "moderately easy," and "very easy." Sometimes a three-point scale of "difficult," "average," and "easy" is all that is appropriate. The principal reference point is the "average" category. Test items so rated are considered suitable for typical pupils in the class under consideration.

Although crude, subjective judgment is useful; in the devising of norm-referenced tests, for example, subjective judgment can prevent any test item from being so easy that all pupils respond correctly or so difficult that none does. Since the purpose of these tests is to differentiate among pupils in terms of their achievement, both extremes should be avoided. In contrast, criterion- and objective-referenced tests often have quite low levels of difficulty.

Reading Level

Because test items are constructed by adults, they regularly include words and expressions more typical of adults than children. This happens despite the most conscientious efforts of the teacher and can be a severe problem in the case of objective test items designed for elementary school pupils. After all, to the teacher these words and expressions seem to express the thought behind the test item very clearly. To the pupil, however, this probably is not true. If he were constructing the test item, he would no doubt choose different words. Often he would use more of them, thereby creating another difficulty. Since there is much to read, the pupil needs more response time for each test item. Consequently, fewer can be included, and the breadth of the sampling of the subject matter decreases.

A pupil with a slow reading rate or a modest vocabulary should not be appreciably penalized in a typical objective achievement test. To prevent any penalty, needlessly difficult terms appearing in the test items should be replaced with simpler synonyms. Complex arrangements of words should be simplified and unnecessary words or phrases removed. Also, ample testing time must be allowed.

Test items must be carefully reread to eliminate improper vocabulary and cut excessive length. If appropriate adjustments are not made, the pupil with superior reading ability and vocabulary may have an undue advantage over his less fortunate fellow pupils. Superior reading ability and vocabulary help him to understand more of the questions more quickly and, as a result, he has more time in which to concentrate on obtaining the correct answers. When such items are included in a poorly timed test, they may actually measure the pupil's reading speed and comprehension more than his achievement in a chosen subject matter area such as science or social studies; the basis on which the test items are differentiating among the pupils has changed.

PROBLEM

9. Goslin (1967, 1967–68) evaluated a number of criticisms of objective tests designed to measure pupil aptitude and achievement, four of which are the following:
   a. They are unfair for "deep thinkers."
   b. They are unfair for culturally disadvantaged pupils.
   c. They are unfair for individuals who lack experience in taking them.
   d. Test scores yielded by them are poor predictors of subsequent performance, e.g., post-academic performance.

Prepare your reaction to these criticisms and compare them with those of Goslin.

ORGANIZING THE OBJECTIVE TEST

So often it is said that a group of test items cannot necessarily be called a test. How true! After each of a group of objective test items has been appraised and edited in the manner described in the foregoing sections, that part of the group that appropriately reflects the balance among the subject matter topics and the behavioral changes established in the table of specifications is organized into an achievement test. For this to be done, we must decide the order in which the items are presented to the pupils and the number to be included. We must also formulate directions for the pupils and draw up a scoring key. Each of these steps must be taken carefully if the test items are to realize their maximum value.

Arranging Objective Test Items

Objective test items should not be arranged haphazardly in an achievement test. Instead, they should be organized on the basis of one or more of three characteristics: the type of item, the subject matter, and the level of difficulty.

When the items of an objective test are grouped according to type, all supply test items are placed together, as are all true-false, multiple-choice, and matching test items. This simplifies the directions given to the pupils. Furthermore, the pupil can no doubt complete a test so arranged more quickly. He acquires a mental set for each type of item and need not change it until all such items have been answered, speeding his progress through the test. Incidentally, it is advisable to restrict the number of different types to as few as conveniently possible.

Arranging the test items according to the subject matter means that the test items are grouped according to a set of subject matter topics, or perhaps according to the cells in a table of specifications. This appeals to the pupil because he sees the test as a miniature of the materials he has learned. It is an integrated, orderly whole to him rather than a disorganized mosaic of unrelated questions. This arrangement may be attractive to the teacher, too, since it may help to reveal any underemphasis in the test.

Objective test items can be grouped according to their levels of difficulty if they happen to vary appreciably, that is, the easy ones first, the more difficult next, and the most difficult last. Such an arrangement has advantages for average and below average pupils. With this kind of test they use the time allowed more efficiently, and morale is improved. When they later encounter the more difficult test items, they no doubt will have time to attack them. Even if they fail to answer some, as will very likely happen, the resulting disappointment will be moderated by the knowledge that they already have answered others correctly.

Certainly we cannot expect to use all three ways of arranging test items simultaneously. In reality, all a teacher can hope to do is find the best possible compromise among the three. Sometimes he can escape partially or wholly from the dilemma by eliminating one of the possibilities. For example, suppose that only one type of test item is used. Now the test can be designed so that the items are grouped according to major subject matter topic, and within each group they can be arranged in order of ascending difficulty. As a second example, suppose that the teacher is building a mastery test, or perhaps a norm-referenced test using test items with levels of difficulties which cluster in a comparatively small zone slightly above the fifty percent level. Now the level of difficulty is unimportant as a basis for arranging test items and should be ignored.

If test items are grouped according to major subject matter topics and, within each group, subdivided according to type of item, the teacher may wish to consider each subject matter group as a subtest. The items in such subtests can be independently numbered and, to ensure that each receives proper emphasis, separate time limits can be imposed.

Length of Objective Achievement Tests

Ideally, the length of an achievement test should be determined by two key factors, representative sampling and reliability. The test should contain as many items as necessary to sample all the verbal and mathematical aspects of the educational objectives on which the table of specifications is based. The smallest sample of test items (in other words, the shortest test) that can be used without jeopardizing reasonable representation varies with the nature of this table. If the subject matter topics and behavioral changes in the table are heterogeneous, then a larger sample is needed. If they are very much alike, a smaller sample can be used. Remember that too short a test may be unsatisfactory because it is impossible to include items based on some less important cells of the table of specifications. Consequently, the degree of content validity is lessened.

The second key factor is that the length of the test is also related to its reliability, that is, the consistency of its results (see pages 241–242). In general, shortening the test decreases its reliability. If, therefore, the use of the test results demands a high degree of test reliability, the length of the test has to be increased. Test results used to diagnose an individual pupil's strengths and weaknesses in an area must be more reliable than those used only to determine differences between groups of pupils in terms of their achievement. In the first case, the test may be so long it is administered in parts and requires several hours. In the second, it may be so short that only one class period or less is needed.

In addition to these two factors governing the length of the classroom achievement test, there is another and very practical one: the time available for the administration of the test. Although this factor lacks the theoretical justification of the first two, it is just as important. Indeed, it often influences the length of the test more than factors of content validity or reliability, because the teacher often has so little control over it. Ordinarily, he must administer the test during a regularly scheduled class period which usually lasts forty to sixty minutes.

In this connection, remember the importance of pupil fatigue. Writing achievement tests can be an exhausting task. For this reason, it is doubtful that time periods longer than one hour should be used for achievement testing even if they were available. Certainly time periods of more than two hours should be discouraged. Any time pupil fatigue is suspected of being a noticeable influence on test performance, the test should be broken into parts with rest periods permitted between them.

The teacher customarily determines the length of his achievement test in a somewhat backward manner. First, he notes the maximum amount of time that administrative routine will allow for giving the test. Then he estimates the number of items to which the pupils should be able to respond in the time allotted. Finally, he selects this number from among those he has constructed. He selects these in such a way that, as a group, they reflect the established relative importance of the various cells of the table of specifications.

As the restrictions on testing time limit the number of items to be included in the test, so also do they weaken its content validity and reliability. All too frequently, there is no convenient way of overcoming this progression of troubles. Instead, the teacher must recognize the situation for what it is, build his achievement test accordingly, and temper his use and interpretation of the results to compensate for whatever degree of content validity and reliability is lost.

Directions for Pupils

To perform to the best of his ability, the pupil must know the purpose of the test and must be thoroughly familiar with its mechanics. The teacher therefore formulates directions that the pupil reads or that are read to him before he responds to any of the test items.

The purpose of most classroom achievement tests is quite clear to the pupils. No doubt the initial announcement of the test is supplemented with remarks concerning the reasons why it is being administered; or, perhaps it is one of a series and the pupils are well aware of its purposes. In both of these instances, the directions need not include statements concerning the purposes of the test. If, however, the teacher doubts for any reason the completeness of the pupil's understanding of the purposes of the test, he should devote the first part of the directions to a brief statement about them. Failure to do so can cause an unnecessary loss of motivation.

The mechanics of the test typically command much more attention in the directions than the purposes. The pupil needs a complete knowledge of the "ground rules" under which he will operate. This means that he must be aware of the time allowed, the manner in which he is to select and record his answers, and the scoring system to be used. He should even be instructed in test-room etiquette if circumstances dictate.

DIRECTIONS FOR SELECTING ANSWERS. Directions for selecting answers must be carefully written. Notice that the sample instructions of this kind given earlier assume that the pupil knows nothing about objective test items. This of course is an extreme assumption and, for the most part, an unnecessary one. Yet, stating the directions with too much detail is far less an evil than stating them with too little. This point is particularly important when novel or semi-novel items are being used.

For assurance that these directions are understood, practice test items may be included. These may consist of a typical item correctly answered in terms of the directions, as well as one or more to be answered by the pupil before beginning the test itself. He is told the correct answers to practice test items so that he can verify his understanding of the directions. Such items can be helpful when testing either elementary or secondary school pupils. The use of this procedure with the former group is quite common.

DIRECTIONS FOR RECORDING ANSWERS. How the pupil is to record his answer is another small detail that cannot be overlooked. When the answer is to be written on

Date _____   Name _____
                                                       Last   First
Subject _____   Scores: Part A _____
                                    Part B _____
                                    Part C _____
                                    Part D _____
                                    Total _____

DIRECTIONS: Read with care the general directions at the beginning of the test and the directions preceding each subpart. Then read each test item and decide which answer is correct. Indicate your answer by filling the blank or circling the number or letter provided below. Be certain that the number of the test item corresponds exactly with the number on the answer sheet when you record each answer.

A: SUPPLY		B: TRUE-FALSE		C: MULTIPLE-CHOICE		D: MATCHING	
Item	Answer	Item	Answer	Item	Answer	Item	Answer
1	_____	1	T F	1	1 2 3 4 5	1	_____
2	_____	2	T F	2	1 2 3 4 5	2	_____
3	_____	3	T F	3	1 2 3 4 5	3	_____
4	_____	4	T F	4	1 2 3 4 5	4	_____
5	_____	5	T F	5	1 2 3 4 5	5	_____

FIGURE 3.1. Section of a Teacher-Designed Answer Sheet.

the same sheet as the question, this is less of a problem. It is necessary to prepare directions such as those already illustrated, and to design a layout of the test items that allows generous space for circling letters, writing numbers, and filling in blanks. When separate answer sheets are used, the directions are not so simple. The relationship between the test copy and the answer sheet must be explained and also any features of the answer sheet that would speed or impair the marking of responses selected or that would increase or decrease the accuracy of scoring.

If separate answer sheets are used, teachers usually design their own. A typical one is shown in part in Figure 3.1. Notice that it can be used with a test having several types of objective items. These have been grouped according to type and each is numbered independently. The manner in which the pupil uses the answer sheet is described in the directions provided.

A wide variety of commercial answer sheets are available. These are designed for machine scoring, perhaps using the IBM Optical Mark Scoring Reader or the Optical Mark Page Reader. An answer sheet for them is shown in reduced size in Figure 3.2. It is quite versatile. In addition to true-false and multiple-choice test items, it can be used for matching test items. The pupil marks his responses with an ordinary soft or medium lead pencil. The scoring machine optically reads the marks at an extremely high rate and prints part and/or total scores. Various scoring formulas (for example,

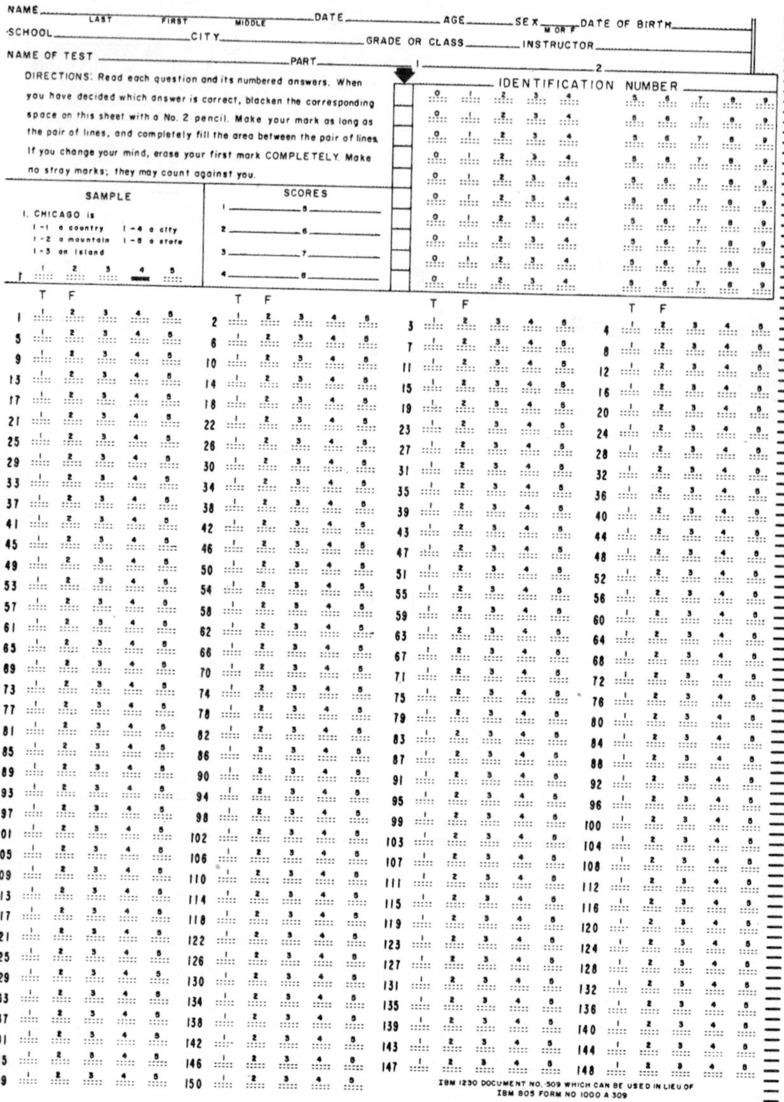
NAME ____ LAST FIRST MIDDLE ____ DATE ____ AGE ____ SEX ____ M OR F ____ DATE OF BIRTH ____
SCHOOL ____ CITY ____ GRADE OR CLASS ____ INSTRUCTOR ____
NAME OF TEST ____ PART ____ 1 ____ 2 ____

DIRECTIONS: Read each question and its numbered answers. When you have decided which answer is correct, blacken the corresponding space on this sheet with a No. 2 pencil. Make your mark as long as the pair of lines, and completely fill the area between the pair of lines. If you change your mind, erase your first mark COMPLETELY. Make no stray marks; they may count against you.

IDENTIFICATION NUMBER

SAMPLE
I. CHICAGO is
1-1 a country 1-4 a city
1-2 a mountain 1-5 a state
1-3 an island

SCORES
1 ____ 5 ____
2 ____ 6 ____
3 ____ 7 ____
4 ____ 8 ____

T F

IBM 1230 DOCUMENT NO. 509 WHICH CAN BE USED IN LIEU OF IBM 805 FORM NO 1000 A 509

FIGURE 3.2. An International Business Machine Answer Sheet, IBM 1230 Document No. 509.
Reproduced by permission of the International Business Machines Corporation.

formulas for correcting for guessing) can be applied by the scoring machine. Also, multiple-response test items can be scored. Finally, it is possible to transfer test score information directly into a computer, which in turn can provide a wide variety of summary data about the test score distribution; for instance, the arithmetic mean of the scores.

Tests involving separate test copies and answer sheets can be successfully administered to pupils as inexperienced as those in the fourth grade. However, if they are used with elementary school pupils, a training period is necessary prior to testing.

Even after this, the pupils cannot handle the separate answer sheet efficiently. No doubt the time limits should be expanded for them. Secondary school pupils familiar with separate answer sheets lose very little time using them.

DIRECTIONS FOR SCORING ANSWERS. The pupil should be informed of the scoring procedure when it is conveniently possible. He is entitled to ask how much credit he will get for each right answer. Usually this can be easily included in the directions because it is constant for each objective item within the subtests or possibly the total test.

Allowing the same number of points for each item is somewhat illogical. After all, they may vary in difficulty and importance, and thus more credit should be allowed for some correct answers than for others. However, attempts to weight the test items in terms of these characteristics tend to be highly subjective. Moreover, research has shown that scores made on an objective achievement test graded with a constant number of points for a right answer correlate very highly with scores obtained on the same test when the right answers are weighted in what is seemingly a more defensible manner. This means that, no matter which scoring procedure is used, the relative position of the pupils within the class remains unchanged in practically all cases. In view of this, most objective achievement tests are scored by means of the simpler method, which is to allow a constant amount of credit for each correct response to a given type of objective test item.

The directions should also include a statement about correction for guessing. Since the possibility of successfully guessing the correct answers appeals to some pupils, teachers may choose to discourage such attempts by penalizing the pupil for any wrong answers he makes. This is known as a correction for guessing. The pupil has the right to know whether one of these methods is to be used. This information could greatly affect his willingness to omit a test item or try to guess the correct answer with little or no information.

PRESENTING DIRECTIONS ORALLY. Writing clear and explicit directions is of little help if the pupil refuses to read them or reads them carelessly. Therefore, a number of teachers read the directions aloud as the pupils read them silently. Any questions the pupils might have are answered, and then the test begins. This is a wise procedure with elementary school pupils. With the primary grade levels it must be carried one step further. Copies of the directions for any objective test items are not given to the pupil. Instead, he is given an answer sheet that is meticulously tailored to the test. After the directions are read and explained, practice exercises are completed. Then the teacher reads the questions one by one, allowing time for a response to each. At the conclusion of the test, he might repeat some or all if time allows. Administering tests in this way removes a serious obstacle to the use of objective test items with elementary school pupils—the reading speed and comprehension problem.

Scoring the Objective Test

To many classroom teachers the least exciting task of achievement testing is the scoring of the pupil responses. To handle this task the pupils are sometimes asked to score their own papers or their neighbors'. Considering the importance of accurate scoring, the limitations of this procedure are obvious. Should the teacher score the papers himself, he commonly takes a blank copy of the test, fills in the correct responses, and compares this key with the responses on the test copy returned by each pupil. The number of correct responses by each pupil is determined and recorded. The total operation may not require much time, but being essentially clerical in nature, it is often viewed with distaste by those who must do it.

Various attempts have been made to reduce the time required for scoring objective tests. These have taken the form of scoring keys designed to assist in hand-scoring individual test copies or separate answer sheets, and machine-scoring procedures using separate answer sheets.

SCORING KEYS FOR HAND-SCORING. Three of the more successful scoring keys for hand-scoring are the fan key, the strip key, and the cut-out key.

The fan key is a sheet of paper on which the correct responses are written in a series of columns. The sheet of paper is the same size as the test copy or the separate answer sheet. Each column corresponds to a page of the test or a column on the answer sheet, and the correct responses are spaced in the column as the pupil responses are spaced on the page of the test or the column on the appropriate answer sheet. The key is folded along vertical lines separating its columns, thus taking the appearance of a fan. It is superimposed on the appropriate page of the test copy or placed next to the appropriate column on the answer sheet and matched with the corresponding responses.

The strip key is similar to a fan key except that the various columns are strips. Each strip is usually mounted on cardboard. It is used like a fan key.

The cut-out key is also a sheet of paper of the same size as the test copy or answer sheet. However, windows are cut in appropriate positions to reveal the correct response if they are made. The key is superimposed on a page of the test copy or the separate answer sheet and the pupil's responses are scored.

MACHINE-SCORING. The machine-scoring procedure now becoming popular for scoring informal objective tests utilizes the IBM Optical Mark Scoring Reader. If the separate answer sheets shown in Figure 3.2 are properly marked, the teacher can, if he chooses, turn over his task of scoring to a skilled clerk operating this machine. Under ideal conditions, the speed and accuracy of scoring can be superior. Furthermore, computers can be programmed to print suggestions for remedial work for pupils whose patterns of error are typical of identifiable learning difficulties (Woods, 1970).

The disadvantages of machine-scoring of this type are well-known. First of all, it cannot be used with supply test items under any circumstances. Secondly, the pupils must be trained in the procedure of marking the answer sheets. The marks in the spaces must be reasonably heavy. Erasures must be complete and stray pencil marks avoided, because they might be recorded by the machine as wrong answers. A third disadvantage is the availability of scoring and computing equipment. Unless one is available on relatively short notice, machine-scoring may prove to be more trouble than it is worth as far as classroom achievement tests are concerned. Finally, there is no indication on the answer sheet as to whether an answer to a given test item is correct or incorrect. The pupil cannot identify his strong and weak areas by examining his answer sheet alone.

CORRECTING FOR GUESSING. A persistent problem encountered with objective achievement tests is the tendency of the pupil to guess when he does not know the correct answer. Sometimes this guess is based on partial knowledge, other times on misinformation, and still other times on no information at all. In the last instance, he may not even have read the test item or, if he did, its answer is a total mystery to him.

If the score is the number of correct responses, any success the pupil had when he guessed will raise it. Obviously, this is not a defensible situation. The test score should reflect his achievement only, rather than this plus the pupil's willingness to guess and the amount of success he happened to have in this case. Therefore, some teachers argue that the pupil must be discouraged from wild guessing and be penalized if he does.

The formula for correcting for guessing in the case of the most common varieties of selection type objective test items is as follows:

$$S = R - \frac{W}{n-1},$$

where

S = the test score;
R = the number of correct responses;
W = the number of incorrect responses;
n = the number of suggested responses from which one is chosen.

R is often called the number of "rights," whereas *W* is thought of as the number of "wrongs."

For a true-false test, *n* is two and the formula reduces to

$$S = R - W.$$

For a multiple-choice test having four suggested responses, the formula becomes

$$S = R - \frac{W}{3}.$$

Notice that to use the formula in any of these cases, the number of omitted test items is ignored.

These formulas assume that all incorrect responses and a chance proportion of the correct ones are the result of wild guessing. This is, of course, not fully justified. The pupils are often taking "calculated risks" when selecting their responses. Rather than making wild guesses they are making more or less intelligent guesses based on sound but incomplete knowledge. Testwiseness is a definite factor.

Because the foregoing assumption is not completely satisfied, the formulas will overcorrect in some instances and undercorrect in others. Consequently, they are persistently criticized by teachers and pupils alike.

There is another disadvantage when a correction for guessing formula is applied.

Informing the pupil that such a correction will be made customarily acts as a deterrent, but its effectiveness varies with the pupil. Some are willing to guess wildly no matter what correction formulas are used. Others are cautious. A correction for guessing will cause them to answer only when they are certain of the correct response, and even intelligent guesses are not ventured. More often than not, the first type of pupil gains higher test scores than the second. Thus, an extraneous personality factor unduly influences achievement tests designed to measure verbal or mathematical ability.

If sufficient time is allowed for the test so that every pupil can attempt every item, and if *every* pupil then answers *every* test item, no correction for guessing is needed for norm-referenced tests. Determining the test score by counting the number of correct responses is perfectly acceptable. Despite the fact that the test scores are different in size when corrected than when not corrected for guessing, the relative position of each pupil in the class is the same in both cases. The relationship between the uncorrected and corrected test scores under these conditions is perfect. If the purpose of an achievement test is to determine the relative position of each pupil in the class, the simpler test score may as well be used.

To ensure that all pupils will answer all test items, they must be instructed to guess when they do not know the answer, even if they must guess wildly. Needless to say, these instructions can hardly be considered good pedagogy. The pupil may lose respect for objective achievement testing, possibly even for the subject matter or the teacher. The full impact of these instructions is difficult to measure. Admittedly unsavory, they probably have no lasting effect upon most pupils. (For a review of research relevant to the correction for guessing formula, see Diamond and Evans, 1973).

PROBLEM

10. Branch-testing or tailored testing is a procedure whereby, with the aid of a computer, the test items to which a pupil is to respond next are determined by his responses on preceding items (Glaser and Nitko, 1971). Hence he is administered a test tailored to his pattern of achievement. Study this procedure and react to it in terms of its potential value in conserving testing time, measuring achievement in depth, and improving educational diagnosis.

SUMMARY

The following are the major thoughts included in this chapter:

1. *An objective test item is one that can be scored so that subjective judgment is practically eliminated when determining the correctness of a pupil's answer.*
2. *There are two types of objective test items, the supply type and the selection type. When responding to the supply type, the pupil has to provide the words, numbers, or symbols necessary. In contrast, the selection type allows the pupil to choose the correct response from the information it provides.*

3. Illustrations of the supply type are the short-answer question and the completion test item. Those teachers who use supply items in achievement tests do so because the likelihood of a pupil's guessing the correct answer is minimized and because of their ease of construction over the selection type. However, they also find that pupil responses to supply test items are more difficult to score, and that often the items measure only the pupil's knowledge of factual details.

4. True-false, multiple-choice, and matching test items all illustrate the selection type. The true-false item in its simplest form is a declarative statement that the pupil must judge as true or false. A test containing this type can sample widely a large amount of subject matter without requiring much testing time. On the other hand, the true-false test item often involves only trivial pieces of information and, because one of two responses must be correct, pupils not knowing the right one frequently guess.

5. A multiple-choice test item is one in which a direct question or incomplete statement is presented and a number of responses are given. The pupil is to choose the correct (or best) answer to the question or expression for completing the statement. This type of objective test is widely used because it is so adaptable. It can be used to measure recall of information or application of a principle in a novel situation in practically any subject matter area with all but the most naive pupils. The principal disadvantage teachers experience is that the items are relatively difficult to build.

6. The typical matching test item consists of two lists of items and a set of instructions for matching each in the first list with one in the second. It can include large quantities of factual information without requiring a proportionately large amount of testing time. However, some subject matter is not well-suited for matching test items.

7. After a group of objective test items have been constructed, they must be appraised and edited prior to being organized into an achievement test. This process involves rechecking the relationship between each item and the table of specifications or objective on which it is based, removing any ambiguity or any irrelevant clues that still remain, establishing relative level of difficulty, and correcting any feature that seriously increases the amount of time needed by the pupil to read and understand it.

8. Organizing objective test items into an achievement test requires a number of major steps:
   a. Proportional representation by the test items of the cells in the table of specifications must be ensured.
   b. The length of the test must be established.
   c. The order of the test items within the test must be determined.
   d. Directions to the pupil must be prepared.
   e. A method of scoring and reporting results must be ready for immediate use.

SUGGESTED READINGS

BLOOM, B. S., J. T. HASTINGS, and G. F. MADAUS. Handbook on formative and summative evaluation of student learning. New York: McGraw-Hill, 1971. Chapter 7.
   Illustrations are given of evaluation techniques for knowledge and comprehension objectives, that is, objectives in the first two classifications of the taxonomy for the cognitive domain.

COFFMAN, W. E. Achievement tests. In R. L. Ebel (ed.), *Encyclopedia of educational research.* (4th ed.) New York: Macmillan, 1969. Pp. 7–17.

    This is a good overview of achievement testing. Attention is given to the history of achievement testing, types of test items, and test construction problems.

EBEL, R. L. *Essentials of educational measurement.* Englewood Cliffs, N.J.: Prentice-Hall, 1972. Chpaters 3, 4, 5, 7, and 8.

    In five chapters, the planning of a classroom achievement test, the construction of true-false and multiple-choice test items, and the administration and scoring of achievement tests are discussed. Numerous faulty true-false and multiple-choice test items are shown and criticized.

EDUCATIONAL TESTING SERVICE. *Making the classroom test, a guide for teachers.* (3rd ed.) Princeton, N.J.: Author, 1973.

    In relatively few pages, the basic rules of test making for both objective and essay tests are developed and illustrated. Elementary and secondary school examples are given.

LIPPEY, G. The computer can support test construction in a variety of ways. *Educational Technology,* 1973, *13,* 10–12.

    This article is an overview of twenty-two articles in the same issue of this journal which describe various successful efforts to engage in computer-assisted test construction.

TINKELMAN, S. N. Planning the objective test. In R. L. Thorndike (ed.), *Educational measurement.* (2nd ed.) Washington: American Council on Education, 1971. Chapter 3.

    In a well-organized manner, the author discusses the steps followed in the development of a table of specifications and the planning for the types of test items, their number, and their level of difficulty. Sound recommendations are given.

WESMAN, A. G. Writing the test item. In R. L. Thorndike (ed.), *Educational measurement.* (2nd ed.) Washington: American Council on Education, 1971. Chapter 4.

    Of the materials available of less than book length that deal with objective test items, this is one of the best. It contains many illustrations of the various forms of objective test items and numerous suggestions for building them properly.

REFERENCES CITED

DIAMOND, J., and W. EVANS. The correction for guessing. *Review of Educational Research,* 1973, *43,* 181–191.

EBEL, R. L. *Essentials of educational measurement.* Englewood Cliffs, N.J.: Prentice-Hall, 1972.

ECHTERNACHT, G. J. Use of confidence testing in objective tests. *Review of Educational Research,* 1972, *42,* 217–236.

GLASER, R., and A. J. NITKO. Measurement in learning and instruction. In R. L. Thorndike (ed.), *Educational Measurement.* (2nd ed.) Washington: American Council on Education, 1971, chapter 17.

GOSLIN, D. A. What's wrong with tests and testing—Part I. *College Board Review,* 1967, No. 65, 12–18.

GOSLIN, D. A. What's wrong with tests and testing—Part II. *College Board Review,* 1967–68, No. 66, 33–37.

MILLMAN, J., et al. An analysis of test-wiseness. *Educational and Psychological Measurement,* 1965, *25,* 707–726.

TINKELMAN, S. N. Planning the objective test. In R. L. Thorndike (ed.), *Educational measurement.* (2nd ed.) Washington: American Council on Education, 1971, chapter 3.

WESMAN, A. G. Writing the test item. In R. L. Thorndike (ed.), *Educational Measurement.* (2nd ed.) Washington: American Council on Education, 1971, chapter 4.

WOODS, E. M. Recent applications of computer technology to school testing programs. *Review of Educational Research,* 1970, *40,* 525–539.

4

MEASURING COMPLEX
ACHIEVEMENT OBJECTIVELY

As part of an assessment of literature achievement, children were asked to tell something about various literary characters such as Thor, Achilles, and Paul Bunyan (National Assessment of Educational Progress, 1972–73, p. 3). Some ran into trouble, as illustrated by the following two responses about Moses:

He opened the sea and when the Russians were coming he closed it—the Jews got through and the rest died.

He was found in the river bank when he was a baby. He was a Baptist.

These and other similar pupil responses resemble strongly those published some years ago (Abingdon, 1952). For instance:

When trying to define the term "adolescence," one pupil responded: "It is the stage between puberty and adultry."

When trying to differentiate between active and passive verbs, one pupil offered the following: "An active verb shows action, as, 'he kissed her'; and a passive verb shows passion, as, 'she kissed him.' "

Aside from the humor present, these and other parts of Abingdon's anthology make an important contribution. They reveal the pathetically inadequate grasp that some people have of simple concepts, meanings, and relationships. Words are only partially understood and, as a result, the pupil commits what might be called "logical errors." In other words, some parts of the pupil's verbal or mathematical achievements are at best superficial.

There are numerous less extreme illustrations of the same problem. In a science class it is generally possible to find a pupil who can quickly and properly define pH as the negative logarithm of the concentration of the hydrogen ion in gram atoms per liter, yet does not know what a logarithm or a hydrogen ion is or of what usefulness pH can be when a farmer tests his soil before deciding whether to spread lime on it. Another pupil can freely quote Newton's laws of motion but fails to see a connection between any of them and the fact that children of various weights travel varying distances when using the same sled on the same hill. A pupil in a modern language class can conjugate a French verb perfectly, but fails persistently to use the proper form of this verb when translating an English passage to French. In a social studies class we find a pupil who can recognize the relationship between latitude and climate north, but not south, of the equator. In a geometry class there are usually several pupils who have difficulty recognizing two parallel lines unless they are drawn vertically or horizontally, or who have trouble solving problems with right triangles if the right angle is not the lower left-hand angle.

These deficiencies have a far-reaching impact on achievement testing. If a test measures only the pupil's ability to recall information, some of the pupils responding to the items may succeed admirably even though they comprehend the subject matter only superficially. Moreover, the teacher may erroneously assume that any pupil who can recall the information is also capable of using it properly, but the consistency of relationship between these two abilities is not large enough to justify this assumption. To identify more closely the perimeters of the pupil's verbal and mathematical achievements, the tests must include items that measure complex cognitive achievement as well as knowledge. Both essay and objective test items can be used for this purpose.

TESTING FOR KNOWLEDGE AND MORE COMPLEX ACHIEVEMENT

For the purposes of this book, a pupil's knowledge is composed of those pieces of information that he commands. He can recall them when he wants to do so. According to this definition, the pupil may, but will not necessarily, have some grasp of the meanings, implications, or significance of his knowledge. In other words, all the facts about people, places, events, and things that he acquired by rote and that he can still recall are a part of his knowledge, whether or not he grasps their meanings.

More complex cognitive achievement, on the other hand, is based on the acquisition of meanings. The pupil gains this when he comprehends the meaning of parcels of knowledge to the point that he can restate them in his own words, grasp the interrelationships among them, and take action intelligently on that basis. Complex achievement is knowledge with its meanings, implications, and significance attached. Now the pupil is able to meet the changing situations thrust upon him every day and to attack intelligently the problems they contain. In other words, we are talking about the five levels of the cognitive taxonomy (Bloom, 1956) called intellectual abilities and skills, that is, comprehension, application, analysis, synthesis, and evaluation.

Testing for Knowledge

Testing for verbal and mathematical knowledge with objective test items is illustrated in the preceding chapter. Most of the test items can be correctly answered by any pupil willing to memorize. If he fails to gain meaning as he memorizes, little is lost as far as these items are concerned.

Since testing for knowledge is comparatively easy, it receives considerable attention in the classroom. The teacher experiences little difficulty in constructing test items requiring the pupil to recall an isolated fact or a series of facts. Consequently, classroom achievement tests and many standardized achievement tests are heavily overbalanced in this direction. This in turn has a profound influence on learning and teaching. Pupils quickly discover the advantages of concentrating on topics on which they are tested. They orient their learning procedures accordingly. Sometimes the teacher is no less susceptible to this pressure, particularly if his pupils are a part of a citywide or statewide testing program. When the tests stress recall of information, he generally teaches accordingly so that the class test results will compare favorably with those of the other classes. In brief, the educational objectives dealing with knowledge become the primary objectives.

The overemphasis on recall of information found in achievement tests today should not be replaced with a fault equally as serious: an underemphasis on testing for knowledge. Knowledge is the raw material for developing more complex achievement. Before a pupil can acquire the latter, he must have all pertinent knowledge at his disposal. A severe deemphasis on educational objectives dealing with knowledge could be as damaging as the present overemphasis.

Testing for Complex Achievement

In knowledge testing, the material the pupil learns is essentially, if not exactly, the same as that included in the test items. Novel material is virtually nonexistent in the test. Appreciably novel test items require more of the pupil than simple recall of information.

It follows that evidence of a pupil's complex cognitive achievements can be obtained by asking him questions about a carefully contrived situation that is new to him. Within this situation he is to apply the appropriate part of his total store of knowledge. To do so successfully, he must know the meanings of his knowledge and be able to reorganize them within a strange but plausible situation. By using a novel situation, the teacher can be confident that the pupil is doing more than merely parroting memorized material.

An illustration of the use of novelty in testing can be found in the mathematics test item shown in Figure 4.1 (adapted from the National Assessment of Educational Progress).

Assume that this situation is new to the pupil but the mathematical procedures involved have been studied. To answer correctly, he must select from his mathematical knowledge the part appropriate to this fictitious but realistic situation and apply it correctly.

What the Test Item Measures

There are instances when we are uncertain as to whether the test item is measuring a pupil's knowledge or a higher order of learning. This is particularly true when the purpose of the test item is to measure knowledge. The teacher building the

Region	Number of Production Workers (♀ = 200 thousand persons)	Amount Paid in Wages ($ = 500 million dollars)
A	♀ ♀	$ $ $
B	♀ ♀ ♀ ♀ ♀ ♀ ♀ ♀ ♀ ♀	$ $ $ $ $ $ $ $ $
C	♀ ♀ ♀ ♀ ♀	$ $ $ $ $ $ $ $ $ $
D	♀ ♀	$ $ $

Directions:

By calculating from the chart, find the region in which the average in-
come per worker was lowest. Select the correct answer from among
the four listed below.

(1) A
(2) B
(3) C
(4) D

FIGURE 4.1. Mathematics Test Item Based on Novel Stimulus
Material. The Chart Shows the Number of Production Workers and the Total Amount Paid in Wages to
Such Workers during One Year in Each of Four Geographical Regions.

test item has no intention of measuring anything except recall of information and, as
far as most members of the class are concerned, he succeeds. Consider, however, the
pupil who for some reason did not acquire the knowledge in question, yet arrives at
the correct answer by a process of deduction based upon related knowledge. For him,
more complex achievement is measured.

The multiple-choice test item shown below is an example:

Which one of these countries was first to have a colony in North America?
(1) Germany   (3) Russia
(2) Italy   (4) Spain

If the class studied the colonization of this continent with any care, the test item
measures recall of information. Yet a pupil who does not know the answer might still
arrive at it by drawing upon related general knowledge about political, economic,
military, and imperialistic aspects of the four countries in the sixteenth century. His
correct response represents a higher level of achievement than simply acquiring
knowledge.

On the other hand, test items designed to measure complex achievement may
measure only recall of information. If the situation on which the test item is based is
familiar to a pupil, the teacher cannot be certain which aspect of the pupil's achievement is reflected in his answer. For example, it is possible in the case in Figure 4.1 that
a pupil had previously memorized the chart and perhaps the answer itself. Certainly

under these conditions he would need only recall this information to handle the test item successfully.

Tests of Knowledge and Complex Achievement Compared

The similarities and differences between tests measuring knowledge and those measuring complex achievement have been repeatedly investigated and reported. The studies have tried to answer two questions:

1. *Are the gains made by pupils, as measured in terms of tests of complex achievement, more permanent than those measured in terms of tests of knowledge?*
2. *Is there a relationship between pupil performance as measured by tests of complex achievement and as measured by tests of knowledge?*

The answer to the first question is an affirmative one. Studies of secondary school and college academic achievement (Tyler, 1934; Wert, 1937; Weitman, 1965) have shown with remarkable consistency that, as the months pass following instruction, pupils retain more of the materials included in a test of complex achievement than those in a test of knowledge. In some studies, tests of both types were administered to classes as pretests at the beginning of the school year and as final tests at the end of the period of instruction. The difference between the scores for each pupil was defined as his gain. Then, without an opportunity to review and relearn the subject matter, the pupils were retested one, two, and sometimes three years later. The gains in knowledge shrank alarmingly; however, the gains in areas of complex achievement showed no such loss. On the contrary, in some instances they actually increased somewhat.

The relationship between pupil performance as measured by tests of complex achievement and by tests of knowledge has been found to be positive and somewhat low (Tyler, 1936). Otherwise stated, the pupil who acquires knowledge in a subject matter area ordinarily acquires more complex learning outcomes too, but this tendency is so imperfect that the second cannot be satisfactorily predicted on the basis of the first. More complex achievement cannot be assessed indirectly by measuring knowledge in a subject matter area; instead, tests specially designed for various levels of the cognitive domain must be used (Solomon, 1965; Smith, 1968).

PROBLEMS

1. Ebel (1972, p. 64) believes there is little evidence that situational test items are more valid measures of command of substantive knowledge than are simpler, more direct test items. Evaluate his position.
2. If a teacher of a class well-known to you built a series of objective test items according to the six principal levels of the cognitive taxonomy, do you think that, working independently, you could properly classify almost every test item

according to its intended level (Stoker and Kropp, 1964)? Even if you and the teacher agree as to the classification, have you necessarily identified the cognitive process that each item is intended to measure?

BUILDING AND SCORING TEST ITEMS MEASURING COMPLEX ACHIEVEMENT

Data concerning complex pupil achievement can be gathered in many different ways. The daily observation of pupil behavior by the teacher can provide a wealth of evidence. Observation can take place in the classroom, on the playground, or in the pupil's home, and the information acquired can be organized by anecdotal records or rating scales. Pupil work products are also useful. An original theme for an English class, a collection or exhibit for a science class, a painting or clay model for a fine arts unit, an apron for a home economics class, or a bookcase for an industrial arts class will quickly reveal some of the pupil's more complex achievements. Also helpful are teacher-pupil interviews, diaries of out-of-class activities, and, of course, paper-and-pencil tests.

A wide variety of possible ways of gathering such evidence was reported some years ago (Henry, 1946). Illustrative procedures are shown for every major school subject. Considerable space is devoted to a measuring technique that is often overlooked: the objective test item. Although by no means a universal solution for the problems of measuring complex achievement, it can be extremely effective in science, social studies, mathematics, and the language arts. In such subjects as agriculture, home economics, and industrial arts, objective test items are used less frequently, but still provide much-needed information.

Procedure for Constructing Test Items

To construct test items that measure more complex pupil achievement, two basic steps must be taken. First, the teacher must decide which pattern of pupil behavior is to be measured. Behavioral patterns include the pupil's ability to apply facts and principles to new situations, and his ability to interpret data and recognize cause-and-effect relationships and assumptions underlying conclusions. Another way to think of these is in terms of the last five levels of the cognitive taxonomy, namely, comprehension, application, analysis, synthesis, and evaluation. Of course only those levels that are important are included in the table of specifications on the basis of which the test is being developed.

Secondly, the teacher must devise a novel but realistic situation with questions that, to be answered correctly, require the pupil to display the pattern of behavior being considered. The situations can be completely original or based on some convenient source such as newspaper or magazine articles or even research reports unfamiliar to the pupils. If possible, they should resemble the everyday environment familiar to the pupil. He is generally impressed with the fairness of a testing approach that requires him to use what he has learned in school to answer questions about situations similar to his out-of-school experiences.

Combining an appropriate pattern of pupil behavior with a suitably novel situation is not simple. Initially, the teacher may be hard-pressed to find the situation he wants and then experience difficulty in reducing it to an objective test item. Finding the situation is a matter of a teacher's sensitivity to the application of what he teaches in the world about him; reducing it to an objective test item is largely a matter of following many of the suggestions for constructing objective test items described in Chapter 3.

In his search for a novel situation, the teacher starts, of course, with a clear notion of the pattern of pupil behavior with which he is concerned. For example, in a mathematics class the pupils have mastered many theorems, one of which is the Pythagorean theorem. To see if they can use this information, the teacher may, in a test item, give them the outer dimensions of a baseball diamond and ask them to compute the distance that the ball must travel when the catcher throws it from home plate to second base. In an elementary school arithmetic unit, the pupils have studied simple areas. Therefore, the teacher might have them compute the number of square pieces of candy of 2 × 2-inch size that could be cut out of an 8 × 10-inch rectangular pan. In a science class the pupils learned of the law of refraction. Hence, the teacher builds a test item in which they must tell how they would judge the position of a rock at the bottom of a fish pond if they, standing on the bank, were to retrieve it. Finally, the ability of pupils to read unfamiliar music could be measured by providing each with a sheet of printed music as a recording of it is played; then, as it stops before the end of the music, having them mark the last note heard. Certainly these and many similar illustrations in other subject matter areas are realistic problems to the pupils.

SINGLE-RESPONSE OBJECTIVE TEST ITEMS. Some teachers prefer to ask only one question concerning the novel situation selected. It can be phrased to conform to any of the types of objective test items already described. Condensing the description of the novel situation and the question concerning it into a single test item can sometimes be accomplished without lengthening the test item excessively. For instance, in a secondary school English class the teacher may want to check on the pupil's skill in the proper use of the words *who, whose, whom, which,* and *that*. To do this he could give the pupil a series of sentences like those below and ask him to select the correct word from the two given, and then write it in the space provided at the right.

1. *The man (which, who) is speaking is our president.*   1. (who)
2. *Do you know the boy (who's, whose) model airplane*   2. (whose)
   is broken?

Sometimes not one but several questions can be asked about the novel situation. These questions can be more or less independent of each other—the response to one does not influence appreciably the response to any other. Each correct response may require the pupil to reveal a different aspect of his ability to use his knowledge.

The following novel situation is one on which a series of test items is constructed. These test items are intended to measure the ability of pupils in a home economics class to apply certain rules for meal planning. Typical menus are shown and proposed changes are to be accepted or rejected by the pupils. Since the rules are summarized for the pupil, these test items demand less recall of information than some of the others included in this chapter.

Directions: *Listed below are the menus of meals for two days and certain meal planning rules. Study them carefully.*

Breakfast

A. *Pear sauce*
   Poached egg on milk toast
   Coffee

D. *Orange slices*
   Soft cooked egg on toast
   Cocoa

Lunch

B. *Tomato soup*
   Bacon, lettuce, and tomato
   sandwich
   Peaches and cookie
   Milk

E. *Chicken soup (broth)*
   Cherry jello salad
   Orange
   Tea

Dinner

C. *Fried pork chops*
   French fried potatoes
   Spinach
   Mince pie
   Coffee

F. *Pea soup*
   Meat loaf
   Baked beans
   Rolls and butter
   Custard pie
   Coffee

Meal planning rules

1. *Balance the different types of foodstuffs in each meal.*
2. *Do not serve the same food twice in the same meal, even in a different form.*
3. *Do not use many rich or hard-to-digest foods in one meal.*
4. *Combine bland or soft foods with those of more pronounced flavor or different texture.*
5. *Plan meals in which the colors harmonize and are appealing.*
6. *Plan at least one food in each meal that has high satiety value.*

Directions: *Keeping in mind the above rules, consider the following changes. If the change would not improve the meal, place a zero in the blank. If the change would improve the meal, write the number of the rule supporting your decision in the blank opposite the change. Judge each change independently of all others.*

(4)   1. *Substitute scrambled egg and cinnamon toast for poached egg on milk toast in Menu A.*

(2)   2. *Substitute cream of mushroom soup for tomato soup in Menu B.*
(3)   3. *Substitute broiled steak for the fried pork chops in Menu C.*
(0)   4. *Substitute pecan pie for mince pie in Menu C.*
(0)   5. *Substitute half a grapefruit for orange slices in Menu D.*
(6)   6. *Substitute cream of chicken soup for chicken soup in Menu E.*
(1)   7. *Substitute baked potato for baked beans in Menu F.*

Observe that the description of the novel situation is quite long. This is to be expected, since it provides ample material for a series of test items. Also observe that the objective test items following the description can be any one of several types. The true-false and multiple-choice types are commonly used.

Building test items such as the foregoing involves a series of revisions if a high-quality product is to be obtained. The teacher begins by writing a description of the novel situation, then constructs test items on the basis of it. It is soon apparent that revision of the description will strengthen one or more of the proposed items. Minor deletions or additions of material may result in a wealth of new test item possibilities. Thus, the construction of test items suggests changes in the description, and changes in description suggest new or better test items. Persistent efforts along these lines by the teacher will produce a description of the novel situation that is virtually unambiguous and that contains no nonfunctional portions of any consequence; with this description will be a series of test items exploiting practically all the possibilities for measuring complex pupil achievement in terms of the situation used.

MULTIPLE-RESPONSE OBJECTIVE TEST ITEMS. Multiple-response objective test items are also used to measure pupil understanding. A common instance of this occurs when the teacher wishes to measure the pupil's ability to apply facts and principles to new situations. In this case the situation is described in some detail. A paragraph or more may be needed. The basic problem within the novel situation is defined and a question asked about it. The pupil answers the question by selecting the correct response from among several listed. Finally, he selects from among many reasons listed those that support his answer. In a sense he views each reason as he does a true-false test item. He must decide whether it is sound or faulty.

An illustration of the above is the following test item intended for use in a secondary school science class.* A knowledge of the principles of reproduction, how they operate in plants, and an ability to apply this information in a novel situation are measured by this test item.

A visitor to a rural area noticed that each apple orchard of any size had beehives located in it. This puzzled him, so he asked one of the local farmers why this practice was followed.

Directions: *Immediately following are three possible answers to the question asked above. Check the one that best answers the question.*
    ____A.   *The bees will be able to get good nectar.*
    ✓ B.   *The number of apples formed on each tree will increase.*
    ____C.   *The apple blossoms will be self-pollinated.*

Directions: *Following is a list of statements that are suggested as reasons for the above answer. Check the statements that are good reasons for the answer you selected above.*
    ____ 1.   *Yield of apples is increased if bees are present.*
    ✓ 2.   *Fertilization makes possible the development of mature fruits.*
    ✓ 3.   *Cross-pollination is necessary for the production of a good apple crop.*
    ____ 4.   *Cross-pollination frequently results in desirable variations.*
    ____ 5.   *Many fruit growers keep bees in their orchards.*
    ____ 6.   *The apple blossoms contain the most desirable type of nectar that can be used in commercial honey.*
    ✓ 7.   *Flowers from which insects have collected nectar are usually pollinated.*
    ____ 8.   *The only completely satisfactory location for beehives is in the orchard from which they can get nectar.*

* *This test item was adapted with modifications from materials prepared in the College of Sciences and Humanities of Iowa State University (1949).*

___✓___ 9. *Even though self-pollination is possible in a flower, it frequently fails to occur.*

_____10. *Bees pollinate apple blossoms in order to aid in the production of a good crop.*

_____11. *All insect-pollinated flowers are cross-pollinated.*

_____12. *Double fertilization increases the yield.*

The construction of test items like the above is, unfortunately, not a simple task. Even after the difficulties of finding a suitable situation and identifying the central problem have been overcome, the teacher must still find two or more plausible answers, each of which is supported by a group of logical reasons. The latter are the most difficult to find. One way of simplifying the task is to submit the situation to groups of pupils as an essay test item, then screen their answers for attractive but wrong answers and logical reasons for them. These answers can be restated so that an objective test item results.

Two additional features of this kind of objective test item deserve mention. Observe that the pupils do not know how many of the suggested reasons are good reasons, and that some that are not relevant to the correct answer are nevertheless essentially true statements. An example of this is the fifth reason listed: "Many fruit growers keep bees in their orchards." To avoid confusion these two points are sometimes mentioned in the directions to the pupils.

Scoring the Multiple-Response Test Item

When a series of more or less independent questions are asked about the same novel situation, the pupil responses can be weighted and scored in essentially the same manner as any other objective test items of the same type; however, when pupil responses to one part of the test item are in some way dependent on responses to another part, the weighting and scoring become more complicated. In the scoring of many of these test items, two questions can be asked:

1. *How much credit should a pupil receive if he answers one part of the item incorrectly and because of this, responds incorrectly to other parts dependent on the first?*

2. *When the pupil is not told how many responses to make, how are his responses scored if he makes too few or too many, some of which are correct and some of which are wrong?*

Both of these questions can be discussed in terms of the multiple-response objective test item concerning beehives in an apple orchard. The pupil must select one of three alternatives as the principal advantage of placing bees in an apple orchard, and then indicate which of the twelve reasons listed support his answer. Suppose a pupil selects the wrong alternative and defends his choice well by checking appropriate reasons for it. How much credit should he receive? According to the scoring key, his responses are totally wrong. He argues, however, that only his first response is wrong. He did check the correct reasons for the wrong alternative. What should the teacher do? Although practices vary, one of the more popular is to allow no credit for any of the reasons checked if the correct alternative is not selected.

The second question deals with the case in which the pupil checks the correct alternative and receives whatever points are allowed for this answer, but does not check the proper reasons. Possibly he checks too many reasons, including the correct ones. Or possibly he checks too few reasons, yet those selected are correct. In either case, how should his choice of reasons be scored? Again, there is no single, widely accepted answer to this question. Sometimes teachers take the point of view that the pupil should be penalized if he checks any unacceptable reasons. Moreover, a pupil who indiscriminately checks *all* reasons should receive no credit.

According to this view, the penalty for any reason erroneously checked will be determined by the total number of reasons listed and the number correct. In the beehives test item, four of twelve reasons are listed on the key as acceptable. Hence, if one point were allowed for each correct reason checked, then one-half of a point would be deducted for every incorrect reason. In this way a pupil who checks all reasons will receive four positive points and four negative points, a net of zero. If more than one point is allowed each correct reason checked, the penalty for each incorrect reason is proportionally increased.

PROBLEMS

3. On the basis of each of the following principles in science, describe a novel situation and construct test items concerning it which will measure a young pupil's ability to apply that principle.
   a. Water tends to seek its own level.
   b. An object floating in water will displace water equal to its weight.
   c. The theoretical mechanical advantage of a lever used in conjunction with a fulcrum is related to the position of the fulcrum.

4. Using a table of specifications in a subject matter area of interest to you, design one or more test items that measure comprehension, application, or analysis. Then cross-refer each test item with the table, that is, indicate the cells in the table with which it is primarily related and those with which it is secondarily related (for example, cells concerning knowledge).

OBJECTIVE TEST ITEMS BASED ON PICTORIAL MATERIALS

A picture is said to be worth ten thousand words. This is just as true in achievement testing as in any other aspect of everyday living. Consider for a moment a teacher who regularly discovers that he needs a large number of words to develop a sufficiently unambiguous test item. Many words, he realizes, increase the pupil's reading load and the time required to answer the test item. Hence, he asks the logical question: Could a diagram, map, photograph, picture, or even a table of data be used to construct the test item? When this is done, the number of words needed to make the item specific and understandable is generally reduced, sometimes to less than half that required when no pictorial or tabular material is used. Furthermore, a well-chosen photograph or table serves as an excellent means of describing a novel situation on which the item is based.

Suggestions for Constructing Pictorial Test Items

Use pictorial material only when it makes a unique and sizable contribution to the quality of the test item. The pictorial material must be functional in an important way. It should represent a central idea much better than words can.

Consider the junior high school test item in Figure 4.2, which is designed to measure the pupil's ability to use his knowledge of angles in a new situation. Certainly it would be most difficult to construct test items of this kind without including a diagram. Furthermore, the number of test items based on the diagram can be increased easily, for example, by adding questions about the areas of the lots.

The pictorial material should be no more complicated than needed to accomplish this purpose. Some of the problems experienced in this regard are illustrated in the

A real estate agent buys the city block shown in the diagram below and divides it into ten lots as indicated by the dotted lines. The lines CD, EF, GH, and IJ are parallel to the streets AB and KL. Street BL meets street AB at an angle of 72°.

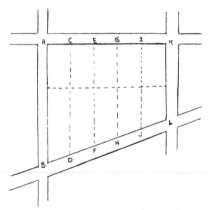

1. *What will the agent find to be the size of angle BCD?* (108) *degrees.*
2. *What will the agent find to be the size of angle IJL?* (72) *degrees.*
3. *Will the lots facing street AK have more, less, or the same frontage as the corresponding lots facing street BL?* (less)

FIGURE 4.2. Mathematics Test Item Based on Pictorial Stumulus Materials.

Teacher: *Draw a line through the number that tells you how many legs this insect has.*

2
4
6
8
10

Teacher: *Draw a line through the number that tells you how many feelers this insect has.*

2
4
6
8

Teacher: *Draw a line through the number that tells you how many wings this insect has.*

0
2
4
6
8

Teacher: *Draw a line through the number that tells you how many eyes this insect has.*

2
4
6
8

FIGURE 4.3. Science Test Item Based on Pictorial Stimulus Material.

test items in Figure 4.3, which is designed for primary-level pupils. Their knowledge of insects is being measured by responding to questions about drawings of insects which they are given. The teacher reads each question at least once and pauses while the pupils draw a line through the answer each selects.

It is difficult to know whether too little or too much detail is included in drawings such as these. The amount used seems to be appropriate, but we cannot be sure of this point without studying pupil responses and questioning the class members about their incorrect answers.

When necessary, use explanatory statements to clarify the meaning of the pictorial material. Often the pictorial material can stand alone, or virtually so. On the other hand, efforts to avoid complex material can produce ambiguities for some pupils. Figure 4.4 is an example of how this might happen.

The purpose of the items is to measure the ability of elementary school pupils to interpret unfamiliar maps. This purpose might not be realized if pupils fail to understand the symbolism used. Also, they are cautioned not to consider the region shown to be any particular place. Since the drawing vaguely resembles the western end of the Mediterranean Sea, a pupil who considers it to be that area may believe the

DIRECTIONS: Carefully study the map below. Do not consider it to be any particular place. The dots represent cities. Each city is identified by a letter. For each of the questions following the map, choose the correct city from among the four listed. Write the letter of that city in the blank provided.

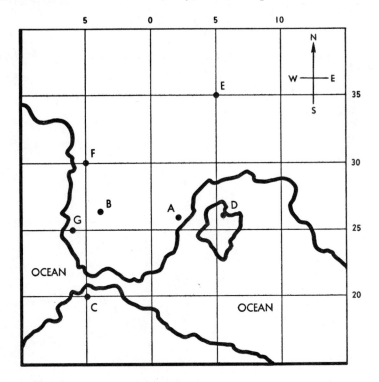

(C)   1. Which city is nearest the equator?
         City C
         City D
         City E
         City G

(D)   2. Which city has the greatest east longitude reading?
         City C
         City D
         City E
         City G

**FIGURE 4.4. Geography Test Item Based on Pictorial Stimulus
          Material.**

cities to be actual localities, thereby adding confusing features to the multiple-choice questions.

Integrate the test items with the pictorial materials so as to reduce the complexity of test items as much as possible. This suggestion is followed in all of the pictorial items shown. Notice that the questions are comparatively short, particularly in Figure 4.4. In addition, the pupil responds to those items by using the letter of the city he selects; numbers for the responses are not provided, thereby streamlining each test item still more.

PROBLEM

5. Excellent illustrations of the use of pictorial and tabular materials as a part of test items to measure more than recall of information have been published by the Educational Testing Service (1973). Select one from this publication and analyze it with respect to the pupil behavioral changes probably involved.

ADVANTAGES OF MEASURING COMPLEX ACHIEVEMENT WITH OBJECTIVE TESTS

The advantages gained by measuring complex cognitive achievement with objective test items are in part the same as those obtained by any other means. In other words, their use enlarges the scope of the achievement evaluation program, which in turn increases the attention paid by both pupils and teachers to the role of educational objectives dealing with a higher order of learning.

Moreover, pupils ordinarily find that objective test items designed to reveal more complex achievement are challenging and practical. Pupil interest can reach the point where more than a few will voluntarily admit that this type of testing is enjoyable and meaningful, a situation particularly probable when pictorial material represents the novel situation. Often we can simulate a natural situation quite well and thereby reduce the degree of artificiality present in the testing situation.

Objective test items measuring complex pupil achievement have several additional advantages. Teachers skilled in objective testing who use it for measuring pupil knowledge find this technique a convenient extension of familiar testing procedures that covers other parts of the table of specifications without sacrificing objectivity of scoring. Unlike the evaluation of pupil work products, for example, the objective test items provide highly structured problems to which the pupils are to react. Each pupil is confronted with the same novel situation and responds in terms of the same list of possible answers. This allows comparisons of pupil performances to be made more easily. Incidentally, the structuring of the problem may also limit the usefulness of objective test items. Complex pupil achievement is reflected in the originality of pupil performance. Responses to objective test items do not reveal this originality, whereas a creative work product does.

PROBLEM

6. Compare the value of information from objective test items with that gained by examining creative pupil products when the degree of complex pupil achievement in the cognitive domain is being evaluated in a subject matter area of interest to you.

LIMITATIONS OF MEASURING
COMPLEX ACHIEVEMENT WITH
OBJECTIVE TESTS

There are three important limitations in the measuring of complex pupil achievement with objective test items. First, the methods tend to be more difficult to devise and execute than those for measuring pupil knowledge. They demand considerable ingenuity on the part of the teacher, especially if he focuses his efforts at the upper levels of the cognitive taxonomy. Secondly, the time needed for pupil response may be excessive. Finally, the results yielded by this procedure cannot be attributed to one—and only one—pupil trait. Instead, they are the products of a combination of pupil traits; prominent among these are ability to recall information and scholastic aptitude.

Difficulty of Construction

The value of the objective test item in the measuring of complex achievement depends directly on the novel situation selected and the description or pictorial material provided. It is already apparent that the selection of the situation is a painstaking operation. Many possibilities are considered before one is selected.

The description of the situation and any pictorial material used must be prepared with equal care. Since the pupils cannot add or change any features of the description, it must be complete and, above all, unambiguous. Several rewritings of the description or reconstructions of the pictorial material are ordinarily necessary before this is accomplished.

Another factor that complicates the problem of construction is the relationship between the description of the novel situation and the basic question contained in the test item. These two parts must be clearly interdependent if the test item is to measure complex pupil achievement. In brief, it must be so designed that it can be answered correctly only if the pupil recalls appropriate facts and uses them in terms of the information contained in the description. Building this interdependence into the test item sounds like a relatively simple task, but it is not. The following is an illustration.

A janitor saw a strange man walking near the high school on the same night that a door was smashed and $400 stolen. He reported this to the police who promptly arrested the man on a burglary charge. Although the man claimed he was innocent, he was held without bail. A fellow prisoner suggested that he should try to obtain a writ of habeas corpus.

Ⓣ F   *1. A writ of habeas corpus is a writ inquiring into the lawfulness of the restraint of a person who is imprisoned.*

Ⓣ F   *2. When a person who is arrested is held without bail, he is allowed to confer with his lawyer.*

Observe that it is possible to answer both true-false test items correctly without reading the introductory material. This item is measuring the pupil's ability to recall information rather than his ability to recall it and then use it effectively. As appropriate as the description of the stranger's troubles seems to be, it is nothing but window-dressing in the test.

Suppose that the last sentence of the introductory material were deleted and that the following two test items replaced the original pair:

Ⓣ F   1. *An effective way to help the stranger would be to obtain a writ of habeas corpus.*

T Ⓕ   2. *The manner in which the stranger was held (i.e., without bail) is a violation of the Tenth Amendment of the Constitution.*

It is difficult if not impossible for the pupil to answer the above questions correctly without reading the description of the novel situation. These changes make the introductory material functional and greatly improve the degree to which the responses reflect higher levels of the cognitive taxonomy rather than knowledge alone.

Response Time Needed

Class time is a precious commodity. The teacher will be pleased with any measuring procedures that require less time and effort than the techniques already known to him, and concerned about any that seem less efficient. Objective test items for measuring complex achievement are usually placed in the latter category.

No doubt you are impressed with the length of many of the objective items in this chapter, especially the multiple-response type. The first reading consumes plenty of time, but the several that are usually required dangerously lengthen the response time. Unfortunately, attempts to shorten test items are only partially successful. The description of the novel situation can be abbreviated only so much. Any inappropriate reading load will penalize the poor reader. This reduces the effectiveness of these objective test items, particularly in the elementary school.

Another factor that increases a pupil's response time is lack of confidence in his answer. Unlike his responses to recall-of-information test items, his answers do not carry the conviction that he is correct. Hence, he rechecks. His relative lack of confidence carries over from item to item and tends to slow his pace.

The limitation of extended pupil response time may have acquired exaggerated importance in some quarters. Although it is true that these objective test items often consume unduly large amounts of testing time and at best reflect a small sample of complex pupil achievement, the teacher can hardly justify not using them on this basis alone, unless he has better means of obtaining as much or more information about these pupil traits. An increase in testing time is, after all, a small price to pay when the reward is a measurement program broadened to obtain evidence of highly important educational outcomes.

Interpretation of Results

Interpretation of results yielded by test items measuring complex achievement is clouded by a variety of traits contributing to the pupil's response. Examination of test items in this chapter shows us that behavioral changes at several levels of the cognitive taxonomy are probably intermixed. After all, knowledge is the building material for more complex cognitive achievement. Therefore a correct pupil response means that several correct steps have been taken. Failure to answer a test item correctly means that the pupil failed to perform one or more steps correctly. Yet the teacher does not know which these are. In a simple case, the teacher might ask whether the pupil failed to give the right answer because he could not recall the necessary information correctly or could not use it in terms of the novel situation after he recalled it.

The manner in which the objective test items discussed here are constructed does not give the teacher any appreciable information with which to answer this question. Nor does it allow him to determine the full meaning of a correct response. If a pupil responds correctly, does this mean that he simply followed a correct procedure, or that he followed the *most efficient* correct procedure? A correct response does not mean that the pupil has full command of the steps required any more than an incorrect response means that he has no command of them.

Testing techniques have been developed that reveal in greater detail the procedures that the examinee follows as he attempts to solve a problem. Prominent among these are the tab item technique (Glaser, Damrin, and Gardner, 1960), a card technique (Rimoldi, 1955, 1963), and simulation exercises (McGuire and Babbott, 1967).

The tab item described is designed to measure a technician's proficiency in detecting the defective unit in a television set that is not operating properly. He is provided with a description of the malfunction, a diagram of the television set, a list of check procedures that might be employed to determine the cause, and a list of possibly defective units. Opposite each check procedure is a tab, under which is a verbal or diagrammatic description of the results the examinee would have obtained if he had actually performed the procedure. The examinee tries to locate the defective unit by making as few check procedures as possible. He begins by selecting one, tearing off the tab, and uncovering the information produced if the procedure is actually followed. He continues to do this until he has diagnosed the difficulty. The pattern of removed tabs reveals all of the steps he had to take; the sequence of the steps can also be recorded. The card technique can be used in a similar manner.

Simulation exercises have also been based on medical problems. They are designed to test the skill of medical students in gathering data about a patient and making judgments for correcting his ailments. A brief verbal description or a short color film is provided, in which the patient's complaints are recounted. The examinee then chooses one of several starting points to be used to alleviate the difficulty, and records his choice by erasing the opaque overlay on an answer sheet. Now he is confronted with a list of possible medical interventions that provide additional information about the patient. He selects those that seem appropriate, again recording his choice by erasing the proper section of the overlay. The results of each of his interventions are reported to him in a realistic verbal, visual, or auditory manner. On the basis of the new data he continues the treatment until his efforts result in the patient's recovery, referral to a specialist, or in some cases death.

Clearly, the simulation exercises differ from the other two techniques in one important way, namely, the problem is modified by the intervening steps taken by the examinee. For this reason these are called *branched* exercises. Several routes may lead to an acceptable outcome. In the first two techniques the same problem is presented to all examinees and it remains the same. This is known as a *linear* exercise.

Certainly none of these techniques has been developed to the point where a teacher can conveniently use them in classroom achievement testing, nor have attempts to establish their worth utilized elementary or secondary school pupils. Nevertheless, these techniques and their variations may appreciably influence future developments in measuring complex pupil achievement.

A final question that is frequently asked is whether objective tests that measure higher order achievement are appreciably different from tests of mental ability. (Madaus et al., 1973). In other words, are these tests achievement tests at all? Certainly the pupil's mental ability plays an important role; there is evidence, however, that these are not the same as tests of mental ability (Furst, 1950; Glaser, 1941). The results yielded by the two types of tests are positively related, but not to a perfect degree by any means.

PROBLEM

7. The first four levels of the cognitive domain (that is, knowledge, comprehension, application, and analysis) can be regarded as convergent thinking, whereas synthesis seems to be a type of divergent thinking (Bloom, Hastings, and Madaus, 1971, pp. 193–194). How does this affect the usefulness of objective test items for measuring complex achievement?

OPEN-BOOK TESTING

Teachers typically administer closed-book tests. The pupil has no source materials at his disposal that would provide him with the correct answers to any of the test items. He depends exclusively on his memory and his ability to manipulate successfully what he remembers. Occasionally the teacher modifies the rules slightly; although access to the textbook and many reference books is forbidden, a restricted number of source materials is allowed. For example, in some mathematics tests the pupils are permitted to use tables of logarithms, tables of trigonometric functions, or tables of squares, square roots, and reciprocals. During science tests the periodic table of elements is prominently displayed, and various chemical, zoological, and botanical handbooks are available to the pupils. In social studies tests, the pupils are sometimes allowed to refer to certain maps and charts. Furthermore, English teachers approve the use of a dictionary during some of their tests. Perhaps these should be called limited closed-book tests.

If the test being administered measures only pupil knowledge, the use of the traditional closed-book approach can be effectively defended. After all, an open-book administration with ample time limits may tell us little more about a pupil's achievement than whether he can use his textbook and other reference materials to find the correct answers to a list of questions. If the test being administered measures primarily complex pupil achievement, however, the use of the traditional closed-book procedure seems to be an unnecessary restriction. An open-book administration is much more realistic. Since a basic purpose of this type of test is to discover whether the pupil can use his knowledge in everyday living, the test situation should simulate the natural situation as much as possible and allow the pupil the use of the normal tools and aids he would have in the natural situation.

The debate on closed- or open-book testing procedures gets complicated when we try to establish the degree to which the test or test item measures primarily complex achievement. It is clear from inspection of the sample test items included in this chapter that a number of levels of the cognitive taxonomy are involved in each, that the relative amount of each varies from item to item, and that this balance can be controlled by the person building it. Furthermore, no matter what the test item may seem to measure on the surface, the learning experiences of the pupils answering the test item must also be known before the behavioral patterns it measures can be determined.

The final decision is, of course, in the hands of the classroom teacher. If he believes that tests for knowledge should be the traditional closed-book procedure and that tests for complex achievement should be open-book, then on the basis of his knowledge of the test items, the pupils, and their experiences, he may separate his test items and administer them accordingly. For those test items about which he is in doubt, he must decide which evidence of a pupil behavioral change is more important and classify the item accordingly.

Building Open-Book Tests

Constructing test items for an open-book test is probably more difficult than constructing those for a closed-book test. Some of the suggestions for constructing objective test items already discussed must be followed with great care. For example, efforts to avoid textbook terminology should be redoubled. Copying verbatim from a textbook, even when designing test items for a closed-book test, is dangerous; for those items to be included in an open-book test, it is very damaging.

Above all, the teacher must construct each test so that the textbook or reference materials will be used in much the same manner as they would be in a similar problem in a natural situation. Although this requirement cannot be fully satisfied, attempts to meet it typically yield good results. For instance, in a mathematics test the textbook may be of little direct help to a pupil as he decides which formula to use to solve the problem, but it does provide an accurate statement of any formula selected. In a social studies test an encyclopedia to which the pupil can refer may serve a similar function. The pupil need not trust his memory here any more than he would in a similar everyday situation in which he wanted to use a given formula or historical fact. In other words, the materials to which the pupil has access in a test should play a supporting role only. The test item should be designed to effect such a condition.

Administering Open-Book Tests

If pupils are to be given an open-book test, they should be forewarned. The reference materials they can use should be carefully listed for them. Perhaps there will be no restrictions, or as some teachers prefer, the list may include only those materials that might be used in a typical out-of-class situation. In any event, the availability of the materials listed will greatly influence the manner in which the pupil prepares for the test. Quite possibly he will concentrate less on factual details and more on broad principles and relationships. Moreover, he may try to become familiar with the reference materials, their content and organization.

Teachers sometimes argue that if an open-book test is to be used and no restrictions placed on the reference materials, class time need not be used for its administration. Instead, the pupil can write the test at home. Although the so-called take-home test has some merit, it suffers from two serious disadvantages. First, the teacher has no certainty that the pupil will work independently. Any assistance destroys the worth of the test results. Secondly, the pupil writing the test at home does not have an opportunity to ask legitimate questions about the items or procedure. Since tests are rarely so well-constructed that no questions are necessary, the pupil should not be denied the chance to ask pertinent questions.

PROBLEM

8. Do open-book tests necessarily measure different pupil abilities from those measured by closed-book tests (Kalish, 1958)?

SUMMARY

The primary points raised in this chapter are these:

1. *A paper-and-pencil achievement testing program measuring only the pupil's knowledge is quite inadequate. Where possible, a testing program should be extended to measure his more complex cognitive achievement as well. In other words, it should determine whether the pupil knows the meaning of his knowledge, grasps the interrelationships among different parts, and can take action intelligently on the basis of them. With enough ingenuity and care, the classroom teacher can construct objective test items capable of eliciting these behavioral patterns from the pupil.*

2. *When a pupil acquires higher order achievement, he can use his knowledge effectively. Therefore, evidence of this fact can be obtained by asking him questions about a carefully contrived situation that is new to him. To answer these questions correctly, he must recall the appropriate part of his total store of knowledge and use it in terms of the novel situation described. If he can do so, he has achieved important, complex educational goals.*

3. *The novel situations are difficult to develop. First, they must involve one or more of the upper levels of the cognitive taxonomy in which the teacher is interested. Secondly, they must be realistic, relatively commonplace, and plausible. Finally, they should require only a short description and/or comparatively simple pictorial material to be understood.*

4. *The question or questions concerning the novel situation can be presented as one or more objective test items. Any type of objective item can be used.*

Integrating the test items with the pictorial material or description of the novel situation requires special care.

5. *Objective test items for measuring complex achievement have the principal advantage of offering the teacher a convenient extension of familiar testing procedures to cover other parts of the table of specifications without sacrificing objectivity of scoring. The principal limitations are that the test items are difficult to build, the pupils need considerable time in which to respond, and the test results are hard to interpret.*

6. *The possibility of using an open-book testing procedure should be seriously explored when more than knowledge is being measured since, in these situations, it is reasonable that the pupil be allowed to use tools and aids normally available to him.*

SUGGESTED READINGS

BLOOM, B. S., J. T. HASTINGS, and G. F. MADAUS. *Handbook on formative and summative evaluation of student learning.* New York: McGraw-Hill, 1971. Chapters 8 and 9.
>Objectives and illustrative test items are given for the highest four levels of the cognitive taxonomy, namely, application, analysis, synthesis, and evaluation. Many of the test items are objective, others are essay questions.

COMMISSION ON UNDERGRADUATE EDUCATION IN THE BIOLOGICAL SCIENCES. *Testing and evaluation in the biological sciences.* Publication No. 20. Washington: Author, 1967.
>After carefully designing a table of specifications, a committee of biologists assembled a large number of test items representing a broad spectrum of both behavioral changes and subject matter. Novel situations are repeatedly used as a basis for item construction.

EDUCATIONAL TESTING SERVICE. *Multiple-choice questions: A close look.* Princeton, N.J.: Author, 1973.
>For the purpose of dispelling the myth that objective test items require no thought or insight by the pupil who responds, twenty-two test items in a variety of subject matter areas are reproduced in their entirety.

HENRY, N. B. (ed.). *The measurement of understanding.* Forty-Fifth Yearbook of the National Society for the Study of Education, Part I. Chicago: University of Chicago Press, 1946.
>Of particular interest are Chapter 3, in which the nature of complex achievement is discussed, and Chapter 4, in which methods of obtaining evidence of complex achievement are described. In Section II are separate chapters devoted to the measurement of complex achievement in social studies, science, elementary school mathematics, secondary school mathematics, language arts, fine arts, health education, physical education, home economics, and agriculture. Methods other than the use of objective test items are also explained.

SMITH, R. B. A discussion of an attempt at constructing reproducible item sets. *Journal of Educational Measurement,* 1968, 5, 55—60.
>Central to this article is a set of eight objective test items based on a novel experiment dealing with the reflection and absorption of light. Each of the six levels of the cognitive taxonomy is represented by at least one item.

WESMAN, A. G. Writing the test item. In R. L. Thorndike (ed.), *Educational measurement.* (2nd ed.) Washington: American Council on Education, 1970, Chapter 4.
>The last portion of this chapter concerns "context-dependent" objective test items, including items based on pictorial or tabular materials. Suggestions for constructing such items and also illustrations of them are provided.

REFERENCES CITED

ABINGDON, ALEXANDER (pseud.). *Bigger and better boners.* New York: Viking Press, 1952.

BLOOM, B. S. (ed.). *Taxonomy of educational objectives: Cognitive domain.* New York: David McKay, 1956.

BLOOM, B. S., J. T. HASTINGS, and G. F. MADAUS. *Handbook on formative and summative evaluation of student learning.* New York: McGraw-Hill, 1971.

COLLEGE OF SCIENCES AND HUMANITIES. *Testing for more than memorization.* Unpublished manuscript. Ames, Iowa: Iowa State University, 1949.

EBEL, R. L. *Essentials of educational measurement.* Englewood Cliffs, N.J.: Prentice-Hall, 1972.

EDUCATIONAL TESTING SERVICE. *Multiple-choice questions: A close look.* Princeton, N.J.: Author, 1973.

FURST, E. J. Relationship between tests of intelligence and tests of critical thinking and knowledge. *Journal of Educational Research,* 1950, *43,* 614–624.

GLASER, E. M. *An experiment in the development of critical thinking.* New York: Teachers College, Columbia University, 1941.

GLASER, R., D. E. DAMRIN, and F. M. GARDNER. The tab item: A technique for the measurement of proficiency in diagnostic problem-solving tasks. In A. A. Lumsdaine and R. Glaser (eds.), *Teaching machines and programmed learning: A source book.* Washington: National Education Association, 1960, 275–285.

HENRY, N. B. (ed.). *The measurement of understanding.* Forty-Fifth Yearbook of the National Society for the Study of Education, Part I. Chicago: University of Chicago Press, 1946.

KALISH, R. A. An experimental evaluation of the open book examination. *Journal of Educational Psychology,* 1958, *49,* 200–204.

MCGUIRE, C. H., and D. BABBOTT. Simulation techniques in the measurement of problem-solving skills. *Journal of Educational Measurement,* 1967, *4,* 1–10.

MADAUS, G. F., et al. A causal model analysis of Bloom's taxonomy. *American Educational Research Journal,* 1973, *10,* 253–262.

NATIONAL ASSESSMENT OF EDUCATIONAL PROGRESS. First results for 1970–71 assessment show literary comprehension limited. *NAEP Newsletter,* 1972–73, *6,* 1–3.

RIMOLDI, H. J. A. A technique for the study of problem solving. *Educational and Psychological Measurement,* 1955, *15,* 450–461.

RIMOLDI, H. J. A. Rationale and application of the test of diagnostic skills. *Journal of Medical Education,* 1963, *38,* 364–373.

SMITH, R. B. A discussion of an attempt at constructing reproducible item sets. *Journal of Educational Measurement,* 1968, *5,* 55–60.

SOLOMON, R. J. New directions in assessing achievement. *Proceedings of the 1965 Western Regional Conference on Testing Problems.* Princeton, N.J.: Educational Testing Service, 1965, 45–51.

STOKER, H. W., and R. P. KROPP. Measurement of cognitive processes. *Journal of Educational Measurement,* 1964, *1,* 39–42.

TYLER, R. W. Some findings from studies in the field of college biology. *Science Education,* 1934, *18,* 133–142.

TYLER, R. W. The relation between recall and higher mental processes. In C. H. Judd et al., *Education as cultivation of the higher mental processes.* New York: Macmillan, 1936, 6–17.

WEITMAN, M. Item characteristics and long-term retention. *Journal of Educational Measurement,* 1965, *2,* 37–47.

WERT, J. E. Twin examination assumptions. *Journal of Higher Education,* 1937, *8,* 136–140.

5

PREPARING ESSAY ACHIEVEMENT TESTS

A skilled trial lawyer in action is a pleasure to watch. With great precision and organization, he carefully extracts information from witnesses—information that, of course, he hopes will be beneficial to his client. He may do this in such a way as to capitalize on any dramatic effects that are present, and he may later summarize the testimony presented to accentuate whatever casts a favorable light on his case and to deemphasize whatever does not.

It is difficult to imagine the amount of preliminary preparation that a lawyer must make before he ever appears in court. Even the framing of the questions to be presented to the witnesses must be carefully planned. The questions need not reveal all the information the witness can recall. Most of this information is irrelevant; some of it may even be damaging to his case. Framing and presenting helpful questions without resorting to leading questions, which the judge might disallow, is a genuine art.

The classroom teacher trying to measure academic achievement with essay tests might tear a page from the lawyer's book. The teacher is also asking questions of reasonably cooperative subjects; he, too, is interested in soliciting certain kinds of information and no other. Therefore, it seems reasonable to expect that the task faced by the teacher as he frames questions for his pupils is essentially the same as that faced by the lawyer as he prepares to examine a witness. Each has in mind distinct purposes that his questions are to serve. If the questions are to serve their respective purposes, they must be prepared deliberately.

Unfortunately, the teacher's questions designed to reveal pupil achievements are usually only partly successful. Consider for a moment oral questioning. Notice how frequently the pupil attempting to answer a question must ask his own questions to clarify his task. He may want to know the definition of some of the terms, or whether a certain basic assumption should be made when answering, or how much detail is desired. Only after this confusion has been dispelled can the original question be answered. The cost in time and frustration is sometimes considerable.

The essay test items included in a paper-and-pencil achievement test are generally a distinct improvement in this respect. Their preparation is much more systematic. Yet there is still unnecessary pupil confusion. In spite of the fact that few questions about the test are asked when it is administered, a review of the pupils' responses customarily reveals considerable uncertainty about one or more questions. Sometimes this review may even lead one to believe that the pupil would have written a correct answer if he had understood the question. In such cases, the questions are clearly not serving the purpose for which they were intended.

When compared with the procedures for constructing objective items, those for constructing essay items seem simple. Nevertheless, you cannot question anyone with consistent success unless the questions are planned. The fact that essay test items are deceptively simple in appearance and hence in construction is the reason why many of their potential values have not been entirely realized.

CHARACTERISTICS OF ESSAY TEST ITEMS

An essay test item is one for which the pupil supplies, rather than selects, the correct answer. More specifically, an essay item demands a response composed by the pupil, usually in one or more sentences, of a nature that no single response or pattern of responses can be listed as correct, and the accuracy and quality of which can be judged subjectively only by a person skilled and informed in the subject, customarily the classroom teacher (Stalnaker, 1951, p. 495). The important features of this description are the freedom of response allowed the pupil, and the difficulty of scoring the responses. The first is used as a basis for classifying essay items; the second indicates the most perplexing problem associated with essay items, a problem treated in detail later in this chapter.

Freedom of Response

The freedom of response allowed the pupil may vary appreciably from one essay test item to another. Consider the following items, both of which are designed for use in a secondary school, the first in an American history achievement test, and the second in an English and world literature achievement test.

In your opinion is the federal government of the United States more or less democratic today than it was at the end of the eighteenth century? Give reasons for your answer.

Explain how the study of English and world literature can help a person to understand better the political, economic, social, and religious aspects of past ages, and how it can influence his present understanding of and attitudes toward modern ways of life.

Both of these test items demand extended responses from the pupils. In fact the typical pupil reaction to each would be ". . .but I could write a book about it." This is justified in both instances. Both items are tapping a higher order of learning than some objective test items; only those pupils who can recall what they have learned, evaluate it in terms of the question, and then organize it into a suitable answer will succeed.

In contrast, examine the following items, one of which is taken from an elementary school test dealing with a health unit, the second from a junior high school general science test.

Bill and Tom are pupils in the sixth grade. They try to take good care of their teeth. Both brush them immediately after their morning and evening meals, but do not brush them after their noon meal or after eating between meals. Both have the dentist inspect their teeth every six months. However, Bill's teeth decay more easily than Tom's. Give possible reasons why this is true.

An athlete wishes to know the amount of time he needs to run 100 yards. He stations one man at the starting line with a revolver and a second at the finish line with a stop watch. In order to time the athlete accurately, should the man at the finish line start the watch at the moment he sees the flash of the revolver or the moment he hears the sound of the shot? Why?

In terms of freedom of response, these two essay items represent the opposite extreme. The correct responses are now quite specific; notice also that, if the two situations described are novel, more than recall of information is required of the pupil.

The variations in freedom of response allowed the pupil offer a crude but useful means of classifying essay test items into types. At least two principal types can be established: the *extended-response* type, as illustrated by the first pair of test items, and the *restricted-response* type, as illustrated by the second pair.

EXTENDED RESPONSE.   The extended response has much to be said in its favor. It can be extremely challenging to pupils. To respond correctly, pupils must display such traits as their ability to organize, evaluate, write clearly, and be creative. Thus, the responses to these test items show how well the pupils have achieved important educational goals, possibly at the synthesis or evaluation levels of the cognitive taxonomy.

Extended-response essay questions are sometimes more suitably used as term paper topics or "take-home" tests rather than as "in-class" tests. Furthermore, they have value as teaching devices or as stimulus material when measuring writing ability instead of achievement in a subject matter area.

RESTRICTED RESPONSE.   The restricted-response essay item is of greater concern to us in the measurement of pupil achievement except as a measure of his writing ability. This type of essay item differs from the first in that the perimeter of pupil response is better defined. A specific problem is presented. It requires the pupil to recall the proper information, organize it in a suitable manner, arrive at a defensible conclusion, and express it in his own words. In several important respects, it requires the pupil to reveal abilities much like those required by a satisfactory answer to an extended-response essay test item; however, this display must occur within well-defined restrictions. These restrictions simplify the scoring problem, thereby greatly improving the reliability of the scoring.

Observe that the restricted-response essay item is far removed from the supply type of test item described in Chapter 3. In the first place, it differs in the amount of freedom of response allowed the pupil. Although the restricted-response essay sets limits in this respect, it does not confine the response to a word or two; on the contrary, a paragraph or more is usually needed if the question is to be answered properly. Secondly, it differs in terms of the behavioral changes reflected. The short-answer test is almost invariably used as a means of measuring pupil knowledge; the restricted-response essay item can be used for this purpose or designed to measure more complex pupil achievement. The latter is a very important function of the essay item.

PROBLEMS

1. Construct a supply item for an objective test and a restricted-response item for an essay test. Design the latter so that it overlaps the scope of the objective test item. Compare the two in terms of the cognitive levels of the pupil behavioral patterns required to respond correctly.

2. Differentiate between essay items designed to measure a pupil's achievement in a subject matter area and those designed to measure his ability to write (Coffman, 1971). Construct a test item of each type.

CONSTRUCTING ESSAY TEST ITEMS

Essay test items are quite popular in the classroom as a method of measuring educational achievement. Objective items are heavily used in standardized achievement tests, but not to the point of excluding the essay type. Essay questions are an important component of the National Assessment of Educational Progress, and have been used as a part of the *Sequential Tests of Educational Progress (STEP)* and some of the achievement testing programs conducted by the College Entrance Examination Board (CEEB).

Preparing and scoring writing ability tests have received considerable attention from teachers and testing specialists (French, 1962; Diederich, 1965, 1967). To measure writing ability, objective and semi-objective items are being used alone and in conjunction with essay items that often require between twenty to forty minutes of testing time. Combinations of these testing methods seem to be satisfactory means of measuring writing ability (Godshalk et al., 1966). Methods of evaluating essays are described in Chapter 7.

With the possible exception of those cases in which evidence of writing ability is desired, the extended-response essay item has limited value as a measuring tool. Therefore, the remainder of this chapter is devoted to the restricted-response type.

Teachers usually consider essay items relatively easy to construct since they require less time and technical skill than objective items. The task, however, is not a simple one. Five important considerations confront the teacher as he constructs essay items:

1. *Relating the essay item to one or more cells of the table of specifications.*
2. *Sampling the pertinent subject matter adequately.*

3. *Adapting the essay item to fit the academic background of the pupils to whom it is to be administered.*
4. *Determining the amount of freedom of response to be allowed the pupil.*
5. *Establishing a suitable time allotment for the pupil's response.*

The five categories overlap each other to some degree and are not of equal importance. However, each is sufficiently important that it cannot be ignored in the process of constructing essay items and arranging them as parts of a test. Failure to comply with the suggestions stemming from any one of the categories will cause otherwise well-designed essay items to fail.

Relating Essay Items to the Table of Specifications

As in the case of the objective test item, the essay test item is a direct outgrowth of one or more cells of the table of specifications. Yet the objective and the essay test items do not merely duplicate each other. Like a station wagon and a sports car, they both perform all the functions demanded, but not with equal ease and efficiency.

As you know, objective test items can be used to measure pupil knowledge with considerable success. Using them, the teacher can sample broadly with a minimum expenditure of time. Measuring complex cognitive achievement with objective test items is an effective approach but not to the same degree as measuring knowledge. The difficulties of item construction and the length of response time pose problems. The essay item, on the other hand, presents a different picture. It is not as efficient a means of measuring pupil knowledge as an objective test, one reason being that the scoring of the answers is a demanding task. As a means of measuring complex pupil achievement, however, it offers many encouraging possibilities.

For these reasons, objective test items are often developed primarily in terms of the cells of the table involving knowledge, and the essay test items in terms of cells involving other levels of the cognitive taxonomy. This means that the achievement test frequently will be composed of both types of items. Such tests offer the pupil some variety. They also distribute the teacher's work load. The construction of the objective item requires more of his time before the test, and the scoring of the essay item requires more of his time after the test.

In addition to differing in the kind of cells of the table of specifications with which they are associated, the objective and essay items commonly differ in the number with which they are associated. Most often, the objective item is primarily related to one cell and perhaps secondarily to another. The essay item quite frequently is related to several in both cases. It deals with a larger whole than the objective item. The correct response to it has several subparts. These may easily involve one group of cells in the table of specifications in a primary manner and another in a secondary manner.

Care must be exercised if we are to maintain a high degree of content validity in an achievement test containing essay items. For instance, suppose that a teacher using an essay item for measuring complex pupil achievement finds that it is primarily related to several cells pertaining to knowledge. In addition, it may be secondarily related to still other cells. If this is true, any objective test items included in the same test for measuring pupil knowledge must be readjusted accordingly. Only when the various subparts of the correct response to an essay test item are identified and analyzed can the relationship between that item and the table of specifications be determined. The contribution of the item to the content validity of the test obtaining it can then be established.

In summary, the teacher follows these steps as he builds essay test items according to the table of specifications. First, he must select the cell or group of cells dealing with complex cognitive achievement (and some dealing with knowledge) to which the item is to be related. With these in mind, he starts his search for suitable item content, most likely a novel situation. When the situation is identified, he frames one or more questions on its basis. Finally, he composes the correct response, separates it into its subparts, and cross-refers them with the cells in the table of specifications. He may discover that the cells he originally had in mind are not involved in the test item in exactly the manner initially intended. Therefore, he may alter the item to support his first plan, or he may expand or contract in an appropriate manner other essay and objective items to be included.

Sampling Subject Matter Adequately

The problems of sampling subject matter for an achievement test are essentially the same as those of a reader selecting a novel in the library. A basic problem in both cases is the size of the sample. How large must it be to guarantee that generalizations based on it will truly represent the population from which it came? Both situations have practical restrictions on the size of the sample. The test cannot have more than a certain number of test items because of limited time. The reader thumbing pages at random will not scan endlessly because it requires too much time and may spoil the novel when he reads it in its entirety.

The variety of the population sampled also affects the size of sample needed. For example, sampling a homogeneous mixture, such as a bottle of milk or a bag of well-mixed inorganic fertilizer, is comparatively simple; a relatively small sample will no doubt be sufficiently representative. On the other hand, sampling a heterogeneous mixture such as subject matter and complex mental processes is difficult. Inevitably, large samples are needed if one is to have confidence in the breadth of the sample.

In the light of this discussion, the inadequate subject matter sampling of the essay test comes into focus. The typical essay achievement test contains only a handful of test items; therefore, despite the fact that each item may have a number of subparts, the test is a distressingly small sample when the variety of most subject matter is considered. The possibility that the sample is unrepresentative is increased. Otherwise stated, its content validity is quite possibly less than satisfactory. There is greater likelihood that a well-prepared pupil might have the misfortune to find that one or more test items touch on his weak areas; hence he responds poorly, and the total test results underestimate his true achievement.

Restrictions on testing time may cause a classroom achievement test dominated by essay items to seem very narrow in scope when judged in light of the table of specifications used. Under such restrictions, it is advisable to replace each essay item requiring a long response with several requiring shorter responses. A careful adjustment will cause the degree of content validity and reliability of the test to rise appreciably.

USE OF OPTIONAL TEST ITEMS. Some teachers try to reduce the sampling limitation of the essay item with optional items. For instance, twelve test items might be listed, and the pupil allowed to answer any eight of them. Rather than improve the sampling, this procedure weakens it. Since many pupils will make partially different selections, they are, in effect, confronted with partially different samples. The content validity depends on the particular combination the pupil chooses, since test content and the meaning of the score varies from pupil to pupil. A direct comparison of the various test scores cannot be defended.

A different use of optional test items is that in which a series to be answered by all pupils is first presented, and a series of paired items follows. The pupil is to choose one of each pair. The members of each pair are considered to be equivalent test items; they are of the same level of difficulty, require approximately the same response time, are based on the same combination of cells in the table of specifications, and so forth. Thus, ideally, the content validity would be the same for all practical purposes no matter what choices the pupil made; yet the test is somewhat more flexible.

The last-mentioned use of optional test items is much more defensible than the first described. Nevertheless, it cannot be recommended. It doesn't relieve the basic difficulty, which is that certain cells of the table of specifications are not represented in the test. The pairs are merely independent test items representing the same combinations of cells. Building equivalent test items is, of course, no simple task. Moreover, they increase the scoring labor because the scorer has a greater variety of items to score.

Adapting Essay Items to the Pupils' Backgrounds

"How much detail should I give?" is a common question asked by a pupil confronted with an essay test item. The answer is particularly important to him if he is well aware of the fact that his response will be scored in terms of exactly what he writes; that is, no credit is allowed for what he seems to have written or for statements that are essentially correct but not pertinent. He recognizes that he will waste valuable testing time by making a very detailed response if detail is not required or that he will lose significant amounts of credit for his response if he erroneously assumes that the teacher allows no credit for minor but important detail.

The teacher also is penalized by any pupil uncertainty as to the amount of detailed information that the correct response should contain. If he expects a great deal but does not make this fact explicitly known, the pupils who did not include the details, but could have, will complain when penalized. If the teacher expects only the major elements but does not make this fact explicitly known, some pupils will include unnecessary information, thus lengthening their responses greatly, and complicating the scoring task.

The problem is illustrated by the following essay test item constructed by a physics teacher for use in a unit examination concerning electricity:

A customer telephones your electrical shop concerning his doorbell, which will not ring when the door button is depressed. He wants to know what the trouble might be. Assuming that the electric current has not failed, describe to him two possible causes of this difficulty and how they could be corrected.

To answer this question the pupils will undoubtedly use such terms as *contact points, armature, magnetic field, hammer, gong,* and so forth. Should they define these terms, or merely use them with the assumption that the teacher will consider proper use of the expressions to signify that the definitions are also known? With the test item stated in its original form, the pupils will vary in their answers.

Suppose that the teacher wants somewhat limited detail; he is willing to assume that proper use of the expressions means comprehension of their meaning. In this event, he could improve the item by adding the following statement:

Assume that the customer is familiar with the basic principles of electricity and magnetism as well as the names and functions of all parts of the common doorbell.

If he did not wish to make this assumption, he could add a statement such as the following:

Assume that the customer has no knowledge either of the basic principles of electricity and magnetism or of the common doorbell. Be certain, therefore, that you define all technical expressions you use.

This illustration emphasizes a broad issue: adapting the essay test item to the academic background of the pupils. Pupils often have a large body of general knowledge. Asking them to reveal this knowledge in a response to an essay test item does nothing but demonstrate that they have it. No differentiation among the pupils has been established. The teacher must decide on how much of this common knowledge is important in the correct response.

If the purpose of a test item is to serve as a means of differentiating among pupils, it is difficult to defend any test item that requires the pupil to repeat great quantities of this so-called common knowledge. Instead, the test item should be built so that the pupils devote most of their response time to, and hence acquire most of their credit from, those aspects that will differentiate among them. This procedure shortens the response time needed and should result in a more efficient use of the testing time.

All these points have a direct bearing on the level of difficulty of the essay item's various parts and, therefore, of the item as a whole. Objective test items are quickly recognized as inadequate if their level of difficulty is very low or very high, a condition not so easily recognized in the case of essay test items. One or more subparts of the essay item may have suitable levels of difficulty but the remainder may not. Adapting the essay item to the academic background of the pupil is equivalent to minimizing those parts of the essay test item that are so easy **or** so difficult that they do not provide a basis for differentiating among the pupils responding.

Determining the Amount of Freedom of Response

How "restricted" is the response to a restricted-response essay item? No definite answer can be given. The illustrations given earlier suggest that the responses are fairly brief. However, they can exceed these limits and still be perfectly acceptable.

The suggestions for the adaptation of the essay item to the background of the pupils indicate some ways in which the freedom of response is restricted. These suggestions help the pupil sort the important elements in the response from the unimportant; nevertheless, the pupil is still confronted with the question of which important elements are wanted. Perhaps the essay test item can be answered from more than one point of view. Although all types of response based on each of several points of view may be correct in a sense, only one is intended.

The essay item must be so framed that each pupil will easily recognize exactly the task he is to perform. He should understand the question in the same way that all other pupils understand it. Any confusion or uncertainty that he may experience should be attributed to his inability to answer correctly rather than his failure to understand the purpose of the test item.

To achieve this clarity in an essay test item is often difficult. On the other hand, violations of this principle can be easily identified and corrected, at least partially. For instance, consider the following essay item, intended for use in a secondary school social studies test:

Today both major political parties of the United States include members representing practically every shade of political conviction between arch conservatism and extreme liberalism. Suppose that a rearrangement of membership took place so that the Republican Party acquired a truly conservative philosophy, and the Democratic Party, a truly liberal philosophy. What would happen to the political situation in this country?

Imagine the great variety of responses that this test item would elicit. The impact of such a drastic rearrangement of the political parties could be discussed in terms of the changes in the sizes of the parties, their financial resources, leadership, appeal to the general public, platforms, and control of state legislatures, governorships, the presidency, and Congress. One pupil could have written successfully about several of these topics, another about several different topics, and yet both could have missed the point of the test item and consequently lost credit. In short, the task to be performed by the pupil is not clearly defined and, as a result, even the well-informed pupil will very likely be penalized.

Suppose the question at the end of the test item is replaced by the following:

Compare the present platforms of the two parties with the platforms that you think

the parties would adopt after the rearrangement of membership. Restrict your comparison to the areas of:
1. *civil rights legislation*
2. *public works legislation*
3. *environmental improvement legislation*

Now the task is better identified. It is only in terms of certain aspects of the platforms that comparisons are to be made between present and hypothetical party composition. A framework for the pupil's response is established. Incidentally, notice that the test item still requires the pupil to select information, organize it properly, and present it as an integrated whole. Although the framework restricts the pupil's freedom of response, it does not do so to the point where the test item elicits only an extremely specific response dealing with superficial knowledge.

Attempts to clearly define the pupil's task have contributed to the general decline in the use of expressions such as "discuss," "tell about," and "give your opinion of." In their place have come a series of different expressions that, when used individually or in combination, tend to clarify the intent of the test item. Typical of these expressions are the following (Stalnaker, 1951, p. 527): "explain," "relate," "interpret," "compare," "discriminate," "select significant ideas," "contrast," and "state the conclusion." The list is suggestive only.

Establishing Suitable Time Limits

Suitable time limits for essay tests are even more difficult to establish than those for objective tests. First, some teachers find it more difficult to estimate the level of difficulty of essay items and overestimate or underestimate the response time needed. Secondly, pupils vary in terms of the speed at which they can write and, as the test progresses, their susceptibility to fatigue. Third, a well-designed test item forces the pupil to marshall his facts and organize them in a suitable manner. To do so he may sketch out the preliminary notes or even a complete outline, then write his answer on the basis of such notes. The amount of time needed for this is another uncertain variable. Finally, if the pupil's response is to be scored partly in terms of organization, spelling, and grammatical accuracy, he will need more response time.

There is a tendency to allow too little response time for essay tests. The pupils must rush through at top speed if they hope to finish. The immediate results are, of course, a steady deterioration in the legibility of the handwriting and the organization of the answer, with consequent complication of the task of scoring.

Suitable time limits can be determined by pretesting the items on a similar group of pupils under normal conditions, and any needed adjustments made on the basis of this trial. Since this can rarely be done, the teacher must rely on his past experience with similar test items and pupils, or he might note the time he needs to *write* a complete model answer for each time. Estimating time allotments for each item and listing them on the test copy helps him pinpoint his judgments. When in doubt, the teacher should allow too much rather than too little time. It is better to have fewer or shorter responses and not have to worry about a speed factor.

PROBLEMS

3. Would the essay item concerning the two political parties (see page 136) be strengthened by stipulating what is meant by a *truly conservative philosophy* and a *truly liberal philosophy?* Why?

4. Criticize and strengthen as you see fit the following essay items which were included in a ninth grade social studies test administered at the completion of a unit devoted to government organization, functions, and services.

    a. An amendment was proposed in the Congress to have the electoral college vote proportionately, according to actual vote of the people.

       1. How would this change the present system?

       2. Would this proposal strengthen the democratic control of the people and would it lead to a probable increased vote? Give reasons for your answers.

    b. The Supreme Court has nine members. Do you feel this number is too large, too small, or just right to carry the responsibilities of the court? Give reasons.

ADMINISTERING THE ESSAY TEST

The administration of the essay test involves many of the same principles and procedures described in the two preceding chapters in connection with objective tests. Hence, these need not be repeated here. Two features of test administration that deserve additional comment for essay tests are the directions to the pupils and the use of open-book testing.

Unlike the directions given in objective tests, those for essay tests are quite simple. Most often the test items are sufficiently self-contained so that few pupils need any additional information to formulate satisfactory responses. The directions are sometimes omitted, or, if given, are no more complicated than the following:

Directions: *Answer the following questions in as brief a manner as possible. Only a few sentences will be necessary in order to cover the important points needed to answer each.*

Special features of the test must be mentioned in the directions. For example, a brief description of the basis for scoring is sometimes included. The classroom teacher can point out if he plans to add or subtract credit for penmanship, style of writing, grammar, or spelling. He should also mention any restrictions on the time allowed or the type of paper to be used, the amount of space on the paper allowed for the response, or the use of pen or pencil.

Using the essay test item primarily as a means of measuring complex achievement suggests an open-book test. If this point of view is accepted, then the question is raised as to whether the pupils could write the answers at home rather than in the classroom. The open-book, take-home administration of essay tests is somewhat common. The task may now fall under the classification of "homework" rather than a test, but, with the proper design of the questions and the cooperation of the pupils, it still can serve as a test with generous time limits.

SCORING THE ESSAY TEST

The scoring of the pupils' responses to an essay test item is unquestionably the most disagreeable task related to the use of these items. In the first place, the teacher is understandably reluctant to allot the great quantities of time that are needed if the job is to be done properly. Also, he is concerned about his ability to recognize the variation of quality in the responses. He suspects that his judgments are highly subjective. Perhaps his state of mind or the name of the pupil at the top of the page are more powerful factors in his determination of the quality of the response than the response itself. These and other doubts cause the scoring problem to be an important one.

The problem is also complicated by the testwiseness of the pupil. This is the same element that reduces the effectiveness of objective achievement tests, but it manifests itself in a different manner here. An imaginative method of faking responses to the essay test item is to practice the art of "precise vagueness." The pupil takes great pains to write at length in a flowing, colorful style. He also takes great pains not to commit himself; he skirts the issue as closely as he can without actually facing it. In short, he wants to impress the scorer without revealing his ignorance. An illustration of this technique is the following response by a pupil to a test item requiring him to evaluate the causes of the fall from power of Napoleon Bonaparte.

There was a day when Napoleon Bonaparte was at the pinnacle of success. People admired him and respected him. He was the outstanding leader in Europe. But this could not last forever. Difficulties arose. These difficulties were political, eco-nomical, social, and, of course, military. Moreover, they were not always obvious. Indeed, some were so subtle that even Napoleon himself was not aware of them. Nevertheless, obvious or subtle, these difficulties were sufficiently powerful that, in combination, they toppled him from power.

The relative importance of these difficulties is hard to determine. It would seem that some were clearly more important than others. This is to say that some contributed more directly to Napoleon's fall than did others.

Paragraph after paragraph, perhaps page after page, the pupil continues to string one vague sentence to the end of another. Each rings of accuracy. Yet the true worth of such an answer is elusive; like a puff of smoke, it seems to disappear as you reach for it. The foregoing response is essentially empty. Yet, in the face of its impressive length and style, it would require a teacher well-schooled in the art of scoring responses to essay test items to recognize this and score accordingly.

Testing specialists have devoted considerable attention to simplifying the task of scoring responses to essay test items and to improving the reliability of the scoring process. Their efforts have been somewhat successful. Well-established general sugges-tions have been formulated and several methods of scoring have been devised and used.

Improving the Scoring of Essay Items

There are four general suggestions for improving the scoring of essay items.
Score the pupils' responses anonymously. It has been demonstrated that the

"halo effect" can appreciably reduce objectivity of scoring. Because a certain pupil has written the response, the teacher expects a certain quality of response and has, in effect, prejudged it. The identical response written by a pupil with a decidedly different reputation will receive a different amount of credit.

To conceal the identity of the examinee is not easy. If the teacher is familiar with the penmanship or style of writing of the pupils, it is virtually impossible. Should this not be the case, the use of numbers, rather than names, to identify the responses, or the practice of having the pupil's name written on the back of the paper, will provide a simple but effective means of maintaining anonymity.

Score all responses to each test item at one time. Only when this is done, and one item is completely finished, should the responses to any other item in the test be examined. This means that, instead of the responses to all test items by one pupil being scored at one time, as is most often true of an objective test, the responses to one test item by all of the pupils are scored at one time.

Two advantages are thereby gained. First, it is easier to maintain a constant or near-constant set of standards on the basis of which each response is to be judged. All details of the completely correct responses can be remembered, and comparisons between and among various pupil responses can be made. Secondly, any "halo effect" that might modify the scoring of all responses by one pupil in a test tends to be minimized. In other words, the way in which a pupil answers one test item will not influence the judgment of the teacher when he scores the pupil's response to a second test item that is more or less independent of the first.

If the spelling, penmanship, grammar, and writing style of the responses are to be scored, it should be done independently of the subject matter content. In other words, how a pupil writes should be judged apart from what he writes. You can easily imagine instances in which one might be of a very different quality from the other, and instances in which the quality of one affects the teacher's judgment of the quality of the other. An all too common occurrence is the case in which accurate spelling, legible handwriting, and pleasant style upgrade the rating of the quality of the content of the response, whereas substandard spelling, handwriting, and style function in the opposite direction (Marshall and Powers, 1969).

The question is frequently asked whether the quality of grammar, spelling, handwriting, and style should be scored at all. The answer is simple. If any or all of these are a part of the educational objectives and hence the table of specifications on which the test is based, they should be scored. If they are not, any deficiencies in these respects can be noted and any superlative achievements can be acknowledged, but no loss or gain of credit can be given. In view of this it is easy to understand why in other tests than those of the language arts, such aspects as grammar, spelling, and writing style are seldom scored, or are scored on a restricted basis. An example of restricted scoring is the marking of spelling for technical words but not for nontechnical words.

If the results of the test are extremely important, have at least one other person score the responses independently. If this is not possible, score them a second time yourself, doing so without knowledge of your first judgments. The time-proven method of improving the scoring of responses to essay items is to average independent judgments made by competent scorers guided by the same set of standards. The feasibility of this practice is questionable. The next best substitute is the procedure in which two independent judgments are made by the same teacher.

Any radical discrepancies between the scores yielded by independent judgments should be immediately investigated and resolved. Perhaps the services of a third scorer are needed. If the differences cannot be resolved, then the opinion of the person who knows the teaching situation best, the classroom teacher, should be followed.

Methods of Scoring Essay Items

A number of different methods of scoring the responses to essay test items have been developed; only two are discussed here. The first is called the *analytical method;* the second is known as the *rating method.*

ANALYTICAL METHOD. To use the analytical method of scoring, the teacher must first write out the correct response to each test item. This is analyzed and its component parts identified. The total number of raw-score points allowed for the correct response is distributed among the various subparts. The points may be distributed equally or unequally among the parts, depending on the teacher's feelings about the matter and the importance of the cells in the table of specifications on which the subpart is based. Finally, each pupil's response to the test item is read, the various subparts of the correct response that it contains are noted, and the raw score determined accordingly. As far as the scoring is concerned, any extraneous material in the pupil's response is ignored, whether it is accurately stated or not. Note that this procedure does not prevent the teacher from marking any inaccuracies in the statements containing unnecessary information. Indeed, he should!

A simple illustration of these procedures can be provided for the test item concerning possible reasons for the differences in incidence of tooth decay of two sixth-grade boys (see page 130). The teacher may decide that the correct response should contain three elements thought to be of approximately equal importance. Therefore, each is allotted one raw-score point.

1. *Recognition that the nature of the boys' diets influences incidence of tooth decay.*
2. *Recognition that heredity factors can partly account for incidence of tooth decay.*
3. *Recognition that all factors causing tooth decay are not known; hence differences between the two boys in terms of the unknown factors could account partly for variations in the incidence of tooth decay.*

A more complex illustration of the analysis of the correct response is Figure 5.1. It is based on an essay test item designed for an achievement test to be administered to agriculture pupils completing a unit concerning dairy cattle. The item is in three parts.

To answer the essay test item correctly, the pupil must recall that the amount of concentrate mixture fed a dairy cow is noticeably influenced by the cow's size, amount of butterfat produced per day, and stage of pregnancy, but is not appreciably

A farmer is undecided whether two of the dairy cows in his herd should be fed the same or different amounts of a concentrate mixture he is using. The following information is available concerning the two cows:

Cow	Breed	Weight	Age	Milk Production	Butter-fat Content	Months in Calf
A	Guernsey	1000 lb	4 yr	37 lb/day	5.1%	4
B	Holstein	1200 lb	5 yr	49 lb/day	3.5%	2

Both cows are fed adequate amounts of the same roughage.
1. Cite reasons why Cow A should be fed more concentrate mixture than Cow B.
2. Cite reasons why Cow B should be fed more concentrate mixture than Cow A.
3. Evaluate all the information and decide whether the farmer should feed more concentrate mixture to Cow A than to Cow B, or more to Cow B than to Cow A, or the same amount to both.

FIGURE 5.1. Test Item Designed to Measure Achievement in Animal Nutrition.

influenced by differences in breed and age such as are shown in the chart. Then he must use this information accordingly.

If eight raw-score points were allowed for the correct response, one possible way of subdividing them among the subparts is as follows:

Subpart 1
  Total points: 3
    A. (2 pts.) Amount of butterfat production is greater for Cow A (1.9 lb/day) than for Cow B (1.7 lb/day).
    B. (1 pt.) Cow A is in a more advanced stage of pregnancy than Cow B.
Subpart 2
  Total points: 1
    A. (1 pt.) Cow B weighs more than Cow A.
Subpart 3
  Total points: 4
    A. (1 pt.) If only the differences in breed and age are considered, both cows should be fed the same amount of concentrate mixture.
    B. (3 pts.) The two reasons for feeding more concentrate mixture to Cow A than Cow B overbalance the reason for feeding more to Cow B than Cow A.

With this analysis of the correct response firmly in mind, the teacher should be able to score pupil responses more quickly and consistently. Moreover, later discussion of the test item, which would include a review of the pupils' responses and the scoring of items, is greatly facilitated when based on such an analysis. Both teacher and pupil are much more certain that the scoring is fair, and, in addition, they have isolated any gaps in each pupil's achievement revealed by the test item.

The analytical method offers several excellent advantages. In the first place, the analysis of the correct response will quite frequently cause the teacher to redesign the statement of the test item. He may realize that the item as originally stated will not necessarily elicit the response he desires, even when the pupil is very well informed. Any reframing of the test item and re-adjustment of the time limits that result from analyzing the correct response are generally distinct improvements. Secondly, the analytical method used by a conscientious grader can yield very reliable scores. This is true when the essay test item is of the restricted rather than extended-response type.

Attempts have been made to train pupils to score essay items using the analytical method. The results are encouraging. In one attempt (Nealey, 1969), the responses for each essay item were separated from the others and those for a specific item were given to several examinees along with criteria for judging the correctness of the responses. Thus, small groups of pupils scored all responses to a given item. Since their pooled evaluations corresponded closely to those of the instructor, it seems reasonable to explore further the possibility of teaching this scoring technique to secondary school pupils, thereby realizing pedagogical gains as well as conserving the teacher's time.

RATING METHOD. The rating method (sometimes called the global or holistic method) also requires that a correct response be written for each test item; however, this is not subdivided as such. The wholeness of the response is emphasized; the scorer attempts to grasp its complete scope. With this in mind, he reads the pupil's responses. On the basis of the wholeness of each response, he classifies it in one of three or one of five categories. The categories represent levels of quality such as, in the first case, good, average, or poor, and in the second case, very good, good, average, poor, or very poor. Although the use of five categories is common in classroom testing, as many as nine can be used with good success (Coffman, 1971).

Once the scorer has read and classified all responses, he reads them a second time, possibly even a third. The answers in each category are compared with each other. Those that don't fit are shifted to a more suitable category. Homogeneity in each category is desirable, even though the scorer realizes that it depends on the number of categories used. The fewer categories used, the more variability exists within each.

When the scorer is completely satisfied that each response is in its proper category, it is marked accordingly. Total, partial, or no credit is allowed, depending on the category checked. The entire process is then repeated for all other essay items in the test.

The rating method of scoring essay items is a distinct improvement over the single hasty reading in the absence of a clearly understood correct answer that some teachers use as a means of scoring pupil responses. On the other hand, it has not yielded the high scorer reliabilities of the analytical method. A scorer often has difficulty differentiating between the various categories and may even find that his basis for differentiating is changing at times.

COMPUTER SCORING. Incredible as it sounds, efforts to use a computer to score essay items measuring writing ability have been rather successful (Page, 1966, 1967;

Slotnick, 1972). As a point of departure, a differentiation was made between intrinsic and proximate variables in an essay. The former are characteristics recognized by the teacher and presumably used in his evaluation. Examples are word usage, spelling, and complexity of sentences. Proximate variables are any which, for whatever reason, happen to correlate with expert judgments of writing quality. These vary widely and include such aspects as the number of commas, apostrophes, dashes, relative pronouns, and prepositions present. As many as thirty of these have been used by a computer as it scans essays and assigns scores to each statistically. Believe it or not, these scores based on proximate variables corresponded closely to those for overall quality based on intrinsic variables used by judges.

Furthermore, evidence exists that a computer can detect the presence or absence of a high degree of opinionation, vagueness, or specificity in an essay (Hiller et al., 1969). For instance, in the case of vagueness, it counted the number of times the examinee used any of sixty key words such as *probably, sometimes, usually,* etc. Computer-derived scores on vagueness correlated negatively with essay scores on characteristics such as content, organization, and style as determined by judges. This is the kind of correlation one would expect.

Can computers be used to score restricted-response essay items in a subject matter area? Undoubtedly. While awaiting better research data on which to base their techniques, a few teachers are moving ahead on a tentative basis. Typically they administer essay items requiring only a three- or four-sentence answer. The pupil prints his answer on a special answer sheet that is converted into a punch card and fed into a computer. Key phrases for each question are specified and assigned various scores so that the computer can compute a total score as it scans each pupil's response. As a check, the teacher selects a small random sample of the responses and gives these intensive personal study. Usually, these checks verify the scores assigned by the computer.

Unreliability of Scoring

Research shows that seemingly competent scorers frequently cannot agree with themselves, much less with each other, concerning the amount of credit to be allowed a pupil's response to an essay item (Coffman, 1972). The subjectivity in the scoring process varies according to the nature of the item but is typically large. When the test item approaches the extended-response type, subjectivity increases and reliable scoring becomes an extremely difficult problem. Unfortunately, the pupil does not always graciously accept any inconsistencies in the teacher's scoring efforts.

The general suggestions for improving scoring that are given in the preceding sections can increase scorer reliability. For this to occur, three conditions must be met. First, the responses must have been elicited by carefully framed test items, which present the pupil with a well-defined task. The problem here resembles that encountered when designing supply items. For instance, consider the plight of the teacher who posed the question: "What is the difference between a king and a president?" One young pupil responded: "The king has to be the son of his father. The president doesn't."

Secondly, the teacher using the analytical or rating method should master and apply it carefully. Among other things, this may mean practicing the method by scoring pupil responses several times independently, then analyzing whatever differences have occurred. He may also wish to tackle his scoring problems in cooperation with his fellow teachers. Such ventures can be profitable (Diederich, 1967). Thirdly, ample time must be allowed. The teacher must be an alert, discerning judge at all times, which is a role he cannot play properly if pressed for time.

PROBLEMS

5. Even though a teacher decides to score responses to essay items on the basis of content without consideration of writing style, he may be influenced, consciously or subconsciously, by the quality of writing (Marshall and Powers, 1969). To what degree do you think this is true? Does the intensity of this problem depend in part on the subject matter used in the item?

6. After an essay test, some teachers ask their pupils to record the reasons for their answers on a 3×5-inch card. This information is then used for diagnosing pupil difficulties and strengthening similar future test items. Identify the advantages and limitations of this procedure.

COMPARISON OF ESSAY AND OBJECTIVE TESTS

At this point, we can identify a number of sizable differences between the essay and objective test as a means of gathering information on which pupil achievement can be evaluated. Seven general characteristics used as a basis for differentiating between the two types of items are as follows:

Difficulty of preparing the test item
Adequacy of the sampling of the subject matter
Relative ease with which knowledge and complex achievement are measured
Study procedures followed by the pupil as he prepares for the test
Originality of the response the pupil must make to the test item
Relative success of guessing correct responses
Difficulty of scoring the pupil responses

The differences between essay and objective tests in terms of these seven characteristics are summarized in Table 5.1. This table reveals the fallacy of the argument that one type of test item is unquestionably superior or inferior to the other. Each has peculiar advantages and limitations. There are testing needs for which each is particularly well suited.

No one should needlessly restrict his measurement program by adhering to one type or the other. Recognizing this situation, many classroom teachers build and administer achievement tests containing both types of items. In these cases, pupils generally prefer to answer the objective items first and the essay items later, thereby making better use of their testing time. This is the order typically followed by national achievement testing programs.

TABLE 5.1.   Comparison of Essay and Objective Tests.

Characteristic	Essay test	Objective test
Preparation of the test item.	Items are relatively easy to construct.	Items are relatively difficult to construct.
Sampling of the subject matter.	Sampling is often limited.	Sampling is usually extensive.
Measurement of knowledge and complex achievement.	Items can measure both, measurement of complex achievement is recommended.	Items can measure both; measurement of knowledge is more common.
Preparation by pupil.	Emphasis is primarily on larger units of material.	Emphasis is often on factual details.
Nature of response by pupil.	Pupil organizes original response.	Except for supply test items, pupil selects response.
Guessing of correct response by pupil.	Pupil is less prone to guess.	Pupil is more prone to guess.
Scoring of pupil responses.	Scoring is difficult, time-consuming, and somewhat unreliable.	Scoring is simple, rapid, and highly reliable.

The choice of whether to build an objective or essay test is usually influenced by one additional consideration, namely, the number of pupils to be tested. If the group is small, less effort may be needed to construct, administer, and score an essay test than an objective one. Sometimes the labor needed to build high-quality objective items can only be justified if they are incorporated in a test file and used several times (see page 162).

PROBLEMS

7. On the basis of your experience, compare the additional time required to build an objective test rather than an essay test with that required to score the essay rather than the objective test.

8. It is said that essay tests encourage the pupil to learn how to organize his own ideas and express them effectively, whereas objective tests encourage him to build a broad background of knowledge and abilities. Do you agree? Why?

SUMMARY

The following are the main ideas presented in this chapter:

1. *An essay test item demands a response composed by the pupil, usually in the form of one or more sentences. The quality of the pupil's response can be judged subjectively by an informed scorer, ordinarily his teacher.*

2. *The freedom of response allowed on an essay item can vary appreciably. In one case, few restrictions are placed on the nature of the pupil's response; such a test item is an extended-response essay test item. Other test items define quite specifically the task to be performed by the pupil; these are restricted-response essay test items.*

3. *Because of the extremely difficult task of scoring answers to extended-response essay test items, their value as a method of measuring subject matter achievement is curtailed. On the other hand, the restricted-response type plays an important role in achievement testing, since its answers can be scored reliably.*

4. *Five important considerations face the teacher when he builds essay test items. First, he must relate the item to one or more cells in the table of specifications; those to be emphasized involve complex cognitive achievement. Second, he must sample the subject matter broadly, favoring those essay items that require comparatively short answers and thereby using more items for a given testing period. Third, he must adapt the item to the academic background of the pupils. Fourth, he must determine the freedom of response to be allowed the pupil. Finally, he must establish suitable time limits.*

5. *Scoring responses to an essay item is usually difficult. To help simplify this task and, at the same time, improve the reliability of the scoring process, four general rules should be followed. First, score the pupils' responses anonymously. Second, score all responses to each test item at one time. Third, if spelling, penmanship, grammar, and so forth are to be graded, score them independently of the subject matter content. Last, if possible, have another person go over them; if this is not possible, score them a second time yourself.*

6. *Two prominent methods of scoring essay test items are the analytical method and the rating method. In the analytical method, the teacher breaks the correct response into subparts, assigns raw-score points to each, and awards points for a pupil's answer insofar as each subpart of the correct response is or is not included. In the rating method, the teacher tries to grasp the complete scope of the right answer, and then, on the basis of the wholeness of a pupil's response, to classify it into one of three or five categories representing various levels of quality.*

7. *It is highly appropriate to use both objective and essay items in the same achievement test. If this is done, the objective items should be administered first, followed by the essay items.*

SUGGESTED READINGS

COFFMAN, W. E. Essay examinations. In R. L. Thorndike (ed.), *Educational measurement.* (2nd ed.) Washington: American Council on Education, 1971. Chapter 10.

   This is a superior discussion of the value of essay test items as a means of measuring pupil achievement. In it are described the limitations of this type of test item, its potential value, suggestions for improving it, and reliable methods of scoring pupil responses.

COFFMAN, W. E. On the reliability of ratings of essay examinations. *NCME Measurement in Education,* 1972, 3, 1–7.

   The sources of error in essay examinations are examined and suggestions are made for reducing rating error.

DIEDERICH, P. B. Cooperative preparation and rating of essay tests. *English Journal*, 1967, 56, 573–584.

> It is the author's opinion that evaluation of pupil writing ability by individual teachers is a failure. A team approach is needed. Five possible objections to the idea are discussed, following which a plan for cooperative efforts by teachers is provided.

EBEL, R. L. *Essentials of educational measurement.* Englewood Cliffs, N.J.: Prentice-Hall, 1972. Chapter 6.

> The differences and similiarities between objective and essay items are recounted, and suggestions are given for the preparation, use, and scoring of essay tests.

HUCK, S. W., and W. G. BOUNDS. Essay grades: An interaction between graders' handwriting clarity and the neatness of examination papers. *American Education Research Journal*, 1972, 9, 279–283.

> Data collected in this study support the hypothesized interaction between the clarity of graders' handwriting and that of the essay they rated. The authors caution those using essay examinations to be aware of extraneous factors affecting test scores.

LA FAVE, L. Essay vs. multiple-choice: Which test is preferable? *Psychology in the Schools*, 1966, 3, 65–69.

> A forceful statement condemning the multiple-choice test as a measuring tool because it is "superficial." Essay tests are held as desirable replacements since they have the potential to be standardized and still measure more than trivial aspects of pupil achievement.

PAGE, E. B. Imminence of grading essays by computers. *Phi Delta Kappan*, 1966, 47, 238–243.

> Initial efforts show that a computer can grade pupil essays about as well as classroom English teachers. These promising results are leading to the study of the use of the computer to score limited response essay items dealing with subject matter.

REFERENCES CITED

COFFMAN, W. E. Essay examinations. In R. L. Thorndike (ed)., *Educational measurement.* (2nd ed.) Washington: American Council on Education, 1971, chapter 10.

COFFMAN, W. E. On the reliability of ratings of essay examinations. *NCME Measurement in Education*, 1972, 3, 1–7.

DIEDERICH, P. B. Reading and grading. In A. Jewett and C. E. Bish (eds.), *Improving English composition.* Washington: National Education Association, 1965, chapter 11.

DIEDERICH, P. B. Cooperative preparation and rating of essay tests. *English Journal*, 1967, 56, 573–584.

FRENCH, J. W. School of thought in judging excellence of English themes. *Proceedings of the 1961 Invitational Conference on Testing Problems.* Princeton, N.J.: Educational Testing Service, 1962, 19–28.

GODSHALK, F. I., et al. *The measurement of writing ability.* New York: College Entrance Examination Board, 1966.

HILLER, J. H., et al. Opinionation, vagueness, and specificity-distinctions: Essay traits measured by computer. *American Educational Research Journal*, 1969, 6, 271–286.

MARSHALL, J. C., and J. M. POWERS. Writing neatness, composition errors, and essay grades. *Journal of Educational Measurement*, 1969, 6, 97–101.

NEALEY, S. M. Student-instructor agreement in scoring an essay examination. *Journal of Educational Research*, 1969, 63, 111–115.

PAGE, E. B. Imminence of grading essays by computers. *Phi Delta Kappan*, 1966, 47, 238–243.

PAGE, E. B. Grading essays by computer: Progress report. *Proceedings of the 1966 Invitational Conference on Testing Problems.* Princeton, N.J.: Educational Testing Service, 1967, 87–100.

SLOTNICK, H. Toward a theory of computer essay grading. *Journal of Educational Measurement*, 1972, 9, 253–263.

STALNAKER, J. M. The essay type of examination. In E. F. Lindquist (ed.), *Educational measurement.* Washington: American Council on Education, 1951, 495–530.

6

APPRAISING CLASSROOM
ACHIEVEMENT TESTS

The use of measuring instruments in our commercial, scientific, and even recreational pursuits is commonplace. This would be a strange world indeed if the desk rulers, bathroom scales, water meters, clocks, thermometers, speedometers, and electrical meters were suddenly removed. These and countless other measuring instruments are constantly feeding information to us that we use to make decisions. Without such information, a significant part of our modern civilization would cease to function.

An interesting result of the dominance of measuring instruments is the great confidence we have in their accuracy. True, we may doubt the readings of an ancient wristwatch or an inexpensive outdoor thermometer, but only infrequently do we entertain doubts as to whether the desk ruler is twelve inches long and divided into twelve equal parts, or whether the water and gas meters are measuring volume properly, or whether the speedometer in our automobile is registering as it should. We assume that, for our purposes, their accuracy is sufficient.

Fortunately our confidence in such instruments is well-founded. Extensive efforts are made by the federal government as well as by industrial and scientific organizations to maintain accurate measuring instruments. For example, the United States Bureau of Standards works actively in this field. Among other functions, it maintains fireproof vaults in which platinum-iridium meter bars and kilogram weights are carefully stored; they are the standards against which some of the instruments for measuring distance and weight can be checked. Governmental officials known as sealers conduct systematic checks of devices such as the scales used in food stores and the meters used in gasoline stations, thereby protecting the consumer. Also, scientists are constantly recalibrating the thermometers, burets, and weights used in their work to be certain that the accuracy of their measurements is maintained.

The perpetual vigilance in commercial, industrial, and scientific fields should be copied by the classroom teacher. He makes numerous measurements and, in so doing, uses instruments in which he has notably less confidence than in the scales and meters mentioned. This is particularly true when classroom achievement tests are used. Although the product of much time and effort, they no doubt contain numerous unsuspected flaws. After all, many tentative decisions are made as they are constructed. Decisions concerning item difficulty, the attractiveness of distracters, or the length of the test, to name just a few, are made on the basis of inadequate evidence and could be at least partially wrong. The teacher will not know the success or failure of these decisions unless the test is carefully reexamined after its administration. Then and only then will he know how worthwhile it was and how meaningful the scores.

In addition to determining the worth of a classroom achievement test after it has been given, reexamining test results has other values. For instance, any errors or inadequacies discovered can serve as warnings to the teacher when he constructs other achievement tests. Although the methods and material used in a class may change from year to year, the important educational objectives are generally stable. Therefore, the classroom achievement testing program changes from year to year but seldom drastically. In view of this, any past failures and successes can assist the teacher immeasurably in future achievement test construction. Furthermore, a careful inspection of pupil responses to individual test items or groups of items has diagnostic value. The areas of strength and weakness for each pupil—or the class as a whole—can be identified.

ITEM ANALYSIS METHODS

Reexamining each test item to discover its strengths and flaws is known as *item analysis*. Item analysis usually concentrates on two vital features: level of difficulty and discriminating power. The former means the percentage of pupils who answer correctly each test item; the latter the ability of the test item to differentiate between pupils who have done well and those who have done poorly.

Essay or objective items from open-book or closed-book tests can be subjected to item analysis. However, it is most useful to us when the items are a part of a norm-referenced test, rather than of a mastery or criterion-referenced test. In other words, the scores are to be used as a basis for ranking pupil achievement. The purpose of a mastery test, on the other hand, is to separate the pupils into two groups, those who have achieved at least as high as a certain level and those who have not. Consequently, the level of difficulty and discriminating power of its items are much less important considerations. The remainder of this chapter is devoted to the analysis of norm-referenced test items, not criterion-referenced ones which pose special problems (Hambleton and Novick, 1973).

Methods of item analysis are essentially mathematical and can take many forms. Various statistical techniques are used, many of them requiring a considerable amount of computing. The methods described in the following sections are, in contrast to many, relatively simple. They are quite satisfactory for classroom teachers. Since teachers do not have the time, facilities, or number of cases often demanded by the more elaborate methods, such methods are of little practical value although widely used in the construction of standardized achievement tests.

Item Difficulty

It is easy to determine a test item's level of difficulty. First a tabulation is made of the number of pupils who successfully answer the item. This figure is then divided by the total number of pupils attempting the item and the quotient is multiplied by 100. These steps are summarized in the following formula:

$$P = \frac{N_R}{N_T} (100),$$

where

P = *percentage of pupils who answer the test item correctly;*
N_R = *number of pupils who answer the test item correctly;*
N_T = *total number of pupils who attempt to answer the test item.*

Suppose that an item in a classroom achievement test is answered correctly by eighteen of the twenty-eight pupils who attempt to answer it. Then the level of difficulty of this test is found as follows:

$$P = \frac{18}{28} (100) = 64.$$

In other words sixty-four percent of the pupils who attempted the test item answered it correctly.

The formula shown does not alert the teacher to two questions that are often ᵣaised about the determination of item difficulty. In the first place, is the number of pupils who attempt to answer the item the same as the total number who are administered the test? If the time limits are too restrictive, it is conceivable that some pupils did not have an opportunity to answer test items appearing near the end. Hence, the number of pupils who attempt to answer the test item is less than the number to whom the test was administered. Secondly, is the number of pupils who know the correct answer the same as the number who answer it correctly? In the case of objective test items, successful guessing may cause the two numbers to be different and thus, to some degree, destroy the value of the computation of item difficulty.

The first question is seldom a problem to the classroom teacher. Sufficient time is allowed for the administration of the test so that each pupil attempts each item. Therefore the denominator of the formula is the same for each test item.

The second question is the source of widespread debate among measurement specialists. The arguments for and against correcting for guessing are concisely summarized elsewhere (Henrysson, 1971). For our purposes it is not necessary to use formulas for computing item difficulty that incorporate a correction for guessing. In the first place, the added computational burden, though not serious, can be troublesome. Also, the assumptions underlying the formula are not fully satisfied, and the pupils' reaction to the warning that a correction for guessing is to be made are so varied that extraneous personality factors influence the achievement test scores. Finally, the teacher ordinarily does not need a very accurate measure of item difficulty. Rough approximations are usually sufficient.

Item-Discriminating Power

The discriminating power of a test item is its ability to differentiate between pupils who have achieved well (the upper group) and those who have achieved poorly (the lower group). To determine the discriminating power of a test item we must first specify the characteristics of the upper and lower groups. Here we have considerable latitude. We may wish to use an independent criterion to classify the pupils. Such a criterion might be the score from a standardized test thought to measure the same aspects of achievement as the classroom test containing the item in question. Or we may wish to use final marks in the same or similar achievement areas, these having been determined without knowledge of the scores yielded by the classroom test. On the other hand, an internal criterion may be used, such as the total scores from the classroom achievement test, the items of which are being studied.

In most cases, the internal criterion is used. This is done not only because independent criteria are customarily unavailable, but also because they are not good measures of the aspects of achievement involved in the classroom test. Achievement tests are, in a sense, "self-defining," that is, the test itself defines what it is to measure. Incidentally, the use of the total test scores as the criterion for classifying pupils into upper and lower groups, followed by the use of these groups to determine an index reflecting the discriminating power of individual test items, is known as the *internal-consistency* method of computing indices of item-discriminating power.

When the total test scores are used in this manner, a decision must be made as to which part of the distribution of scores is the upper group and which part is the lower group. Some choose the upper and lower halves, others the upper and lower thirds with the middle third discarded, and still others the upper and lower twenty-seven percent with the middle forty-six percent discarded. The last has received a great deal of support by testing specialists, and a number of tables designed to assist item analysis are based on this division. However, for the classroom teacher analyzing his own test, use of the upper and lower thirds is probably a suitable compromise. Fewer cases are lost than when the upper-lower twenty-seven percent method is used, and a more distinctive separation between the groups is provided than in the case of the upper-lower halves method.

The rationale behind the scheme for computing an index of item-discriminating power is quite simple. A test item with maximum discriminating power would be one which every pupil in the upper group would answer correctly and every pupil in the lower would answer incorrectly; in short, it can discriminate between every pupil in the upper group and every pupil in the lower group. Thus, this test item produces a maximum number of correct discriminations. Of course, we cannot expect items to discriminate perfectly. The typical test item will yield some correct discriminations—part of the upper group will respond correctly and part of the lower group incorrectly—and will yield some incorrect discriminations in that the remainder of the upper group will respond incorrectly and the remainder of the lower group correctly.

The discriminating power of a test item is the difference between the number of correct and incorrect discriminations expressed as a percentage of the maximum possible correct discriminations. Several reports based on this idea have appeared (Johnson, 1951; Ebel, 1954; Findley, 1956). In simplified form, the formula to compute an index of discriminating power based on this idea is the following:

$$D = \frac{U - L}{N},$$

where

D = *index of item-discriminating power;*
U = *number of pupils in upper group who answer the test item correctly;*
L = *number of pupils in the lower group who answer the test item* correctly;
N = *number of pupils in each of the two groups.*

To use this formula conventionally, one must first find the total raw scores on the test for all pupils. Then the test papers are ranked according to the raw scores, and the top and bottom thirds of the raw-score distribution are found; the middle third is ignored. For each test item, the number of pupils in the upper and lower groups who respond correctly are tabluated. Appropriate substitutions are then made in the formula. For instance, suppose that ten of twelve pupils in the upper third of the raw-score distribution answer an item correctly, and five of twelve in the lower third answer it correctly. The index of discriminating power for this test item is:

$$D = \frac{10 - 5}{12} = +0.42.$$

It is evident that the maximum size of the index is +1.00 and the minimum size is −1.00. In the first case, maximum discrimination occurs in the desired direction; in the second, in the opposite direction. Any negative value means that the test item discriminates—to some degree—in the wrong direction. Hence, the discriminating power of the test item is unsatisfactory. The larger the positive value, the better. Although it is difficult to establish a suitable minimum positive value below which the discriminating power of a test item is considered faulty, certainly values less than +0.20 indicate that the discriminating power of the test item is questionable. A reasonably good achievement test item should have an index of at least +0.30.

Difficulty Levels Near Fifty Percent

It has long been known that the discriminating power of an item is influenced by the difficulty of the item. The manner of influence depends on the relative intercorrelation of the items, that is, the degree to which each test item is correlated with every other. In the case of tests containing items that have low intercorrelation, those composed of items with levels of difficulty near fifty percent will display more discriminating power than those composed of items with widely varying levels of difficulty. In the case of tests containing items with high intercorrelations, the reverse is true. The reasons are beyond the scope of this book; further discussion can be found in any of several standard references (Henrysson, 1971).

Since achievement tests rarely are composed of highly intercorrelated items, the recommendation is frequently made that they include only those test items with midrange levels of difficulty, between forty and seventy percent (Ebel, 1954). This recommendation often disturbs teachers who feel that a wide distribution of levels of item difficulty is necessary to test very good and very poor pupils properly. To separate the very good, the good, the average, the poor, and the very poor pupils from each other, an achievement test with superior discriminating power is needed. To obtain this, it is necessary, strange as it may seem, to avoid the use of test items with widely varying levels of difficulty.

PROBLEMS

1. By means of a simple experimental study, Ebel (1972, pp. 396–399) demonstrated empirically that an inverse relationship exists between the spread of item difficulties and the spread of test scores. Study the three test score histograms he shows. Are the differences among them striking?

2. Do you think that teachers can study multiple-choice test items and successfully predict the level of difficulty and discriminating power of each? Compare your opinion with the findings of a study in which secondary school mathematics teachers were asked to make such predictions (Ryan, 1968).

USING ITEM ANALYSIS RESULTS

The results of item analysis can serve two main purposes. The first and more obvious one is that they can give the teacher a much better view of the worth of the test he built and used; he can also profit by his mistakes in that he should be able to construct noticeably better tests in the future. The second use can be summarized in a single word: diagnosis. By examining the data from item analysis, the teacher can detect learning difficulties of individual pupils or the class as a whole, and can plan more suitable remedial programs. Studying the strengths and weaknesses of pupil achievement will also help him to evaluate more accurately the effectiveness of various parts of the learning situation.

Improving Classroom Achievement Tests

As he administers each achievement test, the classroom teacher is usually plagued by countless questions. Will the distracters of the third multiple-choice item be attractive? Is the ninth item so worded that the superior achievers may misunderstand its intent and respond incorrectly, yet, paradoxically, the poor achievers will not be misled and will tend to respond correctly? Is the last item too difficult? The answers to questions such as these can cause a teacher to view the test results with confidence or doubt.

LEVELS OF ITEM DIFFICULTY. As a first step in the process of answering questions such as the foregoing, item difficulties can be computed. A quick scanning of these data reveals all items to which 100 and 0 percent respond correctly. Since the purpose of a norm-referenced test is to yield scores that will differentiate among the pupils, neither type of item is suitable. On the other hand, a possible use of one or two test items to which 100 percent responded correctly would be to place them at the beginning, thereby letting them serve as a gentle introduction to the remainder of the test.

All items of extremely high or low levels of difficulty should be carefully scrutinized. Since any test items with levels of difficulty that are not in the general vicinity of fifty percent (that is, between forty and seventy percent) tend to reduce the discriminating power of the test, these can be viewed with suspicion. Their indices of discriminating power should be checked since an item which is extremely easy or difficult cannot possibly have a large D value.

Also, the gross failure of certain test items to approximate the anticipated level of difficulty may be information of great value to the teacher. Is the item poorly designed? Is the effectiveness of the learning experience far different from that expected? If so, why? Is the level of difficulty of this test item affected by the presence of other items in the test? If so, which items? These and other avenues of explanation can be explored.

INDICES OF DISCRIMINATING POWER. The second step that can partly answer some of the questions posed by the teacher is to compute and interpret indices of discriminating power. Any D values above +0.40 can be considered very good, any between +0.40 and +0.20 satisfactory, and any between +0.20 and zero poor. It is clear that negative values identify items that differentiate among pupils in the wrong way. Ebel (1954) suggests that, in a well-built classroom achievement test composed of objective test items, more than fifty percent of the test items should have D values exceeding +0.40, less than forty percent should have values between +0.40 and +0.20, less than ten percent should have values between +0.20 and zero, and none should have negative values. Obviously, these are only guides.

EXAMINING ALL RESPONSES TO AN ITEM. An even closer inspection of the effectiveness of test items can be obtained by tabulating and comparing all the responses of the pupils in the upper and lower groups. For example, in the case of a multiple-choice test item the responses to each of the distracters—as well as the correct response—are counted. Incidentally, this tabulation can be made quickly and accurately by a test-scoring machine or a computer if the proper answer sheets have been used (Miller et al., 1967; English and Kubiniec, 1967).

To see the kinds of information that can be obtained by scrutinizing all responses, let us examine several multiple-choice items. In each case the discriminating power is represented by a D value, and the difficulty level is estimated by using data from the upper and lower groups only. Such estimates are usually fairly accurate for our purposes. The middle third often divides itself between correct and incorrect answers much as the other two-thirds combined.

Consider the following test item administered to pupils developing library skills. (The correct response is designated by an asterisk.)

If you wish to find quickly the page on which a particular topic or subject appears in a reference book, to which of the following would you refer?
(1) the appendix
(2) the subject index
(3) the table of contents
(4) the bibliography
The responses of the pupils in the upper and lower groups are as follows:

Option	Upper third	Lower third
1	0	1
*2	10	8
3	1	2
4	0	0
(Omits)	0	0
Total	11	11

This test item is too easy, the estimate of P being eighty-two percent. Moreover, its discriminating power is poor, D being +0.18.

Quite possibly, the weakness in the test item is due to the inclusion of the word "subject" in the second option. This may be a clue to the correct response that is so obvious that the pupils quickly notice it and choose their answer accordingly. The uninformed pupil will profit more by such a clue than the informed pupil who didn't need one in the first place. If this word were deleted, it is conceivable that the differential attractiveness of the distracters would increase, thereby improving the level of difficulty of the item and its discriminating power.

Another illustration is a test item with a satisfactory level of difficulty but negative discriminating power. It appeared in an elementary school social studies test.

The capital of Switzerland is
   (1)Bern
   (2)Zurich
   (3)Lucerne
   (4)Geneva
The responses of the pupils in the upper and lower groups are as follows:

Option	Upper third	Lower third
*1	5	6
2	2	3
3	1	1
4	5	3
(Omits)	0	0
Total	13	13

The estimated level of difficulty is forty-two percent and the index of discriminating power is − 0.08.

We can only speculate as to why more pupils in the lower group than in the upper responded correctly and so many of the pupils in the upper group selected the fourth option. Possibly their familiarity with the League of Nations and the many important international conferences that were held in Geneva caused the pupils in the upper group to think of Geneva as the most important city in Switzerland and thus the capital of the country. The pupils in the lower group, on the other hand, may not have known this about Geneva and therefore were not misled by it. Having no preconceived ideas about the importance of these four cities, almost half of them learned that Bern is the capital and responded accordingly. Perhaps the relative importance of the cities of Switzerland and their relationship to each other and the world are not well taught.

These illustrations make it clear that a rich fund of information concerning his test is available to the teacher who takes the trouble to examine all responses to the test items. Although only multiple-choice items are shown, similar information can be obtained from other types of objective test items and even essay test items of the restricted-response type. At the very least, this information should give the teacher a much more realistic view of the value of his test. Ideally, it should also warn him of some of the pitfalls encountered in achievement test construction and suggest means of overcoming or circumventing these.

Diagnosing Inadequacies in Achievement

As informative as a pupil's total raw score can be in many respects, it does not provide very much information about the sources of his successes and failures. In other words, the raw score of a pupil or the arithmetic mean of the raw scores of a class may be interpreted to mean that one or more pupils are having trouble, but such scores will not tell what the trouble is or where it is located. To locate the nature of the trouble, an item-by-item inspection of the test is necessary.

The first step in diagnosing inadequacies in achievement is to build a chart showing the item-by-item performance by each pupil. A section of such a chart based on an objective achievement test is shown in Table 6.1. The plus signs indicate correct responses, the negative signs incorrect responses, and the zeros, omitted responses. Incidentally, some teachers have their pupils participate in the construction of such a chart as this; others use printed reports prepared by computers (Miller et al., 1967). In the case of multiple-choice tests, the number of the option chosen by each pupil can be used in place of the plus and minus signs, thus providing a summary of the popularity of wrong responses for each test item.

The totals listed at the bottom of the table reveal the number of pupils who responded correctly and incorrectly to each test item. The totals pinpoint the areas of difficulty for the pupils as a class. Notice that, of the first ten test items, these seven pupils found items 2, 3, 4, 6, and 8 to be relatively easy, whereas they found 1, 5, and 10 to be moderately difficult, and 7 and 9 quite difficult. Now the strengths and weaknesses in the achievement of the pupils can be quickly found by examining the areas of achievement involved in the test items identified and noting the cells of the table of specifications on which they are based. Discussing this information with members of the class immediately following the administration of the test can be most enlightening to them.

Very likely the teacher will wish to study the test items that cause difficulty before those that do not. After satisfying himself that there is nothing technically wrong with such a test item and its scoring, he can pose questions as to the reasons why it is difficult: Is little emphasis placed on the point of the test item during the period of instruction? If so, is this lack of emphasis deliberate or accidental? Is there widespread misunderstanding among the pupils in spite of the fact that careful instruction is given? If so, what is the nature of the misunderstanding? Should the learning experiences related to the areas of difficulty be changed in any way?

TABLE 6.1. Sample Chart for Analyzing Pupil Responses to Each Item in an Achievement Test.

Name of pupil	Test item number											Total score
	1	2	3	4	5	6	7	8	9	10 . . . 60		
1. Steve	+[a]	−[b]	+	+	+	−	−	+	−	+	+	39
2. Mary	−	+	+	−	+	−	+	−	−	+	0[c]	21
3. Dick	−	+	+	+	−	+	−	−	+	−	−	18
4. Carol	+	−	−	+	+	+	+	+	−	−	−	37
5. Becky	+	+	+	−	−	+	−	+	−	+	+	41
6. June	+	+	+	+	−	+	+	+	+	−	+	55
7. Sheri	−	+	−	+	+	+	−	+	0	+	−	44
Total No. correct	4	5	5	5	4	5	3	5	2	4 . . . 3		
Total No. wrong	3	2	2	2	3	2	4	2	4	3 . . . 3		
Omissions	0	0	0	0	0	0	0	0	1	0 . . . 1		

[a] Correct response.
[b] Incorrect response.
[c] Omitted response.

There is profit as well in examining test items that the class found to be easy. Again, after a search for technical imperfections fails to reveal any defects, the teacher can raise questions about why the test items are relatively easy: Are the items found to be easy those that primarily measure recall of information rather than more complex cognitive achievement? If so, does this indicate that undue emphasis is being placed on the objectives related to knowledge with a corresponding deemphasis on those involving other levels of the congitive taxonomy? Can the idea behind one or more of the relatively easy test items be traced to a particular learning experience? If so, is there some feature of that learning experience such as a visual aid or supplementary instructional material that is responsible for the pupils' successes and that should be reused with subsequent classes? Is extreme success with a test item caused by unwarranted hints given before or during the administration of the test? If so, should the test be rescored with this item omitted?

After these questions have been answered to his satisfaction, the teacher can turn to the responses of each individual pupil. Just as he attempted to analyze the areas of strength and weakness for the class as a whole, he can now do the same for each pupil. Following a thorough examination of the item-by-item performance of the pupil, other records of his achievement can be consulted, observations of his study habits made, and, in many instances, a teacher-pupil conference held. In this manner, many additional pieces of information come to light as to why the pupil is successful and unsuccessful. These details can be used along with the initial information concerning what the areas are as a basis for building a remedial program. Such a program is individually tailored to the needs of the pupil. If it succeeds, it will not only correct his past inadequacies but also provide him with the means of preventing a number of future difficulties.

SAMPLING PROBLEM. Analyzing the item-by-item performance of each pupil has one serious weakness that must be recognized. This is the problem of adequate sampling—the same problem we encounter with other aspects of educational measurement. According to the procedures outlined in the foregoing paragraphs, the teacher may regularly make decisions concerning the pupil's achievement on the basis of his response to one or perhaps several test items. Frequently these are very small samples of the achievement areas in question; consequently, the probability that they do not present an accurate picture of the pupil's accomplishments is uncomfortably large. This means that the information gleaned from the item-by-item analysis must be considered suggestive rather than definitive.

The sampling problem can be corrected in part without destroying all of the diagnostic features of the analysis by modifying Table 6.1 slightly. Instead of listing the test items individually across the top of the table, we can organize them into meaningful groups and list them in place of the individual items. For instance, in an arithmetic test the test items may be grouped in four categories: those requiring addition, subtraction, multiplication, and division. The number of correct and incorrect responses to each group of items by each pupil can be tabulated.

A recommended scheme for organizing the test items into groups is to use the table of specifications. Items representing the same or similar cells may be combined into one group. The number of groups used, as well as their size, are determined by the teacher and, of course, can vary widely.

Analysis of classroom performance on either an item-by-item basis or groups of similar items can provide, in effect, criterion- or objective-referenced interpretations of norm-referenced test data (Fremer, 1972). To accomplish this, some teachers will establish minimum competency levels for each test item to which actual pupil or class performance is compared.

PROBLEMS

3. Study the steps described by Diederich (1973, pp. 1–3) in which an item analysis is completed by the pupils to whom an achievement test was administered. They performed most of the work involved in the item analysis by raising their hands in response to instructions from the teacher. Demonstrate this procedure with a class which you are now teaching or attending. Evaluate the demonstration.

4. A properly programmed computer can identify the test item missed by each pupil and provide him with printed suggestions as to the material he should review (Miller et al., 1967). Study the illustrations provided. Are the computer print-outs specific enough to help both pupil and teacher? How could the table of specifications on which the test was based assist in this effort?

LIMITATIONS OF ITEM ANALYSIS

Although item analysis data are useful for evaluating an achievement test and diagnosing weaknesses, several serious limitations exist in application of the techniques. In the first place, whereas the internal-consistency method is suitable for tests containing items that measure somewhat the same mental functions, achievement tests generally contain test items that are relatively heterogeneous in this respect. Second, the classroom teacher frequently must base his item analysis on a small number of pupils, forming judgments on limited evidence. Third, analysis of responses to essay test items is less informative that that of responses to objective items. This lessens the utility of the techniques for the teacher using these items. Finally, item analysis results are more relative than some teachers realize. The level of difficulty and discriminating power of a test item are influenced by the test in which the item appears, the conditions under which the test is administered, and the quality of the pupils.

Use of Internal-Consistency Methods

The internal-consistency method for computing indices of item-discriminating power is appropriate when the pupil traits measured by the total test scores are homogeneous for all practical purposes. Successful items in a test of this kind are those that are closely related to each other and, of course, that tend to measure whatever the total test scores measure. They will have large positive D values. As any test items with low discriminating power are eliminated or changed so that their discriminating power increases, the resulting test will become more and more homogeneous.

The total scores of achievement tests typically represent heterogeneous rather than homogeneous aspects of the pupils. They contain test items that measure several different kinds of behavior (that is, various levels of the cognitive taxonomy) in unequal amounts. The total score is actually a composite representation of these behaviors. If one pupil trait stands out in the total test scores, well-constructed items that reflect it will have satisfactory indices of discriminating power. On the other hand, test items reflecting less important and somewhat unrelated traits, even though they are well constructed in many technical respects, will tend to have low indices of discriminating power.

This problem can be easily illustrated. Suppose that an achievement test contains forty-five recall-of-information items that are fairly homogeneous and five application-of-principles items that are noticeably unlike the first group. The total score is found by counting the number of correct responses, regardless of which type of test item is being scored. All other factors being equal, we would expect that the items in the larger group would have markedly higher indices of discriminating power than those in the smaller group, if the internal-consistency method of computation is used.

EFFECT ON CONTENT VALIDITY. The true significance of the foregoing statements comes into focus when the problem of content validity is considered. Certainly maintaining high content validity in each achievement test is the primary goal of the teacher who designs and builds it. Yet indices of discriminating power may actually encourage him to reduce the degree of content validity of future tests. This would occur if, in the illustration of the fifty-item achievement test, the teacher wishes someday to use it again and either eliminates the items with low indices of discriminating power or modifies them in the hope that the indices will improve. In both cases, large or potentially large changes in content validity could take place. Obviously more is lost than gained.

Of course the problem is largely corrected if it is possible to break down an achievement test in homogeneous subtests with reasonably reliable scores and to use each as the internal criterion for computing indices of discriminating power for items within that subtest. Although this is regularly done with standardized achievement tests, such is not the case with classroom achievement tests because it is often impracticable.

Inadequate Numbers of Pupils

Item analyses for standardized achievement tests are often based on hundreds of cases. Contrast this with the usual class size, which places a limit on the number of cases available to a teacher at one time. His sample is extremely small.

Reexamine for a moment the distributions of the responses made by pupils in the upper and lower groups to the two test items shown earlier in this chapter. Note how a shift of one response from one option to another can change your opinion of the power of a distracter, or how it might even change the P or D value noticeably. Remembering that some of the reasons why a pupil selects one option rather than any of the other three can be vague and obscure, you can imagine how easily a shift in choice could have taken place. All of this means that the profile of pupil responses to an item must be considered tentative as long as the number of pupils is so small.

Analyzing Responses to Essay Test Items

Item-analysis technique can be applied to the responses to essay items as well as to objective items; however, it is definitely more difficult, and the results are sometimes considered less meaningful. The difficulty is traced to the problems of reliable scoring of essay responses and tabulating the incorrect responses. Both of these activities are time-consuming. The relative lack of meaning of the data is attributed to the fact that the various subparts of the correct response are frequently related to each other. The level of difficulty of one subpart may affect the level of difficulty of another; the correctness or incorrectness of a pupil's response to one part may affect the correctness or incorrectness of his response to a subsequent part. These are the principal reasons why responses to essay items are analyzed so infrequently.

The analysis of responses to essay items is most successful if they are of the restricted-response type and are scored by the analytical method. If at all possible, each subpart should be separately considered. This is equivalent to considering each an independent test item with its own level of difficulty and discriminating power. When some or all subparts cannot be logically separated, they should be combined as necessary and the composites treated as separate test items. An analysis based on the internal-consistency method can be used here as it is with responses to objective items.

Relative Nature of Item-Analysis Data

We should like to believe that data from item analysis are completely accurate and meaningful. Clearly this is not justified, both because of the limitations introduced by the use of an internal criterion and a small sample of pupils and because of the special circumstances surrounding every test item as it is administered.

Some of those special circumstances relate to the pupils as they respond to the item—their alertness, motivation, and emotional tone. Some relate to the environment in which the test is given—the time of day, the amount of extraneous noise, the temperature of the room and the ventilation. Some relate to the test containing the item in question—its length, the levels of difficulty of the other items, and the order in which they are arranged. Yes, even the attractiveness of a distracter in a multiple-choice item is influenced by the other distracters with which it is used.

It is hard to determine how much these factors influence item analysis data. The influence might be slight, but in a given instance it could be prominent. It must be understood that the P value and the D value are merely representations of the level of difficulty and discriminating power of an item as it appeared in a certain test administered under specific circumstances to one group of pupils. It is clear that if the test or environment is changed, the values can and do change.

General Considerations

Persistent attempts to follow the suggestions for improving test items should directly and indirectly help produce test items with encouraging item-analysis data. There is no guarantee, however, that this will happen. Very careful construction and even ingenious revision based on item-analysis data may fail to improve the P and D values of a test item satisfactorily. This creates a dilemma: considerations of content validity make it necessary to include the material in the test, yet item analysis suggests that the related items are inferior in some respects. Preference must be given to the content validity. Items based on the material must be included and repeated efforts made to improve their quality. If this fails, then the table of specifications can be changed so that the material can be properly excluded from the test. As a result, the meaning of the total score is changed and evaluation of pupil achievement in the area omitted must be made by other methods, that is, nontesting procedures such as rating methods, product scales, and check lists. These are discussed and illustrated in the following chapter.

PROBLEM

5. For classes of about thirty pupils or less, item-analysis data are rather undependable. Demonstrate the degree to which P values and D values will change by systematically altering the response of one pupil in the upper third and one in the lower third of the test item concerning Switzerland (see page 156), and recomputing the two values each time.

TEST ITEM FILE

The teaching notes maintained by many classroom teachers are voluminous. A syllabus, a variety of outlines, numerous references, several study guides, and a quantity of newspaper clippings and miscellaneous pamphlets are usually a part of this collection. Each assists the teacher as he pursues his instructional duties. Some of these are highly prized; they are considered to be proven teaching aids. Although other notes may be of more doubtful value, the practicing teacher would rarely be willing to part with them.

The portion of this mass of teaching notes that often receives the least attention is the evaluation section. Usually it consists of a copy or two of each of the classroom achievement tests administered during the past year or so, and possibly the tables of specifications on which they were based. Nevertheless, more complete materials concerning these techniques could easily simplify the teacher's measurement functions as much as teaching notes simplify his instructional functions. A highly successful means of organizing much of the pertinent information on classroom achievement tests is a test item file.

Item Data Card

A test item file is nothing more than a series of cards that record a great deal of the information obtained by item analysis procedures. Usually the file contains as many cards as there are test items, although sometimes the length of the item or the nature of the information about it requires several cards. The cards are customarily 3 X 5 or 5 X 8 inches in size and are arranged in any order the teacher desires.

The front of a sample item data card is shown in Figure 6.1. Notice that the

---

No. 143

If both the President and the Vice President of the United States are unable to serve, which of the following officials will act as President?

(1) Secretary of State

(2) Speaker of the House of Representatives

(3) Secretary of Defense

(4) President pro tempore of the Senate

Cells in table of specifications:			Reference(s):
Table No.	Primary	Secondary	Doe and Colofort
2	4B	—	American Government Today, Revised Ed. 1975, pp. 273–274.

FIGURE 6.1. Front Side of Item Data Card.

multiple-choice test item shown is typed so that ample space is allowed for revision. Interlinear notations can be made if the item is to be changed; new options can be written to the right of the original ones if desired. Notice also that the item is cross-referenced with the cells of the table of specifications on which it is based. Each cell is identified by the row (the Arabic number) and the column (the English letter) of the table that intersect to form it. Additional useful information is the page or chapter number of a book or other reference directly related to the subject matter of the item. This allows the teacher to check quickly any detail that might be questioned.

The reverse side of the item data card is shown in Figure 6.2. Space is allowed for summarizing the item analysis data for as many as three separate administrations of the test item or a revision of it and for any appropriate comments made by teacher or pupils. For each administration, the name of the test, the class to which it was administered, its size, the date of administration, the test item number, and the type of administration are noted. Below these, the responses to all options by the upper and lower third of the class, and the P and D values of the test item are recorded.

Clearly, maintaining item data cards is a serious clerical problem. Fortunately it is not insurmountable. Item data cards such as the one shown can be easily prepared with a duplicating machine. Once an ample supply is available and the necessary item-analysis tabulation is completed, the item data card can be filled out rather rapidly. Regular attention will prevent a backlog of unrecorded data from accumulating and provide a smooth, permanent, and up-to-date record for every test item used.

Test	Unit 2					Comments:
Class	11th grade					4-22-75—Pupils are confused about the meaning of the expression "unable to serve." Possibly this should be changed to "die while in office."
Date	4-22-75					
Item No.	18					
N_T	33					
Type of Adm.	Closed book					
Options	Upper	Lower	Upper	Lower	Upper	Lower
1	2	4				
2	⑦	②				
3	0	2				
4	2	3				
5	–	–				
Omits	0	0				
P (Est.)	41%					
D	+0.45					

FIGURE 6.2. Reverse Side of Item Data Card.

Some teachers reduce the clerical load by using less elaborate cards. For instance, the data concerning the name of the test, the class to which it was administered, its size, and the type of administration are omitted. If the cards for each test are filed in a separate group, this information need be recorded only once. Others do not fill out cards for all the test items they use. Instead, only very promising test items are filed.

Advantages of a Test Item File

There are significant advantages for maintaining a test item file if you as a teacher intend to reuse test items. On the basis of the item analysis information and the comments made, you can revise the item. A quick check of the table of specifications will reveal whether the relationship between the item and the table of specifications has changed. The fact that the items are on cards facilitates separating and counting them in terms of the cells in the table of specifications. In this way, the degree of content validity of the total test can be estimated. Having the items on cards also simplifies the reproduction of the test. Since the test is built by accumulating a pack of cards, the arrangement of the items in the test can be changed by simply rearranging the cards, and the final copy of the test can be typed directly from them.

Much can be said in favor of using test items again. By constantly reworking his test items and adding new ones as needed, the conscientious classroom teacher can develop some excellent achievement tests. In this way, the teacher's investment of time and effort in maintaining a test item file becomes reasonable and profitable. However, he cannot use test items again if there is any chance that pupils in succeeding classes will be familiar with them before the test is given. To prevent this, some teachers withhold the test copies and answer sheets after the test.

Withholding test materials, however, is neither fair to the pupils nor good teaching procedure. The pupil who is aware of his successes and failures can take action to improve his deficiencies and gain a much more realistic view of his achievements. Therefore, the teacher must, if at all possible, return his tests and discuss the results with him.

Reusing test items, therefore, becomes considerably more difficult. Only after a teacher has developed a large pool of test items over a period of years should he use any of them again. Under these conditions it is unlikely that any pupils will have any unfair advantage worth mentioning. After all, the vast majority of the previous test copies have been discarded or lost. On the other hand, even if a pupil had access to all of them, the task of studying them would be more forbidding than preparing for a test in the normal manner. Finally, the test items that are used again are usually revisions of the original items. Even when the revision is minor, it helps prevent a pupil who may have studied the original item and memorized the answer from gaining a tremendous advantage over others.

Maintaining a test item file also offers advantages to teachers who may not intend to use any of them again. Restudying test items used in the past can provide helpful hints for constructing new ones. The new item may be totally original yet based on the same idea as one in the file, or it might be such a drastic revision of an older test item that its relationship to it is not easily recognized by the pupils.

In addition, restudying the results of earlier tests can alert the teacher to those cells in the table of specifications that very often are the basis of successful test items and those, if any, that are not. If cells of the latter type are found, efforts at item construction can be focused on them. Likely, weaknesses of a new test can be detected before it is given.

Limitations of a Test Item File

One of the chief limitations of maintaining a test item file has already been mentioned, the great clerical involvement. Another limitation is that the method of recording the data is not equally applicable to all types of test items. Although the form shown in Figure 6.1 can be used for many different items, that shown in Figure 6.2 cannot. It is suitable for the common multiple-choice and true-false test items but must be modified if short-answer or some of the longer matching items are used. The essay item presents even more problems, since the scoring and analyzing of the responses are so difficult.

Still another possible limitation is that maintaining a test item file will actually have an adverse effect on the teacher's instructional and measurement efforts. The first part of the argument goes this way: if teachers are very familiar with past test items, and if the same or similar test items are used in the future, they may teach toward the test without knowing it. In reality, they may be coaching the pupils; the instruction may slavishly follow the achievement tests instead of the reverse. The second part is that intimate knowledge of the old test items will tend to dull the teacher's creativity when building new test items. In other words, the teacher falls into a testing rut. The new test items strongly resemble old ones, novel types are typically ignored, and, as a result, the classroom achievement tests become stereotyped.

Certainly these adverse effects are possible. It is difficult to believe, however, that the discerning teacher would tolerate any of them for any length of time. The advantages gained by maintaining a test item file far outweigh these limitations.

PROBLEMS

6. Design a data card for a restricted-response essay test item.

7. Can the data card be used successfully with multiple-response objective test items designed to measure complex pupil achievement, for example, the item concerning beehives in an apple orchard shown on page 113? Give reasons for your answer.

SUMMARY

The principal concepts discussed in this chapter can be expressed as follows:

1. *Each test item should be re-examined after each use by means of an item analysis in order to study its strengths and weaknesses.*

2. *Item analysis concentrates on two vital features: level of difficulty and discriminating power. The former means the percentage of pupils who answer each test item correctly; this is expressed in terms of P values. The latter means the ability of the test item to differentiate between pupils who achieve well and those who achieve poorly; this is expressed in terms of D values. The pupils who achieve well and those who achieve poorly are usually identified by the internal-consistency method. The total scores on the test containing the items to be analyzed serve as the criterion.*

3. *Results of item analysis can serve two significant purposes. In the first place, they provide important information on the basis of which the teacher can gain a much better idea of the value of the test he has built, and he should also be able to construct noticeably better tests in the future. The second use is diagnosis. By examining the data from item analysis, the teacher can detect learning difficulties of individual pupils or of the class as a whole.*

4. *There are four prominent limitations in the application of item analysis. Firstly, the internal-consistency method is suitable for tests containing items that measure somewhat the same mental functions. Achievements typically are not of this type. Secondly, only a very small sample of pupils is available for the analysis. Thirdly, it is difficult to analyze pupil responses to essay items. Lastly, item analysis data are relative in that they are influenced by the remainder of the test in which the item appears and the particular conditions under which it is administered.*

5. *A convenient means of organizing much of the pertinent information yielded by item analysis is a test item file. This file is a series of cards on which are typed the item, information about the test administration, and the item-analysis data. Although maintenance creates a difficult clerical problem, a file can greatly assist the teacher who wishes to use some or all of his original test items in later tests, and also the teacher who plans to build new test items and, in so doing, wants to capitalize on past experiences.*

SUGGESTED READINGS

ANASTASI, A. *Psychological testing.* (3rd ed.) New York: Macmillan, 1968. Chapter 7.
Item difficulty and discriminating power are treated in a complete fashion. Of special interest are the item characteristic curves showing the relationship between the test item and the criterion—in this case, the total scores on the test containing the item.

COX, R. C. Item selection techniques and evaluation of instructional objectives. *Journal of Educational Measurement,* 1965, 2, 181–185.
Empirical evidence is presented indicating that item analysis data may inadvertently cause objective test items related to some educational objectives to be disproportionately eliminated from an achievement test. The first four levels of the cognitive taxonomy were used to classify the objectives.

DIEDERICH, P. B. *Short-cut statistics for teacher-made tests.* (3rd ed.) Princeton, N.J.: Educational Testing Service, 1973. Pp. 1–3.
All needed instructions are given for completing an item analysis of an achievement test by pupils' "show of hands" in the classroom. It is possible to complete an item analysis of a one-period test in ten to twenty minutes.

EBEL, R. L. *Essentials of educational measurement.* Englewood Cliffs, N.J.: Prentice-Hall, 1972. Chapter 14.
The value of item analysis data is explained, followed by illustrations of the use of such data for improving faulty multiple-choice items.

ENGELHART, M. D. A comparison of several item discrimination indices. *Journal of Educational Measurement,* 1965, *2,* 69–76.

> In this somewhat technical report, the *D* index is found to compare favorably with other measures of discriminating power such as tetrachoric coefficients of correlation, phi coefficients, and biserial and point biserial coefficients of correlation.

HENRYSSON, S. Gathering, analyzing and using data on test items. In R. L. Thorndike (ed.), *Educational measurement.* (2nd ed.) Washington: American Council on Education, 1971. Chapter 5.

> The first part of this chapter is a well-written, nontechnical presentation of the methods and principles of item analysis. In contrast, the second part deals with special problems and methods and has a stronger statistical emphasis.

REFERENCES CITED

DIEDERICH, P. B. *Short-cut statistics for teacher-made tests.* (3rd ed.) Princeton, N.J.: Educational Testing Service, 1973.

EBEL, R. L. Procedures for the analysis of classroom tests. *Educational and Psychological Measurement,* 1954, *14,* 352–364.

EBEL, R. L. *Essentials of educational measurement.* Englewood Cliffs, N.J.: Prentice-Hall, 1972.

ENGLISH, H. H., and C. M. KUBINIEC. An objective test analysis program utilizing the IBM 1230 optical mark scoring reader. *Educational and Psychological Measurement,* 1967, *27,* 165–170.

FINDLEY, W. G. A rationale for evaluation of item discrimination statistics. *Educational and Psychological Measurement,* 1956, *16,* 175–180.

FREMER, J. *Criterion-referenced interpretations of survey achievement tests.* Test Development Memorandum. Princeton, N.J.: Educational Testing Service, 1972.

HAMBLETON, R. K., and M. R. Novick. Toward an integration of theory and method for criterion-referenced tests. *Journal of Educational Measurement,* 1973, *10,* 159–170.

HENRYSSON, S. Gathering, analyzing and using data on test items. In R. L. Thorndike (ed.), *Educational measurement.* (2nd ed.) Washington: American Council on Education, 1971, chapter 5.

JOHNSON, A. P. Notes on a suggested index of item validity: The U–L index. *Journal of Educational Psychology,* 1951, *42,* 499–504.

MILLER, C. D., et al. Scoring, analyzing, and reporting classroom tests using an optical reader and 1401 computer. *Educational and Psychological Measurement,* 1967, *27,* 159–164.

RYAN, J. J. Teacher judgment of test item properties. *Journal of Educational Measurement,* 1968, *5,* 301–306.

7

JUDGING OF
PROCEDURES AND PRODUCTS

The full extent of our achievements cannot always be predicted on the basis of information about part of them. For instance, an investor may reveal widespread knowledge about the economic laws of supply and demand, the histories of prominent industrial companies, and the characteristics of economic cycles in the United States and the world, but still fail to realize anything more than an occasional modest profit when playing the stock market. An avid football fan can no doubt quote at length the rules of the game, recall accurately outstanding contests of past seasons, and even diagnose a quarterback's offensive strategy and plan effective defenses to contain it, yet be unable to play the game himself on a par with his twelve-year-old son. The music critic may command extensive knowledge of the musical score, the instruments played, and perhaps the life of the composer, but not be able to play a single note. Likewise, the mechanical engineer may be completely familiar with the principles of an internal combustion engine, the transmission and the suspension system of a modern automobile, yet not be able to drive or repair it with ease.

There are obvious parallels in formal education. A pupil studying general science may be able to cite accurately the laws on which an experiment is based and even draw schematically the apparatus needed to conduct the experiment, yet experience great difficulty when trying to set up the apparatus and reproduce the results of the original experiment. In the language arts, a pupil may quote the rules of English grammar without hesitation, spell a great variety of words, and command a large vocabulary, but be unable to write an acceptable original theme. Pupils in a home economics class may know many facts and principles about food preparation, yet fail in their attempts to prepare a baked custard that is suitable to serve.

It is clear that attempts to predict the quality of a performance involving physical activity on the basis of verbal and mathematical knowledge are often unsuccessful, not only in everyday experiences but also in the classroom. For information about the pupil's ability to perform, direct inspection of that performance is called for. This means that the pupil must be given an opportunity to perform under suitable conditions.

Evaluation of pupil performance all too often is accorded a secondary place in the pupil evaluation program. A quick study of educational objectives reveals, however, that such an attitude is unjustified. Sprinkled liberally throughout the listings of elementary and secondary school educational objectives are those directed toward development of motor skills, ability to create products of approved quality, ability to perform services efficiently, and so forth. These are largely a part of the psychomotor domain.

Note that some of the objectives of physical and biological science require that the pupil be able to manipulate apparatus and create products such as drawings of specimens, logs and diaries, precipitates, and operational mock-ups. In physical education, driver education, art, and music, many of the most important objectives are not verbal or mathematical in nature. The vocational programs, such as business, agriculture, industrial arts, and home economics, also are dominated by educational objectives that stress pupil performance. Finally, in the language arts, handwriting skill and speaking ability are integral parts of the program.

The importance of these objectives cannot be overestimated. Quite regularly, pupil success or lack of success in reaching such goals as these reveals the nature of his higher-order learning. Paper-and-pencil achievement tests are a useful but somewhat limited means of measuring complex pupil achievement. They need to be supplemented. Systematic examination of pupil performance is often an excellent means of doing this.

No doubt the principal reasons that a relatively small part of the teacher's evaluative effort is directed toward the study of pupil performance are that (1) the techniques tend to be more subjective and less dependable than paper-and-pencil achievement testing, and (2) they are aimed at more complex aspects of pupil behavior, and hence are difficult to administer, score, and interpret. In spite of these two problems, a number of useful instruments have been developed in this area. Some are directed primarily toward the procedure displayed by the pupil, whereas others are directed toward a product yielded by that procedure. Therefore, as a first step in examining these measurement efforts, it is convenient to divide pupil performance into two parts—procedures and products.

PROCEDURES AND PRODUCTS

Procedure and product are clearly interdependent, yet in terms of their description they are easily distinguished. Procedures are the sequences of movements executed by the pupil; products are the results of these procedures. A good illustration can be found in typing. The procedure learned by the pupil involves assuming a proper posture, placing the fingers on certain keys before beginning, watching the material to be typed rather than the keyboard, and striking only designated keys with each finger, doing so with the proper stroke. The product can be a typed business letter or several paragraphs or pages of prose. Similar illustrations can be found in art, mechanical drawing, handwriting, home economics, agriculture, and industrial arts.

In some educational areas, however, it is difficult to separate the two. Some of the objectives in music, physical education, and speaking are so stated that procedure and product are inextricably intermixed. The procedures could be singing a song, executing a forehand drive in tennis, or reciting a poem. The corresponding products are identified in the same manner.

Measurable Characteristics of Procedures

The complex nature of many procedures prevents a teacher from measuring all their subtle aspects. Indeed, he often feels fortunate if he can record sufficient data on just their major features. Since the time available is generally short, and a number of the characteristics of many procedures defy measurement for all practical purposes, the teacher is generally faced with a difficult task.

The characteristics that virtually defy measurement may be extremely important. For example, speaking ability should be evaluated in terms of such attributes as rhythm of talking, variety of word usage, and appropriateness of pitch and tone of voice. Shop procedures should display, among other things, an adaptability by the pupil when unforeseen difficulties arise. Performance in a physical education class should often be characterized by grace, ability, and coordination. Since these are essential features of a pupil's performance, they must be judged. But how? Clearly, the teacher must, on the basis of training and experience, establish standards for such features as these and then, in a subjective manner, classify the performance by comparing it with the standards.

The characteristics of measurable procedures can usually be classified in one of two categories—those related to the efficiency of the procedure and those related to its accuracy. Efficiency suggests a smoothness of action coupled with rapidity and a general economy of effort. Very often key data in this category are the speed of performance, as in a typing exercise, or the identification of the sequence of steps followed, as in the use of a microscope. Accuracy means that few errors are committed; moreover, those committed are relatively unimportant. For example, tabulations can be made of the number of words mispronounced and grammatical errors made during a speech. In a singing or instrumental exercise, a similar count could be made of the instances in which the pupil misjudges the pitch of a note or its duration, or the length of a rest. Clearly it is possible for a given pupil performance to have some but not all of the characteristics in each category.

Measurable Characteristics of Products

Since the quality of a product is basically a reflection of the quality of the procedure that yielded it, the tendency of a product to be complex varies directly with the complexity of its related procedure. Again, this factor increases the difficulty of the measurement. On the other hand, the time available is an important difference. Seldom does the teacher feel the extreme pressure of time limitation when examining products, as is often the case with procedures. Moreover, some products can, if necessary, be broken down into their component parts and each part analyzed; many can be subjected to rigorous measurement of various types without such a breakdown—all at a relatively leisurely pace, which simplifies the process.

The study of pupil products is highly subjective. For instance, the teacher must answer questions such as the following: Is the drawing of the biological specimen sufficiently accurate? How "light" must a cake be before it is a good product? Is the woodworking project in question esthetically attractive? What must a typing exercise look like before one can say that it is "professional" work? These and a myriad of similar questions can only be answered by the teacher applying his standards in the same subjective manner as in the case of procedure evaluation.

Measurable characteristics of products are typically numerous. For example, a typing product can be measured in terms of its length and number of errors, a woodworking product in terms of its dimensions and angle sizes. In those cases when the product has been made according to precise specifications (such as blueprint specifications), one can evaluate how closely the product conforms to them. Notice that these characteristics of products tend to be specific rather than general, and that the measurement of them is quite reliable.

Importance of a Natural Situation

Procedures and products are usually studied in a natural situation or one very much like it. This is one of the great strengths of these methods. The elaborate equipment found in the gymnasium, the science laboratories, the industrial and agricultural shops, the art and music studios, the business education rooms, and the home economics kitchens and sewing quarters of the modern school offer realistic settings in which to teach and also to evaluate pupil growth. Certainly samples of pupil behavior concerning procedures and products are being observed in a much more natural situation and much more directly when these facilities are used than when paper-and-pencil tests based upon the same specific educational objectives are administered.

The realism of these observation settings is a function of several factors, one of which is the nature and amount of equipment available. For instance, in vocational education or science courses, the equipment may differ greatly from that later used by the pupil when he leaves secondary school for a job or college. Close liaison with business, industry, and colleges plus a flexible budget for purchasing can prevent any serious gap.

Observation Techniques

The instruments used in the observation of procedure and product are primarily of the nontesting type. In other words, they can but do not necessarily yield quantitative information. Instead, they commonly include qualitative information coupled with personal impressions or opinions. Many times they function as recording devices. They provide a convenient means of organizing and summarizing the teacher's observations of pupil performances and his reaction to them.

The most widely used techniques for procedure and product observation are ranking and rating methods, check lists, product scales, and anecdotal records. Of these, teachers often rely on ranking and rating methods more than any of the others.

RANKING. Ranking is one of the lower levels of measurement. All that is attempted is an ordering of the pupils according to the merits of the procedures they displayed or the products according to their excellence. Under certain circumstances, ranking can be fairly reliable, that is, consistent. This is usually true when a competent judge is ranking a procedure or product on the basis of only one of its characteristics. Thus, members of a driver training class may be reliably ranked according to their ability to brake properly, or the drawings of a mechanical drawing class in terms of the uniformity of thickness of the straight lines. The more clearly defined the characteristic, the more likely that the ranking will be reliable.

As the basis for the ranking broadens, its reliability tends to drop. Rankings of general merit of a procedure or product in which not one but several characteristics are simultaneously considered, can be quite unreliable. Certainly the ranking of pupils' general driving ability (including posture, starting, steering, and stopping) and the general quality of their drawings (including lettering, dimensions, accuracy, and neatness) are no doubt less reliable than the rankings of single characteristics described. This drop in reliability can be traced to two causes. First, it is difficult to define clearly the meanings of these many characteristics. Second, the relative importance of each characteristic in terms of its contribution to the composite rank is rarely, if ever, completely established. Thus, it is clear that successful ranking normally must be based on a single well-defined characteristic. Moreover, if possible, the ranking should be repeated by the same (but without knowledge of the results of the first attempt) or other competent observers.

RATING. Rating scales, which take many forms, are popular devices for summarizing procedure and product information. One of the most common is the continuum form. The basic steps followed in its construction and use are as follows. Characteristics of the performance or product are identified, and a continuum representing degrees of merit is established for each characteristic. The continuum may be divided into as few as two positions or as many as ten or more, each position representing a different degree of merit or quality. The various positions along the continuum are often identified by number and, in the case of the graphic scale, a brief description of the corresponding degree of merit. The observer then rates each characteristic of the procedure or product in question by checking the number or description that corresponds most closely to the degree of merit observed. Illustrations of this type of rating scale are included in the following sections.

Rating based on overall general merit is as difficult a process as ranking on that basis. The failure to define clearly the characteristics to be included and to establish definitely the relative importance of each reduces the worth of this type of rating. Again, successful rating, like successful ranking, usually should be based on a single well-defined characteristic and should be repeated.

CHECK LISTS. Check lists are highly serviceable instruments for recording pupil procedures. Usually they list a series of actions, whether desirable or not, that are a part of a typical pupil's performance. These are arranged in a convenient manner, usually in the order in which you would expect them to occur. For instance, in the case of the check list for softball batting form shown in a following section, the sequence is: (1) grip of the bat, (2) preliminary stance, (3) stride, (4) pivot, and (5) swing.

The type of response for each entry in the check list can vary. Very often, it is simply a check mark indicating that the action listed had occurred. In other cases, a "yes-no" response is required, the "yes" response meaning that the action had been performed in a satisfactory manner, the "no" response meaning the opposite. A third type of response is one in which numbers are placed after the actions. The numbers, starting with "1," indicate the sequence in which the actions occurred. In other words, the completed check list is a step-by-step summary of the procedure followed by a particular pupil.

The development and use of check lists sensitizes the teacher to the subparts of each procedure. In this way, he gains a better view of the totality of the procedure and a more reliable technique for reporting information about it.

PRODUCT SCALES. A product scale is a carefully selected series of products representing various levels of quality. Each product in the scale is usually identified by a number or letter. Generally each scale is composed of five or more products, and an attempt is made to select these so that they are evenly spaced along an "inferior-superior" continuum of quality.

The application of a product scale is quite simple. Each pupil prepares a product of the kind included in the product scale. This is then compared with those of the scale and as close a match as possible is made. The pupil's product is then assigned the letter or number of the one in the scale it most closely resembles. An excellent example of this procedure is found in the case of handwriting, which is described in a following section.

Teachers can build product scales without great difficulty. For instance, pupil products such as drawings involving orthographic projection, sewing samples of hemming, basting, and backstitching, woodworking samples of sawing and nailing, and typing products such as a business letter, can be accumulated over a period of a few years. No doubt their quality will vary widely. Repeated independent attempts to arrange them by quality in equal-appearing intervals will eliminate many products that are near-duplicates or about which there is disagreement. The remainder can serve as a product scale.

ANECDOTAL RECORDS. Anecdotal records are the most informal of the five techniques mentioned here. The teacher does little more than summarize in writing the major actions of a procedure performed by a pupil. A definite attempt is made to produce a factual report. A single such record may mean little; however, a series of related anecdotal records can contribute appreciably to the study of pupil procedures.

Anecdotal records are used most frequently when so little is known about the procedures in question that its characteristics cannot be well defined. Thus, suitable check lists and rating scales cannot be constructed. Anecdotal records are fittingly used in those cases in the fine arts, physical education, social studies, and home economics in which the teacher is interested in expressive educational objectives.

PROBLEMS

1. Identify the measurable aspects of each of the following procedures:
   a. Executing a forehand drive in tennis.
   b. Bending a piece of glass tubing to form a right angle.

    c. Parking an automobile parallel to the curb.

    d. Hemming a dress.

  2. Identify the measurable aspects of each of the following products:

    a. A map that is an enlargement of a professionally drawn map.

    b. A short poem.

    c. An apron.

    d. A set of wooden whatnot shelves.

  3. Five main types of rating scales cited by Wrightstone (1960, pp. 929–931) are descriptive scales, graphic scales, product scales, man-to-man rating scales, and numerical scales. Study each type and determine its merits as a means of gathering data about pupil achievement.

OBSERVATION OF PROCEDURES

Techniques most often used in observation of procedures are ranking procedures, rating scales, check lists, and anecdotal records. Among the many variations of these techniques that have been developed are the following: (1) rating scales for evaluating speaking, (2) a check list for evaluating softball batting form, (3) a check list for recording skill in the use of a microscope, (4) a check list for reporting pupil behavior when engaged in group work, and (5) a sample anecdotal record concerning achievement in social studies.

Rating Scales for Speaking

The characteristics of speaking have been defined quite clearly. Among those usually listed are enunciation, pronunciation, loudness, word usage, rhythm, pitch, rate, and posture and movements. The skilled observer can separate one from another and, with appropriate rating scales, can record his judgments of the quality of a pupil's performance.

Typical of the graphic rating scales constructed and used by teachers are the pair shown in Figure 7.1, the first pertaining to enunciation and the second to pronunciation. Here only a three-point scale is used. If desired, they could be expanded to five points and appropriate descriptions added as required.

The descriptions beneath each number, though brief, are helpful. They add meaning to the numbers; as a result, the rating scales are improved. The space for comments is often an invaluable addition to the scale. Much useful specific information for evaluation and also remediation can be added. If desired, a tally of the frequency of a flaw in procedure can be added as in the case of the "agin" for "again" error in Scale B.

When a pupil is to deliver a prepared speech, some teachers prefer rating scales tailored more closely to this activity than a series such as that in Figure 7.1. For example, scales can be constructed for judging the effectiveness of such elements of the speech as the introduction used by the pupil, the body of the speech, the transition from topic to topic, and the conclusion. Added to these might be scales for judging of gestures and movements, eye contact, voice, and so forth.

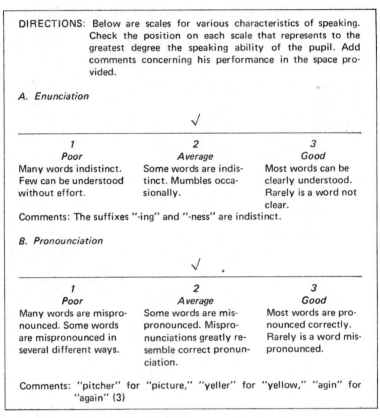

DIRECTIONS: Below are scales for various characteristics of speaking. Check the position on each scale that represents to the greatest degree the speaking ability of the pupil. Add comments concerning his performance in the space provided.

A. *Enunciation*

1	2	3
Poor	*Average*	*Good*
Many words indistinct. Few can be understood without effort.	Some words are indistinct. Mumbles occasionally.	Most words can be clearly understood. Rarely is a word not clear.

Comments: The suffixes "-ing" and "-ness" are indistinct.

B. *Pronounciation*

1	2	3
Poor	*Average*	*Good*
Many words are mispronounced. Some words are mispronounced in several different ways.	Some words are mispronounced. Mispronunciations greatly resemble correct pronunciation.	Most words are pronounced correctly. Rarely is a word mispronounced.

Comments: "pitcher" for "picture," "yeller" for "yellow," "agin" for "again" (3)

FIGURE 7.1. **Sample Rating Scales for Judging Speaking Ability.**

Check List for Batting Form

Check lists and rating scales may not differ as much as descriptions of them would suggest. The "comments" sections frequently included in rating scales allow space in which the observer can note specific features of the pupil's behavior; in a check list the most common of these features would be listed and, hence, checked only when appropriate. On the other hand, some check lists include crude representations of continua much like those found in rating scales.

An illustration of a check list that is based in part on a series of rating scales is that shown in Figure 7.2. This is designed to record observations of batting form (Scott and French, 1959, pp. 421–423). Each time a pupil bats, an observer checks "good," "fair," or "poor" with respect to his grip, stance, stride, pivot, and swing. Then the observer checks in the right-hand column the errors that are committed. The list of errors is expanded if necessary. An experienced observer can complete such a check list as this very quickly and with acceptable accuracy.

Date	Rater's initials	Player's name _____
_____	_____	Captain's name _____

Instructions: Rate the player each time he bats. Place a tally mark in the space which precedes the best description of player's form in each of six categories. Indicate your observation of errors in the right-hand half of the page, again with a tally mark. Write in any additional errors and add comments below.

1. Grip
   _____ good
   _____ fair
   _____ poor

2. Preliminary stance
   _____ good
   _____ fair
   _____ poor

3. Stride or footwork
   _____ good
   _____ fair
   _____ poor

4. Pivot or body twist
   _____ good
   _____ fair
   _____ poor

5. Arm movement or swing
   _____ good
   _____ fair
   _____ poor

6. General (Eyes on ball, judgment of pitcher, etc.)
   _____ good
   _____ fair
   _____ poor

Errors
_____ Hands too far apart
_____ Wrong hand on top
_____ Hands too far from end of bat

_____ Stands too near plate
_____ Stands too far away
_____ Rear foot closer to plate than forward foot
_____ Stands too far forward
_____ Stands too far backward
_____ Bat resting on shoulders
_____ Shoulders not horizontal

_____ Fails to step forward
_____ Fails to transfer weight
_____ Lifts back foot from ground

_____ Fails to twist body
_____ Fails to wind up
_____ Has less than 90° of pivot

_____ Arms held too close to body
_____ Rear elbow elevated
_____ Bat not held so that head is higher than wrists
_____ Fails to use enough wrist action
_____ Wrists are not uncocked forcefully

_____ Jerky movements
_____ Tries too hard
_____ Fails to look at exact center of ball
_____ Poor judgment of pitches
_____ Lacks confidence
_____ Poor selection of bat

FIGURE 7.2. Sample Check List for Softball Batting Form.
From Scott and French, 1959; reproduced by permission of the publisher, Wm. C. Brown Company.

Check List for Operation of a Microscope

One of the better known check lists is that devised by Tyler (1930) for use in reporting a pupil's ability to use a microscope. A small part of it is shown in Figure 7.3. In all, fifty-four "student actions" are included in the master list. A given pupil may perform twenty-five or more when operating a microscope.

The teacher observes operation of a microscope by a pupil who is attempting to find a specified substance present in a culture. All needed materials such as slides, cheesecloth, and lens paper are provided. As the pupil attacks the problem, the teacher records the sequence of actions by numbering them as they occur. He also checks the most obvious characteristics of the pupil's behavior and his mount and the skills in which he needs further training.

The numbers in Figure 7.3 serve as the first part of a description of one pupil's efforts to manipulate a microscope. Only his first seven actions are reported here. The complete check list would show all important desirable and undesirable actions made, and the order in which he made them.

Check List for Behavior in Group Work

Teachers frequently want to determine whether their pupils are acquiring and practicing desirable social habits and attitudes. Some of these are revealed when the pupils are engaged in committee and group work. Of interest in these instances are such pupil behaviors as willingness to cooperate, volunteering for duties, making worthwhile suggestions, and displaying democratic leadership. To provide a situation in which these behaviors can be displayed, a committee of pupils is formed to perform some tasks, such as drawing a map of the playground or planning class observance of a national holiday. The behaviors displayed can be recorded on a check list.

	Student's actions	Sequence of actions
a.	Takes slide	1
b.	Wipes slide with lens paper	2
c.	Wipes slide with cloth	
d.	Wipes slide with finger	
e.	Moves bottle of culture along the table	
f.	Places drop or two of culture on slide	3
g.	Adds more culture	
h.	Adds few drops of water	
i.	Hunts for cover glasses	4
j.	Wipes cover glass with lens paper	5
k.	Wipes cover with cloth	
l.	Wipes cover with finger	
m.	Adjusts cover with finger	
n.	Wipes off surplus fluid	
o.	Places slide on stage	6
p.	Looks through eyepiece with right eye	
q.	Looks through eyepiece with left eye	7

FIGURE 7.3. Partial Check List for Reporting Skill in Using a Microscope.

From Tyler, 1930; reproduced by permission of the Bureau of Educational Research and Service, Ohio State University.

DIRECTIONS: Below are eight kinds of behavior that a pupil might display when participating in committee or group work. Check "Yes" if it occurred; check "No" if it did not. If the evidence available is insufficient or conflicting, check "Uncertain."

BEHAVIOR	YES	NO	UNCERTAIN
1. Starts working promptly			
2. Volunteers for assignments			
3. Displays interest			
4. Cooperates with other pupils			
5. Displays cheerfulness			
6. Makes worthwhile suggestions			
7. Is a follower occasionally			
8. Is a leader occasionally			

FIGURE 7.4. Sample Check List for Reporting Pupil Behavior in Group Work.

A sample check list of the kind that might be used in these situations is shown in Figure 7.4. Eight kinds of behaviors are listed. The teacher is to check whether each occurred. Should the evidence be insufficient or conflicting, he checks the category labeled "Uncertain." Observe that this category is not a middle position between "Yes" and "No." Instead it is a position that indicates that the teacher is unable to make a judgment for any number of reasons. Perhaps the pupil has no opportunity to display the behavior in question throughout the period that the committee is at work. Perhaps the teacher is unable to observe the pupil as long as he desires. Perhaps the pupil behaved inconsistently. The last might be the subject of anecdotal records that would then supplement the check list.

Anecdotal Record in Social Studies

Recording observations of spontaneous procedures is seldom an easy task. Yet much of this behavior is very indicative of learning already acquired, and hence it cannot be ignored. The anecdotal record reports the principal details of the procedures observed, and when a series of them is available concerning related procedures, interesting insights into learning can be gained.

The sample anecdotal record shown in Figure 7.5 concerns a comparatively shy junior high school boy who surprised his teacher by insisting that he make his oral report to a social studies class as scheduled, even though he had accidentally left his written notes at home. His level of performance revealed an unusual degree of knowledge and interest in his topic and offered possible clues with regard to ways to

---

ANECDOTAL RECORD FORM

Date: November 16, 1975　　　　　　　　Pupil's Name: Fred Burke

Observer: R. S. Rover

Description of Incident:

Fred was scheduled to make an oral report to the class concerning cattle branding. Although he forgot his notes, he did not want a postponement. He specifically requested that he report as planned.

He spoke extemporaneously and used the blackboard repeatedly to sketch the various brands he mentioned. Much information was presented, including references to the history of the American West. The class was unusually attentive.

Comment:

This was by far the best report he has given. For the first time he was visibly pleased with his efforts. He evidently knows much about the history of the early West, and enjoys talking about it.

FIGURE 7.5. Sample Anecdotal Record Pertaining to Achieve-
　　　　　　　ment in Social Studies.

involve him to a greater degree in future classroom discussions. Notice the factual nature of the description of the incident as contrasted with the interpretive nature of the comments that follow it.

This case of pupil behavior differs from those previously considered in this chapter. In speaking, batting, and microscope skill, the observer is interested in the efficiency and accuracy with which the procedure is executed. These, too, might be the subjects of anecdotal records. Here, however, the observer is primarily concerned with the fact that this behavior happened at all. In other words, a helpful insight into a pupil's achievement in social studies is obtained by noting what he did and how he reacted to it rather than the level of quality of specific features of his behavior. For example, whether he enunciated clearly or had well-organized material for his oral report is not so important.

PROBLEMS

4. Would the check list for reporting pupil behavior in group work shown in Figure 7.4 be improved if a column entitled "Sometimes" were inserted between the "Yes" and "No" columns and the directions changed appropriately? Why?

5. Using the anecdotal record shown in Figure 7.5 as an example, list the inherent limitations present in this reporting technique.

JUDGING OF PRODUCTS

Ranking procedures, rating scales (including score cards; see Arny, 1953), and product scales are popular means by which pupil products are studied. As illustrations of some of the many possibilities offered by these techniques, three instruments are described here: (1) rating scales for theme analysis, (2) rating scales for judging pupil success in fastening pieces of wood with nails, and (3) product scales used for judging handwriting specimens.

Rating Scales for Themes

Many subjects occasionally require a largely original written product of the pupil. English courses are—and should be—especially demanding in this respect. The well-known English theme calls upon the pupil to select a topic, arrange its subparts in a suitable manner, and develop them in appropriate written form. From a measurement point of view, a theme is both an important and a complex product.

The complex nature of a theme makes its evaluation difficult. To overcome this problem, some teachers divide the characteristics of a theme into two categories, content and matters of form and style. The content categories include the selection of the topic (if topics are not assigned), organization, and the quantity and quality of investigation. The form and style category includes the elements of grammar, punctuation, vocabulary, spelling, capitalization, division of words, documentation, and so forth.

The relative importance of the two categories and their respective subparts no doubt varies radically from teacher to teacher, depending on the purpose of the theme and the maturity of the pupil. For example, themes in a social studies class should be scrutinized more carefully in terms of content than form and style. The reverse may be true for most themes in an English class. In addition, the subparts of a category, such as the quantity and quality of investigation of the topic and the documentation of the theme, will probably lose importance when one is judging themes from lower grade levels.

Sample rating scales for themes are shown in Figure 7.6. Only two are shown, one from each category. Notice that these are five-point scales although only three descriptions are included. An observer vacillating between two of the positions for which descriptions are available may want to select the intermediate position. A series of similar scales for other characteristics in each category can be developed.

Diederich (1964) suggests two sets of five-point rating scales that could be used for judging English compositions. One category deals with general merit and has four scales: (1) quality and development of ideas, (2) organization, relevance, and movement, (3) style, flavor, and individuality, and (4) wording and phrasing. The other deals with mechanics, and its four scales are (1) grammar and sentence structure, (2) punctuation and capitalization, (3) spelling, and (4) handwriting and neatness.

Some doubt exists as to the need for sets of criteria such as those mentioned in this section. There is little evidence that they are consistently used (Fostvedt, 1965). Moreover, other investigations have established that a fast impressionistic reading of essays by several qualified readers is a reliable method of measuring pupil writing ability (Godshalk et al., 1966). This method requires the reader of themes and essays to make "global or holistic" judgments of each paper rather than analytical judgments. The theme is read quickly for total impressions and given one of three ratings: a score of "3" for a superior paper, "2" for an average paper, and "1" for an inferior paper.

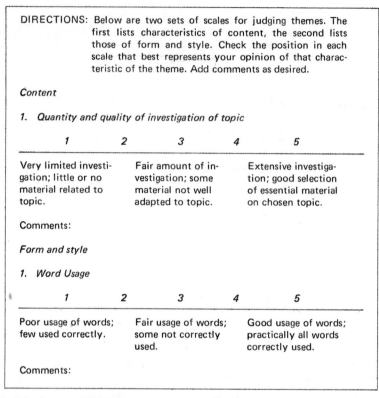

FIGURE 7.6. Sample Rating Scales for Judging Themes.

Attempts to grade essays by means of a computer are described in connection with procedures for scoring responses to essay test questions (see page 143). This work is promising. If the computer can consistently appraise writing ability as well as competent judges can or better, we have made a significant breakthrough in our ability to evaluate this important work product.

Rating Scales for Shop Products

Many shop products must conform to prescribed dimensions and, as a result, mechanical devices can be used as one means of determining their quality. For instance, rules, combination squares, calipers, and gauges of various kinds are employed in this process. In a very direct manner, one or more measurements are obtained that reveal the success or failure of the pupil to develop a product of a certain size, with certain proportions, or within certain tolerance limits.

Helpful as mechanical devices are, they are not capable of measuring all of the important characteristics of a shop product. Anyone who has carefully examined wood, metal, or plastic shop products realizes that two such products may have nearly identical dimensions, but still differ noticeably in workmanship. Characteristics such as esthetic attractiveness, strength, finish, design, and neatness must be judged by other techniques.

A set of numerical rating scales reported by Adkins (1947, p. 231) for fastening edges of pieces of wood with nails is shown in Figure 7.7. Many of these scales are related to the characteristics of strength, attractiveness, and neatness mentioned in the foregoing paragraph. For example, the splitting, spacing, and utility scales are a part of the strength characteristic; the hammer marks and depth scales are a part of the attractiveness and neatness characteristics.

Notice that a ten-point scale is given for each factor. It is quite possible that a teacher will find that he is unable to identify this many degrees of quality. If he finds that fewer than ten points will suffice, the scale should be so revised. Also notice that, unlike the other rating scales included in this chapter, these scales contain a question as a part of each scale and no brief descriptions of the positions. Whether this format is an improvement is for you to decide. Perhaps both techniques could be used to advantage.

Product Scales for Handwriting

Two styles of writing are generally taught in the elementary school. One is the manuscript style, in which the letters are disconnected and made in a form similar to printed letters. The other is the cursive style, in which the letters of each word are connected. The general practice is to teach manuscript writing first, and then change to cursive writing at about the third grade.

The easiest way to gather information about pupil achievement in handwriting,

(1)	Straightness	1	2	3	4	5	6	7	8	9	10

Are nails driven straight, heads square with wood, no evidence of bending?

(2)	Hammer marks	1	2	3	4	5	6	7	8	9	10

Is wood free of hammer marks around nails?

(3)	Splitting	1	2	3	4	5	6	7	8	9	10

Is wood free of splits radiating from nail holes?

(4)	Depth	1	2	3	4	5	6	7	8	9	10

Are depths of nails uniform and of pleasing appearance?

(5)	Spacing	1	2	3	4	5	6	7	8	9	10

Are nails spaced too close or too far apart?

(6)	Utility	1	2	3	4	5	6	7	8	9	10

Will the nails hold?

FIGURE 7.7. Sample Rating Scales for Fastening.
From Adkins, 1947; reproduced by permission of D. C. Adkins.

whether manuscript or cursive style, is to examine specimens that have been obtained under controlled conditions. Both speed and quality can be determined. The speed or rate at which pupils write is the more easily measured of the two. Quality can be defined in many ways. Thorndike, who built the first scale for measuring quality of handwriting, interpreted quality to mean beauty, legibility, and character. Ayres, whose scale is described below, considered quality to mean legibility only.

Speed of handwriting can be measured by a teacher-made test if it is carefully administered. First, the teacher selects a simple statement such as "Mary had a little lamb" or "The quick brown fox jumps over the lazy dog." The statement should be so simple that it can be easily memorized; it should have no unusual words or expressions that will in any way hinder the pupil in his speed test. After the statement has been memorized by the pupils, they are told that, when given a signal, they should start to write the statement as well and as rapidly as they can, and continue to do so until told to stop. Either two or three minutes are allowed. The number of letters written by each pupil is counted and divided by the number of minutes allowed.

One of the most widely used scales for measuring the quality of handwriting is the *Ayres Measuring Scale for Handwriting, Gettysburg Edition*. Before the scale can be used, the pupils must be thoroughly familiar with the first three sentences of Lincoln's Gettysburg Address. Then they are given two minutes in which to copy them. To determine quality, each pupil's handwriting specimen is then compared with a scaled series of printed samples. There are eight samples in all. The comparison is made by sliding each specimen along the scale until a printed sample of the same or very similar quality is found. The number above this sample is the value assigned to the pupil's specimen. The numbers increase as the quality of the specimen improves.

Teachers have not been able to get consistent results when using product scales to study handwriting samples (Feldt, 1962). To improve this situation, at least three handwriting samples should be obtained independently from each pupil and the ratings averaged. This can be repeated each time pupil growth is to be checked in this area of achievement.

PROBLEM

RATING SCALE

5	4	3	2	1
Very neat	Neat	Fairly neat	Somewhat messy	Messy
Words are printed not written	Printed	Some words might not be printed	Written	Written
Has title and key	Both title and key	Might lack correct title or key	Might lack title or key	Lacks both
Has shown rivers and lakes most clearly	Has shown all rivers and lakes	Lacks one or two required items	Lacks several items	Lacks a lot of items

6. Seventh-grade pupils in social studies were required to draw a map showing the principal rivers and lakes in their home state. They were allowed to refer to,

but not copy directly, printed maps. The preceding graphic rating scales were to be used first by each pupil and then by the teacher to judge the product of his efforts. Revise these scales in any manner that, in your opinion, will strengthen them.

RELIABILITY OF JUDGING PUPIL PERFORMANCE

Judging pupil performance is typically less objective and organized than paper-and-pencil testing, and sometimes less satisfying to both teacher and pupil. Many of these problems are associated directly with a serious weakness of judging performance, that is, its relatively high degree of unreliability. A high degree of unreliability means that the procedures frequently yield inconsistent results.

This can be traced both to the performance evaluated and to the observer. In other words, the reliability of the process is directly related to the degree of successful sampling of pupil performance and the consistency of the observer in judging that performance.

Sampling Pupil Performances

Sampling pupil performances is necessarily limited in scope. How many times is it possible for a pupil to deliver a prepared speech, build a pair of bookends, or cut out and sew an apron? The teacher may have only one or two opportunities to observe these performances, and they may not take place under conditions that he can control as much as he would like. Yet he must assume that they are typical representations of pupil achievement.

Some pupil products require considerable quantities of both class and out-of-class time in which to be completed. As a result, unauthorized assistance by a second party is likely. The product then becomes much less useful in terms of judging pupil achievement in that it is a poor sample of his work.

Ideally, then, the teacher should have at least several opportunities to observe an important pupil performance. Such samples should truly reflect the pupil's achievement and his alone, and should take place under suitable conditions.

Observer Reliability

Fatigue, boredom, and indifference can destroy the worth of the observer's attempts to examine pupil performance. To reduce the impact of these factors, the teacher can preplan his observations as much as possible, being certain that he spreads them out over a reasonable period of time. On the other hand, since these and other factors can never be eliminated fully, multiple observation is desirable. This means that, in the case of judging procedures, several competent teachers should observe independently, then reconcile any differences that exist. In the case of judging products, several persons can participate, or one can judge the product more than once without knowledge of earlier decisions.

Unfortunately, consistent results yielded by efforts to judge a pupil's performance do not necessarily mean that a proper analysis has been made. After all, the observer or even a team of observers could be consistently wrong. This, of course, is unlikely if the observers are reasonably competent. On the other hand, such factors as the well-known "halo effect," so often present in efforts of this kind, can make the analyses more consistent but less accurate. For improvement of observer reliability, well-defined reference points are needed. In the case of procedures, these may be careful descriptions of the important aspects of various degrees of quality; in the case of products, they may be a variety of specimen products of known quality.

Use of Performance Tests to Improve Reliability

Performance tests of considerable complexity are sometimes used for improving the quality of procedures and product evaluation. These are tests in which some criterion situation (for example, a job) is simulated to a higher degree than is represented by the usual paper-and-pencil test (Fitzpatrick and Morrison, 1971). On the basis of a careful analysis of the education objectives in question, a great effort is made to design a realistic situation for the examinee within which he can demonstrate his skills.

To develop a performance test, it is necessary to specify exactly what the pupil is to do and the conditions under which he is to do it (Boyd and Shimberg, 1971). One must decide (1) which elements of the task are crucial to success, (2) which of these are to be measured, (3) the equipment and/or materials that are needed, (4) the time required, (5) the standard conditions that should exist, and (6) the instructions to the pupils and the observers. Carefully tailored to the foregoing are appropriate rating and check list forms.

With thorough planning, we can design highly useful performance tests in physical education, foreign languages, industrial arts, music, and many areas of vocational education. Such tests typically combine appropriate equipment arranged in a true-to-life environment with a set of explicit instructions to the examinee. These permit a trained observer to use specially designed rating scales or check lists to report the quality of performance with a comparatively high degree of reliability. The improved reliability is well worth the effort.

The National Assessment of Educational Progress uses test items requiring pupil performance in a wide variety of subject matter areas such as science (e.g., using a balance), music (e.g., singing a standard piece of music), and citizenship (e.g., participating in standardized group situations). These items are individually administered on a national basis and present difficult scoring problems. Nevertheless, high degrees of reliability are obtained. On the basis of this evidence, it is safe to say that classroom teachers can and should do more of this type of testing.

PROBLEMS

7. It has been recommended that, as an aid in judging pupil compositions properly, files of various sorts of pupils' writing should be kept from year to

year (Burrows, 1959, pp. 27–28). Do you think that this procedure would improve the reliability of judging writing ability to any appreciable degree?

8. The closer that a performance test approaches the real criterion situation it simulates, the more likely that the reliability of the measurement of pupil performance will *decrease* (Fitzpatrick and Morrison, 1971). What causes this?

JUDGING BY PUPILS

Pupils as well as teachers can judge performances—their own and also those of their classmates. For example, an audience of pupils can rate a speaker, and he can rate himself. In a food laboratory, all pupils including the cook can examine the roast that is prepared. A pupil who submits a specimen of handwriting can arrive at his own judgment of its merits by following the same procedures the teacher follows.

Much can be said for this type of multiple evaluation as a learning experience. When both pupils and teacher use the same instruments to judge the same performance simultaneously, and the results are examined, the pupils gain a much better perspective of the important features of the performance and the teacher's standards concerning them. Particularly informative is the comparison of the self-evaluation by the pupil with that made independently by his teacher. Certainly the diagnosis of defects and their causes as well as remediation can be based on such a conference. Most important to the pupil is the realistic view of his achievement that he gains.

From the point of view of sound principles of evaluation, there are serious objections to using the pupils' judgments or a composite of them in reporting pupil achievement. Certainly we cannot assume that the average pupil is as competent a judge of the quality of another's performance or of his own as the teacher. This automatically reduces the value of pupil observations to a point where they are normally of minor importance. The successful observer has a maturity of judgment and sense of impartiality rarely found in pupils. Pupils should be regularly allowed to gain experience in observing, but they should not be expected to make sound judgments with great consistency unless carefully trained.

PROBLEM

9. Some teachers believe, that, as pupils become skilled in self-evaluation, they actually raise the standards on which evaluations are made. Do you agree? Why?

SUMMARY

The following are the major points included in this chapter:

1. *Some educational objectives are such that paper-and-pencil measuring instruments cannot reveal the degree to which pupils have achieved them. These goals pertain to pupil performances such as the ability to deliver a speech, write a paragraph, conduct an experiment, or hem a garment. Generally they*

are quite complex, involving both language and nonlanguage aspects, and are a part of the psychomotor domain.

2. Judgments of pupil performance can be based on the procedure displayed by the pupil or the products yielded by the procedure. Both have some characteristics that lend themselves readily to measurement and some that do not. Efficiency and accuracy are the procedure characteristics most often evaluated. Product characteristics can often be measured more easily; in fact, mechanical devices are available for this purpose for such articles as shop products.

3. The instruments used in judging procedures and products are primarily of the nontesting type. For procedures, ranking and rating methods, check lists, and anecdotal records are frequently applied. For products, ranking and rating methods and product scales are used. In all cases, a competent observer is needed.

4. Performance evaluation is not always reliable because pupil performance is not always successfully sampled and the observer not always consistent. Repeated sampling of pupil performances and independent observations by one or more qualified teachers increase the reliability of the process.

5. When pupils judge their own performances or those of their classmates, they gain excellent experience in this process, although their attempts seldom produce superior evaluative data.

SUGGESTED READINGS

AHMANN, J. S., M. D. GLOCK, and H. L. WARDEBERG. *Evaluating elementary school pupils.* Boston: Allyn and Bacon, 1960. Chapters 11, 12, and 13.
    The three chapters cited deal with appraisal in the language arts, mathematics, and the content areas, respectively. A number of rating scales and check lists to be used with elementary school pupils are shown.

BLOOM, B. S., J. T. HASTINGS, and G. F. MADAUS. *Handbook on formative and summative evaluation of student learning.* New York: McGraw-Hill, 1971. Chapters 17, 18, 21, and 23.
    These chapters deal with the evaluation of learning in art, science, writing, and industrial education respectively. Evaluation of pupil performance in these areas is included.

BOYD, J. L., and B. SHIMBERG. *Developing performance tests for classroom evaluation.* TM Reports, No. 4. Princetion, N.J.: ERIC Clearinghouse for Tests, Measurement, and Evaluation, 1971.
    The nature of performance and problems associated with the development of performance tests are discussed.

FITZPATRICK, R., and E. J. MORRISON. Performance and product evaluation. In R. L. Thorndike (ed.), *Educational measurement.* (2nd ed.) Washington: American Council on Education, 1971. Chapter 9.
    Performance tests to measure achievement are described, and a wide variety of illustrations of them is given. Steps for developing and scoring performance tests are presented.

GODSHALK, F. I., et al. *The measurement of writing ability.* New York: College Entrance Examination Board, 1966. Chapters 1 and 2.
    The first two chapters describe the problem of measuring writing ability and measuring devices to be tested. Of particular interest are the illustrations of the objective test items and interlinear exercises used to measure writing ability indirectly. A short description of the "global" and "holistic" method of scoring essays is included.

WRIGHTSTONE, J. W. Observational techniques. In C. W. Harris (ed.), *Encyclopedia of educational research.* (3rd ed.) New York: Macmillan, 1960. Pp. 927–933.
    Research on observational techniques of all kinds is summarized. Separate sections are devoted to time samples, rating methods, and anecdotal records.

REFERENCES CITED

ADKINS, D.C. *Construction and analysis of achievement tests.* Washington: U.S. Civil Service Commission, 1947.

ARNY, C. B. *Evaluation in home economics.* New York: Appleton-Century-Crofts, 1953.

BOYD, J. L., and B. SHIMBERG. *Developing performance tests for classroom evaluation.* TM Reports, No. 4. Princeton, N.J.: ERIC Clearinghouse for Tests, Measurement, and Evaluation, 1971.

BURROWS, A. T. *Teaching composition.* What Research Says to the Teacher, No. 18. Washington: National Education Association, 1959.

DIEDERICH, P. B. Problems and possibilities of research in the teaching of English. In *Research design and the teaching of English,* Proceedings of Conference of National Council of Teachers of English. Champaign, Ill.: National Council of Teachers of English, 1964.

FELDT, L. S. The reliability of measures of handwriting quality. *Journal of Educational Psychology,* 1962, 53, 288–292.

FITZPATRICK, R., and E. J. MORRISON. Performance and product evaluation. In R. L. Thorndike (ed.), *Educational measurement.* (2nd ed.) Washington: American Council on Education, 1971, chapter 9.

FOSTVEDT, D. R. Criteria for the evaluation of high school English composition. *Journal of Educational Research,* 1965, 59, 108–112.

GODSHALK, F. I., et al. *The measurement of writing ability.* New York: College Entrance Examination Board, 1966.

SCOTT, M. G., and E. FRENCH. *Measurement and evaluation in physical education.* Dubuque, Iowa: William C. Brown, 1959.

TYLER, R. W. A test of skill in using a microscope. *Educational Research Bulletin,* 1930, 9, 493–496.

WRIGHTSTONE, J. W. Observational techniques. In C. W. Harris (ed.), *Encyclopedia of educational research.* (3rd ed.) New York: Macmillan, 1960, 927–933.

PART THREE

Characteristics of a Good Measuring Instrument

An unknown wit of several generations ago remarked that the only good thing about error was that it created jobs. The truth of this can be demonstrated in many areas including pupil evaluation. All of our measuring instruments are somewhat inadequate, a number of them to an appreciable degree. To reduce error, the builders of these instruments are striving constantly to refine their products; this is, in a sense, an endless job. These efforts in turn complicate the problems of those who must choose from among many available measuring instruments the ones that are best suited for a particular need. Each new instrument means a repetition of the job of selection by anyone needing an instrument of that type.

The classroom teacher may find himself cast in either or both of the following roles: in one case, he may be constructing a paper-and-pencil achievement test to measure the academic achievement of his pupils; in a second, he may be a member of a teacher committee organized to select a scholastic aptitude or standardized achievement test to be used as a part of the school testing program. In either case the teacher needs standards. He must be familiar with the characteristics of a good measuring instrument and the methods of determining the degree to which a given instrument may possess them.

The characteristics of a good measuring instrument can be classified in many different ways. Here they are grouped under three headings: norms, validity, and reliability. These three headings identify the three chapters that compose Part Three. In Chapter 8, "Using Test Scores and Norms," the need for an instrument to yield information that is easily understood and utilized is discussed. This need is ordinarily satisfied for criterion- and objective-referenced tests by writing statements describing pupil behavior, and for norm-referenced tests by computing norms, that is, by identifying the relative performance of a pupil in terms of a group of pupils much like him. Chapter 9, "The Validity of Measurement Methods," is devoted to the most important of the three characteristics. A measuring instrument is valid to the degree that it serves the purpose or purposes for which its use is intended. In Chapter 10, "The Reliability of Measurement Methods," the need for an instrument to yield consistent or dependable information is discussed. An instrument that strongly reflects this characteristic will yield virtually the same information each time it is used in an unchanging situation.

Chapter 8, concerning test scores, and Chapter 10, concerning reliability, concentrate almost exclusively on norm-referenced tests. The critical feature of criterion- and objective-referenced tests is content validity, which is presented in Chapter 9, concerning validity.

Some statistical methodology must be introduced to describe these characteristics and how they are measured. The arithmetic mean, the median, the standard deviation, and the product-moment coefficient of correlation are discussed at appropriate points in Part Three. In Appendix A is an additional explanation of these statistical measures, as well as a step-by-step description of the easiest means of computing each. Although classroom teachers are seldom required to compute such values, they are often required to interpret them in connection with the validity, reliability, and norm determinations found in test manuals and educational literature.

The purpose of Part Three is to identify the characteristics of a good measuring instrument, to illustrate the most common methods of determining how strongly a specific instrument reflects them, and to provide an adequate background for those statistical techniques commonly used in such determinations. The importance of Part Three can hardly be overemphasized.

8

USING TEST SCORES AND NORMS

Early every morning, practically every radio station in the United States broadcasts a summary of the weather conditons in the locality at that moment and as they probably will be for the remainder of the day. Typical of the kind of announcement that might be heard on a morning in mid-April is the following:

The temperature at 7:00 A.M. this morning was 50°F., the barometric pressure was 29.8, the wind velocity was 10 to 20 miles per hour from the northwest, and the relative humidity was 70 percent. Today will be cloudy and mild, with a high temperature of about 60°F. The probability of measurable precipitation today is 5 percent.

To most listeners, this report, brief as it is, is useful. As he prepares for the day's activities the informed citizen can readily decide such questions as whether he should wear a spring topcoat rather than a winter overcoat, make his son of preschool age button his woolen sweater before leaving the house, or plan an early season golf or tennis match.

The teacher, while he has a common interest with the public in the weather report, may well ponder two additional features of this interpretation of meteorological conditions. These features are involved in the teacher's attempts at describing a pupil to a parent.

In the first place, the complexity of the entity being described is almost overwhelming. A one-word description in either case would be unhappily inadequate. Multiple measurements are involved in a weather report or a well-designed school testing program.

The second feature is the meaning of the measurements when they are reported to a relatively uninformed audience. Here the meteorologist has an advantage over the educator. Each of us learns at a tender age that temperatures in the vicinity of 70° F are comfortable, whereas those in excess of 90° F and less than 60° F tend to be uncomfortable unless appropriate adjustments in dress or physical activity are made. A barometric pressure is almost automatically compared to 30 inches of mercury, the ordinary barometric pressure at sea level. Wind velocities of less than 10 miles per hour are conceded to be practically unnoticeable; velocities between 30 and 75 miles per hour are called gales. Little more need be said to prepare most individuals for the weather. These facts are understood.

Teachers may envy the meteorologist's ability to present succinct, understandable descriptions of something as intricate as the weather. Although the meteorologist has not achieved perfection in his efforts, he can point to notable success. A teacher may well question whether those same individuals who seem to comprehend so much of a brief report on the day's weather would understand comparable amounts of a report on the academic achievement of their child that day in school. It is understandable, therefore, why so much attention is paid to the nature of test scores and their interpretation.

RAW SCORES

The difficulty of meaningfully presenting the results yielded by educational measurement has many illustrations. Assume, for example, that a battery of norm-referenced standardized achievement tests is administered to the pupils in all of the tenth grades of a city school system. One is a vocabulary test composed of 100 words, the meanings of which have to be identified by each pupil. The success of each pupil is then expressed in terms of the number of words correctly identified. Therefore, for each of the 360 pupils who wrote the vocabulary test, a numerical representation of his effort is available, and it can be no smaller than zero nor larger than 100.

Let us consider for a moment the position of a teacher whose pupils are involved in the testing program. One of his pupils correctly identified the meaning of fifty-eight of the 100 words. Hence the teacher records a "58." This he properly calls a *raw score*, that is, the quantitative report that is the immediate end product of scoring the test. In the case of this test and many others like it, each pupil is credited with one point for every correct answer and zero points for any wrong or omitted answer. To be sure, the amount of credit could have varied for each right answer, increasing to two points or more as the words became more difficult. Furthermore, correction for guessing on the part of the pupil could have been made by subtracting points for wrong answers. Had either or both of these procedures been used, the result of the scoring process would still be called a raw score.

Simply labeling the "58" as one of many raw scores does not answer other questions concerning this representation of degree of success. For example, the teacher may wonder whether fifty-eight indicates that this pupil's vocabulary of words is twice as great as that of a pupil whose score on the same test is only twenty-nine. Certainly it is tempting to assume that this is true. Yet the whole idea, in reality, is absurd. Such a comparison of the raw scores cannot, unfortunately, be made unless the units of measurement possess certain characteristics, that is, the characteristics of a ratio scale. Principal among these is the requirement that a raw score of zero represent a total absence of knowledge of word meanings. Of course, such total absence could not be true in this case.

Absolute Zero

The failure of the raw score of size zero to indicate zero knowledge of vocabulary is equivalent to saying that it is not an absolute zero. In other words, unlike the customary measurement of height and weight, the units of measurement of the vocabulary test are relative. Relativity is a common characteristic of test scores.

Like many achievement tests, the vocabulary test is deliberately constructed in such a way that a score of zero is not an absolute zero. If for no reason other than economy of time and energy, such simple words as *dog, house,* and *bicycle* are not included in the test, since they do not differentiate among pupils of a typical tenth-grade class. On the other hand, words like *immaculate, predicament,* and *conscientious* may very likely be of acceptable difficulty for the class and hence are included in the test. Instruments such as the vocabulary test are generally designed to have a relatively small difficulty spread, around the fifty percent level, so that all pupils to be measured will be represented on the scale rather than somewhere below or above it.

This idea can be translated into a diagram such as Figure 8.1. Although this figure is but an approximate representation of the relationship between the raw scores of the vocabulary achievement test and its level of difficulty, it nevertheless illustrates two noteworthy points. First of all, it is evident that a raw score of zero differs from absolute zero by some large and unknown distance. Obviously, the distance between a raw score of fifty-eight and absolute zero is not twice the distance between a raw score of twenty-nine and absolute zero. The second point concerns the level of difficulty of

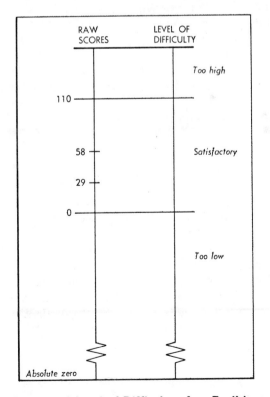

FIGURE 8.1. Raw Scores and Level of Difficulty of an English Vocabulary Test for Tenth-Grade Pupils.

the instrument. Of course, the satisfactory level of difficulty for this achievement test varies with the group of pupils for whom it is designed. It would move up the scale for twelfth-grade pupils and down for eighth-grade pupils. If the test is carefully constructed, its raw-score spread will fall directly opposite the satisfactory level of difficulty as illustrated.

Figure 8.1 resembles the situation that might exist if a school nurse wished to obtain the relative rather than the absolute heights of a group of secondary school girls. To do so she could nail a yardstick vertically to the wall at a position such that every girl would be found to be at least as tall as the distance between the floor and the lower edge and no taller than the distance between the floor and the upper edge of the yardstick. Her knowledge of typical heights of girls of this age group would help her to make a satisfactory approximation of the position. After the yardstick is in place, each girl stands barefooted at a point beneath the yardstick and a reading can be made.

There are two similarities between this determination of relative height and the vocabulary test. In the first place, the relative heights would be very acceptable information for differentiating among the girls in terms of height, just as the vocabulary test scores can differentiate among the tenth-grade pupils. Ratios between these heights, however, like ratios between the test scores, defy interpretation. Certainly a girl with a relative height of twenty-two inches is not twice as tall as a girl with a relative height of eleven inches. Secondly, determining a suitable position on the wall at which to nail the yardstick is essentially the same as selecting the vocabulary test items of satisfactory difficulty. In both cases, changes would be made if different groups of subjects were measured.

The failure of educational measuring instruments to have an absolute zero is not as serious as it may first seem. The continued successful use of the Fahrenheit and centigrade scales to measure temperature is ample evidence that scales without absolute units still have superior utility.

Differences Between Raw Scores

As the teacher examines the raw scores reported for his class, he may find himself grappling with other uncertainties. He notices, for example, that another pupil received a raw score of fifty-nine in contrast to the first pupil's fifty-eight. Does this pupil in fact surpass the first in terms of the vocabulary test? When answering this question remember that this test, like all tests, is somewhat unreliable. In other words, it does not yield completely consistent results. Test unreliability forces us to interpret each score as an interval rather than a point. These intervals, sometimes called *confidence intervals or bands,* are found by using the standard error of measurement (see pages 250–251). Study of such intervals shows that small differences between test scores are no doubt due to chance and hence are uninterpretable.

UNEQUAL UNITS. Further examination of the vocabulary raw scores may reveal a situation such as the following:

Pupil	Raw score
Sheri	88
Carol	68
Arthur	37
Donald	17

Since the raw-score difference between the two members of each pair is twenty in both instances, can it be said that Sheri surpasses Carol in terms of the vocabulary test by the same amount that Arthur surpasses Donald? If the raw-score units are equal, the question can be answered affirmatively. In all likelihood, however, the difference of twenty raw-score units between the two girls is not exactly the same as the difference of twenty raw-score units between the two boys. It is all too true that educational measurement habitually yields somewhat unequal units. A specified difference, such as twenty raw-score units, cannot be identified at any position along the range, as five inches can be isolated in any position on an accurate yardstick. Hence the requirements of an interval scale are imperfectly met.

In all probability, increasing a raw score in a vocabulary test from sixty-eight to eighty-eight represents greater accomplishment than increasing a raw score from seventeen to thirty-seven. Hence, Sheri surpasses Carol to a greater degree than Arthur surpasses Donald. It is typical of achievement tests to find "rubber units."

Interpreting Raw Scores

The individual most vitally concerned about the fifty-eight his teacher wrote in the record book is the pupil himself. When informed of his achievement, he is understandably puzzled. Obviously he lacks reference points against which to compare his information. He needs a raw-score counterpart of "70° F" to help him interpret "58" the way "70° F" helps him interpret temperature reports.

His first reaction might be to convert the number of correct responses to a percent. However, this is not particularly helpful. If the test were composed of simple words, fifty-eight percent might indicate inferior achievement. If the test were composed of difficult words, on the other hand, fifty-eight percent might indicate superior achievement for a tenth-grade pupil.

No doubt the pupil requests information concerning the number of words correctly identified by the other class members. For instance, if the average number of words correctly identified by his classmates is reported, then he can describe his position as "above average" or as "below average" in terms of the vocabulary test.

Three helpful reference points are now available to the pupil. They are the maximum number of words correctly identified by any classmate, the minimum number of words correctly identified by any classmate, and the average number of words correctly identified by the entire class. Meager as this information is, it nevertheless provides the pupil with the opportunity to interpret his "58" in much the same manner as he would a reported temperature.

TABLE 8.1.   Frequency Distribution of 360 Raw Scores.

Raw-score intervals	Frequency	Percent	Cumulative frequency	Cumulative percent
90–94	4	1.1	360	100.0
85–89	6	1.7	356	98.9
80–84	12	3.3	350	97.2
75–79	20	5.6	338	93.9
70–74	28	7.8	318	88.3
65–69	36	10.0	290	80.6
60–64	40	11.1	254	70.6
55–59	46	12.8	214	59.4
50–54	43	11.9	168	46.7
45–49	39	10.8	125	34.7
40–44	32	8.9	86	23.9
35–39	24	6.7	54	15.0
30–34	13	3.6	30	8.3
25–29	9	2.5	17	4.7
20–24	5	1.4	8	2.2
15–19	3	0.8	3	0.8
Total	360	100.0		

FREQUENCY DISTRIBUTION. To provide the pupil with information that will help him interpret his raw score, the teacher must follow several steps. Initially he explains that, in view of the similarity of curriculum and educational environment in general, it is reasonable to compare the raw score of fifty-eight not only with those of other members of his class at his school, but also with those of all 360 pupils of the tenth-grade classes in all schools in the city. Then he decides to show his pupil the scores of all other pupils tested. Needless to say, the columns upon columns of unarranged raw scores (often called the ungrouped data) are hardly informative. On the other hand, the raw scores can be grouped into intervals and a *frequency distribution* constructed. To do so, the total spread of the scores from fifteen (the lowest raw score) to ninety-four (the highest raw score) is arbitrarily subdivided into sixteen intervals of a constant size of five raw-score units. This procedure forms the first column of Table 8.1, which is called the raw-score intervals column. Then each raw score is tallied in the proper interval. Counting the tallies yields the frequencies, that is, the second column in Table 8.1.

The interpretation of the values of the frequency column is by no means difficult. It is clear that three of the pupils have raw scores somewhere between fifteen and nineteen inclusive, whereas forty-six have raw scores between fifty-five and fifty-nine inclusive, one of these being the pupil in question.

To help the pupil understand even more clearly his relative position in the group of 360 pupils, two columns of percentages are added, one based on cumulative frequencies. Approximately thirteen percent of the tenth-graders fall within the same interval as the pupil we are considering, and forty-seven percent fall within the intervals below his. Thus about forty percent of the pupils fall within intervals above the one containing his raw score.

CONSTRUCTING A GRAPH. A further step the teacher may take is to convert the frequency distribution to graphic form. It is common practice to plot the data included in Table 8.1 by spacing the raw-score intervals along a horizontal axis and the frequencies along a vertical axis. In this manner, Figure 8.2 is constructed. The frequency of each interval is plotted directly above the midpoint of that interval.

The curve in Figure 8.2 is fairly characteristic of those resulting from similar plotting of the scores yielded by many different kinds of measuring instruments used in education and elsewhere. Had the pupils involved been infinite in number and unselected with respect to vocabulary, it is expected that the curve would be smooth and symmetrical rather than erratic. The group of 360 pupils somewhat approximates these conditions, and thus the line resulting approximates a smooth symmetrical curve. Measurements made on smaller groups such as the typical class often yield a very erratic curve.

NORMAL CURVE. The curve in Figure 8.2 is shaped, for all practical purposes, like a *normal curve*. The normal curve is distinctively bell-shaped, with the peak of the curve above a point on the horizontal axis corresponding to the average score of the distribution. From the peak, the curve drops rapidly on either side, yielding a symmetrical tapering as it approaches either end of the raw-score distribution.

The fact that the raw scores from the vocabulary test tend to be normally distributed assists considerably in their description. It is immediately possible to say that few pupils have high raw scores, few pupils have low scores, whereas many have scores clustering around the average raw score. This statement can be appreciably strengthened by wording it in terms of the standard deviation and the arithmetic mean of raw scores. If the standard deviation is added to and subtracted from the arithmetic

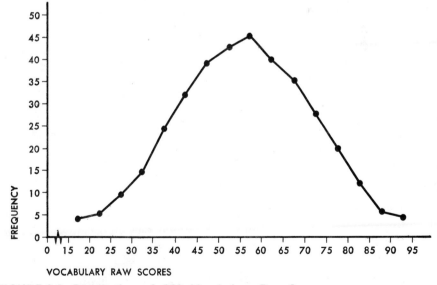

FIGURE 8.2. Distribution of 360 Vocabulary Raw Scores as Presented in Graphic Form.

mean, points along the horizontal axis are found between which fall a fixed percentage of the scores.

MEAN AND STANDARD DEVIATION. The arithmetic mean is often called the "average." It is a measure of central tendency, that is, a point at or near which the test scores are clustering. With ungrouped data, it is computed by adding all the scores and dividing by the number of scores. However, this procedure cannot be followed when they are arranged in a frequency distribution since, in these instances, the exact test score for a particular pupil is unknown. A modified formula for computing the arithmetic mean of scores in a frequency distribution is shown in Appendix A. When this formula is applied to the 360 vocabulary raw scores, an arithmetic mean of 55.7 is found.

Like the range, the standard deviation is a measure of the variability or dispersion present in a distribution of test scores. It is a distance expressed in test-score units rather than a point such as the arithmetic mean. Relatively small standard deviations are obtained when the test scores of a distribution are clustered in the vicinity of the arithmetic mean. As the test scores of a distribution spread widely above and below the arithmetic mean, the size of the standard deviation increases.

As in the case of the arithmetic mean, the standard deviation can be computed for test scores that are ungrouped or for test scores arranged in a frequency distribution. Appropriate formulas are shown in Appendix A. For the 360 vocabulary test scores shown in Table 8.1, a standard deviation of 15.3 was computed.

We can add and subtract the standard deviation (σ) from the arithmetic mean (M) in the following manner:

$$M + \sigma = 55.7 + 15.3 = 71.0$$
$$M - \sigma = 55.7 - 15.3 = 40.4$$

and

$$M + 2\sigma = 55.7 + (2)(15.3) = 86.3$$
$$M - 2\sigma = 55.7 - (2)(15.3) = 25.1.$$

Because the distribution is approximately normal, about sixty-eight percent of raw scores are higher than 40.4 but no larger than 71.0. Of the 360 pupils, we should estimate that roughly 245 have scores between forty-one and seventy-one inclusive. On the other hand, about ninety-five percent of the raw scores are larger than 25.1 and smaller than 86.3. Consequently, we should estimate that approximately 342 pupils have scores between twenty-six and eighty-six inclusive. Only when a normal distribution exists can the foregoing estimates be made.

Because finite groups of raw scores never conform to a perfect normal distribution, it is common to speak of the sixty-eight percent of the scores falling between $M + \sigma$ and $M - \sigma$ as the "middle two-thirds" of the distribution. Thus the two remaining tails of the distribution are identified as the "upper one-sixth" and the "lower one-sixth," respectively. Rough as this subdivision is, it is quite useful. For example, the teacher confronted with these almost normally distributed vocabulary raw scores can quickly add the standard deviation to the arithmetic mean, then subtract the standard deviation from the arithmetic mean, and visualize an ideal diagram such as

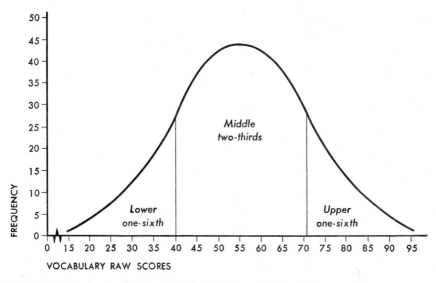

FIGURE 8.3. Theoretical Normal Distribution of Vocabulary Raw Scores.

the one in Figure 8.3. He can accordingly classify any raw score above seventy-one as in the upper one-sixth of the distribution, any raw score larger than forty but no larger than seventy-one as in the middle two-thirds of the distribution, and, finally, any raw score of forty and below as in the lower one-sixth of the distribution. For example, fifty-eight is clearly within the middle two-thirds of the distribution.

SCORES FROM TEACHER-BUILT TESTS. In the case of classroom achievement tests, the teacher typically deals with twenty-five to thirty-five raw scores rather than groups as large as the 360 used here. This means that we cannot safely expect a close approximation to the normal curve to exist, and thus interpretation of the test scores in terms of it is largely lost. Depending on the situation, we may wish instead to interpret these scores primarily in terms of their frequency distribution, mean, range, and highest and lowest values. Furthermore, for such small groups of scores, it is not reasonable to convert them routinely to derived scores like percentile ranks or standard scores.

PROBLEMS

1. On the basis of data shown on page 197, the statement is made that Sheri surpasses Carol in terms of the vocabulary test to a greater degree than Arthur surpasses Donald. Suppose that it required Carol two weeks of study to raise her score twenty points to eighty-eight, whereas it required Donald only one week to raise his score twenty points to thirty-seven. Ignoring possible measurement errors, can we now say that the difference in vocabulary achievement between the two boys is about half of that between the two girls, even though the raw-score difference is twenty in both cases? (For further elaboration regarding this line of reasoning, see Angoff, 1971.)

2. In addition to the arithmetic mean, what other measures of central tendency are commonly computed for raw-score distributions?

IDENTIFYING RELATIVE PERFORMANCE

Attempts to identify the relative performance of a pupil in terms of a test have been numerous. Furthermore, these attempts have yielded procedures that are vastly less cumbersome and casual than the manipulations of the raw-score distribution described above. The gist of the problem of simplifying the identification of relative performance is to convert the raw scores yielded by a test to some kind of derived scores that have, by their very nature, considerably greater interpretability. The many variations of derived scores are classified under the heading of *test norms*.

Test norms are representations of average or common performance, based on the results of testing a normal group of pupils. This group is usually large and supposedly representative of those pupils for whom the test is designed. The test is of course administered under the conditions specified by its author.

Test norms are sometimes confused with test standards. The two expressions are not synonymous. Test norms represent *actual* performance of certain groups of pupils. In contrast, test standards represent *desired* performance in terms of a specific test. In the case of the vocabulary test, for example, the average number of words correctly identified is 55.7, or slightly more than one-half of the total number of items. This value is an indication of average or common performance on the part of the tenth-grade pupils and hence falls within the notion of test norms. However, it is possible that the teachers feel that any raw score below sixty is unsatisfactory. If this position is taken, the teachers have obviously established a standard. Presumably, standards are based on the considered judgment of teachers and supervisors who are intimately familiar with the teaching environment related to the characteristic measured by the test and with the talent of the group of pupils tested.

The most common types of norms can be classified into four groups:

Quartiles, deciles, and percentiles
Standard scores
Grade equivalents
Age equivalents

The very length of this list suggests that none seems to be completely satisfactory. It is common to find test authors and consumers reporting several kinds of norms for the same test. Thus, each type of norm deserves a separate, though brief, description.

Quartiles, Deciles, and Percentiles

Quartiles, deciles, and percentiles are points in a distribution of test scores below which specified percentages of the scores fall. The quartiles are three points dividing the distribution into four equal parts in terms of the number of test scores; deciles are nine points dividing the distribution into ten equal parts; percentiles are ninety-nine points dividing the distribution into one hundred equal parts.

The interpretation of a quartile, decile, or percentile is quite uniform. The first quartile, often identified as Q_1, is the point below which twenty-five percent of the scores fall. The first decile, D_1, is the point below which ten percent of the scores fall. The first percentile, P_1, is the point below which one percent of the scores fall. In a similar manner, the remaining quartiles, deciles, and percentiles are identified symbolically and interpreted.

By definition, equalities have been established between certain quartiles, deciles, and percentiles. For example,

$$Q_1 = P_{25}$$
$$Q_3 = P_{75}$$
$$D_1 = P_{10}, \ldots$$

The most notable equality is

$$Q_2 = D_5 = P_{50}.$$

Interestingly enough, the point in question, namely, the point below which fifty percent of the scores fall, is not known as Q_2, D_5, or P_{50}, but as the median. The median also plays a role in other types of norms described in this chapter.

The computation of any quartile, decile, or percentile can be based on a frequency distribution of raw scores such as the distribution of vocabulary scores shown in Table 8.1. The formula necessary for the determination of any of these values is shown in Appendix A. Repeated application of this formula yields the raw-score equivalents of all of the quartiles, deciles, and percentiles; these values for the first twenty-five percentiles are listed in the fourth column of Table 8.2.

The fact that quartiles, deciles, and percentiles are points and nothing more is reemphasized by examination of the raw-score equivalents. Consider D_1 for a moment. Its raw-score equivalent is 35.8. This value, like the others, is arbitrarily rounded back to one decimal since additional decimal places are of little value. Furthermore, like a great majority of its fellow values, it is not an integer. Hence we can say that a raw score of thirty-five is slightly below D_1, whereas a raw score of thirty-six is slightly above. Note that it is not correct to say that any raw score of less than thirty-six is *in* the first decile. Quartiles, deciles, and percentiles are points, not parts. Raw scores can be above a given one of them, below it, occasionally at it (for example, P_{65} = 62.0), but never in it. To refer carelessly to Q_1 as the lowest quarter, or to D_1 as the lowest tenth of the distribution is inaccurate and unnecessarily confusing.

The raw-score equivalents of the quartiles, deciles, and percentiles as presented in Table 8.2 lack utility to some degree. We might ask, for example, what statement can be made about the raw score of forty-three. Can it be reported that it fell somewhere between P_{21} and P_{22}? Certainly this is true, but it is an awkward way to identify relative performance. Simplification of the wording is not possible if it is necessary to speak of percentiles. However, if *percentile ranks* are to be used, the statement reduces itself appreciably.

PERCENTILE RANKS. Quartile ranks, decile ranks, and percentile ranks are not points, but ranges of raw scores. In the case of percentile ranks, these ranges are

TABLE 8.2.   Percentiles and Percentile Ranks for the Bottom Fourth of a
Distribution of Vocabulary Scores.

Percentile	Decile	Quartile	Raw-score equivalent	Percentile rank	Raw scores
25		1	45.0	25	45
24			44.6	24	
23			44.0	23	44
22			43.4	22	43
21			42.9	21	
20	2		42.3	20	42
19			41.8	19	
18			41.2	18	41
17			40.6	17	
16			40.1	16	40
15			39.5	15	39
14			38.8	14	
13			38.0	13	38
12			37.3	12	37
11			36.5	11	36
10	1		35.8	10	
9			35.0	9	35
8			34.0	8	33, 34
7			32.7	7	32
6			31.3	6	30, 31
5			29.9	5	29
4			28.1	4	27, 28
3			26.1	3	24, 25, 26
2			23.7	2	21, 22, 23
1			20.1	1	20 and below

customarily quite small. By definition, any raw score of the same size as P_1 or less is given a percentile rank of one. Symbolically, this is PR_1. Any raw score larger than P_1 but no larger than P_2 is given a percentile rank of two, that is, PR_2. The process continues until PR_{100} is reached. Thus the distribution is divided into one-hundred percentile ranks.

The last two columns of Table 8.2 list the percentile ranks and the corresponding raw scores. The latter are found simply by inspecting the size of the raw-score equivalents of the percentiles and applying the definition of percentile ranks. A less laborious means of determining percentile ranks is by reading them from an accurately plotted ogive curve, that is, the curve resulting when cumulative percentages are plotted against the raw scores (Cronbach, 1970, pp. 90—91).

Percentile ranks are more commonly reported and used than percentiles. Tables converting raw scores to percentile ranks are standard equipment in many test manuals. Although the last two columns of Table 8.2 perform the conversion function, they are probably not shown in that fashion. Rather, the two columns are rearranged so that the raw-score column is first and the percentile-rank column is second, as in Table 8.3.

Table 8.3 shows the percentile rank equivalent for each raw score. As you can see, a raw score of fifty-eight is equivalent to a percentile rank of fifty-six. This means that a pupil with a score of fifty-eight on this vocabulary test ranks fifty-sixth from the bottom in a standard group of one-hundred tenth-grade pupils.

UTILITY OF PERCENTILE NORMS. The use of percentiles and percentile ranks to represent relative performance is extremely popular. Authors of standardized tests seldom fail to include these norms in their test manuals. Now that teachers, pupils, and even parents have been educated to a point that the term "percentile" has become almost a household word, test authors capitalize on the situation and view percentile norms as a convenient way of communicating with a large, heterogeneous audience.

There is a second reason for the continued use of percentile norms: the tables of norms can always be interpreted exactly no matter what the nature of the distribution of raw scores from which they are derived. This distribution may or may not be normal without changing the interpretation of the percentile norms.

The disadvantages of using percentile norms for representing relative performance of pupils are, however, somewhat damaging. Firstly, and most important of all, the size of units of percentiles and percentile ranks is not constant. Differences between percentiles are not equivalent to differences between raw scores.

Inspection of Table 8.3 reveals this situation in a typical case. Certainly the percentile ranks are hiding large differences between raw scores when they occur at either the high or low extremity of the raw-score distribution, and also are enlarging small differences between raw scores when they occur near the center of the distribution. A pupil with a raw score of fifteen is no different in terms of percentile rank from a pupil with one of twenty. Both are at the first percentile rank. On the other

TABLE 8.3. Percentile Rank Equivalents of Vocabulary Raw Scores.

Raw score	Percentile rank	Raw score	Percentile rank	Raw score	Percentile rank
95	100	68	78	41	18
94	100	67	76	40	16
93	100	66	74	39	15
92	100	65	72	38	13
91	100	64	70	37	12
90	99	63	68	36	11
89	99	62	65	35	9
88	99	61	63	34	8
87	99	60	61	33	8
86	98	59	59	32	7
85	98	58	56	31	6
84	97	57	53	30	6
83	97	56	51	29	5
82	96	55	48	28	4
81	95	54	46	27	4
80	95	53	43	26	3
79	94	52	41	25	3
78	93	51	39	24	3
77	92	50	36	23	2
76	90	49	34	22	2
75	89	48	32	21	2
74	88	47	30	20	1
73	86	46	28	19	1
72	85	45	25	18	1
71	83	44	23	17	1
70	82	43	22	16	1
69	80	42	20	15	1

hand, the raw score of fifty-eight yields a percentile rank of fifty-six. With the present system of scoring the vocabulary test, it is not possible for a pupil to have a percentile rank of fifty-four or fifty-five.

Percentile norms have "rubber units." The extent to which the units have been "rubberized" depends on the nature of the distribution of the raw scores. If that distribution is normal or nearly normal, the amount of distortion is large. In Table 8.3 notice that a pupil at PR_{96} is much farther away from a pupil at PR_{86} in terms of raw-score units than a pupil at PR_{56} is from a pupil at PR_{46}. The difference in raw-score units is nine in the first instance and four in the second. In short, percentile norms form ordinal scales, not interval scales.

The second objection is less serious than the first and sometimes of little concern to teachers. Simply phrased, it states that percentiles and percentile ranks as such cannot be treated arithmetically and a meaningful end product obtained. One cannot legitimately compute an arithmetic mean of these values or correlate them with other measurements by means of a product-moment coefficient of correlation. Percentiles and percentile ranks are, in effect, terminal values. Test norms such as standard scores do not suffer from this limitation.

Standard Scores

Another popular system for representing relative performance on a test is the standard score. The intent of the standard score is to transform the raw score distribution to a derived-score distribution having a desired arithmetic mean and standard deviation. If the arithmetic mean and standard deviation are known, and if the derived-score distribution is normal, identification of the relative performance of individual pupils is a simple matter. The same approach is used here that is described in connection with Figure 8.3 when normally distributed raw scores were involved.

Z-SCORES. There are many types of standard scores, each with its own arithmetic mean and standard deviation. The "parent" of the group is the well-known z score. From this base have sprung the others, three of which are commonly encountered and are described below.

The z scores are computed from the formula

$$z = \frac{X - M}{\sigma},$$

where

> z = *standard score;*
> X = *any raw score of a given distribution;*
> M = *arithmetic mean of the raw-score distribution;*
> σ = *standard deviation of the raw-score distribution.*

Examination of the formula reveals that any raw score smaller than the arithmetic mean of the raw scores yields a z score with a negative sign, whereas any larger than the arithmetic mean yields a z score that is positive. When a raw-score distribution is transformed into z scores, the arithmetic mean of the resulting z scores is zero, and their standard deviation is unity.

To change a raw score to a z score, a table of norms similar to that used for percentile ranks is consulted. Such a table is Table 8.4, the second column of which is constructed by successively solving the z score equation for all obtained raw scores (M = 55.7, σ = 15.3) resulting from the administration of the vocabulary test. Any raw score can be readily converted to a z score merely by glancing at the table. For example, a z score of +0.15 corresponds to the raw score of 58. Note that the practical limits of the z score distribution do not exceed +3.00 and −3.00.

OTHER MULTIPLE-DIGIT STANDARD SCORES. Because z scores have negative signs and decimal points, their usefulness decreases. Clerical errors too easily and too often create havoc when test results are reported. To avoid these difficulties, linear transformations of the original z scores are made and an entire family of standard scores is automatically born. One such transformation is

$$\text{Standard score} = 10\,(z) + 50.$$

This equation produces a distribution of standard scores with an arithmetic mean of 50 and a standard deviation of 10. In Table 8.4 these standard scores are listed opposite the corresponding z score and vocabulary test raw score. It should be noted that this type of standard score is often called a T score, although the original T score as proposed by McCall (1939) is somewhat different.

Another transformation is

$$\text{Standard score} = 20\,(z) + 100.$$

Now the arithmetic mean of the standard scores is 100 and the standard deviation is 20. This type of standard score is used with the *Army General Classification Test* administered during and after World War II.

Also, the equation can read

$$\text{Standard score} = 100\,(z) + 500.$$

The arithmetic mean of these standard scores is 500, whereas the standard deviation is 100. Standard scores of this type are used in connection with the *College Entrance Examination Board Tests.*

The above information is summarized in Table 8.5. In addition to the arithmetic means and standard deviations, the practical limits of the standard-score distribution are given. The practical limits are the points that are three standard-deviation units above the arithmetic mean and three below it.

If the distribution of standard scores is normal, the interpretation is not difficult; if it is not normal, the interpretation is quite uncertain. To assume that standard scores are always normally distributed simply because they are standard scores is a common mistake. If the raw scores are normally distributed, then the standard scores computed from them are automatically normally distributed. The standard-score distribution is the same as the distribution of raw scores on which it is based. Since quite a few raw-score distributions are for all practical purposes normally distributed, the interpretation of many standard scores is based on the normal curve.

TABLE 8.4.   Standard Scores of Raw Scores Based upon 360 Tenth-Grade Pupils.

Raw score	z	Standard score (M = 50, σ = 10)	Raw score	z	Standard score (M = 50, σ = 10)
94	2.50	75	54	−0.11	49
93	2.44	74	53	−0.18	48
92	2.37	74	52	−0.24	48
91	2.31	73	51	−0.31	47
90	2.24	72	50	−0.37	46
89	2.18	72	49	−0.44	46
88	2.11	71	48	−0.50	45
87	2.05	71	47	−0.57	44
86	1.98	70	46	−0.63	44
85	1.92	69	45	−0.70	43
84	1.85	69	44	−0.76	42
83	1.78	68	43	−0.83	42
82	1.72	67	42	−0.90	41
81	1.65	67	41	−0.96	40
80	1.59	66	40	−1.03	40
79	1.52	65	39	−1.09	39
78	1.46	65	38	−1.16	38
77	1.39	64	37	−1.22	38
76	1.33	63	36	−1.29	37
75	1.26	63	35	−1.35	36
74	1.20	62	34	−1.42	36
73	1.13	61	33	−1.48	35
72	1.07	61	32	−1.55	34
71	1.00	60	31	−1.61	34
70	0.93	59	30	−1.68	33
69	0.87	59	29	−1.75	32
68	0.80	58	28	−1.81	32
67	0.74	57	27	−1.88	31
66	0.67	57	26	−1.94	31
65	0.61	56	25	−2.01	30
64	0.54	55	24	−2.07	29
63	0.48	55	23	−2.14	29
62	0.41	54	22	−2.20	28
61	0.35	54	21	−2.27	27
60	0.28	53	20	−2.33	27
59	0.22	52	19	−2.40	26
58	0.15	52	18	−2.46	25
57	0.08	51	17	−2.53	25
56	0.02	50	16	−2.60	24
55	−0.05	49	15	−2.66	23

TABLE 8.5.   Types of Standard Scores.

Type	Arithmetic mean	Standard deviation	Practical limits High	Practical limits Low
z	0	1	+3.00	−3.00
10 (z) + 50	50	10	80	20
20 (z) + 100	100	20	160	40
100 (z) + 500	500	100	800	200

TABLE 8.6. Reference Points for Various Standard Scores.

Standard score characteristics		Middle two-thirds	Upper one-sixth	Lower one-sixth
M	σ	Between	Greater than	Less than
50	10	40 and 60	60	40
100	20	80 and 120	120	80
500	100	400 and 600	600	400

In interpretation of standard scores based on normally distributed raw scores, it is helpful to think of a diagram such as Figure 8.3. For z scores, the middle two-thirds of the distribution falls between +1.00 and −1.00, whereas the upper one-sixth is composed of z scores that exceed +1.00 and the lower one-sixth contains z scores that fail to reach −1.00. For the other three types of standard scores, the reference points are available, and are listed in Table 8.6.

Unlike the percentile rank procedure, no attempt is made here to interpret more exactly the relative performance of each pupil. Occasionally, percentile ranks are criticized for leaving a largely artificial impression of exactness. In any event, the normal curve can be broken into more segments than the three mentioned. Should this be desirable for whatever reason, a table of areas under the normal curve can be consulted. Such a table, along with a description of its functions, can be found in most of the available textbooks devoted to statistical methodology (for example, see page 461 of Dixon and Massey, 1969).

STANINES. The outstanding single-digit standard score used today is the stanine (pronounced *stay-nine*). This word was originally derived from the expression "standard *nine*-point scale," which is the system of standard scores developed during World War II. At that time, a simple and workable type of norm was sought. The stanine scale was found to be satisfactory since it employs a single digit to represent relative performance and yet is precise enough for many practical testing problems. It is used for both standardized and teacher-constructed tests.

When stanine norms are used, raw scores are converted to one of nine stanine scores, which vary from a low of one to a high of nine. The mean of the stanine distribution is five and its standard deviation two. On the other hand, when large numbers of pupils are involved, some measurement specialists will subdivide the two extreme positions on the scale, thereby creating an eleven-point scale with a low of zero and a high of ten.

The determination of stanine scores is simple (Durost, 1961). For example, when working with raw scores from smaller groups of pupils, a teacher can arrange the raw scores from high to low, then determine the median of the distribution, and, with this as a starting point, apply the theoretical percentages of the stanine subgroups. These percentages are as follows:

Stanine	1	2	3	4	5	6	7	8	9
Percentage of Pupils	4	7	12	17	20	17	12	7	4

The median is theoretically in the center of the middle twenty percent of the distribution. This subgroup is given a stanine of five. By working upward and downward from this subgroup, the remaining subgroups are found and the stanines assigned. Certain minor adjustments of the subgroups are usually necessary to bring the actual percentages into the closest possible agreement with the theoretical percentages. This is necessitated by the principle that every pupil having the same raw score will, of course, have the same stanine score.

One word of caution: Remember that the percentages used are derived from the normal curve. Therefore, if the stanine scale is to be used, one must be willing to assume that the trait measured follows this curve reasonably well for the pupils tested.

UTILITY OF STANDARD-SCORE NORMS. After comparing the interpretation of the vocabulary raw scores with that for standard scores based upon those raw scores, you may wonder what advantages standard scores have over raw scores. One is the fact that standard scores have a specified arithmetic mean and standard deviation. Raw-score distributions have a habit of producing arithmetic means and standard deviations that have somewhat quaint sizes and are seldom integers. On the other hand standard-score distributions have arithmetic means that are easily remembered—0, 5, 50, 100, or 500—and a standard deviation that can be speedily added to or subtracted from that mean.

The two disadvantages of percentile norms cannot be attributed to standard-score norms. Because multiple-digit standard scores are nothing but a linear transformation of raw scores, they are a direct reflection of them, both in terms of size of unit and shape of distribution. No "rubber units" are generated as in the case of percentile ranks. Furthermore, standard scores can be treated arithmetically. Finding the arithmetic mean or standard deviation of standard scores is just as legitimate as finding those values for raw scores.

Another important advantage of standard scores is the ease of comparison of scores for a pupil who has been given several tests, and the ease of determining a composite score if desired. For instance, reporting each of a battery of achievement test scores in a subject matter area in terms of stanines permits the teacher to compare levels of achievement from one test to another for a specific pupil, as when a graphic profile of stanines is prepared. He can also combine these stanines to obtain a composite score representing the overall achievement of the pupil. Such a composite score is often the arithmetic mean of the stanines in question. Finding the arithmetic mean weights each test score equally. If desired, various weights can be assigned the stanines before the arithmetic mean is computed.

Percentiles and all types of standard scores are interrelated if the raw-score distribution from which they are computed is normal. The normal distribution restriction is highly important. In Figure 8.4 these relationships are shown in part (Seashore, 1955). Before the relationships shown in this figure can be considered useful, there must be statistical evidence that the distribution of raw scores is essentially a normal one.

The main disadvantage of standard scores is that they are difficult to interpret when they are not normally distributed. This fact, plus the general public's lack of familiarity with them, somewhat restricts their use.

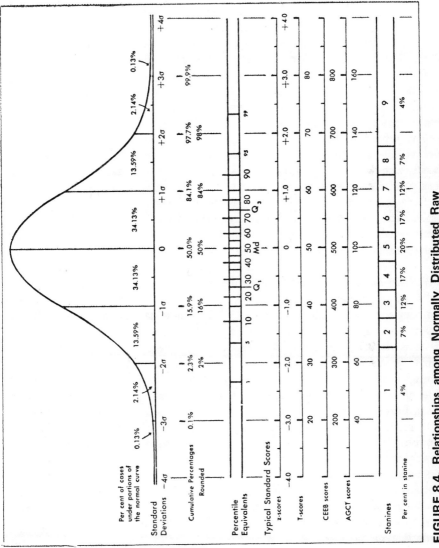

FIGURE 8.4. Relationships among Normally Distributed Raw Scores, Percentiles, and Certain Standard Scores.

Grade Equivalents

Representing the relative performance of pupils with grade equivalents is still another popular method. A grade equivalent of a particular raw score is the grade level of those pupils whose median (or arithmetic mean) is the same as the raw score in question. In other words, if the median raw score happened to be sixty-three for a test administered to sixth-grade pupils just beginning that grade level, all raw scores of sixty-three have a grade equivalent of 6.0.

The generally accepted way of reporting grade equivalents is in terms of two numbers. The first of the two numbers is designed as the year and second as the month. For example, a grade equivalent of 5.4 is the median raw score of pupils tested at the fourth month of the fifth grade. Note that the calendar year is divided into ten parts, nine representing the academic year and one representing summer vacation months.

The process of computing grade equivalents is systematic but not unusually impressive. In the first place, the test is administered to large groups of pupils in consecutive grade levels. This takes place at the same time of year for all pupils. The median raw score of each grade level is found and plotted, on ordinary graph paper, against the grade level. Then the "best-fitting" curve is passed through the points, and sometimes extended (extrapolated) dangerously far beyond the upper and lower grade levels involved in the initial testing. The grade equivalents of raw scores are read directly from the curve.

UTILITY OF GRADE EQUIVALENTS. Despite the limitations of grade equivalents, these scores are amazingly well received, especially in the elementary grade levels. Grade equivalents are easily understood. Contrast these derived scores with standard scores or even percentile ranks. Comparing a pupil's actual grade level with his grade equivalents yielded by tests in various subject matter areas is definitely more comprehensible to many teachers, administrators, and parents than standard scores and percentile ranks. Moreover, grade equivalents offer convenient units for plotting profiles of pupil achievement. Such profiles are graphic representations of a pupil's test scores and typically emphasize the areas of overachievement and underachievement.

Several basic restrictions of grade equivalents must be remembered if they are to be properly used and interpreted. The most important of these is that a grade equivalent cannot always be taken at face value. When the "best-fitting" curve used to determine the grade equivalents of raw scores has been extended to grade levels higher and lower than those used in the initial testing, this trouble becomes pronounced. Suppose, for example, that a pupil beginning the fifth grade is given a fifth-grade arithmetic test and receives a grade equivalent of 8.0. This does not necessarily indicate that he has mastered all of the arithmetic subject matter in the fifth, sixth, and seventh grades. Although he is displaying superior arithmetic achievement when compared to the typical fifth-grade pupil, in all probability he is not sufficiently well trained at that moment to compete successfully in arithmetic with pupils beginning the eighth grade. In other words, had he been tested by an *eighth-grade* arithmetic test, he very likely would have fallen well below the grade equivalent of 8.0.

A second restriction limits the highest grade level to which equivalents may extend. Grade equivalents should not extend beyond the ninth grade since, with the exception of English, there is no continuous and systematic instruction beyond the ninth grade for those subject matter areas taught in elementary school. Remember that the plotting method of determining grade equivalents assumes regular and gradual pupil growth over the period of time selected. Since this does not occur in secondary school in such areas as reading, arithmetic, and spelling, grade equivalents like 10.3 and 11.0 are meaningless. Standard scores or percentile ranks should be used to represent relative performance of secondary school pupils.

Finally, grade equivalents suffer from that ancient malady we call "rubber units." There is no assurance that a given difference between two grade equivalents is comparable to the same difference between two other grade equivalents, even though the same test is involved. However, the seriousness of this difficulty varies with the subject matter area being tested. Within the elementary school levels, grade equivalents yielded by tests in areas such as reading, arithmetic, and spelling tend to have equal units. This is true because the subject matter areas are given a consistent emphasis throughout a relatively long period of time. For other subject matter areas, we should expect grade equivalents to have units of decidedly unequal size.

On balance, one must argue that grade equivalents should be used with great caution. Their simplicity is deceptive; their meaning is often unclear. In many instances standard scores and percentile ranks are superior to them as representations of relative performance by pupils.

Age Equivalents

Age equivalents are very similar to grade equivalents. Years of age have simply replaced grade levels in the method of computation and interpretation. It follows then that an age equivalent of a particular raw score is the chronological age of those pupils whose median (or arithmetic mean) raw score is the same as the raw score in question. For example, a pupil who received a raw score of forty-eight on a certain test finds, on consulting a table converting raw scores to age equivalents, that it corresponds to an age equivalent of 10-4. The median (or arithmetic mean) raw score of pupils ten years and four months of age is therefore forty-eight.

The foregoing illustration lists the age equivalent by means of two numbers separated by a dash, a typical way of reporting these values. The first number represents the number of years, whereas the second represents the number of months. Unlike grade equivalents, the calendar year is divided into twelve parts, so that the second number varies from a minimum of zero to a maximum of eleven.

Computing age equivalents strongly resembles the computation of grade equivalents. Similarly, the utility of age equivalents is severely limited as is that of grade equivalents. They are helpful only when used with pupils at ages at which the trait measured is known to increase noticeably year by year. In other instances, they are inferior to standard scores and percentile ranks.

PROBLEMS

3. Teachers are often interested in pupil growth or improvement in achievement in a given subject matter area and will administer the same test before and

after a period of instruction, hoping that the difference between the two scores will measure pupil growth. Identify the principal measurement problems present in this process (Angoff, 1971). How successfully can the various types of norms reflect pupil growth (Tiedeman, 1951)?

4. When using grade equivalents, a teacher will sometimes confuse norms and standards by saying that his pupils are progressing satisfactorily if they are performing "up to the norm." What does he mean by this statement? What questions would you raise if you were to challenge it?

5. A differentiation is made between "normative" standard scores and a "nonnormative" scale called "content" standard test scores (Wesman et al., 1962). On what basis is this differentiation made and of what significance is it to classroom teachers interested in criterion- and objective-referenced tests?

STANDARDIZATION GROUPS

Throughout the discussion of derived scores, repeated mention is made of the standardization or norm group, that is, the group of pupils whose raw scores are used to identify the raw-score equivalents of the derived scores. The standardization group consists of pupils for whom the test is designed and who are given the test under conditions recommended by its author. For our illustration, this group is more than the tenth-grade class; it is the 360 tenth-grade pupils within the city school system. The appropriateness of interpreting achievement in the light of the results of this larger group must be established before taking the trouble to compute any of the derived scores.

A regularly observed principle is that the expression of a pupil's relative standing in terms of derived scores is meaningful when the standardization group used to determine them resembles that pupil in terms of any of a variety of salient characteristics. It follows, therefore, that comparison of a pupil's vocabulary with that of the 360 pupils is suitable since, within a single city school system, there is appreciable similarity in amount and quality of instruction in any subject matter area among the various component schools, and similarity in the pupils' ability to profit from that instruction.

It is only rarely appropriate to compare a pupil's vocabulary achievement to that of a seemingly very different group. Hence to support the use of the 360 pupils as a standardization group, they should be described in terms of the amount of their previous formal schooling in the area tested, their age distribution, scholastic aptitude distribution, socioeconomic ratings, and so forth. Since the averages of these measures do not differ greatly from the pupil's position, the comparison of his achievement with theirs would seem to make sense. Should the 360 pupils as a group be vastly unlike him, the interpretation of his performance relative to those of this group is less useful, barring unusual reasons.

Sampling Problem

The problem so often faced by teachers who wish to use test norms is that their pupils are not a part of the standardization group. Hence, the teacher must know whether his pupils can be considered a part of the population of which the standardization group is a cross-sectional sample. Unless they can be considered a part of such a population, the tables of norms cannot be used.

In the past, the sampling problem with test norms has been vastly underestimated in some instances. Tables of norms that are labeled "national" or "regional" without bothering to specify the manner in which the nation or region is sampled, are contributing by omission to the fuzzy notion that the worth of a sample is determined only incidentally by the method of obtaining it. More often than not, the size of the sample is impressive and is noted with pride, notwithstanding the fact that it is incidental to the method of selecting its members.

The whimsical nature of some methods of sampling pupils to be used as standardization groups can be neatly illuminated by changing the scene slightly. Suppose you want to find the average body temperature of human adult males. This is a norm, of course, and you already recognize that, if you use the thermometer-under-the-tongue technique, the answer is 98.6° F. In any event, assume that this information is unknown, even though the measurement technique has been perfected. Had you attacked the problem as some test authors have attacked the problem of norms, you would immediately search for a group (preferably large) of readily available and unusually cooperative subjects. What better place is there to find them than in the local hospitals? Hospital authorities will probably cooperate because it means an inexpensive way of acquiring more information about their patients; the patients cannot complain; nurses can be quickly trained to measure temperature reliably. You proceed happily with your research and discover the average body temperature of human adult males to be 99.8° F.

There is a remarkable parallel between the foregoing illustration and the procedure sometimes used in the past for establishing norms of educational tests. However, results of the temperature measurements are summarily rejected by the medical profession and for good reason. The method of measurement is not questioned, but the accurate representation of the sample certainly is. On the other hand, in educational measurement, tables of norms yielded by equally faulty sampling procedures sometimes have been accepted uncritically. Those pupils who serve as standardization groups because they are conveniently available are more likely atypical than typical of the regional and national population that they are supposed to represent.

The task of satisfactorily sampling a group of pupils is admittedly difficult and highly expensive. If there is no evidence to the contrary, national norms should include, in proportion to their numbers, boys and girls, some white and some not, native-born and foreign-born, intelligent and not intelligent, some who live in cities, some in suburban areas, and some in rural areas, those who are wealthy and those who are poor, who attend large schools and small schools, and public and private, and who have received superior and inferior instruction. Even this list is not complete. Any factor that could conceivably affect the test results to an appreciable degree should be considered in the selection of the sample. In recent years, test authors have redoubled their efforts to draw suitable national and regional samples, and the representativeness of their standardization groups has correspondingly increased a great deal.

A number of test authors strengthen the utility of their tables of norms by publishing not one but several such tables, each designed for a relatively homogeneous population. If the sexes are found to differ in terms of a test, such as a paper-and-pencil personality inventory, separate tables of norms for boys and girls are listed. In some instances, separate tables are shown for rural schools and urban schools, for schools in different geographical regions, for various levels of scholastic aptitude within a grade level, and for pupils specializing in various types of secondary school curricula. For each group of pupils so used, the author then reports data concerning the group's age, educational status, and the like. Every pertinent piece of information characterizing the standardization group helps a teacher decide whether his pupils logically belong in the population sampled by the standardization group.

LOCAL NORMS. Even though a variety of tables of norms is available, consideration should be given to the possibility of constructing local norms. These are usually expressed in terms of percentile ranks or standard scores. If several hundred or more test scores from a certain test are available, and if future use is to be made of that test, local norms should be found, and should be revised from time to time as additional raw scores become available. After all, a particular raw score on a test may be equivalent to a standard score of sixty in terms of national norms, fifty-seven in terms of regional norms, fifty-eight in terms of local norms based on one city, or fifty-two in terms of local norms based on one school.

All these indications of relative performance may be helpful, depending on the purpose of the testing and hence the educational decisions about the pupil to be made. For instance, local norms are most helpful when we are looking back at what an individual or class has done, but are less likely to be helpful when we look ahead to what they may be expected to do in the future. Further, they are less often valuable for counseling purposes (Ricks, 1971).

On balance, local norms are valuable. They supplement national norms, and for some purposes they are more appropriate since they are sensitive to atypical conditions (for example, curriculum practices) in the local schools.

PROBLEMS

6. A senior whose percentile rank on a scholastic aptitude test was eighty-five had a percentile rank of sixty on an achievement test in advanced mathematics. His mathematics teacher concluded that he was underachieving. What information must you know about the standardization groups used before you can evaluate the teacher's conclusion on that basis?

7. Study the description of procedures used to select a standardization group and the description of the standardization group finally used for the *Iowa Tests of Basic Skills*. Compare this with similar information provided by any other achievement test battery for the elementary school.

8. In addition to norms for pupil scores, manuals of the *Iowa Tests of Educational Development* provide information concerning norms for school averages. Evaluate the worth of the school norms.

NARRATIVE FORMAT TESTING REPORTS

Are there more understandable ways of reporting test results to unsophisticated audiences than the use of norms? Yes—thanks to computers. Upon scoring a standardized achievement or aptitude test, they are able to print out an appropriate narrative which provides an interpretation of a pupil or class performance (Baker, 1971, pp. 228–229).

Such reports have been prepared for pupils, teachers, and parents following the administration of the *Iowa Tests of Basic Skills* (Mathews, 1973). These are typically several paragraphs in length: in addition to describing each pupil's overall performance as well as his attainment on the subtests, various proficiencies and deficiencies are listed. Suggestions for improving performance are included. Also, the computer formulates growth statements based on a pupil's change of score from the test administration of the previous year.

Increasingly, standardized tests are designed to provide narrative test reports in addition to derived scores. For instance, one can obtain a computer-produced counseling report based on a pupil's *Differential Aptitude Tests* scores and his responses to a career-planning questionnaire. His occupational preferences are compared with the level and pattern of his aptitude test scores, school subjects, and educational plans. The report may confirm his occupational choices or may suggest alternative occupational areas to explore.

Narrative reports about class performance can be produced for some standardized achievement tests, for example, the *Stanford Achievement Test*. As a part of a criterion-referenced interpretation for this battery, an interpretive computer report to the teacher provides an analysis of class achievement on small groups of homogeneous test items. Suggestions are made for placing individual pupils in groups for instructional purposes.

Certainly narrative-test reports are less precise than derived scores, but they offer highly understandable information to pupils, parents, and teachers. They are a superior supplement to norms.

SUMMARY

The highlights of this chapter are:

1. *The results yielded by measuring instruments frequently lack meaning. For instance, raw scores, which are the immediate quantitative end product of scoring a test, defy interpretation until suitable reference points are known. Three such reference points are the arithmetic mean of a group of raw scores and the values of the largest and smallest raw scores.*

2. *Other reference points can be readily located if the distribution of raw scores is normal or practically normal. When this is true, the standard deviation of the raw scores can be successively added to and subtracted from the arithmetic mean to identify distribution points including fixed percentages of raw scores.*

3. *Raw-score distributions are habitually characterized by two inadequacies. In the first place, a raw score of zero does not correspond to absolute zero. This is not a serious deficiency in terms of lessening raw-score interpretability. Secondly, raw-score distributions tend to have "rubber units," that is, unequal units. This deficiency is considerably more serious but hardly disastrous in well-constructed instruments.*

4. *There have been many efforts to improve the meaningfulness of raw scores. Raw scores are changed to derived scores, which more readily show the relative performance of a pupil in terms of the test. Derived scores (better known as norms) are obtained by giving a test to a group of pupils for whom it is designed under conditions recommended by the author and, with a distribution of raw scores available, applying the necessary formulas or plotting the necessary graphs. The group of pupils so used is called a standardization group.*

5. *The most common norms in educational measurement are quartiles, deciles, and percentiles; standard scores; grade equivalents; and age equivalents. Quartiles, deciles, and percentiles are points in a distribution below which specified percentages of raw scores will fall. Standard scores are derived scores with known arithmetic means and standard deviations. Grade equivalents represent the average test performance of pupils of various grade levels, whereas age equivalents represent the average test performance of pupils of various chronological ages.*

6. *The standardization group used to compute tables of norms must be carefully chosen. It is a sample of a population of pupils and, ideally, should be selected in accordance with the sampling procedures designed by a competent statistician. Before tables of norms can be used, a teacher must be convinced that his pupils can legitimately be considered a part of the population represented by a standardization group.*

7. *Many test manuals contain several tables of norms representing various populations, since, for most purposes, norms become more meaningful as the standardization group used to determine them more closely resembles the pupils involved in the comparison. The need for similarity contributes heavily to the importance of local norms.*

8. *In the case of standardized tests, computer-produced narrative-format testing reports should be used whenever possible to supplement derived score reports.*

SUGGESTED READINGS

ANASTASI, A. *Psychological testing.* (3rd ed.) New York: Macmillan, 1968. Chapter 3.
   This chapter includes sections dealing with age norms, percentiles, and standard scores. It concludes with a discussion of normative samples and nonnormative scales, for example, content standard scores.

ANGOFF, W. H. Scales, norms, and equivalent scores. In R. L. Thorndike (ed.), *Educational measurement.* (2nd ed.) Washington: American Council on Education, 1971. Chapter 15.
   Each of the principal types of norms is reviewed in terms of its purposes, computation, and utility. Considerable attention is given to the problem of selecting suitable standardization groups.

CRONBACH, L. J. *Essentials of psychological testing.* (3rd ed.) New York: Harper & Row, 1970. Chapter 4.
   The interpretation of raw scores and various derived scores is systematically considered.

Attention is given to the normal curve and the relationships between standard scores and percentile ranks when raw scores are distributed in this manner.

DOWNIE, N. M. *Types of test scores*. Boston: Houghton Mifflin, 1968.

The seven chapters in this booklet cover a wide range of topics related to norms. One deals with descriptive statistics, the others with various types of popular norms.

JOSELYN, E. G., and J. C. MERWIN. Using your achievement test score reports. *NCME Measurement in Education*, 1971, *3*, 1–8.

All major types of norms are described. Illustrations of standardized achievement test profiles and summary statistics are presented.

RICKS, J. H., JR. *Local norms—when and why*. Test Service Bulletin, No. 58. New York: Psychological Corporation, 1971.

The case for and against local norms is prepared. Scores from the *Differential Aptitude Tests* are used as illustrations.

WESMAN, A. G., et al. Symposium: Standard scores for aptitude and achievement tests. *Educational and Psychological Measurement*, 1962, *22*, 5–39.

The virtues and limitations of various kinds of standard scores are compared and evaluated. Five testing specialists contributed to the symposium.

REFERENCES CITED

ANGOFF, W. H. Scales, norms, and equivalent scores. In R. L. Thorndike (ed.), *Educational measurement*. (2nd ed.) Washington: American Council on Education, 1971, chapter 15.

BAKER, F. B. Automation of test scoring, reporting, and analysis. In R. L. Thorndike (ed.), *Educational measurement*. (2nd ed.) Washington: American Council on Education, 1971, chapter 8.

CRONBACH, L. J. *Essentials of psychological testing*. (3rd ed.) New York: Harper & Row, 1970.

DIXON, W. J., and F. J. MASSEY, JR. *Introduction to statistical analysis*. (3rd ed.) New York: McGraw-Hill, 1969.

DUROST, W. N. *The characteristics, use, and computation of stanines*. Test Service Notebook, No. 23. New York: Harcourt, Brace & World, 1961.

MCCALL, W. A. *Measurement*. New York: Macmillan, 1939.

MATHEWS, W. M. Narrative-format testing approach. *NCME Measurement News*, 1973, *16*, 7–8.

RICKS, J. H., JR. *Local norms—when and why*. Test Service Bulletin, No. 58. New York: Psychological Corporation, 1971.

SEASHORE, H. G. *Methods of expressing test scores*. Test Service Bulletin, No. 48. New York: Psychological Corporation, 1955.

TIEDEMAN, D. V. Has he grown? *Personnel and Guidance Journal*, 1951, *30*, 106–111.

WESMAN, A. G., et al. Symposium: Standard scores for aptitude and achievement tests. *Educational and Psychological Measurement*, 1962, *22*, 5–39.

9

THE VALIDITY OF
MEASUREMENT METHODS

Some years ago, so it is reported, an anthropologist studying the culture of a primitive community wanted to determine the number of children of each age living there. Since birth records were available for only a few children and parental reports were quite undependable, the anthropologist decided to measure the heights of the children to obtain an estimate of their ages. He did this by first measuring the heights of those few children whose ages were known. Then, by comparing the heights of children of unknown age with the heights of children whose ages were available, he estimated the unknown ages on the basis of height. This maneuver by the anthropologist was probably received sympathetically by his colleagues. It is possible that, had he not estimated ages from heights, he would have departed with no information about ages.

The anthropologist's action is not unlike that of a high school senior in his search for a university; he may assess the quality of a university's academic offerings on the basis of the size of its undergraduate student body, or perhaps the number of games won by its football team, or both. In somewhat the same category is the political pundit who evaluates the popularity of his party's agricultural program in terms of the number of unsolicited favorable letters received from the public at large, and also the economic soothsayer who describes the economic health of the nation solely in terms of the rise and fall of the stock market.

Each of the foregoing illustrations may be cynically interpreted by discerning observers, who might ask: Do differences in heights of children always indicate differences in age? Is the quality of a university's academic program necessarily a function of its size? Do unsolicited letters received at a political party's headquarters represent a cross-section of voter opinion? Is the stock market completely sensitive to all of the subtle changes in the economic structure? These and similar questions would undoubtedly tend to yield nothing more than hesitant answers surrounded by embarrassment.

The individuals using the foregoing measurement methods in such potentially dangerous fashions are possibly somewhat innocent. The very accessibility of such data as height, enrollment, number of letters, and stock market reports tempts most investigators. Furthermore, the accuracy of these data is generally considered good. For instance, height can easily be measured to the nearest one-fourth of an inch. The difficulty then is not centered in the accuracy of the data involved, but rather in the interpretation of them. To argue that unwarranted interpretations have been made is to argue that validity, to some degree, is absent.

DEFINITION OF VALIDITY

In educational measurement, validity is often defined as the degree to which a measuring instrument actually serves the purposes for which it is intended. A scholastic aptitude test is a valid measurement of scholastic aptitude if it truly measures scholastic aptitude. An achievement test in spelling is valid to the extent that it assuredly measures achievement in spelling. In the illustration just cited, it is obvious that the measurement of height by means of an accurate tape measure applied under controlled conditions is unquestionably a valid measurement of height, but a doubtful measure of age. Likewise, scores yielded by a scholastic aptitude test may very well be valid indicators of degrees of scholastic aptitude but inadequate representations of emotional stability.

Validity is clearly the most important characteristic of a measuring instrument. No matter what other characteristics an instrument may possess, if it does not adequately serve the purposes for which its use is intended, it is of no value whatsoever.

PROBLEM

1. The claim is made that some definitions of validity are virtually synonymous with that of test value (Ebel, 1961). If this is true, then ease of administration, adequacy of norms, reliability, etc., become aspects of validity. Should the definition of validity be this encompassing? Give reasons for your answer.

TYPES OF VALIDITY

The definition of validity already stated is useful, but still inadequate. To say that a measuring instrument is "valid" in the sense that validity has been defined is not enough. The statement is too vague. An instrument is valid in terms of its purpose or purposes. Examples already have been presented that vividly illustrate the fact that results yielded by a measuring instrument may be highly valid for one purpose and not at all for another. Since the relative validity of an instrument indicates the degree to which its purposes or aims are being achieved, and since the aims of tests vary, somewhat different types of validity are under consideration in various measuring instruments. The types of validity differ with the aims.

The aims of measurement methods are divided into three categories (American Psychological Association, 1974):

1. *To determine how well a pupil performs today in a certain type of situation or subject matter, a cross-sectional sample of which is present in the measuring*

instrument. For example, a teacher might administer a spelling test to his class to determine how much they know at that moment about spelling. In all likelihood, the test would include only a sample of all the words for which the pupils are responsible.

2. *To predict a pupil's future behavior or to estimate his present standing with respect to some characteristic not directly measured by the instrument. For example, in the case of future behavior, a scholastic aptitude test could be given to pupils completing junior high school to predict their academic success in senior high school. In the case of a pupil's present standing, a teacher can administer a paper-and-pencil arithmetic test composed of addition and subtraction problems involving representations of pennies, nickels, dimes, quarters, half dollars, and dollar bills. The size of the test score is intended to show the accuracy with which each pupil can make change when purchasing articles from retail stores.*

3. *To infer the strength of a pupil trait or quality as reflected in the results yielded by the measuring instrument. For example, a teacher might give a memory test to a class to make inferences about each pupil's scholastic aptitude.*

The three types of validity are commonly identified, respectively, as content validity, criterion-related validity, and construct validity. Each can be defined as the degree to which a measuring instrument accomplishes the aim associated with that type.

Of course, an instrument may be designed to meet more than one of the three aims, and hence the person who develops and uses it must investigate more than one type of validity. Also, some types of validity tend to be more vital in certain kinds of tests. For example, content validity plays a key role in achievement testing and criterion-related validity in aptitude testing. To examine these and other ramifications resulting from the classification of validity types, separate consideration of each type is necessary.

Content Validity

Finding the content validity of a measuring instrument is equivalent to showing how well it samples certain types of situations or subject matter. The instrument claiming high content validity clearly attempts to include a cross-sectional sample of a great variety of items representing the area in which the pupil's performance is being measured.

You recall that the primary purpose of achievement measurement is to discover how well pupils have achieved educational objectives. For example, a teacher may wish to know how well his pupils can add whole numbers, or how rapidly they can read. Another may want to determine how much information his class retains from prolonged discussions and readings about the political, economic, and social causes of World War II. These and countless similar illustrations typify the rather well-defined areas of subject matter and behavioral changes in terms of which classroom and standardized achievement tests are constructed. The validity of such a test is determined by the representativeness of its contents. Since all possible questions cannot be included, the test is necessarily a sample. To the degree that the sample is not representative, the test lacks content validity.

Content validity is a useful characteristic of measuring instruments other than achievement tests such as scholastic aptitude tests and personal-social adjustment inventories. In each of these types of instruments, it is generally true that content validity is secondary to another kind. In scholastic aptitude tests, criterion-related validity is paramount, yet content validity is involved in the identification of the great variety of possible test items from which those used are selected.

Criterion-Related Validity

Criterion-related validity can be divided into two parts, namely, the validity of instruments designed to predict future performance, and that of instruments designed to estimate present status with respect to a characteristic different from the test. The former is known as predictive validity and the latter as concurrent validity. The principal difference between these two classifications is the time at which the pupil displays the behavior in question. In the first case we wish to predict the future. In the second, we want to gain information about present performance by using information obtained indirectly.

INSTRUMENTS PREDICTING FUTURE PERFORMANCE. The fact that aptitude tests are designed to predict what a pupil can accomplish with training is another way of saying that aptitude tests, by definition, are fundamentally dependent on the establishment of a high degree of criterion-related validity. The uses of scholastic aptitude scores for sectioning classes, anticipating success in reading, estimating the likelihood of graduating from secondary school, or guiding a pupil toward a career in law, amply illustrate the use of a test score or scores to infer tomorrow's successes and failures. This criterion-related validity of a measuring instrument depends on the accuracy of its predictions of future pupil behavior.

In spite of the fact that achievement tests are constructed for the primary purpose of determining how much a pupil knows or how well he can perform as of that moment, another and less common use is forecasting subsequent achievement. For instance, reading tests are used to section classes in various subject matter areas and to predict academic success in secondary school and college. In these cases, high criterion-related validity is unquestionably necessary.

INSTRUMENTS ESTIMATING PRESENT STANDING. Some measuring instruments try to determine a pupil's present standing indirectly. The pupil behavior elicited by this type of instrument is thought to correspond closely to a certain external behavior criterion. If it does, the instrument has acceptable criterion-related validity of the concurrent type.

Like content validity, this type is usually a necessary attribute of achievement-measuring instruments. Consider, for example, the measurement of reading and arithmetic achievement. A reading comprehension score from a test might be interpreted as the pupil's reading comprehension when he reads for pleasure. The results of an arithmetic test may be interpreted as related to the accuracy with which a pupil can compute his hourly wages when he shovels snow after school. A teacher may wish to interpret scores on a language usage test as closely correlated with a tabulation of the pupil's actual verbal usage at the time.

Criterion-related validity is also important when considering the validity of instruments in personal-social adjustment, particularly so when they are used to classify pupils in groups. For example, an interest inventory may reflect one or more differences between pupils who have hobbies involving manual skills and those who do not. Also, pupils in need of immediate counseling may be detected by personal-social adjustment inventory scores and other evidence.

Construct Validity

To describe construct validity, it is first necessary to establish the meaning of the term "construct." A construct is a characteristic assumed to exist to account for some aspect of human behavior. In psychology, many constructs are used, such as cautiousness, tendency to conform, rigidity, insecurity, dominance, and ability to apply principles. These terms serve the useful purpose of providing a convenient means of identifying the psychological concepts they represent. By themselves, however, they do not explain the concept or any theory underlying it.

Whenever a measuring instrument is believed to reflect a particular construct, its construct validity must be investigated. This amounts to determining how well certain constructs account for pupil performance as measured by the instrument. To make a suitable investigation possible, the construct should be sufficiently well-defined so that verifiable inferences can be drawn from it. Testing the accuracy of the inferences with a measuring instrument is a way of confirming or denying the claim that a certain construct accounts for variations in the performance elicited by the instrument. If the instrument has a high degree of construct validity, its findings will vary from one kind of individual to another, or from one situation to another, as the theory underlying the construct would predict. In many ways, establishing construct validity is the same as validating the theory that defines the construct (Cronbach and Meehl, 1955).

Examples of the importance of construct validity can be found in the measurement of achievement, aptitude, and personal-social adjustment. In the case of achievement measurement, construct validity is a pertinent characteristic of those tests claiming to measure study skills and ability to reason. Is there any proof that the tests actually measure study skills or reasoning ability as defined by the authors of the tests? Aptitude tests can be challenged by questioning whether evidence is available that can describe the complete meaning of the aptitude measured. A teacher using a general mental ability test may demand of its author an explanation of his concept of general mental ability and how the pupil's activities as he writes the test correspond to that concept. Finally, when a personal-social adjustment inventory is thought to reveal the composition of the pupil's personality, the inventory must have a high construct validity.

PROBLEMS

2. Cite arguments for and against the statement that content and construct validity have little in common with criterion-related validity, as well as little in common with each other (Ebel, 1961, p. 640).

3. Cronbach (1970a, p. 125) believes that the central question asked when the construct validity of a test is being determined, is the following: "How can scores on this test be explained psychologically?" What is the full meaning of this question? Illustrate.

DETERMINING DEGREES OF VALIDITY

A given instrument may have more than one purpose, and thus should be characterized by more than one type of validity. The demonstration of high validity, then, is commonly a multiple approach rather than a single attempt. The author is obliged to examine carefully the aims of his instrument and, for each aim, to present evidence that the instrument can validly perform that function. This information can be of immeasurable help to those who wish to use the test for a particular purpose and, most important of all, interpret its scores in the most precise manner possible.

Content Validity

Because content validity is oriented toward achievement testing, which is such a formidable part of pupil evaluation, this section is restricted to achievement testing. Achievement tests are developed on the basis of educational objectives with verbal or mathematical aspects and are designed to show how well pupils have achieved those objectives. Therefore, to construct a test with high content validity, the teacher must begin with the same educational objectives that guided his classroom instruction. On the basis of the objectives chosen, test items are developed for criterion- or objective-referenced tests; for norm-referenced tests, tables of specifications are built, which in turn guide the selection of test items.

When a skilled teacher devises an achievement test for his own class, the probability increases that the level of content validity will be acceptable. Who knows better than he which of many proposed test items are probably "trick" or "unfair" items? Such test-item labels, when attached after considered thought by either teacher or pupil, can be regarded as vernacular expressions equivalent to saying that the test items, and hence the test as a whole, lack content validity to some degree. The teacher's knowledge of the class and its educational objectives are the most important factors accounting for the superior content validity of carefully constructed classroom tests.

NORM-REFERENCED STANDARDIZED ACHIEVEMENT TESTS. To some teachers, norm-referenced standardized achievement tests are unknown quantities. Yet these instruments typically resemble classroom tests a great deal, although they are more highly refined. They usually represent the thinking of teachers, supervisors, subject matter specialists, and others, and have withstood a rigorous statistical assault by professional testing specialists.

The educational objectives of a course of study and their tables of specifications, which are so important in the identification of the content validity of teacher-built achievement tests, are equally important in the identification of the content validity of norm-referenced standardized achievement tests. Hence, for such a test to have high content validity when measuring pupil achievement resulting from a given teaching effort, it must be constructed in terms of the table of specifications evolving from the learning experiences guided by that teacher in that instance. Beyond question, this rarely happens.

Since his test is to be used by not one teacher but hundreds, and since each teacher has his own peculiar set of educational objectives and tables of specifications, despite much common ground in many subject matter areas, the author can hope only to orient his instrument toward those educational objectives that appear to be most prevalent. Each teacher who proposes to use a norm-referenced standardized achievement test is automatically obliged to find convincing evidence that the educational objectives and tables of specifications involved closely correspond to his own.

To aim a standardized achievement test at popularly held educational objectives, the test builders do considerable investigation. A year or more may be spent in the laborious process of scanning lesson plans, state study guides, and widely used textbooks covering the subject matter in question and also in interviewing teachers and supervisors directly involved in the selected field. The process finally yields a core of reference materials thought to be most representative, and possibly a panel of subject matter specialists thought to be well-informed. On the basis of these sources of information, test items are constructed.

If the reference materials are identical with or closely related to those used by a teacher, the possibility of the standardized achievement test having high content validity for that teacher's use is considerably improved. Obviously, the textbooks and courses of study composing the reference materials should be identified for the potential test user. Some, but by no means all, manuals accompanying standardized achievement tests include complete titles and dates of publication of each of the reference materials. If a panel of subject matter specialists in the field is used, either independently of or in conjunction with the reference materials, they should be identified by name and pertinent facts about their professional qualifications listed.

Unfortunately, detailed information about the reference materials and any panel of specialists is not given in some test manuals. The inquiring teacher finds only glib statements about the "careful selection" of the test items and the "popular modern textbooks" that were consulted. This is meager fare indeed for any astute reviewer.

Regardless of the limited data of this kind that might be offered in the test manual, at least two other avenues relative to content validity should be explored. In the first place, manuals usually supply ample statements about the purposes of the test and its limitations in terms of subject matter covered. These statements bear careful perusal for evident reasons. Secondly, the test items themselves should be carefully scrutinized. It is highly recommended that a teacher play the role of pupil and write the answers under similar conditions. Then there should be an additional item-by-item examination. For each item the question must be asked: In view of my educational objectives, the tables of specifications derived from them, and the method of teaching I followed, is this test item appropriate for my pupils this term? Answers will be regularly affirmative if there is acceptable content validity.

The item-by-item examination should not be a casual operation. On the contrary, it should be tied directly to the teacher's educational objectives and his tables of specifications. A tabulation should be made by copying each item number opposite the cell of the table of specifications with which it is associated. If a test item is related to more than one cell, it should be tabulated accordingly. If it is primarily related to one cell of the table and secondarily related to another, a simple coding scheme can identify these differences. Although this process is lengthy, it is necessary if the content validity of a standardized achievement test is to be assessed.

Some norm-referenced standardized achievement tests simplify the tabulation process by including with the test materials a printed outline summarizing the various subject matter areas covered and listing opposite each the numbers of the test items primarily related to that area. An illustration of this can be found in the manual of the *Dunning-Abeles Physics Test* (1967, p. 5). In addition, the fifty items are classified according to subject matter topic and pupil behavioral change. This is summarized in Table 9.1 for *Form E*. Note the comparatively heavy emphasis on the traditional topics of mechanics, electricity, and magnetism, and the comparatively light emphasis on recall of information (that is, knowledge) about each topic.

The balance among the cells in Table 9.1 may or may not be agreeable to a secondary school physics teacher for a given testing situation. Even if it is, it may not be acceptable one term or one year later. The relative emphasis that teachers place on various combinations of topics and behavioral changes is a moving target. It shifts with time. Ideally a standardized achievement test must keep pace, step by step. Content validity can be fleeting.

TABLE 9.1.   Classification of Test Items in the Dunning-Abeles Physics Test (Form E).

Subject matter topic	Behavioral changes			
	Knowledge	Compre-hension	Application	Total
Mechanics	1	9	6	16
Electricity and magnetism	3	4	5	12
Atomic and nuclear physics	3	2	1	6
Wave motion and light	1	7	2	10
Kinetic-molecular theory	0	5	1	6
Total	8	27	15	50

PROBLEM

4. Unlike Table 9.1, the table of specifications for the *Dunning-Abeles Physics Test* lists the number of each test item in the cell in which it is classified. Select five test items from the test at random and, without referring to the item numbers in the table, assign each to a cell. Explain the reasons for your classification and any differences between your decisions and those of the authors.

Criterion-Related Validity

The degree of criterion-related validity for various types of tests can be determined by using aptitude tests as illustrations. The practical value of tests designed to measure mechanical aptitude, clerical aptitude, scholastic aptitude, and similar areas is centered in the accuracy with which a teacher can make predictions on the basis of their scores. It is logical, then, to take a longitudinal approach to the problem of determining criterion-related validity. A scholastic aptitude test can be administered to a group of pupils today and predictions of future academic achievement can be made in one or more subjects. Actual academic success can be measured at that future time by achievement tests or, possibly, final marks. Finally, predicted achievement can be compared with actual achievement, and the criterion-related validity of the scholastic aptitude test as applied in these prediction situations can be evaluated.

Predictions of future academic achievement can also be made in terms of the same units as those of the achievement measurement criterion, but are not always made in this manner. With statistical techniques beyond the scope of this book, a teacher may be able to say, for example, that a pupil whose scholastic aptitude test score is 117 should be expected to score in the vicinity of eighty-two on a particular English test. However, the predictions usually made are informal, thus making it awkward to compare predicted and actual achievement. They are often equivalent to saying that pupils who do well on the scholastic aptitude test will probably achieve well in school, whereas those who do badly will probably achieve poorly. In view of this, comparison of the scholastic aptitude scores and the measures of academic success would yield information concerning criterion-related validity.

Some of the basic steps in establishing the validity of an aptitude test can be examined most directly with an illustration. Suppose that an eighth-grade teacher of social studies wishes to know how satisfactorily achievement in that class can be predicted from scholastic aptitude test scores from a test given one year earlier. For the sake of simplicity, he is willing to define achievement in the social studies in terms of the scores of a comprehensive achievement test given at the end of the term. The result is a double measurement of each pupil, the data from which may be compiled in a fashion similar to Table 9.2.

The twenty pupils are arranged according to their scores on the scholastic aptitude test. Their achievement scores are listed opposite the scholastic aptitude scores. To facilitate interpretation, both sets of scores are ranked from one to twenty according to the position of the pupil in the class with respect to each test. If the scholastic aptitude test possesses high validity, the rank of any pupil in the scholastic

TABLE 9.2. Scholastic Aptitude Test Scores and Achievement Test Scores of Eighth-Grade Social Studies Pupils.

Name	Scholastic Aptitude Test Fall term, seventh grade		Social Studies Test Fall term, eighth grade		Difference in rank
	Score	Rank	Score	Rank	
Jim	135	1	66	9	8
Sam	130	2	90	1	1
Ruth	120	3	68	8	5
Mary	117	4	85	3	1
John	116	5	81	4	1
Louise	114	6	47	17	11
Ralph	113	7	69	7	0
Mae	112	8	77	5	3
Quinton	111	9	65	10	1
Sandra	109	10	56	15	5
Larry	107	11	89	2	9
Norma	106	12	49	16	4
Frank	101	13	57	14	1
Milton	100	14	58	13	1
Dave	97	15	71	6	9
Joe	95	16	60	11	5
Bill	94	17	38	19	2
Sally	90	18	31	20	2
Margaret	88	19	40	18	1
Sue	87	20	59	12	8

aptitude test should be approximately the same as his rank in the achievement test. Table 9.2 shows that the aptitude and achievement ranks of some pupils do not differ by more than one. These cases support the contention that the scholastic aptitude test can predict achievement in eighth-grade social studies. Since other pupils, however, have differences of eight or more, these cases tend to refute the contention concerning the validity of this test.

The foregoing analysis is casual, if not crude. A precise statement of the validity of the test is still lacking. Figure 9.1 was prepared to give a more comprehensive picture of the entire class of twenty pupils. In this figure are plotted twenty points, one for each pupil. The position of a point is found by locating on the vertical axis the scholastic aptitude test score of that pupil, and moving to the right, parallel to the horizontal axis, until his achievement in social studies is located. The points are numbered in terms of the ranks of the pupils on the scholastic aptitude test.

A moment of thought will indicate that, if the scholastic aptitude test has high criterion-related validity in this example, the points should arrange themselves in a straight line. Thus, the greater the tendency of the points to approximate a straight line, then the greater the validity. All points in Figure 9.1 obviously do not fall in a straight line, yet the eye can detect a definite elongated pattern that certainly suggests linearity. It is interesting now to observe the positions of points representing the five pupils whose ranks differ so greatly. The points are numbered 1, 6, 11, 15, and 20, and are represented by squares rather than circles. It is not surprising that they are all found along the perimeter of the pattern, and that their deletion would strengthen the impression that the points tend to form a straight line.

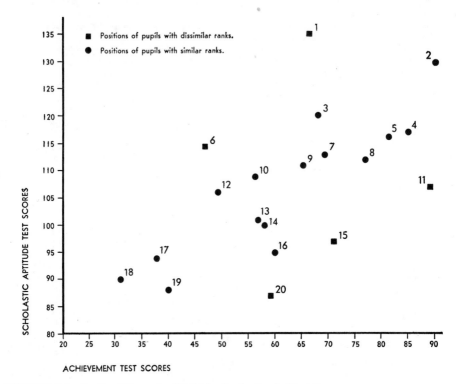

FIGURE 9.1. Scatter Diagram of Scholastic Aptitude Test Scores
and Achievement Test Scores.

Figure 9.1 strongly suggests, as Table 9.2 did, that the scholastic aptitude test has at least some validity in this situation. To identify the degree even more precisely, another step is necessary. This is the computation of the *Pearson product-moment coefficient of correlation*, often known as simply the *correlation coefficient*, and represented by the letter *r*.

THE CORRELATION COEFFICIENT.   The correlation coefficient is a number representing the straight-line relationship between the values of two variables, such as the values of the two variables resulting from double measurement of the pupils listed in Table 9.2. If points are plotted, as in Figure 9.1, and all of them fall in a straight line, the value of *r* will be 1.00. As the points deviate from a straight line, the value of *r* decreases to zero. In addition, when high values of one variable are associated with high values of the second variable, and low values of one variable are associated with low values of the other, as in the data in Table 9.2, the relationship is called positive and the *r* value carries a positive sign. If high values of one variable are associated with low values of the other, and low values of the first are associated with high values of the second, the relationship is called negative and the *r* value carries a negative sign. Thus, *r* values vary from −1.00 to +1.00. The number is indicative of the degree to which the points form a straight line, and the sign reveals the direction of the relationship. It should be noted that positive r values are much more common than negative values in educational evaluation.

The computation of an r value provides a succinct representation of the validity of the scholastic aptitude test in this instance. The extent to which the points plotted in Figure 9.1 tend to form a straight line determines the r value computed from the data, and also shows how efficiently the scholastic aptitude test predicts the eighth-grade achievement in social studies.

Computation of the correlation coefficient is somewhat lengthy, but simple. One formula of r that can be applied to the data in Table 9.2 is shown in Appendix A. With the formula is a complete description of the manner in which the values in Table 9.2 are summarized and substituted into the formula. An r value of 0.61 is found.

The interpretation of this value has, in reality, already been given. It represents the degree to which the points fall into a straight line or, stated differently, the rate of change in social studies achievement test scores compared with a given change in scholastic aptitude test scores. Unfortunately, some uninitiated observers try to improve on the interpretation by considering the r value as a percent. The fact that r values, with the sign ignored, vary from 0.00 to 1.00 undoubtedly encourages this error. In any event, the reasoning follows essentially this path: An r value of 1.00 results from data that, when plotted, yield a perfectly straight line. Hence, prediction of achievement on Test Y from scores from Text X will be 100 percent accurate. On the basis of this evidence, the accuracy of the prediction decreases as the r value decreases in such a fashion than an r value of 0.61 would mean that estimates of social studies achievement test scores based upon scholastic aptitude test scores will be 61 percent accurate. This latter argument is not true.

Although they represent by no means the only method, product-moment coefficients of correlation are popular representations of the criterion-related predictive validity claimed for a test. Other types of coefficients of correlation, discussions of which can be found in many textbooks of statistical methodology, are also used, but in a minority of instances. The computation of some of these is quite simple and rapid. One is the rank-difference correlation coefficient, otherwise known as the Spearman rho. It uses the differences between two sets of ranks such as those in Table 9.2 as a basis for its computation (see Appendix A). In the case of the data in Table 9.2, the rho value is 0.60, a close approximation of the r value. We cannot always expect such a high degree of agreement.

It is clear, certainly, that an adequate grasp of the demonstration of criterion-related validity is highly dependent on an adequate grasp of the meaning of the correlation coefficient. Although teachers generally do not find themselves confronted with computations of an r value, they are regularly obliged to interpret them.

EXPECTANCY TABLES. Rather than trying to make "pinpoint" predictions of future pupil achievement, many teachers wish to predict only in terms of broad categories: that is, whether a pupil will achieve "above average," "average," or "below average" in his class. If this is the intended use of the scholastic aptitude test, the predictive validity of the instrument can be much more realistically appraised by expectancy tables (Wesman, 1949, 1966).

TABLE 9.3. Expectancy Table for Scholastic Aptitude and Social Studies Achievement Test Scores.

Scholastic Aptitude Test scores	Social Studies Achievement Test scores			
	Below average (Below 55)	Average (55–75)	Above average (Over 75)	Total
Above average (Over 115)	0	2	3	5
Average (95–115)	2	7	2	11
Below average (Below 95)	3	1	0	4
Total	5	10	5	20

An expectancy table is merely a condensed version of plotted data similar to that in Figure 9.1. In the figure, each gradation of the scores of each test is shown; in an expectancy table, the scores are grouped into a convenient number of intervals. Table 9.3 is an expectancy table based on the data in Table 9.2 in which each set of test scores is grouped into three intervals. The number within each cell of the table represents the number of pupils who have scholastic aptitude and social studies achievement scores within the limits indicated.

The interpretation of Table 9.3 is straightforward. For instance, we can say that none of the pupils whose aptitude score is "below average" (less than 95) has an achievement score that is "above average" (greater than 75). Moreover, none of the pupils with "above average" aptitude scores (greater than 115) receives a "below average" achievement score (less than 55). More inclusive statements could be made in a slightly different manner. Pupils with aptitude scores of 95 or greater rarely (2 out of 16) receive achievement scores of less than 55.

Generally the interpretation of the expectancy table is simplified if percents are used. This requires a larger number of cases than twenty but can be illustrated by using the data from Table 9.3. By computing percents for each row separately, as in Table 9.4, we can estimate the probability of different levels of success in social studies for pupils having a given level of scholastic aptitude. For example, if a pupil has "average" scholastic aptitude, the probability of his having "below average" achievement in social studies is 18 in 100. His probability of having "average" achievement is 64 in 100; for "above average" achievement, it is 18 in 100.

DEGREES OF CRITERION-RELATED VALIDITY. It is certainly clear at this point that the scholastic aptitude test in question does not have the greatest possible predictive validity. On the other hand, although the r value is no larger than 0.61 and the expectancy table shows some pupils classified in cells other than the ones desired, we cannot automatically say that the validity of the instrument is unsatisfactory. On the contrary, the instrument may be judged as useful for prediction purposes if, in spite of its inaccuracies, it can predict future achievement of these pupils better than other means.

TABLE 9.4. Expectancy Table Based on Percents.

Scholastic Aptitude			Social Studies Achievement Test scores		
Category	Test score	Number of cases	Below average	Average	Above average
Above average	Over 115	5	0	40	60
Average	95–115	11	18	64	18
Below average	Below 95	4	75	25	0

Actually the *r* value of 0.61 is comparatively large in this case. When attempting to predict future academic achievement we often must work with scholastic aptitude tests with lower *r* values. This does not mean that they are extremely poor. On the contrary, tests yielding *r* values as low as 0.30 can be quite useful for screening groups of candidates for an educational program or a job.

Predictions of future achievement based on aptitude test data must be viewed in much the same manner as the predictions of life expectancy made by insurance companies. Life insurance companies can predict with striking accuracy the percentage of thirty-year-old men who will be living twenty-five or fifty years from now; yet they cannot predict with similar accuracy which *members* of the group will be alive or dead at these future dates. This is also true of achievement predicted from aptitude-test data. If predictions are made for a group, the accuracy is customarily quite good; a prediction made for an individual member of that group may be distressingly inaccurate.

TEST MANUAL AS A SOURCE OF INFORMATION. The primary source of information for most teachers as they investigate the validity of standardized aptitude tests and personal-social adjustment inventories is the test manual. Although this compilation is usually highly abbreviated, it regularly provides sizable amounts of data about the author's attempts to establish acceptable validity and perhaps lists references to research conducted by other interested investigators. Examination of the test manual by the potential test purchaser is always sound practice.

The test author who wishes to present the most comprehensible discussion of his test's validity is certain to find it an exacting task. Among other things, he must carefully describe the criterion with which his test is correlated and the nature of the pupils who cooperated in the validation attempt. Both of these descriptions emphasize the fact that the determination of validity as it is outlined is relative to the criterion used and the pupils measured. To the degree that the criterion is weak or the standardization group inadequate in any way, the determination of validity becomes less meaningful.

PROBLEMS

5. What is cross-validation (Anastasi, 1968, pp. 181–184)? Of what significance is it in the determination of the relative validity of a scholastic aptitude test? Give an illustration to support your answer.

6. When homogeneous groups of pupils are used, the predictive validity of aptitude tests is low. In other words, the r values are small compared with those for the same test used with heterogeneous groups. Explain why this is so (see Kaufman, 1972).

7. What major types of expectancy tables are being used? Study the illustrations shown by Schrader (1965) and compare them with Tables 9.3 and 9.4.

Construct Validity

Many of the methods used to determine the relative validity of the first two types are also suitable when construct validity is being investigated. An analysis of construct validity is supported by total available knowledge of the validity of the instrument in question. In other words, demonstrating what constructs account for variations in the performance elicited by a measuring instrument is a difficult task.

The basis on which the investigation of construct validity proceeds is provided by the theory underlying the construct supposedly involved in the measuring instrument. On the basis of the theory, predictions are made: one group of individuals will differ from another in terms of the data yielded by an instrument involving the construct, or individuals will or will not change in terms of an instrument involving the construct after they have experienced certain environmental conditions. The measuring instrument is then used to test the predictions. If the predictions and the data produced by the instrument concur, evidence in support of the construct validity has been found. If they do not, a state of uncertainty exists. Either the instrument does not involve the construct, or the theory is not sound. In any event, the degree of construct validity is in doubt (Cronbach and Meehl, 1955).

COMPARISONS WITH OTHER INSTRUMENTS. One method of determining construct validity is to correlate the data from the instrument under study with a second instrument thought to measure the same construct. This is sometimes done with group tests of general mental ability of the type regularly used in elementary and secondary schools. For example, an experimental group test of general mental ability and the *Stanford-Binet Scale, Form L-M*, are administered to a sample of pupils. The scores from the experimental test and the *Stanford-Binet* test are then correlated. If the *Stanford Binet* test is an acceptable measure of general mental ability, and its scores are closely correlated with those of the experimental test, the experimental test is said to have high construct validity.

Since complete agreement is seldom obtained as to the quality of the test serving as a standard, the correlation process is often repeated with several tests. When a group test of general mental ability is being studied, the standards are usually individual tests or well-known group tests of this trait. In areas other than general mental ability testing, there is a similar tendency, rightly or wrongly, to use popular tests reputed to measure the same construct as the test under investigation.

COMPARISONS WITH JUDGES' RATINGS. The use of judges is another means of assessing construct validity and has been used in connection with a variety of tests. For example, suppose that a paper-and-pencil inventory has been constructed to measure the social adaptability of junior high school pupils. Each of the 100 items included in the inventory requires the pupil to select one of the five alternatives that best approximates his behavior should he be confronted with the social situation described. The author defines social adaptability as the ability of a person, when participating in a social situation, to adjust his behavior in accordance with the nature of the situation and to do so easily.

To discover whether this inventory actually measures social adaptability, the author may employ a group of judges who are to observe independently—and somewhat surreptitiously—the social behavior of a group of pupils. The judges are, of course, ignorant of the pupils' scores determined by the paper-and-pencil inventory. They may use rating scales and check lists to record each pupil's behavior at such events as a school dance, a class picnic, a basketball game, and a concert. If the scores correlate well with the ratings, then the paper-and-pencil inventory has acceptable construct validity.

Serious doubts have been raised about the use of ratings of individuals as criteria against which to validate test scores (Guilford et al., 1962). These ratings are thought to be valid in that it is assumed that the raters know what they are measuring. Unfortunately, ratings regularly measure different traits from those intended.

PROBLEM

8. When two testing instruments are compared to estimate the construct validity of one of them, and the second is considered a standard, is the investigator engaging in a "circular" argument?

General Considerations

Determining the relative strength of any one of the three types of validity in a measuring instrument is sometimes frustrating. If the instrument is commercially distributed, the teacher may faithfully scan the test manual and doggedly sift the references to articles in professional journals in which the instrument is mentioned. Yet it often happens that even this effort leaves the investigator unsatisfied. The information gleaned from the process is often too vague and too limited.

VAGUE TERMS. The complaint of vagueness is traceable in part to the widespread use of a handful of terms that are not as meaningful as often supposed. Expressions such as "face validity," "statistical validity," and "curricular validity" fall into this category. Even the expression "validity coefficient" is applied too generally to contribute much to a discussion of validity.

A paper-and-pencil test has "face validity" when it seems to be valid to someone reading it. In other words, if a person unsophisticated in achievement measurement is handed an English vocabulary test for high school seniors and, after reading it, agrees that it appears to be a "valid" vocabulary test for that group, "face validity" is claimed. Admittedly, this is important to the pupils writing a test. Certainly they will tend to cooperate more readily if they sense that the nature of the items logically corresponds to the overall purpose of the test. Nevertheless, a flat claim for "face validity" of an instrument does not release its author from the responsibility of establishing the relative strength of one or more of the three types of validity.

"Statistical validity" is not a meaningful expression. As the title suggests, validity determinations in which correlation coefficients of some kind are computed are labeled determinations of "statistical validity." Within this loose framework are many determinations of validity, particularly criterion-related and construct validity. The expression is, therefore, unnecessary.

The expression "curricular validity" suggests the same type of validity as content validity. In achievement measurement both are acceptable. In aptitude and personal-social adjustment measurement, however, "curricular validity" becomes an awkward identification because the term "curricular" suggests only that an academic curriculum is implicated in some fashion. To speak of content validity does not inject any such restrictions. Therefore, the expression "curricular validity" is not so flexible and thus less satisfactory than "content validity."

THE MENTAL MEASUREMENTS YEARBOOKS. Fortunately, there is a yet unmentioned source of information about standardized instruments of all kinds. This helps fill the voids one typically finds when searching for definitive evidence about degrees of validity present. This source is known as *The Mental Measurements Yearbook,* the first volume of which was published in 1938. Additional volumes are published at fairly regular intervals.

The largest section of each *Yearbook* is entitled *Tests and Reviews* and contains—among other items—materials related to validity. This section assists in the appraisal of measuring instruments by providing frank, critical reviews of them and comprehensive bibliographies of references concerning each. For a given instrument, it is common to find such information as its complete title, age or grade levels of the individuals for whom it is designed, date of publication, cost, time limits, and the names of the author and the publishing company. In addition, one or more reviews is usually included, and the author identified. Pertinent references are listed without comment and may be numerous, in a few instances as many as one hundred. These contain information on the construction, validity, use, and limitations of the instrument.

The magnitude of the yearbooks is somewhat startling. For instance, *The Seventh Mental Measurements Yearbook* (Buros, 1972) alone contains information on over 1,000 tests and 12,000 references on the construction, use, and validity of specific tests. When it is remembered that this yearbook supplements rather than supplants the preceding six volumes, it is eminently clear that these volumes form a colossal body of material.

Several significant companion volumes to the *Yearbooks* have been published. One is *Tests in Print II* (Buros, 1974), which contains information about currently available tests and is cross-referred with the *Yearbooks*. Two monographs have been issued, *Reading Tests and Reviews* (Buros, 1968) and *Personality Tests and Reviews* (Buros, 1970). These contain a wealth of information about reading tests and personality inventories respectively, part of which appeared originally in the *Yearbooks*.

Counselors, supervisors, and research workers, as well as classroom teachers, find the *Yearbooks* and their companion volumes of inestimable value in their instrument appraisals. As a readily accessible compilation of facts about, and considered criticisms of, measuring instruments, they are unmatched. Certainly no validity appraisal other than that of a teacher-constructed instrument is complete without including whatever information the *Yearbooks* can provide.

PROBLEMS

9. Study the reviews in *The Mental Measurements Yearbooks* of two tests or test batteries of interest to you in the area of (a) academic achievement, (b) scholastic aptitude, or (c) interest patterns. On the basis of the evidence presented, compare each pair of tests or test batteries in terms of their various kinds of validity.

10. In the last analysis, the responsibility for valid use of a test rests on the individual who interprets it (Cronbach, 1970b). Do you agree? If so, what are the responsibilities in this regard for authors of standardized tests?

SUMMARY

Here are seven outstanding ideas presented in this chapter:

1. *Validity, the most vital attribute of any measuring instrument, is commonly defined as the degree to which that instrument actually serves the purposes for which it is intended. Since the purposes of measurement are divided into three categories, validity is classified into three types: (1) content validity, (2) criterion-related validity, and (3) construct validity.*

2. *Content validity is defined as the degree to which an instrument can be used to measure the present performance of a pupil in a certain type of situation or subject matter of which its items are a cross-sectional sample.*

3. *Criterion-related validity exists (1) to the extent that it can be used to predict a pupil's future performance, and (2) to the degree that the behavior elicited by a measuring instrument corresponds to external but concurrent pupil behavior.*

4. *An instrument has construct validity if a specified construct accounts for the variations in pupil performance it elicits.*

5. *The demonstration of a measuring instrument's validity is almost invariably a lengthy and laborious task. It may be necessary, for example, to ascertain*

whether a given instrument is characterized by more than one of the three types of validity, perhaps all three. Furthermore, suitable criteria and samples of pupils must be found before the validity determination can be completed. This is particularly true of criterion-related validity investigations.

6. *The end product of a validity determination may or may not be quantitative in nature. Studies of content validity typically do not yield quantitative evidence, whereas studies of criterion-related and sometimes construct validity do yield quantitative evidence, such as a product-moment coefficient of correlation.*

7. *Before a teacher uses any measuring instrument, he is obliged to conduct a thorough investigation of its validity. This appraisal commonly is based on the material presented in the instrument's manual, the information provided by The Mental Measurements Yearbooks and their companion volumes, and the considered judgment of the teacher.*

SUGGESTED READINGS

AMERICAN PSYCHOLOGICAL ASSOCIATION. *Standards for educational and psychological tests.* Washington: Author, 1974.
> This bulletin is the result of the third important attempt by the American Psychological Association and other organizations to develop an authoritative statement concerning test standards. Content, criterion-related, and construct validity are defined carefully and illustrations are provided.

ANASTASI, A. *Psychological testing.* (3rd ed.) New York: Macmillan, 1968. Chapters 5 and 6.
> Chapter 5 includes descriptions of various types of validity and is nonquantitative in nature. In contrast, Chapter 6 emphasizes quantitative representations of validity and their interpretation. One section deals with expectancy tables, another with the net gain in selection accuracy resulting from the use of a test.

CRONBACH, L. J. *Essentials of psychological testing.* (3rd ed.) New York: Harper & Row, 1970. Chapter 5.
> Within this chapter are discussions of the three types of validity. Steps for computing a product-moment and a rank difference coefficient of correlation are given.

CRONBACH, L. J. Validation of educational measures. *Proceedings of the 1969 Invitational Conference on Testing Problems.* Princeton: Educational Testing Service, 1970.
> Primary emphasis is given to content and construct validity. A useful summary of types of validation is given in table form.

EBEL, R. L. Must all tests be valid? *American Psychologist,* 1961, *16,* 640–647.
> This is a provocative article. The author argues that all tests need not be "valid" if the term "valid" is not to be made synonymous with the term "good," and if validity is a clearly defined concept that can be quantified by correlating test scores and data from an independent criterion.

WESMAN, A. G. *Double-entry expectancy tables.* Test Service Bulletin, No. 56. New York: Psychological Corporation, 1966.
> Since predictions of future achievement are often made on the basis of two predictors rather than one, a double-entry expectancy table is needed. In this bulletin, such tables are described and illustrated.

REFERENCES CITED

AMERICAN PSYCHOLOGICAL ASSOCIATION. *Standards for educational and psychological tests.* Washington: Author, 1974.

ANASTASI, A. *Psychological testing.* (3rd ed.) New York: Macmillan, 1968.

BUROS, O. K. (ed.). *Reading tests and reviews.* Highland Park, N.J.: Gryphon Press, 1968.

BUROS, O. K. (ed.). *Personality tests and reviews.* Highland Park, N.J.: Gryphon Press, 1970.

BUROS, O. K. (ed.). *The seventh mental measurements yearbook.* Highland Park, N.J.: Gryphon Press, 1972.

BUROS, O. K. (ed.). *Tests in print II.* Highland Park, N.J.: Gryphon Press, 1974.

CRONBACH, L. J. *Essentials of psychological testing.* (3rd ed.) New York: Harper & Row, 1970a.

CRONBACH, L. J. Validation of educational measures. *Proceedings of the 1969 Invitational Conference on Testing Problems.* Princeton: Educational Testing Service, 1970b.

CRONBACH, L. J., and P. E. MEEHL. Construct validity in psychological tests. *Psychological Bulletin,* 1955, 52, 281–302.

DUNNING, G. M., and S. ABELES. *Manual, Dunning-Abeles Physics Test.* New York: Harcourt Brace Jovanovich, 1967.

EBEL, R. L. Must all tests be valid? *American Psychologist,* 1961, 16, 640–647.

GUILFORD, J. P., et al. Ratings should be scrutinized. *Educational and Psychological Measurement,* 1962, 22, 439–447.

KAUFMAN, A. S. *Restriction of range: Questions and answers.* Test Service Bulletin, No. 59. New York: Psychological Corporation, 1972.

SCHRADER, W. B. A taxonomy of expectancy tables. *Journal of Educational Measurement,* 1965, 2, 29–35.

WESMAN, A. G. *Expectancy tables—a way of interpreting test validity.* Test Service Bulletin, No. 38. New York: Psychological Corporation, 1949.

WESMAN, A. G. *Double-entry expectancy tables.* Test Service Bulletin, No. 56. New York: Psychological Corporation, 1966.

10

THE RELIABILITY OF MEASUREMENT METHODS

Prodded by his teenage son, the proud owner of a near-new automobile decided to determine the number of miles that it traveled for each gallon of gasoline consumed. During a week in early May he carefully tabulated the gasoline consumption and the miles traveled, and computed the gasoline mileage to be 15.2 miles per gallon. Later that same month the owner selected another week, determined the gasoline consumed and miles traveled, and found that the gasoline consumption was 15.0 miles per gallon. The procedure was repeated during the first week of June, and a gasoline mileage of 15.4 miles per gallon was the result.

It is not surprising that the gasoline mileages varied by only small amounts. Because the three one-week periods were separated by relatively short periods of time, and because such factors as weather and traffic conditions were, for all practical purposes, uniform during all three trials, it seemed reasonable that the results should be consistent if these measurements of gasoline mileage were at all accurate. No doubt the owner ignored the minor differences among the three values and concluded that the gasoline mileage produced by his automobile under the existing traffic and weather conditions was fairly well identified. He might have even averaged the three measurements, and then used this value as the final product of his investigation.

Had he known that the true gasoline mileage had remained unchanged during the three trial periods and was really 15.3 miles per gallon, he would not have been dismayed. On the contrary, he might have been quite pleased with the accuracy of his estimates. Furthermore, if he had been pressed for an explanation as to why his three estimates varied while the true value did not vary, he might have shrugged his shoulders and attributed the small fluctuations to "chance" errors.

The chance errors that he had in mind are many. First of all, the measurement of the gasoline delivered by the pump might have been in error. Thus, exactly ten gallons of gasoline drawn from the pump might not necessarily have been registered on the meter as exactly ten gallons. Secondly, the reading of the meter introduced a possibility of error. The gasoline was measured to the nearest one-tenth of a gallon, and since the amount necessary to fill the tank probably fell somewhere between two such points, it had to be estimated to the nearest one-tenth of a gallon. Thirdly, the attendant might have filled the gasoline tank to varying degrees of "fullness" each time the owner began and completed the measurement of the gasoline mileage. Lastly, the odometer might not have registered the miles traveled with perfect accuracy, and the reading of it also might have involved certain amounts of estimation.

Despite these possibilities of error, the gasoline mileages were fairly consistent. Such consistency of measurement is equally desirable in education. A good measuring instrument must yield dependable information; in other words, if it is possible to use it repeatedly in the same unchanging situation, the information yielded by each administration of the instrument should be similar to that yielded by any other administration. For instance, the typing teacher who gives a speed test to his pupils on Friday would hope that the typing rates determined would be the same, for all practical purposes, as those obtained from such an exercise administered on Monday, if the pupils did not study or practice during the weekend. Likewise, the scholastic aptitude scores yielded by a test given to pupils at 10:30 *A.M.* on September 18th are assumed to be essentially the same as those that would be obtained were the test administered at 9:30 *A.M.* on September 19th.

Should there be no assurance that tests such as these do yield reasonably consistent results, their value would be severely limited. Before any measuring instrument should be used, therefore, the question might be asked: If repeated attempts are made to obtain information about an unchanging pupil attribute with this instrument, will the results tend to duplicate each other? The question can be stated much more simply: Is the measuring instrument highly reliable?

DEFINITION OF RELIABILITY

Reliability means consistency of results. Unfortunately, all instruments are unreliable to some degree, that is, they are subject to *chance errors.*

Chance Errors

Chance errors, or compensating errors as they are sometimes called, have one vital characteristic: they have a tendency to cancel each other when the instrument is used many times. There are a number of possibilities of chance error in the gasoline mileage determinations, one of which can be traced to the meter on the gasoline pump. Although a given withdrawal of precisely ten gallons from the pump may be recorded on the meter as slightly more than ten gallons, a second attempt might be recorded as slightly less. Were the process to be repeated an infinite number of times and the tendency to overestimate and underestimate found to be equal, then the error is a chance error and affects the reliability of the measurement.

There still remains, of course, the possibility that the meter consistently overestimates or consistently underestimates; no canceling takes place no matter how many measurements are made. This is obviously an error of measurement, but not a chance error. It does not lessen the reliability of the measurement, but it does lessen the validity. Thus, the degree of validity of the gasoline mileage measurement is reduced if the readings on the gasoline meter were always, say, one percent less than the actual amount of gasoline delivered by the pump. In the case of the typing speed test and the scholastic aptitude test, similar errors are possible. Either one could have yielded erroneous measurements to the extent that, say, every typing rate is seven percent too low or every scholastic aptitude score is four percent too large. These errors are classified in the second group of errors called *biased errors*, or *constant errors*, and affect only the relative validity of these instruments.

PUPIL-CENTERED AND INSTRUMENT-CENTERED FACTORS. Many factors affect the reliability of measuring instruments. Some are associated with the pupils themselves, whereas other factors arise from the instrument itself. Pupil factors ordinarily mentioned are state of health, fatigue, motivation, emotional strain, and the like. Two factors associated with the instrument itself are prominent in the paper-and-pencil test. First of all, the test is only a sample of an immense number of possible test items; secondly, the scoring of the test, particularly those with essay test items, may not be consistent, a factor known as lack of scorer reliability. Many additional factors related both to the pupils and to the instrument and its administration have been listed elsewhere (Stanley, 1971, pp. 363–369).

Certainly the importance of these factors as they affect the information yielded by a measuring instrument is not uniform from pupil to pupil or instrument to instrument. The pupil-centered factors may easily fluctuate from day to day, perhaps from forenoon to afternoon, and, for many pupils, play only a small role in terms of influencing an instrument's results. Instrument-centered factors tend to be less damaging when, for example, a paper-and-pencil test is lengthened by adding suitable items and when the scoring becomes more objective. Trivial as some of the sources of trouble may seem to be, they can drastically reduce the value of a measuring instrument.

Perhaps it is disconcerting to find such factors as those listed classified as the originators of chance errors. Admittedly they may not fit as neatly into the scheme as the gasoline meter and its errors do. Yet we can argue that the errors from the sources listed would cancel out if it were possible to measure an unchanging pupil attribute many times with each of many tests for this attribute, tests in turn scored independently by many judges.

PROBLEMS

1. On the basis of your experiences, order the following in terms of the degree of reliability that probably exists:
   a. Using a common yardstick to measure the height of basketball players.
   b. Using a quart bottle to measure volume of bath water.
   c. Using a bathroom scale to measure the weight of loaded suitcases.

2. Suppose that you were confronted with the problem of estimating the degree of reliability with which a small group of English literature teachers could score pupil answers to a certain limited-response essay test item. Describe the steps you would take to meet the problem.

DIFFERENTIATING BETWEEN
VALIDITY AND RELIABILITY

The terms "validity" and "reliability" have too often been used as though they were synonymous or nearly so. Though the concepts are somewhat related, they are by no means identical. The validity of a measuring instrument is the degree to which it actually serves the purposes for which its use is intended; the reliability of an instrument is its capacity to yield consistent information regardless of whether it serves the purposes in question. Thus a highly reliable instrument is not necessarily an equally valid instrument. For example, the heights of male college seniors majoring in education can be measured with considerable reliability. Yet this fact would in no way support the statement that the tall male college senior will be a better classroom teacher in future years than a short one. Educational tests may likewise have superior reliability and still be woefully lacking in validity. An arithmetic achievement test used to measure qualities of leadership is one of many possible examples.

It is timely to reemphasize that high validity is the most important characteristic of an instrument. The role of reliability is a vital but secondary one when a measuring instrument is being appraised. The importance of both characteristics can be summarized in the statement that the perfect instrument must serve the purpose or purposes for which it is intended and, in doing so, must produce consistent information.

DETERMINATION OF DEGREES OF RELIABILITY

Testing specialists concerned with methods for estimating the validity of a measuring instrument often search for external evidence and try to appraise the instrument's validity in terms of such evidence. Reliability determination, on the other hand, is not based on evidence of this kind. Instead, the instrument is compared with itself or some equivalent form. These procedures can be illustrated readily in the case of paper-and-pencil tests.

The determination of test reliability is based on one central method. The instrument to be investigated is used (perhaps in conjunction with an equivalent form) to obtain one or more attribute measurements of each member of a group of pupils. Each measurement identifies the position of each pupil in terms of the attribute measured. The consistency with which he maintains his position within the group from measurement to measurement is a reflection of the reliability of the test. This consistency can be translated into a product-moment coefficient of correlation, called a *coefficient of reliability*. Moreover, a coefficient of reliability can often be interpreted more easily by converting it to a *standard error of measurement*. This is an attempt to estimate the size of the errors of measurement caused by the unreliability of the test.

Determination of Coefficients of Reliability

Coefficients of reliability can result from four separate processes known as the stability method, the equivalence method, the stability and equivalence method, and the internal-consistency method. The first three are classical methods in that they call for correlating two sets of scores.

According to the stability method, a test is administered once, then a short period of time is allowed to pass and it is administered a second time to the same pupils. A coefficient of reliability is computed from the two sets of test scores. The equivalence method requires two equivalent forms of the test. They are given consecutively to a group of pupils, and a coefficient of reliability is computed. If a time interval of some size (for example, one week) occurs between the administration of the two equivalent forms, then the reliability determination follows the stability and equivalence method. Lastly, it is possible to analyze the data obtained from a single administration of a test and compute a reliability coefficient. This is the internal-consistency method.

In the past, the coefficients of reliability resulting from the application of the four methods have been identified, respectively, as the coefficient of stability, coefficient of equivalence, coefficient of stability and equivalence, and coefficient of internal consistency. Although these are useful labels, they do not adequately describe the kind of reliability determination that yielded the coefficient of correlation. It is recommended that in their place more complete statements be used to describe the coefficient of correlation such as "coefficient of reliability representing stability of measurements obtained by administering two different forms of the test one week apart."

STABILITY METHOD. We can easily determine the reliability with which we can assess such dimensions as the length or weight of a block of wood. Repeated measurements of the object are made and compared. A similar procedure is sometimes applied when the reliability of educational measuring instruments is under study. Suppose that a test author constructs a 100-item norm-referenced test designed to measure eleventh-grade pupils' knowledge of American history, and that this test has satisfactory content validity. To determine the reliability of his instrument, the author may give the test to a sample of eleventh-grade pupils, tabulate the results, allow an interval of time to pass, and finally readminister the instrument to the same pupils under the same conditions as before. Unless there is evidence to the contrary, it is assumed that the group has not changed with respect to their knowledge of American history during the time interval. Ideally then, each pupil would receive the same test score the second time as the first. In reality, the most the author can hope for is that pupils who received high scores on the first test administration will receive high scores on the second test administration and that those who received low scores the first time will receive low scores the second time.

Plotting the results of the two test administrations is most profitable. Figure 10.1 is a partial reproduction of the kind of configuration that might occur if the test were highly reliable. Many more cases (perhaps 200 or more) would be used than are shown in Figure 10.1. Observe that in this figure, as in the case of Figure 9.1 shown in Chapter 9, the points arrange themselves in an elongated manner so as to approximate a straight line. If the test were very unreliable, the points would scatter considerably, even to the extent that no straight line could satisfactorily represent the total number of points.

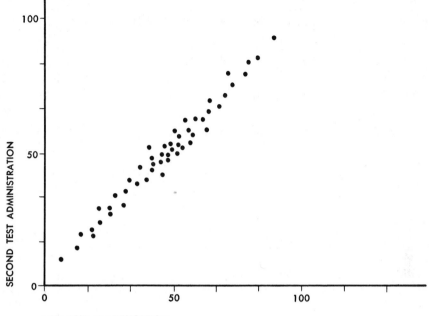

FIRST TEST ADMINISTRATION

FIGURE 10.1. Scatter Diagram of Achievement Test Scores Resulting from Two Test Administrations.

Once again the product-moment coefficient of correlation is the most convenient and suitable means of representing the degree to which the points conform to a straight line. The scores of the two test administrations are substituted in the appropriate formula (see Appendix A) for the coefficient of correlation, and a coefficient of reliability is computed. For a test such as the one described in this illustration, the r value might be 0.90 or more. A value of 1.00 would represent perfect test reliability in terms of this method, whereas a value of 0.00 would represent no test reliability.

The scores from the second test administration are generally slightly higher than those from the first, because of the practice effect that results from the first test administration. Unlike a block of wood, which can be measured endlessly without any noticeable effect on the block, a pupil will probably change as a result of the measurement. In the case of achievement tests, the change is customarily slight but discernible.

The length of time allowed between test administrations is critical and must be selected with care. If it is too short, pupils will remember the answers given at the first test when they answer the questions the second time; if it is too long, the pupils may change with respect to the characteristic measured. In many cases, a week or two is judged to be an appropriate compromise. Obviously there is no single, widely accepted time interval suitable for all types of tests with all varieties of pupils.

The stability method is not considered the most defensible for establishing test reliability. Some of its weaknesses have been mentioned. Three apparent defects are the practice effect that may result from the first test administration, the difficulty of establishing a suitable interval of time between test administrations, and the failure to have identical testing conditions both times. More serious in the eyes of some, however, is the fact that the coefficient of reliability reflects pupil-centered chance errors but not one of the most vital instrument-centered chance errors, namely, the fact that tests are samples of an immense number of possible items. Repetition of a test at different times will reveal inconsistent pupil behavior, but, since the same test is used twice, the sampling of the items is held constant. Consequently, an important instrument-centered chance error is ignored and the coefficients of reliability tend to be unduly *high*. Some writers recommend that these coefficients not be computed for achievement tests.

EQUIVALENCE METHOD. Rather than involve administration of the same test twice to a group of pupils, as in the case of the stability method, the equivalence method utilizes the scores from each of a pair of equivalent tests. The two equivalent tests are given to a suitable group of pupils with little or no time allowed between the two administrations. For each pupil two scores are available, one from each form of the test. When the scores are correlated, a coefficient of reliability results. If the two forms of the test were administered with an intervening time interval as in the test-retest method, then the stability and equivalence method is being followed. In many such cases, the time interval is at least a day and no longer than a week.

The requirement that a measuring instrument be available in two equivalent forms is, of course, a severe limitation. Equivalent forms of classroom tests are seldom found. Teachers usually do not construct them except in the case of "make-up" tests, which are supposed to be equivalent to the tests they replace. Standardized tests, on the other hand, are often published with two equivalent forms, sometimes more. Suppose that the test author who developed the 100-item norm-referenced achievement test in American history wants to construct an equivalent form. The problem he faces is not incidental. One danger to be avoided is the designing of the equivalent form to be so "equivalent" to the original that it is essentially identical. Then he still has but one test in spite of his efforts. The second danger is to design the equivalent form to be so "unequivalent" that it is measuring something at least slightly different from the original. A satisfactory equivalent form is somewhere in between.

The problem of building an equivalent form of the American history achievement test can be attacked systematically. First of all, as emphasized in the discussion of content validity of achievement tests, the test author must have identified certain specific educational objectives and developed one or more tables of specifications on the basis of them. To measure the degree to which these selected objectives have been achieved, he had to compose a vast number of test items. Pretesting the items at various times with appropriate pupils has helped screen them. In all likelihood, only part of the surviving items are included in the original form of the test. The balance are available for an equivalent form. Then the test author might dip into this supply in search of a second cross-sectional sample of test items that represent the same level of difficulty and the same relative importance of the cells of the table of specifications as the set of test items composing the original form. Evidence concerning the equivalence of the two forms can be obtained by methods beyond the scope of this book (Gulliksen, 1968).

Assume that the test author completes an equivalent form of the American history test and labels it Form B. The original test, now called Form A, and Form B can be administered consecutively to a group of 200 eleventh-grade pupils for whom the test is designed. The result is a pair of scores for each pupil, which in turn can be plotted and will yield a scatter of points very much like that in Figure 10.1. A coefficient of correlation computed from the data is a coefficient of reliability and will, of course, fall somewhere between 1.00 and 0.00. An r value of 0.91 is found in the case of the history test.

This coefficient of reliability is clearly not the same representation of test reliability as the coefficient yielded by the stability method. The chance errors involved in the two methods are different. In the equivalence method, the pupil-centered chance errors are not reflected in the coefficient of reliability. This is because the time interval between the two test administrations is virtually nonexistent. On the other hand, the instrument-centered chance error, associated with the fact that the test is necessarily a sample, is manifest in this method. Each form of the test is assumed to be a cross-sectional sample of the same group of items. The opposite is true in the case of the stability method: the pupil-centered chance errors are operative, whereas the instrument-centered chance error is not.

The test author may choose to give the two forms consecutively to an appropriate group of pupils, or he may choose to allow a time interval between the two tests. By the latter process, many pupil-centered as well as instrument-centered chance errors will influence the reliability estimate. Therefore, since reliability is defined as the relative absence of chance errors in the measurement results, the most logical procedure for estimating test reliability is the stability and equivalence method. Remember that its coefficient of reliability represents stability of performance by the pupil over a short period of time. This is essential information, since we often want assurance that the pupil would have obtained a similar test score had he been tested on a different day or with an equivalent instrument.

INTERNAL-CONSISTENCY METHOD. The practical difficulties in the test-retest and equivalent-forms methods of determining reliability emphasize the desirability of estimating test reliability with a single administration of a single form of the test in question. The savings in time and labor are obvious. In this undertaking, however, new formulas are necessary and new assumptions must be made.

There are two basic procedures for analyzing the results of a single administration of a test to assess the reliability of the instrument. The first, sometimes known as the split-half procedure, arbitrarily divides the total test into two halves, scores them separately, thereby yielding two scores per pupil, and correlates the pairs of scores. The resulting coefficient of correlation is a coefficient of reliability of one-half of the test rather than the total test, and is adjusted to be applicable to the total test. The second procedure, sometimes known as an analysis-of-variance procedure, involves examination of the responses to each test item in terms of the number of pupils who successfully answered the item and the number who failed it.

Usually the first controversy concerning the application of the split-half procedure is centered around the selection of the two halves. Imagine the number of possible halves that could be obtained by splitting the 100-item achievement test in American history previously mentioned. The most satisfactory set of all possible halves would be that pair composed of the two most equivalent members. In other words, the level of difficulty of the test items and the manner in which the items reflect the relative importance of the cells of the table of specifications involved should be the same in both halves. Dividing a test haphazardly into halves without thought of equivalence reduces the split-half process of reliability determination to busy work of dubious value.

If two equivalent halves of a test are to be found in the same way as two equivalent forms of a test are constructed, little has been gained in terms of conserving time and labor when the split-half method is used. Therefore, some compromises generally are made. Again the achievement test in American history can illustrate a typical situation. Let us assume that this achievement test, like many norm-referenced achievement tests, follows two general principles of construction. In the first place, the levels of difficulty of the test items cluster closely around the fifty percent level. Secondly, the test items are crudely grouped according to content; items relating to each cell in the table of specifications are clustered in a systematic fashion. Under these conditions, a convenient way of selecting two halves that would tend to be equivalent is to separate the odd-numbered items from the even-numbered items. The level of difficulty of the items in the odd half will approximate the level of difficulty of those in the even half. So also will the content of the test items in the odd half approximate that of the items in the even half. Note that had the author decided to divide his test so that the items numbered from 1 to 50 composed one half, whereas the items numbered from 51 to 100 composed the second half, the second would sample different material. The lack of equivalence would be striking.

The odd-even division is a popular method of separating a test into two halves of approximate equivalence. If the test author chooses to use this method, the remainder of the reliability determination is simple. First he gives the complete test (with odd and even test items in their proper order) to a representative group of eleventh-grade pupils for whom the test is designed. Then he separately scores the odd- and even-numbered items. A correlation coefficient can be computed by substituting the odd-half and even-half scores into the appropriate formula. The correlation coefficient between their scores is 0.73. This is the coefficient of reliability for one-half of the test rather than for the total test. To estimate the expected coefficient of reliability of the total test, an adjustment formula known as the Spearman-Brown "Prophecy Formula" (Spearman, 1910) is used.

In modified form the formula is

$$r_{xx} = \frac{2r_{oe}}{1 + r_{oe}} ,$$

where

r_{xx} = coefficient of reliability of the total test;

r_{oe} = coefficient of correlation between the odd-half scores and the even-half scores

In the American history achievement test the coefficient of reliability is

$$r_{xx} = \frac{(2)(0.73)}{1 + 0.73} = 0.84.$$

Observe here the increase in the size of the coefficient of reliability as the length of the test is doubled. The main assumption underlying the applicability of the Spearman-Brown formula is that the two halves are indeed equivalent. As they fail to be ideally equivalent, so the coefficient of reliability of the total test is an underestimate. Since the equivalence of the two halves is probably somewhat inadequate, the coefficients of the Spearman-Brown formula are conservative estimates of test reliability.

Computation of a coefficient of reliability by an analysis-of-variance method most often utilizes one of the Kuder-Richardson formulas (Kuder and Richardson, 1937). This formula, identified as K-R #20, is relatively easy to apply, although its derivation is intricate and beyond the scope of this book. An important category of information necessary for solution of the formula is the proportion of pupils passing and failing each test item. This procedure estimates test reliability on the basis of consistency of pupil performance from item to item within the test. In the case of achievement tests, the r values computed are usually smaller than expected because the item content of this type of test is not homogeneous.

The Kuder-Richardson and Spearman-Brown formulas are appropriate only for tests which are so administered that practically all pupils have an opportunity to attempt every test item. The r values that will result from use of these formulas with a single administration of a pure speed test will be inflated, perhaps substantially. The amount of overestimation is difficult to establish, but tends to decrease as the number of unattempted test items becomes smaller. The preferred procedure for determining the reliability of a speeded test is the stability and equivalence method.

Internal consistency methods of the analysis-of-variance type are becoming increasingly more popular. A number of variations are now being used, for example, the alpha coefficient (Cronbach, 1970, pp. 160–161). This kind of evidence of internal consistency is found in the technical manuals of many unspeeded standardized tests.

PROBLEMS

3. To what degree would one expect the problem of the "practice effect" to reduce the value of a coefficient of reliability from the stability method as a representation of the reliability of a test? Is "practice effect" also a problem when the equivalence method is used? Explain your answer.

4. Serious objections have been raised with respect to the usefulness of the test-retest correlations as representations of degrees of reliability (Cureton, 1969, p. 795). Do these objections justify the position that this type of reliability determination should be avoided?

5. It is argued that, in spite of evidence presented by the test author, so-called equivalent forms of an achievement test may be far from equivalent for a particular pupil population, and therefore comparisons based on these forms of the test may be distorted (Howell and Weiner, 1961). Study this argument and the supporting data. Of what significance are they in terms of the equivalence method?

Determination of the Standard Error of Measurement

Since every test is somewhat unreliable, each score obtained for a pupil must be considered as an estimate of his "true score," which would have been found had the test been totally reliable. Useful as the coefficients of reliability are when test reliability is being appraised, they do not directly offer an estimate of the actual magnitude of the error present in scores because of test unreliability. The standard error of measurement, on the other hand, attempts to do this. In other words, the standard error of measurement affords the test consumer some indication of the size of the difference between an obtained score for a pupil and his "true score" on the test. This difference is expressed in the same units as the test scores are. Observe that, when using the expressions "obtained score" and "true score" in the description of the standard error of measurement, considerations of validity are temporarily ignored.

COMPUTING STANDARD ERRORS OF MEASUREMENT. The computation of the standard error of measurement is not difficult. Its formula is:

$$S.E._m = \sigma\sqrt{1 - r_{xx}},$$

where

$$S.E._m = \text{standard error of measurement;}$$
$$\sigma = \text{standard deviation of total test scores;}$$
$$r_{xx} = \text{coefficient of reliability.}$$

The standard error of measurement of the achievement test in American history is 3.2. To obtain this value, we use the coefficient of equivalence of 0.91 along with the standard deviation, which is computed in accordance with a formula shown in Appendix A. The standard deviation value of 10.5 and the coefficient of equivalence are substituted in the standard error of measurement formula as follows:

$$S.E._m = \sigma\sqrt{1 - r_{xx}} = (10.5)\sqrt{1 - 0.91} = 3.2.$$

INTERPRETING STANDARD ERRORS OF MEASUREMENT. It is *not* appropriate to say that, in the case of the American history achievement test, a pupil's "true score" differs from his obtained score by no more than 3.2 raw-score points. Rather, it can be said that the "true scores" will not differ from their respective obtained scores by more than 3.2 raw-score points in approximately two-thirds of the measurements we might make with this test. Or, the standard error of measurement can be doubled and the statement made that the "true scores" will not differ from their respective obtained scores by more than 6.4 raw-score points in approximately ninety-five percent of the measurements we might make. Finally, we could triple the standard error of measurement and say that the "true scores" will not differ from their respective obtained scores by more than 9.6 raw-score points in approximately ninety-nine percent of the measurements.

Although the foregoing interpretations still do not offer a direct, unequivocal statement of the error caused by test unreliability in a given pupil's obtained score, teachers still consider the standard error of measurement to be a highly meaningful measure of test reliability. The fact that it is expressed in the same units as the test scores contributes greatly to its popularity. Teachers repeatedly argue that it offers a good basis for judging how satisfactory the reported test reliability is for a given testing function.

Because of test unreliability, scores must be interpreted as regions rather than as points. Such regions, often known as "bands," are determined by the standard error of measurement of the test. Since a pupil's "true score" does not differ from his obtained score by more than the standard error in approximately two-thirds of the measurements we make, it is customary to find the limits of the "band" by adding the standard error of measurement to and subtracting it from the obtained score. Suppose that a pupil obtained a test score of 70 on a test with a standard error of measurement of 3. The "band" often used would have a lower limit of 67 and an upper limit of 73. A pupil with a score of 75 would have a 72–78 "band." By the way, because the two "bands" overlap, we can say that there is probably no difference between the two pupils in terms of this test. Should the two "bands" fail to overlap, there probably is a genuine difference between the pupils in question. This use of the standard error of measurement, crude as it is, serves to inject caution into the interpretation of small differences between raw scores.

PROBLEMS

6. Study the procedure for scoring and interpreting the *School and College Ability Tests*. Why does the width of the percentile bands vary?

7. Describe a practical classroom situation in which knowledge of the standard error of measurement would be useful to you. Using layman's terms, how would you explain to a pupil that his test score should be interpreted as a region (or band) rather than as a point?

APPRAISING ESTIMATES OF RELIABILITY

The test manual accompanying the standardized achievement test and *The Mental Measurements Yearbooks* are extremely valuable sources of information in a study of reliability determinations, as they are in connection with the topic of validity. One or both sources often provide sufficient information to allow the teacher to make at least tentative judgments. Particular attention needs to be given those aspects of the determination that may influence negatively the interpretability of the reliability coefficient or standard error of measurement reported.

Coefficients of Reliability

Evaluation of the coefficients of reliability reported for a standardized test should include a searching look at (1) the test itself, (2) the characteristics of the group of pupils involved in the reliability determination, and (3) the testing conditions.

CHARACTERISTICS OF THE TEST. Examination of the test itself to find helpful evidence for appraising a coefficient of reliability requires attention to at least three characteristics. These are the tendency of the test to be speeded, the homogeneity or heterogeneity of its content, and the length. The role of speededness as it affects the size of coefficients yielded by the internal-consistency method and the role of homogeneity of test content when the Kuder-Richardson formula is applied are mentioned earlier. The importance of test length in determining the size of coefficients of reliability is dramatically illustrated by the Spearman-Brown formula. If the number of items in a test is increased by adding items equal in quality to the original ones, the reliability of the test will improve noticeably. With use of the Spearman-Brown formula, it is necessary to assume the items added are indeed equal in quality to the originals. Unfortunately this assumption is not always remembered, and an overgeneralized statement results, namely, the longer the test, the more reliable it is. Although it is true that longer tests tend to be more reliable in repeated instances, lengthening a test does not automatically assure us of greatly improved reliability.

Test items in a test that is comparatively homogeneous usually have higher indices of discrimination (D values) than those from tests of a heterogeneous nature. Furthermore, there is a close relationship between indices of discrimination of a test and its reliability coefficient (Ebel, 1967). To improve the degree of reliability of a test of a given length, use test items with relatively high indices of discrimination.

CHARACTERISTICS OF THE PUPIL GROUP. The group of pupils cooperating in the reliability determination is a second source of information. As in the case of the determination of criterion-related validity, the test author should characterize this group as to any attribute conceivably related to the dimension being measured. For example, the 200 eleventh-grade pupils involved in the experimental use of the American history achievement test should be identified as to grade level, average scholastic aptitude score on some well-known instrument, previous training in history, and geographic location. These and other pieces of information will help the teacher immeasurably in reaching his decision as to whether the 200 eleventh-grade pupils are comparable to his class for whom the test is being selected. If his class and the 200 eleventh-grade pupils seem to be the same, he can assume that the reliability estimates listed closely reflect the reliability of the measurements he will make.

The variability of the 200 eleventh-grade pupils with regard to the attribute being measured by the achievement test must never be ignored. A key value in describing the variability of the group in terms of this test is the standard deviation, in this instance 10.5. As the variability in American history achievement increases, so will the standard deviation. Moreover, as the variability increases, so will the coefficient of reliability. An extreme illustration involving the achievement test under consideration can readily illuminate the problem. Suppose that the 200 pupils had been drawn in about equal numbers from tenth, eleventh, and twelfth grades, in spite of the fact that the test is designed for eleventh-grade pupils who are completing a course in American history. The tenth-grade pupils may know relatively little about the material covered in the test; the eleventh-grade pupils know more; the twelfth-grade pupils, now having completed both American history and probably world history courses, supposedly command even more knowledge. If this is true, the new group of 200 pupils is extremely variable in terms of American history achievement, and the standard deviation will exceed 10.5. Hence the coefficient of reliability will be larger. Obviously the robust size of a coefficient of reliability based on a highly variable group of pupils does not indicate the reliability of measurements made on a more uniform group. Therefore, to interpret a coefficient of reliability, one should study the standard deviation of the test scores. Coefficients of reliability become more and more interpretable as the standard deviation of the standardization group, the 200 eleventh-grade pupils, approaches that of the teacher's class.

STANDARDIZATION OF TESTING CONDITIONS. The uniformity or lack of uniformity of the testing conditions is another point of concern when reports of reliability determination are appraised. Certainly the testing conditions at the time the standardization group is measured must be essentially the same as those recommended by the test author. This prerequisite is generally attained without difficulty. A persistent problem, however, is pupil motivation. An appropriately oriented pupil who is to be given the test only once may be highly motivated throughout the measurement process. In contrast, a pupil who is the unwilling victim of double measurement, be it by test-retest or equivalent forms, and who is measured at some inopportune time for no reason known to him, is undoubtedly less motivated. These differences introduce error. They will, for example, tend to lower the coefficients of stability that might be computed.

MINIMUM COEFFICIENTS OF RELIABILITY. Thoughtful consideration of the test itself, the characteristics of the standardization group used, and the testing conditions inevitably lead to a more intimate grasp of the meaning of the coefficient of reliability. The question is often posed, however, as to what minimum a coefficient of reliability must attain before the test can be used under any condition. The answer is not straightforward. For instance, tests whose reliability coefficients are near 0.50 are used. Either the teacher applied an instrument of limited reliability or he did not measure at all, since, as happens periodically in the measurement of personality traits, no other more satisfactory instruments exist. Needless to say, interpretation of scores from instruments with such low reliability coefficients must be made with extreme caution.

There is no single minimum size a coefficient of reliability must reach, since the minimum alters with the purpose for which the test scores are to be used. The minimum size is comparatively low when the level of *group* accomplishment is being measured. It rises for the measurement of the level of *individual* accomplishment. In any event, coefficients of reliability of about 0.85 and higher are regularly found for many standardized achievement and aptitude tests distributed by well-known publishing companies. Values for personality inventories vary considerably but frequently are lower.

RELIABILITY OF THE DIFFERENCE BETWEEN TWO MEASUREMENTS. An important sidelight of the problem of appraising coefficients of reliability is revealed when the purpose of the measurement is to identify differences between two measurements rather than to interpret each measurement as such. Determining the difference between two measurements is relatively common. A teacher may wish to know how much progress his pupils made as a result of a particular learning experience. He could measure the class before the learning experience, then again after it, and interpret the difference between the two scores. In another case, a test battery composed of three, four, or more achievement and aptitude tests may have been given to a class. Then a test profile for each pupil is found. Among others, the question might be raised as to whether a pupil or a class is more competent in English than in general science. Differences between the scores of the two appropriate tests would be most helpful.

Although the coefficient of reliability indicates the reliability of individual measurements, it does not directly show the reliability of the difference between two measurements. This, however, can be computed when we know the coefficients of reliability of the two tests involved in the determination of the differences in question, and the intercorrelation between these tests.

It is unfortunately true that, if there is any important correlation between the two tests yielding scores from which difference scores are obtained, the reliability of these difference scores is substantially lower than average reliability of the two tests in question. All users of tests should be keenly aware of this fact. In Table 10.1 notice the striking drop in the reliability of the difference scores as the correlation increases between the two tests used.

Standard Errors of Measurement

The foregoing discussion of the coefficients of reliability is appropriate in part to the standard error of measurement. Appraising the significance of standard errors of measurement embodies a searching examination of the test itself, the characteristics of the standardization group of pupils, and the testing conditions. However, fluctuations in the variability of the group with respect to the characteristic being measured are considerably less important when standard errors of measurement are being considered

TABLE 10.1.   Reliability of Difference Scores for Tests Having Various Degrees of Reliability.

Coefficient of reliability		Correlation between Test A and Test B	Reliability of difference scores
Test A	Test B		
0.90	0.90	0.60	0.75
		0.40	0.83
		0.00	0.90
0.80	0.80	0.60	0.50
		0.40	0.67
		0.00	0.80
0.70	0.70	0.60	0.25
		0.40	0.50
		0.00	0.70

instead of coefficients of reliability. Whereas differences in variability of the character-istic measured cause considerable fluctuations in the coefficients of reliability, the standard errors of measurement are, for all practical purposes, independent of fluctua-tions in the variability of the test scores. Hence, the standard error of measurement is a desirable way of comparing the reliability of a particular test administered to two different groups of pupils. This is precisely what happens when a teacher compares the reliability of a test given to a standardization group with its reliability when it is given to his class.

There are no readily applied suggestions as to how big a standard error should or should not be to ensure that the test is useful for a given purpose. Since it is expressed in the same units as the test scores, and since these units typically vary from test to test, a standard error of measurement of a specific size may be considered small in the case of one test and large in the case of another. Evaluation of standard errors of measurement is largely centralized in the teacher's concept of the importance of score difference in terms of the purposes for which the test has been administered. If a test author reports more than one standard error of measurement and identifies them as being applicable to certain different score levels, the foregoing principle still holds.

PROBLEM

8. Study the procedure for scoring and interpreting the *Differential Aptitude Tests*. Compare the interpretation of pupil profiles plotted on the individual report form to the foregoing discussion of the unreliability of difference scores.

SUMMARY

The primary ideas in this chapter can be summarized as follows:

1. *Reliability is defined as the tendency of a measuring instrument to yield consistent information. It is secondary to validity as a desirable test character-istic.*

2. *A test is reliable to the degree that chance errors do not influence the information produced when it is given. Common chance errors in educational measuring methods are (1) pupil-centered errors, such as fluctuations in level of health, emotional strain, and motivation, and (2) instrument-centered errors, which arise from the fact that, for example, a paper-and-pencil test is actually a sample of an immense number of possible items, and it may not be scored consistently.*

3. *Reliability is practically always expressed in quantitative terms, either as a coefficient of reliability or as a standard error of measurement. The coefficient of reliability, as discussed in this chapter, is a product-moment coefficient of correlation that can be determined in one of several ways. These are the stability method, the equivalence method, the stability and equivalence method, and the internal-consistency method.*

4. *According to the stability method, the coefficient of reliability is computed when a test is administered twice (with an intervening period of time) to a*

group of pupils, and the pair of scores correlated. This representation of reliability has serious limitations.

5. *For the equivalence method, the coefficient of reliability is found by administering (with no intervening period of time) two equivalent forms of a test to a group of pupils, then correlating the pairs of scores. When a time interval is allowed, the stability and equivalence method is being applied.*

6. *For the internal-consistency method, several procedures may be followed, the split-half method or an analysis-of-variance method. The split-half method may utilize the Spearman-Brown "Prophecy Formula." One analysis-of-variance method is the Kuder-Richardson Formula # 20.*

7. *The standard error of measurement affords some indication of the size of the error caused by test unreliability. It is considered a useful indicator of test reliability because it is expressed in the same units as the test score and it is relatively independent of fluctuations in group variability in terms of the characteristic measured.*

SUGGESTED READINGS

AMERICAN PSYCHOLOGICAL ASSOCIATION. *Standards for educational and psychological tests.* Washington: Author, 1974.

> One section of this set of standards lists essential and desirable information needed for evaluating the reliability of a test.

ANASTASI, A. *Psychological testing.* (3rd ed.) New York: Macmillan, 1968. Chapter 4.

> The chapter cited contains sections dealing with the types of test reliability, the reliability of speed tests, the dependence of test reliability upon the sample used, and the interpretation of the standard error measurement.

CRONBACH, L. J. *Essentials of psychological testing.* (3rd ed.) New York: Harper & Row, 1970. Chapter 6.

> Strictly speaking, only part of this chapter is devoted to reliability (which the author prefers to call "generalizability"). Analysis-of-variance methods are stressed.

DIEDERICH, P. B. *Short-cut statistics for teacher-made tests.* (3rd ed.) Princeton, N.J.: Educational Testing Service, 1973. Pp. 3–12.

> The three chief topics considered are the standard error of a test score, reliability, and correlation. Simple methods of computing needed statistical values are demonstrated.

EBEL, R. L. The relation of item discrimination to test reliability. *Journal of Educational Measurement,* 1967, *4,* 125–128.

> An important generalization is demonstrated, namely, if one is to achieve a high degree of reliability for a test of a given length, use test items that are high in discrimination as measured by the *D* index.

WOMER, F. B. *Basic concepts in testing.* New York: Houghton Mifflin, 1968. Chapter 2.

> Topics such as errors of measurement and the computation and interpretation of reliability coefficients are covered in a brief and straightforward manner.

REFERENCES CITED

CRONBACH, L. J. *Essentials of psychological testing.* (3rd ed.) New York: Harper & Row, 1970.

CURETON, E. E. Measurement theory. In R. L. Ebel (ed.), *Encyclopedia of educational research.* (4th ed.) New York: Macmillan, 1969, 785–804.

EBEL, R. L. The relation of item discrimination to test reliability. *Journal of Educational Measurement,* 1967, *4,* 125–128.

GULLIKSEN, H. Methods for determining equivalence of measures. *Psychological Bulletin*, 1968, 70, 534–544.

HOWELL, J. J., and M. WEINER. Note on the equivalence of alternate forms of an achievement test. *Educational and Psychological Measurement*, 1961, 21, 309–313.

KUDER, G. F., and M. W. RICHARDSON. The theory of estimation of test reliability. *Psychometrika*, 1937, 2, 151–160.

SPEARMAN, C. Coefficient of correlation calculated from faulty data. *British Journal of Psychology*, 1910, 3, 271–295.

STANLEY, J. C. Reliability. In R. L. Thorndike (ed.), *Educational measurement*. Washington: American Council on Education, 1971, chapter 13.

PART FOUR

Standardized Tests, Scales, and Inventories

The purpose of Part Four is to acquaint the reader with the nature and availability of various instruments designed to measure achievement. aptitude, and aspects of personal-social adjustment. Considerable attention is given to norm-referenced standardized measuring instruments. Chapter 11, "Standardized Achievement Tests," discusses the construction of such tests, and attempts to give the reader an understanding of their general nature. Selected achievement tests and batteries are used to illustrate their contribution to the evaluation program.

Chapter 12, "Measuring Pupil Aptitudes," is devoted to an explanation of the various kinds of aptitude instruments. It discusses selected tests to clarify the different purposes for which each should be used, and outlines procedures for their effective use in the classroom and with individual pupils. A large part of the chapter is concerned with a discussion of scholastic aptitude and its testing both by individual and group instruments. The concepts of mental age and intelligence quotient are developed, and precautionary measures for their use discussed. Differential testing is also explored and its advantages are delineated.

Chapter 13, "Evaluating Personal-Social Adjustment," is devoted to the third general area of evaluation. Emphasis is laid upon the strengths and weaknesses of the personal-social adjustment inventories, and suggestions are given for their use in conjunction with less formal methods of evaluation, including observation with use of anecdotal records, rating scales, check lists, and interviews. Measurement of attitudes and interests is treated as an important aspect of understanding pupil growth.

11

STANDARDIZED ACHIEVEMENT TESTS

When a golfer "breaks seventy-five" for eighteen holes, he is considered an outstanding performer. The athlete who runs a mile in four minutes has finished a superlative race. The major league baseball player with a batting average of over 0.300 will be surpassed by relatively few. On the other hand, the golfer who requires more than 100 strokes to complete eighteen holes is considered a duffer and the miler who is clocked over 4' 30" would not be likely to make a good college track team. Certainly a baseball player whose batting average is below 0.225 isn't considered a good hitter.

These performances are evaluted in terms of norms generally accepted as representing various degrees of competence. It makes no difference whether the game is played or the mile run in Kansas City or Seattle. The performances are regulated by specific rules so that the degree of excellence is affected by the ability of the performer. Even though an athlete may be considered outstanding when compared with limited competition, his performance may be mediocre on a national scale.

A similar situation exists when norm-referenced standardized tests are administered. There are prescribed conditions for testing. Norms are established. It follows that the examinee's performance can be evaluated by comparing it with that of a large number of his peers from many schools. No such comparisons are made in the case of criterion- and objective-referenced tests.

If you have studied the foregoing chapters carefully, you already know a great deal about standardized achievement tests. To understand the concepts of validity, reliability, item analysis, test scores and norms, the place of educational objectives in testing, and the building and appraisal of classroom tests means that you already know about the framework on which standardized achievement tests are constructed.

ACHIEVEMENT VS. APTITUDE TESTS

Both achievement and aptitude tests measure the effects of learning. Therefore, one finds considerable similarities among them. The difference lies in the degree to which the relevant experiences prior to taking the tests are uniform. Aptitude tests measure the effects of learning under relatively uncontrolled and unknown conditions, whereas achievement tests measure the effect of learning that occurred under partially

260

TABLE 11.1. A Continuum of Tests of Developed Abilities.

Specificity . . . . Generality

Course-oriented achievement tests	Broadly oriented achievement tests	Verbal-type intelligence and aptitude tests	Non-language tests	Culture-fair tests

From Anastasi, 1968, p. 392. Reprinted by permission of the Macmillan Company.

known and controlled conditions (Anastasi, 1968, p. 391). Achievement tests are designed to inform the teacher about what a pupil knows and can do now whereas aptitude tests are designed to predict future performance. But one must exercise care in making absolute classifications. For example, achievement tests are very useful in predicting subsequent performance. If a pupil does well on an arithmetic achievement test, the score is a good predictor of performance in algebra or geometry.

The different names for the two kinds of tests have led to confusion. Long ago, Kelley (1927) coined the terms "jangle fallacy" and "jingle fallacy" in discussing the problem. The "jangle fallacy" refers to the assumption of difference between two tests with different names. He used "jingle fallacy" when two tests with the same name, for example, Scholastic Aptitude Test, are thought to measure the same thing.

Actually, achievement tests and scholastic aptitude tests form a kind of continuum in terms of the degree of specificity of experiential background that they presuppose, as shown in Table 11.1. Course-oriented achievement tests, including teacher-made tests, are very specific; in contrast, nonlanguage aptitude tests emphasize generality of learning.

Other continua have been developed, for instance, a spectrum for comparing tests of scholastic aptitude (see p. 297). Here again, aptitude tests at one end of the continuum are very similar to achievement tests because they measure knowledge and skills that require direct training. As you can see, there is no simple way of differentiating between the many types of achievement tests on the one hand and all of the various kinds of aptitude tests on the other.

STANDARDIZED VS. TEACHER-CONSTRUCTED TESTS

The term *standardized* actually refers to specific instructions for administration and scoring. In the case of norm-referenced tests, norms are subsequently prepared that represent performance for similar groups. These give the teacher an independent yardstick for checking the achievement of his pupils. While his own tests can measure only the relative performance of the pupils in his class, norms provide the opportunity to compare their achievement with that of pupils in other schools. The college-bound pupil particularly needs to know how well he does in comparison with future competitors. The teacher, too, can use norms to judge the effectiveness of his teaching.

Most of the factors that distinguish standardized from classroom achievement tests relate to better test making. Planning and construction are probably more careful and thorough for standardized achievement tests, which are handled by specialists, than for teacher-constructed tests. There is also a much more critical analysis of the objectives on which the measurement is based. Exacting procedures are followed in the construction and appraisal of individual test items for standardized tests, and extensive statistical analyses are applied to determine their level of difficulty and discriminating power. Often there are comparable forms of the instrument so the test can be administered periodically to measure growth.

In building a classroom test, teachers can take advantage of the individuality of the local community and the pupils in the classes, having pupils study that which best relates to their experiences. Appreciation of literature can be taught with different literary selections, and scientific method can be taught through different subjects. Obviously, individual variations in study materials cannot be considered on a test designed for wide use in many schools, and it becomes necessary to include the materials on which questions are based. This results in many short selections with a definite limitation on achievement measurement; it is impossible to ask an examinee to criticize complete literary works or determine his recall on wide reading. At the classroom level, however, teachers must be better trained in test construction so that they will avoid using assigned materials to measure memorization of content for its own sake; they should instead use these materials as a vehicle for evaluating the lasting results of instruction.

PROBLEMS

1. What arguments might you, as a teacher, offer your school principal to justify using a standardized achievement test as a final examination in your course?

2. Standardized tests are generally recognized as superior in planning and construction to tests prepared by classroom teachers. What techniques used by standardized-test builders could be easily and profitably used by the classroom teacher?

USES OF STANDARDIZED ACHIEVEMENT TESTS

Standardized achievement tests play an important role in strengthening the instructional program. One function is to provide the teacher with a criterion for checking his own emphasis in teaching. Of course, the use of norms implies that comparisons made between and among pupils or classes are restricted by the content of the test. If a class has a high mean score on an American history test, it has not necessarily achieved more in this subject matter area than another class with a lower score. Emphasis in one class may have been on facts and details, while the other stressed critical thinking and broad relationships. Test content must be analyzed before final judgment is made. However, when a test proves to include important and generally accepted areas of knowledge and skills, a teacher ought to make a critical evaluation of his own educational objectives and instruction if a class does poorly in relation to individual pupil ability.

A second use of standardized tests is for determining pupil progress. Generally there are comparable forms of the test, which allows the administering of one at the beginning of the year and another at the end. Although cautious interpretation should be made on the basis of individual test scores, group scores representing progress or the lack of it may reliably emphasize particular strengths or weaknesses.

It must also be remembered that pupils' mental ability is positively correlated with achievement. Effective teaching cannot always be inferred just because the class average is at the median. On the other hand, a class average below the median may actually represent excellent progress in one case, whereas in another, achievement above the median may still be far below the potential of the group.

A third function of standardized tests is to provide a comparison of achievement between various subject matter areas and specific phases of a particular area. It is often desirable to determine how a pupil's arithmetic skill compares with his reading ability or to compare achievement in vocabulary, comprehension, and rate of reading. Obviously these comparisons can be made on an individual or group basis. If the group has a particular weakness, then an evaluation of class learning experiences is in order. When problems seem to relate to individual pupils, then the teacher must provide individual attention.

A fourth use of standardized tests is for diagnosis of difficulties in achievement. Often the source of pupil difficulty may be determined through one or a number of very effective standardized instruments. Because test items have been constructed on the basis of studies that have determined frequent sources of difficulty, it is possible to analyze the adequacy of performance in crucial areas. In diagnosing a reading disability, for example, one can discover whether the pupil knows the initial consonant sounds, whether he can break words into syllables, and whether he makes use of punctuation for improved comprehension. Naturally, the teacher will also use his own tests in diagnosis, but standardized tests are helpful in providing a systematic approach. Criterion- and objective-referenced tests are particularly helpful in this regard.

Finally, a fifth use is for purposes of selection and classification. Achievement tests can serve as aptitude tests predicting performance in a given subject area. Not only are achievement-test results helpful in grouping for instruction, but scores are useful in determining whether pupils can be expected to do well or poorly in given courses.

PROBLEM

3. A principal use of standardized tests is that of grouping pupils for instruction. Would you consider achievement or scholastic-aptitude-test results more appropriate for this purpose? Explain your choice.

STANDARDIZED ACHIEVEMENT TEST CONSTRUCTION

The expense and effort of building a norm-referenced standardized achievement test demand a very careful appraisal of the need for a particular kind of instrument.

First, it may be determined whether there is a group of individuals that provides a potential test market. Ideally, there should be a need for an instrument and no satisfactory test is available to meet this need. Unfortunately, the criterion for the construction of a new test sometimes becomes the soundness of a business venture, even though several good instruments that can serve the same purpose are available.

Nevertheless, once it has been decided that a new instrument will be constructed, representatives from the population of test consumers are consulted to formulate specifications for the instrument. The purpose of the test must be spelled out clearly. Is it to be a survey or a diagnostic test? Is it to be primarily for individual or group guidance? Will there be subscores or just a total score? For what population of pupils is the test to be designed? Is it for a group of homogeneous ages or for grades three through twelve? Does it require reading ability? What will be its general contents? All of this must be answered before actual test construction begins.

Pretest Construction and Administration

In the discussion of paper-and-pencil achievement tests in Chapter 2, three steps were outlined for construction: (1) identifying educational objectives with verbal and mathematical aspects, (2) developing tables of specifications reflecting the relative importance of the objectives, and (3) building the test items on the basis of the tables of specifications. A similar approach is used in developing standardized achievement tests, though test items are generally constructed by several subject matter specialists and examined by test specialists for technical considerations. Practical considerations, such as typical length of school class periods, help determine test length. Although at times improving the reliability and validity of a test by increasing its length would be desirable, it is not always possible because test administration must be fitted into existing school schedules.

In the development of the better tests, more items are initially constructed than will be used in the final form of the test. These items are assembled into a form called a *pretest*. Before the pretest is administered, the individual items are carefully scrutinized by other subject matter specialists and test experts for inaccuracies and technical flaws.

Directions and accessory materials must be prepared and provision made for recording answers on either separate sheets or the test booklet itself. When the test has been cast into its final form, these accessory materials, including scoring stencils, must be revised to fit it.

Analysis of Pretest Data

When the pretest form is ready, it is administered to a group of pupils comparable to those for whom the test is being designed. The results of the pretest administration are studied to determine which items should be kept. If the test is to discriminate among pupils, the items should be neither so difficult that some will answer them all incorrectly, nor so easy that some can make a perfect score. In neither case is it possible to obtain a true measure of the individual's achievement. It is absurd to conclude that he has achieved nothing; it is equally erroneous to assume that an individual has achieved the ultimate or that two individuals with a perfect score have equal achievement. Therefore, the levels of difficulty of the test items retained should be such that both zero and perfect scores will rarely, if ever, occur.

Items should also be chosen on the basis of their power to discriminate between good and poor pupils. Therefore, those items are retained that are answered correctly by more good pupils than poor. By the same token, the distracters or foils should be chosen more often by the poor than the good pupils.

The total number of items selected for the final form of the test depends on how many can be answered by the pupils in a given amount of time. One general rule of thumb is that about ninety percent of an average class should have an opportunity to attempt all the items in the time allowed. If careful attention has been given to the level of difficulty of these items, an average pupil should answer somewhat more than fifty percent of them correctly.

Developing Norms

On the basis of the criteria discussed above and the tables of specifications, items are selected for the final form of the test. It is then given to groups of pupils typical of those for whom the test is designed but who have not taken the pretest. Their scores provide the basis for setting up the norms of the test by which a teacher or school administrator can compare pupils' performances. These norms usually are standard scores, percentile ranks, or grade equivalents. Often several different kinds of norms are reported.

Equivalent, Parallel, and Comparable Test Forms

It is often helpful to have two or more forms of a test so that a pupil may be tested more than once—perhaps at the beginning and end of a term of instruction. A second test may be helpful at times when there is reason to doubt the validity of a pupil's first test score—because of illness, for example.

Parallel forms of a test may be developed simultaneously. This is sometimes done by constructing pairs of items that measure the outcome of specific objectives and are of approximately the same level of difficulty. Obviously, the administration procedures and format of both tests should be alike. Parallel forms administered to a large population of pupils and yielding scores with identical distributions are *equivalent* forms. *Comparable* forms of a test are illustrated by the various subtests of the *Differential Aptitude Tests (DAT;* see p. 301). Unlike the approach in equivalent forms, various mental traits are measured. In the *DAT,* all comparisons are based on the same norm group. The raw scores of each test can be converted into the same type of derived scores.

Accessory Materials

In addition to the test booklet, there may be special scoring stencils and, with all of the better tests, a manual. A set of test standards (American Psychological Association, 1974) recommends that certain kinds of information be placed in the manual. Procedures in administration and scoring should be stated so that it is possible to duplicate the conditions under which the test was standardized. The directions should be clearly phrased so the examinee will understand how the author intended him to perform. Although most standardized tests can be scored objectively, whenever there is an element of subjectivity, scoring variations leading to error should be discussed.

Because the name of a test does not always clarify its purpose and sometimes may even misrepresent what the test actually measures, the manual should state the objectives to be measured and assist in the correct interpretation of test results. Competencies required in administration, scoring, or interpretations beyond the typical classroom teacher should be indicated.

Detailed information on reliability and validity should include evidence that can be used in judging whether it is pertinent to the teacher's and the examinee's problems. The method of determining the reliability coefficient should also be reported. Discussion of validity should be specific in terms of whether it is content, criterion-related, or construct validity (see Chapter 9). The nature of any validating criteria and their desirability for a specific test purpose should be reported fully. Statistical data for determining any validity coefficients should be so adequate that the test user may judge their worth.

The manual should contain a discussion of the development of the test norms. Norm groups must be defined, the method of population sampling reported, and the time and conditions under which norm data were secured should be included. It is imperative that measures of central tendency and variability be reported.

PROBLEM

4. You have an appointment with your principal to present a request to purchase and use a certain standardized achievement test. What specific information about this test should you have prior to the conference? What will be your chief selling point?

SELECTED STANDARDIZED TESTS

There are many standardized achievement and diagnostic tests available to the classroom teacher. They attempt to measure a wide variety of areas, including such skills as critical thinking, reading, and listening. There are also tests in subject areas such as arithmetic, physics, and history. A discussion of a few selected tests and batteries is included here. The survey test, test battery, and diagnostic test are illustrated.

Survey Tests

Whether a test can be labeled as a survey test depends partly on the purpose for which it is used and also on the number of its subscores. Although generally a test yielding only one score is not thought of as being inherently diagnostic, it could well be used for diagnostic pupposes if one were to analyze the performance of the examinee on individual questions. As the number of subtests is increased, the instrument begins to assume a diagnostic flavor.

Tests generally thought of as survey instruments are often used along with scholastic aptitude tests to determine whether pupils are underachieving. For example, the underachieving reader is one who does not read as well as he should for his ability. He may be reading above his grade level, but if he is a bright child, he still may be an underachiever. Likewise, a child who reads below his grade level is not necessarily underachieving; his performance may be adequate for his mental capacity. The reading survey test actually provides a measure of the level of difficulty at which the pupil can read. In general it contains at least two measures, one of vocabulary and the other of comprehension. A measure of reading rate is often included. A useful illustration of a reading survey test is the *Gates-MacGinitie Reading Tests.*

GATES-MACGINITIE READING TESTS. The *Gates-MacGinitie Reading Tests* is a series of tests replacing the well-known *Gates Primary Reading Test, Gates Advanced Primary Reading Tests,* and the *Gates Reading Survey.* The plan of the tests is as follows:

Primary A—*Vocabulary and comprehension for grade 1 (Forms 1, 2)*
Primary B—*Vocabulary and comprehension for grade 2 (Forms 1, 2)*
Primary C—*Vocabulary and comprehension for grade 3 (Forms 1, 2)*
Primary CS—*Speed and accuracy for grades 2 and 3 (Forms 1, 2, and 3)*
Survey D—*Speed, vocabulary, and comprehension for grades 4 through 6 (Forms 1, 2, and 3)*
Survey E—*Speed, vocabulary, and comprehension for grades 7 through 9 (Forms 1, 2, and 3)*
Survey F—*Speed, vocabulary, and comprehension for grades 10 through 12 (Forms 1, 2, and 3)*

Both *Survey D* and *Survey E* contain thirty-six short paragraphs of approximately the same level of difficulty as in the *Speed and Accuracy Test.* These paragraphs end in a question or incomplete statement. From four words, the pupil chooses one that best answers the question or completes the statement. Vocabulary tests contain fifty items, each of which has a word to be defined from a choice among five other words. Items become progressively more difficult. The comprehension test contains twenty-one passages with fifty-two blank spaces. From five choices, the pupil picks the completion that best fits the passage meaning. In this test, too, difficulty increases progressively.

The vocabulary tests in *Primary A, Primary B,* and *Primary C* consist of items of four printed words and a picture that illustrates one of these words. *Primary C* has, in addition, items of a test word followed by four others, one of which means the same as the test word.

Comprehension tests are designed to measure a pupil's ability to read and grasp the meaning of whole sentences and paragraphs. In *Primary A* and *Primary B,* passages are matched with a four-picture panel, one of which best conveys the meaning of the paragraph. In *Primary C,* there are two multiple-choice test items for each paragraph.

Primary CS, Speed and Accuracy Test, is similar in construction to this kind of test in surveys *D* and *E.* Short paragraphs of uniform difficulty end in a question or an incomplete statement followed by four words, from which the pupil chooses one.

Additional information about the tests is available in a *Technical Manual.* Among other topics, there is a discussion of item selection, establishment of norms, reliability, and correlation between subtest scores and reading and IQ scores. Validity information is not given. Nor does the manual indicate how an interpretation of the score should be translated to classroom practice. Unfortunately such interpretation is seldom done for any reading test.

PROBLEM

5. What kinds of information should the subtests of a good reading survey test yield? Which of these do you consider most significant?

Test Batteries

In any survey of pupil strengths and weaknesses, information is needed concerning relative achievement in the basic skills and the various subject areas. Does the pupil excel in reading but do poorly in arithmetic? Is he a high achiever in the physical and biological sciences but lacking information and skill in dealing with problems in social studies? Standardized tests can provide information for evaluating a pupil's relative status. However, scores from single tests standardized on different populations are not necessarily comparable. For example, the standardization group for one test may have higher achievement or aptitudes than that for another, resulting in more exacting norms for the first test; representativeness of the normative sample may vary in terms of size of school, type of location (urban or rural), geographical area, and so forth. Norms may also vary according to time of year when the test was administered. Recency of norms might also affect a pupil's standing. Over time, there are discernible upward and downward national trends in achievement (National Assessment of Educational Progress, 1974, pp. 5–7).

This limitation inherent in the use of separate tests is overcome through the use of test batteries standardized on the same population. By comparing subtest scores, it is possible to determine whether a pupil has any real differences in his achievement pattern.

PROFILES. We have seen that the raw scores pupils earn on a test can be converted to derived scores such as percentile ranks, standard scores, and grade equivalents. If a

CLASS RECORD SHEET

Iowa Tests of Basic Skills

Grade __6__   Semester (1st or 2nd) __2nd__   County __Cherry__   School Building __Pleasant View__   Date __May 3, 1975__   Form __1__

City, or District __Chalsea, New York__   State __New York__   Teacher __Susan Allison__

Each cell shows the grade equivalent (top) and the percentile rank (bottom).

Names of Pupils	SEX (Write B or G)	AGE: Age in Years at Last Birthday	AGE: Months Since Last Birthday	TEST V Vocabulary	TEST R Reading Comprehension	L-1 Spelling	L-2 Capitalization	L-3 Punctuation	L-4 Usage	L TOTAL TEST L	W-1 Map Reading	W-2 Reading Graphs and Tables	W-3 Knowledge and Use of Reference Materials	W TOTAL TEST W	A-1 Arithmetic Concepts	A-2 Arithmetic Problem Solving	A TOTAL TEST A	COMPOSITE V, R, L, W, A (C)
Adams, John				6.3 / 40	7.4 / 66	6.5 / 42	5.6 / 18	6.1 / 22	5.9 / 34	5.8 / 27	7.2 / 63	5.9 / 26	6.9 / 54	6.7 / 48	5.3 / 6	5.7 / 12	5.5 / 5	6.3 / 35
Baker, Alvin				8.4 / 80	7.0 / 56	6.5 / 42	6.6 / 64	6.6 / 47	9.7 / 93	7.6 / 67	8.5 / 85	6.6 / 44	7.1 / 60	7.2 / 68	6.5 / 40	6.9 / 65	6.7 / 46	7.4 / 68
Bell, Betty				8.5 / 86	8.6 / 88	8.4 / 71	7.6 / 64	9.5 / 91	10.3 / 97	9.0 / 89	7.8 / 80	9.9 / 99	9.5 / 98	9.2 / 91	8.8 / 98	7.8 / 80	8.2 / 83	8.7 / 93
Carter, Susan				8.7 / 77	7.6 / 70	5.8 / 23	8.8 / 83	6.1 / 47	8.1 / 97	7.5 / 65	6.5 / 40	8.1 / 89	8.2 / 82	7.5 / 76	8.8 / 86	7.4 / 74	7.6 / 81	7.7 / 76
Chenworth, Ellis				9.2 / 91	9.0 / 93	4.9 / —	8.2 / 74	8.1 / 47	8.1 / 72	6.0 / 54	7.7 / 78	6.1 / 19	7.4 / 69	7.6 / 76	7.5 / 77	6.1 / 24	6.7 / 50	8.0 / 82
Corson, Margaret				8.7 / 87	7.5 / 68	8.0 / 79	9.8 / 98	10.1 / 97	9.1 / 86	9.6 / 95	6.5 / 40	8.3 / 83	8.5 / 90	7.6 / 78	9.4 / 99	9.4 / 99	9.4 / 98	8.5 / 91
Daig, Herbert				10.6 / 96	9.1 / 87	9.4 / 94	10.8 / 98	10.0 / 94	8.6 / 76	9.6 / 95	7.5 / 72	8.8 / 88	8.7 / 92	8.7 / 89	8.0 / 91	8.9 / 89	8.4 / 75	8.7 / 93
Dall, Amy				10.5 / 98	9.8 / 97	8.5 / 87	9.7 / 92	9.5 / 91	10.3 / 97	9.4 / 94	7.8 / 80	9.5 / 95	9.7 / 98	8.9 / 95	8.0 / 90	8.5 / 95	8.2 / 83	9.1 / 97
Fels, Ann				10.3 / 97	9.8 / 97	8.5 / 87	11.2 / 99	10.5 / 99	10.6 / 98	10.2 / 98	7.7 / 78	9.9 / 97	9.7 / 98	8.9 / 96	8.1 / 91	8.1 / 93	8.2 / 95	9.5 / 98
Green, Carter				5.6 / 25	6.2 / 35	5.9 / 35	6.8 / 50	5.4 / 27	6.8 / 44	6.2 / 36	6.3 / 34	6.6 / 26	6.7 / 48	6.3 / 33	6.1 / 54	6.4 / 35	6.2 / 42	6.2 / 32
Gould, Robert				6.2 / 38	6.5 / 43	7.1 / 71	8.2 / 74	7.3 / 58	10.1 / 97	8.0 / 80	6.3 / 34	7.1 / 71	7.6 / 76	7.1 / 64	8.4 / 91	8.5 / 97	8.4 / 87	7.3 / 65
Hall, William				7.0 / 54	4.5 / 42	6.5 / 42	5.3 / 11	5.1 / 21	5.4 / 44	5.2 / 27	7.8 / 78	6.4 / 64	7.4 / 74	6.9 / 75	5.3 / 70	6.1 / 24	5.1 / 46	6.8 / 51
Heald, Joe				8.4 / 80	8.5 / 87	8.0 / 79	8.2 / 82	8.2 / 82	9.1 / 86	8.4 / 81	8.0 / 85	6.6 / 97	7.7 / 63	7.8 / 86	8.0 / 77	8.5 / 95	8.0 / 90	8.3 / 88
Julson, Patricia				8.5 / 82	7.5 / 74	7.3 / 54	8.2 / 74	6.9 / 73	9.8 / 86	7.9 / 73	8.0 / 85	6.6 / 44	7.6 / 60	7.6 / 68	5.6 / 58	9.5 / 95	6.5 / 50	7.6 / 73
Larson, Alfred				6.9 / 52	6.8 / 41	5.9 / 15	5.9 / 27	6.6 / 52	8.8 / 82	6.7 / 47	6.0 / 26	7.4 / 71	6.9 / 54	6.8 / 52	6.1 / 26	6.7 / 46	6.4 / 34	6.6 / 45
Metz, Connie				7.7 / 70	7.8 / 80	8.3 / 83	8.9 / 89	8.4 / 73	5.3 / 30	7.8 / 71	8.0 / 80	7.1 / 71	5.4 / 82	8.0 / 80	7.3 / 73	7.8 / 80	7.5 / 75	7.3 / 73

HOUGHTON MIFFLIN COMPANY   BOSTON   Printed in the U.S.A.

FIGURE 11.1. Class Record Sheet Showing Grade Equivalents and Percentile Ranks.

From Lindquist and Hieronymous, 1955; reproduced by permission of Houghton Mifflin Company.

battery of tests is given, a pupil's raw scores cannot be compared, but his derived scores can if all norms are based on the same standardization group. The pupil may, for example, have a percentile rank of eighty in vocabulary and a percentile rank of ninety in spelling. It appears that his achievement in spelling is greater than that in vocabulary. But this is not necessarily so. Neither test has perfect reliability, and the reliability of the difference between two scores is less than the reliability of either test. In the better standardized tests, information is included in the manual that will help the test user determine when real differences exist.

When the raw scores of a battery of tests are changed into common derived scores, the result is a pupil's score profile. Profiles may be reported in various ways. A number of batteries have a class record sheet on which all pupils in the class have their profiles presented in tabular form (see Figure 11.1). Also, they may provide profile sheets for individual pupils (see Figure 11.2).

Note that Alice White's profile (Figure 11.2) is recorded in percentile bands. Her *School and College Ability Test* scores include performance on the *Verbal* and *Quantitative* parts plus a combination of the two. She has earned a percentile rank of sixty-eight in *Reading.* However, because this test, like others, is somewhat unreliable, we cannot be certain that she would earn the same score if she took the test again. On the other hand, we can say that approximately two-thirds of the time her "true-score" will lie within the percentile band limits of fifty-six and seventy-eight.

How, then, does one compare a pupil's standings in the various areas recorded in the profile? Can we infer that Alice White's score in *Reading* is higher than her scores in *Spelling* and *Social studies*? No, because these bands overlap. On the other hand, it is reasonable to infer that her scores in *Reading, Spelling,* and *Social studies* are greater than her scores in *Science* and *Mathematics computation*.

ELEMENTARY SCHOOL TEST BATTERIES. There are a number of achievement test batteries available for elementary school use. Those batteries listed in Table 11.2 are widely used. The table presents a rough classification of the emphasis in the different areas of achievement for the intermediate grades. In some cases, this includes grades four, five, and six, and in others, only grades five and six. Time limits allotted to the various subtests are used in determining the percentages listed. Because the total time of test administration varies, caution should be exercised in comparing percentages between tests. They can best be used in noting the degree of emphasis. Another point in interpretation is that, in some batteries, areas were combined. For example, in the *Metropolitan Achievement Tests* we placed *Mathematical concepts* and *Mathematical computation* under *Mathematical fundamentals*.

Note that the *California Achievement Tests* and the *Iowa Tests of Basic Skills* do not include social studies and science. Emphasis is placed on diagnosis in fewer areas. Only two of the batteries listed, the *Metropolitan Achievement Tests* and the *Stanford Achievement Test*, include subtests in social studies and science.

Note that content of test batteries is based on what is considered important on a national scale. Certain local objectives may be deemphasized or even omitted. For example, the "new" mathematics is taught by some schools but is not adequately sampled in every test battery. However, even though a school may teach the new mathematics, the objective of developing an understanding of the basic mathematical

Name White, Alice Jane			Testing Date Fall 1974 Grade 11		
Test	%ile rank	%ile band	Test	%ile rank	%ile band
SCAT Series II:			**STEP Series II (continued)**		
Verbal	78	66-90	Mechanics of Writing:		
Quantitative	63	52-71	Spelling	60	47-73
Total	70	59-80	Capitalization and Punctuation	51	36-65
STEP Series II:			Total	57	45-68
Mathematics Basic Concepts	33	21-47	Social Studies	64	47-77
Reading	68	56-78	English Expression	65	52-76
Science	21	10-34	Mathematics Computation	29	21-36

1. Your score on each test is reported as a percentile rank. Each percentile rank shows the percentage of students whose scores were lower than yours. For example, a percentile rank of 76 means that, for every 100 students tested, 76 earned lower scores than you did.

2. The meaning of your percentile ranks becomes clearer if they are entered on the graphs below. On each graph draw a vertical line corresponding to your percentile rank on that test.

3. Your standing is indicated by the area of the graph in which your percentile rank falls. For example, a percentile rank of 84 falls in the area marked High.

4. If you took a number of similar tests in the same subject, you would not get exactly the same score on all of them. Most of your scores would fall within a percentile band. If you have been given percentile bands, draw two vertical lines across each graph to show the range of your percentile band.

5. To compare your scores on any two tests look at the two percentile bands. Only if they do not overlap is it likely that you are better in one subject than the other.

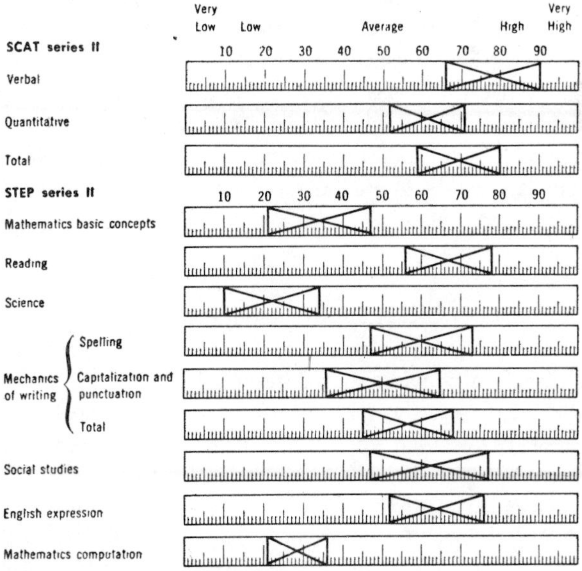

FIGURE 11.2. Pupil Profile Chart.
From *Student Bulletin.* Copyright © 1970 by Educational Testing Service. All rights reserved. Reproduced by permission.

271

TABLE 11.2.   Elementary School Test Batteries and Percentages of Total Testing Time Allotted to the Various Areas.

	California Achievement Tests	Iowa Tests of Basic Skills	Metropolitan Achievement Tests	Stanford Achievement Test
Reading comprehension	14.0	19.7	9.2	10.9
Vocabulary	26.3	6.1	5.5	7.8
Fundamentals of arithmetic	12.2	10.7	22.2	17.1
Arithmetic reasoning	14.9	10.7	9.2	10.9
Language	23.6	19.7	18.5	10.9
Social studies	0.0	0.0	16.6	9.3
Science	0.0	0.0	12.9	9.3
Spelling	8.0	4.3	5.5	6.2
Study skills	0.0	28.7	0.0	0.0
Word study skills	0.0	0.0	0.0	6.2
Listening comprehension	0.0	0.0	0.0	10.9
Total working time (minutes)	114	279	270	320

concepts found in the typical test battery would be maintained. A number of the test batteries now have supplementary tests for the "new" mathematics.

Another problem that plagues us is the comparability of scores from subtests in different test batteries that purport to measure the same thing. For instance, suppose a pupil took the *Iowa Tests of Basic Skills* in the fall and the *Metroplitan Achievement Tests* in the spring. Could we compare directly his two reading comprehension scores? Normally this would not be possible, but thanks to the *Anchor Test Study* (Jaeger, 1973), one can translate a pupil's reading comprehension or vocabulary subtest score from one test battery to an equivalent score on the corresponding subtest of another test battery. This massive study was based on the four test batteries included in Table 11.1, as well as the *Comprehensive Tests of Basic Skills, SRA Achievement Series, Sequential Tests of Educational Progress*, the *Gates-MacGinitie Reading Tests*. The tables for equating scores are limited to grades four, five, and six. How helpful it would be if similar tables were available for other elementary grade levels and in learning areas such as arithmetic and language!

IOWA TESTS OF BASIC SKILLS. Representative of the many well-developed achievement test batteries for the elementary school are the *Iowa Tests of Basic Skills*. The original multilevel edition is designed for grades three to nine. Two additional levels have been added, one for grades 1.7–2.5 and the other for 2.6–3.5. The primary battery contains tests of listening, vocabulary, word analysis, reading comprehension, and skills in language, work-study, and mathematics.

In the original multilevel edition there are eleven separate tests, with five basic skills emphasized: *Vocabulary, Reading comprehension, Language skills* (the mechanics of correct writing), *Work-study skills*, and *Arithmetic skills*. Pupils of only one grade level take the same test. Although there is overlapping, the tests are designed for specific grade levels. There are no tests in the content subjects. These are not course-oriented achievement tests.

The battery is unusual in that all levels are bound in a single booklet. There are actually six batteries, one for each of grades three to eight; grades eight and nine use the same battery. Therefore, pupils at different grade levels can be tested simultaneously, since the time limits and directions are the same for all levels.

Instructions for administration are written very clearly, and the mechanics of the test booklet are simple. A test schedule of four sessions is suggested. Some schools administer the battery in four consecutive sessions, one each half-day. Others choose to give the test in the mornings of four consecutive days. The authors rightly recommend that under no circumstances should the entire battery be administered in one day.

The *Vocabulary* subtest is composed of items requiring the examinee to select from four choices a word having most nearly the same meaning as one designated in a brief context. As in all vocabulary tests of this kind, the examinee needs only to recognize a synonym superficially; there is no measure of the breadth and depth of his concepts.

Reading comprehension is measured by a series of multiple-choice questions on brief selections. The authors are to be commended for including a variety of questions unrelated to fact or detail. For example, there are a number of items on organizational pattern, main ideas, summarizing, and tone and intent. True measures of reading comprehension must determine whether the reader understands more than the sense meanings. Also, he must not be able to select the correct answer by a process of matching words in the test item with those in the selection. Another very strong point of this reading test is the variety of the subject matter and style of the chosen selections, which give a better overall measure of comprehension than simple narrative material alone. Furthermore, the selections appear to be sufficiently difficult to provide for individual differences at each level.

The *Language skills* test actually measures the skills of correct writing, spelling, capitalization, punctuation, and usage. The spelling test uses recognition items. There are five choices, the fifth one in each case being "No mistakes." The pupil's task is to determine if any word is misspelled, and if so, which one. The incorrect spellings are selected from children's frequent errors.

The tests on *Capitalization, punctuation,* and *usage* have four choices in each item, the last choice being always "No mistakes." Pupils are directed to determine whether an error occurs, and if so, to indicate the choice where it is to be found. Various kinds of materials are used, such as letters and conversation. The skills chosen appear in general to be consistent with what is taught at the various levels.

Work-study skills are divided into three subtests—*Map reading, Reading graphs and tables* and *Knowledge and use of reference materials.* The subtests represent important aspects of reading skill in addition to development of vocabulary and comprehension of narrative material. Items in the map-reading test determine a pupil's knowledge of direction, distance, symbols, and specific concepts such as latitude, parallels, and elevation. Measurement of ability to read graphs and tables includes use of pictures; bar, circle, and line graphs; the calendar; and a various assortment of tables. The test is organized so that several items refer to one graph or table. In general, the material is meaningful and should result in greater pupil motivation. *Knowledge and use of reference materials* is concerned with those skills required in locating words in a dictionary, using an index and table of contents, using an encyclopedia, and locating information through the selection of correct references. There are also items on the interpretation of diacritical markings in the dictionary.

Arithmetic skills are divided into two subtests, *Arithmetic concepts* and *Arithmetic problem solving.* Among the concepts included are cardinal and ordinal numbers, directional orientation, geometric figures and component parts, telling time, our monetary system, linear measurement, reading a thermometer, size of fractional components, common denominators, Roman numerals, and some simple algebra. All of the items in *Arithmetic problem solving* are problems requiring the pupil to set up his own operations. The items have four choices, the last choice being "Not given." The problems require the pupil to use addition, subtraction, multiplication, and division for whole numbers and fractions. Items on percentage are also included. The various skills are introduced at the grade levels where they are generally taught. Problems tend in general to be related to the meaningful activities of children and their families. Readability is geared to the particular grade level for which the problem is designed. A supplementary modern mathematics test is available.

Grade and percentile norms are available for each of the eleven tests and for the composite of all tests. There are also percentile norms for interpreting individual pupil achievement and school averages. Norms for school averages are presented for the beginning, middle, and end of the year.

A great deal of planning and careful consideration was given to the validity of this battery of tests. Instructional procedures, courses of study, and textbooks were analyzed. The skills tested and subject matter content included were identified and studied with considerable care. The manual includes a complete analysis. Proper grade placement received particular attention. Cruciality and discriminating power served as the main criteria for items finally selected, items that emphasize the pupils' ability to use the skills, in line with the test's objective. Tests are longer than usual to provide as adequate a sample in each area as was practically possible.

SECONDARY SCHOOL TEST BATTERIES. Although achievement test batteries have been constructed for secondary school pupils, meaningful norms for the content subjects are difficult to develop. This is so because the populations are different for each subject area and often pupils included in the norm group have not studied the subject in question. Pupils enrolled in physics have not necessarily completed a course in world history. When the same pupils constitute the norm group for all subject areas whether or not they have received instruction in them, the norms are meaningless; the test is invalid for those who have not received instruction.

Two popular test batteries are the *Iowa Tests of Educational Development* and the *Sequential Tests of Educational Progress.* The latter battery has an unusual approach in measuring achievement in the content fields. This series of achievement tests, originally known as *STEP I,* which was subsequently replaced by *STEP II,* is designed to measure critical skills in application of learning in the fields of reading, mathematics, writing mechanics, science, and social studies. A serious attempt is made to measure the ability of pupils to use what they have learned in the classroom, rather than merely to recall it.

STEP II is composed of seven subtests, five of which are available at four levels (grades four through fourteen), whereas the remaining two have only three levels (grades four through twelve). The five are *Reading, English expression, Mathematics–basic concepts, Science,* and *Social studies.* The two subtests not included in the battery at the college level are *Mechanics of writing* and *Mathematics–computation.*

The following brief descriptions of each subtest reveal the broad scope of the battery:

Reading

Measures ability to read and understand a variety of materials including stories and poems as well as literary selections from the sciences, social studies, and humanities. In addition to sentence-comprehension questions, the tests include sets of analytical and interpretive questions based on passages of various lengths.

English expression

Evaluates ability to deal with English sentences in terms of their correctness and effectiveness. The materials measure proficiency in standard written English by providing an editorial exercise in which the pupil is asked to detect errors in grammar or usage, or to choose between various recastings of a given sentence.

Mechanics of writing

Evalutes mastery of such fundamental composition skills as spelling, capitalization, and punctuation. Measures ability to identify misspelled words and to detect errors in capitalization and punctuation in the context of given sentences.

Mathematics–basic concepts

Measures the elementary mathematical concepts that are part of the general education of all pupils. The major strands are: number and operation; measurement and geometry; relations, functions, and graphs; proof; probability and statistics; mathematical sentences; sets; and applications.

Mathematics–computation

Measures a wide variety of computational skills ranging over such topics as the fundamental operations with integers, fractions, decimals, and percents; evaluation of formulas and solving simple inequalities; and manipulation with exponents.

Science

Measures knowledge of important topics in science, the comprehension and application of this knowledge, and the mastery of science skills. Major emphasis is placed on biology. Physics and chemistry are moderately emphasized, while astronomy, geology, and meteorology are the least emphasized.

Social studies

Tests skills in organizing, interpreting, and evaluating information as well as many major concepts of history and social sciences. Questions are based on such stimulus materials as maps, graphs, cartoons, pictures, and passages drawn from the fields of history, geography, economics, government, sociology, and anthropology.

STEP II and the *School and College Ability Tests (SCAT II)* have been normed on the same pupil samples, and between- and within-series comparisons of scores can be made. *SCAT II* is a scholastic aptitude test measuring verbal and quantitative skills. Like *STEP II*, it is designed for continuity of measurement, having four levels of instruments extending from fourth grade through the college sophomore year. *STEP II* is also linked with the *Cooperative Primary Tests* in order to establish an inter-related testing program from grades one through fourteen.

STEP II is a high-quality achievement-test battery. There is ample evidence that its reliability is adequate, and considerable attention has been given to the development of suitable content validity. For instance, qualified persons were asked to evaluate the relationship of the test items to current curricula and teaching objectives. Each test item in each test form has been classified according to the knowledge and skill it is designed to measure. Finally, various types of norms are provided, including percentile bands and stanines for individual pupil interpretation, and for group interpretation, norms for school means.

PROBLEMS

6. What, in your opinion, are the outstanding advantages of using the *Sequential Test of Educational Progress* or the *Iowa Tests of Basic Skills* for the purpose of measuring pupil achievement in the elementary school?

7. Thelen (1960, p. 19) says that "our tests teach pupils that academic status, not learning, is the goal of education." Do you agree? Why?

Diagnostic Tests

Survey tests, whether individual or battery, help the teacher screen out those pupils who have serious learning disabilities. They provide some diagnostic information. The teacher, however, needs many more data on the specific difficulties of a pupil to be able to provide adequate remediation. Diagnostic tests serve this purpose.

Such tests must, therefore, be considerably longer than the typical survey test to make the necessary subtests sufficiently reliable. Instead of the three scores typical of reading survey tests—vocabulary, comprehension, and rate—they may provide numerous scores. A reading diagnostic test may give scores in syllabication, knowledge of consonant sounds, blending, reversals, wrong beginnings, and endings. Whereas an arithmetic survey test may provide two scores, computational and reasoning, a diagnostic arithmetic test may provide information on the difficulties encountered by a pupil in each of the fundamental processes as well as in fractions and decimals. For example, one pupil may have difficulty in long division because he makes mistakes in subtraction. Another makes errors in multiplication that give him an incorrect answer. Still a third has difficulty in his placement of zeros in the quotient. A good diagnostic test will reveal to the teacher the source of the pupil's difficulty.

The more detailed diagnostic tests are individually administered and require greater administrative skill than survey tests. Interpretation is also more complex. Norms are not always provided. Although norms are useful, they are not nearly so important as the careful tabulations and analysis of the pupil's performance in the varied tasks presented.

Finally, because diagnostic tests often tend to be subdivided into numerous subtests, sampling is frequently limited, and doubt is thereby cast on the adequacy of their reliability. Such scores should be supported by further data if the test is to realize its potential usefulness.

DIAGNOSTIC TESTS AND SELF-HELPS IN ARITHMETIC. A good illustration of this type of test is the *Diagnostic Tests and Self-Helps in Arithmetic* for use in grades four, five, and six. Three kinds of material are provided: *Screening Tests, Diagnostic Tests,* and *Self-Helps* exercises. Three screening tests enable the teacher to survey the pupils' achievement in whole numbers, fractions, and decimals. A fourth screening test, designed for use in grade six and above, is general in nature and contains more difficult examples than the other three. The author suggests that when a pupil makes one or more errors in a screening test, the proper diagnostic tests be administered.

There are twenty-three diagnostic tests in all:

Addition facts	*Subtraction of like fractions*
Subtraction facts	*Addition of unlike fractions*
Multiplication facts	*Subtraction of unlike fractions*
Division facts	*Multiplication of fractions*
Uneven division facts	*Division of fractions*
Addition of whole numbers	*Addition of decimals*
Subtraction of whole numbers	*Subtraction of decimals*
Multiplication of whole numbers	*Multiplication of decimals*
Division by one-place numbers	*Division of decimals*
Division by two-place numbers	*Percent*
Regrouping fractions	*Operations with measures*
Addition of like fractions	

The tests are also cross-referenced to each other. For example, those related to *Multiplication of Whole Numbers,* Test 8, are Tests 1, *Addition Facts,* 3, *Multiplication Facts,* and 6, *Addition of Whole Numbers.* When a pupil makes a mistake in a problem such as 986 × 357, he may have one of several difficulties. He may place the products of the various steps incorrectly. Possibly he does not know how to carry. Perhaps he does not know his addition facts or understand how to do column addition. Some of these difficulties will be obvious after administering Test 8. By assigning the related tests, the teacher can locate the source of error.

The *Self-Helps* guide the pupil in overcoming his difficulties in a particular skill. Each diagnostic test has its companion self-help material. For example, if a pupil has difficulty in multiplying numbers with zeros in the multiplicand, there are exercises showing all the work required in this type of skill:

760	806	900
× 59	× 48	× 67
6840	6448	6300
38000	32240	54000
44840	38688	60300

The pupils are instructed to study the work to determine how the answers are found. They are then advised to cover the work and answers and solve the exercise on their own.

No coefficients of reliability or validity are reported. However, the author points out that rows of examples testing each step were included to increase reliability. For example, in testing a pupil's ability to deal with one-place multipliers where no carrying is involved, we have the following exercises:

$$
\begin{array}{ccc}
34 & 213 & 111 \\
\times 2 & \times 3 & \times 6 \\
\hline
\end{array}
$$

Content validity is stressed. The tests are based on an analysis of the underlying skills involved in the various operations. These are organized systematically in terms of the development of each skill.

PROBLEM

8. Would different methods be used to ensure a high degree of content validity in a diagnostic test than in a norm-referenced survey achievement test? Explain.

Criterion-Referenced Tests

There are somewhat fewer criterion-referenced standardized achievement tests commercially available than norm-referenced ones. Most of these focus on the basic skills, such as the *Prescriptive Mathematics Inventory* and the *Prescriptive Reading Inventory,* aimed primarily at the elementary grade levels. Their worth is more difficult to evaluate since it is troublesome to produce the counterpart of such standard indicators as reliability coefficients used with norm-referenced tests.

Furthermore, a test-design issue must be squarely faced. Given that the total testing time is fixed and that one wishes to measure pupil competencies associated with a large number of specific objectives, we have the choice of measuring a small number of competencies well or a large number less precisely (Hambleton and Novick, 1973). Choosing the second alternative is somewhat common, resulting in the use of a very small sample of test items for a given objective. Attention to this point is crucial when examining and interpreting criterion-referenced tests.

SUMMARY

The following are the major points included in this chapter:

1. *The different names for aptitude and achievement tests have led to confusion, since there are considerable similarities among them.*
2. *Standardized tests are typically of the norm-referenced type. Fewer criterion-referenced standardized tests are available.*

3. *Standardized achievement tests are, in general, more carefully constructed than teacher-built achievement tests, with greater attention given to technical considerations.*

4. *The strength of standardized achievement tests lies in their use as an added criterion of measurement against which the teacher may judge the adequacy of his content selection and the effectiveness of the learning experiences he has organized.*

5. *Achievement-test batteries at the secondary as well as the elementary leve. are being used as survey tests administered to identify areas of individual and group weakness.*

6. *A distinct advantage of the achievement battery is the availability of a profile providing a more adequate interpretation of a pupil's educational strengths and weaknesses.*

7. *Diagnostic tests can be administered to further analyze areas of weakness emphasized by the survey achievement test.*

8. *The frontier in standardized achievement testing lies in the development of instruments measuring complex cognition and affective behaviors rather than specific information taught.*

SUGGESTED READINGS

ANASTASI, A. *Psychological testing.* (3rd ed.) New York: Macmillan, 1968. Chapter 15.
Uses and limitations of achievement tests and batteries and problems in construction are emphasized. A number of achievement tests in special areas are described, and some of the items are illustrated.

BLUM, S. H. Group test administration: Promise and problems. *Educational Forum,* 1969, *33,* 213–218.
An interesting, nontechnical, practical article on the important factors to consider in test administration.

BURRILL, L. E. *How a standardized achievement test is built.* Test Service Notebook, No. 125 New York: Harcourt Brace Jovanovich, Undated.
Typical steps taken when building a standardized achievement test are described, including the development of the test items, their preliminary tryout, the computation of norms, and the preparation of a manual.

EBEL, R. L. What do educational tests test? *Educational Psychologist,* 1973, *10,* 76–79.
According to the author, tests should measure the pupil's command of some segment of knowledge, particularly verbal knowledge.

KATZ, M. *Selecting an achievement test: Principles and procedures.* (3rd ed.) Princeton, N.J.: Educational Testing Service, 1973.
This monograph is designed to help laymen make a more intelligent choice among the many available tests. The basis for test selection consists of certain universal elements, namely, pupil population, school objectives, purposes in testing, and use of the test scores.

TRAXLER, A. Some misconceptions about standardized testing. *Education,* 1967, *87,* 407–410.
The author discusses five misconceptions about testing. These involve the definition of psychological tests, the use of tests for screening purposes, the focus of interest on individual responses to specific questions, and limiting an individual's freedom of choice.

REFERENCES CITED

AMERICAN PSYCHOLOGICAL ASSOCIATION. *Standards for educational and psychological tests.* Washington: Author, 1974.

ANASTASI, A. *Psychological testing.* (3rd ed.) New York: Macmillan, 1968.

HAMBLETON, R. K., and M. R. NOVICK. Toward an integration of theory and method for criterion-referenced tests. *Journal of Educational Measurement, 1973, 10,* 159–170.

JAEGER, R. M. The national test-equating study in reading—the anchor test study. *NCME Measurement in Education, 1973, 4,* 1–8.

KELLEY, T. L. *Interpretations of educational measurements.* Yonkers, N.Y.: World Book, 1927.

LINDQUIST, E. F., and A. N. HIERONYMOUS. *Iowa Tests of Basic Skills.* Boston: Houghton Mifflin, 1955.

NATIONAL ASSESSMENT OF EDUCATIONAL PROGRESS. *National assessment achievements: Findings, interpretations and uses.* Denver: Author, 1974.

THELEN, H. A. The triumph of "achievement" over inquiry in education. *Elementary School Journal, 1960, 60,* 190–197.

12

MEASURING
PUPIL APTITUDES

Visit any classroom with a democratic social climate and you will observe as many kinds of behavior as there are pupils. Within a fifth-grade class you find some pupils working arithmetic problems while another group turns, fascinated, to the production of a play they have written. One boy is building a model to illustrate the operation of a machine studied in a science unit; one of the girls is writing a poem. Other children are reading and seem to be totally absorbed in a story. You see one pupil staring out the window; occasionally he will try to work at an assignment, but he seems to give up easily. Another child is buzzing around the room enjoying a series of social calls, and is soon called back to his seat.

You also notice that performance varies considerably. Some children seem adept at manipulating scissors or blocks. Others paint very well, though the art work of their peers seems immature. Certain pupils offer many ideas as they work with others; some tend to follow and do as they are told.

The many individual differences you observe reflect interests, attitudes, experience backgrounds, and innate ability. All these factors form the basis for the pupil's ability to learn. His ability to learn is his aptitude; his achievement refers to what he has learned. As we shall see, tests that measure aptitude and achievement differ not so much in their content but in the functions they perform.

Certain inherited traits are basic to specific aptitudes. Early studies of individual differences revealed that some people react to stimuli more quickly than others. Take, for example, the case of a certain astronomer engaged in recording the instant at which he saw the images of stars as they crossed the field of his telescope. When a consistent time-lag appeared in his reports, his employers discharged him promptly, thinking him simply careless. This occurred before scientists discovered that individuals react to stimuli with varying rapidity. Those who react quickly have an advantage in some kinds of work. Certain manual skills require long fingers and a deftness of manipulation. In those areas an individual with short stubby fingers that he uses awkwardly will find himself at a definite disadvantage.

In most instances, aptitude represents more than innate ability. Two individuals with identical inherited capacities, like identical twins, may have quite different aptitudes because their experiences have been different. One may learn or perform a task with ease; he has a high aptitude for that work. The other may find the task difficult; he is inept at improving his skill, and has little aptitude for the work. Theoretically, each could develop this special genetically based aptitude to the same degree, but this may not happen because of the important part achievement plays in aptitude potential.

High general ability is necessary for the development of superior specific aptitudes. The concert pianist has not only high musical aptitude, but high general ability as well. An individual with superior native endowment is also more likely to have a wider range of aptitudes than his peer who is less intellectually mature and may be talented in the graphic arts, exhibit physical prowess, and show high scholastic achievement.

Knowledge of a pupil's aptitudes is of value in counseling him on vocational plans and preparation for jobs in which he is likely to succeed. It is also helpful in organizing learning experiences for the individual. For example, low achievement may be the result of lack of effort or ability; we want to know how much a pupil can achieve. Of course, reliability of prediction is dependent on the stability of the aptitude. If an aptitude is unstable, it cannot be measured reliably and will have low correlation to achievement. The findings of research dealing with constancy of aptitudes indicate some disagreement among psychologists, but, in general, aptitudes seem to be fairly stable. Many seem to become crystallized in childhood and develop in a predictable, relatively constant way.

In developing instruments for evaluating aptitudes, investigators have emphasized proceeding from general to "purer" aptitudes. Any list of aptitudes we choose will be arbitrary, depending on the extent to which we find measurement of discrete aptitudes helpful as opposed to lumping them together for practical purposes. For instance, it is often useful to know a pupil's mechanical aptitude in addition to having a measure of his general mental ability. Yet mechanical aptitude is a composite of spatial visualization, perceptual speed and acuity, and mechanical information. At the present time it is probably more generally useful to take a global approach to aptitude measurement than an "atomistic" one such as making a separate analysis of mechanical aptitude.

The discussion that follows is centered around those aptitude tests of particular importance to school personnel. Hence special attention is given to individual and group scholastic aptitude tests and differential aptitude test batteries that include other aptitudes, such as clerical aptitude and mechanical reasoning.

SCHOLASTIC APTITUDE

Someone once quipped that intelligence is what intelligence tests measure. Unfortunately most other definitions do little more to clarify the concept, and though many have been offered, they all fail in some sense. Since intelligence, unlike a muscle, cannot be described, definitions delineate an individual's inherited capacity. Because intelligence can only be inferred from the behavior of the organism, test scores imply a quantity or quality of intelligence rather than a direct measure.

In measuring achievement, we sample areas of learning, and if our test and testing situation are adequate, we can arrive at some fairly defensible conclusions about the pupil's skills. But in measuring intelligence, we must consider unequal educational opportunities. Since we cannot measure intelligence directly, we establish problem situations that represent important intellectual functions. Though we try to exclude problems whose solutions have been taught in school, the tools the pupil uses are learned. If he is to answer questions on a group intelligence test, he probably will have to know how to read. Some items will demand arithmetic; others, the development of specific concepts, such as liter, quarter, capital, civil war, and so forth. Because a pupil's ability to do well on these tests is so closely related to success in school, the commonly used measures of general intelligence are known as scholastic aptitude tests. There is a high correlation between scores on these tests and achievement tests. Test items are often similar.

Glaser and Nitko (1971) suggest that our scholastic aptitude tests are designed to predict achievement in situations where instruction is relatively nonadaptive; it is the kind of instruction directed at the total group that one finds in the average classroom; it is not generally adjusted for maximum effectiveness on an individual basis. Nonadaptive instruction assumes that all pupils can develop a certain degree of proficiency in a given task. However, adaptive instruction demands a different approach to prediction. In essence, it involves determination of specific instructional methodology for each learner and prediction of success from each learner's characteristics.

Individual Tests

The individual scholastic aptitude test, as the name implies, is designed for face-to-face administration to the individual pupil. Commonly used instruments in this category are the *Stanford-Binet Scale (Form L-M), Wechsler Preschool and Primary Scale of Intelligence (WPPSI), Wechsler Intelligence Scale for Children (WISC),* and *Wechsler Adult Intelligence Scale (WAIS).* Of these, the *Stanford-Binet Scale* and the *WISC* deserve the most attention.

STANFORD-BINET INTELLIGENCE SCALE, FORM L-M. The first Binet scales appeared at the turn of the century in France. Terman and his co-workers prepared American revisions, the most recent of which is *Form L-M* published in 1960. It is grouped into twenty age levels, each composed of a group of tests, usually six.

Beginning at Year II the levels are placed at six-month intervals up to Year VI. This grouping allows for the assessment of the rapid growth of preschool children. Each level has six tests; one month of credit toward the mental-age score is allowed for each test. From Year VI to Year XIV, twelve-month intervals are used. Since there are also six tests in each of these levels, each receives two months of credit. Topping the scale are four increasingly difficult levels, the Average Adult, the Superior Adult Level I, Superior Adult Level II, and the Superior Adult Level III. *Form L-M* reflects the conclusions of longitudinal studies that improvement in performance on the test continues after sixteen years of age. It recognizes improvement to age eighteen.

The tests demand both verbal and nonverbal performance. In some cases, simple memory is sufficient; in others, reasoning is necessary. The pupil must rely on his past experiences as well as his talent to solve problems in new situations. Test materials consist of toy objects, printed cards, a test booklet for recording responses, and the test manual.

Below are samples of some of the tests from various age levels:*

Year II—*Identifying Objects by Name (Alternate)*
  Material: Card with dog, ball, engine, bed, doll, and scissors attached.
  Procedure: Show the card with the six small objects attached and say, "See all these things? Show me the dog." "Put your finger on the dog." "Where is the dog?"
Year VI—*Mutilated Pictures*
  Material: Card with mutilated pictures.
  Procedure: Show subject the card with mutilated pictures and pointing to each in turn, ask, "What is gone in this picture?" or "What part is gone?"
Year XIV—*Orientation: Direction I*
  Procedure: Read the following directions distinctly, emphasizing the critical words:
      (a) "Which direction would you have to face so that your left hand would be toward the east?"

The authors emphasize three requirements for a valid test administration (Terman and Merrill, 1973):

1. *The standard procedures must be followed.*
2. *The pupil's best efforts must be enlisted by the establishment and maintenance of adequate rapport.*
3. *The responses must be correctly scored.*

The examiner must have special training in test administration and scoring before he can meet these criteria. He must also have background information in testing and a considerable amount of practice with the instrument to administer it well. Any variation of the standardized procedure invalidates the test results somewhat. Too much attention to details excludes continuing rapport with the pupil and may result in a less-than-adequate performance. Test administration is further complicated by the fact that scoring is simultaneous with administration. Cues for the next step in the procedure are dependent on the pupil's success or failure.

No pupil takes all the tests. He tries only those items that determine the upper and lower limits of his ability. Provision is made for the spoiling of tests by making an alternative test available at each of the age levels. About one hour is usually needed for test administration; the time required may vary from as little as thirty to forty minutes for younger children to an hour and one-half or more for older children.

The test manual specifies the desired performance on each test for credit at a particular level. For example, in *Identifying Objects by Name* for Year II, the child must correctly identify at least five of the six objects to pass. Scoring is on an all-or-none basis. The child who identifies three objects correctly receives no more credit than one who identifies two. Both children fail.

Some tests are used at more than one age level and require higher standards of performance for success at the higher age levels. If a test is administered at a lower

* *Sample items from the* Stanford-Binet Intelligence Scale, Form L-M: Manual for the third revision. *Copyright © 1973 and 1960 by Houghton Mifflin Co. Reproduced by permission.*

level, it is not given again at the higher level, but is scored and credited for the proper age level at that time. For example, consider one of the test items from the *Opposite Analogies I* test of Year IV:*

"Brother is a boy; sister is a_____."

For Year IV, the child needs to have only two of such items correct; however, if three or more are right, he is given credit for the same test in Year IV-6.

The mental age of a child is determined by scoring his successful responses to the various tests. Traditionally, the intelligence quotient (IQ) had been found by dividing his mental age (MA) by the chronological age (CA) and multiplying by 100. However, this method prevents IQs having the same meaning at different age levels. At one CA an IQ of 120 may be the highest score of eighty-five percent of the age group while, for another age group, an IQ of 115 may be the top figure for the same percentage of that population. To overcome this problem, in *Form L-M* of the *Stanford-Binet*, a deviation or standard score IQ (sometimes known as DIQ) is found by entering a table with the proper MA and CA values for the pupil in question. In essence, DIQs are standard scores with an arithmetic mean of 100 and a standard deviation of sixteen.

Like any other aptitude test, the *Stanford-Binet* does not measure pure native capacity, but innate ability and the effect of learning. Only if we could assume that the test is completely valid and reliable and that influencing environments are identical could we infer that the pupils tested have the same native capacity. At that, it would be sounder to infer only that they had the same ability to learn. But no psychological test has perfect reliability or validity; rapport and effective tapping of a pupil's maximum potential are always problems. He may know the answer to a question and refuse to respond; he may give an incorrect answer for many reasons. Pupils with academic disabilities may have a particularly strong dislike or even a fear of the kinds of items included in the *Stanford-Binet*.

The improbability that children will experience the same environments extends even to siblings. The older children may be asked to assume more responsibility, to supervise younger brothers or sisters. Perhaps more sharing is demanded of them. Because older children serve as models of behavior, younger members of the family are likely to participate in certain activities at an earlier age than their older siblings.

Differences also exist among family environments. One home may provide a great deal of social interaction, another almost none. Reading may be a central interest of all members of one pupil's family; his classmate's family may lack even a daily newspaper. Bilingual homes present a special problem for children. Because the *Stanford-Binet* is highly verbal, a pupil from a bilingual home is likely to be severely affected by lack of verbal stimulation. Although he may have other types of ability, they are not effectively sampled by this test.

It should also be noted that the *Stanford-Binet* is not designed to differentiate among the various aspects of intelligence. There are no separate scores, only a composite.

Despite these limitations, the *Stanford-Binet* has proved over the years to be a

---

* *Sample item from the* Stanford-Binet Intelligence Scale, Form L-M: Manual for the third revision. *Copyright © 1973 and 1960 by Houghton Mifflin Co. Reproduced by permission.*

valuable instrument. Although superior performance on the test is dependent on success in school, the test may also be the instrument for predicting such success, since verbal ability is an important factor in school success and this highly verbal test enables an examiner to assess the pupil's verbal facility. It also helps spot deficiencies in arithmetic, problem solving, and the fund of information.

During the administration of the *Stanford-Binet*, one can observe a child's reactions. Although the quality of his performance should be interpreted cautiously by an experienced examiner, a pupil's problem-solving ability, his work habits, and his reaction to success and failure can be examined. When he fails, the examiner seeks to determine whether he is disturbed, irritable, argumentative, or depressed. When he is successful, his reaction is also observed. Reaction time should be noted; it can be indicative of certain personality problems. Is it delayed, blocked, or irregular? Is there any indication of negativism, or are the responses given quickly and impulsively? On the basis of this and other evidence, the examiner can gain insights into the personality of the pupil.

THE WECHSLER SCALES. *Form I* of the original *Wechsler Intelligence Scale* was published in 1939 and was called the *Wechsler-Bellevue Intelligence Scale. Form II* was adapted from a scale developed during World War II. Scales of both forms were designed for adults rather than children. The tasks in existing instruments, such as the *Stanford-Binet*, do not hold enough interest to motivate many adults. In addition, the speed factor is particularly detrimental in assessing adult intelligence when a test is standardized on children.

The items in these scales reflect Wechsler's specific objective, namely, to construct an instrument that would enable him to understand better his adult patients at New York's Bellevue Hospital. Because he had to determine their intelligence and personality aberrations, he needed an instrument with diagnostic properties in addition to those measuring "global" intelligence.

From this work were developed three scales, namely, the *Wechsler Intelligence Scale for Children (WISC)* for ages six to sixteen (introduced in 1949 and revised in 1974), the *Wechsler Adult Intelligence Scale (WAIS)* for older subjects (introduced in 1955), and the *Wechsler Preschool and Primary Scale of Intelligence (WPPSI)* for ages four to six and a half (introduced in 1967). The pattern of subtests in each of the three scales is quite similar. As displayed in Table 12.1, the scales are organized into subtests, five or six composing a verbal score and another five designed to yield a performance score. Note that, in addition to subtests used regularly (indicated by check), there are alternate tests to be used if, for instance, the administration of one of the regular subtests was poor.

Unlike the age scales used in the *Stanford-Binet*, the *Wechsler* tests are a series of point scales. In other words, each test item is assigned points for a correct response. Points for each test represent raw scores which are changed to scaled scores by means of a table. The respective subtests in the *Verbal Scale* and the *Performance Scale* are added to secure the verbal and performance scores. By the use of tables, the intelligence quotients may be determined.

The pupil's IQ is found, therefore, by a comparison of the score representing his test performance with those scores earned by the individuals in the standardization

TABLE 12.1. Subtests for Three Wechsler Scales.

Subtest	WPPSI (Ages 4 to 6½)	WISC-R (Ages 6 to 16)	WAIS (Adult)
Verbal			
Information	✓	✓	✓
Comprehension	✓	✓	✓
Arithmetic	✓	✓	✓
Similarities	✓	✓	✓
Vocabulary	✓	✓	✓
Digit span		Alternate	✓
Sentences	Alternate		
Performance			
Picture completion	✓	✓	✓
Block design	✓	✓	✓
Picture arrangement		✓	✓
Object assembly		✓	
Mazes	✓	Alternate	✓
Digit symbol			
Animal house	✓		
Geometric design	✓		
Coding		✓	

sample of a single age group. If the standard deviation of IQs is held constant and the total mean score for each age group equated, the IQ is made comparable for pupils of different ages. An individual is assigned an IQ on the basis of the amount that he deviates from the average performance of those in his own age group.

It should be noted that the *Wechsler* IQs are deviation IQs as in the case of the *Stanford-Binet*. One difference exists, however. The *Wechsler* scores have a standard deviation of fifteen in contrast to the sixteen used for *Stanford-Binet* scores. Therefore, for comparably bright pupils, the DIQ on the *Stanford-Binet* will be slightly higher than on the *WISC*. With comparably dull children, the DIQ on the *Stanford-Binet* will be a little lower.

The *Wechsler* manuals emphasize that the test examiner must be well-trained and have access to a quiet testing room and proper materials. The directions for test administration must be followed specifically. Rather than change the wording of the questions, the teacher should read the instructions from the manual. The conditions under which the child performs certain tasks have been carefully standardized; norms of performance have been prepared under the conditions of the instructions. As in the administration of the *Stanford-Binet*, the examiner has an opportunity to note any unusual behavior that bears on the child's personality.

The examiner must always be concerned with securing optimum performance, and very skillful questioning is required. Often the child's response needs clarification, which can be accomplished by nonevaluative querying. For example, the examinee may be asked "Please explain further," or "Tell more about it." Also, in maintaining rapport it is sometimes necessary to encourage with supporting statements, such as, "This is a little difficult; you will find it easier when you are older." One should not build up an expectancy for approval within the child, because he may come to interpret no comment as disapproval. On balance, the *Wechsler* scales are more easily administered than the *Stanford-Binet*. Moreover, the child does not undergo the frustrating situation he experiences in the latter when he encounters a series of failures as he approaches his ceiling.

Unlike the *Stanford-Binet*, which provides only one IQ score, the *Wechsler* scales have separate verbal and nonverbal IQs. This feature is often valuable in diagnosing educational problems of some pupils. As you might expect, many studies have compared performance on the *WISC* with that of the *Stanford-Binet*. Coefficients of correlations usually found vary between 0.60 and 0.80. Correlations based on the *Performance scale* alone tend to be somewhat lower than those based on the *Verbal scale* alone.

PROBLEMS

1. Teachers usually look only for the actual IQ score when an individual psychological test has been administered. Few bother to read the detailed report prepared by the examiner. What dangers are inherent in this practice? What information should you as a teacher look for and expect to find in a psychological report? In what respects might a psychological report of a *Stanford-Binet* test differ from one on the *WISC* in terms of the kinds of information given?

2. How might one account for the low correlations between scores on ability tests for very young children and later measures of intelligence in terms of validity?

Group Tests

In most school situations, neither time nor trained personnel is available for the administration of the individual tests described. Group tests, therefore, are much more extensively used, since they may be administered to a large group of pupils by an examiner with minimum training. In general, they are verbal, and if they do not require reading, the examinee must at least be able to understand the verbal instructions of the examiner. Therefore great care must be taken in interpreting test scores, for a low score may indicate a lack of verbal facility rather than intellectual immaturity.

Although many good group intelligence tests are available for school use, all of them cannot be discussed here. We take the logical alternative of mentioning briefly several tests that represent somewhat different approaches to the measurement of mental ability. In addition, a summary of the important college aptitude tests is included.

OTIS-LENNON MENTAL ABILITY TEST. In 1918, publication of the *Otis Group Intelligence Scale* marked the development of the first group test of mental ability for school use. During the intervening years various forms and editions have been published. The *Otis-Lennon Mental Ability Test* represents the fourth principal edition. The authors continue to emphasize the *g* or general factor as the most meaningful assessment of scholastic aptitude. Therefore, a broad range of cognitive abilities is measured by the spiral omnibus form; instead of using subtests of homogeneous items, the designers introduce all easy items first, whatever the nature, proceeding in the same way through the more difficult ones.

Six levels of tests have been developed for pupils in kindergarten through the freshman year in college. They are as follows:

Primary I Level *(K)*
Primary II Level *(Grade 1)*
Elementary I Level *(Grades 2 and 3)*
Elementary II Level *(Grades 4–6)*
Intermediate Level *(Grades 7–9)*
Advanced Level *(Grades 10–13)*

The first three levels measure the ability to classify, follow directions, reason quantitatively, conceptualize, and reason by analogy; items contain both pictorial and geometric material. The authors indicate that the upper three levels contain verbal and nonverbal items that sample *fourteen* different mental processes designed for a power measurement of abstract reasoning. However, they present no factor-analytic evidence to support these claims.

The deviation IQs reported have a mean of 100 and standard deviation of sixteen. They provide an index of a pupil's relative brightness when compared with others of his own age, regardless of grade. According to the authors, they "reflect, at a given point in time, the pupil's ability to deal with abstract relationships involving the manipulation of ideas expressed in verbal, numerical, figural, or symbolic form." The authors recommend that DIQs be translated into percentile ranks and stanine scores for proper interpretation.

CALIFORNIA TEST OF MENTAL MATURITY. The 1963 edition of the *CTMM* (Long Form) is available for six levels, covering all grade levels as well as college and adult groups. There are twelve subtests listed under five factors: *Logical reasoning, Spatial relationships, Numerical reasoning, Verbal concepts,* and *Memory.* Tests results yield a language, nonlanguage, and total IQ. Actually, here again nonlanguage is not accurate terminology since the examinee must understand the verbal instructions of the examiner in the nonlanguage tests.

Probably the total test IQ is the most valid measure to be derived from this instrument. The language and nonlanguage IQs, however, can aid in educational diagnosis. If the pupil is poor in reading, he is likely to make a lower language IQ score than a nonlanguage IQ on this test, and knowledge of this fact can help prevent wrong classification.

The manual contains an Intellectual Status Index for determining anticipated achievement for a pupil in his actual grade placement. This index enables one to predict, for example, whether a pupil can be expected to do average, below average, or above average work in accordance with his score on the *CTMM* series. When used with scores on the *California Achievement Tests,* it roughly indicates the status of a pupil's performance in various subjects.

A short form of the test is available. Again, language, nonlanguage, and total IQs can be determined. However, only four out of the five factors in the long form are included: *Logical reasoning, Numerical reasoning, Verbal concepts,* and *Memory.* The short form requires only thirty-four to forty-three minutes of actual testing time for administration, whereas the long form demands forty-eight minutes to one hour and twenty-three minutes depending on the particular test level.

LORGE-THORNDIKE INTELLIGENCE TESTS. The initial edition of the *Lorge-Thorndike Intelligence Test (LTIT)* was published in 1954. Like the editions that followed, it provides verbal and nonverbal measures of ability for a wide age range, basically kindergarten through secondary school.

It is a multilevel battery, originally having five levels, each a separate booklet designed for two or three grade levels (for example, grades four to six). Now available is a single booklet multilevel battery for grades three through thirteen. It has eight subtests, five for the verbal score, three for the nonverbal:

Verbal	Nonverbal
Vocabulary	Figure classification
Sentence completion	Number series
Arithmetic reasoning	Figure analogies
Verbal classification	
Verbal analogies	

The so-called "multilevel edition" of the *LTIT* tries to use the pupil's time efficiently. Since the items in each subtest increase noticeably in difficulty from the beginning to the end, each subtest is, in effect, divided into eight different but overlapping scales. Each higher level scale is created by eliminating the first items of the preceding scale and adding the easy ones from the next higher level. As a result, each pupil takes items suitable for his grade level, neither wasting time on items he is certain to pass nor experiencing excessive frustration by attempting items much too difficult for him.

The language and nonlanguage scores are typically expressed as deviation IQs. The correlation between the two IQs is substantial, sometimes approaching an r value of 0.75. They also correlate highly with the scores of other mental ability tests as well as standardized achievement tests.

PROBLEM

3. Compare the *California Test of Mental Maturity* to the *Lorge-Thorndike Intelligence Test* in terms of (1) validity evidence, (2) standardization groups, and (3) interpretability of scores.

SCHOLASTIC APTITUDE TEST. As more and more high school pupils become interested in going to college, many admissions offices are relying heavily on test scores as one of the criteria for selecting students. To provide these scores, several independent testing agencies develop tests, arrange for their administration, score the answer sheets, and report information to the pupil and the college to which he wishes to gain admission.

The College Entrance Examination Board *Scholastic Aptitude Test (SAT)* is probably the oldest test for this purpose. Generally, the pupil takes these tests during his senior year in high school. However, because there were demands to have these test scores before the last high-school year, the *Preliminary Scholastic Aptitude Test* was made available to juniors in secondary schools. This test also serves as the qualifying test for the National Merit Scholarship Program.

The *Scholastic Aptitude Test* has three parts, the *Verbal* and *Mathematical,* each seventy-five minutes in length, and a thirty-minute section to measure mastery of English grammar and sentence structure. Each of the first two parts is graded in a range of 200 to 800. The third section is marked between 20 and 80. The last segment, the newest of the three, is designed for use in placing individuals in freshman English and not for selection for admission. It is directed toward the person who is likely to need more specialized attention in English composition.

The candidate who has read widely, so that his vocabulary and skill are well-developed, has a definite advantage in the verbal section over a peer with the same native ability but inadequately developed verbal skill. Performance on this test depends on developed skills rather than knowledge of specific information. The quantitative part of the test is also a measure of ability for dealing with concepts rather than mathematical achievement. Although a knowledge of elementary mathematics is necessary, emphasis is on the pupil's application of basic knowledge in the solution of problems. The ceiling of this test is high enough to discriminate among able pupils even though their training in formal mathematics may be limited.

AMERICAN COLLEGE TESTING PROGRAM. Another program for testing college-bound pupils has been developed under the auspices of the Measurement Research Center in Iowa. The American College Testing Program (ACT) offers a basic battery of four tests in the field of English, mathematics, social studies, and the natural sciences. This battery can predict college success, and like other widely used scholastic aptitude tests, it includes items sampling the intellectual skills of solving problems that require mathematical reasoning and interpreting of passages.

DECLINE IN COLLEGE SCHOLASTIC APTITUDE TEST SCORES. Reports have been widely publicized about the lowering trend of the *ACT* and *SAT* test scores. Speculation as to the causes has stimulated considerable debate. Some of the causes suggested are changes in the test, more high school juniors taking the tests, and the quality of education in the first twelve years. These possibilities have been largely rejected by many knowledgeable measurement specialists. For instance, careful scale equating precludes year-to-year variability in test difficulty. Also, the scores of high school juniors are adjusted so they are comparable to those that they would make if they were seniors. Finally, score data are obtained from college-bound individuals and so do not reflect the competency of the total graduating population. Therefore, it is not possible to determine from these data whether the schools are in fact responsible.

Evidently no one knows for sure the nature of the reasons for the lower scores (Munday, 1974). Perhaps the most plausible explanation is that the pool of college-bound youth has changed. More individuals in the lower half of their high school class are probably attending college now than in the past. Furthermore, many of these lower scoring pupils are attending community colleges. To be sure, some have not had the traditional college preparatory work, nor do they have the academic goals of youths attending college in previous years.

PREPARING FOR THE TESTS. Teachers wonder if they can prepare pupils for these tests by tutoring them. The effect of coaching for the College Entrance Examination Board's *Scholastic Aptitude Test* has been studied extensively (College Entrance Examination Board, 1968). Scores obtained by groups coached in private and public schools and by groups given intensive individual tutoring were compared with scores obtained by matched control groups with no special training. Results show that special coaching increased test scores only very slightly. On the average, the increase was ten points or fewer. Remember that the scale extends from 200 to 800; the gains in question are much less than the standard error of measurement of the test.

These findings are not strange. Scholastic aptitude tests require both innate ability and achievement. To demonstrate this fact, solve the problems below:

If 5 post cards cost y cents, how many cents will 15 post cards cost? (A) 3y (B) 15y (C) 5y (D) 75y (E) 16y.

The answer is 3y. However, the purpose of the problem is not to determine whether the pupil can multiply 3 by y, which is one computation that might be used in determining the answer, but to determine if he knows how to attack the solution of the problem—finding the cost of one post card and then 15. Nevertheless, it is obvious that if he cannot divide 15 by 5 correctly and then state the product of 3 and y, his answer will be wrong. Therefore, achievement in mathematics is basic to success in this test.

The following analogy is similar to those found in the *Verbal* section of the *SAT* (College Entrance Examination Board, 1965):

Trigger: Bullet::	*(A) handle: drawer*	*(B) holster: gun*	
	(C) bulb: light	*(D) switch: current*	
	(E) pulley: rope		

The purpose of the item is to determine the examinee's ability to see the relationship among these words rather than to measure his understanding of each. However, the examinee has to know the meanings of trigger, bullet, switch, and current to select response *D* as the correct answer.

Teachers can do nothing to increase the innate intellectual capacity of their pupils, but can do much to improve their effective intelligence. Verbal and mathematical facility are based on good intellectual ability, but poor achievement in language and mathematics precludes the use of this ability. If it were possible to select two pupils of equal capacity, the one who had read more widely, had a broader vocabulary, and had developed more critical skills in reading and thinking than the other would be at an advantage in taking the various scholastic aptitude tests. Pupils pay a penalty for a meager educational environment, since with their deficiencies they may not do so well in further school work, and are rightfully steered to other paths.

Individual vs. Group Tests

The individual intelligence test can be administerd to only one person at a time. The only numerical limitation on a group intelligence test is the number of facilities and proctors available. Administering group tests is not difficult in most instances, although certain problems arise when young children are being tested.

The examiner must cope with their short attention span and their difficulties in following instructions. However, he can be trained rather quickly for group test administration. The same is not true for the individual test; special training is necessary if the examiner is to capitalize on the testing situation to learn something of the individual's work habits and personality. One of the most important factors in any test administration is motivating the examinee to optimum performance. It is much easier to obtain good motivation when the examiner's attention can be concentrated on one person. In group testing, disinterest, with lapses of attention and effort, are more difficult to determine.

Scoring of responses on individual tests tends to be more subjective than on group tests. Although scoring guides are furnished, the examiner must interpret the correctness of the response. For example, in the *Stanford-Binet Vocabulary* the examinee is asked, "What is an orange?" The response "tree" is listed as a correct answer but "lemon" is not. The *Memory for Designs* test at years nine and eleven requires the examinee to reproduce two designs after looking at them for ten seconds. In scoring, he is allowed full credit for the *A* designs but only one-half credit for the *B* designs shown in Figure 12.1. On the other hand, a group test is generally scored in terms of the number of items right and, in most instances, no such fine interpretation need be made. Ordinary clerical or machine scoring can be employed.

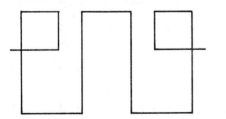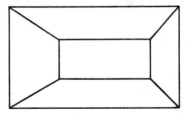

The examinee looks at these designs for ten seconds.
He must then reproduce them.

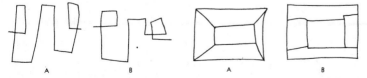

A   B   A   B

**FIGURE 12.1. Memory for Designs—Stanford-Binet Scale Years
             IX and XI.**

Sample item from the *Stanford-Binet Intelligence Scale, Form L-M: Manual for the third revision.* Copyright © 1973 and 1960 by Houghton Mifflin Co. Reproduced by permission.

Each type of test has advantages and disadvantages. The group test is used more in the schools because it does not require highly trained personnel for administration and is more economical in time and cost to administer. An individual intelligence test should be administered when one suspects that group-test results are invalid. Because the group test emphasizes reading ability more than the individual test, considerable caution should be exercised lest a low score be interpreted as lack of native ability rather than as low reading achievement.

PROBLEM

4. Bill received an IQ of 107 on the *Otis-Lennon* and 107 on the *Stanford-Binet*. What justification can you see for the additional time and expense involved in the use of the individual test?

Verbal vs. Performance and Nonlanguage Tests

Performance tests generally require the subject to manipulate some object, put parts of a figure or picture together, set up a color design, and so forth. Generally they call for individual administration; they are often designed for those individuals with some physical anomaly, and are exemplified by speech and hearing tests for illiterates or those who cannot speak English. Scoring procedures vary. In some instances, only the time to complete the test is recorded. In other tests, the examiner scores the number of moves in addition to keeping a time record, and sometimes tabulates false movements.

Nonlanguage tests are paper-and-pencil tests designed for group administration. No knowledge of written or spoken language is necessary, and although some test instructions are given orally, they are very simple and can be translated into another language without affecting test validity. Pantomime is often used to clarify instructions. Test items may require a subject to complete paper-and-pencil mazes, determine the number of cubes in a pile, complete a series in which X's and O's have different patterns of arrangement, mark identical pairs of numbers, draw in missing parts of pictures, and solve a spatial relations test.

One test requires the examinee to determine which geometric figure cuts another into parts of a certain shape; find missing parts on reversed geometric figures; determine the resulting design of a pattern synthesis, in which two geometric figures are superimposed; determine the next position of a sequence of geometric figures in a movement sequence; determine spatial relations in a manikin test, in which the position of the manikin is changed and the correct figure in terms of hand placement must be determined; and identify, in paper folding, how the paper would look after it had been folded, cut, and opened again.

It should be understood that both the performance and nonlanguage tests measure different aspects of intelligence from those measured by verbal tests. It is doubtful if they tap higher order abilities, since the verbal tests demand the manipulation of verbal symbols through thinking. Performance and nonlanguage tests rely on spatial and perceptual abilities.

The tests are useful in supplementing data obtained from verbal tests on certain occasions. A child who has failed in school may not be motivated to do items on a verbal test so similar to school work. On the contrary, he may find the tasks in performance and nonverbal tests novel and exciting. Performance tests are also helpful to the clinician in his observation of a child's behavior, but require training beyond that of the average teacher. Despite certain limitations, the verbal test is a better instrument for prediction of academic success.

PROBLEM

5. What place would you allocate to performance and nonlanguage tests in a public school testing program? Defend your answer.

Culture-Fair Tests

This type of test is sometimes spoken of as a *culture-free* test, which, of course, is not an accurate description. Every individual's development bears the imprint of some culture. The concern is that the typical scholastic aptitude test is unfair to those reared in a deprived environment. We often question whether our commonly used tests give a valid indication of a pupil's intelligence when he comes from an unstimulating environment where verbal communication is not valued.

Various kinds of items have been utilized in an attempt to avoid penalizing this kind of pupil. Mazes, symbol copying, classification of pictures, explaining the essence of a picture, and identification of similar drawings have been employed. Because speed is a cultural factor, it has been deemphasized. Tests placing a premium on quick recall have not been used.

Despite an attempt to eliminate cultural bias, studies in general show that lower-class children do not perform any better on this type of test than on other tests of mental ability.

Stroud (1957, p. 85) writes that:

. . . We may find that the problem is really too big for the test author. It may turn out that the kinds of cultural impact associated with social class differences affect the course of mental development of children as well as their performance on intelligence tests.

Social class differences are real differences, substantial psychological phenomena with which schools and society must deal. It may be that we cannot build valid intelligence tests which will not at the same time discriminate among the social classes. Or, if we start the other way round by designing tests which will not discriminate among social classes, we may find that the tests are poor predictors of academic achievement.

But there is another aspect to the use of scores from our typically culturally biased aptitude tests. A number of children coming from "disadvantaged" environments and having values and classroom behavior at variance with that of their teachers, do well on the tests, in contrast to their daily academic performance. Without objective test results, some of these nonconforming children would be categorized adversely by the typically middle-class professional staff.

There is other evidence supporting the use of our commonly used standardized tests. If the criterion of validity of our scholastic aptitude tests is the prediction of academic success, then we can have some satisfaction in the findings of studies investigating the problem. Cleary (1966) studied the relationship of scholastic aptitude test scores and achievement in three integrated colleges. In two of these institutions there was no significant difference in over- or underprediction of academic success by the *SAT*. However, in the third college the *SAT* overpredicted grades of the black students.

However, Fishman et al. (1964) urge us to look for the different meanings in the scores of minority children. They ask that we not use their scores as evidence of fixed potential but that we plan activities that will help to free the child from his handicaps. Furthermore, interpreting their scores may well be complicated by the influence of certain nonintellective factors on test performance by disadvantaged pupils, such as familiarity of the examiner and the materials used (Kinnie and Sternlof, 1971).

INCREASING MENTAL ABILITY.   Because of government programs such as Head Start, designed to improve the aptitude for learning of culturally disadvantaged children, there has been considerable discussion about the possibility of increasing mental ability and scholastic achievement. Jensen (1969a, 1969b) argues forcibly that compensatory education efforts have failed to make permanent gains on children's IQ and achievement. He questions the rationale on which these programs have been based—that variance of the environment and the cultural bias of scholastic aptitude tests are the main causes of IQ differences. Finally, he concludes that genetic factors are of greater importance in producing these differences than is environmental influence.

The Jensen position has generated vigorous debate. Some seriously question his conclusions (Hunt, 1969; Sanday, 1972), whereas others believe they are valid at least in part and suggest further research (Crow, 1969; Shockley, 1972). Unsurprisingly, many questions have been raised. For instance, if variations in environment are gradually reduced, will the effect of heritability on mental ability correspondingly increase (Bereiter, 1969)?

How much then can we boost mental ability and scholastic achievement? Hunt (1969, p. 297) concludes: "As I read the evidence, the odds are strong that we can boost both IQ and scholastic achievement substantially, but we cannot know how much for at least two decades." Longitudinal studies will be necessary to answer the question (see National Council on Measurement in Education in the Suggested Readings at the end of this chapter).

PROBLEM

6. What are the major common fallacies about heredity, environment, and human behavior existing today (Anastasi, 1973)? Identify possible reasons for each.

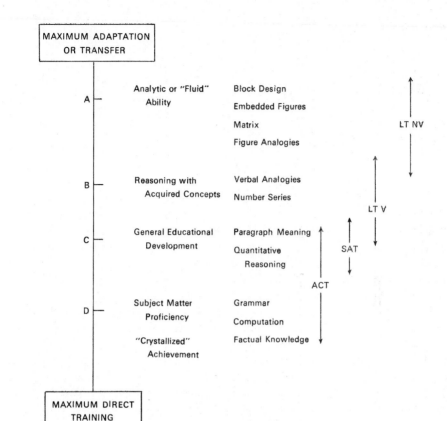

FIGURE 12.2. Spectrum for Comparing Tests of Scholastic Aptitude or General Aptitude.

From *Essentials of Psychological Testing*, 3rd ed., by Lee J. Cronbach (Harper & Row, Publishers, Inc., 1970). Reprinted by permission of the publishers.

(Note: Tests with which you are unfamiliar are discussed in Buros' Mental Measurements Yearbook. Symbols in figure above represent the following tests: LT, Lorge-Thorndike; SAT, Scholastic Aptitude Test; ACT, American College Testing Program. V signifies verbal score; NV is the nonverbal score.)

Educational Loading

Cronbach (1970, p. 282) has constructed a chart for comparing various tests of scholastic aptitude (see Figure 12.2) by establishing a continuum ranging from those sampling school work content directly to those utilizing analytic tasks. Those tests at the bottom of the chart sample trained abilities; they make few demands for adaptation or transfer. The analytic tasks at the other end of the chart, however, require little use of specific knowledge and much transfer.

The *A* tasks in the spectrum seldom demand advanced knowledge; analysis and reasoning are required. Verbal concepts may aid the examinee but he does not need to understand the examiner's language. At the *B* level tasks, the subject is required to use familiar words in novel combinations. In the *C* or *D* categories, the difficult items could, for instance, use uncommon words.

Note the similarity between the spectrum and the continuum of tests of developed ability shown in Table 11.1 (p. 261). Both are oversimplifications. Yet both have utility when we try to understand how aptitude and achievement tests are the same and different.

Mental Age

When buying clothing for school-age children, we do not ask for something to fit a ten-year-old; we ask for a definite size because children of the same age vary. Intelligence testing is the same; pupils of the same age do not have the same amount of intelligence. The outstanding feature of the *Stanford-Binet Scale* is that the tests are grouped according to the age at which a majority passed. For example, if a child passes the items at the ten-year level and fails those at the eleven-year level, he has a mental age of ten. If his chronological age is less than ten, he is bright; if his chronological age is greater than ten, he is duller than average. In actual testing practice, a child may receive a mental age of ten and yet miss some items in the scale below the ten-year level and pass some above this level.

Mental age may be determined in other tests from the raw score, such as the total number of items correct. The mean raw score earned by a particular age group in the standardization sample would represent the mental age for the group. If the group were seven-year-olds, the mental age would be seven. A child who makes a raw score equal to the average of seven-year-olds would, therefore, have a mental age of seven. It should be emphasized that the mental age in itself tells us nothing about the brightness of the child. It refers only to the level of mental development.

Other characteristics inherent in the concept of mental age make interpretation difficult. Unlike the measurement of height or weight, no absolute zero point exists, and it would be difficult to define the point of no intelligence in a human being. Moreover, mental age units are unequal. As the individual grows older, the mental age units represent decreasing development. Since the increase in mental age units compared to the increase in the CA is quite small, the concept of MA becomes meaningless for pupils in their late teens. Actually, the growth pattern is not unlike that for height. Between two and four years of age, there is a much greater increase than between the years of sixteen and eighteen. It is for this reason that percentile ranks and standard scores, rather than IQs, are used for older pupils.

Another problem is in the interpretation of identical mental ages of two pupils who have different chronological ages. If mental age is assumed to represent a pupil's level of mental capacity, than an MA of eight represents the same degree of intellectual maturity no matter if one child has a CA of six and another a CA of ten. However, these two pupils are quite different intellectually. Further difficulties in the interpretation of the MA must be dealt with when extrapolating to determine an IQ value for the superior pupil. How does one interpret a mental age of twenty-two obtained from the norm table when the mean adult mental age on the test is fifteen years?

We should not conclude from this discussion or from the use of the DIQ that the

MA has no value. When the teacher recognizes the limitations, the concept of mental age can be of help in suiting a learning task to the pupil's ability. We know that the understanding of concepts of number, time, and distance requires a certain degree of mental maturity. Much research about teaching children to read has established that general intelligence is the most important factor in reading readiness; mental age is closely related to the pupil's success or failure. Harris (1970, p. 26) summarizes the evidence as follows:

1. *There is a substantial relationship between mental age and ease of learning to read; most children who fail in reading in the first grade have mental ages below six years. The more mature children not only learn more easily but also retain what they learn better than the less mature children.*

2. *Most children who have IQs within or above the normal value and are free from special handicaps can be successfully taught to read in the first grade. However, a delayed start does these children no harm.*

3. *It is not possible to set a definite minimum mental age for learning to read because too many other factors are involved. Children with mental ages as low as five years can be taught to read first-grade materials. There seems to be no lasting advantage in such an early start, however, and many of these children fail to make any headway when the pace of instruction is geared to the progress of older or brighter children.*

Intelligence Quotient

Information concerning a child's rate of mental development is also useful to the teacher. He needs to know whether the child is maturing more or less rapidly than the average child. If his mental age is greater than his chronological age, he is brighter and will eventually be more mentally mature than his duller peers. Other things being equal, he will be a more rapid learner.

Levels of intelligence have been classifed in relation to IQ intervals, as listed in Table 12.2. These descriptive levels are helpful in communicating about individuals with different degrees of intelligence and in roughly predicting job success. It is well to remember that these classifications are useful guides, not rigid divisions.

TABLE 12.2. Distribution of Deviation IQs for the Stanford-Binet Scale.

IQ	Percent	Classification
Above 148	0.1	Near genius
124–148	6.5	Very superior
112–123	16.0	Superior
88–111	54.7	Normal
76–87	16.0	Dull
64–75	5.5	Borderline defective
Below 64	1.2	Mentally defective

Adapted from Pinneau, 1961, p. 70; reproduced by permission of Houghton Mifflin Company.

CONSTANCY OF THE IQ. How stable is the IQ of an individual? Does it effectively predict an individual's ability over a long period of time? This question is of great importance in educational and vocational planning. Test intelligence demands achievement as a means for sampling innate ability; inherited capacity cannot be measured directly. If heredity is highly significant, and if we could measure it accurately, it might yield a more stable score. If environment were more important, its influence could vary from time to time and change measurement. We have reason to believe that both heredity and environment influence effective intelligence. Someone has said that "heredity sets the limit, while environment determines how closely an individual approaches this limit." In other words, probably no individual fully develops his innate capacity.

What are some of the other reasons why the IQ seems less stable than is really warranted? Unreliability of measuring instruments is one prime reason. Also, few instruments are effective for measuring the entire range of abilities found in the typical classroom. Less able pupils will be crowding the "floor," while the "ceiling" will be too low for the able.

Another reason is that mental growth is uneven (Bayley, 1949, 1955). Possible causes could be transitory psychological or physical conditions, such as illness or rapport between the examiner and the subject. On the other hand, the irregularities might reflect real changes in intellectual maturity.

It should be noted that a pupil tends to change in his relative position in the group in relation to the amount of time between tests (Hopkins and Bibelheimer, 1971). Less shifting of relative positions occurs with increasing age (Bayley, 1933, 1949). Reporting the age of the pupil at the time of testing, along with the name of the test, is therefore important in considering the constancy of the IQ.

There are two other reasons that may affect the stability of the measured IQ score. One is caused by the different variabilities of scores for a given test for different ages (Pinneau, 1961). Secondly, for a given pupil, test scores from different scholastic aptitude tests may vary greatly. Hence, the report of an IQ should always include identity of the test from which it was derived, e.g., IQ *(Otis-Lennon, Form J, Intermediate Level):* 93.

CONCLUSIONS. After analyzing the data from numerous studies, we may conclude that the IQ of an individual is quite stable throughout his life if we consider it to be a rough classification. Certainly, the child with a high IQ will tend to remain an individual with considerable intellectual prowess. A pupil who has an IQ well below 100 will probably become an adult who functions on a lower intellectual level, unless the score is the result of poor academic efficiency. We are assuming also that the IQ is not based on an infant test since such tests are quite unreliable. Because of the numerous factors that may influence test scores, a teacher should never rely on the results of a single test. In addition to other test scores, data obtained through observation, for example, should be used to evaluate mental maturity.

PROBLEMS

7. An elementary school is grouping pupils in the intermediate grade levels according to the total scores from a well-developed group scholastic aptitude test. Is this defensible? Explain.

8. There is much current controversy concerning making school records available to parents, including the reporting of actual IQ scores. Should this be done? Can you justify your answer?

DIFFERENTIAL TESTING

The basis of multiple measurement is rooted in trait and factor psychology (Cooley, 1971). A trait is an enduring pattern of behavior that is exhibited by everyone in varying degrees. We should use the multiple-trait approach in studying individual differences. After all, we are attempting to change behavior along several dimensions, for example, verbal as well as quantitative. Furthermore, the affective domain as well as the cognitive must be considered in predicting a pupil's performance. Motivation, to mention one such trait, is obviously a factor in achievement.

Useful insights into a pupil's strengths and weaknesses may be found through a battery of tests standardized on the same population. A profile of aptitude scores can be determined and comparisons made among an individual's cognitive, perceptual, and sensorimotor aptitudes. Recently, batteries of tests standardized on the same population have made a comparison of scores more meaningful. Representative of this kind of test battery are the *Academic Promise Tests (APT)* designed for grades six through nine, the *Differential Aptitude Test (DAT)* for use in the secondary school, and the *General Aptitude Test Battery (GATB)* for ages sixteen and over. We shall discuss only the *DAT* to illustrate differential testing instruments.

Differential Aptitude Test Battery

The *Differential Aptitude Tests* is a battery of eight tests: *Verbal reasoning, Numerical ability, Abstract reasoning, Clerical speed and accuracy, Mechanical reasoning, Space relations, Spelling,* and *Language usage.* These abilities are defined as follows:

Verbal reasoning: *To understand, think, and reason with words.*

Numerical ability: *To reason with numbers and solve mathematical problems.*

Abstract reasoning: *To think logically without words or numbers; to see and manipulate mentally the relationships among things, objects, patterns, diagrams, or designs.*

Clerical speed and accuracy: *To compare and mark simple letter and number symbols quickly and accurately.*

Mechanical reasoning: *To understand mechanical principles and devices and apply laws of everyday physics—to understand how appliances work and how tools are used.*

Space relations: *To "think in three dimensions" or picture mentally the shape, size, and position of objects.*

Spelling: *To recognize correct and incorrect spellings of common English words.*

Language usage: *To be sensitive to language structure, to recognize correct and incorrect word usage, grammar, and punctuation.*

Content overlapping is minimized in the various tests, and the level of difficulty is related to the particular age group. The tests are essentially power tests, except *Clerical speed and accuracy,* which is actually a speed test. In addition to the norms for each subtest, there are norms for a composite of the *Verbal reasoning* and *Numerical ability* scores, which is considered a good indicator of general scholastic aptitude.

A pupil's pattern of aptitude scores can be integrated with his responses to a career planning questionnaire, yielding a computer-produced career planning report (see page 217). The appropriateness of his occupational choice might be confirmed or, if it is not, suggestions made for further exploration.

PROFILE CHART. Two types of profile charts are available, with basic design identical for each. Only the orientation varies. For computer printing the profile is horizontal. The hand-plotted profile illustrated in Figure 12.3 is vertical. Through statistical formulas the authors arrived at a convenient method for approximating the significance of the differences between test scores (see "How Big a Difference is Important" in Figure 12.3).

It is important that the individual tests in a battery have high reliability; it is also essential, however, that tests not correlate highly with each other if important differences among the abilities of an individual are to be determined. The *DAT* subtests meet these criteria.

VALIDITY. The Differential Aptitude Tests represent a model of attention to detail of test construction and interpretation. The care that has been exercised in their development is so well presented in the test manual that by studying these discussions, you can readily develop an understanding of the important considerations of test construction in general. However, despite this commendation, one must be aware that many of the reported validation coefficients are low and differential prediction of performance must be made carefully.

PROBLEM

9. Study Jane's *DAT* profile as displayed in Figure 12.3. Is she a potential college student? What additional major features might a counselor point out to Jane and her parents?

USE OF APTITUDE TESTS IN SCHOOL

The Scholastic Aptitude Test

The commonly used tests of scholastic aptitude differ greatly. Choosing the right test for a given purpose requires careful consideration. Test specialists are not in agreement on their utility. Some believe that tests of general mental ability are of limited value, and argue that most of the uses to which they have been put can be better served by

DIFFERENTIAL APTITUDE TESTS

G. K. Bennett, H. G. Seashore, and A. G. Wesman

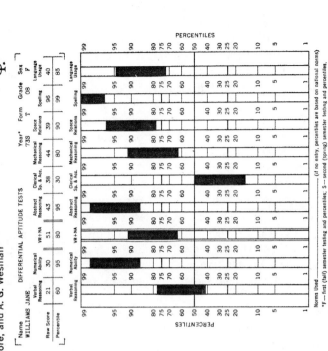

PROFILING YOUR DAT SCORES

The numbers that tell how you did on each test are in the row marked "Percentile." Your percentile tells where you rank on a test in comparison with boys or girls in your grade in numerous schools across the country. If your percentile is 50, you are just in the middle — that is, one-half of the students in the national group did better than you and one-half did less well.

If your percentile on one test is 80, you are at the top of 80 percent of the group — only 20 percent made higher scores than yours. If you scored in the 25th percentile, this means about 75 percent of the group did better than you on the test. These percentiles indicate your relative standing among students of your sex and grade. They do NOT tell you how many questions (or what percent of them) you answered correctly.

Using the information printed in the "Percentile" row, you can now draw your aptitude profile on the chart provided. There are nine columns to be marked; in each of these make a *heavy short line* across the column at the level corresponding to your percentile on that test. (In some cases, the line you draw will coincide with a dotted or solid line already printed on the chart.) Then blacken each column for a distance of one-half inch above and one-half inch below the short line you have drawn, so that you end up with a solid black bar in each column. (For extremely high or low percentiles, you will not be able to blacken one-half inch in both directions without running off the chart.)

HOW BIG A DIFFERENCE IS IMPORTANT?

Since tests cannot be perfectly accurate, you should not overestimate the importance of small differences between two percentiles in comparing your aptitudes. The bars on your profile help by indicating the more important differences.

Look at the bars for any *two* tests and notice whether or not the ends of the bars overlap. If they do not, chances are that you really are better in the kind of ability represented by the bar that is *higher* on the profile chart. If the bars overlap, but not by more than half their length, consider whether other things you know about yourself agree with this indication; the difference may or may not be important. If they overlap by more than half their length, the difference may be disregarded; so small a difference is probably not meaningful. This method of looking at the overlap of bars works for any two abilities you want to compare, whether they are listed next to each other or several columns apart on the chart.

FIGURE 12.3. Sample Profile from the Differential Aptitude Tests.

Reproduced by permission. Copyright © 1973 by The Psychological Corporation, New York, N.Y. All rights reserved.

using properly constructed achievement tests of more specialized abilities (Davis, 1964, p. 137). Nevertheless, a pupil's academic potential must be determined and the scholastic aptitude test is helpful for this purpose.

Group, rather than individual, tests of verbal mental ability are probably the most useful and can provide helpful information in any school testing program. Because of their economy and practicality, they do not require a trained examiner, and yet they tend to be as reliable as individual tests. For school use their degree of validity is satisfactory.

It must be emphasized, however, that at times a pupil does not give his optimum performance, and this invalidates the score. If the score seems to deviate widely from other data available, a teacher may want a child retested on an individual basis with an instrument such as the *Stanford-Binet* or the *WISC*. In administering the individual test, the examiner can observe the pupil and better evaluate the validity of the test. If personnel trained for administering individual tests are unavailable, another form of the group test already used or a different group test should be administered. The nonlanguage test is a helpful supplementary instrument for discovering pupils whose scores are affected by poor reading or general lack of verbal facility. Some tests give a language and a nonlanguage IQ in addition to a composite IQ, and are popular in some schools. However, in interpreting these scores, one must realize that differences may be due to measurement error.

The usefulness of the typical scholastic aptitude test for inner-city schools is often questioned. In fact, their use has been discontinued in some large cities (Loretan, 1965), and other programs installed. For instance, New York City uses common sets of material for both instruction and assessment entitled *Let's Look at Children*. In this program, children are taught and given an opportunity to practice those tasks on which they are to be later evaluated, thus increasing the opportunity for equality of exposure. The primary objective of the project is to help teachers better understand and assess the intellectual development of each entering school child, so that they may teach every child more effectively (Bussis, 1965, p. 7).

In order to accomplish this goal, three steps were taken. First, a guide for teachers, entitled *Let's Look at First Graders*, was written. It illustrates logical concrete behavior in six different areas: *Basic language skills, Concepts of space and time, Beginning logical concepts, Beginning mathematical concepts,* the *Growth of reasoning skills,* and *General signs of development.* The second step was the development of tasks for eliciting intellectual behavior. The tasks not only allow the child to demonstrate his understanding and the teacher to observe it, but they also have instructional value. They are game-like situations for the child to discover new concepts and develop new skills in thinking. The final step is the development of a series of written exercises, which are designed to determine the child's understanding and developed ability in the areas of *Shapes and forms, Spatial relations, Time concepts, Mathematics, Communication skills,* and *Logical reasoning.* They provide practice for the child before any record is made of the measurement.

The unique aspect of the entire program is the attempt to make instructional materials and "test" materials one and the same thing. This is quite unlike other readiness tests such as the various reading readiness tests. Furthermore, the developmental progress of the child is presented only through qualitative descriptions rather than norms. Additional modifications and improvement of programs of this type are most certain to come.

Grouping

The classroom teacher and guidance staff can use the scores on the scholastic aptitude tests to understand the pupil better in teaching and in planning his educational and vocational goals. Likewise, the test scores may be administratively helpful in class grouping and occasionally for problems of promotion. It should be emphasized, however, that no group determined by one criterion is homogeneous. A typical scholastic ability test contains both verbal and quantitative problems. Pupils making the same total score may vary considerably in their abilities. Pupils with identical scores also may have quite different motivations and interests. As one psychologist concluded, "The only way it is possible to have a homogeneous group is to have one pupil—and he continues to change." Grouping alone is not the answer to effective learning.

The teacher must plan in terms of materials and method to meet the needs and potential of each group. Furthermore, he must make special provisions for the deviate within a group, whether this individual is very bright or very dull, or has problems of an affective nature. Most schools are unable to organize special classes for these individuals.

It is perhaps easier to group for academic achievement in high school than in the elementary school. In the latter, many subjects are taught in one class. In high school, subjects are typically separated and an achievement test can be used along with an aptitude test for grouping.

Differential Testing

At the secondary school level, differential aptitude testing may provide some information for educational as well as vocational counseling; yet testing alone should not be used as the only criterion for determining the aptitude of boys and girls. The alert teacher is aware of their interests, their performance in and out of the classroom, the kinds of questions they ask, and so forth. Complete evaluation is necessary for valid interpretation.

An increasing number of secondary schools are realizing the importance of obtaining information about other aptitudes of their pupils. With the advent of differential testing, such instruments as the *Differential Aptitude Tests* have provided a means to identify the aptitude patterns in areas other than those most generally measured by the typical scholastic aptitude test. This added information provides many more data for the school to help all pupils plan their studies.

To be specific, a few of pupils' special problems more readily identified by differential testing are listed below:

1. *The boy who is failing the verbally oriented courses, but who has excellent mechanical ability.*

2. *The boy from a bilingual home with few cultural opportunities who makes high scores on the* Numerical ability, Mechanical reasoning, *and* Space relations *tests, but is failing in school.*

3. *The girl whose tested abilities are below average except for* Clerical speed and accuracy.

4. *The boy who aspires to be a physicist but whose* Numerical ability *score is low.*

The school must have adequate information about its superior pupils if it is to help them achieve. The gifted pupil is too often overlooked or unmotivated to continue his education. School authorities should identify such pupils and exercise every effort to appreciate and develop their talents.

It is also important to identify accurately the aptitude patterns of those who are less able. The common practice is to direct them into vocational courses without regard for any other criterion except that they are doing poorly in their academic classes. Yet the chances of a pupil's succeeding in a commercial course are not good if his score on the *Clerical speed and accuracy* test is valid and low. In addition, the mechanically inept are not served best in a shop course. It is necessary to assign courses that correspond with the interests and abilities of all students.

Overachievement and Underachievement

A concern of the teacher is determination of a pupil's achievement in terms of his ability. One may well question how a pupil can overachieve. The concept refers to a pupil achieving more than is predicted for a person of his academic ability. That is, he is not achieving more than is possible for him to achieve but more than is expected of him based on the past performance of pupils with like ability. On the other hand, the underachiever is so labeled because his performance in comparison with others of his ability is not measuring up to expectations.

Before such conclusions are drawn about pupils, several considerations should be taken into account. First of all, a prediction of achievement made from performance on a scholastic aptitude test score alone is insufficiently based. Probably only verbal and mathematical skills have been measured. Secondly, although aptitude and achievement are not perfectly correlated, they are highly related and not at all independent; there is not a one-to-one relationship between ability and achievement. Thirdly, one must also consider that, in addition to this problem, tests measuring these components are not perfectly reliable; they contain errors of measurement.

A much more effective way to predict achievement, and thus determine whether pupils are performing adequately, is to judge achievement on the basis of achievement expected from an individual with his aptitude. In the past, teachers have attempted to estimate performance without any real basis for doing so. What they have done in many instances is to label pupils underachievers when they haven't measured up to the average performance of all pupils. This could be grossly unfair to a given pupil.

Some test publishers now provide a joint-norms table that indicates the expected achievement of a pupil who performs at a given level on an aptitude test. The *Iowa Test of Basic Skills* is such an instrument; tables indicate the percentile rank equivalent for a grade equivalent score for pupils falling at various IQ levels on the *Lorge-*

Thorndike Intelligence Tests. The *California Achievement Test* also has tables for relating achievement to ability. Nevertheless, one must interpret these norm tables with care because adequacy of achievement is determined by many factors and not the score on a scholastic aptitude test alone. It should also be remembered that when predictions are made from data on relatively homogeneous groups such as these, the reliability of the difference scores is not high.

The causes and characteristics of underachievement are suggested by a wealth of labels such as free-floating anxiety, negative self-value, hostility toward authority, high dependence-independence conflict, and negative interpersonal relations. Also, underachievement is usually defined arbitrarily by the investigator. As a result, depending on definition, underachievement is found among both gifted pupils (Ewing and Gilbert, 1967) and low-ability pupils (McGowan, 1968).

PROBLEM

10. In advising pupils about curriculum choice, what relative weights would you assign to aptitude scores as compared with school marks? Why?

SUMMARY

In this chapter, a number of significant points have been developed:

1. *Scholastic aptitude tests are often verbal and mathematical in nature and closely related to school work. They measure not only aspects of innate ability, but also the effects of learning.*
2. *Measuring aptitude can be useful in planning programs to help children attain their growth potential. However, care must be exercised in predicting achievement from aptitude test scores because many factors determine achievement.*
3. *Individual mental ability tests provide a wealth of information about the pupil but are only occasionally used in schools because of administration and cost considerations.*
4. *Aptitude tests may be classified as verbal, performance, or nonlanguage tests. To perform successfully on verbal tests, the subject must understand oral and often written language. Performance tests are individual tests and emphasize the manipulation of objects rather than verbal skill. Nonlanguage tests are constructed as paper-and-pencil tests and, unlike performance tests, are designed for group administration. Although some oral instructions in the administration of a nonlanguage test may be required, in general no written or spoken language is necessary to obtain correct responses.*
5. *For all practical purposes, the ratio IQ has been replaced by the deviation IQ for translating scores of children's mental ages.*
6. *A rough classification of a child's IQ generally holds throughout life; that is, dull, normal, or bright children tend to become dull, normal, or bright adults.*
7. *Differential aptitude tests are helpful for measuring specific aptitudes such as mechanical, spatial, and clerical. A series of such tests are standardized on the*

same population so that meaningful profiles can be constructed to interpret a pupil's strengths and weaknesses.

8. *Culture-fair tests have been constructed to deemphasize the role of the examinee's environment because aptitude is affected by achievement as well as innate ability. These tests vary in the degree to which they achieve their purpose; there are substantial relationships between scores on these tests and typical scholastic aptitude tests. Nevertheless, we must look for different meanings in many of the aptitude scores of disadvantaged children.*

9. *The use of scholastic aptitude tests has been terminated in some cities and as a result new types of instruments have been developed. One such attempt is to make instructional materials and test materials one and the same thing. The program is designed to determine the child's understanding and developed ability in specific areas and then to provide practice for the child before any record is made of the measurement.*

SUGGESTED READINGS

ANASTASI, A. *Common fallacies about heredity, environment, and human behavior.* ACT Research Report No. 58. Iowa City, Iowa: The American College Testing Program, 1973.
  A discussion of the controversy of the environment-heredity issue and the place of test scores for developing human potential.

BERSOFF, D. N. Silk purses into sows' ears: The decline of psychological testing and a suggestion for its redemption. *American Psychologist,* 1973, *28,* 892–899.
  After reviewing some of the problems associated with psychological tests, the author suggests remedies, emphasizing naturalistic observation of behavior.

CRONBACH, L. J. *Essentials of psychological testing.* New York: Harper & Row, 1970. Chapters 7, 8, 9, 10, 11, and 12.
  Extensive discussion of the appraisal of general ability and the research and theory on which it is based will be found in these chapters. Group and individual test instruments are included as well as the use of ability profiles in guidance.

NATIONAL COUNCIL ON MEASUREMENT IN EDUCATION. *Untangling the tangled web of education.* Princeton, N.J.: Educational Testing Service, 1969.
  The papers presented in a special symposium dealing with the problems of evaluating early schooling for disadvantaged children are included in this research memorandum.

TUDDENHAM, R. D. Intelligence. In R. L. Ebel (ed.), *Encyclopedia of Educational Research.* (4th ed.) New York: Macmillan, 1969. Pp. 654–667.
  A thorough review of basic research concerning intelligence, including intellectual development during the life span.

TYLER, F. T. Readiness. In R. L. Ebel (ed.), *Encyclopedia of Educational Research.* (4th ed.) New York: Macmillan, 1969. Pp. 1062–1069.
  Readiness is of prime consideration in aptitude for learning. The author presents a thorough review of the research on all facets of this topic, including readiness as it relates to maturation, Piaget's theories, learning theories, cognitive structure and style, and structure of knowledge.

ZACH, L. The IQ debate. *Today's Education,* 1972, *61,* 40–43.
  Discusses the problems in using scholastic aptitude tests with disadvantaged children.

REFERENCES CITED

ANASTASI, A. *Common fallacies about heredity, environment, and human behavior.* Iowa City, Iowa: The American College Testing Program, 1973.

BAYLEY, N. Mental growth during the first three years. A developmental study of 61 children by repeated tests. *Genetic Psychological Monographs,* 1933, *14,* 1–92.

BAYLEY, N. Consistency and variability in growth of intelligence from birth to 18 years. *Journal of Genetic Psychology*, 1949, 75, 165–196.

BAYLEY, N. On the growth of intelligence. *American Psychologist*, 1955, 10, 805–818.

BEREITER, C. The future of individual differences. *Harvard Educational Review*, 1969, 39, 310–318.

BUROS, O. K. (ed.). *The seventh mental measurements yearbook*. Highland Park, N.J.: Gryphon Press, 1972.

BUSSIS, A.M. *From theory to the classroom*. Princeton, N.J.: Educational Testing Service, 1965.

CLEARY, T. A. Test bias: Validity of the Scholastic Aptitude Test for Negro and white students in integrated colleges. *Educational Testing Service Research Bulletin*, 1966, RB-66-31.

COLLEGE ENTRANCE EXAMINATION BOARD. *A description of the College Board Scholastic Aptitude Test*. Princeton, N.J.: Author, 1965.

COLLEGE ENTRANCE EXAMINATION BOARD. *Effects of coaching on Scholastic Aptitude Test scores*. Princeton, N.J.: Author, 1968.

COOLEY, W. W. Techniques for considering multiple measurement. In R. L. Thorndike (ed.), *Educational measurement*. (2nd ed.) Washington: American Council on Education, 1971, chapter 16.

CRONBACH, L. J. *Essentials of psychological testing*. (3rd ed.) New York: Harper & Row, 1970.

CROW, J. F. Genetic theories and influences: Comments on the value of diversity. *Harvard Educational Review*, 1969, 39, 301–309.

DAVIS, F. B. *Educational measurements and their interpretation*. Belmont, Calif.: Wadsworth, 1964.

EWING, T. N., and W. M. GILBERT. Controlled study of the effects of counseling on the scholastic achievements of students of superior ability. *Journal of Counseling Psychology*, 1967, 14, 235–239.

FISHMAN, J. A., et al. Guidelines for testing minority group children. *Journal of Social Issues* (Supplement), 1964, 20, 129–145.

GLASER, R., and A. J. NITKO. Measurement in learning and instruction. In R. L. Thorndike (ed.), *Educational measurement*. (2nd ed.) Washington: American Council on Education, 1971, chapter 17.

HARRIS, A. J. *How to increase reading ability*. (5th ed.) New York: David McKay, 1970.

HOPKINS, K. D., and M. BIBELHEIMER. Five-year stability of intelligence quotients from language and nonlanguage group tests. *Child Development*, 1971, 42, 645–649.

HUNT, J. M. Has compensatory education failed? Has it been attempted? *Harvard Educational Review*, 1969, 39, 278–300.

JENSEN, A. R. How much can we boost IQ and scholastic achievement? *Harvard Educational Review*, 1969a, 39, 1–123.

JENSEN, A. R. Reducing the heredity-environment uncertainty: A reply. *Harvard Educational Review*, 1969b, 39, 449–483.

KINNIE, E., and R. E. STERNLOF. The influence of nonintellectual factors in IQ scores of middle- and lower-class children. *Child Development*, 1971, 42, 1989–1995.

LORETAN, J. O. The decline and fall of group intelligence testing. *Teachers College Record*, 1965, 67, 10–17.

MCGOWAN, R. J. The effect of brief contact interviews with low ability, low achieving students. *School Counselor*, 1968, 15, 386–389.

MUNDAY, L. A. What does it mean if the scores are falling? *Activity*, 1974, 12, 3.

PINNEAU, S. R. *Changes in intelligence quotient, infancy to maturity*. Boston: Houghton Mifflin, 1961.

SANDAY, P. R. An alternative interpretation of the relationship between heredity, race, environment, and IQ. *Phi Delta Kappan*, 1972, 54, 250–254.

SHOCKLEY, W. Dysgenics, geneticity, raceology: A challenge to the intellectual responsibility of educators. *Phi Delta Kappan*, 1972, 53, 297–307.

STROUD, J. B. The intelligence test in school use: Some persistent issues. *Journal of Educational Psychology*, 1957, 48, 77–85.

TERMAN, L. M., and M. A. MERRILL. *The Stanford-Binet Intelligence Scale: Manual for the third revision*. Boston: Houghton Mifflin, 1973.

13

EVALUATING PERSONAL-SOCIAL ADJUSTMENT

The Greek myth of Daedalus and his son Icarus tells how Icarus met his death because he could not adjust to a new situation. When Daedalus, who had been held captive, made his escape from prison, he found no other way to flee the heavily guarded island but by air. Rarest of craftsmen, he set to work making great feathered wings for himself and for his son, binding the large feathers with thread, the small with wax. When all was ready for flight, he gravely cautioned the boy Icarus always to fly close to him in a moderate course between sky and sea, warning that if they flew too low the weight of sea spray in their feathers would drag them down, and if too high, the heat of the sun would melt the wax that bound them.

All went well until Icarus, lacking his father's realistic caution and giddy with the joy of flight, soared away into the heavens. The blazing sun melted the wax bonds of the wings and feathers and as they fell away, nothing was left to hold the boy in the air but his flailing arms. Suddenly missing his beloved son, Daedalus cried out to him but was answered only by the terrible sight of scattering feathers swirling in the sea beneath.

Icarus' behavior seems to defy explanation. What foolhardiness caused him to behave so? Men have always concerned themselves with human behavior. It was once believed that patterns of adjustment were entirely inherited, and personality traits passed on to children in the same way as blue eyes and red hair. Even today we hear people say of nonconforming children: "Well, he comes by it honestly; he's a chip off the old block," assuming, however unconsciously, a hereditary basis for atypical behavior.

Modern psychology has shown that personal-social development depends on the interplay of many factors, not only on learned patterns of adjustment, but on such elements as the chemical function and physical structure of the body, and the general level of intelligence. The small boy may become aggressive to compensate for his size, or withdraw from physical contact and compensate through intellectual prowess or fantasy. The dull girl with high standards may resort to atypical actions in an attempt to adjust to an impossible situation, but her reaction is learned, not inherited.

The maladjusted individual is no longer assumed to be immoral or suffering over his sins. Neither is he accused of deliberate nonconformist behavior. The clinician accepts the individual and approaches his problem with sympathy, but objectifies the situation and tries to determine its antecedents. Instead of focusing on symptoms, he seeks causes.

Yet some parents and teachers still subject "different" children to sarcasm, and believe that if these children would only "try," they would improve. The shy child is urged to show more spunk; daydreamers are asked to wake up. Too often this approach convinces the child that he is right in his estimation of himself, that he is indeed inadequate, and, too often, he accepts the situation as hopeless. Thus, his behavior may actually be reinforced by exhortations to reform. Admonishing or ridiculing are not effective ways to initiate a positive change in behavior.

The process of adjustment is the individual's attempt to create a more congruous relationship between himself and his environment. The process may consist of an attempt to change the environment or his behavior, or to modify both. The teacher should play a very important role in helping the child manage the adjustment. Certainly, he cannot assume that the burden to adjust rests entirely on the individual alone. Yet, if he is careless of his responsibility, he may establish a social climate in which it is impossible for his pupils to meet even their basic personality needs. A teacher who stipulates equal requirements for all is frustrating many pupils by denying them any opportunity for success. Equally, when able children are forced to repeat much that they have already experienced and learned, the teacher is denying them the challenge that comes through new experience and that stimulates new learning and growth. The authoritarian taskmaster who expects everyone in his classroom to conform is stifling not only creativity but also the satisfaction that comes through self-expression.

TEACHERS' CONCEPTS OF ADJUSTMENT

One of the most difficult problems in evaluating the personal-social adjustment of pupils lies in the teacher's understanding of adjustment. Just because certain kinds of behavior disrupt the well-oiled machinery of a carefully controlled classroom is no defensible reason to label them maladjustment. Yet a number of studies indicates that teachers fail to differentiate between behavior that disturbs the activities of the classroom and behavior that may lead to serious emotional difficulty.

In one study (Sparks, 1952), teachers were asked to rank fifty-five problems, those most serious for the pupil and those most troublesome to the teacher. Table 13.1 shows clearly that the participating teacher did not have an accurate concept of what constitutes evidence of serious adjustment problems. Apparently they considered traits that violate society's social and moral code as most likely to produce adjustment problems in the individual. They listed as most "serious" the traits that proved troublesome to them as teachers, not symptoms related to the emotional conflicts of children. They tended to make little differentiation between academic success and emotional health. In general, they considered pupils who did satisfactory academic work to be well-adjusted individuals, whereas if a pupil's achievement was low they were inclined to think of him as a behavior deviant or just stupid.

Do teachers and psychologists perceive types of pupil behavioral patterns in the same way? No, not to the degree one might hope. In one study, elementary school

TABLE 13.1.   Traits Ranked Most Troublesome to the Teacher and Most Serious to the Pupil.

	Traits	
Rank	Most troublesome to teacher	Most serious to pupil
1	Interrupting	Stealing
2	Carelessness in work	Untruthfulness
3	Inattention	Unreliableness
4	Restlessness	Cruelty and bullying
5	Silliness, smartness	Cheating
6	Whispering and note writing	Heterosexual activity
7	Tattling	Impertinence
8	Thoughtlessness	Imprudence
9	Disorderliness	Selfishness
10	Inquisitiveness	Laziness

Adapted from Sparks (1952). Copyright 1952 by the American Psychological Association. Reprinted by permission.

teachers and psychologists were asked to indicate whether various types of behavior were normal or abnormal for children and adolescents (Tolor, Scarpetti, and Lane, 1967). The results are summarized in Table 13.2.

Teachers and psychologists responded much differently, particularly when classifying regressive, aggressive, and affective behavior. When ratings by experienced teachers and inexperienced teachers were compared with those by psychologists, the experienced teachers did not differ nearly as much from psychologists in ascribing abnormality as the less experienced teachers did. The following behaviors regarded as normal by the experienced teachers and abnormal by the inexperienced teachers are illustrative:

Cries or whimpers

Plays with or fingers his mouth

At the slightest upset, coordination becomes poor

TABLE 13.2.   Types of Behavioral Patterns That Teachers and Psychologists Perceive Differently.

Category	Number of behaviors	Percentage of items disagreed upon
Physical-psychosomatic	71	10
Phobic	18	6
Aggressive	56	38
Affect	58	33
Communication	21	14
Regressive	15	40
Inefficiency	25	12
Fantasy-withdrawal	31	19

Adapted from Tolor, Scarpetti, and Lane (1967). Copyright 1967 by the American Psychological Association. Reprinted by permission.

Is frightened in crowds
Is afraid of being alone in a wide open space
Lying

PROBLEM

1. Are you surprised by the degree of difference between the perceptions of pupil behaviors by teachers and psychologists as shown in Table 13.2? Postulate reasons why they exist and suggest steps to rectify the situation.

METHODS OF EVALUATING
PERSONAL-SOCIAL ADJUSTMENT

The discussion in this chapter is confined to personal-social adjustment rather than personality. The latter is much broader in meaning:

Personality does not depend on one or a few characteristics only, but on the interplay of practically all of an individual's qualities. Physical structure, chemical functioning, learned motives, and habits of adjustment all contribute to personality, and not as separate entities but as interacting aspects of an organized system (Shaffer and Shoben, 1956, p. 310).

Of course, the individual must adjust to his physiological needs; he eats when he is hungry, he seeks warmth if he is cold. But much broader dimensions of adjustment are assumed than this simple adaptive behavior. We must consider the pupil's relationship to his social environment as well as his behavior in relation to his own psychological needs.

In the lives of most civilized people, social adjustments are more significant than responses to physiological wants. Human beings are social persons as well as biological organisms. Social interactions among people and between groups of people are required to fulfill even some of our most elementary needs. On the other hand, people often work in competition or at cross purposes so as to thwart one another's satisfactions. When a child feels insecure and unwanted by his family, when a student feels isolated from his fellows, or when a man is unsuccessful in his work, adjustments are required to mediate between the socially defined needs and the socially determined frustrations (Shaffer and Shoben, 1956, p. 4).

Behavior patterns such as these are partial reflections of the degree to which some important educational objectives have been achieved in the pupil, and it is necessary, therefore, to attempt to evaluate them.

A variety of instruments for evaluating personal-social adjustment is available to the teacher. Some of these are based on formal observations, some are paper-and-pencil inventories to be administered to a group of pupils, others are individual instruments designed primarily for use by clinicians. The following outline is indicative of the variety of useful instruments and techniques in this area of evaluation.

Evaluation methods based on observation
   Anecdotal records
   Rating scales
   Check lists
   Interviewing

Projective techniques
   Inkblot and picture presentation
   Use of graphic and art materials
   Doll play
   Presentation of verbal stimuli

Sociometric and related techniques
   Sociograms
   Social-distance scales
   "Guess who" questionnaires

Self-report inventories
   Biographical data blank
   Personal inventories
   Interest inventories
   Attitude scales and questionnaires

Neither the standardized instruments nor less formal ones are as reliable or valid as the better standard achievement and scholastic aptitude tests. As there are extremists who harbor an indefensible degree of enthusiasm for the measurement possibilities of these tests, there are many prophets of gloom who mistrust them altogether and advocate a "hands-off" policy. It seems reasonable to adopt a middle-of-the-road position. The following discussion emphasizes the limitations of various methods and techniques included in the outline above, but goes on to suggest some practical approaches to this area of evaluation.

Evaluation Methods Based on Observation

What a teacher can learn from observation of pupils in natural situations is generally useful to him, and is, for many reasons, a valuable addition to the study of personal-social development.

First, the results of such observation supplement information gathered elsewhere. A pupil may do well on a mechanical aptitude test, but be awkward and uninterested in the shop. Another may give the desired answers on an adjustment inventory, but be unable to work cooperatively with any of his peers.

Second, they provide the teacher with information unobtainable in other ways. He has an opportunity to notice numerous significant incidents and attitudes in the daily activities of the pupil, an opportunity which may be lacking in artificial situations. When a pupil answers "yes" to the question "Is it fun to do nice things for other boys and girls?" his behavior may not be indicative of his adjustment to a peer group; the teacher may observe that the child is really self-centered.

Third, they afford an opportunity to sample the pupil's actual behavior. Under informal observation, a pupil is not asked to conform to what he might feel in an artificial situation, as in answering a questionnaire, and is not requested to report on his own behavior. Direct observation will, therefore, be more valid in certain instances.

Finally, the results of such observation benefit the observer. It is important that the teacher develop proper relationships with the pupils. When he observes pupils objectively, bias can be lessened and understandings deepened. Too often teachers judge their pupils in terms of their own feelings and prejudices and therefore find it impossible to help them. It should be said, however, that the teacher may need help in developing the skill of accurate reporting. A serious limitation of observation may lie within the observer himself, for what a person sees or hears depends in part on what he is predisposed to see or hear (Froehlich and Darley, 1952, pp. 84–87).

WHAT THE TEACHER OBSERVES. What should the teacher observe in the behavior of children in a natural situation, such as in the classroom? Does the pupil volunteer or offer to share experiences, or does he withdraw and fail to participate? What kind of questions does he ask? Does the nature of his questioning indicate that he has a genuine interest in learning, or is he more interested in his marks? What does he like to talk about? Does he ever mention his interests, problems, or family? How does the group react to contributions by individual members? The teacher will find that the group will support certain individuals, contradict some, and ignore others.

The teacher should also observe the interactions within a group. Which pupils are aggressive, withdrawn, or hostile? Which lead and which follow? Does group behavior within the freedom of the playground differ from that in the classroom? The pupil who appears listless and uninterested in the classroom may come alive in a ball game. Are some pupils more aggressive when freed from the teacher's control? Do they exhibit leadership characteristics in the rough-and-tumble of sports while they are withdrawn in the classroom?

Finally, a great deal is revealed about a pupil's personal-social development through observation of his creative activity, which enables him to translate his feelings into action. Does he prefer working with abstract symbols or concrete objects, enjoy participating in dramatics and role playing? Is he overly anxious when he appears before others? What emotions does he tend to express in his drawings and paintings?

DANGER OF BIAS. Bias in observation is common. Take, for example, the commonly accepted fallacy that "only" children are spoiled. Teachers often interpret negative behavior in pupils without siblings as being a direct result of having their own way at home. This may or may not be the cause underlying the behavior. Mere knowledge that a pupil is an only child, without further examination of his actual relationship with his parents, is not grounds for assuming that his "onlyness" will result in a handicap.

Bias may also result when an observer does not admit his own feelings and weaknesses to himself. Failing to do so, he may attribute his inadequacies to others, and a pupil's behavior will be interpreted as similar to his own inhibited desires.

This same projective type of weakness in reporting may also be reflected in a "Pollyanna" attitude toward all pupils. While it is commendable to look for strengths in children, their total behavior must be evaluated objectively, and that is not easy. Many people well-versed in factual knowledge of human behavior have never learned to apply this information to themselves or to others. An astute observer is able to analyze his feelings toward others as they relate to his own behavior, and attempts to discover their causes through an objective approach. Why does he dislike certain pupils and champion others? What makes him unhappy with the behavior of some students? Observation alone cannot yield valid answers. Lack of objectivity makes it possible to report behavior truthfully.

Objectivity in reporting may be improved by separating description from judgment. "Johnny is undependable," and "Mary will assume no responsibility" are judgments that do not specify what happened and how, nor do they specify the responsibilities Mary failed to assume. As they stand, there is no way to check their validity; possibly they express only the teacher's dislike for a child. The following illustrates a more useful description of behavior.

> I said, "Eddie, you haven't done the work assigned you this period. Don't you understand it?" Eddie answered by saying, "I don't know." When I checked to see if he understood, he knew the answers to all of my questions relating to the assignment. Eddie seldom completes more than one assignment per week during the allotted time.
> On the playground I overheard Susie say, "Don't choose Eddie, because he won't try hard if he doesn't like the game." Janie said, "But someone has to choose him."

Note that this is a report; it injects no judgment. This is what the teacher said, how Eddie answered, and what was done as a result. In the same manner, the playground incident consists simply of the children's conversation.

SAMPLING. Adequate sampling is also important for valid observation. The teacher who concerns himself only with classroom behavior may have a very biased picture of pupils' total personal-social adjustment. The same boy who is hostile and aggressive in English class may be a cooperative and respected leader in the chemistry club, or have a helpful attitude toward his mathematics classmates.

To improve sampling, one must make observations in varied situations. However, care should also be given to timing. A pupil under observation may have a toothache on the day you have chosen to make mental notes about his actions, or perhaps difficulties have arisen in his home, and what you see or hear may not be at all typical of his behavior. Naturally, the more you observe him in a variety of situations, the more likely you are to synthesize an accurate picture of his problems of adjustment, and the more reliable your observation will become.

The teacher must plan for reliability and economy of effort. It is not practicable for him to use the technique, valuable in certain researches, of planning a schedule of short observations in advance where, by *randomizing* the schedule, numerous pupils are seen in more or less comparable situations. Nevertheless, the teacher can schedule, and, through a conscious effort, somewhat avoid the bias resulting from observation of a nonrepresentative or improperly timed situation.

PROBLEM

2. Elementary school teachers who remain with the same children all day have ample opportunity to obtain a wide variety of behavior samples. In what specific ways might junior and senior high school teachers meet the problem of less opportunity to sample behavior?

PURPOSE IN OBSERVATION. The teacher always seeks information that will help him promote learning; this is a very general objective, however. It is more helpful to look for something specific. Why does one pupil seem to have difficulty in getting along with other boys? Why does another refuse to make reports or enter class discussion? An intelligent search for the answers will be guided by what we already know. It may be necessary to arrange some special occasions in which there is an opportunity to test guesses and hypotheses about the source of difficulty. Some simple structuring can elicit reactions to social stimuli that are encountered in the normal course of events—perhaps assigning certain pupils specific responsibilities, formulating key questions, or organizing games that present some individual and social problems.

ANECDOTAL RECORDS. Observation techniques function most effectively when the information is written. One way of recording such information is in anecdotal records, systematic and significant records of the pupil's behavior, which generally form part of the permanent record passed on with him from grade to grade. In studying a behavior problem, it is important to look for signs of its development, because change can be evaluated only through knowledge of previous happenings.

A sample anecdotal record is shown in Figure 13.1. Notice that the description of the incident is separated from the teacher's comments about it. In both instances, more details can be added if necessary. Incidentally, a copy of this anecdote could be placed in the files of both girls mentioned.

ANECDOTAL RECORD FORM

Date: 1/23/75   Pupil's Name: Sue Collings

Observer: Dorothy Larson

Description of incident:
    Sue had won our first essay contest. When she was offered a prize for her second success, she gave it to Marlene, who was runner-up. Marlene accepted it without any expression of appreciation.

Comment:

    Sue seems to be a very well-adjusted child and quite sensitive to the needs of the other children. It was a particularly noble gesture for her to give Marlene the prize since Marlene is very selfish and uncooperative with her peers.

FIGURE 13.1. Sample Anecdotal Record.

Deviant behavior may appear periodically among some pupils. Possibly certain taxing school events, like issuing report cards, coincides with this behavior. The amount of security that home life affords a child varies as it does in school. Therefore, adequate sampling is necessary for a valid interpretation of behavior. Extended observation also provides an opportunity to detect improvement or lack of it in an individual's behavior.

PROBLEM

3. An important use of the anecdotal record is to serve as a reference, along with other data, when the teacher is making inferences and formulating hypotheses about behavior. What other important uses can you see in this technique?

RATING SCALES. Rating scales are also useful in the making and recording of observations. These instruments are popular in many schools because they emphasize important aspects of adjustment and provide data that can be treated statistically. They also make it possible for several judges to rate the same pupil, a procedure that usually increases the reliability of the rating.

Most of the rating instruments used in the elementary and secondary schools are graphic scales, constructed so that the rater can mark any point along a continuum. For example:

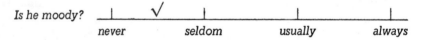

Is he moody?

never   seldom   usually   always

The foregoing scale can be improved by substituting brief behavioral statements for the more general terms like "seldom" or "usually." For example:

Is he even-tempered or moody?

Generally very even-tempered	Is happy or depressed as conditions warrant	Stolid, rare changes of mood	Strong and frequent changes of mood	Has periods of extreme elation and depression

If some of these items, such as "even-tempered," were defined more specifically, they would provide a more common basis on which to evaluate the pupil. Specific examples of behavior will do much to offset disparity of judgment that arises because different raters employ different criteria in judging pupils according to general descriptive terms.

There are several types of error affecting the reliability and validity of ratings, namely: (1) rating all pupils either too high or too low ("personal bias" or "personal equation"); (2) rating everyone near the central point of the scale (error of central tendency); (3) inaccurate rating because of ambiguity in the scale or misunderstanding on the part of the raters; and (4) allowing one's general impression of the pupil to affect the rating ("halo effect"). The fourth type of error results if the rater is favorably impressed by a pupil and so tends to give him a higher evaluation than he deserves on many items. Lower ratings may result for a pupil of whom the rater is not particularly fond (Wrightstone, 1960, p. 931).

The reliability of ratings can be improved by increasing the number of judges. This poses a practical problem in the elementary school where a child generally has only one teacher. In secondary school, the large pupil-teacher ratio prevents teachers from knowing all their pupils well, but because each pupil has contact with a number of teachers, there is a better opportunity to get reactions from several observers. It should be emphasized that rating pupils without sufficient evidence to make a highly reliable and valid opinion is a waste of time.

One might well be skeptical of the relative validity of ratings because of the many human errors attributable to the rater. However, some recent studies of the validity of rating scales definitely support their use. For instance, rating of aptitude for military service proved to be more highly related to ratings of performance in the field than any other information (*Technical Research Report*, 1953).

An interesting variation of the common rating scale is that involving the forced-choice technique. This, in its simplest form, requires the rater to choose between two descriptive statements, deciding which is more characteristic of the person rated. In one instance, both paired choices may represent desirable behavior; in another instance, undesirable behavior. In either case, the members of the pair appear to be equally acceptable in terms of desirability, but actually they represent different kinds of behavior. Instruments have been developed using groups of three, four, and even five statements.

Below is a pair of statements concerning one aspect of a pupil's social relationships:

A. Shares his interests with the group.
B. Listens attentively while others relate their experiences.

Since the rater must choose between what appears to him to be equally complimentary statements, the "halo effect" is counteracted, and the judge is prevented from giving only cursory attention to the items. Actually, as determined by validity studies, the choices do not represent equal degrees of personal-social development. Choice A might reflect more maturity than choice B.

Although there is still much research to be done and many problems to be resolved, the forced-choice technique may prove to be helpful in developing more adequate instruments for evaluating personal-social adjustment in our schools. This technique is also being used successfully in self-report inventories, such as the *Gordon Personal Profile*. In completing the items, the pupil himself determines which statements best describe his behavior.

PROBLEM

4. The United States Armed Forces have made use of the "man-to-man" type of rating scale in evaluating officers. The individual doing the rating is first asked to think of the best, the poorest, the average, etc., officer in his experience. Each

man to be rated is then compared with these models. Could this procedure be successfully adapted to the classroom situation?

CHECK LISTS. Check lists make it possible to record aspects of behavior rapidly. They are simply lists of personality descriptions or traits that the recorder notes as present or absent in individual pupils. Some schools construct their own, and a particularly valuable device is developed when the whole staff cooperates under a leader who is well-informed about child growth and development. The experience of constructing a check list may then prove to be effective in in-service training.

Standardized check lists have been published, for example, the *Vineland Social Maturity Scale*. The items are arranged in the order of their increasing average difficulty and represent progressive maturation in self-help, self-direction, locomotion, occupation, communication, and social relations. Below are some excerpts from the scale, ranging from those designed for very young children to those for an adult:

"Crows"; laughs
Follows simple instructions
Relates experiences
Goes to school unattended
Makes telephone calls
Performs responsible routine chores
Buys own clothing
Looks after own bath
Assumes responsibilities beyond own needs
Shares community responsibility

This scale has many possible uses. It can serve as: (1) a standard schedule of normal development to be used repeatedly for the measurement of growth or change; (2) a measure of individual differences and, consequently, of extreme deviation that may be significant in such problems as mental deficiency, juvenile delinquency, and child placement or adoption; (3) a qualitative index of development variation in abnormal subjects such as the maladjusted, the unstable, the psychopathic, the epileptic; (4) a measure of improvement following special treatment, therapy, and training; and (5) a schedule for reviewing developmental histories in the clinical study of retardation, deterioration, and rates of growth and decline.

INTERVIEWING. An interview with a pupil often *supplements* and *verifies* other information about his adjustment. Since the teacher is able to observe a child in only a limited variety of situations, a face-to-face encounter with no peers present provides an opportunity to observe his reactions closely and with greater attention than is possible in the classroom. Since the interview is less objective and reliable than paper-and-pencil inventories, it should not supplant them. Furthermore, its lack of economy precludes its use with all pupils. At times it is most helpful with those pupils having special problems.

Several schools of thought exist concerning the interview approach. Part of the disagreement concerns the degree to which the pupil is allowed to dominate the interview, in other words, the degree of permissiveness the teacher exercises. Despite differences of opinion on this point, a number of suggestions will serve as guides for effective interviewing.

1. *Be certain that you have a desirable purpose for the interview. With a purpose in mind, you can prepare for the interview by checking relative available data and formulating what you hope to accomplish.*

2. *Rapport must be established. Certainly a teacher cannot expect to get helpful information if he calls in a pupil after a misdemeanor and uses this as the basis for a conference. Good relationships between the pupil and the teacher can hardly be expected if the discussion revolves around an interpersonal difficulty. What the teacher says in establishing rapport is not nearly so important as how he says it and whether he is encouraging good feeling between the pupil and himself. Try to help the pupil to see that you are sincerely interested in him and his problems.*

3. *Guide the discussion so the pupil has an opportunity to express his feelings. If you ask questions that can be answered with a "yes" or "no," he may respond with the expected answer.*

4. *Avoid communicating a note of finality at the end of the interview. Suggest that there will be opportunities for other conferences if they seem desirable. The pupil should feel that the interview has been helpful and satisfying to him. If it appears that he does not, set a time for another interview.*

5. *After the pupil has left, make a short written summary of the salient points of the interview to place in his cumulative record. Do not trust your memory.*

Interviews with parents can also yield useful information for evaluating a pupil's personal-social adjustment. As in interviewing the pupil, it is important to have a purpose in mind. Know what gaps of information you need to fill; parents can be an excellent source of missing information about behavior problems.

There are advantages in having the parents come to the school for interviewing as well as in visiting them at home. As a home visit gives the teacher a picture of a pupil's home life, a school visit lets the parent see how his child spends the day. Some parents may feel more secure in their homes because many of them recall painful childhood experiences that are, unfortunately, associated with school. Among the disadvantages of visiting the home are the shame some parents may feel about their home's physical appearance and the possibility of other family members interrupting the interview.

In learning to know the father and mother, a teacher may come away with a better understanding of the pupil in the light of parental reactions. One teacher wrote of a home visit:

The time could have been spent to no better advantage. I developed an insight into Ann's problems that I've never had before. It will be much easier for me to be sympathetic with her at school now. I'm certain that I shall conserve considerable emotional energy. Frankly, I wonder how Ann has been able to adjust so well to our classroom environment. Coming from a middle-class home, I'm afraid I didn't realize how some people live.

PROBLEM

5. What symptoms of the pupil might indicate the need for a home visit? What factors should the teacher keep uppermost in his mind when interviewing parents? How might you proceed with the hostile or withdrawn parent?

Projective Techniques

The general idea of projective techniques is to present the pupil with some unstructured and ambiguous situation and then to note his reaction to it. Since the individual has no clues from the examiner, he will tend to react to the situation in terms of his own personality. Whatever he does or says in such a situation will be influenced by his experiences and his state of mind at the moment.

Two very common projective tests used by highly trained specialists in clinical diagnosis are the *Rorschach Inkblot Test* and the *Thematic Apperception Test,* commonly called the *TAT.* The *Children's Apperception Test (CAT)* is similar in type to the *TAT* and is designed for children of ages three–ten. The *Rorschach* is composed of ten inkblots that serve as unstructured and ambiguous stimuli, exciting the individual to a performance giving expression to the pattern of his personality. They are presented to the subject in a given order and he tells what he sees in each. The *TAT* consists of a series of pictures that may be interpreted in many ways. The subject is asked to tell a story about each picture, emphasizing how the scene was initiated, what is happening, how the characters feel, and what will probably result. The test is based upon the well-recognized fact that when a person interprets an ambiguous social situation, he is likely to expose his own personality as much as the phenomenon under scrutiny. Absorbed in his attempt to explain the objective occurrence, he becomes naively unconscious of himself and of the scrutiny of others and, therefore, less vigilantly defensive. To a trained ear, he is disclosing certain inner tendencies and cathexes,* wishes, fears, and traces of past experience (Murray et al., 1938).

Cronbach (1970, p. 651) emphasized the difference between the two kinds of test. He classifies the *Rorschach* as a stylistic-type test and the *TAT* as a thematic type. In other words, the stylistic type indicates the style with which a pupil handles a problem, while the thematic type emphasizes the content of his thoughts and fantasies. He indicates, however, that the specific strengths are not mutually exclusive and that of the two, the thematic test more nearly examines "the whole person" yielding possible information on emotions, attitudes, and cognitive processes.

Numerous other projective procedures are less well-known than the above instruments. Several of these are quite similar to the *TAT.* Some present pictures as does the *TAT* while others require the examinee to draw his own pictures and interpret them. Varied approaches employ the use of finger painting, clay modeling, and doll play in unstructured situations with an opportunity for the pupil to project himself.

Another procedure in projective testing is the use of verbal materials such as word association; a list of stimulus words is read and the subject responds with another

* *Webster's Third International Dictionary defines a cathexis as an "investment of libidinal energy in a person, object, idea, or activity."*

word. When he responds with unusual words or slowly, it is indicative of problem areas.

An additional example of the use of verbal materials is the sentence completion test. Partial sentences are presented such as:

My greatest difficulty is _____.
In working with other people I _____.

The completed sentences may be scored for the content as in the case of the *TAT* or the responses may be coded in terms of healthfulness of adjustment.

Rarely is the classroom teacher trained to use these instruments and procedures. Their administration and interpretation require the knowledge and experience of the trained clinician; he will be familiar with the limitations of validity and reliability of these instruments and the bases for their use and interpretation. Schools fortunate enough to have psychologists on their staffs may find that they will employ projective testing for certain difficult behavioral problems. In skilled hands, these procedures may provide helpful information with a comparatively small outlay of time and effort.

Sociometric and Related Techniques

One of the most valuable sources of information about the personal-social adjustment of pupils is their peers. Instruments that cause pupils to rate their classmates in various ways are known as sociometric techniques. Teachers will find it helpful to use these means to verify their judgment of pupils for a number of reasons. First, the teacher has an opportunity to observe boys and girls only in a limited number of situations. Second, the relationship between teachers and pupils is different from that between pupils and their peers; teachers represent authority and children respond to authority in different ways. Third, a teacher may lack objectivity in his observation.

Teachers may look on sociometric techniques as a lot of unnecessary bother, feeling that very little additional information can be obtained through their use, since, on the whole, good teachers have been quite successful in determining the degree of a pupil's adjustment to the group. There continue to be some very bad misjudgments, however. As an example, a pupil who carefully cultivates the friendship of his teacher may be rated quite differently by that teacher than by his peers.

Teachers who use sociometric techniques are quick to admit that they have at times misjudged the relationship among pupils. Social interaction is so complex a process that many feelings are expressed in such a way that even the keenest observer cannot detect them. Pupils may admire certain traits in each other that completely overshadow behavior the teacher considers undesirable. It is also possible that the observer may, because of his own background, emphasize undesirable characteristics disproportionately.

SOCIOGRAMS. The sociometric test is a device for getting preferences among associates to determine the social structure of a group. One method of administering the test is to ask pupils to list, in order of preference, the three persons in the class with whom they would most like to work on a project. A sociogram is constructed by drawing a map showing, by means of names and lines, the choices of each pupil. This depicts the social structure of the group for a particular moment in a particular situation that prompted the members' choices. To obtain a complete picture of the social interaction in the group, it is necessary to give several tests involving varied situations. Pupils do not always choose the same persons for work on different assignments. The choices expressed by a pupil represent what he would like. They do not necessarily indicate what the situation is. For example, several students may indicate by their choices that they would like to be a part of the group populated by two or three leaders. If one were to observe them in the classroom, however, he would find no interaction between them and the pupils of their choice. This explains why the sociometric test can provide information that may not be available to an observer.

A natural circumstance should be selected to initiate the test, such as reseating a group, forming committees, or a similar activity. The teacher should emphasize that he will keep the pupil's preferences confidential. They must understand they may choose anyone; in some schools, where separation of boys and girls is encouraged, children may think that they must choose only from their own sex. Finally, sufficient time should be given for all pupils to make their choices.

The following is an effective way of wording the sociometric question (adapted from Jennings, 1973):

Our next unit is on the western movement in the United States. You have decided that you would like to take certain projects and work on them in committees. Each of you knows with whom you would like to work. Now I am going to pass out some cards. Print your name in the upper right-hand corner and then number from "1" to "3" on the left-hand side of the card like this. (Illustrate on the blackboard.) Beside the "1" write the complete name of the person with whom you would like most to work in a committee. After "2" indicate your second choice and after "3" your third choice. You may choose either a boy or a girl, but of course the person must be in this class. I will arrange the committee members so that you will be with at least one of those whom you have chosen.

It is also possible to ask the children to list at the bottom of the card the name of anyone with whom they would prefer not to work. This procedure has serious limitations, however, since it is in contradiction to the social philosophy that the teacher should wish to develop in his class. When a group of eleventh graders was asked to list classmates whom they preferred not to have on their committees, a number of parents said that the pupils were disturbed by the request. Even though there were a number of cliques that operated among them, the pupils were unhappy about having to "blackball" someone.

The primary-grades teacher may let the children give their choices orally if they cannot write. One second-grade boy reported that he had chosen Tom because he couldn't write Marjorie, the name of his best friend. A problem also arises when children do not know each other's names. Pupils must be well acquainted before the sociometric test can be used effectively.

Figure 13.2 is an illustration of a sociogram of a fourth-grade class of twenty-five

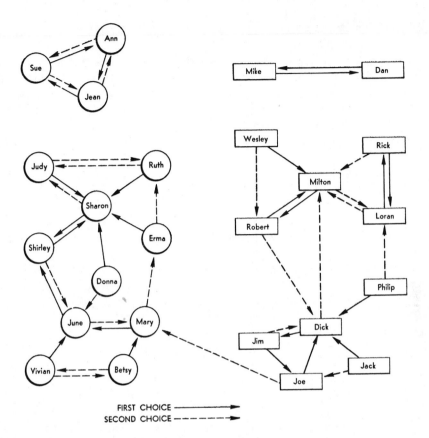

FIRST CHOICE ——————▶
SECOND CHOICE ———————▶

FIGURE 13.2. Sociogram of a Fourth-Grade Class.

pupils. Only first and second choices are shown; the solid lines indicate first choices and the broken lines, second choices. The boys' names are enclosed by boxes, the girls' by circles.

Notice the sex cleavage in this class. Only one pupil, Joe, has chosen another of the opposite sex. Sue, Ann, and Jean form a clique. There are a number of mutual choices. Prominent among these are Mike and Dan, Rick and Loran, Sharon and Shirley, and Milton and Robert. There are also several isolates—pupils whom no one has chosen: Donna, Wesley, Philip, and Jack. Complete directions for constructing a sociogram such as this are given by Jennings (1973).

After the sociogram is constructed, it should be evaluated. The individual pupil should be considered first: Who are his preferences? Who has chosen him? The pupils should then be considered as a group: Who was chosen most often, very seldom, or not at all? Are there any small groups who have chosen each other and seem to stand apart from the class as a whole? Does the group tend toward cleavages, boys choosing boys and girls choosing girls? Do urban children fail to choose rural children and vice versa? The answers to these questions may prove surprising when the teacher compares them with his own reactions.

The sociometric interview, a by-product of the sociometric test, is used to obtain information and explanations from children. For example, John, a high-school junior, said that he chose Bill because he wasn't as cocky as Tom. Actually, the sociogram indicated that Tom was well liked and had shown his effectiveness as a leader many times. John and Tom were rivals for high marks as well as for social position in the school, and this struggle had had its effect on John's feeling toward his rival. Tom, on the other hand, had given John his first choice for committee work. When queried about his reasons for this choice, he said simply, "John has good ideas."

Care must be taken in the interview not to place the pupil on the defensive because of his choices. The teacher should not say, "Why did you choose Bill?" but "How did you decide to choose Bill?" If the teacher finds that his duties do not leave him time to interview the whole class, he may select those few about whom he is most concerned. He might also get from all pupils written statements of the reasons for their choices. Of course, he must assure them of his intent to keep the information confidential. Written statements of this kind are seldom effective unless the teacher has excellent rapport with his class.

Jennings (1973) gives specific suggestions for using the sociogram. However, a teacher will be wise not to use set formulae for dealing with group problems. Rather he should use the information as a basis for formulating hypotheses concerning procedures for helping isolates, coping with cliques, and improving the cohesiveness of a group.

PROBLEM

6. In a junior high school, sociograms of each seventh- and eighth-grade section were constructed by the guidance counselor on the basis of choices made in group guidance sessions during the fall semester. These data were then released to the teachers. Evaluate this procedure.

SOCIAL-DISTANCE SCALES. The sociogram is limited in the degree to which it can show the complete social structure of the group. Since each pupil typically has only three choices, we have no information on why he failed to choose other classmates. As one fourth grader said, "I didn't have enough choices to choose Sally." However, she did not choose Billy because "He is such a tattletale."

The social-distance scale overcomes this particular weakness. It is possible to use this instrument to determine the degree to which the individual accepts or rejects the group as well as the degree to which the group accepts or rejects him. Table 13.3 shows how thirty-two elementary school pupils reacted to two classmates in terms of certain social situations. The number of checks for each item on the scale received by the most accepted child and the least accepted child are listed. Interestingly enough, every pupil is usually accepted by at least one classmate, and even the most popular are not approved by everyone.

The questions used in this technique have certain limitations. For example, if our objective is to promote peer acceptance, we may wonder about the effect of an item like "Wish he were not in our room." Some teachers prefer not to use social-distance scales because items of this kind are in opposition to their goals.

TABLE 13.3. Social Acceptance of Two Pupils.

Item on scale	Checks for pupil 1 (Most accepted)	Checks for pupil 2 (Least accepted)
1. Would like to have him as one of my best friends.	20	2
2. Would like to have him in my group but not as a close friend.	7	15
3. Would like to be with him once in a while but not too often or for a long time.	3	4
4. Do not mind his being in our room but do not want to have anything to do with him.	1	3
5. Wish he were not in our room.	1	8

From Cunningham et al., 1951, p. 172; reproduced by permission of the publisher, Teachers College Press. Copyright 1951 by Teachers College, Columbia University.

"GUESS WHO" QUESTIONNAIRES. Another method of obtaining reports from pupils is to have them match their peers with a list of behavioral characteristics. The teacher makes a list of characteristics ranging from complimentary to unfavorable. The pupils then indicate those classmates who, in their opinion, fit each description. Since pupils often know each other better than the teacher does, it is possible to get a great deal of information about many aspects of their adjustment. The following examples illustrate the kind of item that has proved helpful.

Here is someone who likes to talk a lot, always has something to say ＿＿ .
Here is someone who waits for somebody else to think of something to do and always likes to follow the suggestions which others make ＿＿ .
Here is someone who is very friendly, who has lots of friends, who is nice to everybody ＿＿ .*

Children may list themselves or as many pupils as fit the description. It is also possible that some pupils will feel that certain items apply to no one in the class. When the teacher tabulates the number of times each pupil is mentioned for each description and finds some individuals referred to by a large number of the class, it is significant information. No doubt he should disregard mention by only one or two, although possibly some children are not well-known and are mentioned infrequently for this reason.

Self-Report Inventories

Since no one has an opportunity to observe an individual under as many or as varied situations as he himself, a biographical data blank elicits important factual information. The self-report test attempts to tap the wealth of information that a

* From Cunningham et al., pp. 419, 420, 422; reproduced by permission of the publisher, Teachers College Press. Copyright 1951 by Teachers College, Columbia University.

person has about his feelings, interests, and attitudes. If a number of standardized questions are chosen that can be relied upon to show differences among individuals, one has the basis for the so-called paper-and-pencil "personality," interest, and attitude inventories. It is obvious that the reliability and validity of these instruments depend to a great degree on how adequately the individual can or will report the facts. It is possible that some pupils with severe emotional problems cannot satisfactorily interpret their feelings and behavior to make a valid report.

BIOGRAPHICAL DATA BLANK. Factual information about an individual's past history has been found helpful in predicting a pupil's future success on the job or in higher learning. Hobbies, special activities in and out of school, skills, success with past education, etc., can be used by an evaluator to make a clinical judgment about an individual. In some cases, items have been analyzed to determine the relationship of responses to future behavior of the individual. For example, it may be that in a question such as

How many things have you built out of wood?
   (a) none
   (b) several
   (c) many

the pupil answering *many* probably is more successful in shop class than one answering *none* or *several*. On the other hand the question may have no predictive value for success in general mathematics.

Serious efforts have been made to use biographical data to predict pupil achievement. For instance, data yielded by a biographic blank (Schaefer and Anastasi, 1968) were used to predict creativity in adolescents. A 165-item inventory was grouped into five sections: Physical characteristics, family history, educational history, leisure-time activities, and miscellaneous. *Project Talent* also employed numerous questions of the biographical-data-blank type in the nationwide inventory of human talent. Typical of the questions used are the following:

How many times have you been president of a class, a club, or other organization (other than athletic) in the last 3 years?
   (a) none
   (b) once
   (c) twice
   (d) three times
   (e) four times
   (f) five or more times
How many books are in your home?
   (a) none, or very few (0–10)
   (b) a few books (11–25)
   (c) one bookcase full (26–100)
   (d) two bookcases full (101–250)
   (e) three or four bookcases full (251–500)
   (f) a room full–a library (501 or more)

Instruments of this type probably have predictive value because they reflect interests, personality traits, and certain abilities related to performance.

PERSONALITY INVENTORIES. One of the typical personality inventories designed for school use is the *California Test of Personality.* This instrument was developed in five series so that it can be administered to pupils from kindergarten to adulthood. According to the authors, the primary purpose of the inventory is to reveal the extent to which the pupil is adjusting to the conditions facing him and is developing a normal, happy, and socially effective personality.

Each series is divided into two sections. The first part indicates the pupil's feelings about himself (personal adjustment), and the second reflect social adjustment. Each division is further subdivided into six headings having an equal number of questions: eight in the primary series, twelve in the elementary series, and fifteen in the intermediate, secondary, and adult series. Such questions are asked of primary children as: "Do the children think you can do things well?" "Are you asked to play in other people's yards?" Older pupils are queried as follows: Do you visit with several young men and women in your neighborhood?" A "yes" or "no" response is made to each question. The authors suggest that a profile be made for each pupil so that serious deviations may be determined and dealt with. This is a questionable recommendation.

The foregoing inventory is designed to be a measure of traits or components of adjustment. Another approach to the evaluation of personal-social adjustment is through the determination of problem areas. The *Mooney Problem Check List,* which can be used with junior and senior high school pupils, is a self-report instrument whose purpose is to help individuals express their personal problems. The pupil reads through the check list and underlines the problems that concern him. After completing the first step, he is asked to go back over the items he has underlined and circle the numbers of those of greater concern to him. In the high school form there are 330 items representing common problems of adolescents that were collected from reports of pupils. Some of the items in this form are:

Getting sick too often
Awkward in meeting people
Not being attractive to the opposite sex
Being different
Too little freedom in class
Worrying about grades
Afraid of the future

The items are set up in problem areas to facilitate counseling. For the high school form there are eleven areas: health and physical development; finances; living conditions and employment; social and recreational activities; social-psychological relations; courtship, sex, and marriage; home and family; morals and religion; adjustment to school work; the future: vocational and educational; and curriculum and teaching procedures.

It would appear offhand that the pupil who has checked the most problems would be in serious need of counseling. However, an individual may check an item even though it bothers him very little. Since the number of problems checked depends on the willingness of the pupil to express himself, some individuals may not check their most serious problems. It is also possible that one problem may be more difficult for one pupil than a series of problems for another. It should be noted that what may not seem to be a problem to an adult, or at least one of little importance, may be a very real source of concern to the pupil.

Extensive investigations of the reliability and validity of the adjustment inventories, particularly of the type represented by the *California Test of Personality,* have been made. One reviewer (Ellis, 1953, p. 48) states that:

> . . . *In most instances the inventories are not measuring the independent traits they are supposed to be measuring; they do not agree too well with each other nor with the results of Rorschach and projective tests; they are easily faked; and they usually do not give significant group discriminations when used with vocational, academic, sociometric, and disabled and ill groups. It was especially found that in none of the areas in which they are commonly employed, do personality inventories consistently show significant group discriminations.*

If these instruments are used, the data must be interpreted with extreme care. Subtest scores are quite unreliable. Total scores might be used for screening, that is, selecting some individuals for further study. Answers to specific questions on these inventories occasionally may furnish tiny hints with respect to further diagnosing a child's problems. However, under no circumstances should scores from these inventories be the basis of educational or vocational decisions without further corroborating evidence.

ETHICAL CONSIDERATIONS. Questions have been raised about the ethics of requiring individuals to answer very personal questions included in some personal-social adjustment inventories. These have caused some to inquire as to whether such questions constitute an invasion of privacy. Particular attention has been focused on requiring individuals who are not thought to be emotionally ill to answer questions about private feelings in such areas as religion, family relationships, patriotism, and so forth.

Psychologists defending the use of personal-social adjustment inventories stress their present basic limitations, but emphasize their usefulness when the results yielded by them are considered along with other data. Self-regulation by the psychological profession is helpful, but a basic conflict exists. At the same time the psychologist believes firmly in the dignity and worth of the individual, he is committed to increasing man's understanding of himself and others. Hence, is the use of personal-social adjustment inventories in a given instance an invasion of privacy or a legitimate investigation of man's behavior (Messick, 1965)?

The concern for the problem of privacy in behavioral science research supported by government funds has been so acute that a federal panel was established to study the matter. Because the use of tests has been one of the concerns of this panel, its recommendations are important to us. They are (Clark, 1967):

1. *Those who are doing human research with government funds are to accept responsibility for its ethical propriety.*

2. *Institutions are to determine their own methodology of review relative to ethical considerations.*

3. *When consent of subjects and confidentiality of information cannot be met, there must be an explanation included in fund applications.*

4. *The onus of the burden to protect privacy falls on agencies and scientists and their institutions who receive government research monies; government agencies should not be responsible for reviewing research instruments or designs in this regard.*

5. *Support of education on the ethics of research is a primary responsibility of institutions and professional associations that are recipients of research money.*

Concern has also been expressed about the collection, maintenance, and dissemination of pupil records, particularly data from personal-social adjustment inventories. Guidelines have been prepared that protect the privacy of the pupil and his family without seriously inhibiting the school's efforts to help the child (Goslin, 1970).

PROBLEM

7. Three major issues associated with the invasion of privacy question are (1) respecting the dignity of those tested, (2) the permissibility of deception in the procedures, and (3) the limits on freedom of scientific inquiry (Cronbach, 1970, pp. 509–515). Evaluate each. In view of your evaluations, should schools routinely gather personal-social adjustment data about pupils?

INTEREST INVENTORIES. The experienced teacher knows that interest plays an important part in the personal-social adjustment of children. The boy who likes sciences and has books available to him in this area will be motivated to read, thereby developing his basic reading skill and his sense of adequacy at the same time. The teacher who involves his pupils in a project that interests them will find that facility in social situations will develop much more readily than if they are made to do uninteresting or irrelevant work.

Informal methods (for example, interviews) of obtaining information about pupil interests are commonly used. In addition, standardized interest inventories are comparatively popular. Two of these are Strong's *Vocational Interest Blank* (sometimes called the *VIB* or the *Strong*) and the *Kuder Preference Record–Vocational (Form C)*. Both have been used repeatedly for vocational guidance in the secondary schools.

A number of *Kuder* inventories are available. The *Kuder General Interest Survey (Form E)* is a revision and downward extension of *Form C*. It is designed for grades six–twelve. Two other inventories, the *Kuder Preference Record–Occupational (Form D)* and the *Kuder Occupational Interest Survey (Form DD)*, are similar to the *VIB* in that they compare a pupil's response with those of a number of occupational groups. With *Form DD*, which uses the same items as *Form D*, there are direct item-by-item comparisons between an individual's responses and those in numerous occupational and college-major groups. Unlike *Kuder Form D* and the *VIB, Kuder Form DD* makes it possible to compare each individual's interest pattern with that of a given occupational group. It eliminates the general reference group of men-in-general or women-in-general. This procedure has proved to be a great improvement in scoring.

The *Kuder Preference Record—Personal (Form A)* reflects an individual's personal and social preferences rather than those related to vocations. It is therefore more like an adjustment inventory than the other *Kuder* forms. Its five scales reflect the following personal and social preferences: (1) preference for being in active groups; (2) preference for familiar and stable situations; (3) preference for working with ideas; (4) preference for avoiding conflict; and (5) preference for directing or influencing others. Only the *Strong Vocational Interest Blank* and the *Kuder Preference Record—Vocational (Form C)* are discussed in this chapter.

STRONG VOCATIONAL INTEREST BLANK. In developing the *Strong Vocational Interest Blank (VIB)*, a number of items relating to an individual's everyday living was selected. There are 399 items for men and 398 items for women, each grouped into eight parts. For the first five parts men respond by indicating whether they like, dislike, or are indifferent to a series of occupations, school subjects, amusements, activities (repairing a clock, adjusting a carburetor, etc.), and types of people (progressive, conservative, energetic). In Part VI they order a preference for activities by indicating from a series of groups those three that they like to do best and those they like to do least. They indicate a preference for items in Part VII (airline pilots versus airline ticket agents; outside work versus inside work). In Part VIII the respondent signifies whether an ability or characteristic typifies him (I win friends easily, I discuss my ideals with others). In the women's form, items relevant to feminine interests are similarly grouped.

Both men's and women's forms have four types of scales. The *Basic Interest Scales* focus on specified types of activities, such as sales, agriculture, teaching, and science. The respondent can compare his score with individuals in a relevant occupation. For example, occupations scoring high in the science scale are physicists, chemists, biologists, psychologists, etc.

In the *Occupational Scales* the respondent's score represents the degree of similarity with the scores of those in different occupations. It was found, for example, that engineers tended to express similar likes and dislikes. Persons in other fields showed the same tendency to have common interests within the occupational group and to differ from persons of other occupational groups. Thus, an individual could be questioned about his interests to determine how closely they compared to those of individuals who were successful in their chosen fields. The inventory is scored for more than fifty different occupations.

There are a number of *Non-Occupational Scales* developed by comparing responses of two contrasting groups on the *VIB*, namely *Academic Achievement* (those who do well in school versus those who don't), *Age-Related Interests* (men's profile: scores on scale increase with age), *Masculinity-Femininity* (contrast of scores of men and women working in the same occupation), *Managerial Orientation* (men's profile: good versus poor managers), *Occupational Level* (men's scale: represents socioeconomic level of one's intersts), and *Specialization Level* (men's profile: those who score higher have more education in the field).

The *Administrative Indices* aid in detecting problems in administering and scoring the instrument. For example, the *Total Responses* of the individual should be within two or three of the total number of items. The *Form Check* indicates whether he was using the old or the revised booklet. *Unpopular Items* may indicate that numerous unpopular responses have been selected for one reason or another. The respondent may have eccentric interests; he may be using the wrong booklet; he could have misunderstood the directions; or he may have lost his place on the answer sheet.

A great amount of research has been done with this instrument. Strong (1943) found that interests change very little from age twenty-five to fifty-five, that there is a little change from twenty to twenty-five years of age, but that the shifts are considerable between the ages of fifteen and twenty. He therefore suggests that it would be wise not to use the test with boys under the age of seventeen unless they are unusually mature; in any event, an allowance should be made for their youth. Interest scores may be helpful to high school juniors and seniors if the emphasis is on the general direction of a career rather than in a specific vocation.

The *VIB* is oriented toward those occupations that college students enter. The *Minnesota Vocational Interest Inventory* provides information about "blue-collar" vocational interests.

THE KUDER PREFERENCE RECORD—VOCATIONAL. This instrument illustrates another method of construction. As in Strong's *Vocational Interest Blank* a large number of items were collected describing everyday life. However, instead of emphasizing the interests of those in the various occupations and then attempting to determine if a person's interests were like theirs, Kuder sought to describe the interests of a subject through a logical grouping of items. If a pupil showed an interest in a certain group of items, it could be said that he had an interest in activities related to that group. Altogether there are ten areas of interest and a verification scale to identify those who answer the items carelessly or without understanding.

The *Kuder Preference Record—Vocational* has 168 items organized in groups of three. The pupil decides which of the three he likes most and which he likes least. He is forced to choose even though he likes or dislikes them equally. In the first example shown in Figure 13.3, the examinee has punched a hole in the left-hand circle in front of the letter R. In this way, he has indicated that of the three activities, P, Q, and R, he would most like to visit a museum. By punching the hole in the right-hand circle beside letter Q, he indicates that of the three activities he would like least to browse in a library. Similarly, in the second example, he would like most to collect autographs and would least like to collect butterflies.

A sample *Kuder* profile is shown in Figure 13.4. This profile of Jim Spencer, a high school junior, shows that he has very little interest in the computational and scientific areas. Jim's father is an engineer and holds an important executive position in his firm. Both parents are anxious that their son choose engineering as a vocation. Jim's record throughout elementary school has been satisfactory. His IQ on the *Otis-Lennon Mental Ability Test* administered at the end of the eighth grade was 130. His scores on the *Iowa Tests of Basic Skills* showed no difficulty in the basic subjects.

Directions:

A number of activities are listed in groups of three. Read over the activities in each group. Decide which of the three activities you like *most*. There are two circles on the same line as this activity. Punch a hole with the pin through the left-hand circle following this activity. Then decide which you like *least* and punch a hole through the right-hand circle.

P	Visit an art gallery	O	P	O
Q	Browse in a library	O	Q	◉
R	Visit a museum	◉	R	O
S	Collect autographs	⊘	S	O
T	Collect coins	O	T	O
U	Collect butterflies	O	U	⊘

FIGURE 13.3, Instructional Examples of the Kuder Preference
Record—Vocational, Form CH.
From Kuder, 1951; reproduced by permission of Science Research Associates. © 1948, G. F. Kuder.

However, in high school his final marks in algebra, plane geometry, and general science were below average. He had to repeat biology during the summer session. During his junior year he was in serious difficulty with his mathematics and science courses, though he had completed one of the best projects in social studies. He had also become a behavior problem and was absent from school quite often. Because he refused to cooperate at band practice, he was suspended from that organization.

Although the preceding data do not represent a complete case history, it seems apparent that Jim's interests are more closely related to other vocational fields than to engineering. His superior academic ability will probably be wasted if he is forced to continue his present course of study. Quite possibly a career in a social science would be appropriate for him.

The descriptive nature of the *Kuder* provides a suitable basis for counseling. Through statistical analysis, it has become possible to translate *VIB* scores into descriptions of traits as well. The form for the *Kuder* is also the same for both sexes, while the *VIB* for women is less complete than the men's form. The scoring of the *VIB* is complex and time-consuming, although it can be scored commercially for a nominal fee. On the other hand, the pupil can score his own *Kuder* record in a few minutes and the results are available immediately. It is not surprising, therefore, to find the *Kuder* used in the secondary school much more extensively than the *VIB*.

Faking is an important consideration in the test validity of interest inventories, just as it is in the personal-adjustment inventories. An examinee suitably motivated can successfully fake the *Kuder Preference Record*. Because the intent of the items is not so obvious in the *VIB*, it is less easily faked. When tests are given for employment purposes, apparent motives could promote untruthful answers, but when used with secondary school pupils, it would seem that little is gained from faking.

The stability of the interest patterns of adolescents has been questioned repeatedly. For instance, a considerable shift of high school pupils' low and high interest scores has been found when there is a difference of several years between two

NAME Spencer James R. AGE 16 SEX M GROUP Grade 11 DATE OF TEST 1-9
Print Last First Initial M or F

First Revision, February 1951
REPRODUCTION BY ANY MEANS STRICTLY PROHIBITED

PROFILE SHEET

for the
KUDER PREFERENCE RECORD
VOCATIONAL
Forms CH, CM

MEN and WOMEN

DIRECTIONS FOR PROFILING

1. Copy the V-Score from the back page of your answer pad in the box at the right. [40]

If your V-Score is 37 or less, there is some reason for doubting the value of your answers, and your other scores may not be very accurate. *If your V-Score is 45 or more,* you may not have understood the directions, since 44 is the highest possible score. *If your score is not between 38 and 44,* inclusive, you should see your adviser. He will probably recommend that you read the directions again, and then that you fill out the blank a second time, being careful to follow the directions exactly and to give sincere replies.

If your V-Score is between 38 and 44, inclusive, go ahead with the following directions.

2. Copy the scores 0 through 9 in the spaces at the top of the profile chart. Under "OUTDOOR" find the number which is the same as the score at the top. If your score is not shown, draw a line *between* the scores above and below your own. Use the numbers under M if you are a man and the numbers under F if you are a woman. Draw a line through this number from one side to the other of the entire column under OUTDOOR. Do the same thing for the scores at the top of each of the other columns. If a score is larger than any number in the column, draw a line across the top of the column; if it is smaller, draw a line across the bottom.
3. With your pencil blacken the entire space between the lines you have drawn and the bottom of the chart. The result is your profile for the *Kuder Preference Record—Vocational.*

An interpretation of the scores will be found on the other side.

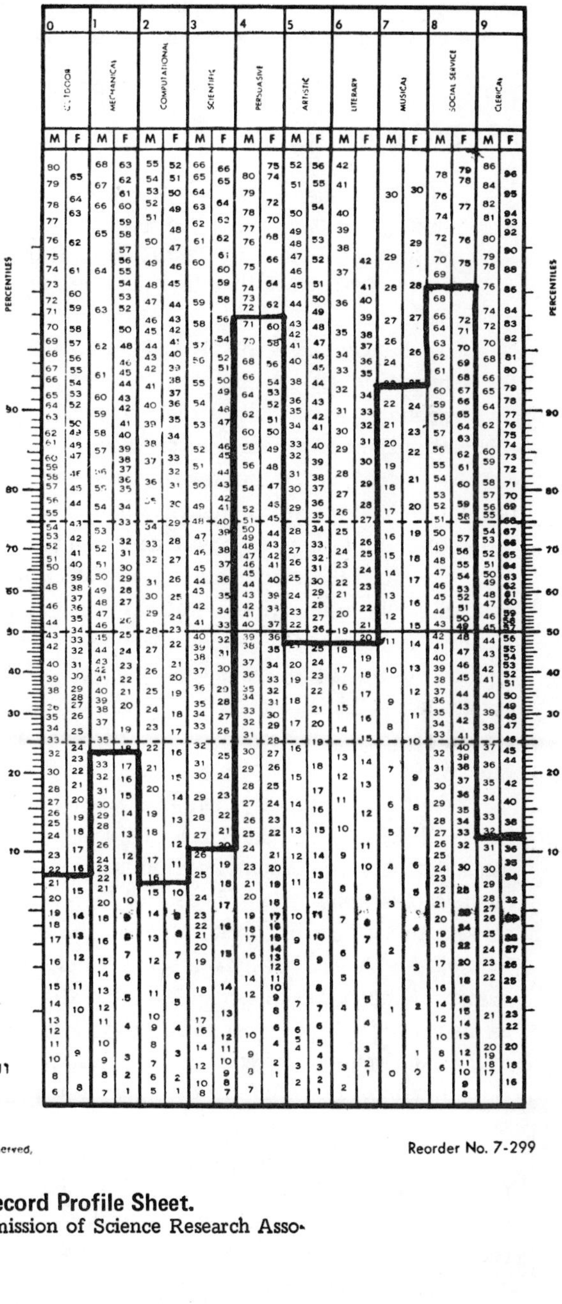

SRA Science Research Associates, Inc.
259 East Erie Street, Chicago, Illinois 60611

A Subsidiary of IBM

Reorder No. 7-299

FIGURE 13.4. Kuder Preference Record Profile Sheet.
From Kuder, 1951; reproduced by permission of Science Research Associates. © 1951, G. F. Kuder.

administrations of the *Kuder Preference Record—Vocational* (Millinson and Crumrine, 1952). Nevertheless, this instrument is of some help to the counselor and teacher, since it focuses attention on general fields of interest rather than on the interests of successful people in various occupations, as in the case with the *Vocational Interest Blank*. However, the teacher or counselor needs to exercise caution against over-interpretation. Effective evaluation must include the use of other data gathered from varied sources as an adjunct to the interest inventory scores.

PROBLEM

8. The *Kuder Preference Record* is often administered during the ninth grade as an aid in the selection of high school courses and for prevocational planning for the pupil. Although counselors know that interests may shift, they find the inventory useful. Why?

ATTITUDE SCALES AND QUESTIONNAIRES. The concept of attitude refers to the way individuals act and think toward and about people, objects, and situations they encounter, as a result of their previous experiences. The school is committed to the development of certain basic social attitudes in its pupils. Among the attitudes that can be learned are those toward race prejudice, bigotry, consideration, religion, democracy, and quality of man. Evaluation of attitude formation and change becomes just as important, then, as achievement in the basic skills.

The formal instruments for attitude measurement fall into two categories: opinion polling and attitude scales. Neither is very useful to the classroom teacher. Their value lies chiefly in their utility as research tools. The Gallup poll is a typical opinion survey. A person is generally approached with a single question that he is usually asked to answer with "Yes," or "No," or "Undecided." The results are typically reported in terms of the percentages of answers given in each of those categories.

Attitude scales are generally of the Thurstone (Thurstone and Chave, 1929) or Likert (1932) types. The Thurstone scales are designed so that an attitude can be measured on a continuum from unfavorable to highly favorable. A number of state-ments representing various degrees of favorableness give the subject an opportunity to express his feelings. For example, in measuring attitude toward the law, the excerpt in Figure 13.5 shows that a favorable attitude is given a higher value. Those with low numerical values suggest an unfavorable attitude. The subject identifies those state-ments with which he agrees and those with which he disagrees. His score is the average of the scale values of the statements toward which he is favorable.

A subject's position on the scale of attitude toward the law is then determined by finding the average of all the scale values of statements with which he agrees. Suppose that out of the twenty items on this scale he checked statements having the following values: 10.1, 10.5, 9.1, and 6.1. He would then have the average of $35.8/4 = 8.95$ or 9. The items on Thurstone scales are generally on a continuum from one to eleven. Therefore, this individual appears to have a favorable attitude toward law.

In the Likert method, statements are never neutral toward the object in question but are favorable or unfavorable in varying degrees. The subject reacts to each

Directions:
Put a check mark (√) if you agree with the statement.
Put a cross (X) if you disagree with the statement.

			Value
( )	6.	I believe in the use of force to overthrow the law.	0.2
( )	15.	The law is made in response to the pressure of lobbies in Washington.	2.9
( )	16.	Some laws command our respect while others are mere regulations.	6.1
( )	9.	The law is more than enactments of Congress; it is a sacred institution.	10.5

FIGURE 13.5. Excerpt from Thurstone's Scale for Measuring Attitude Toward the Law.
From Thurstone and Katz, 1931; reproduced by permission of the University of Chicago Press.

statement on a five-point scale, indicating that he either strongly agrees, agrees, is uncertain, disagrees, or strongly disagrees. His score is computed simply by weighting the responses from five to one for a favorable statement beginning with strong agreement. Values are assigned in reverse order for unfavorable statements.

The Likert method is illustrated by the following two items taken from a scale designed to measure a pupil's attitude toward science education.

Encircle one of the symbols preceding each of the following statements: A stands for "Agree," SA for "Strongly Agree," D for "Disagree," SD for "Strongly Disagree," and "?" for "Uncertain."

SA Ⓐ ? D SD   *Science books are very interesting to study.*
SA Ⓐ ? D SD   *Laboratory work in science classes is drudgery.*

Note that both items have the A circled, which means that the subject agreed with both statements. However, since the first item is favorable to science education, the "Agree" has a value of four. The second item is essentially unfavorable, and so the reverse order of scoring gives it a value of two. The total score on the scale is the sum of the values of all items. The maximum possible score is five times the total number of items.

Determining the relative validity of attitude scales has been a difficult problem, chiefly because of a lack of adequate criteria by which to judge test scores. The question arises as to whether verbalized opinions actually represent attitudes. Although behavior can be checked, of course, individuals behave in different ways for different reasons. A pupil may say that he likes school and show outward signs of full cooperation. He may nonetheless dislike teachers and his classwork intensely, but find it expedient to foster good will so that he can stay on the basketball team. As is true of other self-report techniques, attitude evaluation is likely to be most valid when the pupil has no reason for falsification.

Unfortunately, standardized instruments for attitude measurements have not developed to the point where they can be practically useful to the classroom teacher, who must in large part depend on other evidences of attitude formation and change.

Through observation and sociometric data, he will be able to evaluate these changes if he directs his attention toward them and systematizes his approach.

To obtain objective data, a teacher must look for attitudes in pupil behavior. Pupils may say that honesty is the best policy, but do they cheat, lie, or steal? Do they accept other pupils despite their social status? Are they responsive to the needs of others? Do they have a scientific attitude? Do they get all the facts? Do they draw logical conclusions? The teacher who has stated his educational objectives in terms of changes in pupil behavior will be able to infer attitude development and change from the modified actions of his pupils. If he then records this development in anecdotal records, if he files some of the answers to open questions, and if he summarizes these data for the group, he will make progress toward effective evaluation of attitudes.

PROBLEM

9. There is common agreement that the degree of validity of attitude scales is generally low at best. Nevertheless, describe possible uses of these instruments in a classroom or in a group guidance session.

SUMMARY

The main thoughts included in this chapter can be condensed as follows:

1. *Fostering achievement in the affective domain is as important a responsibility for our schools as is teaching the basic skills.*

2. *Teachers must be able to differentiate between adequate adjustment and atypical behavior if they are to provide effective learning situations leading to maturity. They must determine causes and facilitate solutions.*

3. *Anecdotal records are helpful in providing a means for recording observational data in evaluating the personal-social adjustment of children. To prevent bias, it is well to separate reports of behavior from interpretations of it.*

4. *Rating scales and check lists direct and objectify observation, and can provide quantitative data as a basis for pooling the evaluations of several observers.*

5. *Teacher-parent and teacher-pupil interviews are useful means of gathering data about pupils' personal-social growth, provided a high degree of rapport is established.*

6. *Standardized projective instruments to evaluate affective characteristics of children are designed chiefly for specialists such as clinical psychologists. The teacher's role relative to these instruments is to be informed of their utility and to be alert to refer pupils when a need arises.*

7. *Still another source of information comes from children themselves. The use of such devices as the sociogram, social-distance scale, and "guess who" questionnaire can indicate how well a pupil is accepted by his peers and can reveal specific strengths and weaknesses of his personality. Follow-up interviews for interpretation are recommended.*

8. *Further information from children can be garnered by the use of self-report tests such as personal inventories, interest inventories, attitude scales, and*

biographical data blanks. Care should be exercised in the interpretation of data—faking can occur.

9. There is genuine concern expressed nationwide about the ethics involved in privacy. Some school systems have adopted carefully formulated procedures to avoid abuses.

10. Because personal-social adjustment is such a complex process, it demands extensive and varied approaches to evaluation. There is a fine line between the dictum that a teacher should collect as much information about a pupil from as many sources as possible, and the problem of ethics in doing so.

SUGGESTED READINGS

AMRINE, M. (ed.). Testing and public policy. *American Psychologist*, 1965, *20*, 857–993; 1966, *21*, 401–478.
> These two issues of the *American Psychologist* contain testimony presented to committees of the Congress that were investigating the criticism of the use of psychological tests, particularly paper-and-pencil personality inventories. Invited comments from government officials and other individuals are also included.

CARTWRIGHT, C. A., and G. P. CARTWRIGHT. *Developing observation skills.* New York: McGraw-Hill, 1974.
> The authors emphasize the need for observation and then delineate the principles, procedures, and problems that can be applied to all observational situations. Finally, they deal with specific types of records used for observation: behavior tallying and charting, check lists, rating scales and participation charts, and anecdotal records.

CRITES, J. O. Interests. In R. L. Ebel (ed.), *Encyclopedia of Educational Research.* (4th ed.) New York: Macmillan, 1969. Pp. 678–686.
> The topics of dimensions of interests, development of interests, and correlates of interests should provide meaningful additional information.

CRONBACH, L. J. *Essentials of psychological testing.* (3rd ed.) New York: Harper & Row, 1970. Chapters 14, 15, 16, and 17.
> Extended discussions will be found on interest inventories, personality measurement, and systematic observation. The author compares, contrasts, and criticizes various procedures and instruments.

SHAW, M. E., and J. M. WRIGHT. *Scales for the measurement of attitudes.* New York: McGraw-Hill, 1967.
> The authors list the items in 176 attitude scales covering forty years of scientific work. In addition to describing the subjects, and commenting on technical data, they delineate the strengths and weaknesses of each scale.

TYLER, R. W. Assessing educational achievement in the affective domain. *NCME Measurement in Education,* 1973, *4*, 1–8.
> Affective behavior is described, and attention is given to selecting objectives and appropriate evaluation techniques in this important domain.

WEITZ, H. Some practical problems in interest measurement. *Measurement and Evaluation in Guidance,* 1968, *1*, 56–62.
> Examples and practical solutions are given various problems calling for the use of particular interest inventories.

REFERENCES CITED

CLARK, K. E. Privacy and behavioral research: Preliminary summary of the report of the panel on privacy and behavioral research. *Science,* 1967, *155*, 535–538.

CRONBACH, L. J. *Essentials of psychological testing.* (3rd ed.) New York: Harper & Row, 1970.

CUNNINGHAM, R., et al. *Understanding group behavior of boys and girls.* New York: Bureau of Publications, Teachers College, Columbia University, 1951.

ELLIS, A. Recent research with personality inventories. *Journal of Consulting Psychology*, 1953, *17*, 45–49.

FROEHLICH, C. P., and J. G. DARLEY. *Studying students.* Chicago: Science Research Associates, 1952.

GOSLIN, D. A. *Guidelines for the collection, maintenance, and dissemination of pupil records.* New York: Russell Sage Foundation, 1970.

JENNINGS, H. H. *Sociometry in group relations.* Westport, Conn.: Greenwood Press, 1973. (Reprint.)

KUDER, G. F. *Kuder Preference Record-Vocational, Form C.* Chicago: Science Research Associates, 1951.

LIKERT, R. A technique for the measurement of attitudes. *Archives of Psychology*, 1932, No. 140.

MESSICK, S. Personality measurement and the ethics of assessment. *American Psychologist*, 1965, *20*, 136–142.

MILLINSON, G. G., and W. M. CRUMRINE. An investigation of the stability of interests of high school students. *Journal of Educational Research*, 1952, *45*, 369–383.

MURRAY, H. A., et al. *Explorations in personality.* New York: Oxford University Press, 1938.

SCHAEFER, C. E., and A. A. ANASTASI. Biographical inventory for identifying creativity in adolescent boys. *Journal of Applied Psychology*, 1968, *52*, 42–48.

SHAFFER, L. F., and E. J. SHOBEN, JR. *The psychology of adjustment.* (2nd ed.) Boston: Houghton Mifflin, 1956.

SPARKS, J. N. Teachers' attitudes toward the behavior problems of children. *Journal of Educational Psychology*, 1952, *43*, 283–291.

STRONG, E. K., JR. *Vocational interests of men and women.* Palo Alto: Stanford University Press, 1943.

TECHNICAL RESEARCH REPORT, PRB 1077. Personnel research for the United States Military Academy. Washington: The Adjutant General's Office, 1953.

THURSTONE, L. L., and E. J. CHAVE. *The measurement of attitude.* Chicago: University of Chicago Press, 1929.

THURSTONE, L. L., and D. KATZ. *The measurement of social attitude toward the law.* Chicago: University of Chicago Press, 1931.

TOLOR, A., W. L. SCARPETTI, and P. A. LANE. Teachers' attitudes toward children's behavior revisited. *Journal of Educational Psychology*, 1967, *58*, 175–180.

WRIGHTSTONE, J. W. Observational techniques. In C. W. Harris (ed.), *Encyclopedia of educational research.* (3rd ed.) New York: Macmillan, 1960, 927–933.

PART FIVE

Using Evaluation
to Improve Learning

Part Five attempts to help the reader apply his under-
standings of measurement and evaluation in the classroom. Chapter 14, "Diagnosis and
Remediation of Problems," is devoted to outlining procedures and suggesting materials
and tests to aid in diagnosing and prescribing remediation in severe learning difficulties. Practical examples are included to provide the teacher with information for the
selection of tests and interpretation of test data. Specific difficulties in such subjects as
reading, arithmetic, and writing are treated. The philosophy of diagnostic teaching as
effective teaching directs the discussion throughout.

Chapter 15, "Determining and Reporting Growth," focuses attention on the
pupil's development and how we can best use the results of measurement to aid the
school and the home in helping him achieve his potential. In this context, the purposes
of final marks for informing pupils, parents, and school personnel are discussed. It is
suggested that specific evidence of pupil progress should be based on the school's
educational objectives, among these being data on test performance, procedure and
product evaluation, class participation, and projects and reports. Various methods of
marking and reporting these data are given, such as the letter-number systems, check
lists, written correspondence, and teacher-parent conferences. Finally, suggestions for
improving marking and reporting are outlined. The chapter concludes with a discussion
of promotion as it relates to final marks.

The last chapter is Chapter 16, "A Schoolwide Program of Evaluation." It
stresses the importance of organizing a program of evaluation rather than one of
testing alone. It also emphasizes that we must be concerned with the inputs and
operations of the educational program rather than the outputs alone. The program
should be developed democratically rather than imposed on the teachers by administrative officers.

14

DIAGNOSIS AND REMEDIATION OF PROBLEMS

There is more to gardening than having a "green thumb." When the expert gardener's plants do not grow well, he knows there is a reason, and he tries to determine the source of the trouble. Is an insect, a fungus, or an improper soil condition causing the damage? He searches for evidence that will help solve his problem. When he has identified the parasite or disease, he determines the treatment, which may consist of spraying fungicides or insecticides on the affected plants. The gardener knows, however, that all insecticides are not lethal to all insects, that a certain fungicide will not destroy all fungi, and that plants differ in their tolerance of various kinds of chemicals.

The gardener's approach is like that of the teacher who realizes that all members of the group of pupils he is teaching do not have the same abilities. Some of them are not growing well scholastically, and the causes must be found and remedies applied. He knows that the textbook for the class will be too difficult for some pupils, too easy for others. Some children are not able to do long-division exercises because they lack skill in multiplication, addition, and subtraction. Others are proficient in long division and can be challenged only by more advanced work in mathematics. The teacher tries to avoid the mistake of frustrating the slower pupils or boring the more able. With a range of ability and achievement from three to nine grade levels in most classes, he knows that good teaching must begin with information about the ability and achievement of each pupil.

MEANING OF DIAGNOSIS AND REMEDIATION

If a school is to reach its educational objectives, each teacher must recognize and understand the complex aspects of behavioral changes. Since a pupil's development tends to be sequential, schools must provide the most effective sequence of experiences, that is, those that will bring about behavior consonant with the abilities of the individual. Because growth patterns differ among individuals, causing various degrees of maturity at the same age, and because a developmental sequence in behavior is necessary, the teacher must determine where the individual pupil stands in this sequence, and what marks the limits of his potential.

342

The teacher sees each individual within the group as having different problems. In practice, of course, pupils in a class have many common difficulties and can be grouped for instruction. For example, in a class where a few advanced pupils know how to multiply common fractions, those who do not can be taught as a group. And certainly, as a gardener waters the whole garden, there are many opportunities to bring the entire class together for instruction, like listening to a poem or story, watching a demonstration, or discussing initiation of a project.

In helping the individual, the teacher must determine the stage of his development and his peculiar learning difficulties. This is educational diagnosis. Some years ago, educational diagnosis was confined for the most part to academic knowledge and skills, but its scope has kept pace with the modern concept of education, which emphasizes all aspects of development. Thus the development of the nonintellectual aspects of the pupil's personality is as much the legitimate concern of his teacher as his academic knowledge and skills. Indeed, research has shown that personal-social adjustment and personality development cannot be divorced from learning knowledge and skills.

Remediation, which is nothing more than good teaching, is possible only when the teacher understands the basis of a pupil's difficulty, and seeing his needs, teaches to meet them. Good teaching implies several things: first, that we meet the child at his own level of achievement and start from there; second, that we know something of the experiences and problems he has met in reaching that level; third, that we are aware of how present learning relates to the future sequences. The child who has suffered agonies of frustration and humiliation in arithmetic classes will present a more complex problem of remediation than his friend who simply does not understand long division.

DIAGNOSIS

Educational diagnosis centers on three questions. Which pupils have learning difficulties? What are the strengths and weaknesses in their achievement? What factors have caused their unsatisfactory achievement?

Identifying Pupils Having Difficulty

There are a number of ways to locate pupils with learning difficulties. One of the most effective is the survey approach. Survey achievement tests of the kind included in a school testing program are specifically designed to find pupils who need remediation. When a serious lack of achievement shows up, the teacher will need information about the pupil's scholastic aptitude to make the achievement score more meaningful. Perhaps the child is achieving as well as can be expected in terms of his potential; a pupil is not retarded simply because his score is lower than the class average. Perhaps some pupils, particularly at the secondary level, need to change their educational and vocational goals. Others may have average or above average achievement but are still below their potential. It is these brighter pupils who generally benefit most from remediation because there is a wider disparity between their achievement and their ability.

A teacher will often discover from test data that his entire class has a specific weakness. One fifth-grade teacher found that all of his pupils were below the grade norm in rate of reading, although they were above average in scholastic ability. Another uncovered a weakness in study skills; a third, difficulties with fractions; a fourth, spelling.

Many sources of information are helpful in locating the pupil who needs help. One may contact a child's former teacher, because past achievement must be evaluated. Attendance records and data on personal-social adjustment may provide clues. Information in a pupil's cumulative record, such as an anecdotal record, perhaps, may prove helpful. For example, some of the highest academic achievers are in serious need of guidance in their social relations. Case histories show that some pupils, having no friends, strive for high scholastic achievement as a means of compensating for lack of personal-social development.

PROBLEMS

1. Define retardation with regard to academic achievement. Illustrate with specific examples.

2. A high school biology teacher who meets with 150 pupils per day, along with being responsible for a tenth-grade homeroom, maintains that, under these circumstances, individual pupil diagnosis is an impossible task. What arguments would you use to refute the position he is taking?

Determining Strengths and Weaknesses

The pupil's improvement is the goal of all diagnosis and remediation, and to achieve it, a good teacher helps the pupil correct his weaknesses by building on his strengths. For example, if he has a reading disability, it is just as important to know that he is good in his word attack skills as it is to know that he is poor in his use of context clues. One of the basic principles in effective remediation is that the pupil must experience success, and building on his strengths makes this possible.

COMPETENCIES IN DIAGNOSIS. Determining a pupil's strengths and weaknesses requires essential diagnostic skills that a teacher must develop even though he is not a trained clinician. He should first understand the principles of learning and their application. Second, he should be able to recognize behavioral symptoms that suggest the causes of specific difficulties. Third, he should be able to apply diagnostic and remedial techniques.

Before a teacher can be a successful diagnostician, he must be familiar with the psychology of learning in general, and with regard to specific subject areas. He can formulate useful hypotheses about the nature of a child's difficulties far more readily if he has a grasp of the way learning normally develops in a subject area and is aware of the difficulties most frequently encountered in it.

Take, for example, the problem of transfer of learning. If we learn how to shift gears in a Chevrolet, most of us can then shift gears in a Ford. Learning from the original task has transferred to the new. But if we are then asked to drive a Volkswagen with a four-forward-speed shift, our previous learning tends to interfere with the new task, and this psychological process is known as the negative transfer effect.

Research in transfer of learning indicates that though considerable transfer occurs from some learning tasks to others, there are cases in which there is little transfer unless we teach for it. In one such instance, a teacher discussed word endings and rhyming with his class. He followed the prescribed procedures carefully; *Jane* rhymes with *rain, cane, train.* A little girl went home and announced, "We learned about rhyming today. Try me. You say *Jane.*" When the parent dutifully obeyed, the child responded with a triumphant "rain, cane, train." Asked whether other words rhymed with *Jane,* the child said no, only the three she had just given them. Clearly her concept of rhyming was the relationship among four specific words and no useful learning transfer was gained.

We can further illustrate the importance of understanding in learning as it applies to concept formation. A teacher cannot *give* a pupil a concept; concepts can only be formed by the individual out of his own experiences. Research shows, for instance, that difficulties in all arithmetic processes can be traced to a failure to understand basic number concepts. Too often understanding is evaluated on the basis of the products of learning without considering learning processes. When a pupil's answers are correct, does he understand the problem? He may not. It is possible that he got the correct answer by coincidence or, having dutifully learned a method, followed it blindly down a corridor of computation to the proper reply. Can you explain why you invert and then multiply when you divide by a fraction? If you cannot, you were probably taught how to perform the operation without understanding the process. Understanding number concepts comes through many experiences in which the pupil is required to think through the reasons for performing an operation. Therefore, diagnosis in mathematics should begin with a study of the pupil's concept of a number as it relates to his particular difficulty.

A second competency in diagnosis is the ability to recognize symptoms related to the physical and psychological aspects of growth. Sometimes the underlying causes of a pupil's difficulty are so complex that the teacher will need to rely on the services of a specialist for diagnosis, but he should be familiar with symptoms of poor vision, inadequate hearing, and lack of energy. Further, the informed teacher understands the common mental mechanisms used by poorly adjusted children to reduce their tension. Pupils with severe anxieties are not ready for learning. Remediation is, after all, exceedingly demanding of the pupil, requiring both concentration and a high degree of motivation.

The psychological bases of a problem may be hard to reach. One pupil of above average intelligence was having great difficulty with arithmetic. His achievement in subjects demanding verbal facility was high, relationships with his peers appeared satisfactory, and his rapport with his teacher was excellent. The teacher tried every approach he could think of to help the pupil but made little progress. Finally, in a case history, he discovered the child's mother had always done poorly in arithmetic and persisted in talking about it. The youngster had identified with his mother, building up a self-concept of his inability that completely negated his efforts.

The third competence is the ability to use the various diagnostic and remedial techniques, devices, and materials with understanding. Among these devices are standardized and classroom tests and practice exercises. Detailed discussions of specific difficulties, particularly in arithmetic and reading, can be found elsewhere, and suggested remedial procedures are outlined in detail. The teacher can do much diagnosis and remediation without a clinical specialist. Available printed materials help him in the classroom, and this experience expands his knowledge.

Factors Causing Unsatisfactory Achievement

The teacher who knows the more common causes of unsatisfactory achievement has some basis for making intelligent hypotheses about the difficulties of his pupils. Lack of achievement may be attributed to personal and/or environmental factors reflected in scholastic aptitude and physical development and health, with special emphasis on visual and auditory abilities, and personal-social adjustment.

SCHOLASTIC APTITUDE. If a child has low scholastic aptitude, lack of achievement cannot necessarily be interpreted as the result of faulty teaching or lack of application. He may be doing as well as he can. Many pupils who are poor in reading and mathematics have low scholastic aptitude scores, but a low score does not necessarily mean that a pupil has low innate mental ability. His score on most group tests of scholastic aptitude can be seriously affected by poor reading ability, lack of motivation, or distractions from poor test administration. Therefore, a principal diagnostic problem is to get as accurate an estimate of the pupil's ability as possible. The teacher should not conclude that a pupil has a low scholastic aptitude unless he has considered various data. If at all possible, an individual intelligence test should be administered to those pupils who have low achievement and low group scholastic aptitude scores. It is often surprising to learn that some of these pupils have higher mental ability than some of the high achievers. Too often teachers equate ability to pass tests, conformity, good grooming, and verbosity with high intelligence. Many shy, withdrawn, poorly groomed or nonconformist pupils excel intellectually.

HEALTH. A pupil's health influences his ability to achieve, because learning is hard work. Many things cause inadequate stamina: malnutrition, glandular difficulty, or improper rest. In one fourth-grade class a teacher discovered that forty percent of the pupils were consistently watching television until after ten o'clock on school nights. It is understandable that this group was difficult to teach. Poor health may also cause excessive absences, which are especially detrimental to achievement in such subjects as arithmetic and reading, with their requirement of cumulative sequences of skills.

There is no unequivocal evidence that visual anomalies are a primary cause of educational disability. While some pupils with good vision are poor readers, others who fail to pass vision tests read well, but the latter perform with considerable discomfort. Many cannot attend to print and can only read for short periods of time. If a pupil is nearsighted, and if his teacher uses a visual approach, the pupil may miss basic instruction.

Poor hearing is a distinct disadvantage. Pupils may successfully camouflage hearing anomalies with apparent attention and go unnoticed by the teacher. Even pupils who pass common hearing tests may have serious auditory deficiencies. If there is a high tonal frequency loss, it is difficult to differentiate among consonant sounds so that an oral approach to beginning reading distinctly handicaps such a pupil.

An alert teacher can often detect symptoms of poor hearing. Pupils so handicapped may speak without expression and with the voice pitched unnaturally. Because they cannot differentiate among sounds, they are often poor spellers, and their speech and pronunciation lack clarity and precision. When they cannot understand what is being said, their attention often wanes; they may stare out the window or disturb other students. Others may frequently request that statements or questions be repeated. Whether speech defects result from loss of hearing or some other cause, they seriously impair a pupil's achievement.

There are also organic symptoms of poor hearing, such as earache, sinus condition, and ear discharge. Because such disorder can be corrected, teachers can prevent permanent disabilities by referring these pupils for medical attention.

Motor coordination is another physical factor to which the elementary teacher in particular should be attentive, since it can have a detrimental effect on handwriting. Because handwriting is important in developing other skills, a disability may have far-reaching effects. If a student writes slowly, he may understand test items but find it impossible to complete them within the time limit. His score implies low achievement but the real deficiency lies in the handwriting.

PERSONAL-SOCIAL ADJUSTMENT. The emotionally disturbed pupil dissipates his energy before he can apply it. It is difficult to determine whether emotional difficulties are causing learning difficulties or vice versa. Learning difficulties can at times be cause or effect. Indeed, a pupil may become an outstanding achiever to compensate for some emotional problem. But too often the child with an emotional disturbance finds himself caught in a vicious circle, anxious over lack of achievement, and performing poorly because of the emotional disturbance.

Harris (1970) lists ten kinds of emotional problems that contribute to reading disabilities, but which can also be applied to other subjects.

1. *Conscious refusal to learn.*
2. *Overt hostility—because some children have built up intense feelings of resentment, they find it difficult to exercise control of their emotions. Pupil-teacher relationships are not conducive to learning.*
3. *Negative conditioning to reading—reading has been associated with something the child dislikes intensely like a teacher or punishment. Therefore, he learns to dislike reading.*
4. *Displacement of hostility—suppose a child dislikes or fears a parent or a teacher. The child realizes that this person enjoys reading. Since it may arouse feelings of anxiety and guilt to direct his hostility toward this individual, he expresses these hostile feelings toward reading.*
5. *Resistance to pressure—when an overambitious parent pressures his child to achieve, the reaction of the child may be a disinterest in reading.*

6. *Clinging to dependency—to avoid growing up a child may cling to a symbol of early childhood—inability to read.*

7. *Quick discouragement—because some children lack a feeling of security, they become quickly discouraged. They have little confidence and respect.*

8. *Success is dangerous—success may symbolize entering adult society and competing as a rival with a parent. There is an implication for the child that this competition will result in extreme retaliation.*

9. *Extreme distractability or restlessness—when a child has a high degree of tension, he finds it difficult to control his physical activity. This results in inattention and inability to learn.*

10. *Absorption in a private world—daydreams, through which some children fulfill their wishes, result in lack of concentration and inability to learn.*

The teacher should be continually aware of symptoms. If a pupil cannot solve his problems in the classroom, he may need to be referred for clinical treatment. Symptoms of aggression, withdrawal, and general problem behavior are often indicative of personal-social adjustment problems. Sometimes antisocial behavior results from a particular incident and passes quickly. Serious and deep-seated problems, however, can be identified by persistence of symptoms.

ENVIRONMENTAL FACTORS. Although it is difficult to identify outside causes of a pupil's learning difficulties, the difficulties quickly show up in the pupil. A poor home environment, where the parents are separated or the child is rejected, may cause personal adjustment difficulties in the child in short order.

Some pupils are handicapped by a lack of intellectual interests in the home. Their parents provide few, if any, books or magazines for them. Lack of travel and other cultural opportunities make it difficult, if not impossible, for them to develop the concepts so readily attainable by those with broader experiences.

Poor teaching may be the cause of learning problems. The pupil may have learning disabilities that become cumulative. He may be underequipped to learn and be emotionally disturbed. Suffice it to say that in diagnosing learning difficulties, one must investigate a pupil's environment to find if the principal cause lies there.

SPECIFIC SUBJECT DIFFICULTIES. Learning difficulties often stem from the subject itself. The complex skills demanded by mathematics, language, spelling, and reading present learning problems. Considerable research on learning disabilities has indicated typical and specific errors and has resulted in the design of many diagnostic instruments to help locate them. But the teacher need not always administer a standardized instrument in diagnosis, because informal techniques are effective when used competently. Criterion- and objective-referenced test items are particularly helpful when trying to identify specific learning difficulties.

A variety of common errors can be observed in the work of children as they solve problems in basic arithmetic skills. For example, they make mistakes in carrying, counting, and subtracting because of inability to cope with zeroes. The interrelationships among the fundamental processes must be taken into account in any diagnosis concerning them. For example, if a child is struggling with long division because he cannot subtract or multiply, giving him more division problems to work without analyzing his difficulty is an inefficient way of helping him. Learning to subtract will make him competent in long division.

Oral language provides its share of common errors, such as misplaced accents, confusion with silent letters, and incorrect vowel and consonant quality. Also, failure to write legibly often requires attention. Illegibility of handwriting can often be traced to a few improperly formed letters repeated many times. The lower case e is written with a closed loop resembling an i, or the i is written with a loop to resemble an e. Often letters like o, s, a, and b are not closed, thereby making them illegible. If legibility is to be improved, the teacher must concentrate on letters causing the most difficulty. It is a waste of valuable time to have pupils drilling on every letter of the alphabet.

Spelling errors may be related to mispronunciation, speech disability, or inability to use phonic skills. A classification of typical spelling errors can reveal this relationship and give the teacher a basis for helping the pupil. Spache (1940) analyzed the errors made by poor and average spellers in the third, fourth, and fifth grades and showed that the average spellers make more phonetic substitutions (that is, a vowel, consonant, diphthong, or syllable) than poor spellers who, in turn, are inclined to make more nonphonetic substitutions. Also, average spellers add fewer letters than poor spellers, which may be accounted for by greater use of phonics by the average spellers. Mistakes occur because English words are not always spelled as they are pronounced.

Pupils having difficulty with spelling often have difficulty with reading and vice versa; the skills are closely related. Another, and subtler, cause of reading disability is lack of background, a difficulty in all grades and areas. A first-grade pupil may not have had the visual and auditory experiences to acquire a sight vocabulary. A pupil in secondary school may lack the vocabulary to comprehend his assignments in social studies and physical science. One gifted pupil thought that a cow was about the size of a large dog. He had never seen a cow, though he could very well talk about one. Field trips provide experiences that help make classroom learning meaningful. A lesson in conservation will be much more effective if pupils have actually seen the results of erosion. A discussion of city government will be aided by a visit to the municipal buildings. Words have no intrinsic meaning; they trigger associations from the experiences of the individual. When he has no experiences to associate with the symbol, he can only memorize.

Another cause of poor reading is lack of the systematic development of the basic skills in reading, such as a sight vocabulary, techniques of word recognition, comprehension, and the work-study skills. For example, if a child has not developed an adequate sight vocabulary, he may become overanalytical in his reading and break words apart without learning how to blend the syllables or use meaningful phrases and the context to help him understand. In other cases, structural analysis, syllabication, phonics, etc., have been too little emphasized, and the pupil finds himself handicapped in attacking new words. Independent reading demands a system of word-attack skills.

Failure to transfer reading skills to other assignments is another difficulty. Teaching reading without applying it to assignments in, for example, biology, too often results in the pupil's inability to do everyday reading tasks. The science teacher needs to discuss main ideas of paragraphs with his students. He should show how skimming, thorough reading, and rapid reading can be applied to his assignments. He should help his pupils initiate vocabulary development programs for themselves, because skills must be applied, not allowed to remain in isolation.

PROBLEMS

3. A sixth-grade teacher reports that his pupils can do arithmetic computations fairly well but that they are experiencing frustration in the areas of arithmetic reasoning and problem solving. Apply the principles of diagnosis to this situation by outlining specific steps for this teacher to follow to gain a thorough understanding of the learning problems he faces.

4. Common learning difficulties in the basic skill subjects have been presented. How might teachers in the following curriculum areas approach similar analyses?
   a. Junior high school physical education
   b. Elementary art
   c. Tenth-grade biology
   d. French I

REMEDIATION

In addition to recognizing what a child needs to learn, the teacher must also determine how he can best learn (Rutherford, 1972). Remediation would be much simpler if we could apply a trusted formula to each learning disability—a notion as sadly impossible as every other cure-all. Pupils differ, and learning disabilities are rooted in different soils. The source of one pupil's difficulty may be emotional while another suffers from faulty teaching. One pupil's handwriting is illegible because of inadequate motor development while his neighbor is simply careless.

Despite the different techniques and methods for remediation, certain guiding principles apply to all subjects and provide an operational framework.

1. *Remediation should be accompanied by a strong motivational program.*
2. *Remediation should be individualized in terms of the psychology of learning.*
3. *A continuous evaluation which informs a pupil of results is vital.*

Providing Motivation

No remedial technique will be successful unless the pupil can see the relationship between the purposes of the technique and his own needs. Many failing pupils have acute feelings of inadequacy and feel they are unable to succeed, that they are different. Some of them withdraw, and refuse to try; others rationalize by thinking that success is unimportant and that whatever they might learn will never be useful.

The teacher is the catalyst for changing these attitudes. Such pupils long to be understood. Many of them have been lectured, threatened, and rejected until often the first task is to help them rebuild self-confidence. Good remedial teaching has all the hallmarks of good teaching anywhere. The teacher lets the pupil know that he is liked and appreciated; above all he is optimistic and stays optimistic during the pupil's "downs" as well as his "ups." By accepting the pupil, the teacher helps him to build a self-security which is vital for effective learning.

Since a pupil develops confidence when he experiences success, it is important that the teacher know his strengths as well as his weaknesses, for the teacher must build on those strengths, starting at the child's level of achievement. It helps if the pupil's first success is dramatized. Presenting progress concretely is effective, particularly for younger children. Charts, graphs, and pictures can all be used successfully, though the device must be attuned to the maturity of the pupil. A device that lets him see his improvement works well. When he competes with himself, he can better his past record and this proves highly motivating.

To sustain motivation, the teacher should stimulate interest in the remedial program and monotony should be avoided like smallpox. Different approaches prevent mental fatigue, and so do materials with high motivational value. If the pupil can help plan his program by selecting materials and procedures, his involvement will often generate a permanent interest basic to the development of his independence.

A pupil's interest may droop if he is forced into remedial activity because some pupils honestly feel that their skills are adequate in spite of painful indications to the contrary. Sometimes allowing them to take a standardized test and helping them analyze the results produces the desired effect. Ingenious teachers use many methods to help a student want to improve, and social recognition is not the least of them. Most pupils find it rewarding to demonstrate progress to their peers and parents. Above all, remedial activities should not be scheduled when they conflict with other things the pupil would like to do. To be required to work a sheaf of arithmetic exercises while a "big game" is going on is hardly motivating.

Evaluating the Program

No remedial program can be based on initial diagnosis without consistent follow-through. In the first place, the pupil's needs will change as he overcomes his learning difficulties. Just as his problems have been cumulative in nature, remedial instruction will be cumulative in its impact. The new is learned in terms of the old.

Secondly, the teacher will want to judge the success of his program. He may have to shift methods and materials to help the pupil learn; all pupils do not respond equally to the same treatment. Only a continual evaluation can determine progress and future procedure.

In the third place, evaluation is important because it lets a pupil know how he is progressing. Motivation to learn goes up when the pupil knows the results of his effort. The less mature the child, the more it is necessary to depict results graphically.

Using Clinical Personnel

Although most teachers are responsible for remedial work, special teachers are occasionally employed to help them with their problems and often to work with pupils who show severe retardation. Because reading problems are the source of much educational retardation, a number of schools employ reading specialists. Although they are most often found in the elementary schools, some secondary schools are also providing their services. In other schools, a subject specialist handles problems in all basic skill or curriculum areas rather than reading alone.

Another specialist who can substantially contribute to a child's improvement is a school psychologist. Although a great share of his work will be corrective in nature, much of it will also be preventive. His task is to sensitize school personnel to the needs of pupils, and to diagnose individual problems and make the proper referrals when necessary. In this role, he serves as a coordinator for all the special services in the school as well as the community. Through him, the varying contributions of remedial teachers, mental health clinics, social agencies, and the home can be effectively utilized.

PROBLEMS

5. Imagine that you are a foreign language teacher. Three of your pupils are having difficulties. Robert works hard but stumbles desperately in dictations and oral work. Al has a natural ear for the language but seemingly cannot understand the grammar. Donna is a rote learner who memorizes long vocabulary lists with ease, but cannot grasp the essential meaning when translating. Describe how you would provide individualized remediation for these pupils.

6. Some teachers do not report standardized test scores to their pupils as they fear that poor results may be discouraging. Do you agree?

SURVEYING CLASS ACHIEVEMENT

A good way to identify pupils with learning difficulties is to administer a survey achievement test and a scholastic aptitude test. Pupils who appear to be underachieving may then undergo thorough diagnosis and remediation. The discussion that follows is based on the results of seven of the eleven subtests of the *Stanford Achievement Test* and the *Lorge-Thorndike Intelligence Test (Verbal)* administered in October to twenty-three pupils of a fifth-grade class who attended an elementary school in a small city. Their families varied in socioeconomic status. In analysis of the data, description is given of the use of the class record and the class analysis chart in identifying group as well as individual strengths and weaknesses. Suggestions for individual diagnosis and remediation are presented through a discussion of one pupil's difficulties.

Class Record

A class record was prepared on the basis of the test scores from both tests and is shown in Table 14.1. The pupils' names are listed in the order of their overall achievement, as represented by a composite value for all eleven subtests in the total battery. The sex of the pupil is recorded in the first column following the name. His age is listed in the next two columns, his *Lorge-Thorndike IQ* in the fourth column,

TABLE 14.1. Class Record of Stanford Achievement Test Scores for a Fifth-Grade Class.

Pupil's name	Sex	Age (yr–mo)	Lorge-Thorndike	Vocabulary	Reading comp.	Math concepts	Math comp.	Math applic.	Spelling	Language
1. Mary Jones	G	10–2	132	8.8–9[a]	9.3–8	8.4–9	7.8–9	9.5–9	7.0–7	8.5–8
2. William Seeber	B	10–1	128	8.8–9	9.3–8	8.4–9	6.5–7	8.6–8	8.1–8	9.0–8
3. Mary Hillhouse	G	9–8	125	8.8–9	7.9–8	5.2–5	5.2–5	5.4–5	8.1–8	9.5–9
4. Ann Chitwood	G	9–10	130	8.3–8	9.3–8	7.5–8	5.9–6	7.4–8	6.0–6	8.7–8
5. Celia Graham	G	10–4	120	7.3–7	6.7–7	5.2–5	5.6–6	5.6–6	7.3–8	9.5–9
6. Carol Smith	G	10–5	125	6.8–7	6.2–6	6.5–7	6.9–8	7.4–8	6.3–6	6.4–6
7. Gloria Behrens	G	10–7	122	6.1–6	6.4–6	5.8–6	5.6–6	7.4–8	8.1–8	7.4–7
8. Sandra Black	G	10–4	123	6.8–7	7.3–7	5.2–5	4.6–5	5.6–6	6.3–6	9.5–9
9. June Nelson	G	9–10	128	6.8–7	5.1–5	6.0–6	4.1–4	7.4–8	6.3–6	6.4–6
10 Trudy Lincoln	G	10–4	115	7.0–7	6.2–6	5.6–6	5.1–5	5.4–5	6.3–6	7.4–7
11. Joe Sills	B	10–3	110	6.3–7	5.9–6	5.2–5	4.6–5	5.6–6	6.4–7	7.4–7
12. Albert Uken	B	9–11	115	5.7–6	6.2–6	5.6–6	4.6–5	5.1–5	6.3–6	7.8–7
13. John Sevaar	B	10–2	110	6.3–7	5.3–5	4.9–5	3.0–2	5.1–5	5.3–5	6.2–6
14. Cindy Bockwitz	G	10–5	104	4.4–4	2.7–2	4.7–5	5.1–5	5.4–5	7.3–8	4.8–5
15. Florence Weber	G	10–6	98	5.7–6	4.6–5	3.7–3	3.9–3	4.0–4	4.8–5	4.5–4
16. Meg Adams	G	10–8	102	4.4–4	5.1–5	4.0–4	4.1–4	4.4–4	4.3–4	2.8–3
17. Stanley Seward	B	10–4	98	4.1–4	4.4–4	3.7–3	3.5–3	4.4–4	3.2–3	4.9–5
18. Beverly Hill	G	10–8	122	3.8–3	3.6–3	6.2–6	4.6–5	6.2–6	3.6–3	3.5–4
19. Carol Jones	G	10–6	94	3.8–3	3.3–3	3.2–3	3.0–2	4.0–4	4.5–4	3.5–4
20. Peter White	B	9–10	98	3.8–3	3.6–3	3.2–3	3.0–2	4.0–4	3.2–3	3.5–4
21. Floyd Echart	B	9–9	90	3.8–3	2.7–2	3.7–3	3.0–2	3.5–3	3.2–3	2.3–3
22. Oscar Biggs	B	10–1	88	2.7–2	2.5–2	2.0–1	3.0–2	2.9–3	2.7–2	2.3–3
23. Helen Brown	G	10–7	85	2.4–2	2.5–2	2.0–1	2.7–2	2.9–3	2.7–2	2.6–3

[a]The first score is the grade equivalent; the second score is the stanine based on the standardization group.

and the grade equivalent and stanines for the seven subtests of the battery in the following columns.

Class Analysis Chart

The numbers preceding the pupils' names serve as identification numbers when preparing a class analysis chart, such as that shown in Table 14.2. A column is available for each subtest score. Note that these scores are in terms of stanines. The distribution of stanines for each column is found by writing the identification number of each pupil in the box on the same line as his stanine score. For example, Meg Adams (#16) has a stanine score of three for the *Language* test. Therefore, a "16" is written in the language column in the box opposite the stanine score of three. The remaining twenty-two numbers are similarly recorded in this column.

For each column, the median stanine score was determined by locating the twelfth score from the top or bottom, and plotted by placing a rectangle at the appropriate stanine in each column. As you can see, the class analysis chart is a summary of the test results for the entire class. At a glance, the teacher can identify the areas in which the best and poorest work is being done. There is considerable variability in all areas of achievement. Few pupils have scores at the very top or bottom of the class in all subtests.

TABLE 14.2.   Class Analysis Chart for a Fifth-Grade Class.

Stanine	Vocabulary	Reading comp.	Math concepts	Math comp.	Math applic.	Spelling	Language
9	1,2, 3		1,2	1	1		3,5, 8
8	4	1,2, 3,4	4	6	2,4,6, 7,9	2,3,5, 7,14	1,2, 4
7	5,6,8,9, 10,11,13	5,8	6	2		1,11	7,10, 11,12
6	7,12 15	6,7,10, 11,12	7,9,10, 12,18	4,5, 7	5,8, 11,18	4,6,8, 9,10,12	6,9, 13
5		9,13, 15,16	3,5,8, 11,13,14	3,10,11 14,18	3,10,12, 13,14	13,15	14,17
4	14,16, 17	17	16	8,9, 12,16	15,16,17 19,20	16,19	15,18, 19,20
3	18,19, 20,21	19,18, 20	15,17,19, 20,21	15,17	21,22, 23	17,18, 20,21	16,21, 22,23
2	22,23	14,21, 22,23		13,19,20, 21,22,23		22,23	
1			22,23				

Notice that the low point in achievement for this class is in mathematics computation. Obviously, certain computational skills are not being mastered. The class does somewhat better in mathematics application because needed skill in computation in this subtest is on an easy level.

Finally, the highest points of achievement are in vocabulary, language, and spelling. Vocabulary is related to good scholastic ability. In this connection, note that the median IQ of the group is 115, which is above average. Spelling ability can be attributed to the school staff's special emphasis on this subject.

As the teacher studies the class analysis chart, he becomes aware of other problems. For instance, Cindy Bockwitz (#14) has a much higher score in spelling than in other parts of the achievement test. Is this an indication that Cindy could improve in other areas? Does it mean that her parents have been drilling her in spelling and find that she excels in this skill? Spelling is not as high level a verbal skill as is reading for comprehension. Cindy's IQ supports the idea that she may be giving spelling special attention.

The teacher cannot assume that two pupils with about the same average (or composite) achievement are alike in terms of their patterns of achievement. This is true of Meg Adams (#16) and Stanley Seward (#17). Even though their average achievement differs little, Meg is at the third stanine in language usage, while Stanley is at the fifth. There are also differences in spelling and reading comprehension, but in the opposite direction (see Table 14.1).

Item Analysis

Another useful aid is an item-analysis chart constructed from the right and wrong answers to each item in a subtest. Table 14.3 lists the responses of the fifth-grade class on the mathematics computation subtest of the *Stanford Achievement Test*. This diagnostic device gives the teacher a more detailed picture of the area of his pupils' lowest achievement. For example, the content represented by items like 1, 4, and 6 is fairly well learned by the class as a whole, while several items missed by a large percentage of the group represented areas of low achievement.

Items 24, 25, 29, and 37 require information about how to cope with zeros in the minuend when subtracting. The results indicate that only a few of the pupils have mastered these skills. Poor performance on some of the other items reveals that many pupils had trouble with mathematical computations involving fractions.

In a multiple-choice test, it is possible to determine the number of pupils choosing each of the distracters as well as the number answering correctly. When items are machine-scored, the test-scoring machine can easily run the analysis. Because a good test item included plausible distracters, a study of pupils' choices will often give the teacher insight into their difficulties. He will be in a better position to diagnose and, as a result, to prescribe effective remediation.

Table 14.3 provides information about how well the class as a whole performs specific tasks. In a sense, we are now using data from a norm-referenced test in an objective- or criterion-referenced way (Fremer, 1972). Certainly a well-constructed criterion-referenced test would provide better information in these instances. Yet an item analysis as shown in Table 14.3 has much value.

TABLE 14.3. Item Analysis of the Mathematics Computation Subtest of the Stanford Achievement Test.

Test item	Right No.	Right %	Wrong No.	Wrong %	Test item	Right No.	Right %	Wrong No.	Wrong %
1	19	83	4	17	21	13	56	10	44
2	17	74	6	26	22	10	44	13	56
3	16	70	7	30	23	17	74	6	26
4	19	83	4	17	24	4	17	19	83
5	16	70	7	30	25	7	30	16	70
6	18	78	5	22	26	3	13	20	87
7	16	70	7	30	27	5	22	18	78
8	16	70	7	30	28	9	39	14	61
9	14	61	9	39	29	7	30	16	70
10	14	61	9	39	30	4	17	19	83
11	11	48	12	52	31	4	17	19	83
12	5	22	18	78	32	12	52	11	48
13	8	35	15	65	33	7	30	16	70
14	3	13	20	87	34	6	26	17	74
15	5	22	18	78	35	9	39	14	61
16	12	52	11	48	36	8	35	15	65
17	11	48	12	52	37	3	13	20	87
18	10	44	13	56	38	8	35	15	65
19	11	48	12	52	39	8	35	15	65
20	16	70	7	30	40	9	39	14	61

It should be further noted that, in working with the learning disabled where instruction must be individualized, norm-referenced measurement devices are of use in determining how deviant from the "normal" a child is. However, after his problems are evaluated, they provide less flexibility for making the frequent measurements of educational progress needed for this type of child (Proger and Mann, 1973).

PROBLEMS

7. Can you find specific instances of retardation in achievement in the fifth-grade class in question? Are any of the pupils overachievers? In your opinion, what is the chief problem confronting the teacher of this class? What additional information about the pupils would be highly useful to him?

8. What advantages would criterion-referenced tests have over norm-referenced instruments in working with severely disabled learners?

INDIVIDUAL DIAGNOSIS AND REMEDIATION

At this point it is clear that group strengths, weaknesses, and range of ability can be determined from the class record and the class analysis chart. Some individual problems also become apparent. Consider the case of Beverly Hill (#18), who is significantly below the average achievement in language skills of a normal fifth-grade child in the second month of the school year. Beverly has ability that surpasses the average child. Her verbal score on the *Lorge-Thorndike Intelligence Test* is 122 (see Table 14.1). Despite her superior scholastic aptitude, she is definitely below the point a pupil with average mentality should be, except in mathematics. Even her mathematics scores represent some retardation considering her scholastic aptitude.

Inability to Read

Because there was evidence that inability to read might be the cause of Beverly's difficulties, the teacher wanted to explore several related elements, but needed more information about her specific reading difficulties. Many teachers like to use an informal oral reading test for this purpose. Beverly's teacher selected several interesting narrative passages, each about 200 words long, from material that Beverly had not read. The reading level of the first passage was of first- or second-grade difficulty, the others of increasing difficulty.

This procedure threw considerable light on Beverly's reading problems. Typical questions asked in an informal reading test are: Does she know the sounds of the vowels and consonants? Can she break a new word into syllables? Can she blend individual sounds together so that she can recognize the word? Does she read with expression, indicating that she is using the context to help identify new words? Does she rely too much on context and fail to recognize certain words, substituting those that make sense but distorting the meaning?

TABLE 14.4. Scores on the Gates-McKillop Reading Diagnostic Tests, First Administration.

Subtests	Beverly's grade score	Highest possible grade score
Oral reading	3.8	7.5
Reversals	Poor score	
Recognizing and blending common word parts	Very low score	
Syllabication	Low score	

In addition to the informal reading test, the teacher administered the *Gates-McKillop Reading Diagnostic Tests*, a standardized instrument to analyze reading difficulties. Table 14.4 contains some of Beverly's grade scores on these tests. Her oral score is 3.8, approximately the same as her silent reading score. The other scores indicate her serious weakness in reading fundamentals.

Beverly had developed no systematic method for attacking words. She tended to concentrate on words themselves, rather than on the relationship among them, and thereby lost the train of thought. Even her word-by-word reading was marked at times with considerable confusion. Not only did she make a considerable number of reversal errors, but she had difficulty in blending word parts. A number of letter sounds were confused, particularly *a* and *e*. Recognition of syllables and phonograms was weak and because of her undue attention to word parts and units, she made very little use of context to aid her in pronunciation or comprehension.

SURVEY VS. DIAGNOSTIC TEST DATA. What are the differences between a diagnostic and a survey test? A survey test provides a general appraisal of overall achievement in some subject area such as reading. It is not designed to give a detailed picture of deficiencies; that is the province of the diagnostic test. Nor is it constructed to indicate possible causes of inadequate achievement; a good diagnostic test should provide cues for the formulation of hypotheses concerning lack of growth and possible remedial procedures.

The survey test showed Beverly Hill to be very low in achievement of language skills, but it required a diagnostic test to emphasize weakness in syllabication, recognizing and blending common word parts, and so forth, which are the bases of low performance in the language arts.

Determining the Cause

The teacher found from Beverly's cumulative record,* Figures 14.1 and 14.2, that she had a long history of retardation. She had complained of headaches during her first year of school and, in the second grade, was required to wear glasses for close work. Also, during that year her father had been killed in an accident and her mother had been compelled to work. Beverly had symptoms of anxiety and insecurity, and her early school experience probably accounts for the reading difficulty. She was severely

* For additional information about cumulative records, see pages 422–426.

1. IDENTIFICATION DATA

CALIFORNIA CUMULATIVE RECORD ELEMENTARY FORM

Confidential Information for use by Professional Personnel

PHOTOGRAPHS

FILE No. (Pencil)

LAST NAME	FIRST NAME	MIDDLE NAME	NICKNAME (Pencil)	CHECK SEX
Hill	Beverly	Jane		M / F X

BIRTH DATE	BIRTH DATE VERIFICATION	PLACE OF BIRTH CITY (OR COUNTY)	STATE (OR NATION)
2/20/64	Birth Certificate	Suburban	New York

DATES PHOTOGRAPHED (Pencil) _____ SCHOOL DISTRICT _____

HOME				
NAME	ADDRESS	TELEPHONE (Pencil)		
Mary L. Hill	101 Olds Ave.	748-3218		

IN CASE OF EMERGENCY NOTIFY

NAME	ADDRESS	TELEPHONE (Pencil) (OR)	NAME	ADDRESS	TELEPHONE (Pencil) (OR)
Joe S. Brown	1805 Lotus St.	748-4532	Dr. Ralph Ogden	16 Main Street	744-8072

COMMENTS

2. GROUP SCHOLASTIC CAPACITY TESTS (LABEL OTHER SUB SCORES USED, e.g. PERFORMANCE, PERCEPTION, ETC. DOUBLE SPACES PROVIDED.)

DATE TEST GIVEN	GRADE	NAME OF TEST	FORM	LEVEL	C.A.	M.A.	Total	Verbal	Non-Verb.	8	9	10	11	12	13	COMMENTS	EXAMINER
10/70	1	Otis-Lennon		Prim II			124										
10/74	5	Lorge Thorndike (Verbal)		Multi			122										

COMMENTS

3. INDIVIDUAL TESTS

DATE TEST GIVEN	GRADE	NAME OF TEST	C.A.							RESULTS AND REMARKS							EXAMINER
11/74	5	Revised S-B, L-M		130 I.Q. Had trouble with tests demanding reading skill.													A. J. Smith

4. GROUP ACHIEVEMENT TESTS (Including Reading Readiness) (LABEL VARIOUS SUB SCORES, e.g. VOCABULARY)

DATE TEST GIVEN	GRADE	NAME OF TEST	FORM	LEVEL	1	2	READING		5	6	ARITHMETIC			10	11	LANGUAGE		14	15	COMMENTS	EXAMINER
11/71	2	Stanford	J	Prim			Par M Word M 1.1 1.5				Reas Comp 3.1 1.8					Spell 1.5					
10/72	3	Stanford	W	Prim			Par M Word M 1.8 2.3				Comp Conc 2.9 2.9					Spell 2.5					
10/73	4	Stanford	W	Inter I			Par M Word M 2.4 2.8				Appl Comp Conc 5.1 3.8 5.0					Spell Lang 3.6 3.6					
10/74	5	Stanford		Inter I			Read Voc 3.6 3.8				Appl Comp Conc 6.2 4.6 6.2					Spell Lang 3.6 3.5					

5. PERSONALITY AND INTEREST INVENTORIES, APTITUDE TESTS, AND OTHER TESTS (LABEL VARIOUS SUB SCORES, e.g. EMOTIONAL, SOCIAL)

DATE TEST GIVEN	GRADE	NAME OF TEST	FORM	LEVEL	Pers. Adj. %ile	Soc. Adj. %ile	4	5	6	7	8	9	10	11	12	13	14	15	COMMENTS	EXAMINER
11/74	5	Calif. Test of Personality	AA	Elem	50	60														

6. INFORMATION CONCERNING INDIVIDUAL ADJUSTMENT

YEAR AND GRADE	INTERESTS, ACTIVITIES, LEADERSHIP	FAMILIES AND HOME RELATIONSHIPS OUT OF SCHOOL RESPONSIBILITIES	ATTITUDES AND FEELINGS ABOUT: SELF; PEERS; SCHOOL	REFERRALS TO SCHOOL SERVICES AND/OR COMMUNITY AGENCIES
YEAR 1969-1970 KINDERGARTEN	Quiet child. Very cooperative.	Shares family experiences. Close family ties.	Has adjusted well to school and to her peers.	
YEAR 1970-1971 GRADE 1	Likes to do activities with hands. Doesn't choose books in free time.	Family watches television a great deal.	Sometimes appears to be daydreaming.	
YEAR 1971-1972 GRADE 2	Seems withdrawn since death of father.	Mother is now working. Does not spend as much time with Beverly.	Retarded in reading. Seems un-interested.	
YEAR 1972-1973 GRADE 3	Evidences of some leadership. Has several close friends.	Seems to be a close relationship with the Mother.	Has shown considerable interest in arithmetic.	
YEAR 1973-1974 GRADE 4	Continues to be liked and accepted by her peers.	Has done some baby sitting with neighbor children during the day hours.	Has applied herself to her school work.	
YEAR 1974-1975 GRADE 5				
YEAR 19 -19 GRADE				
YEAR 19 -19 GRADE				
YEAR 19 -19 GRADE				

FIGURE 14.1. Inside Half of an Elementary School Cumulative Record.
Reproduced by permission of Carlisle Graphics Division, Litton Industries.

7. GROWTH AND DEVELOPMENT THROUGH SCHOOL EXPERIENCES

INDICATE MAJOR CURRICULUM UNIT, DESCRIPTION OF EXPERIENCE, AND DURATION. INITIAL EACH ENTRY. THIS SPACE MAY ALSO BE USED FOR INDICATING DEGREE OF SUCCESS IN SCHOOL EXPERIENCES AND READERS USED

FORM L.M.—A. Carlisle & Co., S.F., 1955

YEAR 1969-1970 KINDERGARTEN	YEAR 1970-1971 GRADE 1	YEAR 1971-1972 GRADE 2	YEAR 1972-1973 GRADE 3	YEAR 1973-1974 GRADE 4
Works well with group and plays independently. Neat; follows directions. Sings in tune; knows many nursery rhymes. Knows the letters of the alphabet, names of the colors. Can write her name. Cooperative Seems ready for first grade work	Reading: S-F series. Readiness bks, 3 pre-primers, Jr. primer and primer completed. Also 3 pre-primers of supp (H-M) rdrs. Did not start first reader, but should be ready for it in Sept. Did all bks. Math: Knows combinations and understands meaning of concepts	Readers: S-F series. 1^1 reader ...11/20 1^2 " (H-M) ..2/2 1^2 " 4/15 L-C phonics bks, A & B Cowboy Sam, 1 & 2 (started 2^1 reader in May, but finds it difficult. Cannot concentrate. Wears glasses, but forgets them) Math: Understands add. & sub., knows basic facts. S-B bk.	Readers: S-F series. 2^1 of S-F and of H-M; workbooks Eye & Ear Fun,1, 2, 3 L-C phonics, bk C Completed S-F 2^2 and began 3^1. but finds it difficult. Dislikes reading. Social Studies: Local history, Indians Math: Average in class S-B bk 3; knows all combinations and 4 processes; accurate and neat.	Readers: In lowest group. S-F 3^1 & 3^2 Workbooks: S-F & Readers Digest, Skill Builders, 2, 3, 4 Merrill Skilltexts: Nibs, Nicky, Uncle Funny Bunny Math: S-B bk 4. Neat, accurate. Understands problems but has trouble reading them. Social Studies — Foll. Regional studies. Can't read text. Does not participate in disc. Science: enjoys experiments, can't read text.
YEAR 1974-1975 GRADE 5	YEAR 19 -19 GRADE	YEAR 19 -19 GRADE	YEAR 19 -19 GRADE	YEAR 19 -19 GRADE

Requirements of U.S. Constitution, American History, State and Local Government satisfactorily completed.

Date Certified _____ INITIAL

8. SCHOOL HISTORY

DATE ENTERED	HOME ADDRESS & TELEPHONE	CITY OR COUNTY	SCHOOL & SCHOOL DISTRICT	GRADE	TEACHER	ATTENDANCE	TRANSFERRED TO:	DATE LEFT
9/69	101 Olds 748-3218	Suburban	Suburban Central	K	Shapiro	Perfect		
9/70	"	"	"	1	Wilson	1st week — trip		
9/71	"	"	"	2	Eddy	1 week — death of F.		
9/72	"	"	"	3	Wood	Periodic absences		
9/73	"	"	"	4	Bannar	No absences		
9/74	"	"	"	5	Green			

COMPLETED GRADE 6 OR 8 OR ( ) ON   CIRCLE   Month   Day   Year

9. PARENTS' EDUCATIONAL AND/OR VOCATIONAL PLANS FOR PUPIL: (Pencil)

	HOME ADDRESS (Pencil)	SPECIFIC OCCUPATION (Pencil)	BUSINESS ADDRESS AND TELEPHONE (Pencil)
10. FATHER'S NAME Deceased			
11. MOTHER'S NAME Mary L. Hill	101 Olds Ave.	Teacher	Elmwood School
12. OR GUARDIAN'S NAME			

13. CHILDREN OF FAMILY

NAMES	Year of Birth	RELATIONSHIP TO PUPIL	Living at Home
Beverly Hill	1964		

14. ADULTS OTHER THAN PARENTS LIVING CONTINUOUSLY IN PUPIL'S HOME (Pencil)

NAME	RELATIONSHIP TO PUPIL
DATE	

CIRCLE   CIRCLE (Pencil)

Pupil Living With   Yes (No)   Living?   Yes (No)
Pupil Living With   (Yes) No   Living?   (Yes) No
Pupil Living With   Yes No   Living?   Yes No

15. SIGNIFICANT HEALTH FACTORS

DATE	RECOMMENDATIONS OF HEALTH ADVISER	ADVISER'S NAME
9/71	Classes prescribed	Jones
	Audiometer reading normal	Jones

DATE	TEACHER'S COMMENTS ON PUPIL'S HEALTH CONDITIONS	TEACHER
11/71	Symptoms of extreme anxiety	

FIGURE 14.2. Outside Half of an Elementary School Cumulative Record.

Reproduced by permission of Carlisle Graphics Division, Litton Industries.

handicapped because learning basic skills is cumulative and she lacked a foundation on which to build. Beverly's mother remarried, and both parents expressed concern about the child's achievement. They asked for a conference, so the teacher had an opportunity to enlist their help.

The teacher realized the importance of involving the parents in learning and giving them a positive role in the process. He understood that parental nagging, forcing children to forego normal social activities, or a lack of genuine parental interest in the child can prevent a remedial program from being a success. He also knew that he must give parents specific instructions before they can help. If possible, he must avoid telling them that there is nothing they can do, that everything will work out all right.

Of course it is sometimes difficult if not impossible to elicit parental cooperation. Some parents' own lack of personal-social adjustment prevents them from being close to their children. Some are so absorbed in their own interests and professional lives that they find it impossible to become involved in their children's problems.

During the conference with Beverly's parents, the teacher explained that their child was bright and that her difficulty stemmed from immature word-recognition skills and lack of concentration on the meaning and the relationship among the words. It was decided that Beverly should have individual remedial reading instruction each day. Her parents were helped to realize the need for supporting the child emotionally and were asked to praise her liberally for any improvement. They were advised against exerting pressure either overtly or through expression of concern about her progress.

The teacher was also able to discuss television and its relation to Beverly's reading problem. He helped her parents to see that if their own chief interest was television, not reading, it would be impossible to convince the child of the importance of improving her reading, that their habits would have a marked effect on Beverly's. They were advised to discuss both television programs and their reading, drawing Beverly into the conversation, thereby signifying the importance of both in acquiring and formulating ideas.

Providing Remedial Instruction

Removing the cause of a learning difficulty is only the first step. Now Beverly had to be taught to read. In her case, stress was placed on recognition of sounds, syllables, and blending. She was given opportunity for practicing a systematic attack on unfamiliar words and helped to use context for determining meanings. Her left to right orientation was developed.

Attention was also given to improving her reading rate. Beverly was encouraged to time herself on short easy exercises and to keep a record of her progress. To keep her abreast of class work, the teacher made available easy materials on topics under study.

A pupil who has had difficulty in such a basic skill as reading is probably short on confidence. Beverly was given an opportunity to read an easy passage to the class occasionally, but first her teacher made sure that she was well-prepared. Recognition of this kind provided a high degree of motivation.

At the end of the year, several tests from the second form of the *Gates-McKillop Reading Diagnostic Tests* were administered to Beverly. The scores are listed in Table

TABLE 14.5.   Scores on the Gates-McKillop Reading Diagnostic Tests, Second Administration.

Subtests	Beverly's grade score
Oral reading	7.2
Reversals	Normal progress
Recognizing and blending common word parts	Normal progress
Syllabication	Normal progress

14.5. Notice the vast improvement. The total score in oral reading increased from 3.8 to 7.2 All other scores are now satisfactory. Moreover, her scores on the *Gates-MacGinitie Reading Tests* are as shown in Table 14.6.

Beverly kept a record of the books she read during the year, and at the last count, she had over forty to her credit. Although some were very short and easy, she also had read a number of considerable substance.

All remedial teaching does not have to be done on an individual basis. Elementary school teachers can group pupils in various ways so that special help can be given for special difficulties. More secondary school teachers need to utilize these grouping procedures. The teacher might begin with two groups. Four or five pupils who excel in the course may be grouped for special projects while the teacher works with the majority of the class. Gradually, as the teacher's skill and confidence increase, he can increase the number of groups.

Instructional Placement Reports

Help for relating diagnostic findings in reading to remedial procedures is provided by means of a computer program used with the *Stanford Diagnostic Reading Test, Level II.* It is known as the *Instructional Placement Report (IPR).* The IPR provides an initial grouping for instructional purposes based on pupil needs as evidenced by the diagnostic test scores. Needs are defined in terms of scores and patterns of scores. Pupils with similar profiles are grouped and instructional suggestions are provided.

The results of administering the *Stanford Diagnostic Reading Tests* are sorted and reported to the teacher in terms of stanines as Diagnostic Reading Tests in Table 14.7.

TABLE 14.6.   Scores on the Gates-MacGinitie Reading Tests.

Test	Grade level
Vocabulary	6.8
Speed and accuracy	6.3
Comprehension	6.5

TABLE 14.7.   Stanine Scores on the Stanford Diagnostic Reading Tests.

Group 2	Reading comprehension			Vo-cabu-lary	Syl-labica-tion	Sound disc.	Blend-ing	Rate of read-ing
	Lit.	Inf.	Tot.					
Christner, Anthon	2	3	3	3	3	3	2	4
Costa, Norman J.	4	2	3	5	3	3	4	3
Gordon, Lawrence	2	3	3	3	2	2	2	4
Haman, Dorothy E.	3	4	3	4	4	4	3	4
Holland, Winifred	2	2	2	2	3	2	3	1

Note that these five pupils have been classified in Group 2. For this group and all others, the teacher is provided with a general group description and instructional suggestions. In the case of Group 2, they are:

GROUP DESCRIPTION.   The reading skills of pupils in Group 2 are generally very weak. Their comprehension is low; most of them probably have a poor vocabulary; they lack decoding skills; and they read very slowly. They will need intensive, individualized instruction throughout the school year. Careful study will often show that these pupils also have extensive learning problems in other school subjects, especially spelling.

INSTRUCTIONAL SUGGESTIONS.   These pupils should be placed in a developmental reading program at their level. Such a program should cover these facets of reading:

1. *The decoding skills should be taught systematically, including grapheme-phoneme relationships, variant spellings of the phonemes, syllabication, and blending of sounds and syllables.*
2. *Some instructional time should be devoted to vocabulary development, especially listening vocabulary. Such instruction should include lexical meanings, word parts and derivations, slang and dialects, and idiomatic expressions.*
3. *These pupils should read books of high interest and low reading level, to develop comprehension skills and interest in reading. This aspect of the program should be given extra emphasis with pupils who lack motivation. The books should be primarily interesting, not challenging in difficulty. Books that are extremely easy to read help to develop reading fluency.*
4. *These pupils have reading problems of such magnitude as to require more time and assistance than is ordinarily possible in the normal reading program.*

Eleven groupings are provided. It is expected that, in the case of most classes, several of the groups will contain three or more pupils, some groups only one or two, and others none. By the way, Group 11 is typically a very small group, containing only unclassified pupils, that is, pupils having a pattern of scores that the computer system could not classify.

Properly used, the *IPR* and similar efforts should offer important help to classroom teachers. They should improve the interpretability of diagnostic test data and strengthen remedial instruction.

PROBLEM

9. An analysis of Beverly's reading scores has been presented. Does the interpretation given indicate a need for a certain degree of sophistication on the part
of the teacher to make maximum use of these tests? How would you explain the
meaning of the *Gates* subtest scores to a parent?

SUMMARY

These are the highlights of this chapter:

1. *Good teaching implies that each pupil should achieve in terms of his interests,
   needs, and potential. "Lockstep" teaching forces some children to repeat what
   they already know and confronts others with tasks too difficult for them. It
   precludes effective learning.*
2. *The first step in diagnoses of learning difficulties is to ascertain strengths and
   weaknesses of the pupil. Underlying causes of the difficulty should be largely
   or totally eliminated before remedial instruction begins.*
3. *Although the teacher is not expected to develop the proficiency of a clinician,
   he must have several competencies in diagnosing and providing for remediation:*
   a. *An understanding of the psychology of learning as it applies to specific
      subject areas.*
   b. *An ability to recognize those physical and psychological aspects of human
      development related to learning.*
   c. *An understanding of the important diagnostic techniques and the remedial
      methods and materials in various subject areas.*
4. *A number of factors affect pupil achievement—scholastic aptitude, health,
   vision, hearing, motor coordination, personal-social development, and environment.*
5. *Difficulties peculiar to a specific subject may be responsible for learning
   problems, and such elements have been identified in arithmetic, language,
   handwriting, spelling, and reading.*
6. *The following considerations should be emphasized in remediation:*
   a. *motivating the learner*
   b. *individualizing learning*
   c. *evaluating continuously*
7. *A school testing program is an excellent way to initiate a sound program of
   diagnosis and remediation. Both norm-referenced and criterion-referenced
   instruments are useful.*
8. *Analysis of test scores and use of cumulative records are the basis on which to
   build a remedial program.*

SUGGESTED READINGS

BLAIR, G. M. *Diagnostic and remedial teaching.* (Rev. ed.) New York: Macmillan, 1956.
This book is designed for both elementary and secondary teachers. In addition to discussing

the problems of diagnosis and remediation in reading, arithmetic, handwriting, spelling, and English fundamentals, the author outlines remedial programs for elementary, junior high, and high schools.

DAVIS, J. A. Use of measurement in student planning and guidance. In R. L. Thorndike (ed.), *Educational measurement.* (2nd ed.) Washington: American Council on Education, 1971. Chapter 18.

The selection of measures for the individual's use and the interpretation of the information they provide are principal topics in this chapter.

HAMMELL, D. D. Evaluating children for instructional purposes. *Academic Therapy,* 1971, 6, 341–353.

Today considerable attention is being focused on children with learning disabilities. The author of this article suggests a helpful bibliography to aid the teacher in coping with these problems and he delineates methods for translating diagnostic information into remediation procedures.

HARRIS, A. J. *How to increase reading ability.* (5th ed.) New York: David McKay, 1970.

This is one of the best and most widely used references in the field of diagnosis and remediation in reading. The author bases his discussion on research and practical experience. The book is a thorough and practical source of information.

WILSON, R. M. *Diagnostic and remedial reading for classroom and clinic.* (2nd ed.) Columbus, Ohio: Charles E. Merrill, 1972.

A diagnostic-teaching-oriented volume with practical suggestions for the teacher. Suggestions given are also helpful for subject areas in addition to reading.

REFERENCES CITED

FREMER, J. *Criterion-referenced interpretations of survey achievement tests.* Test Development Memorandum. Princeton, N.J.: Educational Testing Service, 1972.

HARRIS, A. J. *How to increase reading ability.* (5th ed.) New York: David McKay, 1970.

PROGER, B. B., and L. MANN. Criterion-referenced measurement: the world of gray vs. black and white. *Journal of Learning Disabilities,* 1973, 6, 72–84.

RUTHERFORD, W. L. From diagnosis to treatment of reading disabilities. *Academic Therapy,* 1972, 8, 51–55

SPACHE, G. Characteristic errors of good and poor spellers. *Journal of Educational Research,* 1940, 34, 182–189.

15

DETERMINING AND REPORTING GROWTH

Suppose you have asked your physician to give you a thorough physical examination. He runs through a complex series of clinical and laboratory examinations, evaluates them, and says "Well, I guess you're worth about a *B+.*" You leave cheerfully enough—a *B+* always sounds good when you are told achievement test results—but a bit puzzled. Perhaps it means that there are not many people as physically able as you. But these seem to be the only conclusive judgments you can come to. You do not know how to improve your health, because you do not know what deficiencies kept you from getting an *A*.

Clearly a letter grading system is inadequate for summarizing the results of a physical examination. If your physician discovers circulatory difficulties, he discusses the ailment with you. Often he must interpret extensively before you understand the meaning of the evaluation. Many bits of information are related and balanced. Furthermore, a physician relates his diagnosis to remediation, and is likely to modify your activities or diet.

Similarly, evaluating a pupil's competence requires careful reflection on many aspects of his personality and abilities. Much more is examined than his knowledge of subject matter; his teachers are concerned with his personal-social adjustment, the way he represents his school, and the quality of his response to the learning situations he experiences.

Composite evaluation of something as nebulous as human behavior must be highly complex. Not all evidence can be completely objective. Every source of data available for assessing both psychological and physical characteristics must be tapped. It is impossible to summarize the evaluation with a single symbol.

Teachers agree that giving and reporting marks (or "grades") is one of their most uncomfortable responsibilities. Some lack confidence in the marks they assign; others believe their marks are fair, but find them difficult to defend. Behind these negative attitudes lies the fact that the basis for assigning marks is often unclear. Should the intelligent pupil who loafs be given a low mark? Should the pupil who works very hard but whose mental capacities are limited be upgraded in spite of his below-average performance on tests and assignments? Should the pupil who adjusts well to his peers but receives failing marks be promoted? What would be the effect on this child's future development if he were held back? Should marks be eliminated entirely? There are very strong advocates for doing so. With so many factors to consider, it is small

367

wonder that teachers regard giving final marks as a chore and wish that they could be relieved of the responsibility.

In many modern schools, there is a definite trend toward revising methods of marking and reporting. Child psychology and a redefinition of the objectives of the school have had their influence. Attention has been centered on the whole child, emphasizing his achievement in relation to his own potential for development. The complexity of this kind of evaluation is reflected in changed methods of reporting, leading to such devices as check lists, personal letters, teacher-parent conferences, pass/fail grading, criterion-referenced marking, and contracting for grades.

Marks can make a positive contribution to learning. They can serve an evaluative function that cannot be served or served as well by other forms of evaluation (Feldmesser, 1972). Unfortunately, marks have not always represented valid measures of achievement, because the meaning of marks and the evidence for determining them have not been carefully determined. The elimination of marks will not guarantee the elimination of undesirable competition in the classroom, nor will this act alone foster the elimination of conformity and the development of creativity. There seems to be agreement on all sides that evaluation of learning is important. Disagreement focuses on how it should be reported.

There is no method of reporting that will prevent all of the problems inherent in the evaluation of pupils. However, certain flagrant violations can be eliminated by a knowledge of acceptable procedures. Furthermore, newer methods of marking and reporting, such as criterion-referenced marking, can be used in association with traditional methods. They may eventually be more widely used as teachers become more knowledgeable about them and as certain problems in their use are solved.

It is possible that newer methods of reporting may solve yet another problem, namely, the apparently modest relationship between college grades and adult accomplishment reported for many vocational fields (Hoyt, 1966). College grades have even been found to have little relationship to postcollege participation in community affairs, politics, cultural activities, and interest in current events (Mann, 1968; Lewis, 1970; Munday and Davis, 1974). It appears that grades are not measuring those kinds of successful behavior valued in our society.

PURPOSES OF REPORTING

The purposes of marking and reporting can best be defined in terms of those who use them—pupils, parents, teachers, school administrators, and employers. In the final analysis, reports should serve the paramount purpose of facilitating the educational development of each pupil in relation to his ability, and their effectiveness should be judged by this criterion. Reports succeed insofar as they help each pupil realize his potential.

Informing the Pupil

Originally, one of the purposes of reports was to exhort pupils to greater effort in school. Fear of failure, it was argued, would produce greater achievement, while if the pupil knew he would be passed on automatically from grade to grade, he would work less.

It has been found that certain pupils will be challenged to work for higher marks. Although they may have little interest in the subject matter at first, it may develop through feelings of accomplishment and success. Yet there are dangers in working for marks. A pupil who conforms rigidly to a teacher's set standards for an *A* may sacrifice his creativity and imagination in the process. Another, lacking the mental ability to meet the standards set by his teacher, is not motivated to learn when he knows he cannot succeed despite his efforts. Yet if marks represent his improvement rather than status alone, he may have incentive to strive for them.

Final marks must be interpreted in terms of the quality of instruction and the general ability of the pupils in the class. In some schools where there may be a lack of talent among the pupils, it is possible for high marks to give a distorted picture of a pupil's achievement. The lower marks of some pupils in our better schools may depict more achievement than an *A* in schools inadequately staffed and equipped. A final mark of *C* in an honors class may represent greater achievement than an *A* in an average class.

The interpretation of marks, then, is very important. The value of the report increases as the pupil is helped to understand what it means. This implies that the teacher is prepared to defend its accuracy and show its significance. There are teachers who make it a practice to explain the meaning of marks and other data to pupils before the reports go home. This procedure also provides an opportunity to review the school's objectives with the pupils.

Informing Parents, School Personnel, and Employers

Parents must understand the school's objectives to advance cooperation between home and school; otherwise, there is likely to be conflict. Not until a parent can accept the educational objectives of the school is he in a position to support and supplement the educational program for his child; but he can neither accept nor support without understanding. A truly informative system of reporting is formulated in terms of these objectives and of his child's growth and progress toward them, and provides a basis for understanding and the intelligent cooperation of the parent with both teacher and child.

A composite evaluation of a pupil's achievement and growth should be available for his future teachers and the administration. The cumulative record is most helpful. Periodic reports should be filed therein, since they represent evaluations of much of the data. Whether or not the pupil remains in the same school system, his teachers will have information about his progress in previous grades.

The school administrator or guidance officer often must evaluate the competence and potentiality of the school's graduates. As more pupils continue their formal education, colleges and universities exercise stringent selection, and well-organized evaluations of college-bound pupils should be available for them.

Pupils who do not go to college generally seek employment. Because the tendency to practice social promotion has changed the meaning of a high school diploma, their prospective employers often request information about them. While competence in secretarial or machine-shop skills are important for certain types of jobs, employers also want people who can get along with others, assume responsibility, have leadership potential and an attitude of cooperation. Periodic reports over the years provide an indication of the future pattern of behavior that an employer might expect of an individual.

PROBLEMS

1. If we accept the premise that report cards and final marks exist to help each pupil develop according to his ability, how then can we justify the use of rigid standards of passing and failing?

2. If standardized test scores yield information comparable to secondary school marks, could we then abolish report cards and concentrate on thorough interpretation of the achievement test results in individual conferences with the parents and child? Explain your answer.

BASES FOR REPORTING

Objectives of the School

If evaluation is to be made in terms of all of the school's objectives, general and specific, then marking and reporting become very complex. In the first place, evaluation of some parts of a pupil's behavior cannot be as adequate as we would like, yet even so may be more valuable than a paper-and-pencil test indicating only what the pupil says he will do. If one of our objectives is to develop effective citizenship, statements such as "He votes in all elections for which he is eligible," and "He assumes responsibility in group work," give some direction and basis for evaluation. Secondly, it is impractical to sample enough behavior of every pupil to obtain an adequate evaluation. This is especially true for the secondary school, where a teacher meets many pupils every day. Third, to report on each one of a great number of behavioral patterns would give the false impression that valid judgments can be made in every instance. A fourth problem would arise in presenting such a report to parents, since it would be too long and complex to be interpreted easily; certainly the evaluation could not be given in a single number or letter.

So the teacher faces something of a dilemma. On one hand, he wants to base his marking and reporting on all pertinent educational objectives, general and specific. On the other, the list of these objectives is so long, and sometimes the evidence concerning them so difficult to obtain, that he faces an almost impossible task. To make his reporting task more manageable, he compromises, however reluctantly. Rather than try to report pupil progress in terms of all educational objectives each time a report is to be made, he may select a group of objectives, perhaps reporting on a different group on the next occasion. Or he may report on each pupil on each reporting occasion in terms of a group of basic objectives of special importance to the pupil and the school. Each of these may really be a combination of related specific objectives. But typically, however, grading is done more simply. Marks are awarded on what can be easily measured, namely, subject content. Too often the subject content is factual information, and skills such as problem solving, critical thinking, application, and so forth, are not emphasized in the report. Unfortunately even these marks reflect a teacher's bias in such factors as amount of work completed, neatness, and correctness of expression.

Growth and Achievement

Reports may depict growth or achievement, or both. These are distinct concepts. Growth means change or gain. To interpret it adequately, we must consider the individual, his ability, background experience, present environmental stimulation, and so on. Achievement means the pupil's present status—what he knows or can do now. Achievement is generally judged against norms or teacher's standards, and all too often is evaluated without respect to ability and prior experiences.

Differences between the two concepts can be described by use of diagrams. Figure 15.1 is a record of John's and Bill's growth and achievement in reading comprehension. The top line is a description of John's progress, the bottom line describes Bill's. Clearly there was a point in the life of each boy when his achievement in this basic skill was zero; this is represented on the far left of the two lines by the position labeled absolute zero. Proceeding to the right represents an increase in achievement. Let us assume that John and Bill have just entered the fifth grade. Each boy's achievement in reading comprehension at this particular time is represented by a point called prior achievement. Bill's prior achievement in reading comprehension exceeds John's considerably.

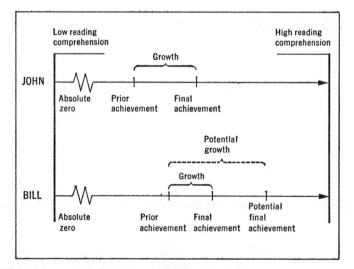

FIGURE 15.1. Diagram of Growth and Achievement in Reading Comprehension of Two Fifth-Grade Pupils.

If we examine the boys' achievement at the end of the academic year (final achievement), we find that Bill still surpasses John. Their growth in reading comprehension is represented by the difference between prior and final achievement. Both boys have grown in this skill, but John has made a tremendous spurt. Several interpretations are possible, depending on the other information we have about these pupils. Suppose that they have equal potential in reading. We might then conclude that Bill is an overachiever who could not be expected to make tremendous growth strides whereas John may be achieving according to his ability. It is more likely that John was retarded in the earlier grades and, through good teaching, was able to make great strides in the fifth grade. Bill, on the other hand, may or may not have shown adequate growth during the year. But suppose that Bill is a brighter boy than John. His actual growth is then inadequate; his potential growth may then be as great as that shown in Figure 15.1. Although his final achievement may be the highest in the class, it is still unsatisfactory in terms of what he could do.

We see from the above illustration that both growth and final achievement guide the teacher in evaluating pupil progress. However, it is questionable whether to assign marks on the basis of achievement gains rather than present status. First, gains are very unreliable because they include the errors of both the initial and final achievements. Second, if initial scores are obtained from instruments that are too easy, able pupils will have little opportunity to improve on the final assessment. Third, it is much more difficult to raise a high score even higher than to raise a low score. A gain of one-half standard deviation from a score below the mean may not be of the same substance as a gain of one-half standard deviation above the mean. The regression effect is operating.

The problem confronting teachers is psychological. How does one prevent a pupil who receives only low marks from getting discouraged? One way, of course, is to have him compete against himself; that is, to evaluate him on the basis of his gains. However, if this is not defensible, then we can give all pupils opportunities within the school and the class to excel in some way even though it is not through overall achievement status in the subject matter. The hard facts of life dictate that all pupils must learn eventually that present status rather than growth is what counts for the most part.

IN THE ELEMENTARY SCHOOL. During the elementary school years, the teacher is concerned with helping each individual achieve as much and as rapidly as possible. Studies in child development inform us that children mature at different rates; every child is different and has environmental problems peculiar to him that affect his learning. Thus, it is not always possible to predict which pupils will eventually lead the group in specific areas of achievement. The elementary school teacher is in a position to manipulate the school environment so that pupils are not thwarted and stunted in their growth before they reach a degree of maturity at which they can evaluate their own strengths and weaknesses realistically. Therefore, the teacher often emphasizes self-improvement—growth, in other words. Emphasis on growth stresses the child in relation to the subject matter to be learned. It can apply to all kinds of learning situations, academic and nonacademic.

IN THE SECONDARY SCHOOL. Even in the secondary school, evaluation based on final achievement alone does not tell the whole story of the pupil's development.

Achievement scores, for example, do not indicate whether he is at a particular level from lack of effort or talent. Neither does a single achievement score give an indication of whether there has been improvement or not. A teacher should consider pupil growth in evaluating his teaching. But in the secondary school, the pupil is looking forward to higher education and professional life, and it is imperative that his grades reflect achievement status. The standards that students must meet for the professions of medicine, law, and teaching, for example, exist as much to protect society as to select qualified students.

Standards and Ability to Learn

Whether to evaluate pupils in terms of standards or of achievement in relation to learning ability is a part of the growth-versus-achievement question. Standards of achievement are often thought of as the teacher's estimate of the level of achievement that a pupil must reach before he has done acceptable work. The use of such standards is sometimes defended in the following manner (Green, 1956, p. 72):

> When I pass a student in this course I am certifying to his next instructor that he has covered the material of the course, and that if he works reasonably hard he is capable of continuing with the next course in this field at least approximately at the level indicated by his letter grade. In the first place, I will not give a fraudulent certification. In the second place, it would be no kindness to your child to let him get into college or into a job only to find out that he is not prepared to do good work. Moreover, if I lower the standards, the result is a disservice to your children and your community, handicapping all future students by making colleges and universities reluctant to accept them or give them scholarships, and prospective employers mistrustful of them.

This issue may be, for all practical purposes, a "straw man." In many instances, standards are derived from the observed performances of the pupils themselves, which means that they are relative and not absolute measures of subject matter achievement (Ebel, 1972, p. 322).

But there are other clear-cut issues that at best are difficult to resolve. If the teacher does in fact employ norm-referenced grading (for example, grading "on the curve"), are certain pupils doomed always to receive low marks? Furthermore, if grading is done on a relative basis, are standards compromised? Flexible marking systems exist that can prevent the low-ability pupil with excellent achievement from not receiving an *A*, or the high-ability pupil with equally high achievement from not receiving an *A* just because he is in an honors class (see p. 376). This is not a flawless solution to our first question, but it does a better job of solving the problem than does marking on what are called "standards" with inevitable maneuvering of marks that results in order to produce some kind of acceptable grade distribution. Those who would eliminate grades, however, suggest that this is one of the criticisms that they have of grades. They would use another kind of reporting system (see criterion-referenced marking, p. 394).

The second question is more easily answered. There is no evidence that the quality of learning need suffer with relative marking. The concern should be focused rather on improved instruction and providing experiences for all pupils with varied individual differences. This may require regrouping into more homogeneous classes and, of course, differential instruction within the classroom.

Specific Evidence of Pupil Progress

The specific evidence needed for accurate assessment and reporting of a pupil's progress must come from the many measuring instruments and techniques discussed in detail in other chapters. Certainly data from both teacher-constructed and standardized paper-and-pencil tests, ranking and rating scales, and check lists, must be used. Data from observation of class participation and pupil success in projects and reports are helpful as well.

The key to success is the use of a wide variety of evidence. In some ways paper-and-pencil achievement tests, particularly standardized ones, provide the most impressive looking data about pupil achievement. But these have a verbal or mathematical emphasis only. In contrast, sample products like an essay written by the pupil are more difficult to interpret, yet serve well as a means of explaining to him and his parents the degree of his achievement. Furthermore, reports of class participation often reflect pupil attitudes and even interpersonal relationships. Use of all of the foregoing will strengthen the marking and reporting effort.

PROBLEM

3. If there are to be multiple standards of achievement in the interests of healthful psychological development on the part of the pupil, is there a need to revise the high school diploma system as it now exists in many schools? Why?

METHODS OF MARKING AND REPORTING

Typical procedures for marking and reporting are letter-number systems, check lists, correspondence with parents, and teacher-parent conferences. It is important that these methods be critically evaluated in terms of purposes, bases, and the sources of information available for reporting. Whatever system is used must be established as the best possible under existing circumstances.

Letter-Number Systems

The letter-number system has been and remains a popular method of reporting pupil progress. In essence, it is an effort to summarize a variety of information about such characteristics of a pupil as his growth, final achievement, effort, ability, and general deportment. The summary is given in the form of a letter, usually A through E or F, or a number, usually 100 through 0, reported for each subject matter area each report period.

There are two reasons why these marks are difficult to assign. First, the teacher cannot be certain whether appropriate credit is being given to growth and to final achievement for each educational objective considered. Second, since the mark represents pupil progress in terms of a combination of objectives, the teacher is uncertain whether each objective within the combination is being appropriately weighted.

MULTIPLE MARKING SYSTEMS. An interesting variation of the traditional letter-number system is the use of two or more marks for each subject matter area. One may represent the pupil's final achievement in relation to the teacher's standards. Another is often an evaluation of effort put forth by the pupil; in some school systems it represents pupil growth in the area of achievement listed. A three-point letter system is sometimes used for recording the pupil's effort: *H* if the pupil exceeds what is expected of him, *S* if his level of work corresponds approximately to his level of ability, and *U* if he is capable of better work. Pupils evaluated according to this system might receive marks such as *A/S* or *91/S*, each indicating high final achievement and normal effort. Marks such as *C/H* or *83/H* mean that the pupil is average in terms of final achievement, and that his effort is superior.

Clearly the success of multiple marking systems depends on a teacher's ability to evaluate final achievement and effort by a letter or number. Some teachers find evaluation of effort particularly troublesome since satisfactory judgment requires more accurate evaluation techniques than are available. If a second mark represents growth rather than effort, an extensive pretesting program must be set up to establish achievement levels before instruction begins and then careful consideration must be given to the problems of interpreting gains.

In actual practice, Halliwell and Robitaille (1963) found a halo effect on assigning good marks to bright students on their relative achievement as well as on subjective factors such as effort. Teachers tended to equate effort with achievement disregarding individual differences of intelligence.

These are central issues. In theory, multiple marking systems should be expected to give a clearer picture of a pupil's progress than a single mark. However, multiple reporting often presents an oversimplified picture of the teacher's evaluation. Each subject matter area encompasses many educational objectives. It is difficult, at best, to obtain enough evidence to give one valid mark. When the number of marks is increased, the problem is compounded.

RELATIVE VS. ABSOLUTE STANDARDS FOR MARKING. Because there is no absolute zero for achievement test scores, it is impossible to assign marks on an absolute scale or standard. If a pupil responds correctly to all items on a test, it does not necessarily mean that he knows one-hundred percent of what is to be learned in the subject, and a mark of fifty percent does not mean that he has learned half of the subject matter. Test items are a sampling of what is learned in the subject. Furthermore, whether a pupil receives credit for having mastered a particular concept depends on how understanding of it is measured by a particular test item. Even a question about a difficult concept may be answered correctly by almost all pupils if the question requires only superficial understanding. In other words, the difficulty of an item often depends as much on how a concept is measured as what is measured.

Actually, teachers who convert raw scores or percentages directly into final marks usually adjust them near the end of the year by giving bonus points, by constructing an easy or difficult test as the situation may warrant, or some such procedure, until the raw scores or percentages will convert to a distribution of final marks that was largely predetermined. This distribution involves an arbitrary decision. It may be determined by school policy, the ability and vocational plans of the pupils, gaps in the distribution of composite scores, and so forth. In a high ability class, for example, a teacher might give thirty percent As, forty percent Bs, twenty percent Cs, and ten percent Ds. Rarely are there as many Fs as there are As; the median final mark in many classes is often B rather than C.

Regardless of the marking system adopted, it is important that the marks present a clear message to pupils, parents, employers, and college admission officers. The meaning of marks is much clearer when school personnel agree on the criteria for choosing the percentage of pupils in a given class who will be assigned a particular mark.

To illustrate how final marks may be assigned unfairly, imagine three English classes taught by different teachers. Classes 1 and 2 are made up of college-bound pupils of comparable ability, Class 3 of pupils of lesser ability. The teacher of Class 1 assigns sixty percent As and Bs. The teacher of Class 2, who is less liberal, gives only forty percent As and Bs. Consequently a pupil whose English achievement is typical of college-bound pupils would probably receive a B if he were in Class 1, a C if in Class 2, and an A if he were a member of Class 3, in which he would probably be one of the best pupils.

One way of rectifying this situation is to obtain some common and relevant measure by which the three English classes could be compared. Scores from a scholastic aptitude test or from standardized or teacher-constructed English achievement tests with acceptable degrees of content validity might be used. Suppose it is decided that fifteen percent of the pupils will receive As. Then the cutoff score, above which only fifteen percent of the pupils score on the common measure, would be determined. The number of pupils in a particular class who surpass this cutoff score provides the approximate number of As to be given in that class. The same is true of the percentages of Bs, Cs, and so on. Note that the final mark a particular student receives depends on his total performance in his class, not on his scholastic aptitude score. The scholastic aptitude tests serve here to determine percentages of letter grades assigned, not the pupils to whom they will be assigned. Some pupils will receive higher final achievement marks than their fellows who scored higher on the scholastic aptitude test.

Ebel (1972, pp. 338–342) reports a method of marking with a simplified procedure designed to promote uniformity in marking. Consideration is given to scholastic aptitude and/or prior achievement of the class to which a pupil belongs. Ebel believes that more high marks should be assigned to a class with a higher mean scholastic aptitude score or total grade-point average. The procedure is defended on the basis of the relationship between aptitude and prior achievement with future achievement.

In the procedure, a five-unit letter system is used with each letter encompassing the same interval on the score scale. This replaces percentage assignment of marks that considers only ranks and disregards score differences. It also provides an alternative that differentiates among marking levels by looking for "natural breaks" in the distribution.

The result is that each letter mark covers the same range of achievement on the scale. There will be more C pupils, but the C will encompass the same "distance" on the scale as an A, a B, or an F. Although for a given class there will be no fixed percent of each mark assigned, over a period of time final marks given to a number of diverse classes will tend to conform to the normal distribution. The arithmetic steps to be followed to determine the cutting point for each letter mark for each class are not difficult (see Ebel, 1972, pp. 338–342).

Michael (1960) reports another system to prevent able pupils from being penalized in terms of final marks because of ability grouping. He describes how, in a subject such as English, pupils are usually grouped into three to five categories. There may be a top section designed to prepare pupils for advanced placement. A number of classes either homogeneously or heterogeneously grouped are the designated standard college preparatory sections. Then there may be several low ability classes of pupils who in general do not intend to go to college.

In Michael's system, when a school reports letter marks, it is common to assign a certain number of points to a letter: A-5 pts; B-4 pts; C-3 pts; D-2 pts. A multiplying factor that varies according to the ability category is applied to each pupil's mark. Suppose there are three categories. The pupil in the highest group will have his A multiplied by 6; an A received in the middle group will be multiplied by 5; As in the low section are multiplied by 4. The plan has the effect of raising marks in the top section by one letter grade while lowering those in the bottom section by one letter grade.

Michael emphasizes that the point system affects only class rank. It does not appear on the report card. However, because rank is one important criterion determining college admission, pupils in the higher groups are compensated for possible lower marks than pupils receive in lower ability groups.

WEIGHTING DATA. One of the problems the teacher encounters in giving final marks is weighting the data gathered from such various sources as informal quizzes, final examinations, and reports to obtain a valid composite score for ranking his pupils. There is no consensus on the emphasis each of these types of data should receive in the total evaluation. Some teachers maintain that a final examination should count far more than the quizzes and other tests given during the course. They point out that since the final examination measures long-term retention, and the ability to organize and deal with large units of subject matter, this score should logically be weighted more heavily than others. Other teachers are quick to retort that it is unfair to the pupil to determine such a large proportion of his final evaluation from his performance at a specified time within an interval of several hours at most. They also object to the limitations of most final examinations that preclude measurement in terms of many important educational objectives.

The last point is vital. The weighting of various data must be determined in terms of the educational objectives of the specific grade level or class. Those data that reflect pupil progress in terms of the most important objectives must be given greater

TABLE 15.1.   Variability of Scores on Tests and Assignments.

Source of points	Nominal weight	Range	Standard deviation
Class reports	1	26	5.1
Daily assignments	1	46	8.6
Quizzes and unit tests	1	110	20.8
Final examination	2	90	16.4

weight when computing a composite mark than those relating to less important objectives. This is equally true whether the data come from a final examination or from any other measuring instrument.

There is a precaution that must be taken in determining a composite mark no matter what weightings are chosen. Suppose we wish to base one-fifth of the final mark for a course on class reports, one-fifth on daily assignments, one-fifth on quizzes and unit tests, and two-fifths on the final examination. Inspection of the ranges and standard deviations of these measures in the preceding table reveals a definite lack of uniformity. If we hope to maintain the weighting scheme originally chosen, we must take into consideration these differences in variability. A failure to do this will result in inequities.

To illustrate this point, let us suppose that Mary made a total of fifty-five points for class reports, the highest number of points for this category. However, on quizzes and unit tests her score was the lowest, thirty points. For daily assignments and the final examination she earned sixty-one and ninety-one, respectively. Frank, on the other hand, did the poorest of anyone in the group on class reports; his score was twenty-nine. On the quizzes and unit tests he had a high score of one hundred forty. It happens that he also made the same scores as Mary on daily assignments and the final exam, namely sixty-one and ninety-one. (See Table 15.1.)

If we weight Mary's and Frank's scores for each source and add them to obtain a composite, we have Table 15.2.

Note that although class reports, quizzes, and unit tests are to have the same weight, Mary is penalized because of the lesser variability of scores of class reports when compared with that of quizzes and unit tests. In other words, class-report scores with a relatively low standard deviation ($\sigma = 5.1$) have less influence than scores of quizzes and unit tests ($\sigma = 20.8$) in determining the class rankings on the composite score.

TABLE 15.2.   Weighting of Pupils' Scores without Consideration of Score Variability.

	Mary	Frank
Reports	55 × 1 = 55	29 × 1 = 29
Assignments	61 × 1 = 61	61 × 1 = 61
Quizzes	30 × 1 = 30	140 × 1 = 140
Final exam.	91 × 2 = 182	91 × 2 = 182
Total points	328	412

A procedure for avoiding errors like the one above would be to convert the raw scores into standard scores so that the variability of the scores for each category would be the same. When the scores for each category are converted into stanines the following formula to compute the composite is appropriate:

$$C = \frac{\Sigma WS}{\Sigma W},$$

where

C = composite average;
Σ = the sum;
W = weight for a particular category;
S = standard score for that category for each pupil.

To illustrate the use of the formula let us assume that Mary received stanine scores of 9, 5, 1, and 7 for class reports, daily assignments, quizzes, and unit tests, and the final examination respectively. Frank's stanine scores were 1, 5, 9, and 7. The composite averages would be:

Mary

$$C = \frac{(1 \times 9) + (1 \times 5) + (1 \times 1) + (2 \times 7)}{1 + 1 + 1 + 2} = \frac{29}{5} = 5.8;$$

Frank

$$C = \frac{(1 \times 1) + (1 \times 5) + (1 \times 9) + (2 \times 7)}{1 + 1 + 1 + 2} = \frac{29}{5} = 5.8.$$

Although these composite averages are not stanines, they do provide means for the ranking of pupils that reflects the desired weightings of the scores for the several categories. On the basis of this distribution, the teacher may assign final marks.

PASS/FAIL MARKING. The surge of reaction against grading with letter or numerical marks on a scale of five or more points has prompted a number of colleges and universities to provide the option of *Pass/Fail* marking for at least some of the courses in the curriculum. In various modified forms, this two-point procedure has also been used in secondary schools. The most common justification for the *P/F* plan is the provision it offers for pupils to take courses which they may omit from their schedules for fear of failure. Other reasons supporting the plan are that it reduces pupil anxiety, provides for his own control of study time, and places emphasis on learning rather than "grade getting."

Studies of the *P/F* plan reveal that pupils report that they feel less anxious in *P/F* courses and they reduce study time in those courses in order to concentrate on others. There is also reason to believe that they do not perform as well in *P/F* courses as in other courses.

The weakness of *P/F* marking is that it does not promote learning and it does not provide the pupil with an adequate record of his achievement. It is questionable whether motivation to learn would be equalized in a system where all courses were graded on a *P/F* basis. It is possible, then, that the level of learning in all courses would deteriorate. This question can only be answered if and when *P/F* marking is used more extensively.

GRADE CONTRACTS. Contracts are agreements between a teacher and each of his pupils, spelled out in writing, as to what is to be achieved over a period of time for a particular grade. Everyone does the work required to earn a *D* for the course. A *C* grade demands additional accomplishments. To earn a *B* the pupil must first complete the requirements for the *D* and *C* marks. An *A* can be earned by doing *D, C,* and *B* contracts and then completing the additional *A* requirements.

The principles underlying the idea are as follows (Frymier, 1965, pp. 252–264):

1. *Clarification of expectations and limitations.*
2. *Emphasis on success and teaching.*
3. *Use of the pupil's aspiration levels.*
4. *Provision for democracy in action.*

The contract idea has some of the characteristics of criterion-referenced marking (see page 394) in that there is at least an attempt to specify achievement, albeit in a rather global fashion. Instead of representing relative standing, the marks of *A, B, C,* and *D* represent specified achievement. There should be no failures since the pupil continues to work until he at least has done satisfactory *D* work.

RELIABILITY AND VALIDITY. The reliability of scores from paper-and-pencil tests is sometimes not as great as we wish it to be. Reliability of data from a teacher's observations of a pupil's procedures and his personal-social adjustment is usually even lower. Yet both are used to determine final marks. Consequently, the reliability of final marks is often less than desired.

Such evidence as is available suggests that the usual reliability coefficients of semester marks may be as high as 0.70 to 0.90. This means that in many, if not all, cases it is difficult to defend the practice of interpreting such differences as those between an *83* and an *84* or a *91* and a *92*. For that matter, the difference between a *C+* and a *B−* may be due purely to chance. This evidence raises the question of the number of divisions that should be used in a marking system. The more categories one makes, such as *90, 91,* and *92,* the more errors in placement of pupils is likely. The fewer the categories, such as *Pass/Fail,* the smaller the number of pupils who will be given an incorrect mark, but the more serious the error. These facts must be balanced with concern for the amount of information a mark reveals; *S* and *U* reveal less than *90, 91,* and *92*.

Evidence of the validity of final marks is also limited. They seem to be quite valid as a measure of mastery of subject matter by the pupil, the correlation coefficient estimated to be 0.70 or possibly higher. This estimate was arrived at by summarizing the results of a number of studies concerning the correlation between the final marks in question and (1) other marks in the same subject matter area, (2) test scores from appropriate standardized tests, and (3) the pupils' estimates of the marks they deserved.

The validity of final marks has been investigated with respect to a number of different criteria, such as college entrance examination scores, college marks, economic success, and success on the job. The correlation coefficients vary a great deal. The most widely investigated use of secondary school final marks is that of predicting academic success in college. The correlation coefficients are often as high as 0.50 and seldom higher than 0.70. It has been repeatedly shown that final marks in secondary school are one of the best means of predicting college success, whether used alone or as part of a prediction battery.

INTERPRETATION. The typical letter or number system of marking is based primarily on final achievement. Confusion results when a teacher also attempts to include an evaluation of effort and other personality traits in this single mark. Interpretation becomes almost impossible. There is no way to determine whether a low mark is the result of lack of achievement or effort. Even when a single letter mark is used to report final achievement alone, it is very difficult to make a valid interpretation. What does a B in general science mean? Does it show that the pupil did A work in quizzes, C work in laboratory, B work in class participation? Or more important still, does it mean that the pupil achieved at an A level with respect to one educational objective, a B level with respect to another, and a C level with a third? We have no way of knowing. Therefore when letter or numerical marks are used, there must be additional data in the report that provide diagnostic information.

The mark is also influenced by other factors, one of which is the nature of the pupil population. Too often pupils who have been graduated magna cum laude from their high schools find to their dismay when they face competition in a university that they do not have exceptional ability. Another factor is the peculiarity of the individual teacher who does the marking. Some teachers give consistently high marks, while others pride themselves in never being so easy as to give an A or a 95. A pupil may find it very difficult to identify a criterion by which he can judge the value of his marks.

Marks as they are now generally assigned are far from being as meaningful as people think. They are being overinterpreted; they reveal far less about the pupil than is commonly supposed, and their meaning is often ambiguous. Hence it is imperative that standardized test scores be used to supplement final marks whenever possible. It is particularly important for secondary school pupils to have this objective basis for comparing their own capacity and achievements with a broader sample of pupils, giving them a better opportunity to interpret their potentialities for future academic work.

TYPES OF REPORT CARDS. The report cards used to record the assigned marks can take many different forms. Commonly they provide for the recording of marks for all marking periods during the school year. Parents or guardians are requested to sign the card before it is returned at the end of each marking period.

Reports of academic achievement are often accompanied by a check list of personality traits and attitudes. The teacher may generally place a check in any one of several categories, such as "unsatisfactory," "satisfactory," or "improving." If these check lists are carefully worded, the instrument can save the teacher time and effort.

Reporting must not become a stereotype procedure. In the past, many pupils have been checked "satisfactory" in every characteristic from kindergarten through the sixth grade. The "halo effect" seems to keep some teachers from making a realistic evaluation of the pupil. This can be eliminated if the teacher bases his report on adequate data, carefully compiled and critically interpreted. Space left on the check list form for comments on pupils' problems will help individualize the method.

At the secondary level, check lists are usually used to supplement numerical or letter marks, both providing information not discernible from the mark alone, and helping to clarify the mark itself. In elementary school, check lists are often the only report given. The example shown in Figure 15.2 represents the type that can be used for this purpose. Observe that all main aspects of the academic program are included, and also health, music, art, and personal development. The common three-point letter system is used to represent the teacher's judgment of the pupil's success. In this case, the letters are O for outstanding, S for satisfactory, and N for not satisfactory. Such a check list can give a great deal of information about the pupil's school life.

REPORT CARD FORM

What the letters mean:

O—Outstanding for your child; commendation for special effort and achievement.

S—Satisfactory for your child; achievement consistent with ability.

N—Not Satisfactory for your child; improvement needed.

Note: Any further information in regard to the standing of your child may be secured in personal conference.

Growth in Skills	1st Report	2nd Report	3rd Report
Reading			
Understands what he reads			
Works to develop independent reading habits			
Writing			
Expresses himself well			
Uses basic writing skills			
Writes legibly			
Spells correctly			
Uses good sentence structure			
Learns to use new words			
Arithmetic			
Knows arithmetic facts			
Understands arithmetic processes (addition, subtraction, multiplication, division)			
Applies skill in solving problems			
Social studies			
History, geography, civics, government, development of American ideals			
Works to develop a knowledge and understanding of home, community, state, country, world			
Works to develop skill in the use of materials (newspapers, maps, encyclopedias, etc.)			
Science			
Works to develop keen observation			
Is growing in scientific knowledge			
Listening			
Understands what he hears and responds wisely			

Health
Works to develop good health habits _____   _____ _____ _____
Helps to maintain safety _____   _____ _____ _____
Plays and enjoys games _____   _____ _____ _____
Works to develop skill in physical education   _____ _____ _____

Music
Takes part in group singing _____   _____ _____ _____
Responds to rhythm _____   _____ _____ _____
Works to develop basic music skills_____   _____ _____ _____

Art
Expresses ideas creatively _____   _____ _____ _____
Works to develop a variety of skills _____   _____ _____ _____

Personal development
Is developing a variety of interests _____   _____ _____ _____
Is courteous and considerate _____   _____ _____ _____
Respects the rights and property of others   _____ _____ _____
Shares outside experience, skills and mate-
    rials with others _____   _____ _____ _____
Accepts responsibility _____   _____ _____ _____
Works to the best of his ability _____   _____ _____ _____

FIGURE 15.2. Modified Form of Check List.
From Heffernan and Marshall, 1955, pp. 75–76; reproduced by permission
of the California State Department of Education.

A number of schools, wishing to conserve time, are employing computers for reporting marks and organizing and analyzing data about them. In one school system (Crisler and Wogaman, 1963) each school's master class schedule and individual pupil programs are converted into punched cards. There is a deck of cards for each class with one mark-sense card for each pupil (see Figure 15.3). All the decks are arranged alphabetically by teacher name and each teacher's decks by period sequences.

At the time of reporting, a teacher receives a deck of mark-sense cards for each of his classes. He marks these in the space representing the final mark earned by each pupil. One to four comments, such as "excellent," "satisfactory," etc., from a list of nine on each card are also marked.

The cards are then returned to the processing center where the teacher's marks are printed on the report card (see Figure 15.4). Four copies of this report are available. The original is given to the pupil to take home and the other three copies are for office use. The reports are cumulative during a semester; that is, the pupil's previous marks also appear on successive reports. Parents do not sign these cards and pupils do not return them.

This system of reporting provides readily available data about marks to the school staff. The number of times each pupil received each letter mark and each comment is totaled along with his average mark. Data on teachers include the number of times they made a comment such as "excellent," or "inattentive." The average mark of each teacher's class and the average for all his classes are tabulated. Marks are also available for each class grouped by subject matter area, as are the comments marked, the percentage of each mark given, and the average mark for the class.

With information showing how teachers mark, this school has the basis to set up

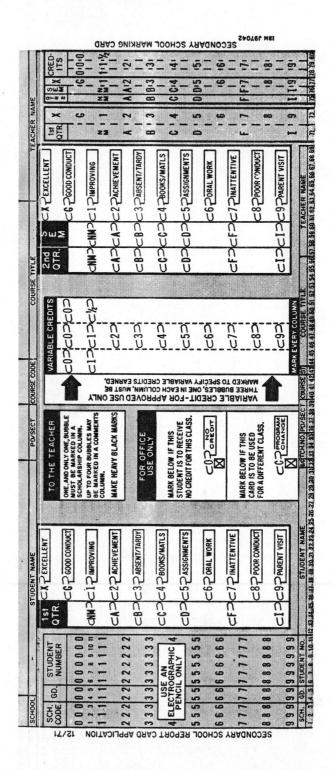

Figure 15.3. Pupil's Mark-Sense Card.
Reproduced by permission of the Richmond (California) Schools.

RICHMOND UNIFIED SCHOOL DISTRICT

REPORT CARD

School Name	School Term	Counselor	Gd.	Adv.	Student Name

Per./Sect.	COURSE	MARKS 1	MARKS 2	Sem.	Comments	TEACHER	Credits

EXPLANATION OF MARKS

A — Outstanding achievement
B — Good achievement
C — Satisfactory achievement
D — Minimum achievement
F — Failure due to unsatisfactory achievement
I — Incomplete due to justifiable absence

EXPLANATION OF COMMENTS

X — Excellent progress
G — Good attitude/conduct
1 — Showing some improvement
2 — Achievement is not up to apparent ability
3 — Absences/tardiness affecting school work
4 — Books/materials are not brought to class
5 — Assignments are incomplete or unsatisfactory
6 — Oral participation needed
7 — Inattentive/ wastes time/ does not follow directions
8 — Conduct in class is not satisfactory
9 — Please contact teacher through counselor

Normal credits for a semester are 30.   You may keep this card for your records.

R |

Figure 15.4. Report Card.
Reproduced by permission of the Richmond (California) Schools.

guidelines for assigning marks and give the teacher feedback on his own marks and also those of his colleagues. There is an excellent opportunity to make marks more meaningful to pupils and their parents.

USE OF REPORT CARDS. The two most widely used methods for reporting pupil progress to parents are teacher-parent conferences and a classified scale of letters, that is, *A, B, C,* etc. (National Education Association, 1971). More elementary teachers use the conference, while the letter classification is employed to a greater extent in the secondary school. The majority of the teachers feel that the conference is more effective in the elementary school. Opinion seems to be divided among secondary school teachers among a classified scale of letters, teacher-parent conference, and a *Pass/Fail* system. A number of teachers use more than one method of reporting to parents. For example, sometimes reports are accompanied by a check list.

PROBLEM

4. What difficulties might parents face in interpreting information from a check list? How can these be minimized?

Correspondence with Parents

Communications sent to parents may range from a little notation on a report card to a long letter discussing many aspects of their child's school experiences and growth. It is possible to emphasize both pupil development and subject matter achievement. With an adequate cumulative record, the teacher has evidence to interpret patterns of development. He may discuss problems and emphasize factors pertinent to the individual pupil. If some phases of his work would profit from help at home, this can be explained to the parents. Parental comments should be requested, to provide for two-way communication. The interchange of information may lead to some fruitful conferences between teachers and parents.

One of the serious weaknesses of letters to parents is that they tend to be generalized and stereotyped, all too often appearing to have been run off an assembly line, with little variation in wording to relate to a particular pupil. For instance, the following letter is far less helpful to the parent than it might have been:

> *Mary is an exceptionally likeable child. In general her progress has been quite satisfactory in all phases of her school work. She seems to be interested in all activities and is purposeful in the tasks she undertakes. Her personal-social adjustment is proceeding at a very normal rate.*

What has the parent learned? Do Mary's peers accept her, or is she just liked by the teacher? Perhaps the teacher likes her because she is retiring and does not bother anyone. Certainly there must be some strength or weakness in her academic progress that could be emphasized. Does she question what she reads or is she inclined to accept it without critical evaluation? Do her reports show imagination or does she tend to string together some of the words she has read in the encyclopedia? What does the teacher mean by "purposeful?" What is "normal" personal-social adjustment?

Often the reason for inadequate reporting can be traced to vaguely stated objectives. Objectives like the following do not ensure that the teacher understands the criterion behavior. There is no suggestion of how he is to determine whether an objective has been achieved (see Chapter 2).

To develop good citizenship.
To improve health habits.
To understand the scientific method.

Even with sharpened objectives, communicating with parents by letter is not easy. In one community, a parent received among other comments the statement "Your child is nervous." He reacted at once with concern about the youngster's mental health, a notion the startled teacher had not meant to convey at all. Letters may annoy the parent or fail to express what the teacher means. The following note concerning a fifth-grade pupil is not helpful in cementing effective relations between home and school:

Dear Mr. and Mrs. Knowles:
John has been a real problem in our class this year. Unlike most of the children in the group, he doesn't enjoy working with others. He is really a lone wolf. Instead of cooperating, he seems to find satisfaction in disturbing others, and he. . . .

This could be changed to a much more effective report for securing parental cooperation. For example:

Dear Mr. and Mrs. Knowles:
We find that it is difficult to summarize in a single mark the things we would like to share with you about John's development this year. In addition to achievement in academic skills, there are many other aspects of growth that we feel are important.
John can be depended upon to see a task through to completion. In preparation for a recent play, he volunteered to get a number of props and he had them for us on time. When he offered to interview several city officials about our town's history, he brought back information that was exceptionally well organized and interesting. Even in activities that require considerable effort, John will finish the task. I recall a particularly long assignment in fractions with which he had some difficulty. He worked longer than he usually has to, but the paper he handed in was well done.
John seems to have no serious trouble in mastering the basic skills. He reads with understanding and he has learned how to make effective use of source materials for research reports. He is a good speller and has missed no words on our weekly spelling tests. In class discussions, he expresses himself well and reflects a background of reading and travel.
We have been trying to help John this year in associations with his classmates. He tends to prefer working by himself rather than with others. At times he is quite aggressive in a group and finds it difficult to cooperate with his classmates on a

project. We feel, however, that he has made considerable progress in this respect. Of late he has commented favorably on the good ideas of his group members. He was also chosen as chairman of the entertainment committee for the last day of school.

John tells us that most of the children in his neighborhood are younger than he. It might be helpful if John had some opportunities this summer to play with children of his own age. This would enable him to enter into the "give-and-take" that is so important for his continued development.

I have enjoyed working with John this year. We anticipate that he will have a good relationship with his sixth-grade teacher and class group.

Sincerely,

Because poorly written letters may cause serious troubles, many principals supervise this type of reporting closely. Some schools have provided such suggestions as the following:

SUGGESTIONS FOR WRITING LETTERS TO PARENTS*

I. Begin the letter with encouraging news.

II. Close with an attitude of optimism.

III. Solicit the parents' cooperation in solving the problems, if any exist.

IV. Speak of the child's growth—social, physical, and academic.

    A. Social (Citizenship traits)

        1. Desirable traits: attention, attitude toward school, care of property, cooperation, honesty, effort, fair play, neatness, truthfulness, obedience, promptness, reliability, self-control, self-reliance, concentration, courtesy and consideration, thrift, patience, appreciation, kindness, sympathy, orderliness, interest in associates, discrimination, politeness, respect for the rights of others.

        2. Undesirable traits: selfishness, wastefulness, untruthfulness, dishonesty, spitefulness, slow to respond, impudence, carelessness, untidiness, rudeness, noisiness, insolence, cheating, inattention, lack of self-reliance, discourtesy, tattling, snobbishness, conceit, impatience, stealing.

    B. Physical (Health conditions): posture, weight, vitality, physical handicaps, cleanliness (personal), muscular co-ordination, nervousness, emotional traits.

    C. Academic

        1. Interests: (a) in school activities; (b) in extra-school activities.

        2. Methods of work: (a) methods of attack; (b) purposing; (c) planning; (d) executing; (e) judging; (f) consistency in finishing work.

        3. Achievements: (a) growth in knowledge, appreciation, techniques; (b) subjects in which the child is making progress and those in which he is not making progress; (c) relationship of his accepted standards to his capacities.

V. Compare the child's efforts with his own previous efforts and not with those of others.

VI. Speak of his achievements in terms of his ability to do school work.

VII. Remember it is our professional duty to know the reason why if the child is not making what, for him, is normal progress. (Some possible reasons for lack of progress—late entry; absence; lack of application; health defects, such as hearing, sight, undernourishment.)

* Reproduced by permission of the Santa Monica City (California) Schools.

VIII. Teacher's advice to parents in matters pertaining to health in which the home is a vital factor; such as diet, rest, clothing, exercise, etc.

IX. Please remember that every letter is a professional diagnosis, and as such is as sacred as any diagnosis ever made by any physician.

Obviously it requires a great deal of time to compose a thoughtful and helpful letter and the teacher is faced with an enormous task if he must report on thirty or forty pupils. Some elementary schools have abandoned reporting by letter for just this reason. It is impractical in most secondary school situations.

The problem can be eased if reports are sent out in staggered lots rather than on all pupils at once. The number of letters for each pupil can be limited. It is better to have one good letter than three poor ones, and to use other methods for other reporting periods. Perhaps some pupils will benefit more than others by frequent letter reports, and the load can thereby be reduced.

Time spent on reporting is never lost and often produces rich dividends in parental cooperation. If the report concerns a problem child, the energy saving from better relations may be very rewarding. Too often teachers become so involved in unimportant details that they overlook more fruitful approaches.

PROBLEM

5. What is the most serious limitation in reporting both positive and negative pupil behavior by means of a letter? If a school system requires this type of evaluative procedure, what steps can be taken to avoid poor public relations?

Teacher-Parent Conferences

The conference method of reporting is most generally used in the elementary school, although for special situations it should be more widely employed at the secondary level. It has potential for providing more information and better understanding between home and school, for misunderstanding can be eliminated far more readily when either conferee is able to raise questions than when communication is by letter. Certainly there are optimum conditions for conferences. They should not be called only when a special problem arises—rapport can hardly be at its best if this is the only basis for meeting. They should be planned periodically to serve as a regular report on the child's progress.

Sufficient time must be allowed—a minimum of thirty minutes. Attempting to rush through one interview to be prompt for the next is unfair to parent and teacher. Conferences are just as much a part of a good instructional program as teaching the multiplication table, and the teacher should be given time to prepare and hold them during his working schedule. Some schools dismiss classes for half-day periods; others provide substitutes to relieve the teacher of classroom responsibilities. Because conferences involve a great deal of time, some schools arrange only one per pupil during the school year, using other methods for the remaining report periods.

CONFERENCE PREPARATION. Preparation is basic to an effective conference. Some school systems orient their teachers in the conference technique by distributing bulletins describing the conference purpose, policy, records to be kept, time and preparation. These typically contain numerous illustrations suggesting ideas for preparation. The following are examples: *

> *Bobby Bates, in second grade, an only child, is 7 years, 6 months. He is sturdy and well-developed physically, energetic and active. He seems to have superior mental ability, reads very well and possesses distinct creative language ability. He loves music and the arts, expressing himself creatively and freely. He is doing very satisfactory number work. Bobby has never been able to get along in a group—he exhibits a quarrelsome and domineering attitude and a tendency to be very aggressive with his peers. He also evidences a negative and often openly resistant attitude toward adults. His parents need to give him more experience in children's groups, and gradually add responsibility for certain home tasks. They have a "perfectionist" attitude, and want him to excel.*

Show Mrs. Bates puppet stage (point out Bobby's ideas)
Refer to room-mothers' meeting
Growth in skills
  Reading (books, reading records)
  Language arts (sample stories—dictionary—broad writing vocabulary)
  Doing two-column addition, gaining mastery of facts
  Attendance records
  Help in broadening interests
Group adjustments
  Home interests and attitudes
  Seems resistant to suggestion (examples)
  Sometimes domineering—aggressive (examples), makes group acceptance difficult—good ideas
  Plans for helping Bobby—home—school (boys' groups? hobbies? help to share his ability)
Individual work habits
  Perfectionist
  Sharing and helping others is difficult (examples—games, books, Monday play)
  How can we help him accept and profit by occasional failures?
  Parents' support and encouragement (suggestions)

> *James, age 12-8, entering junior high school, has reached sixth grade with normal physical and social growth and development. His academic achievement ranges from a year to a year and one-half beyond normal sixth grade as per the fall testing scores.*

Safety Patrol work—fine job
Review academic progress Kgn through 6
Indicate seventh-grade adjustment problems
Emphasize adequate social growth for age
Successful six years of growth
Meeting of sixth-grade parents and junior high school guidance teachers on May 20.

---

* Reproduced by permission of the Schenectady (New York) Public Schools.

Some schools have organized workshops and various kinds of training sessions for their teachers. Role playing, in which teachers assume the roles of both parent and teacher, is helpful. Writing a script of a hypothetical conference and inviting criticism from colleagues develops insight into conference skill. Often bulletins are issued outlining suggestions including "do's and don'ts." They include such helpful materials as the following (Weckler, 1955, pp. 120–121):

1. *A teacher's guide sheet for each child, with appropriate headings, to be filled in prior to the conference.*
2. *Lists of characteristics of boys and girls at different age levels. Such lists are most helpful if these characteristics are described in terms of specific behaviors. They help teachers to identify possible problems in their early stages and to find strengths in pupils that might otherwise be overlooked.*
3. *An outline of the school program to help parents understand the goals of the school and the ways in which the school works to attain these goals.*
4. *A reminder sheet of effective and ineffective conference techniques.*
5. *A form to report what actually took place at the conference. Ample space is provided for the contributions made by parents. One copy of this report is often given to the parents, the other is retained in the cumulative folder.*

It is helpful to foresee some of the questions parents may ask in a conference. A list of such inquiries and suggested answers is usually included in the conference bulletins for teachers. The following are typical:

Why can't my youngster sound a strange word? He's in the third grade now.

Answer: This is what he can do. He can recognize beginning consonant sounds. He is beginning to be able to sound consonant combinations. I am working with him toward . . . (an opportunity here to present a phonetic program grades one through six). It takes some children longer to reach various stages.

My older boy's first year in junior high school leads me to believe that he wasn't ready for the seventh grade. Do you send children to junior high school who aren't ready for seventh grade?

Answer: It is the policy of this school system to accept a pupil at his level of achievement in each succeeding grade level and bring him along from there. Perhaps your boy was doing arithmetic, shall we say, below seventh-grade achievement level. His seventh-grade teacher will recognize this from information sent along in the boy's folder and record and will begin his instruction where he is . . . (opportunity for interpretation of variances in the promotion policy).

I like marks. I want to know whether my youngster is an A or B student.

Answer: We have discussed the work of your child and find that he works hard and with understanding at easy material for his grade. We're satisfied with what he is doing and the effort he is putting forth. At present, he is working at a lower level of achievement than the average student in the class. If you want to think of his work in terms of marks with which you are familiar, you can apply a letter or a grade to the usual three divisions of a group such as A, B, C, and thereby indicate to your satisfaction the mark that you are giving your child.

One reason why teachers do not get as much information as needed from parents is that they do not ask good questions. Typical questions like the following lack the sharpness so necessary to get at specific behaviors that would be helpful for teachers to know about.

Is Jimmy generally good-natured?
Does Nancy like mathematics?
Does Jack seem to be in good health?

Parents can and will provide, under adequate stimulation, information that will help the teacher determine how effective his teaching has been in transferring to pupils' behavior outside of school. Note the questions below:

Is Nancy interested in graphs printed in the local newspaper?
Does she ask questions when cost-of-living data are broadcast?
Does Jack accept food that he has disliked or ask for a substitute to maintain a healthful diet?

Parents can also provide information to aid in remediation. Too often in answer to queries about their child's difficulties they have been told that everything is all right. They are advised not to concern themselves with instructional problems. Nothing is more frustrating to the interested and intelligent parent than this approach.

In addition to his skill, the teacher's attitude about the conference determines its success to a large degree. He has to accept the parent and look objectively at his problems and their relationship to the child's welfare. Resenting the parent for his treatment of the child is more likely to reinforce the parental attitude than to change it.

USING SPECIFIC INFORMATION. The mother of one kindergarten child must have been perplexed to hear the teacher sum up a conference during the eighth month of school by saying, "You know, I just haven't learned to know Ann very well." This teacher violated an important rule of a good conference, namely, always have specific information available on each pupil. Anecdotes and dated illustrative examples of daily work and quizzes can mean the difference between a generally unproductive visit, however friendly, and a purposeful, helpful conference. Rather than saying "Bill is a very cooperative child," how much more informative to report "Bill is always willing to help out with class activities. He's dependable. The other day he mentioned that he could bring a book on trucks from home, and he didn't forget." Or instead of "Mary is a well-adjusted child," it is far more meaningful to the parent to hear "Children are always choosing Mary for their games and activities. She is very thoughtful of other pupils. Yesterday she helped Jim and Sally clean up their paints so they could go out to recess with the rest of the group."

Rather than comparing elementary school pupils with each other, discuss the child's progress in terms of his past achievement, and his own strengths and weaknesses. Instead of "Jack is the best reader in the room," the comment would be better phrased, "Jack reads a great many books during his free-reading period. He's always willing to discuss what he's read, and really enjoys recommending books to other children. You may be interested in this list of books that he's read since the beginning of school. Notice how varied his interests are. You may remember he wasn't nearly so interested in books last year." Try to be constructive and positive in discussing pupils. For example, rather than stating, "Sally lacks the ability to do independent reading," say "Sally is slowly becoming interested in reading books on her own. She told me you had given her a very exciting book for her birthday. It was clear that your family discussion of the hero of the story impressed her. I'm pleased to learn of your interest in this aspect of Sally's work."

A teacher can report a great deal more on children's reading if he has data to draw on. Evaluation of the child's reading rate, the adequacy of his oral reading, and the grade level of the reader he comprehends present objective data for reporting. Many of the basal reading series provide tests that can give a still clearer picture of his progress. Numerous standardized tests, both norm-referenced and criterion-referenced, provide information on achievement that can be meaningfully interpreted to the parent. Areas like music and art can also be reported specifically. Can the pupil match tones, keep rhythm, and follow a tune? Does he read musical notes? How effective is he in handling specific media such as crayons and watercolors? Does he show indications of creativity and originality? Can he show perspective? Does he have a grasp of the vocabulary?

Along with information about his academic work, there should be reports on a pupil's health, attendance, tardiness, and personal-social adjustment. It is important to relate these data to his scholastic achievement, for they are part of the total picture of his progress.

LIMITATIONS. Conferences have several important limitations, one of which is the time factor. Yet as in the case of letters to parents, this time can be very important in developing learning readiness. Educating the parent may be as important as working with his child in the classroom. Teachers also find that the information gathered and the thinking they must do in preparing for the conference may be very useful in class instruction. Often they are forced by a conference to collect information they should already have.

Another limitation sometimes mentioned is that parents will not come to conferences. A great deal of the blame for this can be attributed to the school administrators, and to teachers ill-trained in the technique. The effective administrator will involve the community leaders as well as his staff in affairs of the school, and is concerned about the community's understanding of the purpose of conferences. Of course he and his staff need to exercise the greatest care that the conferences prove worthwhile and do not degenerate into sheer generalizing and passing of pleasantries. The inadequately trained teacher can do more harm than good, for the parent is often antagonized and refuses to cooperate readily in the future. In such a case, the usefulness of conference-type reporting is greatly reduced.

A third limitation is that the conference technique is difficult to use in the secondary school. It is true that most experimentation with conferences has been in the elementary school. Moreover, there is reason to believe that secondary school pupils do not want their parents to participate in formal teacher-parent conferences.

On the other hand, as the educational level of parents increases over the years, parental concern about pupil growth in the secondary school will undoubtedly be as great as for the elementary grades now. Such a trend appears to be developing. Nonetheless, a very practical problem must be solved before there can be extensive conferences at the secondary school level, namely, the large pupil-teacher ratio. In many instances, the guidance staff is able to alleviate the teacher's load by conferring with some of the parents.

PROBLEM

6. The teacher-parent conference is often more helpful to the teacher than to the parents in terms of understanding the child. If you were allowed only one conference each year, during what month would you prefer to schedule these meetings? Support your answer.

Criterion-Referenced Marking

Typical marking systems are norm-referenced, that is, they tend to rank an individual in relation to other pupils such as those in his class, his school, or some other specified norm group. Two major trends in education, namely, individualized instruction and the emphasis on criterion-referenced instruments, invite a different format for reporting school progress known as criterion-referenced marking (Millman, 1970). If the key task of schools is to maximize the amount of each learning area that a pupil has mastered, then one must know whether the pupil can perform in ways specified by the objectives.

The essential features of a criterion-referenced report are a list of objectives (or an abbreviated description of tasks), spaces for indicating whether proficiency has been demonstrated, and a system to identify objectives achieved since the previous report (Millman, 1970). Figure 15.5 is an example of such a report card.

Of course, one of the important tasks in the marking system is the formulation of objectives and the construction of test items to measure the criterion performance. This has already been done commercially for a number of curricula to aid school personnel in this arduous undertaking.

Criterion-referenced testing (which is the basis for criterion-referenced marking), is clearly not a panacea for all the grading and sorting problems that exist in education (Airasian and Madaus, 1972). More thoughtful reflection and research is required before all the difficulties associated with criterion-based measurement are resolved. However, the criterion-referenced approach serves two very valuable functions within the instructional context. First, it directs attention to the performances and behaviors that are the main purpose of instruction. Secondly, it rewards pupils on the basis of their attainment relative to these criterion performances rather than to their peers. Under this system, it is conceivable that intrinsic pupil motivation will dominate over the extrinsic, which has been the result of common marking and reporting practices (Van Hoven, 1972).

MATHEMATICS
Grade Two

Skill	*Date*
Concepts	
Understands commutative property of addition (e.g., 4 + 3 = 3 + 4)	9/27
Understands place value (e.g., 27 = 2 tens + 7 ones)	10/3
Addition	
Supplies missing addend under 10 (e.g., 3 + ? = 5)	10/8
Adds three single-digit numbers	
Knows combinations 10 through 19	
*Adds two 2-digit numbers without carrying	
*Adds two 2-digit numbers with carrying	
Subtraction	
Knows combinations through 9	10/4
*Supplies missing subtrahend — under 10 (e.g., 6 − ? = 1)	
*Supplies missing minuend — under 10 (e.g., ? − 3 = 4)	
*Knows combinations 10 through 19	
*Subtracts two 2-digit numbers without borrowing	
Measurement	
Reads and draws clocks (up to quarter hour)	
Understands dollar value of money (coins up to $1.00 total)	
Geometry	
Understands symmetry	
Recognizes congruent plans figures — that is, figures which are identical except for orientation	
Graph Reading	
*Knows how to construct simple graphs	
*Knows how to read simple graphs	

*In Jefferson Elementary School, these skills are usually learned toward the end of grade two. Some children who need more than average time to learn mathematics may not show proficiency on tests of these skills until they are in grade three.

FIGURE 15.5. Report Card Based on a System of Criterion-Referenced Measurement.
From Millman, 1970, p. 228; reprinted by permission of J. Millman and *Phi Delta Kappan.*

Mastery Learning

Mastery learning is closely related to criterion marking. Usually we distribute our grades according to the normal curves on the assumption that pupils will achieve in varying amounts because of different amounts of aptitudes. However, Bloom, Hastings, and Madaus (1971, pp. 43–57) believe that most pupils can master what we have to teach them, if they receive the kind, quality, and amount of time for learning needed to meet their needs. Aptitude and achievement should then have a relationship approaching zero.

Typically in mastery learning, a course is broken into small learning units, involving a week or two of learning activity. Formative evaluation of a diagnostic nature provides continuous feedback for pupil and teacher while learning occurs; it paces and motivates the pupil. Furthermore, it is designed to reduce the negative effect associated with evaluation by reducing judgmental aspects. Grades or quality points should not be assigned. Formative tests should be marked to show *mastery* and *nonmastery* with respect to specified instructional goals.

For pupils who lack mastery of a particular unit, the formative tests should reveal the particular points of difficulty—the specific ideas, skills, and processes they still need to work on. It is most helpful when the diagnosis shows the elements in a learning hierarchy that the pupil still needs to learn. Pupils respond best to the diagnostic results when they are referred to particular instructional materials or processes intended to help them correct their difficulties. The diagnosis should be accompanied by a very specific prescription if they are to do anything about it.

As in any instructional methodology, it is important in mastery learning that objectives of instruction be carefully specified in terms of products and processes the pupil is expected to learn. These must be used in summative evaluation for the purpose of judging and grading the pupil's achievement. Summative evaluation is a summing up of the pupil's achievement that has been attained over an entire course or some substantial part of it.

One of the most difficult tasks is to set the standards for mastery. Some suggest that at least eighty to eighty-five percent of the skills be mastered in each learning unit. Numerical procedures for setting passing scores for domain-referenced tests have been devised, and all require the use of judgment at some stage of their execution (Millman, 1973, p. 214).

If grades are to be given, we must go one step further than criterion-referenced marking previously described. This can be done by using standards from nonmastery teaching of the subject. For example, Block (1971) suggests using scores earned by pupils receiving *As* and *Bs* with this type of instruction as the grading standard. The procedure will result in many more pupils receiving *As* and *Bs* with mastery learning. Under the latter type of instruction, pupils have an opportunity to take parallel tests if they do not attain mastery under a particular test administration.

Mastery learning presents several issues. Its proponents (Block, 1971; Bloom, Hastings, and Madaus, 1971) claim that it improves the self-concept and mental health of the pupil. This is not always true. Considerable frustration and hostility can be developed among pupils when they must continue to work on tasks that were easily accomplished by their classmates. Another issue that is not resolved even in the minds of mastery-learning proponents is whether mastery learning is effective for all subjects. Some (Block, 1971; Bloom, Hastings, and Madaus, 1971) believe that the strategy is most effective for learning areas whose content is stable (closed) and where the emphasis is on convergent rather than divergent thinking. For this reason, among others, the concept of mastery is criticized as too limiting (Cronbach, 1971, p. 52).

Self-Evaluation

Because of self-directed learning, there is greater emphasis on pupils evaluating themselves. Research does not provide evidence to show that self-evaluation is a valid part of a marking and reporting system (Russell, 1953; Sawin, 1969). Somewhat consistent over- or underestimation of achievement levels is a common fault of pupils.

Self-evaluation is an important educational objective. Pupils should be able to interpret their achievement and to understand reports sent to parents. Special instruction to help pupils to improve these abilities is needed (Sawin, 1969).

Marking and Reporting in the Open Classroom

New methods of organizing the schools based on some British ideas of education are now found with increasing frequency in this country. Designated by such terms as "open" education, "informal" classroom, "Leicestershire plan," and "integrated day," these methods produce classrooms quite different from the typical American model. The British system is child- rather than teacher-centered. The learner is responsible for directing his activities. Many and varied kinds of materials in the classroom provide the pupil with a laboratory to explore, create, and learn. Furthermore, proponents of "open" education believe that evaluation of children's achievement should be mediated by these materials rather than by the teacher. For instance, if the child is studying levers and he seeks an answer about how to balance his heavier classmate with himself, he can answer the question when he finds that the distance between himself and the fulcrum must be greater than that for his classmate.

Permeating the "open" classroom philosophy is the belief that children learn from their errors and that these errors may be only a temporary condition. Proponents do not believe that the teacher needs to find and correct all mistakes that children make. They maintain that teachers must learn to accept the idea that when consequences of children's mistakes become known to the children themselves, their behavior will change. The teacher must learn to accept children's expression of mathematics and reading like they accept artwork, namely, as only temporary manifestations of a pupil's thinking.

Obviously this type of classroom organization presents special challenges for evaluating pupils' work that are different from those in the classroom in which the teacher directs the entire class or a very few groups in a sequence of activities. First, in the "open" classroom, pupils are completing many and varied tasks so there are few comparable products to evaluate. Secondly, "open" classrooms place greater emphasis on such qualities as initiative, independence, social skill, curiosity, and creativity, in addition to the basic skills. Development of these personal characteristics is much more difficult to measure.

Evidence of learning is typically assessed by direct observation, or perhaps by criterion- and objective-referenced test items. Even norm-referenced tests are sometimes appropriate as well. No matter which techniques are used, it is particularly important that teachers in "open" classrooms keep detailed records that chronicle the pupil's work. It is these records, rather than the commonly used report card, that provides information to the child and his parents, and gives organized feedback to the teacher himself. Records that are kept carefully day by day might be similar to the following:

Alice Blue: *Week of May 1*
Worked on fractions. Measured various storage boxes to determine the amount of decorative paper necessary to cover them.

Read several plays. Began writing one of her own.
Assigned her Task Card #1 on electricity. Worked one hour with the materials and read from several references to find the answers to a number of questions raised.
Observations:
Needs more practice in subtracting fractions. Has difficulty in work syllabification. Shows signs of developing a greater sense of personal worth. Is able to accept praise and criticism in stride.

In addition to teacher records, children maintain logs of their activities. These often include pictures, essays, graphs, charts, and the like. With these data, one of two methods or a combination of the two are sometimes used in more formal reporting. One method is the use of a criterion-referenced-type report card. School learning is analyzed and the desired outcomes indicated. Personal characteristics such as dependability, leadership, and persistence are listed as well as cognitive and psychomotor skills. Another method is to report to parents using anecdotal records. Needed skills in writing such reports are basically the same as those for preparing correspondence with parents.

PROBLEM

7. Outline a specific program in your subject matter area for implementing self-evaluation procedures. What are your underlying objectives for following this program?

BY-PRODUCTS OF MARKING AND REPORTING

Emotional Problems

Invariably a cartoonist playing on some aspect of reporting will emphasize the defensive behavior of the pupil or his fear of adult disapproval. The judgment always seems to be punitive, and the implication that life would be wonderful if report cards could somehow vanish. Certainly in many instances parents do withhold privileges or administer corporal punishment when their child brings home a bad report. Some offer prizes and rewards for an A; then the child's problems may be overlooked and the mark becomes all important. Other parents identify with their children and may blame the school for bad reports, and the necessary cooperation between the home and school is hard to come by.

In other cases, the pressures for getting high marks result in cheating, or, at best, in conforming to a teacher's wishes as a ploy in working for marks. Some pupils develop feelings of inferiority and their resulting self-concept keeps them from trying to solve their difficulties. It is not uncommon for gifted children with specific difficulties in arithmetic or reading to be convinced of their general lack of intellectual prowess.

Marking and reporting need not cause these reactions. In many school systems, children are eager for reporting time. The spirit is one of helpful cooperation, with the child standing to gain. Prevailing attitudes promote helpfulness rather than criticism.

Effect of Marking on Teaching

Some teachers present marks in the light of rewards or prizes, but even with this approach there will be pupils who face failure. Trying to motivate through marks seems an easy way out for the teacher, eliminating the need to provide interesting and worthwhile learning experiences. The typical textbook assignment with equal requirements for all can be followed regardless of individual differences in learning ability. Academic achievement can be emphasized while other aspects of pupil growth are ignored. It is a simple process to evaluate only in terms of test averages, marks on papers, and participation in recitation, much simpler than trying to understand each pupil and evaluate his growth in terms of his own inherent characteristics and environmental problems.

When marks are used for motivation, they too often degenerate into being an end in themselves. They should be a tool for improvement of learning, not a crutch for ineffective teaching. The process of determining them should result in feedback of a diagnostic nature for the teacher as well as the pupil.

PROBLEM

8. A high-school teacher felt that Johnny was lazy, and was concerned about his sloppy work in algebra. He reasoned that this boy needed a good jolt. Knowing that Johnny's father held rigid, high standards for his son, the teacher assigned his pupil a particularly low mark. Evaluate this decision by the teacher.

IMPROVING MARKING AND REPORTING

The following seven steps include various suggestions advanced by schools that have studied their marking and reporting systems seriously and initiated programs of effective improvement (Strang, 1955, pp. 15–17).

Have teachers, parents, and pupils study the problem cooperatively. *Involving representatives of all groups who will be concerned with marks and reports is the best way to ensure understanding and cooperative effort for continued critical analysis and improvement of the system. This means calling on teachers from a range of grade levels and subjects and also a variety of specialists among school personnel, such as administrators and guidance staff. There should be representatives from the parent-teacher association and other interested organizations. It is important to provide a hearing for a cross section of the pupils, and for parents from several socioeconomic backgrounds, as their goals for their children will differ.*

Begin by studying the present reporting system. *The experience of all representatives with the existing marking practices of the school will generate interest, should produce profitable discussion, and do much to involve all members of the group. They should determine the effectiveness of communication under the current reporting system and the usefulness of the information that reports give to pupils and parents. Certainly the group will be concerned with how well the marking and reporting evaluate in terms of the educational objectives of the school. This provides an excellent opportunity to interpret the school program to parents and pupils.*

Determine what marking and reporting should accomplish. *The answer to this problem will evolve from the previous discussion. The group must decide what it believes important to know about the pupil, and whether it is feasible to report it. Furthermore, they should decide on suitable measurement tools and procedures. There must be exploration of such issues as the use of universal standards in marking and marking achievement in terms of the pupil's ability. The breadth of achievement and growth must be determined. If only final achievement is to be assessed, the group's problem is comparatively simple; if there is a desire for some of the reporting to be based on pupil growth, then serious consideration must be given to the problems involved.*

Explore the marking and reporting systems of other schools. *The group can often glean helpful ideas from the experiences and reports of other schools. Though no two school systems have identical problems, there is enough similarity to make it helpful to examine effective methods, difficulties that have been met, and suggestions made for improvement elsewhere.*

Prepare a tentative form. *The starting point for a reporting system is always the objectives of the school. The group must select those objectives on which they wish reports made, examine the feasibility of various methods of reporting in terms of those objectives. It is important to consider such factors as time available to the teacher. Possibly there should be time released from teaching to prepare and make the reports. If a printed form of some kind is to be used, specific suggestions should be made for its construction.*

Present the tentative form to pupils, teachers, and the general public. *A considerable amount of study may be necessary if a basic change in reporting is involved. Questions that may not have been considered in the representatives' group will surely be raised on general presentation. Another meeting of the group may be necessary to resolve some of them. Possibly teachers will find it helpful to meet in special session to study means of administering the system effectively. Understanding and agreement should be reached. If there is a change to teacher-parent conferences or the writing of letters, in-service training conferences will undoubtedly be needed. Possibly some basic curriculum changes will be recommended if educational objectives are reformulated. A new look at school and community relationships may be in order, and some aspects of the school program may have to be revised, such as promotional policies, guidance services, and curriculum offerings.*

Give the tentative form a trial. *When the basic groundwork has been completed, the new system is ready for its trial run. Plan on several semesters to appraise its strengths and weaknesses. Set up machinery to collect all possible suggestions and criticisms from pupils, parents, teachers, and the general public. Emphasize the growth of the pupils as the criterion for judgment. Has his attitude toward learning been improved? Has his personal-social adjustment matured? Is there a better relationship among pupils, teachers, parents?*

We should not stop here. The new system must always be subject to revision. Parents and pupils should be involved continuously in a study of the educational program of the schools. This includes evaluation of the extent to which the program achieves the educational objectives. It also means that evaluation must keep pace when objectives are changed.

Schools and communities that follow the seven steps above to the best of their ability will not necessarily arrive at the same system of marking and reporting, for there is no single system that is best for schools of all types or for all grade levels within these schools. Because of differences, however slight, in educational objectives, pupil talent, and points of view about the function of reports, the reporting systems selected vary from place to place and time to time. Furthermore, it is common to find variations within a school system. Different combinations of several of the reporting techniques may be used.

Regardless of which reporting system or combination of systems is chosen, it is most important that the result should receive widespread approval and that its purposes should be clearly understood by all concerned. If understanding and approval exist, cooperation among teachers, pupils, parents, and school administrators will come more easily, and the likelihood of misinterpretation (usually in the form of overinterpretations) of the reports themselves will be greatly lessened.

PROBLEM

9. A suggested program of improving marks and reporting has been outlined. Choose one of the seven steps, and assume that you are to head a committee that is to carry out this phase of the program. Describe in detail the procedures you and your committee would follow.

PROMOTION AND FINAL MARKS

Problems and Principles

If the philosophy of the school is concerned with the most effective development of the whole pupil, policies for promotion must be consistent with the criterion of "what is best for the pupil." Widely different practices are currently in effect in an effort to meet this criterion. Pupils in some schools must meet or exceed a "passing level" of achievement before they are promoted. Other schools have the policy of "social promotion," or one-hundred percent promotion. Both approaches have serious limitations.

Requiring all pupils, without respect to their talents and goals, to reach a "passing level" before promotion creates a threat of failure that can in some cases do great harm to the pupil. To a pupil of modest ability, it becomes a perpetual threat of failure that can undermine his confidence in himself, creating feelings of inadequacy and insecurity that can do irreparable damage to his personality. Moreover, failing him not only leaves the cause of his difficulty unchanged, but aggravates the situation by his feelings of inadequacy. Some pupils are doomed to repeat failure because they do not have the intellectual capacity to meet certain standards necessary for promotion. The bad effect on their mental health is obvious.

The very nature of today's school population greatly complicates the mental health problem. The schools are committed to accept all children with few exceptions and to give them twelve or thirteen years of free education. State laws force the children to stay in school for most of these years. Great heterogeneity results. Unfortunately the curriculum of many schools has not been expanded to meet the different needs of their pupils. Consequently those placed in classes in which they may have no interest and for which they are ill-prepared, are faced with failure. The result may be boredom, apathy, anxiety, belligerence, or hostility. The teacher is confronted with a complex teaching situation.

Thus the use of a "passing level" is not the source of the problem. A much more basic cause is the limited nature of the curriculum in many schools. Until they are placed in classes better suited to their needs and talents, some pupils will experience a series of failures. To assume that every pupil should receive the same dosage of subject matter in a particular grade level is to ignore the fact that, at any grade level, there are pupils at all levels of achievement with a wide range of learning capacities. There must be appropriate levels of instruction with appropriate standards.

Yet "social promotion" is not the answer. In the first place, there are some pupils who profit by repeating a course or grade level. A pupil who is generally immature might find considerable satisfaction in being with a younger group of children and a teacher who instructs accordingly. A second and more important factor is that pupils do not become a homogeneous group by some magic after they are promoted. The fact that they are all now fourth graders or sophomores in high school does not suddenly emulsify heterogeneity. Pupils must still be taught on the basis of their experience, backgrounds, and learning capacities. Data show that there are from three to nine grades of achievement levels in any one grade level. Indeed, effective teaching tends to make a group more heterogeneous relative to achievement. Therefore, if we are to promote pupils regardless of achievement, considerable attention must be given to the individual pupil and the problems peculiar to him.

IMPROVING PROMOTION POLICIES. Trying to establish the best promotion policy is about as difficult as trying to find the best marking and reporting system. In fact, there are many problems common to the two issues. In both cases, differences among schools in terms of educational objectives, pupil populations, and the opinions of all parties concerned can be reasons for differences in policies.

Six basic principles that can be used as the basis for a policy for promotion are the following (National Education Association, 1931, pp. 18–22):

1. *Promotion should be decided on the basis of the individual pupil.*
2. *Promotion should be on the basis of many factors. The final decision as to whether a particular pupil should be promoted should rest not merely on*

academic accomplishment, but on what will result in the greatest good to the all-around development of the individual.

3. In order that promotion procedures may be more or less uniform throughout a particular school system, a definite set of factors should be agreed upon, which each teacher will take into consideration in forming his judgment as to whether or not a particular pupil should be promoted.

4. Criteria for promotion must take into consideration the curriculum offerings of the next higher grade or unit and the flexibility of its organization, its courses of study, and its methods.

5. It is the duty of the next higher grade or unit to accept pupils who are properly promoted to it from the lower grade or unit and to adapt its work to fit the needs of these pupils.

6. Promotion procedures demand continuous analysis and study of cumulative case history records in order that refinement of procedure may result, and guesswork and conjecture be reduced to a minimum.

The principles above were stated a number of years ago, and then only as a basis for discussion. However they are sound and applicable in today's classrooms. Notice that they stress the individual child as the central factor. In many instances, uniform promotion is the answer, yet to make this a blanket policy would work against the needs and interests of some pupils. There can be no substitute for the careful study of the individual. Decisions must be made on the basis of what is best for him.

PROBLEM

10. Nancy has failed four seventh-grade subjects. She is of average mental ability and has a stable home background. She is physically immature, has low vitality, and has grown very little in the past few years. This year she has been absent a great deal due to illness. The seventh-grade teachers have made the decision that she should repeat the seventh grade. What other information would you like to have before you could evaluate their action?

The Ungraded School

Much criticism has been leveled at the present patterns of school organization that foster common expectations for all pupils, both in content of what is to be learned and in the time given to learn it. Nonpromotion is labeled as an adjustment mechanism to counteract problems resulting from specified graded content, graded materials, and limited provision for individual differences.

As a remedy, nongrading is proposed, that is, the removal of grade levels, as a device for breaking this lockstep (Goodlad and Anderson, 1963). Nongrading is in tune with the realities of individual differences; it provides for both the slow-moving pupil and the high achiever. It facilitates pupil progress, in terms of his readiness, by using sequentially organized subject matter with closely related instructional materials and evaluation based on individual progress rather than comparison with others. Pupils can be placed, not simply because they pass or fail, but on the basis of whether they "fit" into the group.

In one ungraded high school (Brown, 1963) pupils are placed in temporary learning situations that they can leave at any time depending on their ability to move into the next higher "phase." These "phases" are designed to group students in terms of their skill level, namely, low, minimal, medium, high, superior.

The challenge of the ungraded system is for the teacher to take advantage of a school organization that focuses on meeting individual needs. An opportunity is provided for him to break the lockstep that too often persists in the graded school.

SUMMARY

The following are the key points presented in this chapter:

1. *No other teacher activity has greater potential for interpreting the school program, for securing cooperation between home and school, and for promoting pupil development than determining and reporting pupil progress.*

2. *Reporting exists to inform pupils, parents, school personnel, and employers on the degree to which teachers judge the pupil to be achieving certain educational objectives.*

3. *The chief sources of information used for evaluating the pupil are classroom and standardized tests, procedure and product evaluation, class participation, and projects and reports.*

4. *Common methods of marking and reporting are the letter and number system, check lists, Pass/Fail marking, correspondence to parents, and teacher-parent conferences. Criterion-referenced marking is gaining attention. Mastery learning is also being emphasized.*

5. *The best plan of reporting is a combination of different methods, tailored to meet the needs of the pupils, school, and community.*

6. *Parents should be active participants in the evaluation process. They have opportunities to observe many phases of their children's development that the teacher does not see, and are in a position to provide helpful information.*

7. *Promotion policies should be based on what is best for the pupil. Although there are tendencies toward social promotion, promoting all pupils does not solve all the problems of organizing effective learning experiences.*

8. *A suggested solution to the problems of failure and promotion is nongrading. A pupil progresses in terms of a curriculum arranged sequentially, rather than on expectations for a particular grade level.*

SUGGESTED READINGS

ANDERSON, R. H., and C. RITSHER. Pupil Progress. In R. L. Ebel (ed.), *Encyclopedia of Educational Research.* (4th ed.) New York: Macmillan, 1969. Pp. 1050–1060.
    Related research on promotional policies for children is discussed. Reporting on pupil progress is included as part of the discussion.
BAILARD, V., and R. STRANG. *Parent-teacher conferences.* New York: McGraw-Hill, 1964.
    The setting and conditions necessary for successful parent-teacher conferences from kinder-

garten through high school are considered. Illustrative interviews from elementary, junior, and senior high schools are reproduced and evaluated.

CURETON, L. W. The history of grading practice. *NCME Measurement in Education*, 1971, 2, 1–8.
> A well-documented history of marking and reporting pupil achievement, which concludes with a list of five major problems that still perplex us.

FELDMESSER, R. A. The positive function of grades. *Educational Record*, 1972, 53, 66–72.
> The author believes that grades serve an evaluative function that cannot be served or served as well by some other form of evaluation.

GRONLUND, N. E. *Stating behavioral objectives for classroom instruction.* New York: Macmillan, 1970. Pp. 45–50.
> The last chapter of the volume gives suggestions on how to use instructional objectives in marking and reporting. Goal report cards are illustrated.

MARSHALL, M. S. Why grades are argued. *School and Society*, 1971, 99, 350–353.
> A discussion of the relative merits of using grades, emphasizing their limitations.

THORNDIKE, R. L. Marks and marking systems. In R. L. Ebel (ed.), *Encyclopedia of Educational Research.* (4th ed.) New York: Macmillan, 1969. Pp. 759–766.
> A thorough review of marking and reporting. Such topics as objections to marks, substitutes for marks, what a mark should represent, and proportion awarded each symbol are included.

REFERENCES CITED

AIRASIAN, P. W., and G. F. MADAUS. Criterion-referenced testing in the classroom. *NCME Measurement in Education*, 1972, 3, No. 2.

BLOCK, J. H. (ed.). *Mastery learning: Theory and practice.* New York: Holt, Rinehart and Winston, 1971.

BLOOM, B. S., J. T. HASTINGS, and G. F. MADAUS. *Handbook on formative and summative evaluation of student learning.* New York: McGraw-Hill, 1971.

BROWN, B. F. *The non-graded high school.* Englewood Cliffs, N.J.: Prentice-Hall, 1963.

CRISLER, R. D., and T. D. WOGAMAN. Educational data processing at Richmond. *Journal of Secondary Education*, 1963, 38, 71–76.

CRONBACH, L. J. Comments on mastery learning and its implications for curriculum development. In E. W. Eisner (ed.), *Confronting curriculum reform.* Boston: Little, Brown, 1971, 49–55.

EBEL, R. L. *Essentials of educational measurement.* Englewood Cliffs, N.J.: Prentice-Hall, 1972.

FELDMESSER, R. A. The positive function of grades. *Educational Record*, 1972, 53, 66–72.

FRYMIER, J. R. *The nature of educational method.* Columbus, Ohio: Charles E. Merrill, 1965.

GOODLAD, J. I., and R. H. ANDERSON. *The non-graded elementary school.* New York: Harcourt Brace Jovanovich, 1963.

GREEN, C. D. What shall we do with the dullards? *Atlantic Monthly*, 1956, 197, 72–74.

HALLIWELL, J. W., and J. P. ROBITAILLE. The relationship between theory and practice in a dual reporting program. *Journal of Educational Research*, 1963, 57, 137–141.

HEFFERNAN, H., and L. E. MARSHALL. Reporting pupil progress in California cities. *California Journal of Elementary Education*, 1955, 24, 67–77.

HOYT, D. P. College grades and adult accomplishments. *Educational Record*, 1966, 47, 70–75.

LEWIS, J. W. A study of the achievements and activities of selected liberal arts graduates. Unpublished Ph.D. dissertation, University of Iowa, 1970.

MANN, M. J. Relationship among certain variables associated with college and post-college success. Unpublished Ph.D. dissertation, University of Wisconsin, 1968.

MICHAEL, K. E. What are some of the new trends in reporting student growth and achievement to parents? *National Association of Secondary School Principals Bulletin*, 1960, 44, 146–149.

MILLMAN, J. Reporting student progress: a case for a criterion-referenced marking system. *Phi Delta Kappan*, 1970, 52, 226–230.

MILLMAN, J. Passing scores and test lengths for domain-referenced measures. *Review of Educational Research*, 1973, *43*, 205–216.

MUNDAY, L. A., and J. DAVIS. Varieties of accomplishments after college: Perspectives on the meaning of academic talent. *ACT Research Report Series*, No. 62. Iowa City, Iowa: American College Testing Program, 1974.

NATIONAL EDUCATION ASSOCIATION. Pupil promotion problems. *Five unifying factors on American education*. Ninth Yearbook. Washington: Author, 1931.

NATIONAL EDUCATION ASSOCIATION. Reporting pupil progress to parents. *National Education Association Research Bulletin*, 1971, *49*, 81–82.

RUSSELL, D. H. What does research say about self-evaluation? *Journal of Educational Research*, 1953, *46*, 561–573.

SAWIN, E. I. *Evaluation and the work of the teacher*. Belmont, Calif.: Wadsworth, 1969.

STRANG, R. *How to report pupil progress*. Chicago: Science Research Associates, 1955.

VAN HOVEN, J. B. Reporting progress: A broad rationale for new practices. *Phi Delta Kappan*, 1972, *53*, 365–366.

WECKLER, N. Problems in organizing parent-teacher conference. *California Journal of Elementary Education*, 1955, *24*, 117–126.

16

A SCHOOLWIDE PROGRAM OF EVALUATION

The football coach has one overall objective—to win as many games as possible. To have a successful season, he must accomplish numerous other objectives centering around individual performance and team play. Blocking, running, tackling, and passing should develop as closely as possible to each player's potentialities. Then these skills have to be orchestrated to form a smooth-functioning team.

The coach will measure progress in various ways. This is important to him. He wants to note continuous improvement. Evaluation of the success of his program is based on data collected in various ways at various times. Speed can be timed. Effects of blocking can be visually judged. Distance and accuracy of passing can be measured. But data are not so easily obtained for other important performance objectives. On what basis does the coach measure motivation and eagerness? How can he judge player morale? How will he estimate sensitivity to, and ability to profit from, suggestion? How may he determine the team's confidence in the quarterback? He relies on reports, observations, a sensitivity to certain cues, and comparative mental images of past performance. From this information he evaluates progress. These evaluations continue throughout the season and into the following year.

To evaluate the school's total educational program is even more complex than the task of the coach. We sometimes lose sight of the broad range of our goals and how difficult it is to measure change in such areas as attitudes, interests, and personal-social adjustment. To collect data for evaluation, many types of instruments and procedures, in addition to tests, must be used. But we must not lose sight of the fact that these are all selected on the basis of measuring degree of attainment of the school's objectives. One does not ask the question "What is the best achievement test?" Rather, one asks "What is the best test for obtaining data about my school program under the conditions that it must operate?"

PURPOSES OF AN EVALUATION PROGRAM

Evaluation is the discovery of the nature and worth of something. We can evaluate pupils, teachers, curricula, administrative systems, teaching materials, etc. Evaluation contributes to understanding substance, function, and worth.

The ultimate goal of a pupil evaluation program is to inform the school how to assist each pupil in the development of his potential. We must be able to translate measurement data into teaching prescriptions (Fleming, 1971). To accomplish this, the school must know the pupils' capacities, interests, and achievement. Furthermore, it must have instructional objectives that lend themselves to the evaluation process. Stated objectives like "To develop good citizenship" are of limited value if good citizenship is not defined and delineated so that the degree of the pupil's development can be determined. It is much less bewildering to assess progress toward the following objective, representing one facet of good citizenship: "The pupil does not destroy, or mutilate in any way, property that does not belong to him."

A schoolwide program of pupil evaluation is based on the complete set of educational objectives held by that school. The task is exceedingly complex. Too often testing is confused with evaluation, and the school initiates a testing program per se. Though an important part of the evaluation program, testing is still only one part. Many kinds of evidence are needed, and from various sources. Because we do not have effective tests to measure all aspects of behavior, many other approaches including observation, rating scales, questionnaires, and interviews must be used. Evaluation that considers a variety of data can also focus on the process of learning rather than on the product alone. Data collected can then be the basis for evaluating individuals in terms of their abilities and needs.

But there should be more to a schoolwide program of evaluation than pupil evaluation. It can be vastly strengthened by the presence of program and product evaluation (see pages 5–8). Now we can take steps to evaluate the inputs and processes as well as the outputs of the instructional program. What programs are effective for learning? What procedures can be used to overcome specific weaknesses? We need information to aid in selecting among various competing instructional approaches.

Unfortunately, we are more able to predict from test scores the possible success or failure of a pupil than we are able to suggest instructional procedures to prevent failure and ensure success. We are much more sophisticated in using measurement techniques that determine a pupil's rank in a particular norm group than we are in describing what he can and cannot do, as in the case of objective- and criterion-referenced testing. We need instruments and methodology that will aid us in identifying barriers to learning, barriers related to specific instructional techniques.

PROBLEMS

1. The board of education of a small community hired a team of educational specialists from a nearby university to evaluate the testing program of the school system and to make specific recommendations for improvement. The team prepared a comprehensive report, which was then presented to the faculty. Although this report was complimentary for the most part, there was a general feeling of dissatisfaction among both faculty and administration. Criticize the procedure followed by the board of education. Suggest a better approach.

2. Prepare a list of general educational objectives for a secondary school program in a slum area in a large city, and another list for a secondary school

program in a small rural community. In what respects are your lists similar? Are the differences sufficiently large to cause the schoolwide evaluation program at one school to be greatly different from that of the other school?

INITIATING THE PROGRAM

Since a program of evaluation cannot be separated from the total educational program, school personnel in administration, guidance, and instruction must participate in its inception, organization, and promotion. It should be a truly cooperative venture. The authoritarian principal who dictates a program may compel his staff to comply mechanically. They may administer, score, and record the results of tests, but it is doubtful that they will be motivated to understand pupil behavior and motivation. Such understanding only comes through in-service education and democratic participation of a staff; it is the basis of a good evaluation program.

In a small school, the general staff meeting should involve all teachers and specialists; everyone should have a chance to ask questions and discuss procedures. The administrator should probably assume leadership to stimulate interest, perhaps by posing such a problem as "Why do our pupils always do better on the mathematical parts of standardized achievement test batteries than on the verbal parts?" Perhaps community criticism of achievement may prompt the staff to evaluate its educational program. It is also possible to interest the staff by showing them the results of the administration of a standardized achievement test, like a reading survey test; from this they can determine the strengths and weaknessses of the pupils. When properly directed, this approach will stimulate thinking about the total evaluation problem in the school.

In the large city system it is impractical, if not impossible, to involve the entire staff in the initial evaluation discussions, so a representative committee should work out preliminary details. However, as in smaller schools, one person should be responsible for coordinating the program. He should be adept in working with people and sophisticated in measurement and statistics; it is important that he be given time to do the assignment effectively. Nevertheless, before any final action is taken in test selection or evaluation procedures, the entire staff should discuss and evaluate the proposals, a necessity if the evaluation is to be integrated with the total educational program.

In the initial discussions, teachers should understand that evaluation is a comprehensive process requiring continuous administrative and guidance functions in addition to the more obvious instructional ones. Suggestions of the kinds of evidence needed for evaluating in terms of a group of related objectives, and where that evidence can be sought, can be made meaningful if presented in chart form, as illustrated in Table 16.1. This will help prevent the limited approach of paper-and-pencil testing alone.

The objectives concerning communication shown in Table 16.1 are adapted from Kearney (1953). Although it is desirable to refine the wording of some of the objectives in this table in terms of the discussion in Chapter 2 concerning the guidelines for stating specific objectives (Mager, 1962), note that these are not vaguely phrased. Rather than a vague statement "to develop comprehension," the objective

TABLE 16.1. Educational Objectives in Communication for the Primary Period and Means of Evaluation.

Educational objective	Means of evaluation
Knowledge and Understanding	
He can recognize basic reading sight-vocabulary.	Standardized oral reading tests Informal word recognition tests Standardized word lists
He can define common words that he uses orally.	Standardized word meaning tests Observation: teacher listens to his use of words Informal tests: Pupil writes definitions of words
He can read orally in a meaningful way.	Standardized oral reading tests Informal tests Check lists: smooth reading, good phrasing, correct interpretation of punctuation marks
He has developed an acquaintance with children's literature.	Check lists: books checked out of library, brought to school Observation: talks about books
He understands that many words "pair off" as opposites, e.g., yes-no, little-big.	Informal and standardized tests Workbook exercises Informal questioning during group instruction
He can distinguish between the names of persons and things and action words.	Informal tests Observation: ability to act our directions, to make up directions for others to follow Classification lists
Skill and Competence	
He does assigned reading independently.	Informal questioning during group instruction Observation: independent reading Written work
He can recall the sequence of a story or the facts read in a story.	Standardized reading tests Informal reading tests: recalls and writes facts Observation: answers well-phrased questions during group discussion, illustrates sequence in pictures, acts out sequence
He reads simple informational material with comprehension.	Informal reading tests Written work: brief written reports Observation: discusses material read
He reads third-grade material with a comprehension of 80 percent.	Standardized reading tests Informal tests
He can read seven out of ten paragraphs of third-grade material and recognize many of the main ideas.	Standardized reading tests Informal tests Working with him independently and questioning him
He can read from 95 to 120 words silently each minute.	Standardized reading tests Informal tests (timed)

TABLE 16.1. Continued

Attitude and Interest

He enjoys reading for recreation or information.	Observation: talks or writes about his reading, anxious to read new books, brings in objects about what he has read
He likes to recite poems and retell favorite stories.	Observation: reflects interests by what he says and does
He is interested in the sounds of words in word-families, in rhymes, and in secret languages and codes.	Observation: questions asked by him indicate this interest; knows how to determine word-families

Educational objectives adapted from N. C. Kearney, *Elementary school objectives*, 1953, pp. 102–110; by permission of the Russell Sage Foundation, copyright 1953.

listed is "he reads third-grade material with a comprehension of 80 percent." Rather than "to read rapidly," the objective is stated "he can read from 95 to 120 words silently each minute." The last objective could be improved by adding "and is able to answer correctly 80 percent of the comprehension questions sampling the passage." The criterion of acceptable performance is now definite. A few other objectives could be more crisply stated in behavioral terms.

In Table 16.1, the statement of objectives is followed by a suggested means for gathering information to be used as a basis for evaluation. Although teacher-constructed and standardized tests are often very helpful, there are some areas of achievement where they are inapplicable. For example, no test can determine whether a pupil does his assigned reading independently. Certainly improved skill will be reflected in test results, but the teacher can only observe him in the classroom for effective evaluation of this achievement. Incidentally, not all pupils will be limited to the specific objectives stated in Table 16.1, which are only general guides for primary teachers. A number of pupils should be able to read more difficult material than those at third grade level, just as some will read faster than 120 words per minute.

PROBLEM

3. Choose one or more of the educational objectives that you have stated for your subject matter and devise reasonably reliable and valid methods by means of which you might systematically and objectively evaluate each pupil in a class.

USE OF STANDARDIZED TESTS

Although standardized tests represent only one means of obtaining data for evaluation, they are very important tools in measurement. Therefore their selection, administration, scoring, and interpretation are significant aspects of educational evaluation. Selection of the wrong test, its improper administration or scoring, or inadequate interpretation of the results can waste time and money, and harm pupils.

Scope of the Program

INFANT AND PRESCHOOL TESTS. There has been a resurgence of interest in infant and preschool tests largely because of concern for retarded children and the establishment of compensatory school programs for culturally disadvantaged boys and girls. These tests are either performance or oral tests and must be individually administered. Generally, infant tests are designed for children up to eighteen months of age and preschool tests are considered applicable to the eighteen-to-sixty month period.

Some of these instruments are rating scales rather than tests to aid in the observation of children (Gesell and Amatruda, 1969). Others are downward extensions of the *Binet* scales such as the *Cattell Infant Intelligence Scale*. At the lower end of these scales, the required responses are largely perceptual, such as following a moving object or focusing on sounds. There may be some motor tasks requiring movement of parts of the body or changing an object from one hand to another. Of course, as one proceeds up the scale the tasks become more complex. Some verbal responses are required and manipulative tasks require added skill.

Regarding use of infant and preschool tests, we must conclude that infant tests have no validity in predicting future intelligence test performance. Beginning with the age of twelve months, however, there is a constant increase in predictive power so that the preschool tests have a moderate correlation with subsequent intelligence test scores. One may conclude that the value of infant tests is to aid in the diagnosis of children who may later be judged mentally defective.

ELEMENTARY AND JUNIOR HIGH SCHOOL. A minimum testing program for the elementary and junior high school consists of periodic measurement of scholastic aptitude and yearly achievement testing. Although authorities differ about the best grade level for administering scholastic aptitude tests, they generally agree that four or five administrations should occur between the time the child enters school and his completion of high school. A suggested sequence is at the beginning of the first, fourth, seventh, and tenth grades. Some schools add two more administrations in the second and eighth or ninth years. These are transitional points in the pupil's educational life, representing the beginning of formal study and of the intermediate, junior high, and senior high periods. In addition to the administrations suggested above, the pupil should be tested again whenever results are at variance with the teacher's judgment.

Another argument for frequent administrations of scholastic aptitude tests is the variation in the test results that typically occurs. IQs commonly vary as much as ten or more points when two or more tests are given. A pupil may therefore be penalized unless previous test results are continually checked. Fluctuations tend to be greater in the primary grades.

Achievement batteries should be administered yearly. The minimal program should emphasize tests of basic skills. The basic responsibilities of the school at this level are proficiency of work-study skills, language arts, and arithmetic. These are of greater importance than content areas.

An optimum program for the elementary and junior high school would include access to all available tests that would help the pupil. In addition to survey tests of achievement, diagnostic tests would be administered whenever necessary. Special reading tests, such as readiness tests, could be added to the first-grade battery. An optimum program might also include interest inventories administered late in the junior high school program.

SENIOR HIGH SCHOOL. The minimum program in the senior high school should include a test of scholastic aptitude or a differential aptitude test and measures of achievement in various subjects. It is particularly important that college-bound pupils know their adequacy in such areas as mathematics, social, biological, and physical sciences, and the language arts. Every program should also include a recheck of the basic skills. It is especially important to administer a reading test. Whether or not a pupil is college-bound, reading is important.

The optimum program for the secondary school might employ personal-social adjustment inventories, problem check lists, and interest inventories. These can be used for screening purposes or educational and vocational guidance. In this regard, the limitations of adjustment inventories should be carefully considered.

GUIDELINES FOR TESTING THE DISADVANTAGED. Attention has been given to the problem of obtaining valid scores for disadvantaged pupils in aptitude testing (see p. 294). In addition, test scores from achievement and personal-social adjustment instruments may need special interpretation for the disadvantaged. Fishman et al. (1964) elaborate on three critical issues in testing the disadvantaged: (1) unreliability of differentiation within their range of scores, (2) the possible difference in predictive validity between disadvantaged groups and standardization groups, and (3) the importance of understanding the group's social and cultural background. They believe that it is important to compare the disadvantaged child's test performance with his previous test performance. Such a child's progress can best be judged by using himself as his own control and employing the norms as "benchmarks."

However, numerous attempts to discuss the special problems of testing the disadvantaged have not been unusually helpful. Certain considerations are undoubtedly important for testing those children from lower economic groups, but we know too little about them. Nevertheless, they are probably not nearly so important as those factors that we do know a lot about for adequate testing in general: clarity of instructions, appropriate test selection in terms of use, rapport with the pupil, validity, reliability, and so on. The informed test user is sensitive to the various characteristics of a given test, the testee, and the interpretation of test scores. If he is knowledgeable about general test use, he is not likely to make gross errors with any specific individual or group.

AN ILLUSTRATIVE SCHOOL TESTING PROGRAM. School testing programs often vary considerably in terms of the tests used. In Table 16.2 are shown the various types of tests included in a well-developed program. For each type, some of the tests commonly used are listed. These lists are by no means complete.

Note that many of the tests are only used for special purposes with a few pupils. For instance, individual intelligence tests would be given only when group mental ability tests produce questionable results. Diagnostic tests would be administered when there is need to study basic problems of learning experienced by certain pupils.

TABLE 16.2.   An Illustrative School Testing Program.

Testing area	Age or grade level of the instruments[a]	Recommended grade level												
		K	I	II	III	IV	V	VI	VII	VIII	IX	X	XI	XII
ACHIEVEMENT														
Reading Achievement:														
Gates-MacGinitie Reading Tests	I–XII		X	X	X	X	X	X						
Davis Reading Test	VIII–XI										X			
Basic Skills Battery:														
California Achievement Tests	I–XIV			X	X	X	X	X						
Comprehensive Tests of Basic Skills	II–XII			X	X	X	X	X						
Iowa Tests of Basic Skills	III–IX													
Content Achievement:														
Cooperative Tests	I–College							X						
Metropolitan Achievement Tests	I–IX										X			
Sequential Tests of Educational Progress	IV–XIV													
Diagnostic Tests:		(As needed)												
Gates-McKillop Reading Diagnostic Test	II–VI													
Stanford Diagnostic Arithmetic Test	II–VIII													
Stanford Diagnostic Reading Test	III–VIII													
APTITUDE														
Group Mental Ability Tests:														
California Test of Mental Maturity	I–Adult		X											
Lorge-Thorndike Intelligence Tests	III–XIII					X								
Otis-Lennon Mental Ability Test	K–XII								X					
School and College Ability Test	IV–XIV											X		
Differential Aptitude Test:														
Differential Aptitude Test	VIII–XII									X				
General Aptitude Test Battery	IX–XII													

TABLE 16.2. Continued

College Admissions Tests:			
CEEB Scholastic Aptitude Test	XI–XII		
American College Testing Program	XI–XII		X
		(As needed)	
Individual Intelligence Tests:			
Stanford-Binet Intelligence Scale	3–18		
Wechsler Preschool and Primary Scale			
of Intelligence	4–6½		
Wechsler Intelligence Scale for Children	6–16		
Wechsler Adult Intelligence Scale	Adult		
PERSONAL-SOCIAL ADJUSTMENT		X	
Interest:			
Kuder Preference Record—			
Occupational	IX–Adult		
Minnesota Vocational Interest Survey	IX–Adult		
Strong Vocational Interest Blank	17 and over		
General:		(As needed)	
California Test of Personality	K–Adult		
Mooney Problem Check List	VII–Adult		

[a]Age levels are given in Arabic numbers, grade levels in Roman numbers.

Also, some tests are designed for special groups only. Examples are the *General Aptitude Test Battery* and the *Minnesota Vocational Interest Survey*, which are designed for non—college-bound youth.

Overtesting should be avoided at all costs. Any nonfunctional tests should be eliminated. The staff should be satisfied that each part of the testing program is contributing new and useful information each time it is used.

PROBLEM

4. At what levels would you administer reading tests in the elementary and junior high school program? When might an aptitude battery such as the *DAT* be most useful?

Selecting the Test

Tests should be selected on the basis of their contribution to evaluation in terms of the school's educational objectives. Therefore, a test must be studied carefully to determine both its content and its relationship to other tests and information available. The best way to do this is to take the test oneself. This indicates the processes required for correct responses, makes clear the obvious content, and enables the teacher to anticipate difficulties in administration.

In selecting tests, the teacher should consult Buros' *Mental Measurements Yearbooks*. These references are revised continually and provide quantities of information about all types of tests. At least one specialist discusses the strengths and weaknesses of most of the popular tests. Often individual items are criticized, and sometimes problems in administration and scoring are discussed. As well as being helpful in selection, these volumes provide a great deal of general learning about tests.

It is important to keep the continuity of a testing program in mind for all the grades from kindergarten through high school. The cumulative record (see page 422) is more meaningful if related tests are used at the different grade levels. If the *Stanford Achievement Tests* are selected, for example, the norms from level to level would be based on similar populations, and the relative emphasis on various types of content in the tests would tend to be similar, thereby making it easier to assess achievement. Likewise, the scores from a given scholastic aptitude test would be more comparable from level to level than comparisons made between tests having different authors.

After tests have been selected, administered, and proved functional for a school, they should not be replaced unless it appears that other instruments will be more effective, since it is necessary to compare results from year to year if the cumulative record is to be meaningful. A more recent copyright date on another test does not necessarily guarantee a better test. At times, because of the development of new instruments, it is wise to make a change. Then study of the results of groups of pupils will be helpful in making comparisons with previous test data.

In selecting the test, special attention must be given to its degree of validity and reliability, the adequacy of its norms, its ease of administration and scoring, and its cost in time and money. Furthermore, tests with equivalent forms are necessary for testing different classes at different times or multiple testing of one class. Aids for test interpretation such as class charts and profile blanks ease and clarify recording and interpreting test results.

PROBLEM

5. A junior high school is using a new battery of achievement tests this year. A faculty committee has been appointed to evaluate the usefulness of the new tests and to recommend either retaining or discontinuing them. Outline a procedure for the committee to follow.

Administering the Test

If test results are to be successfully interpreted, they must be carefully administered according to the specific instructions. Results from various classes cannot be compared unless administration is standardized, nor can norms be of any value. This applies not only to reading printed instructions carefully, but to motivating the pupils to do their best on a test. Time limits must be followed rigidly. Proper administration requires very careful planning from ordering tests on time to their distribution to the classrooms.

THE TEST ADMINISTRATOR. Who should administer the tests? Some individual tests will be given by the school psychologist. In large school systems, a testing specialist may be employed to administer group tests. In most instances, however, the teacher gives tests, and to some advantage. Not only does it identify the teacher with the testing program, since he must familiarize himself with the tests, but because he knows his pupils, he can motivate them more effectively, interpret their reactions, and establish the necessary rapport.

Those who criticize teacher administration usually focus their arguments on inaccurate timing or improper instructions. Teachers should be given instruction in the administration of the tests. The first step is to familiarize them with standardized test construction, for they must understand the importance of standardized procedure. Group instruction is advised when provision can be made for a question period. Instruction had best be given by a specialist in testing, whether from the local school or from a college or university.

If the instructions are particularly complex, teachers should be encouraged to give the test to each other. Many a test has been spoiled because instructions were not completely understood.

Special emphasis should be given to proper timing. Instructions generally appear quite simple, but when an ordinary watch is used as the timing instrument, it is easy for the examiner to err in finding the termination point. When possible, the teacher should use a stopwatch that he has operated with checks on his readings before he administers the test. When a regular watch is used, the starting time should be recorded in minutes and seconds. Then the testing time should be added to record the exact moment to stop the test. Memory should never be trusted in timing any more than in memorizing instructions. Record the time and read the instructions.

GIVING THE TEST. Scheduling is one of the biggest problems in a testing program. On the surface it may appear simple, but when test booklets are being reused for economy, when IBM answer sheets are used on which all the answers for several sittings are recorded, or when test length does not coincide with the length of the class periods, some complicated situations can arise. For example, since the test booklets must be checked for marks after each administration, the same booklets cannot be used in consecutive periods. Getting pupils started at the right place when their answer sheets are collected at the close of one sitting is another problem. When testing time is longer than class periods or a combination of them, it is probably wise to set up a testing timetable.

Proper physical conditions for testing will allow pupils to work with freedom without crowding, poor lighting, or interruptions. A sign should be placed on the door indicating that a test is in progress. All testing equipment must be in the room and readily available, along with extra pencils and erasers, and carefully spaced functional chairs. Cheating should not be tolerated, but dealt with firmly without emotional outbursts to disturb the other pupils.

An additional factor requiring planning is the allowance of the proper amount of time for passing out test booklets, answer sheets, and pencils; they must also be collected. Too often the time requirement for these procedures is underestimated.

Even though details are carefully provided for, directions carefully followed, timing accurately completed, and interruptions eliminated, test results may not be highly valid if the pupil is not motivated to do his best. The pupil must be confident that testing is for his own welfare and not for determining promotion or for assigning final marks. He must understand the purpose of the test and the demands it will make on him. Unless testing is of value to him, he may not do his best work.

On the other hand, overstimulation produces anxiety, which interferes with good performance. It is particularly aggravated among those pupils who have the greatest need to earn high marks. The test administrator provides the best testing atmosphere for dealing with anxiety when he establishes a relaxed, businesslike atmosphere with a touch of humor. He encourages the pupil to do his best, but does not threaten.

Furthermore, pupils need to have a certain amount of sophistication or testwiseness to give evidence of their best performance. Teachers should exhort pupils to listen carefully to instructions, mark their papers neatly and accurately, plan wise use of their time, leave enough time to recheck their answers, and understand when to omit or answer a question.

TIME OF YEAR FOR TEST ADMINISTRATION. An important decision in any evaluation program is the time for test administration. Should standardized tests be administered in the spring or fall? Fall administration has a number of advantages:

1. *With today's itinerant population, fall administration assures the teacher a record for each pupil. Transfer pupils may not bring adequate records with*

them from other schools. If tests are administered in the spring the teacher is more likely to have inadequate data for some pupils throughout the year, a deficit which prevents him from focusing his attention on pupil needs rather than on what is supposed to be taught in a certain class. If pupils have specific weaknesses and the teacher knows about them, he can plan remedial work. If they rank high in achievement, he won't make the serious mistake of having them repeat what they already know just because it appears in the syllabus. The information enables him to meet the needs of individuals through grouping or through any other practical approach.

2. Fall testing provides a more realistic measure of pupils' achievement. During the summer vacation, certain skills may improve; others may deteriorate. If the child does know arithmetic, he may not be as proficient in September as he was in June. On the other hand, he may have done considerable reading during the summer, thereby improving his skill in this area.

3. Testing can be helpful to pupils in self-evaluation. If the results are used wisely, they can provide aid in formulating goals. The objective data from standardized tests can give the pupil direction and purpose for the new school year.

4. Too often it appears that tests are administered to determine the effectiveness of the teacher rather than the status of the pupils. This may result in coaching the pupils for tests or in invalid administration such as lengthening the time limits. Fall testing lessens this possibility.

5. Testing in the spring is generally done under pressure of time. As the school year draws to a close, teachers are busy filling out reports and completing final details. Testing may tend to be more of a chore than an aid to good teaching.

Although fall testing is generally recommended, certain conditions may require spring testing. This is particularly true when ability grouping requires that data be available for determining programs of the pupils for the following year.

PROBLEMS

6. Imagine that you are in charge of a schoolwide achievement testing program in which classroom teachers will administer the tests. What steps would you take to ensure standard testing procedures? What difficulties would have to be anticipated?

7. Some school systems do not tell pupils in advance when standardized tests are to be administered, in the hope that undue anxiety and absenteeism will thereby be avoided. Evaluate this practice.

Scoring the Test

Although essay and objective tests of the supply type are generally scored by hand, many standardized and classroom objective tests can be machine-scored. Central agencies providing this scoring service at a nominal fee offer some definite advantages:

1. Accuracy is greater; machine-scoring results in fewer errors.

2. It saves time for the busy teacher, who can spend his time more profitably than

doing clerical work. For some tests a pressure-sensitive label, containing each pupil's scores, is available to attach to the cumulative record. Scores are easily recorded without retyping.

3. *Item-analysis data can be quickly prepared when needed.*

Hand-scoring by the teacher also results in certain benefits:

1. *Results are generally more quickly available.*
2. *It is possible that by scoring some tests the teacher will gain better insight into a pupil's strengths and weaknesses. However, this is not as likely to occur in the case of the objective test as it is in the case of the essay test.*

The advantages and disadvantages of hand-scoring notwithstanding, the fact remains that many test papers are scored in this manner, so the scorer must avoid injustice due to inaccuracy. This is so important a matter that school officials must exert considerable effort and care in training teachers and checking scoring accuracy.

Two types of errors are frequently made: compensating and biased. In the first category are those errors made by carelessness in checking, adding, or using formulas; they score too high in one instance and too low in another. The other type of error is a misinterpretation of a scoring formula, which slants scores all in one direction, high or low. There is no opportunity for them to be cancelled out.

How should these errors be prevented? Teachers must be taught how to score, and carry out the scoring instructions to show they have understood them. A discussion of procedures is not enough. The papers first scored should be rescored. When high accuracy is maintained, only a sampling of papers need be checked. One out of five or ten papers may be selected for this purpose. Because biased errors prove to be so serious, the second scoring should be done by a different person. In some schools all papers are scored twice with different colored pencils. One helpful idea is to have one or more teachers responsible for each subtest. They can then become thoroughly proficient in their task; scoring becomes much more efficient and accurate.

Another check is to see if any extreme scores show up in a pupil's profile. It is possible that they are valid, but if such scores occur, these subtests should be scored again. Also, if scores seem unrealistic in terms of a pupil's past achievement, the corresponding parts or the entire test should be rescored.

PROBLEM

8. Some argue that, if each teacher scores the tests of those pupils whom he meets every day, test results become meaningful to the teacher; in the process of scoring, the teacher will become conscious of specific areas of subject matter difficulty. Evaluate this position.

Interpreting and Using the Testing Results

Regardless of the care with which the tests have been selected, administered, and scored, little value will accrue from them unless the results are used in the evaluation program. This means that they must be available to teachers, counselors, and school administrators. In Chapter 14, summarization and interpretation of group and individual test scores provide information for improving diagnostic and remedial programs. In Chapter 15, suggestions are given for the use of test scores in reporting to pupils and their parents.

It is sometimes advantageous to use test scores in interpreting the school program for the public or special community groups; presenting information comparing pupil achievement with national norms of those having comparable ability is one procedure. It may focus attention on a school's educational objectives to portray achievement in various subjects, and at different grade levels. Such a summary may, on the other hand, reveal specific weaknesses that should be remedied through increased financial support by the community.

Test data should be presented in the most meaningful ways. The use of numerical or graphic charts is clearer than a narrative. Figure 16.1 shows the distribution of mental ability scores of a senior high school class compared with national norms. Information about achievement in various subject areas would be helpful. Insight could also be gained from comparing achievement in various subject areas for specific groups through several grades. Groups could vary in terms of racial and socioeconomic characteristics. It is possible that comparisons of groups exposed to different curricula would also be timely. In Figure 16.1 it would also have been possible to graph the achievement of the group to provide a comparison with their ability. Note that stanines are employed.

The group of pupils from School X tends to be above the national norms. No pupils have a stanine score of 1, and fewer have stanine scores of 2, 3, 4, and 5 than is

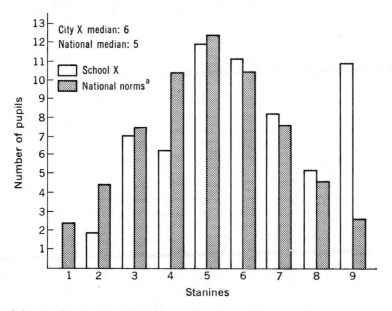

[a]Expected frequencies of a representative sample; the same number of pupils were selected from the standardization group.

FIGURE 16.1. Distribution of the School and College Ability Test, Total Score, for a Twelfth-Grade Class.

true of those from the national norm group; there is a larger proportion of pupils from School X having stanine scores of 6, 7, 8, and 9.

THE CUMULATIVE RECORD

The cumulative record is a device for recording and filing all pertinent data that will lead to a better understanding of the pupil for educational and vocational guidance purposes. Various kinds of data from many sources are more helpful than data obtained from a single source. A systematic, long-range accumulation of data clearly produces more intelligent interpretation than data collected at one time.

Cumulative records take various forms, the most common of which are the card, the folder, or a combination of them. The folder is printed for recording data, and any pertinent materials such as anecdotal records may be placed inside. A typical cumulative record of the folder type for the elementary grades is shown in Chapter 14 (pages 358–361). Notice the information required, the recording method, and the insert for recording additional health data. A surprisingly large amount of information can be permanently recorded on such a form.

If possible, the school staff should plan the record form cooperatively. The following are guiding principles for its construction (Traxler, 1971, pp. 74–75):

1. *It should agree with the educational objectives of the local school.*
2. *It should be the result of the group thinking of the faculty members.*
3. *It should either provide for a continuous record of the development of the pupil from the first grade to the end of the junior college or be one of a series of forms which make provision for such a record.*
4. *It should be organized by time sequence; that is, it should be set up by yearly divisions which run throughout the form.*
5. *It should contain ample and carefully planned space for a record of the results of all types of tests and for an explanation of the norms in terms of which the results were interpreted.*
6. *It should provide for the annual recording of personality ratings of behavior descriptions, which represent the consensus of the pupils' counselors and teachers.*
7. *While it should be as comprehensive as possible it must be simple enough to avoid overwhelming the clerical resources of the school.*
8. *It should be accessible to the teachers as well as to the counselors and principal. Highly confidential information that the counselor may possess should be filed elsewhere.*
9. *The record form should be reevaluated periodically and revised as needed to take account of educational change and progress.*

Information Needed

One of the best ways to select data to include in the cumulative record is to determine the usefulness of each in understanding the pupil. In general, the following information is thought helpful.

1. Identifying data. *These include items such as name, address, age, and date of birth.*

2. Scholastic achievement and mental development. *This would include not only information about the pupil's achievement in various areas but data concerning his general and special aptitudes. Some of this information can be recorded in anecdotal form. Other data can be tabulated as the results of classroom and standardized tests and as school marks.*

3. School attendance record. *Many factors, such as the suitability of the curriculum, home conditions, and the pupil's health, are related to a poor attendance record. These should be reported as well as the source of this information.*

4. Home and family background. *The educational and cultural backgrounds of the parents should be noted. It is also important to know the father's occupation, whether parents are living together, and any other information about home conditions that may be reflected in the pupil's behavior.*

5. Personal-social development. *Such factors as a pupil's degree of self-confidence, emotional stability, predominant moods, relationship to peers and authority figures, and his general mental health should be recorded.*

6. Health. *Under this category, items such as a history of medical and dental care, disabilities, and special information on vision and hearing are included. If a pupil has a disability, it is also wise to record his attitude toward it.*

7. Special activities and interests. *Discovering how a pupil uses his free time in and outside school often provides answers to important questions about his behavior. Any skills in athletics, music, or art, and any other special talents, and also any work experience that he had, should be reported.*

8. Educational and vocational plans. *For the pupil in secondary school, this item becomes a prime factor in his selection of subjects and in his decision for the future. As his plans develop they should be noted, even though the pupil may be somewhat vague about them.*

Interpretation and Use of the Cumulative Record

The cumulative record will be useful to all school personnel concerned with educational and vocational guidance. The three key persons involved are the teacher, the counselor, and the school administrator.

THE TEACHER. The teacher facilitates learning through improved instruction. Though he must consider the individual differences in his class, the practical demand is that he instruct the group. The discussion of the class record and class analysis chart in Chapter 14 shows how an orderly presentation of data enables the teacher to analyze the needs of his class and know the strengths and weaknesses of the group as a whole For example, a large percentage of the class may be having trouble with decimals, finding the main idea in a paragraph, or problem solving in science. Knowing this, the teacher can use group instruction effectively. Those pupils who do not need help can explore new material.

But the teacher must go further than release pupils from areas they have already mastered. He must help them select projects and materials. The direction the pupils need should be readily available in the cumulative record from achievement and aptitude scores, samples of their work, and indications of their interests.

The cumulative record can also aid in finding a pupil's weaknesses. For example, a child often appears to succeed, but only in comparison with his lackluster classmates. A mediocre performance often looks good if the competition is weak. Because the pupil seems to be doing all right, the teacher attends to those whose difficulties are more obvious and who are generally the less able. But when the teacher matches achievement with ability, and notices from the record of the able pupil that he does poorly in areas hitherto unnoticed, instructional problems are seen that would otherwise have gone overlooked.

After the teacher has located learning difficulties, he must prescribe remediation and try to prevent such difficulties in the future. Chapter 14 includes a discussion of the process of identifying group and individual difficulties, and suggests remedial help. Again, in the attacking of remedial problems, the importance of data from the cumulative record is emphasized.

The cumulative record may be expanded for records of individualized instruction programs. Evaluation is central to the effective functioning of these plans. Pretests, posttests, and continuous monitoring of each pupil become integral parts of the systems. In some instances, computers are used to collect and systematize the data for feedback.

To be sure, the cumulative record can play an important role in teacher-parent conferences. To make these conferences helpful, the teacher must have such data as objective test scores, illustrative work samples, and reports of critical behavioral incidents.

THE COUNSELOR. Darley and Anderson (1951, pp. 74–75) list seven significant measurements needed in the counseling process:

1. *General scholastic ability*
2. *Differential measures of achievement*
3. *Evidence of special aptitudes or disabilities*
4. *Interests*
5. *Personality structure and dynamics, including attitudes and beliefs*
6. *Socioeconomic and cultural derivation and relations*
7. *Health and physical attributes*

They also give four types of questions with regard to counseling pupils that may be answered by data obtained from the above measurements.

1. *Questions regarding vocational planning*
2. *Questions regarding underachievement*
3. *Questions regarding personal development and adjustment*
4. *Questions regarding motivation and interest*

The choice of a vocation should depend on the pupil's ability, often with emphasis on scholastic aptitude. In certain cases, vocational choice must be made on the basis of past achievement, health, physical attributes, or the ability to adjust to people. Jobs are classified into families; if the pupil is interested in a particular area, he may select a vocation appropriate to his talents. The low-IQ pupil who is interested in medicine can, after all, be a hospital orderly.

Although the pupil may have excellent academic potential, and be a well-adjusted individual, his lack of interest can result in underachievement. For a determination of the causes, it is helpful to turn to interest inventory scores, notations of hobbies, leisure-time activities, and anecdotal records. Possibly a pupil's parents may be insisting on a particular course of study because they think it is prestigious or, thwarted in their own lives, are trying to live through their children. Parents may exhort their children so violently to greater effort that the child refuses to try at all.

To be most effective, counselors and teachers must cooperate. Evaluation is improved as additional data are added to the record available to both. Teachers, through observation of pupil behavior, can give important information to the counselor, just as the counselor can share interpretations of test scores and other information found in the pupil's cumulative record.

An important objective for the counselor is to develop in the pupil a capacity for self-evaluation. Society is competitive and each pupil must have an understanding of his behavior to cope effectively with it. It is encouraging that more and more tools and information are becoming available so that counselors can advise all pupils, no matter what their level of occupational interest (see Berdie, 1969). The pupil should see test scores and other discreetly selected portions of information in the cumulative record to help him understand his strengths and weaknesses; decisions must be based on adequate data.

THE SCHOOL ADMINISTRATOR. Data from cumulative records prove helpful to the school administrator in organizing class groups, and in providing information to colleges, prospective employers, and schools to which pupils may transfer. Some of the data can be used in a public relations program, particularly such elements as recorded results of standardized achievement and aptitude tests.

As our population increases, even small schools must have more than one class at each grade level. Combination grades, such as a fifth and sixth, may be formed. At other times, particularly at the secondary level, pupils may be grouped into more or less homogeneous groups on the basis of their educational and vocational aims, or of scores from standardized scholastic aptitude tests. Achievement is related to these variables, though not perfectly correlated. In other cases some pupils may be grouped because of such factors as lack of basic skills in English.

As applications for higher education increase, college officials must have data on which to base selection, and one source is systematic records of standardized tests. Because final marks given in small schools are often not comparable to those assigned in larger ones, and because the quality of instruction varies from school to school, standardized test data provide a basis for comparison of candidates across the country. Though many colleges use college entrance examinations, the data from a school testing program represent a child far more completely than the single test administration.

Many pupils work after high school. As recently as fifty years ago, graduation from secondary school was a measure of achievement, but when most children receive high school diplomas and variability of achievement becomes the rule, the wise employer must contact the high school administration about a prospective employee. As requests of this kind increase, the administrator must have a well-kept cumulative record.

But this is not the whole of the administrator's informational obligation. He must also interpret the school program for the general public, a task that may involve the publishing of brochures, speech-making, and instigating public discussion.

Accountability in education is a very important concern of schools as hard-pressed taxpayers and parents are demanding that schools provide evidence about their degree of effectiveness. In fairness to teachers, we must realize that the input from pupils is a big factor in the end product. Teachers have little control over their "raw material." Therefore, accountability must be tempered in terms of those outcomes which can be affected by teachers' and administrators' actions and decisions (Barro, 1970).

Furthermore, the purpose of accountability should not be punitive, but for the improvement of instruction and learning (Campbell, 1971). In order to do this, the school must have its goals clearly in mind. It makes a great difference as to how resources are allocated. For instance, should the responsibility of the school be to try (1) to bring all pupils up to some basic minimum level of achievement, or (2) to help each child develop his potential?

The latter is the better choice, even though, with our present state of knowledge and restricted resources, our efforts are limited. It is very difficult for schools to guarantee a specific level of pupil performance. Educators can only keep themselves informed of pupil needs, then try to meet those needs within the limits of what they know about the teaching-learning process (Dyer, 1970).

PROBLEM

9. The cumulative record folder accompanies the pupil as he moves from elementary to junior high school and also when he enters senior high school. At the transfer points, many counselors go through the folders and discard materials which, in their opinion, are no longer useful or which might jeopardize the child in a new setting. What kinds of material might they prefer to discard? Is this a wise practice?

SUMMARY

The principal ideas in this chapter can be summarized as follows:

1. *A sound evaluation program should be based on measurable objectives of the school. The data gathered should reflect the educational program and include information about the personal characteristics of the pupil and his environment. Too often what is measured may be only a trivial and inconsequential part of the total educational outcome.*
2. *All school personnel—teachers, counselors, and school administrators—should be involved in the evaluation program from its initiation throughout its*

integration with other activities of the school. Staff members should receive training to prepare them for their roles in the program.

3. *A minimal testing program includes tests of scholastic aptitude and achievement. The optimum program adds other aptitude tests as well as interest and personality inventories.*

4. *Standardized achievement tests are most helpful when administered yearly. Scholastic aptitude tests car be scheduled at the beginning of the first, fourth, seventh, and tenth grades.*

5. *In selecting a test, the first consideration should be its usefulness to the evaluation program as a whole. Attention should be given to its degree of validity and reliability, the adequacy of its norms, and the complexity of its administration and scoring. Consideration should also focus on ease of interpretation by selecting one test series for all grade levels if possible. Buros'* Mental Measurements Yearbooks *prove helpful guides in test selection.*

6. *Valid test results depend on effective administration and scoring. This includes proper training of personnel and good judgment when selecting the time and place of test administration.*

7. *Test and inventory scores transformed into charts and diagrams are helpful in a public relations program, but they are only one source of data. Rating scales aid in observation, and are an effective technique for collecting certain kinds of information.*

8. *The use of cumulative records is recommended for making data available for diagnostic teaching and guidance.*

9. *The school administrator not only needs data for interpreting the school program to the public to satisfy its concern for accountability, but also to supply information to colleges, prospective employers, and schools to which pupils transfer.*

SUGGESTED READINGS

BERDIE, R. F. The uses of evaluation in guidance. In R. W. Tyler (ed.), *Educational evaluation: New roles, new means.* Sixty-Eighth Yearbook of the National Society for the Study of Education. Part II. Chicago: University of Chicago Press, 1969. Pp. 51–80.
> An excellent discussion on evaluation and its use in terms of a counselor's philosophy. The chapter includes references on recent research dealing with predictive data.

DENTON, D. E. Cumulative records: Invalid and unethical. *Educational Forum,* 1968, 33, 55–58.
> The author criticizes the cumulative record on three counts: metaphysical, statistical, and civil libertarian. Cumulative records can be helpful, but unfortunately they are sometimes misused.

FINDLEY, W. G. (ed.). *The impact and improvement of school testing programs.* Sixty-Second Yearbook of the National Society for the Study of Education. Chicago: University of Chicago Press, 1963.
> Highly useful information is contained in this volume. Particularly pertinent are Chapter 10, which deals with the selection and use of tests, and Chapter 12, which contains recommendations concerning the interpretation of test scores.

Memos to a test director. *NCME Measurement News,* 1973, 16, 5–14.
> Three helpful memos to aid a direction of a testing program describe how to organize and supervise a school testing program.

Testing program. *Childhood Education,* 1973, 49, 338–372.
> A symposium on testing and accountability is summarized. Included are such topics as the assessment of young children, the use of norms, and decision-making based on accountability data.

WOMER, F. B., and N. K. WAHI. Test use. In R. L. Ebel (ed.), *Encyclopedia of educational research.* (4th ed.) New York: Macmillan, 1969. Pp. 1461–1469.

A good review of the research and writings on the development of testing programs, test administration, scoring and interpretation, and test norms.

REFERENCES CITED

BARRO, S. M. An approach to developing accountability measures for the public schools. *Phi Delta Kappan,* 1970, *52,* 196–205.

BERDIE, R. F. The uses of evaluation in guidance. In R. W. Tyler (ed.), *Educational evaluation: New roles, new means.* Sixty-Eighth Yearbook of the National Society for the Study of Education. Part II. Chicago: University of Chicago Press, 1969, 51–80.

CAMPBELL, R. E. Accountability and stone soup. *Phi Delta Kappan,* 1971, *53,* 176–178.

DARLEY, J. G., and G. W. ANDERSON. The functions of measurement in counseling. In E. F. Lindquist (ed.), *Educational measurement.* Washington: American Council on Education, 1951.

DYER, H. S. Toward objective criteria of professional accountability in the schools of New York City. *Phi Delta Kappan,* 1970, *52,* 206–211.

FISHMAN, J. A., et al. Guidelines for testing minority group children. *Journal of Social Issues* (Supplement), 1964, *20,* 129–145.

FLEMING, M. Standardized tests revisited. *The School Counselor,* 1971, *19,* 71–72.

GESELL, A., and C. S. AMATRUDA. *Developmental diagnosis: Normal and abnormal child development.* New York: Harper & Row, 1969.

KEARNEY, N. C. *Elementary school objectives.* New York: Russell Sage Foundation, 1953.

MAGER, R. F. *Preparing instructional objectives.* Palo Alto, Calif.: Fearon Publishers, 1962.

TRAXLER, A. E., et al. *Introduction to testing and the use of test results in public schools.* Westport, Conn.: Greenwood Press, 1971. (Reprint.)

APPENDICES

APPENDIX A: STATISTICAL METHODS*

Part One

Measure of central tendency: the arithmetic mean. The arithmetic mean is a measure of central tendency. In other words, it is a value that attempts to represent the clustering that is so commonly found in test-score distributions. In the cases in which the test scores are for all practical purposes normally distributed, the arithmetic mean corresponds closely to two other measures of central tendency, the mode (the most common score) and the median (the point below which fifty percent of the test scores fall).

The arithmetic mean is the sum of all test scores in a distribution divided by the number of test scores. Many people call it "the average." This definition can be translated into the following equation:

$$M = \frac{\Sigma X}{N},$$

where

M = *arithmetic mean;*
Σ = *the sum;*
X = *any test score;*
N = *number of test scores.*

This formula can be applied to any set of ungrouped data to determine the arithmetic mean, for example, the following mental ability scores of twenty fifth-grade pupils.

107	123	112	97	100
93	88	83	109	91
101	96	98	114	106
115	105	85	118	111

* For those who wish to engage in independent study of statistical concepts useful in tests and measurements, a programmed textbook is available entitled Statistics and Measurement: A Programmed Introduction, *2nd ed., by L. A. Schoer, Allyn and Bacon, Inc., 1971.*

The sum of the twenty values (ΣX) is 2052. The arithmetic mean is 2052 divided by 20, or 102.6. The substitution in the formula is as follows:

$$M = \frac{2052}{20} = 102.6.$$

Test scores are not always available in the ungrouped fashion illustrated in the foregoing table. Occasionally they are grouped in a frequency distribution, as in the case of the 360 vocabulary scores shown in Table 8.1 (see p. 198). In a frequency distribution, the exact test score for any particular pupil is unknown, and the formula for the arithmetic mean as presented above cannot be applied.

One method of computing the arithmetic mean of test scores included in a frequency distribution is to guess the arithmetic mean and then correct the guess. The only requirement for a guessed mean is that it be the midpoint of one of the intervals of the frequency distribution. The guessed mean is corrected by a simple coding operation.

The first steps of the computation of the arithmetic mean of the 360 vocabulary scores included in the frequency distribution cited are shown in Table A.1.

The guessed mean is 57, the midpoint of the 55–59 interval. The values in the deviation column are found by counting, in terms of the number of intervals, how far each interval deviates from the interval containing the guessed mean. Thus, the d value of the 60–64 interval is +1 because it is one interval above the 55–59 interval; the d value of the 50–54 interval is −1 because it is one interval below the 55–59 interval. The fd values are determined by multiplying each frequency by the corresponding d value.

The complete formula for finding the arithmetic mean of a frequency distribution is as follows:

TABLE A.1. Frequency Distribution of 360 Vocabulary Test Scores.

Raw-score interval	Frequency (f)	Deviation (d)	fd
90–94	4	7	28
85–89	6	6	36
80–84	12	5	60
75–79	20	4	80
70–74	28	3	84
65–69	36	2	72
60–64	40	1	40
55–59	46	0	0
50–54	43	−1	−43
45–49	39	−2	−78
40–44	32	−3	−96
35–39	24	−4	−96
30–34	13	−5	−65
25–29	9	−6	−54
20–24	5	−7	−35
15–19	3	−8	−24
Total	360		−91

$$M = G.M. + (h)\left[\frac{\Sigma fd}{N}\right],$$

where

    M = *arithmetic mean;*
  G.M. = *guessed mean;*
     h = *size of the intervals of the frequency distribution;*
  Σfd = *algebraic sum of the entries in the* fd *column;*
    N = *number of test scores.*

The expression following the plus sign corrects the guessed mean by increasing it if it is too small or reducing it if it is too large.

The appropriate values can be readily taken from the table and substituted in the equation as follows:

$$M = 57 + (5)\left[\frac{-91}{360}\right] = 55.7.$$

The fact that the guessed mean is slightly higher than the actual arithmetic mean causes the sign of the Σfd to be negative.

The formula for computing the arithmetic mean of test scores arranged in a frequency distribution is nothing more than a convenient substitute for the definition formula for the arithmetic mean that is applied to ungrouped data. The frequency distribution formula is none too satisfactory at times. It often yields inacccurate answers when the number of cases in the frequency distribution is small.

The formula for computing the median of test scores included in a frequency distribution is shown in Part Four of Appendix A. For the frequency distribution of 360 vocabulary test scores the median is 55.8. Since the distribution of test scores is approximately normal, it is very close to the arithmetic mean.

Part Two

Measure of variability: the standard deviation. The standard deviation, like the range, is a measure of variability, or dispersion, as it is sometimes called. It is a distance expressed in test-score units rather than a point such as the arithmetic mean. If the test scores of a distribution are widely scattered above and below the arithmetic mean of the scores, the standard deviation is large; the distribution has considerable variability. If the test scores of a distribution cluster closely around the arithmetic mean, the standard deviation is small; the distribution has little variability.

Like the arithmetic mean, the standard deviation can be computed for un-grouped data or test scores arranged in a frequency distribution. The formula for computing the standard deviation of ungrouped data can serve as a definition of the standard deviation. The formula for computing the standard deviation of test scores arranged in a frequency distribution is a somewhat imperfect substitute for the first formula.

To compute the standard deviation of ungrouped test scores, the following formula is used:

$$\sigma = \sqrt{\frac{\Sigma X^2 - [(\Sigma X)^2 / N]}{N}}$$

where

σ = standard deviation;

Σ = the sum;

X = any test score;

N = number of test scores.

This formula was used to determine the standard deviation of the 200 American history achievement test scores cited in Chapter 10. In Table A.2 are a few of the 200 test scores, and opposite each is its square.

Summing the two columns yields the two values needed for the numerator of the standard deviation equation. Substitution of all values gives the following equation:

$$\sigma = \sqrt{\frac{585,979 - [(10,620)^2 / 200]}{200}} = 10.5.$$

Finding the standard deviation of test scores arranged in a frequency distribution is a simple extension of the process used to compute the arithmetic mean of those test scores. A convenient interval is selected, the deviations of the remaining intervals from the selected interval are identified, and a systematic series of multiplications follow.

The frequency distribution of vocabulary test scores shown in Table 8.1 (see p. 198) is reproduced in Table A.3.

The 55–59 interval is chosen as the starting point and all other intervals are identified in the deviation column according to the number of intervals they happen to be above or below the selected interval. The entries in the fd column are found by multiplying each frequency by the corresponding d value. The entries in the fd^2 column are determined by multiplying each fd value by the corresponding d value.

TABLE A.2.   Array of American History Achievement Test Scores.

Pupil	Test score (X)	X^2
1	80	6,400
2	21	441
3	62	3,844
4	76	5,776
5	32	1,024
6	47	2,209
.	.	.
.	.	.
.	.	.
200	75	5,625
Total	10,620	585,979

TABLE A.3. Computation of the Standard Deviation of a Frequency Distribution.

Raw-score interval	Frequency (f)	Deviation (d)	fd	fd²
90–94	4	7	28	196
85–89	6	6	36	216
80–84	12	5	60	300
75–79	20	4	80	320
70–74	28	3	84	252
65–69	36	2	72	144
60–64	40	1	40	40
55–59	46	0	0	0
50–54	43	−1	−43	43
45–49	39	−2	−78	156
40–44	32	−3	−96	288
35–39	24	−4	−96	384
30–34	13	−5	−65	325
25–29	9	−6	−54	324
20–24	5	−7	−35	245
15–19	3	−8	−24	192
Total	360		−91	3,425

The sums of the fd column and fd^2 columns are needed if the standard deviation is to be found. The complete formula for the standard deviation is as follows:

$$\sigma = (h)\sqrt{\frac{\Sigma fd^2}{N} - \left(\frac{\Sigma fd}{N}\right)^2},$$

where

σ = standard deviation;

h = size of the intervals of the frequency distribution;

Σfd^2 = sum of the entries in the fd^2 column;

Σfd = algebraic sum of the entries in the fd column;

N = number of test scores.

Substitution of the values computed in the table yields the following:

$$\sigma = (5)\sqrt{\frac{3425}{360} - \left(\frac{-91}{360}\right)^2} = 15.3.$$

A simpler method of determining the size of a standard deviation is available provided that the distribution of the test scores is approximately normal. All that is necessary is to (a) sum the scores for the top sixth of the group of pupils, (b) sum the scores for the bottom sixth, (c) find the difference between these two values, and (d) divide the difference by half of the number of pupils in the total group. The formula is as follows:

$$\sigma = \frac{\Sigma X_t - \Sigma X_b}{N/2},$$

where

σ = standard deviation;

ΣX_t = sum of scores for top sixth;

ΣX_b = sum of scores for bottom sixth;

N/2 = half of the number of pupils in the total group.

Values yielded by this formula are often quite satisfactory for the needs of a classroom teacher.

Part Three

Measure of relationships: the product-moment coefficient of correlation. The Pearson product-moment coefficient of correlation represents the degree of straight-line relationship between two sets of measurements, such as those of two characteristics of each of a group of pupils. The correlation coefficient reflects the tendency of these pupils to have, in some systematic manner, similar relative positions or dissimilar relative positions in the two distributions. If pupils who are high in one distribution tend to be high in the second, and if pupils who are low in one distribution tend to be low in the other, the correlation coefficient is positive: a direct relationship exists between the two characteristics. If pupils who are high in one distribution tend to be low in the other, and if pupils who are low in one distribution tend to be high in the other, the correlation coefficient is negative: an inverse relationship exists between the two characteristics.

The amount of straight-line relationship between two characteristics is indicated by the size of the correlation coefficient. If the correlation coefficient is +1.00 or −1.00, the straight-line relationship is perfect, that is, plotting one measurement against the other will yield a series of points that can be joined by a single straight line. If the correlation coefficient were 0.00, there would be absolutely no straight-line relationship between the two characteristics. Thus, correlation coefficients can vary in size from +1.00 to −1.00, the sign reflecting the direction of the relationship and the size reflecting the amount of the relationship. The fact that two characteristics are correlated does not necessarily mean that one is the immediate cause of the other.

A correlation coefficient is useful in situations such as that described in Chapter 9 in connection with the discussion of criterion-related validity. Table 9.2 (see p. 229) shows the test scores of the scholastic aptitude and social studies achievement of each of twenty pupils.

The following formula is used to compute the coefficient of correlation:

$$r = \frac{\Sigma XY - [(\Sigma X)(\Sigma Y)/N]}{\sqrt{\left[\Sigma X^2 - \frac{(\Sigma X)^2}{N}\right]\left[\Sigma Y^2 - \frac{(\Sigma Y)^2}{N}\right]}},$$

where

r = product-moment coefficient of correlation;

Σ = the sum;

X = *any test score of one characteristic (i.e., any scholastic aptitude test score);*
Y = *any test score of the other characteristic (i.e., any social studies test score);*
N = *number of pupils.*

Solution of the formula can be simplified by preparing a worksheet. Table A.4, based upon Table 9.2, is such a worksheet.

The new entries in the worksheet are products, either the square of a test score or the cross-product of two test scores for a pupil. The sums of these products as they are listed in the last row of the table are the values necessary to solve the r formula. The following needed values can be taken from the table:

$$\Sigma X = 2,142 \qquad\qquad \Sigma Y = 1,256$$
$$\Sigma X^2 = 232,750 \qquad\qquad \Sigma Y^2 = 84,188$$
$$\Sigma XY = 137,085 \qquad\qquad N = 20$$

Substitution of these values into the formula for the correlation coefficient yields the following:

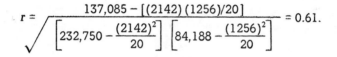

$$r = \frac{137,085 - [(2142)(1256)/20]}{\sqrt{\left[232,750 - \frac{(2142)^2}{20}\right]\left[84,188 - \frac{(1256)^2}{20}\right]}} = 0.61.$$

TABLE A.4. Computation of a Coefficient of Correlation for Un-grouped Data.

Pupil	Scholastic aptitude test (X)	Social studies test (Y)	XY	X²	Y²
Jim	135	66	8,910	18,225	4,356
Sam	130	90	11,700	16,900	8,100
Ruth	120	68	8,160	14,400	4,624
Mary	117	85	9,945	13,689	7,225
John	116	81	9,396	13,456	6,561
Louise	114	47	5,358	12,996	2,209
Ralph	113	69	7,797	12,769	4,761
Mae	112	77	8,624	12,544	5,929
Quinton	111	65	7,215	12,321	4,225
Sandra	109	56	6,104	11,881	3,136
Larry	107	89	9,523	11,449	7,921
Norma	106	49	5,194	11,236	2,401
Frank	101	57	5,757	10,201	3,249
Milton	100	58	5,800	10,000	3,364
Dave	97	71	6,887	9,409	5,041
Joe	95	60	5,700	9,025	3,600
Bill	94	38	3,572	8,836	1,444
Sally	90	31	2,790	8,100	961
Margaret	88	40	3,520	7,744	1,600
Sue	87	59	5,133	7,569	3,481
Total	2,142	1,256	137,085	232,750	84,188

As in the case of arithmetic means and standard deviations, coefficients of correlations can be computed by use of measurements arranged in frequency distributions as well as of ungrouped data. The formula must be altered somewhat to do this. A complete description of the computation of a correlation coefficient from a two-way frequency distribution can be found in most introductory textbooks of statistical methodology.

A simple means of obtaining a somewhat accurate estimate of the size of the product-moment coefficient of correlation is to compute a Spearman rank-difference coefficient of correlation, known as rho (ρ). It represents the tendency of the pupils to have similar or dissimilar ranks in terms of two variables. Rho values are computed by means of the following formula:

$$\rho = 1 - \frac{6 \Sigma D^2}{N(N^2 - 1)},$$

where

ρ = rank-difference coefficient of correlation;

Σ = the sum;

D = difference between a pair of ranks;

N = number of pupils.

In Table 9.2 are shown the ranks of each of the twenty pupils for both a scholastic aptitude test and a social studies achievement test. When the differences between these pairs of ranks are squared and added, a sum of 526 is found. Hence,

$$\rho = \frac{(6)(526)}{20(400 - 1)} = 0.60.$$

Another quick way of obtaining an estimate of the degree of relationship that exists between two variables is to compute a tetrachoric correlation coefficient. Such coefficients can be determined by finding the percentage of pupils who are in the top half of the class in terms of both sets of test scores being correlated, and then looking up the correlation coefficient corresponding to this percentage in a table (see Table A.5) published by the Educational Testing Service.

Unfortunately, the tetrachoric correlations yielded by this table are not precise. At best they can be thought of as a rough approximation of the size of the product-moment coefficient of correlation for the data in question.

TABLE A.5.   Simplified Method for Estimating the Size of Tetrachoric Correlation Coefficients.

%	ρ	%	ρ	%	ρ	%	ρ	%	ρ
45	0.95	37	0.69	29	0.25	21	−0.25	13	−0.69
44	.93	36	.65	28	.19	20	− .31	12	− .73
43	.91	35	.60	27	.13	19	− .37	11	− .77
42	.88	34	.55	26	.07	18	− .43	10	− .81
41	.85	33	.49	25	.00	17	− .49	9	− .85
40	.81	32	.43	24	− .07	16	− .55	8	− .88
39	.77	31	.37	23	− .13	15	− .60	7	− .91
38	.73	30	.31	22	− .19	14	− .65	6	− .93

TABLE A.6. Computation of Quartiles, Deciles, and Percentiles Based on a Frequency Distribution.

Raw-score intervals	Frequency (f_w)	Cumulative frequency (f_c)
90–94	4	360
85–89	6	356
80–84	12	350
75–79	20	338
70–74	28	318
65–69	36	290
60–64	40	254
55–59	46	214
50–54	43	168
45–49	39	125
40–44	32	86
35–39	24	54
30–34	13	30
25–29	9	17
20–24	5	8
15–19	3	3
Total	360	

Part Four

Measure of relative performance: the quartile, decile, and percentile. Quartiles, deciles, and percentiles are points in a distribution of test scores. The first quartile, often identified as Q_1, is the point in the distribution below which twenty-five percent of the test scores fall; the first decile (D_1) is the point below which ten percent of the test scores fall; the first percentile (P_1) is the point below which one percent of the test scores fall. Other quartiles, deciles, and percentiles are similarly defined and symbolically identified.

Quartiles divide the test-score distribution into four equal parts in terms of the number of test scores. Deciles divide such a distribution into ten equal parts, and percentiles divide it into one-hundred equal parts.

A computation of any quartile, decile, or percentile can be based on a frequency distribution of test scores such as that shown in Table 8.1 (see p. 198). This frequency distribution contains vocabulary test scores obtained by testing 360 pupils. It is reproduced in Table A.6.

The formula for determining any quartile, decile, or percentile is as follows:

$$Q, D, \text{ or } P = 1 + (h)\left[\frac{(F)\,(N) - f_c}{f_w}\right],$$

where

1 = *theoretical lower limit of the interval containing the quartile, decile, or percentile desired;*

h = *size of the intervals in the frequency distribution;*

F = *a fraction that varies according to which quartile, decile, or percentile is
     desired;*

N = *number of test scores;*

f_c = *cumulative frequency below the interval containing the quartile, decile, or
         percentile desired;*

f_w = *number of test scores within the interval containing the quartile, decile, or
         percentile desired.*

Two of the values used in the formula, l and F, deserve further explanation. That l is a theoretical lower limit of an interval and not a reported lower limit simply recognizes the fact that all measurements are limited in accuracy. Although test scores are reported to the nearest whole number, theoretically each score represents the interval that extends from 0.5 below the test score in question to 0.5 above it. A reported score of 50 represents an interval from 49.5 to 50.5 in a test-score distribution. Whenever test scores are reported to the nearest whole number, the value of l is 0.5 less than the reported value of the lower limit of the frequency distribution interval containing the quartile, decile, or percentile to be computed.

The value of F is defined as the size of a fraction associated with the quartile, decile, or percentile. For the median, the point below which fifty percent of the scores fall, the fraction is 50/100, or 1/2. For the third decile (D_3), the point below which thirty percent of the scores fall, the fraction is 30/100 or 3/10. For the sixty-third percentile (P_{63}), the fraction is 63/100. All other fractions can be found in a similar manner.

Suppose that P_{32} is to be computed. The first step is to find the interval containing P_{32}. The most rapid way of doing this is to determine F, which is 32/100, and multiply it by N, which is 360. The answer, 115.2, is entered in the cumulative frequency column of the table. Observe that 86 pupils have test scores of 44 or less, whereas 125 pupils have test scores of 49 or less. Therefore, P_{32}, which corresponds to 115.2, falls somewhere within the 45–49 interval.

Now that the interval is identified, three of the required values can be quickly identified. The number of test scores within the interval (f_w) is 39; the cumulative frequency below the interval (f_c) is 86; the theoretical lower limit of the interval (l) is 44.5. Substitution of these and other needed values yields the following equation:

$$P_{32} = 44.5 + 5 \left[\frac{32/100(360) - 86}{39} \right] = 48.2.$$

The determination of a decile or quartile is equally simple. The steps needed to compute D_6 are as follows:

1. $F = 60/100$, or 6/10
2. $(F)(N) = 6/10(360) = 216$
3. Therefore, the interval containing D_6 is the 60–64 interval.
4. $f_w = 40$
5. $f_c = 214$
6. $l = 59.5$

Therefore

$$D_6 = 59.5 + 5 \left[\frac{6/10\,(360) - 214}{40} \right] = 59.8.$$

A quartile, such as Q_3, is computed as follows:

1. $F = 75/100$, or $3/4$
2. $(F)\,(N) = (3/4)\,(360) = 270$
3. Therefore, the interval containing Q_3 is the 65–69 interval.
4. $f_w = 36$
5. $f_c = 254$
6. $l = 64.5$

Therefore

$$Q_3 = 64.5 + 5 \left[\frac{3/4\,(360) - 254}{36} \right] = 66.7.$$

Quartile, decile, and percentile ranks can be determined by inspecting the appropriate quartiles, deciles, and percentiles; inspecting an appropriate ogive curve; or computing from ungrouped test scores arranged according to size from low to high. These techniques are described in many introductory textbooks of statistical methodology.

APPENDIX B: FREE AND INEXPENSIVE MATERIALS ON MEASUREMENT AND EVALUATION

I. Test Bulletins Published at Irregular Intervals

Test Data Reports, *Harcourt Brace Jovanovich, Inc.*
Test Service Bulletins, *The Psychological Corporation*
Test Service Notebook, *Harcourt Brace Jovanovich, Inc.*
Testing Today, *Houghton Mifflin Company*

II. Newsletters Concerning Measurement

ACTivity, *American College Testing Program*
Educational Researcher, *American Educational Research Association*
ETS Developments, *Educational Testing Service*
Measurement in Education, *National Council on Measurement in Education*
Measurement News, *National Council on Measurement in Education*
Memo to a Test Director, *National Council on Measurement in Education*
NAEP Newsletter, *National Assessment of Educational Progress*

III. Educational and Psychological Journals

American Educational Research Journal

Educational and Psychological Measurement

Journal of Educational Evaluation

Journal of Educational Measurement

Journal of Educational Psychology

Measurement and Evaluation in Guidance

Psychological Abstracts: "Psychometrics and Statistics" and "Educational Psychology"

Review of Educational Research

IV. Annual Reports and Proceedings

Annual Reports, *College Entrance Examination Board*

Annual Reports, *Educational Testing Service*

Proceedings, *Annual Invitational Conference on Testing Problems, Educational Testing Service*

Proceedings, *Annual Western Regional Conference on Testing Problems, Educational Testing Service*

V. Miscellaneous Paperback Books and Bulletins

Tests and Measurement Kit. *Educational Testing Service, 1973.*

Making the Classroom Test: A Guide for Teachers

Multiple-Choice Questions: A Close Look

Selecting an Achievement Test: Principles and Procedures

Short-Cut Statistics for Teacher-Made Tests

Guidance Monograph Series, Set III: Testing. *Houghton Mifflin Company, 1968.*

    Modern Mental Measurement: A Historical Perspective

    Basic Concepts in Testing

    Types of Test Scores

    School Testing Programs

    Intelligence, Aptitude, and Achievement Testing

    Interest and Personality Inventories

    Tests on Trial

    Automated Data Processing in Testing

    Controversial Issues in Testing

TM Reports. *ERIC Clearinghouse on Tests, Measurement, and Evaluation; Educational Testing Service.*

NAME INDEX

A

Abeles, S., 227, 239
Abingdon, A., 105, 126
Adkins, D. C., 183, 189
Ahmann, J. S., 8, 33, 188
Ahrens, M. R., 36, 63
Airasian, P. W., 394, 405
Amatruda, C. S., 412, 428
Amrine, M., 339
Anastasi, A., 24, 33, 167, 218, 234, 238, 256, 261, 279, 280, 296, 308, 328, 340
Anderson, G. W., 424, 428
Anderson, R. H., 403, 404, 405
Angoff, W. H., 201, 214, 218, 219
Arny, C. B., 180, 189

B

Babbott, D., 122, 127
Bailard, V., 404
Baker, F. B., 217, 219
Barro, S. M., 426, 428
Bayley, N., 300, 308, 309
Berdie, R. F., 425, 427, 428
Bereiter, C., 296, 309
Bersoff, D. N., 308
Bibelheimer, M., 300, 309
Blair, G. M., 365
Block, J. H., 396, 405
Bloom, B. S., 4, 19, 32, 33, 36, 38, 40, 41, 62, 63, 103, 123, 126, 127, 188, 395, 396, 405
Blum, S. H., 279
Bounds, W. G., 148
Boyd, J. L., 186, 188, 189
Brown, B. F., 404, 405

Buros, O. K., 23, 33, 236, 237, 238, 239, 297, 309
Burrill, L. E., 279
Burrows, A. T., 187, 189
Bussis, A. M., 303, 309

C

Campbell, R. E., 426, 428
Cartwright, C. A., 339
Cartwright, G. P., 339
Chave, E. J., 336, 340
Clark, K. E., 330, 339
Cleary, T. A., 296, 309
Coffman, W. E., 104, 131, 143, 144, 147, 148
Cooley, W. W., 301, 309
Cox, R. C., 167
Crisler, R. D., 383, 405
Crites, J. O., 339
Cronbach, L. J., 14, 21, 32, 33, 204, 218, 219, 224, 225, 234, 237, 238, 239, 249, 256, 297, 308, 309, 322, 331, 339, 396, 405
Crow, J. F., 296, 309
Crumrine, W. M., 336, 340
Cunningham, R., 327, 339
Cureton, E. E., 249, 256
Cureton, L. W., 405

D

Damrin, E. E., 122, 127
Darley, J. G., 315, 340, 424, 428
Davis, F. B., 303, 309
Davis, J., 368, 406

441

SUBJECT INDEX